TIDEWATER TOWNS

WILLIAMSBURG ARCHITECTURAL STUDIES

TIDEWATER TOWNS

City Planning in Colonial Virginia and Maryland

by JOHN W. REPS

Published by
THE COLONIAL WILLIAMSBURG FOUNDATION, Williamsburg, Virginia

Distributed by
THE UNIVERSITY PRESS OF VIRGINIA, Charlottesville, Virginia

Library of Congress Catalog Card No. 77-154342
Colonial Williamsburg ISBN 0-910412-87-1
University Press of Virginia ISBN 0-8139-0332-7

PRINTED IN THE UNITED STATES OF AMERICA

To my daughter and son
Martha Christine and Thomas William Reps

Contents

Preface

THIS book, like my earlier works, deals with the forms and designs man has used in planning American towns. It focuses on the region that saw the earliest permanent English settlements in America—the tidewater area of Virginia and Maryland around Chesapeake Bay and along its river estuaries. Although the colonial period is treated in greatest detail, the subsequent development of certain towns has been traced into the nineteenth century in an effort to discover to what extent later growth followed or diverged from colonial patterns.

Previous research for a general study of the history of American town planning had served to introduce me to the region, but I had not realized the amount of material that was available. What I first conceived of as a rather modest and compact monograph has grown into a book of substantial size. I suspect, however, that far from exhausting the subject I have merely tapped some of the richer veins of the vast research resources that still remain to be worked over in greater depth. If what appears here suggests directions for future more specialized studies the book will have served at least one useful purpose.

Many, perhaps most, Americans seem to believe that our cities somehow arose more or less spontaneously and that urban planning is an invention of the present era. This misconception is nowhere more erroneous than in the tidewater region. From the first day of settlement town planning played an important role in colonization. For reasons we shall explore in the text, towns were slow to grow. Yet those that were established took the forms determined consciously by individuals or groups to whom this responsibility was delegated by colonial officials.

In devising these early plans the colonists relied heavily on tradition, although the physical environment of the New World and the roles that towns were expected to play differed substantially from those of the mother country. The first chapter of this book summarizes the English planning tradition so that the reader will have some understanding of the concepts of towns and their designs brought to North America by the colonists. The second and third chapters examine the earliest communities in the two colonies of Virginia and Maryland, beginning with the unsuccessful attempt on Roanoke Island and followed by the founding of Jamestown and St. Mary's.

Two chapters then deal with the evolution of town planning policy in the seventeenth century. A remarkable series of laws in both colonies during that period represented efforts to implement a determined policy that towns should be created as an essential, even predominant, element of colonial life. While this policy proved far more difficult to carry out than English administrators anticipated and can be regarded as only partly successful, it resulted in the founding of a number of communities and the partial balancing of a plantation economy by urban activities.

At the end of the seventeenth century new capital cities were planned in both colonies. Their designs, the work of the energetic Francis Nicholson, were quite different in character from anything yet created in North America. The chapter dealing with Annapolis and the two on the founding and subsequent growth of Williamsburg describe and analyze the unusual designs Nicholson employed and their possible sources in European baroque principles and practice.

The eighteenth century brought a shift in urban planning policy. Instead of attempting to create many towns at once by general town and port legislation, the two colonial assemblies established individual towns as the need arose. This period also saw, especially in Virginia, a number of communities founded and planned by individuals seeking speculative gain. The rise of private entrepreneurship in tidewater town development foreshadowed what was to occur on a much greater scale throughout America in the nineteenth century. Two chapters trace the events in Virginia and Maryland during this era. That dealing with Maryland also explores the founding of the national capital. While not a colonial venture, the District of Columbia was intimately related to the other tidewater communities by location, and it represented at the end of the eighteenth century, as did Annapolis and Williamsburg nearly a hundred years earlier, a major innovation in urban design.

Two very important cities of the colonial Tidewater were Richmond and Baltimore. The former succeeded Williamsburg as Virginia's capital. The latter became the dominant mercantile city of the Chesapeake region and one of the major communities of the country. Because of their size and prominence in the life of the two colonies, a separate chapter has been devoted to their planning and growth. The final chapter is a brief evaluation of the town planning achievements in the Tidewater with relation to the other English colonies and to subsequent developments in what became the United States.

As important as the text in this investigation are the numerous illustrations showing original or early plans and views of the towns discussed. A large number of these are manuscript drawings, many of which have not heretofore been reproduced. In addition to whatever value this book may have as history it also can serve as a kind of town atlas for the region under examination. The notes on the illustrations, which the reader may find toward the end of the volume, contain full carto-bibliographical information concerning the maps, plans, and views that have been used. I am aware of occasional variants in the spelling of names and places in the illustrations from those in the text; in these instances the modern and more familiar forms appear in the text.

In my discussion of individual towns I have relied heavily on historical investigations by earlier scholars. Fortunately for my task, the tidewater region has been the subject of research almost from the first years of colonization. The bibliography lists my principal sources of information, but I have also visited virtually every town or site mentioned in the text or represented in the illustrations. For the town planning historian, field inspection is indispensable, and in walking through the towns themselves I gained a number of insights that would not have been possible from a mere examination of drawings and documents.

I am under no illusions that this book is free from errors. Some of the sources are themselves in conflict, and it was necessary in a number of cases for me to choose the account that appeared more likely to be accurate. It should be made clear that those persons whose help is acknowledged elsewhere in this book should not be held responsible for any erroneous statements of facts or mistaken interpretations, for which I alone am to blame.

With this book I am beginning a number of regional studies that will extend, correct, and supplement the research and conclusions in the history of American town planning that appeared in my *Making of Urban America*. The years ahead will be interesting indeed if the other regions of the country prove to be as rewarding to study as has that of the Virginia and Maryland Tidewater. I can only hope that the reader will find this subject, largely neglected until now, as fascinating as it has proved to the author.

Acknowledgments

In my research for this book I have been fortunate in having the assistance of many persons and institutions whose aid has been indispensable. It is with deep gratitude that I acknowledge their help.

Through the initiative of Carlisle H. Humelsine, its president, Colonial Williamsburg provided substantial financial support that made it possible for me to devote both summers of 1967 and 1968 to field studies, library research, and writing. Edward P. Alexander, vice-president and director of the Division of Interpretation of Colonial Williamsburg, administered this grant in a manner that left nothing to be desired from an author's standpoint.

Many staff members of Colonial Williamsburg patiently and skillfully answered my questions and supplied me with helpful material. I owe a special debt to Edward M. Riley, director of research, and Paul Buchanan, director of architectural research for such assistance. Others who provided essential aid or suggestions include George H. Reese, formerly assistant director of research, and Susanne Neale, Marylee McGregor, and Jane Carson.

In the two state historical societies I found much valuable material with the help of efficient members of their staffs: In the Virginia Historical Society at Richmond my thanks go to John Melville Jennings, director, and Waverly Winfree, assistant curator of manuscripts. In the Maryland Historical Society at Baltimore I was assisted by Harold R. Manakee, director; P. W. Filby, librarian; Henry G. Klingel, reference librarian; and Richard H. Randall, chairman of the Committee on the Maritime Collection, among others.

The public archives of Virginia and Maryland also contained research resources of great value to this study. In the Virginia State Library I had the help of John W. Dudley, the assistant state archivist, and Thomas J. Headlee, assistant archivist. Morris L. Radoff, director, and Gust Skordas, assistant archivist, rendered similar assistance in the Maryland Hall of Records.

For material on Baltimore I had the invaluable aid of Wilbur H. Hunter, Jr., director of the Peale Museum, who generously gave me access to his unpublished study of the city. In locating and selecting illustrations to document Baltimore's founding and development Paul Amelia, archivist of the Peale Museum, provided informed guidance.

In the Mariners Museum at Newport News the following persons helped my research: Harold S. Sniffen, assistant director; Mrs. Agnes M. Brabrand, curator of prints and paintings; and Mrs. David E. Hendrix, assistant to the librarian. Margaret Cook, curator of manuscripts of the Swem Library of the College of William and Mary, also assisted me in locating various maps and plans in the manuscript collection there.

Helen Wallis, superintendent of the Map Room of the British Museum, located and arranged to have photographed a number of maps and plans. In the Library of Congress I received similar aid from Walter W. Ristow, chief, and Richard Stephenson, Andrew Modelski, and Alberta Koerner of the Division of Geography and Maps; and from Milton Kaplan of the Division of Prints and Photographs.

I am also grateful to the following: Howard Rice, Jr., assistant university librarian for Rare Books and Special Collections at Princeton University;

Mrs. Stuart Gibson, librarian of the Valentine Museum in Richmond; Mrs. Howard A. Keith, president, and Mrs. J. M. P. Wright, first vice-president of Historic Annapolis, Inc.; Mrs. Elizabeth Werner and Constance Werner of Annapolis; William Kerr; James A. McAllister, Jr., librarian of the Dorcester County, Maryland Historical Society; George H. S. King of Fredericksburg; Virginia Baer, librarian of the John Work Garrett Library in Baltimore; and F. G. Emmison, county archivist of the Essex Record Office, Chelmsford, England.

Also to Charles Hatch and Paul Hudson of the National Park Service; Edward F. Heite, managing editor of *Virginia Cavalcade;* Robert D. Cheesman, chief ranger of the National Park Service at Manteo, North Carolina; Marshall Butt, director of the Portsmouth Naval Shipyard Museum; Calvert W. Tazewell, executive vice-president of the Norfolk Historical Society; Dallas H. Oslin of the Richmond City Planning Commission; David Beers Quinn of Liverpool University; and Mary Dewar of the University of Texas.

The staff of Olin Library at Cornell University efficiently responded to my numerous requests for assistance. Barbara Berthelsen, map librarian, and Caroline Spicer, reference librarian were particularly helpful. I am also indebted to the following faculty colleagues at Cornell who generously shared with me their specialized knowledge of a number of matters beyond my competence; Michael Kammen, James M. Smith, Frederick Marcham, Stephen Jacobs, and Michael Hugo-Brunt.

Three of my graduate students in a seminar on the history of American city planning listened to and commented on presentations of several chapters in the book. They also prepared research papers on subjects related to my research. For that help I am grateful to Richard Anglin, Cornelia Griffin, and Lawrence Parker.

The painstaking care with which James Rourk photographed many of the plans and drawings reproduced in this book is deeply appreciated. His skillful work in increasing the contrast between the faded lines and darkened paper of many old drawings has made them far more legible than appeared possible. I am indebted also to Mrs. Kay Page who corrected many errors in proofreading the first draft and who typed the final manuscript with unusual care and accuracy. For careful, sensitive, and understanding editing of the manuscript I am thankful to James R. Short of Colonial Williamsburg whose knowledge and help were invaluable.

Finally, as has been appropriate on previous occasions, I acknowledge with deep appreciation the encouragement of my wife, Constance Reps, whose ability to manage family affairs during my travels away from home in the course of my research allowed me the luxury of uninterrupted concentration on scholarly matters.

John W. Reps

I. *The English Town Planning Tradition*

In the English colonization of America town planning played an important role. Very few of our urban communities with colonial origins began as spontaneous settlements of two or three dwellings clustered around a church, a fort, or a crossroads and then grew without conscious effort to guide development. Contrary to popular belief, virtually all of the villages, towns, and cities of the colonial period began as planned communities. Some individual, corporate group, or governmental body conceived of a pattern of streets, dwelling sites, and locations for public or institutional activities and stamped this design on the virgin land.

Nowhere in the English colonies was town planning pursued with more attention than in the tidewater region—that area of deep, wide rivers flowing into the great inland sea of Chesapeake Bay. These planned towns of the Tidewater, the great majority of which were deliberately created by governmental action, were intended to provide a wide variety of functions. Some were designed as garrison communities. Others were expected to serve as ports through which would flow colonial exports to England and manufactured goods from the home country. Other towns were planned as centers of agricultural activity and marketing or as places for the first stages of industrial processing of mineral resources. Still others came into being as havens for religious communities or to accommodate refugees from discrimination or persecution in Europe.

Those responsible for the creation of these towns did not need to invent new forms and designs for this purpose. Ample English precedents helped to guide the hands of colonial officials called on to plan the new communities expected to form the basis for tidewater settlement. In some cases direct evidence links the plans of an American town with an earlier venture in town planning under English auspices. In others, the influence of prior experience or an earlier theoretical proposal must remain a matter of conjecture.

In the earlier period of colonization one should not expect to discover much innovation in town layout. In all periods of colonization since the time of the Greeks, those responsible for the creation of new urban centers have found it easier and more convenient to apply on the settlement site what had been tested by experience in the motherland. Perhaps the most consistent in this respect were the Romans, who established in the lands under their control hundreds of almost identically planned towns. An American example that well illustrates the point is the first plan by the Dutch early in the seventeenth century for the settlement of New Amsterdam on the rocky tip of the island of Manhattan. That settlement pattern, which quickly proved so impractical, was an echo of a typical Dutch town built on flat land where canals and streets were of almost equal importance.[1]

This is not to suggest that English colonial administrators always followed blindly what had been accomplished or proposed in their native country. Nor can one assume that those who created the planned towns of the Tidewater were students of the history of town planning in England or abroad. But we must beware of the contrary belief that English colonizers were ignorant of the precedents existing in their own country. One late American colonial example is revealing. In 1732 there appeared in London an anonymous tract, *A New and Accurate Account of the Provinces of South Carolina*. This has been attributed to General James Oglethorpe, then preparing to launch his Georgia colony. The work was designed to silence critics of the project, and the author appealed to history for his answer to them. There is, he said,

> a Precedent of our own for planting Colonies, which perhaps, in Part, or in the Whole, may be worthy of our Imitation. England was more than four Hundred Years in Possession of a great part of Ireland. . . . In the Days of King James the First, the Londoners were at the Charge of sending into the most dangerous Part of that Kingdom more than four Hundred poor Families. There were a City, and a Town built, as had been agreed on: The City of London-derry contained three Hundred, the Town of Colerain a Hundred Houses; these were fortified with Walls and Ditches, and established with most ample Privileges.[2]

It is not strange that when Oglethorpe came to lay out his chief city of Savannah he introduced into its plan a repeating pattern of open squares that closely resembled the market square of Coleraine. Nor should one wonder that his garrison community of Frederica resembled a typical new town of Ulster in Northern Ireland with its castle, fortified courtyard or bawn, and house lots for the settler-soldiers laid out nearby in rectangular order. Oglethorpe was a meticulous planner, whether of towns, military expeditions, or systems of land tenure. In neither versatility nor knowledge of history, however, did he surpass some of his countrymen under whose jurisdiction the towns with which we are concerned came into being.

We should, therefore, cast our net far in attempting to capture those historical precedents that may have served as models, even unconsciously, for the town planners of colonial Virginia and Maryland. Our search begins in medieval times at a period when English town planning activities resulted in the creation of several dozen new communities. It was then that the English tradition of town design began, to continue, though with periods of inaction, through the era of American colonization.[3]

When Edward I became king in 1272 on the death of his father, Henry III, he was on a crusade in the Holy Land. He returned to England by way of France, where he remained for two years consolidating his control over the Duchy of Guienne. This area of southwestern France had come under English jurisdiction through the marriage of Henry II to Eleanor of Aquitaine. The territory centered around Bordeaux as the principal military stronghold, port, and administrative headquarters. To strengthen his domain and to make it more productive Edward set about planning a series of new towns on strategic sites dominating transportation routes and the fertile land of the river valleys.

In this policy Edward was simply following a practice long in use in this and adjoining regions by the kings of France and the counts of Toulouse. In some cases new towns were planned and built by royal decree on land already available. In perhaps the majority of the cases, however, the town resulted from a treaty of *paréage* between the king or count and the owner of the land, who might be a lesser lord or an abbey. In the latter case the landowner provided the site and the king or count constructed the walls and fortifications. The profits were then shared between the two. New settlers were attracted by grants of town lots and agricultural land and, usually, through the offering of certain market and other privileges. A common stipulation, much later to be used in many of the new towns of the Tidewater in America, required those receiving town lands to construct a house on the site within one or two years.[4]

These towns of southwestern France were known as *bastides*. More than two hundred still exist, most of them dating from the latter part of the thirteenth century. Whether of French or English origin, their plans were similar in broad outlines but exhibited a good deal of variety in their internal arrangements.[5] Except on very steep and restricted sites the street system is generally rectangular though not always of geometric regularity. Virtually all of them have a market square near the center of the town, many of these squares being surrounded by buildings with overhanging second floors to provide an arcaded walkway around the square. While the church in a few of the *bastides* fronts directly on the central square, its site in most cases can be found on a second open square, either touching one corner of the market place or located one or two blocks away.

The open spaces in the grid street pattern are invariably of the "medieval" type. That is, they are bordered on all four sides by streets. The square, then, becomes merely an unbuilt-on block in the normal grid. While most of the "squares" are, in fact, square, in some of the *bastides* they take the form of elongated rectangles and in fewer cases are distinctly irregular in shape.

These communities followed the normal medieval practice of containing all of the dwellings of those farming the lands in the immediate surroundings. There were few if any isolated farmsteads. Those who tilled the fields or cared for the cattle returned to the *bastide* in the evening to dwell behind the security of the walled and ditched perimeter, which was interrupted at intervals by gates and watchtowers.

One of Edward's *bastides* was Monpazier, founded for him by Jean de Grailly in 1284.[6] Its orthogonal plan (figure 1) is defined by streets twenty-four and sixteen feet wide and a system of six-foot lanes or alleys serving the rear of the rectangular building plots. Monpazier was a royal *bastide,*

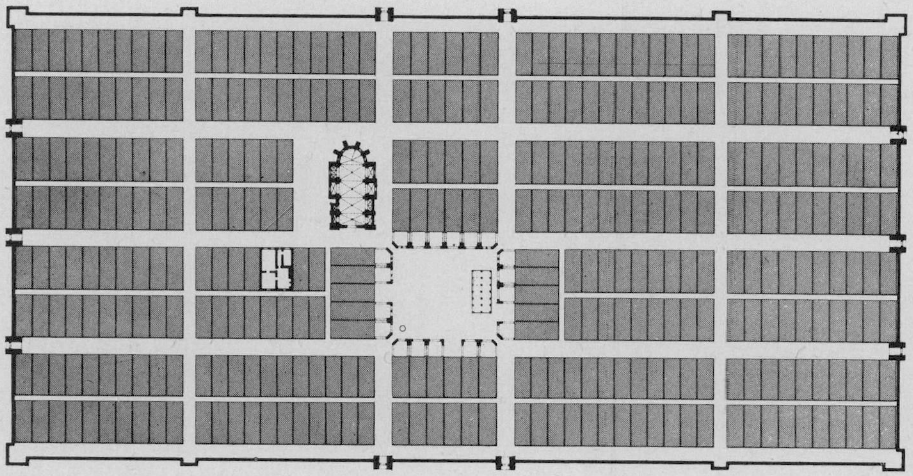

Figure 1. Plan of Monpazier, France: 1284

created solely by the initiative of Edward who granted its charter and put it in the charge of a bailiff or *senéchal.* Beaumont-en-Périgord, the central portion of which is shown in figure 2 was created, on the other hand, through a treaty of *paréage* with the Abbé de Cadouin in the first year of Edward's reign. Here the market place is slightly irregular in shape, although essentially rectangular. The plan very clearly shows the arcades around the market place, so characteristic of the *bastides.* These were but two of many created by Edward and of numerous others resulting from similar activities by the French.[7]

When he returned to England, Edward put to good use the experience gained in Gascony. The collapse of Welsh resistance on England's western border led eventually to a program of internal colonization. Edward constructed or rebuilt a series of castles as centers of English power and near many of them planned new towns to be peopled by trustworthy English who could be counted on to assert control over the newly won province. The first of these towns apparently was Beaumaris. This was soon followed by the planned communities of Flint, Carnarvon, Conway, and others. The layout of Flint (figure 3) closely resembles the earlier *bastide* plans in France, with a market square and a separate site for the church fitted into its tidy rectangular street system. The main street of the little town runs from the wall and ditch at the southwestern end of the community, past the church, then to the market square and guildhall, and through the gate at the other end of town to the castle on the shore. The plan of Carnarvon (figure 4) appears to depart from the

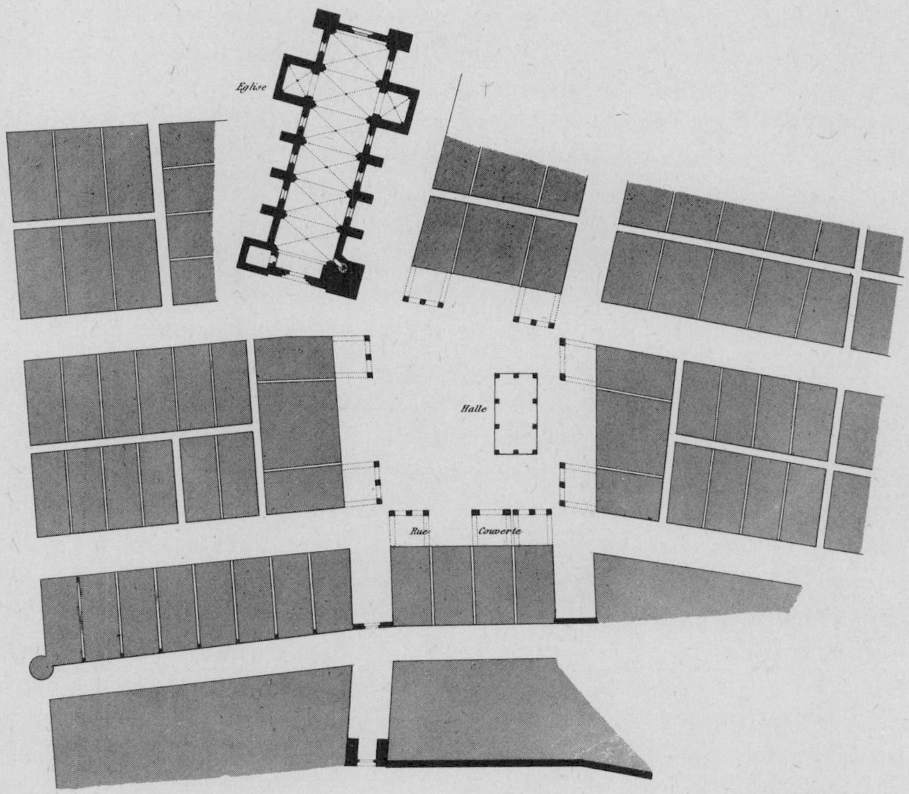

Figure 2. Plan of a Portion of Beaumont en Perigord, France: 1272

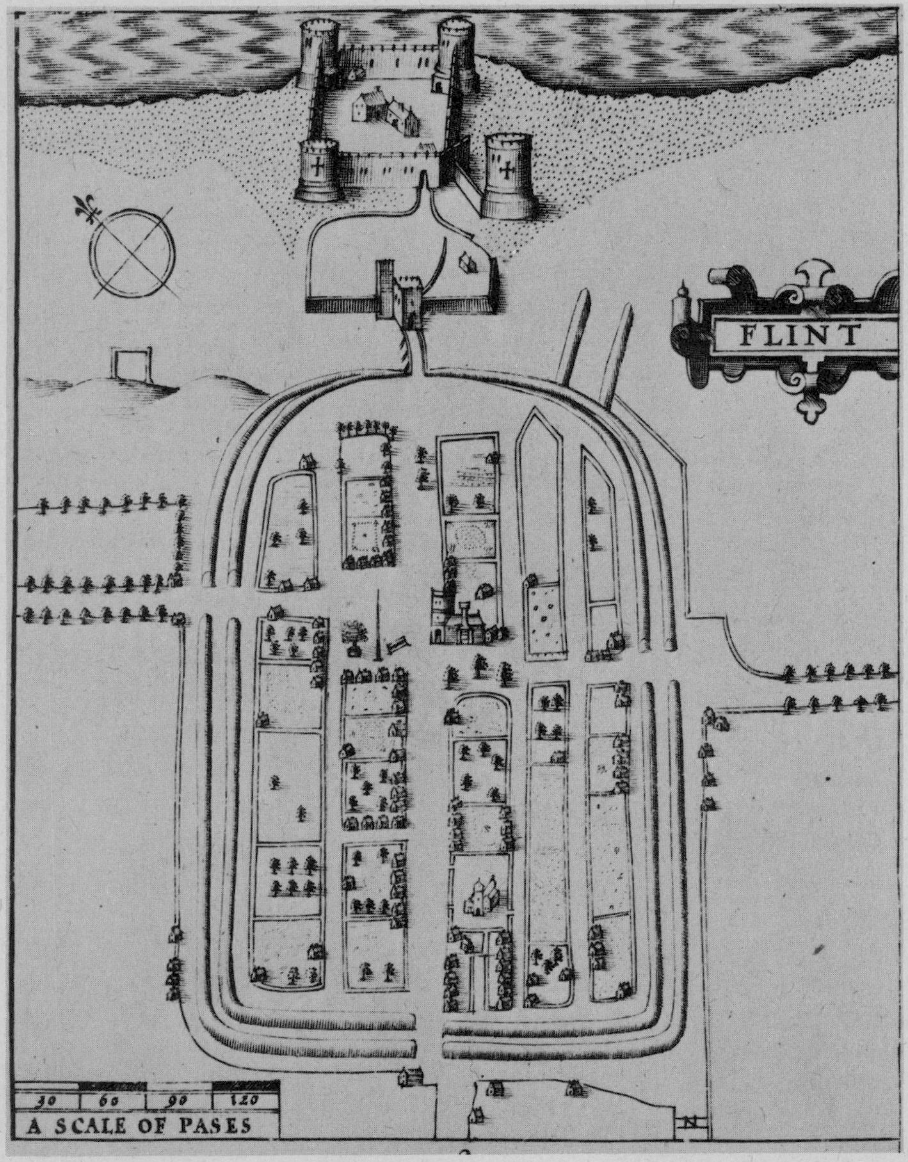

Figure 3. Plan of Flint, Wales: 1610

bastide pattern. Although the streets are rectangular, no separate market square apparently was provided in the original design.

In size and importance in the modern era the most prominent of Edward's new towns was Hull. Its site on the eastern coast of England was already occupied by a small settlement, but in 1293 the lands passed to the king, who proceeded to create a much larger community with a generally regular street pattern and many new and reconstructed buildings (figure 5). A few years later, in 1296, Edward attempted the founding of another new town not far away at Berwick-on-Tweed. To a meeting at Bury St. Edmunds Edward directed the City of London to send "four wise men of the most knowing and most sufficient who know best how to devise, order and array a new town to the most profit of the king and of merchants."[8] A short time later the king issued a series of writs to no less than twenty-three other cities and boroughs to send two representatives each with identical qualifications. This remarkable action indicates that town planning was a subject of considerable interest and an activity well known in medieval England.

Although the Berwick plan never materialized, an earlier and rather different project in the south of England was carried out under Edward's direction by a team of experts summoned for the purpose of advising him on town planning. This project was for Winchelsea, a new community to replace one of the same name, the site of which was suffering serious erosion by the sea. Three miles away on the estuary of the river Brede stood a rise safely above flood level but still suitable for port facilities. Among the town planners was one Itier of Angoulême, a Gascon on whom Edward had previously relied for similar help in France.[9] The design of the town (figure 6) incorporated thirty-nine square blocks in its geometric grid, and soon the residents of Old Winchelsea began to build in this new port. The town today has a certain charm, though its intended function as a port was never fully realized. The river estuary gradually silted up, and the town, deprived of its economic justification, lost most of its population.

The Edwardian towns of thirteenth-century Britain were not the first planned communities in the country. The Norman castle of Ludlow was built by Roger de Lacy not long after the Conquest. Early in the following century the town itself was planned in a series of parallel and cross streets creating a little gridiron of elongated blocks.[10] Richard I was evidently responsible for the founding of Portsmouth in 1189, entrusting the task of preparing its plan to his sheriff, Gervase of Southampton.[11]

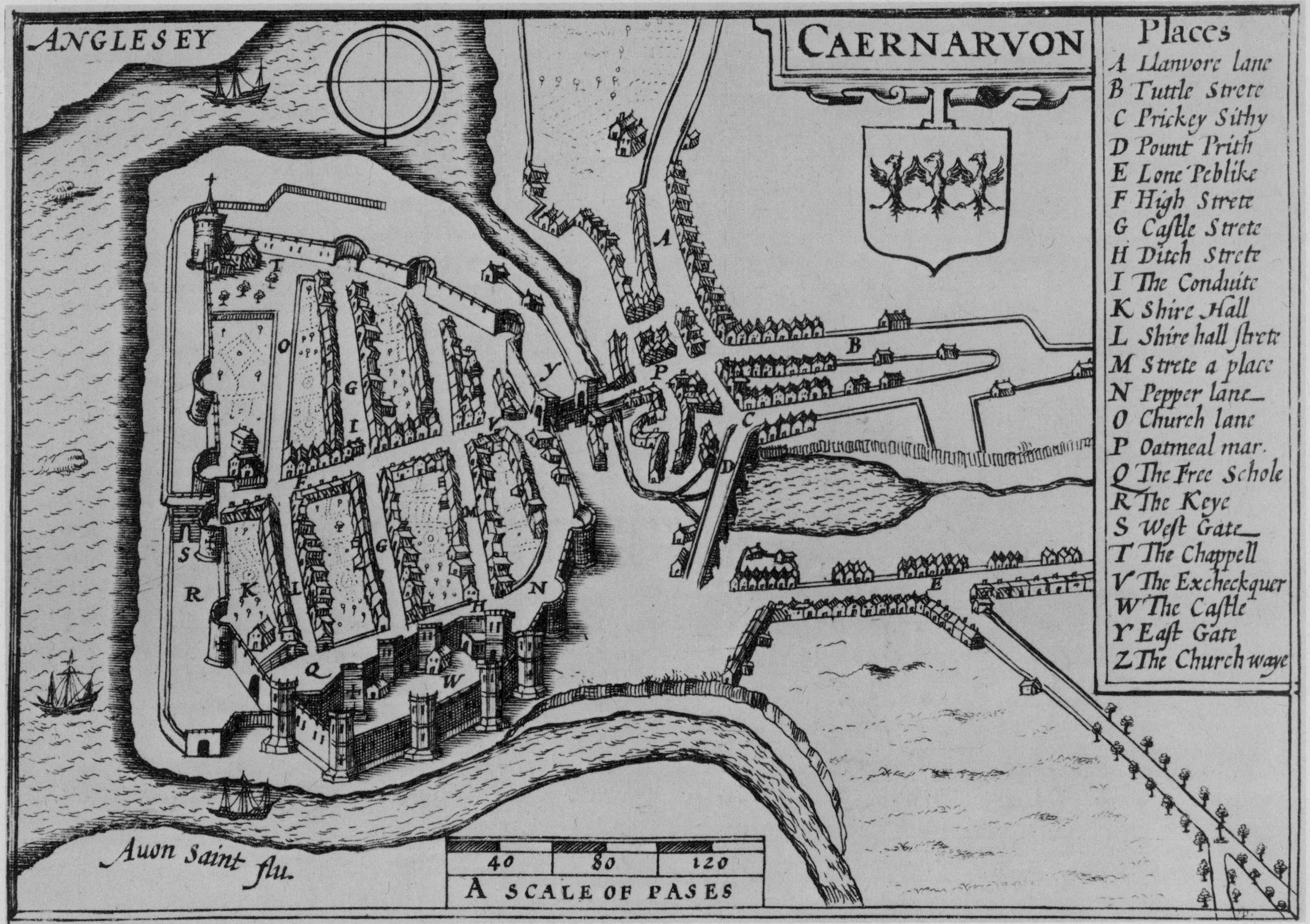
ANGLESEY
CAERNARVON
Places
A Llanvore lane
B Tuttle Strete
C Prickey Sithy
D Pount Prith
E Lone Peblike
F High Strete
G Castle Strete
H Ditch Strete
I The Conduite
K Shire Hall
L Shire hall strete
M Strete a place
N Pepper lane
O Church lane
P Oatmeal mar.
Q The Free Schole
R The Keye
S West Gate
T The Chappell
V The Excheckquer
W The Castle
Y East Gate
Z The Church waye
Auon Saint flu.
40
80
120
A SCALE OF PASES

Figure 4. Plan of Caernarvon, Wales: 1610

Figure 5. Plan of Hull, England: 1610

Perhaps the most important of these pre-Edwardian ventures in town design was that for New Sarem or Salisbury early in the thirteenth century. Old Sarem, now an archaeological park, had developed on a hilltop site. In 1220 Bishop Richard le Poer decided to move the cathedral to the valley two miles to the south. There he built one of the architectural glories of England set in a spacious close and with the bishop's palace nearby. To induce settlement at the new location he planned a town to the north of the cathedral on a checkerboard pattern that included a large market place. John Speed's plan of 1610 (figure 7) shows the prosperous town much as it must have looked within a short time after its founding. The drawing reveals one interesting feature that may have been part of the original design—the system of streams, supplied by water from the Avon River, running down most of the streets. Founded for commercial and ecclesiastical purposes, Salisbury had no surrounding ring of fortifications. The size of the cathedral close also far exceeded in area the more restricted sites for churches set aside in the French and Welsh *bastides*. In its other aspects, however, Salisbury conformed generally to the patterns employed in other medieval new towns at home and abroad.[12]

While the intensive creation of new towns that marked the reign of King Edward I did not continue for long, there was never a complete break in the tradition of English planning. If we find few examples of planned town development in the fifteenth and sixteenth centuries, we must not ignore achievements in creating well-designed portions of cities. In particular, the construction of many of the quadrangles of Oxford and Cambridge universities may be cited as evidence that order and beauty in large-scale organization of urban space had not been forgotten.

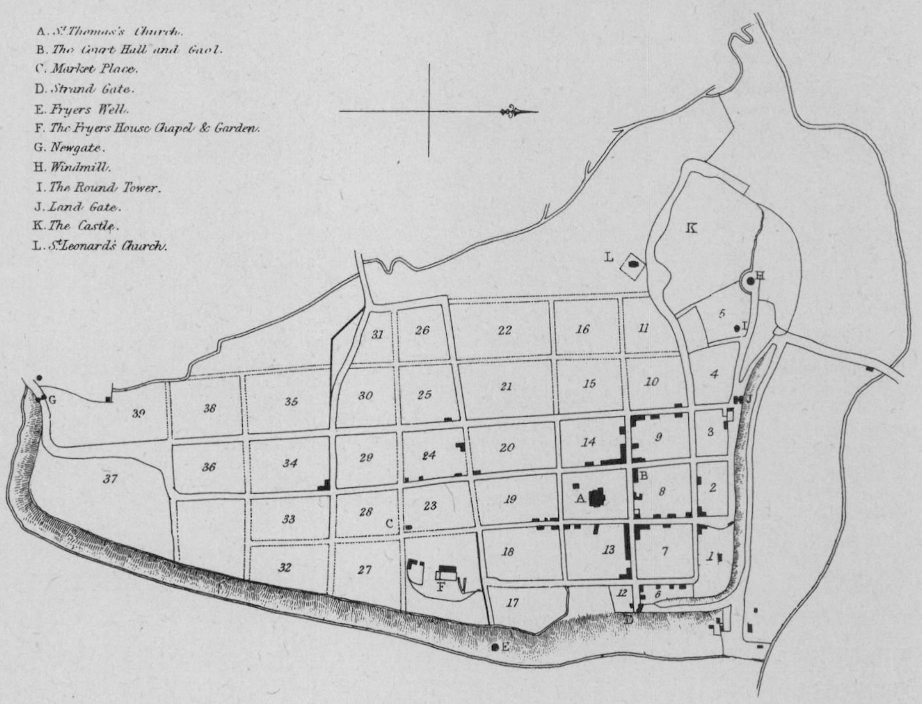

Figure 6. Plan of Winchelsea, England: 1853

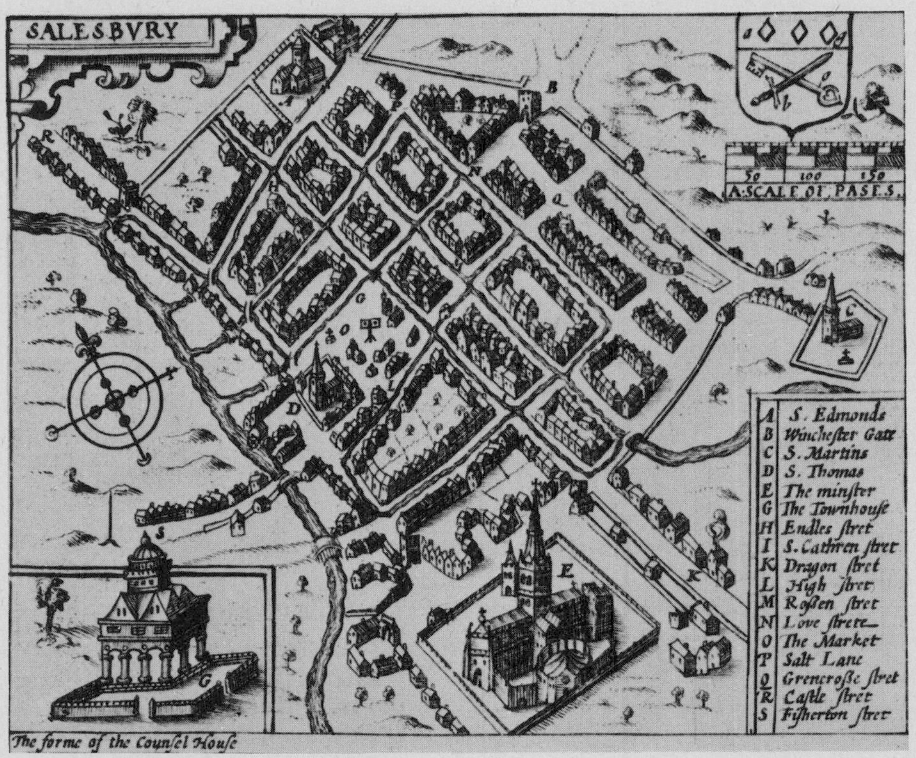

Figure 7. Plan of Salisbury, England: 1610

There was, in addition, the city of Calais, planned by Edward III, grandson and namesake of Edward I, in 1347. This mighty fortified port is shown in figure 8 as it appeared about 1557. The plan represents an elaboration on the simpler and much smaller *bastide* designs, but the underlying structure of the town was essentially similar to those earlier English communities laid out in France.

Earlier than all of these planned towns were, of course, the many carefully designed settlements established in England by the Romans, first as military camps and then as civil communities. While medieval encroachments had begun to blur the geometric precision of these gridiron settlements, many of them still exhibited substantial portions of their original plans. Perhaps the most regular was Chester, but Colchester, Gloucester, and Chichester, among others, also showed in their generally rectangular street system the Roman origins so clearly indicated by the incorporation into their names of *castra,* the Latin word for camp.[13]

Coinciding with the beginning of attempts to colonize the New World a number of English publications appeared that recalled this tradition of town founding. Two are of particular importance and must have been familiar to virtually everyone engaged in colonization activities. The first was William Camden's elaborate history, *Britannia,* first published in 1586 and reissued in at least six editions before 1607, with still later versions translated into English from the original Latin.[14]

With the exception of the first Edward's work in southern France, the whole English tradition of town development was recalled in this gigantic work. Camden included a discussion of the birth of English cities in Roman forts as well as a review of how the Romans went about establishing cities as an essential part of building their empire. Edward's

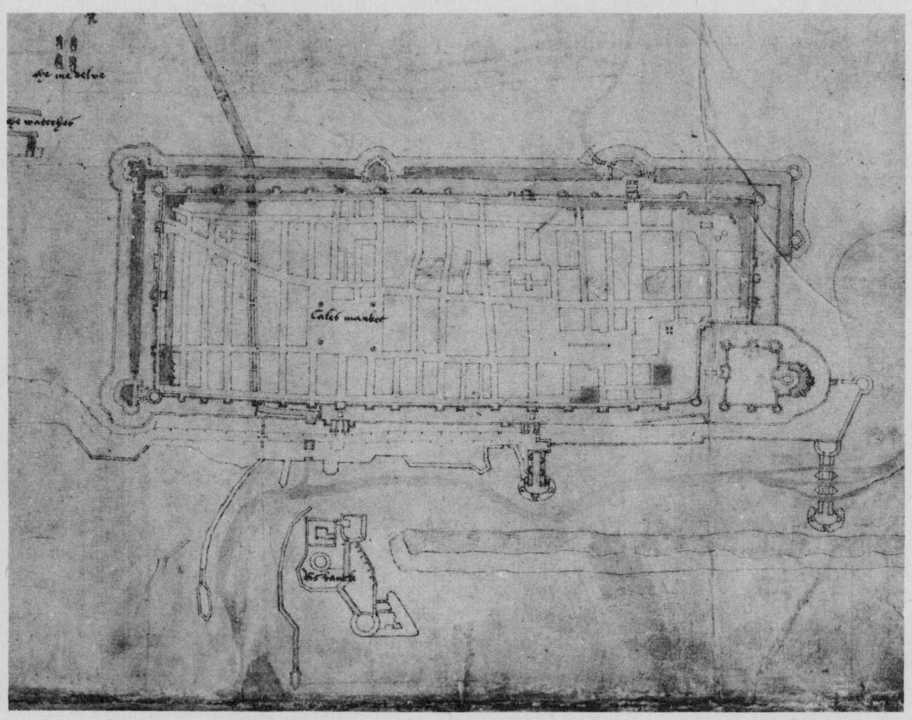

Figure 8. Plan of Calais, France: ca. 1557

founding of Carnarvon, Conway, Hull, and Winchelsea appears, along with an account of how the new town of Salisbury was developed. The large number of editions indicates the popularity with which this work was received. Those who read its pages must have come away with a clear and strong impression of the essential role of towns and cities in the development of their civilization.

The second of these works was published only four years after the first settlement of Virginia and came at a time when the thoughts of the leaders of that enterprise must inevitably have turned to the functions, forms, and locations that towns should take. This was John Speed's *Theatre of the Empire of Great Britaine* published in 1611. Although it had almost certainly not been the intention of its author, this atlas and geography of the British Isles provided a handy catalogue of town plans for any who had the imagination to use it in this manner.

The book was composed of folio atlas sheets showing maps of each county. It also provided for the first time a printed collection of town plans for the major cities of Britain. These appeared as inset plans on the county sheets. (Figures 3, 4, 5, and 7 are examples.) The *Theatre* thus also indirectly reviewed the great period of new town planning in Britain that had seen the creation of these communities. Text on the back of the atlas sheets described the circumstances of the founding of some of these towns. In addition, the plans of such cities as Chichester, Colchester, York, and Chester plainly showed a regular street pattern, suggesting their Roman origins. Oxford, which may well have been a Roman town, was also depicted with its two major streets crossing at right angles at Carfax. This Oxfordshire map with the inset town plan of Oxford had been issued earlier by Speed as a separate sheet in 1605.[15]

Other printed town plans had been published prior to this time. The Elizabethans and Tudors possessed an insatiable appetite for knowledge of the world in which they lived, and the demand for maps and town plans was substantial. John Norden, for example, anticipated Speed in providing an inset plan of the shire town in his county map of Sussex issued in 1595. Norden's inset plan of Chichester (figure 9) clearly shows the rectangular street pattern of that town whose origins stem from the Roman occupation of Britain.[16] It was Speed's *Theatre,* however, that marked the beginning of widespread publication of plans of British cities.

The many subsequent reprintings of Speed's work attest to the attention it received. The importance of the publication, appearing almost simultaneously with the first successful efforts to settle Virginia, is obvious. At the very beginning of attempted urban development in the tidewater colonies virtually every English colonial administrator must have known something of the variety of urban patterns existing in the home country. At least some of them must also have been curious enough to inquire about the origins of those towns with geometric patterns and to ponder the applicability of such plans in the settlement of North America.

The rediscovery of the English tradition in town planning, aided by the publication of such volumes as Camden's and Speed's, may have influenced the planning of towns in the English settlement of Northern Ireland. It was here that a new era of town founding began and provided experience that could be utilized in the more extensive colonies of North America. One cannot understand English colonization in America, including the development of town planning theory and practice and the role that towns were expected to play, without some knowledge of the earlier overseas colonial venture. The real frontier for English colonization in the latter part of the sixteenth century and the first decades of the seventeenth lay in nearby and familiar Ireland rather than on the strange and distant shores of North America.

Among those most prominent in the attempts to settle Englishmen in the New World, many had first-hand experience in similar efforts in Ireland when the English mounted a concerted program to re-establish their hegemony over this rebellious land. Some, like Thomas Hariot and John White, succeeded in Ireland where they had failed in Carolina. Others, including Richard Grenville, Walter Raleigh, and Humphrey Gilbert, acquired their earliest colonial experience in Ireland before turning their attention to the greater prize across the North Atlantic. Many, perhaps the majority, of those most active in the Virginia Company, which was responsible for the ultimate founding of Jamestown and other early Virginia settlements, were deeply involved in Irish colonization as well.[17]

Indeed, as David Quinn suggests, the failure of Raleigh's own Roanoke colony in 1586 may have been caused in part by the attention devoted by Grenville and Raleigh to their individual interests in the Munster County colonization project in Ireland that same year. Settlement in Ireland and final subjugation of the Irish preceded the effort in America both in point of time and in resources mobilized for the purpose.

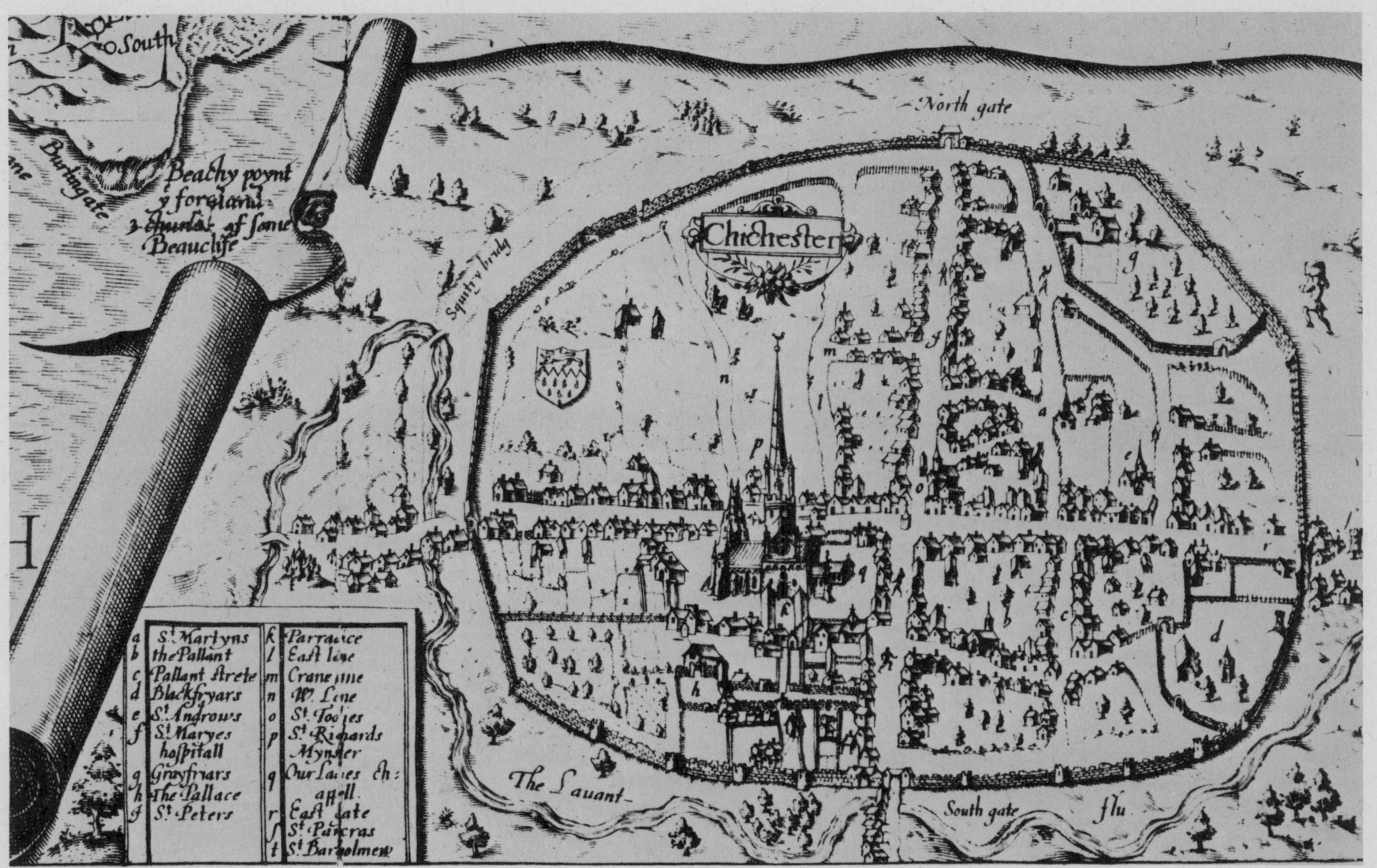

Figure 9. Plan of Chichester, England: 1595

It is useful as a guide to understanding the settlement policies and techniques employed by the English in North America to look briefly at certain aspects of that other earlier and nearer frontier. Two features of English colonial policy in Ireland are of particular importance. These are the role that towns were expected to play in the whole enterprise and the forms that their plans took.

In the middle of the sixteenth century English control of Ireland was at best precarious. Between 1520 and 1547 the island had been partially reconquered, but numerous military posts were necessary to keep the uneasy peace. It became apparent that English settlers in fairly large numbers would be required to establish some kind of stability. In 1551 Sir James Croft suggested settling a colony of English soldiers and their families in the province of Munster.[18] In 1565 Sir Henry Sidney, lord deputy of Ireland, advocated the creation of a series of privately financed colonies in Ulster, the most northerly province of the island.[19] These suggestions, among several of the period, did not stem entirely from considerations of how best to pacify Ireland. They were based as well on the desire for property, for personal power, and for the wealth that might be gained by systematic exploitation of the land, its native population, and English colonists who might be induced to settle there.

Sir Thomas Smith, public official, scholar, and philosopher, advanced a proposal for an Irish settlement that is of special interest. Smith's knowledge of history strongly influenced his scheme for colonization, and it is fitting that his ideas were to affect in indirect ways the subsequent course of English colonization.[20] In the year 1571 he petitioned the queen for a land grant in Ireland to be settled at his own expense. He issued a broadside to advertise his colonization plan, appealing for support from adventurers, and he also published a book describing a proposed policy for Irish settlement. In that volume we find his first and rather brief references to towns. He proposed to develop "one haven [port] with common granyers [granaries] made upon the key, sufficient for the receipt of the corne of the Cuntry, and one Poste Town builded, as soon as we may begin to be any thing settled."[21]

Elizabeth approved the requested grant of land late in 1571 but then dispatched Smith to France as ambassador, and responsibility for organizing the details of the project fell to his son. From France, however, Smith wrote a steady flow of letters of advice and criticism. On April 10, 1572, he instructed the younger Smith of the first requirement: "For the first year there, and peradventure the second, ye shall do well to take one sure and convenient place to make a fort, as Byrsa was to Dido, and Mons Aventinus to Romulus, and there to fortify yourself; and that being strong and provided to live and defend, may master the country about."[22] A month later he wrote again about the "principal city, which I would were called *Elizabetha*. . . ." Here he proposed that each "assistant," the chief investors in the scheme who were to participate in governing the territory with Smith and his son,

> have a place of ground, to make his palace or chief residence, of our giving . . . with condition to maintain in the chief castle or citadel of the city Elizabetha, one tower, against all the Queen's Majesty's enemies. I reckon that you can do nothing till you have a strong town, as a magazine of victuals, a retreat in time of danger, and a safe place for the merchants. Mark Rome, Carthage, Venice and all other where any notable beginning hath them.

The town was to be "so large that within it, in time, walls, towers, streets and market places may be made, and in the mean, the magazines of victuals and munitions, and all the merchants and traffickers may be in surity."

The colony, therefore, was to have one central city to serve both as a strong point for military purposes and as a center for the necessary civil activities of administration and commerce. Smith summed up the advantages of compact rather than dispersed settlement: "This habitation together engendereth civility, policy, acquaintance, consultation, and a firm and sure seat."[23] This policy was to be echoed again and again by those ultimately responsible for the administration of the American tidewater colonies throughout the seventeenth century.

The Smith proposal was well received in England. In May, 1572, some eight hundred persons gathered in Liverpool ready to sail to Ireland under the leadership of the younger Smith. Then everything began to go wrong. The Irish learned of the expedition and threatened violence. Elizabeth postponed the sailing date, and by the time she decided to allow the party to depart most of the would-be colonists had dispersed. When the younger Smith finally left for Ireland toward the end of August his force numbered only about a hundred persons. In Ireland they discovered that the hostility of the native population made their bold plans impossible to execute. Smith's son proved an inept leader, and his own men turned against him.

Reinforcements sent from England never arrived. Finally young Smith was assassinated by his Irish servants.

Still Sir Thomas clung to his ideas of colonization and mounted a second effort in 1574. He prepared a highly detailed program setting forth all aspects of the colony's government, financial support, and methods of land disposition.[24] Included was a plan of the chief city. It called for a rectangular street system with a central market place and a broad street around the perimeter giving ready access to the protective fortifications.[25] Doubtless Smith drew on his knowledge of Roman colonization and the methods of castremation or military encampment design. It is not improbable that he knew something of the history of the English *bastide* towns in southern France of the thirteenth century, and he surely was aware of the similar towns established by Edward I in the home country. Calais, as planned by the English under Edward III, may also have served as a source of ideas.

But Elizabetha was never to be established. Smith's second expedition reached Ireland in August and at first was successful in establishing a base of operations. In November, 1574, however, the Irish rose against the English and were able to drive them from the area. In the spring of 1575 Smith conceded that his project had failed and surrendered his claims to the earl of Essex. It was not to be the last attempt at foreign colonization that collapsed when faced with the harsh realities of a strange land, a hostile population, and lack of adequate support from the mother country.

Subsequently the English erected a number of forts in Ireland as strong points from which military force could be used to subdue the natives and settle the land with yeoman from the home country. In this respect Ireland and Virginia came to be viewed by the English in much the same light. One of these forts bears a strong resemblance to the form given by the settlers at Jamestown to the first town of Virginia. This is reproduced in the lower portion of figure 10, one of a series of recently discovered manuscript plans and views executed by Richard Bartlett for Charles Blount, lord deputy Mountjoy, who succeeded the earl of Essex as head of the English forces in Ireland in 1600.

The drawing shows the fort at Blackwater erected by Mountjoy in July, 1601. The enclosure is a modified triangle, with two of the sides bent outwards at their middle, while that facing the river angles inward toward the group of structures surrounding the triangular mustering ground at the

Figure 10. Plan of Armagh and the Fort at Blackwater, Northern Ireland: ca. 1601

center. Three bastions at the corners of the fort provided emplacements for cannon. As will be discussed in the chapter to follow, this plan was to be duplicated almost exactly at Jamestown, and it is far from inconceivable that this Irish fortification only a few years earlier may have served as a model for the stockaded James Fort.

Eventually, of course, Ireland was conquered. In the process a number of towns were newly planned as military, administrative, and market centers. Some of this experience was to be influential in the English colonization of North America, the first period of which largely coincided with the pacification of Ireland and the creation of many of its towns. Most important of the new towns in Ireland was Londonderry on the River Foyle in Ulster. One of the last of the Irish outposts, it was captured temporarily in 1600 by an English force led by Sir Henry Docwra. That attack and the earlier explosion of a powder magazine in 1568 had left the town severely damaged. Docwra's reconstruction plan included a proposed extension to the south (figure 11). Here we see an attempt to provide rectangular order through the creation of six additional blocks served by straight streets intersecting at right angles. This was apparently never executed, as Londonderry was retaken by the Irish in an engagement that virtually destroyed the town and made its complete rebuilding necessary.[26]

In September, 1607, the flight of the Irish earls, O'Neill of Tyrone and O'Donnell of Tyrconnell, marked the end of organized Irish resistance to the brutal conquest by the English. A program of wholesale colonization was now possible, and it was Ulster that became the center of English activities toward this end. The vast lands of the earls were declared forfeit, confiscated by the crown, and made available for settlement. Sir Arthur Chichester, the lord deputy of Ireland, supervised a survey of the new royal domain. The results of the survey reached London in 1608 where a committee immediately went to work on a plan for the disposition of the lands and related matters.[27] Their recommendations, dealing almost entirely with county Tyrone, were made to the council on December 20, 1608. They were supplemented shortly by proposals affecting all six of the Ulster counties.

The plan envisaged land grants to private "undertakers," subject to certain requirements. Grantees receiving two thousand acres had to construct a castle and a "bawn," or fortified courtyard. Persons granted

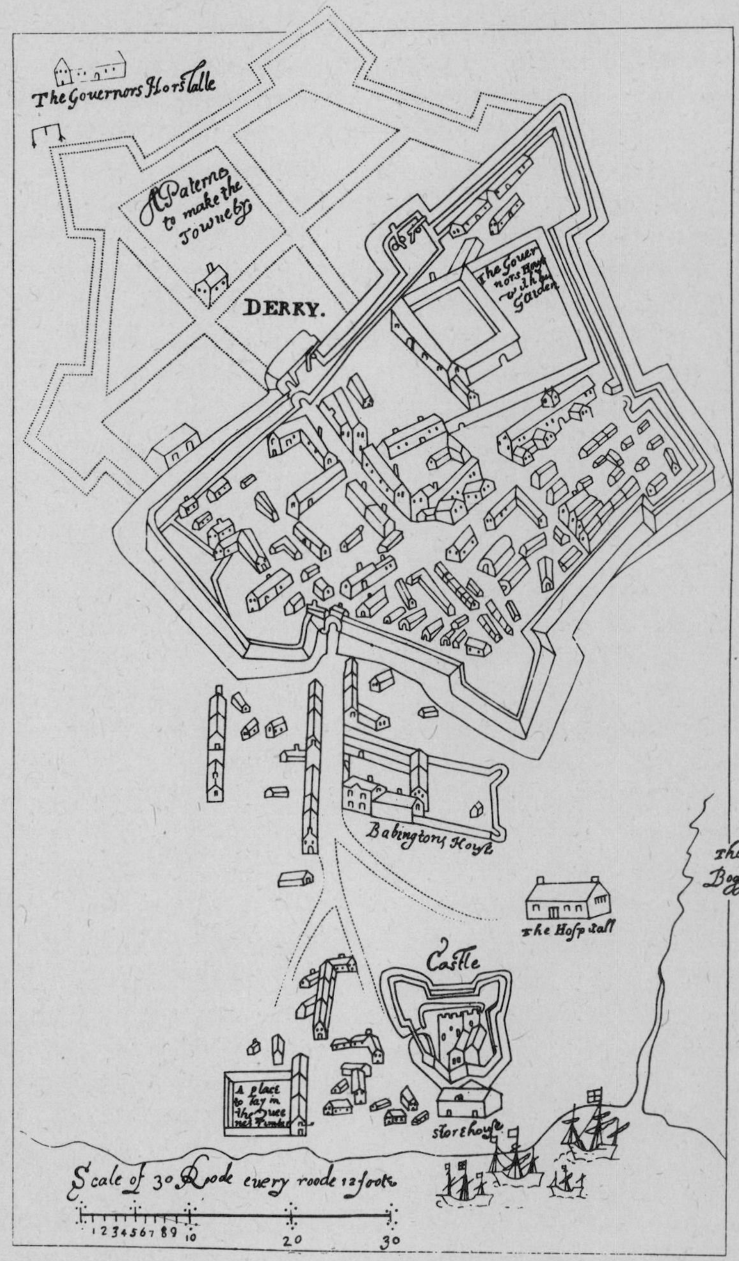

Figure 11. Plan of Londonderry, Northern Ireland: 1600

fifteen hundred acres were to build a house of brick or stone and a bawn. Those offered a thousand acres had to agree only to the erection of a bawn. All buildings were to be completed within two years, during which period the undertakers were to bring as settlers an adequate number of Scottish or English tenants to work the land. The houses for these tenants were to be grouped in small villages. Finally, a number of sites for "corporate towns, or boroughs" were designated: five in Tyrone, two in Coleraine, six in Donegal, three in Fermanagh, three in Cavan, and four in Armagh.

This proposal, either in draft form or as completed shortly thereafter, was reviewed in 1608 by Francis Bacon who submitted his observations to James I in January of the following year. Bacon's recommendations are of interest because they foreshadow later English policy proposed for the tidewater colonies in America—proposals that, as will be discussed in a later chapter, were to prove essentially unworkable.

Bacon criticized the concept of scattered settlement in small villages and recommended "that the building be altogether in towns, to be compounded as well of husbandries as of arts." He gave several reasons for this position. In a smaller number of larger settlements craftsmen could be used more efficiently since "one of them will the better supply the wants of another." Fewer roads would be required, and these could be "made more passable for carriages to . . . towns than . . . to a number of dispersed solitary places." Bacon also asserted that it would be far easier to provide an adequate supply of food for a few towns than for many villages. Finally, he suggested that a limited number of well-fortified towns would provide better and less costly protection against attack than the "bawns" that were to be constructed "about every castle or house."

Anticipating the argument that this policy of exclusive settlement in towns might be regarded as undesirable by farmers who would be forced to travel some distance from towns to their fields, Bacon proposed that the number of towns could be increased. He recommended that these be located in the center of the "portions assigned to them: for in the champion countries of England, where the habitation useth to be in towns, and not dispersed, it is no new thing to go two miles off to plough part of their grounds; and two miles compass will take up a good deal of country."[28]

There were other objections to the proposal, including those of Sir Arthur Chichester under whose authority as lord deputy much of the colonization scheme would fall. The project was therefore postponed, Chichester and others were directed to prepare a modified plan, and the crown at the same time began a series of negotiations with the city of London to secure the financial backing of the city companies for at least a portion of the colonization program. After further preparations, proposals, and modifications a final plan of action materialized by 1610.

By articles of agreement signed on January 28 of that year the London companies received all of the county of Coleraine and large portions of several adjoining counties, the new territory being known as county of Londonderry. The companies and the city of London agreed to build two new towns, Derry (or Londonderry) and Coleraine. Work on this project was to begin immediately. Two hundred houses were to be constructed at Londonderry with space left for three hundred more; at Coleraine one hundred houses were to be completed with room set aside for an additional two hundred. Sixty houses in Derry and forty in Coleraine were to be finished by November 1, 1610.[29] Within a year from that date the entire number of dwellings and the town fortifications were to be provided. By separate action the city of London created a corporate body known as the Irish Society, under whose responsibility the planning and construction of the two towns was to be carried out.

In the five remaining counties the earlier plan of land grants to private individuals was followed with some slight modifications. The various sites designated for towns were separately conveyed to some of the private undertakers who agreed to design and construct the new urban settlements. Lord Deputy Arthur Chichester, for example, was himself one of the undertakers and was responsible for the development of Belfast in Antrim at the end of Belfast Lough. As early as 1611 the commissioners appointed by the king to oversee the Ulster program could report that "the town of Belfast is plotted out in a good form, wherein are many families of English, Scotch and some Manx-men already inhabiting, of which some are artificers who have built good timber houses with chimneys."[30] Sir Arthur was also responsible for the development of Dungannon in Tyrone, and during the first years of the settlement many other private undertakers were busily engaged in planning and building new towns and villages.

The city companies were also at work. The plans of their two towns, intended as the chief settlements of the entire region of Ulster, are believed to be the work of one Thomas Raven, although Sir Edward Doddington may have been responsible for their design with Raven carrying out the

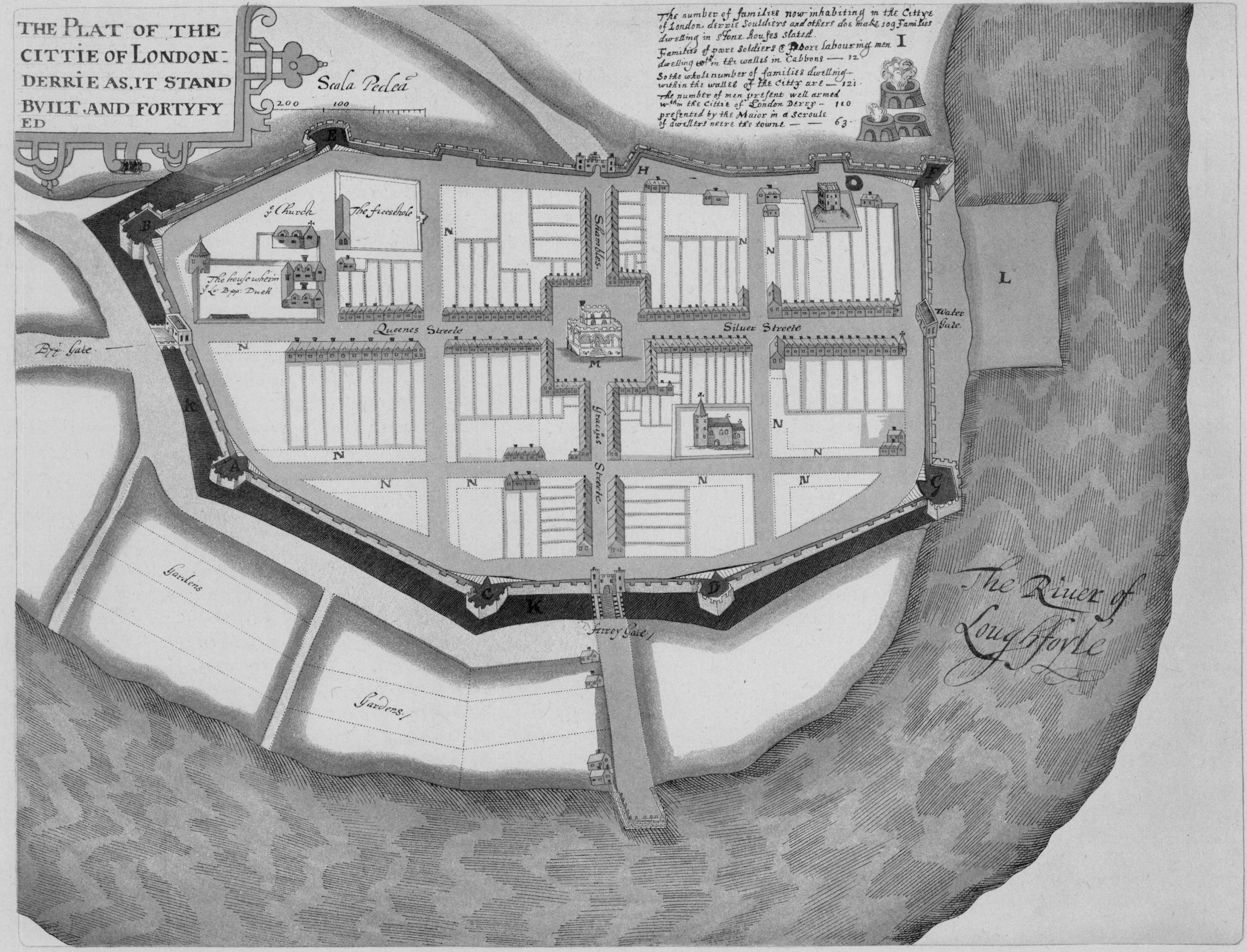

Figure 12. Plan of Londonderry, Northern Ireland: 1622

necessary surveys.[31] The plan of Londonderry in 1622, as originally laid out eleven years earlier, is reproduced in figure 12. This was the most formal and elaborate of the Ulster towns, befitting its intended function as the chief city of the province. Captain Nicholas Pynnar, appointed by the crown to inspect the progress of the city, submitted the following report and description of it in 1619:

> The city of London-Derry is now compassed about with a very strong wall . . . being all good lime and stone; the circuit whereof is two hundred and eighty-four perches and two-thirds at eighteen feet to the perch; besides the four gates which contain eighty-four feet; and in every place of the wall it is twenty-four feet high, and six feet thick. . . . All things are very well and substantially done, saving there wanteth a house for the soldiers to watch in, and a centinnell house for the soldiers to stand in in the night to defend them from the weather. . . . Since the last survey, there is built a school, which is sixty-seven feet in length, and twenty-five feet in breadth, with two other small houses. Other building there is not any within the city. The whole number of houses within the city are ninety-two, and in them there are one hundred and two families.[32]

This plan is certainly one of the earliest expressions in Britain of Renaissance urban design concepts. The central open space is perfectly square, with the four principal streets entering it at the mid-points of each of its four sides. This followed Renaissance planning theory as developed much earlier on the continent of Europe by Leone Battista Alberti in his *De Re Aedificatoria,* published in 1485, and Andrea Palladio in his *I Quattro Libri dell' Architettura,* which appeared in 1570. They and lesser known but still important architects advocated symmetrical street patterns and the use of squares and plazas as devices to terminate imposing vistas along principal avenues. On the plan of Londonderry the large structure in the center of the square is elsewhere identified as "The forme of a citadell fitting to have beene built in the market place." A less impressive building was eventually constructed to serve as a town hall, market building, and jail.

Londonderry's plan is an almost exact duplicate of one of the few completely new towns of Renaissance France, Vitry-le-François, designed for Francis I by the Italian Hieronimo Marino in 1545. In the numerous books on military encampment there were other possible precedents available in the drawings of ideal military communities. One of these, Robert Barret's *Theorike and Practike of Modern Warres,* had appeared in London in 1598 and contained a design for a garrison community not too unlike the plan used at Londonderry.[33]

The form of Londonderry's square was to be repeated many times in the urbanization of North America. Champlain had already employed the same device in his abortive plan for the French settlement on Sainte Croix Island off the coast of Maine in 1604. It is not surprising that in some of the tidewater towns, as in such large cities as Philadelphia, it would be used by English colonial town planners.

Coleraine's plan, dating also from 1611, incorporated a different design for the central place (figure 13). The market was reached by four streets

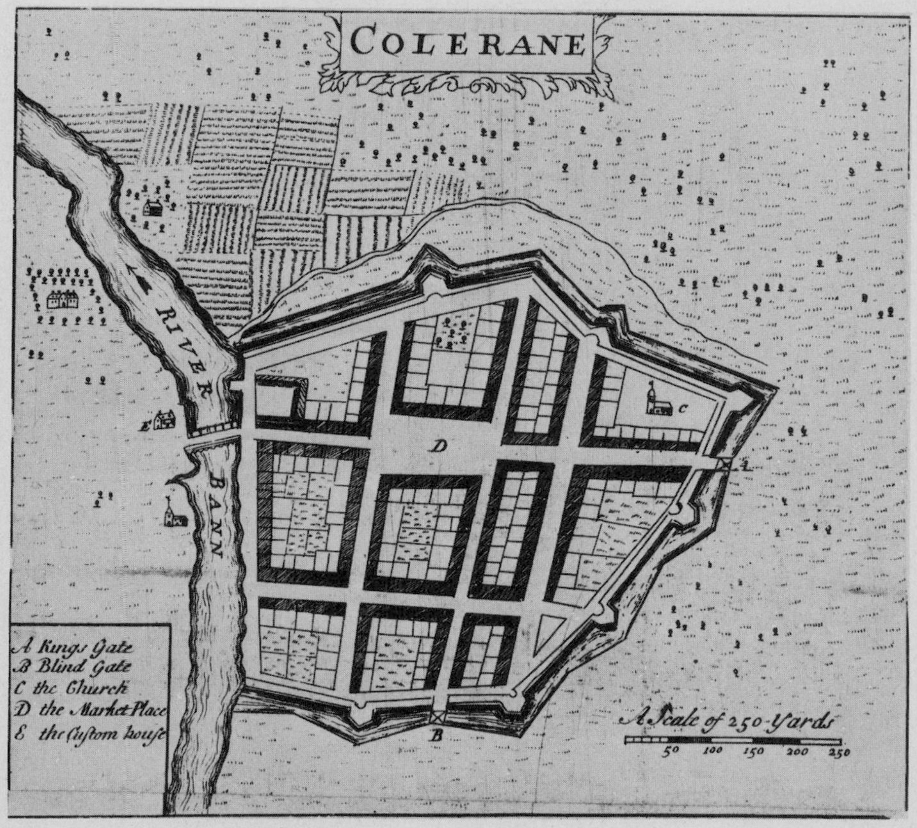

Figure 13. Plan of Coleraine, Northern Ireland: 1683

entering at its corners, and two streets intersecting the shorter sides of its rectangular shape. This pattern is a curious combination of the typical medieval English *bastide* square of southern France and the much newer Renaissance-type square of Vitry and Londonderry. It is quite obvious that far less attention had been given to possible aesthetic effects in Coleraine than in its sister town developed by the London companies.

The construction techniques employed are of considerable interest. Many of the houses were of prefabricated design, their wooden frames having been built in England. These were assembled quickly on the site and finished off in the conventional manner with roofs, chimneys, and brick or plaster filling for the walls.[34] A price was paid for speed in construction, however. In 1619 Pynnar reported that many of the buildings were in unsatisfactory condition and that portions of the fortifications had fallen into disrepair.[35]

While Londonderry and Coleraine were planned and developed by the London companies acting in concert, individual companies were responsible for the founding of many other smaller communities. Each company was assigned a portion of Ulster to be settled under its jurisdiction (figure 14). The Drapers, Vintners, Salters, Cloth Workers, Fishmongers, Goldsmiths, Skinners, and others all played a part in this colonization scheme, and the boundaries of the land under their jurisdiction can be seen on the map.

Figure 15 shows the plan of Moneymore, developed by the Drapers' Company. For more than three hundred years this organization has maintained an interest in the towns established on its lands, engaging in urban redevelopment and improvement of this ancient settlement in the middle of the nineteenth century.[36] The original plan was for a neat little crossroads community at one end of which stood the castle and fortified courtyard, or bawn, called for in the program of Ulster settlement. Two dozen houses appear on the drawing, three of them marked "void" or empty at the time this depiction of the little town was prepared in 1622.

This regular and not unimposing town contained one unusual feature. In 1615 it could boast of a piped water system that brought water underground through wooden pipes from its source a quarter of a mile away. This innovation did not last long. The wooden conduits soon began to leak, and the inhabitants complained that their rents were too high because of the cost of this unaccustomed luxury service.[37] Pynnar's report on Moneymore three years before this drawing is worth quoting because it is so typical of his descriptions of dozens of the new village communities he observed in Ulster:

> There is a strong bawn of stone and lyme an hundred feet square, fifteen feet high, with two flankers. There is a castle within the bawne of the same wideness, being battlemented, the which hath also two flankers, and near finished. Right before the castle, there are built twelve houses whereof six are of lime and stone very good, and six of timber, inhabited with English families and this the best work that I have seen for building; a water mill and a mault-house also.[38]

These lesser towns of Ulster exhibited considerable variations in their plans. The crossroads design of Moneymore was one general pattern used by the several companies and by individuals who acquired settlement rights under the same obligations. Sir James Hamilton, for example, used this plan when he founded Holywood.[39] Linear plans were also popular. The castle and bawn stood at one end of the town. Leading away from this protective enclosure, a single street provided access to the dwellings, church, and other structures of the village. Magherafelt, Salterstown, Articlave, and Bellaghy all followed this system.[40] Some of the contemporary drawings of the period omit the spine road of the settlement, as on the drawing (figure 16) of "The Fishmongers Buildinge at Ballekelle," suggesting that some of the towns at least were less precisely surveyed into the streets and that the open space between the two rows of houses was not clearly demarcated.

In the second phase of the development of Jamestown after about 1614, that Virginia community must have resembled closely these linear Ulster villages. The triangular "James Forte" served as the equivalent of the Ulster bawn, located at one end of a street of detached houses stretching away in the other direction. By the time the Jamestown settlers planned this first extension to the original small and cramped community many such linear towns existed in Ireland and may consciously have been imitated by those first Virginians.

In 1619 Pynnar could report what would appear to be substantial progress in colonization. Although he pointed out that he had not visited all the new settlements in the areas he had inspected, "there are now built within the counties of Ardmogh [*sic*], Tyrone, Donagall, Fermanagh, Cavan, and London-Derry, 107 Castles without Bawnes, 42 Bawnes without Castles or Houses, 1897 Dwelling Houses of Stone and Timber."[41] The king and his advisors, however, had expected much greater accomplishments, particu-

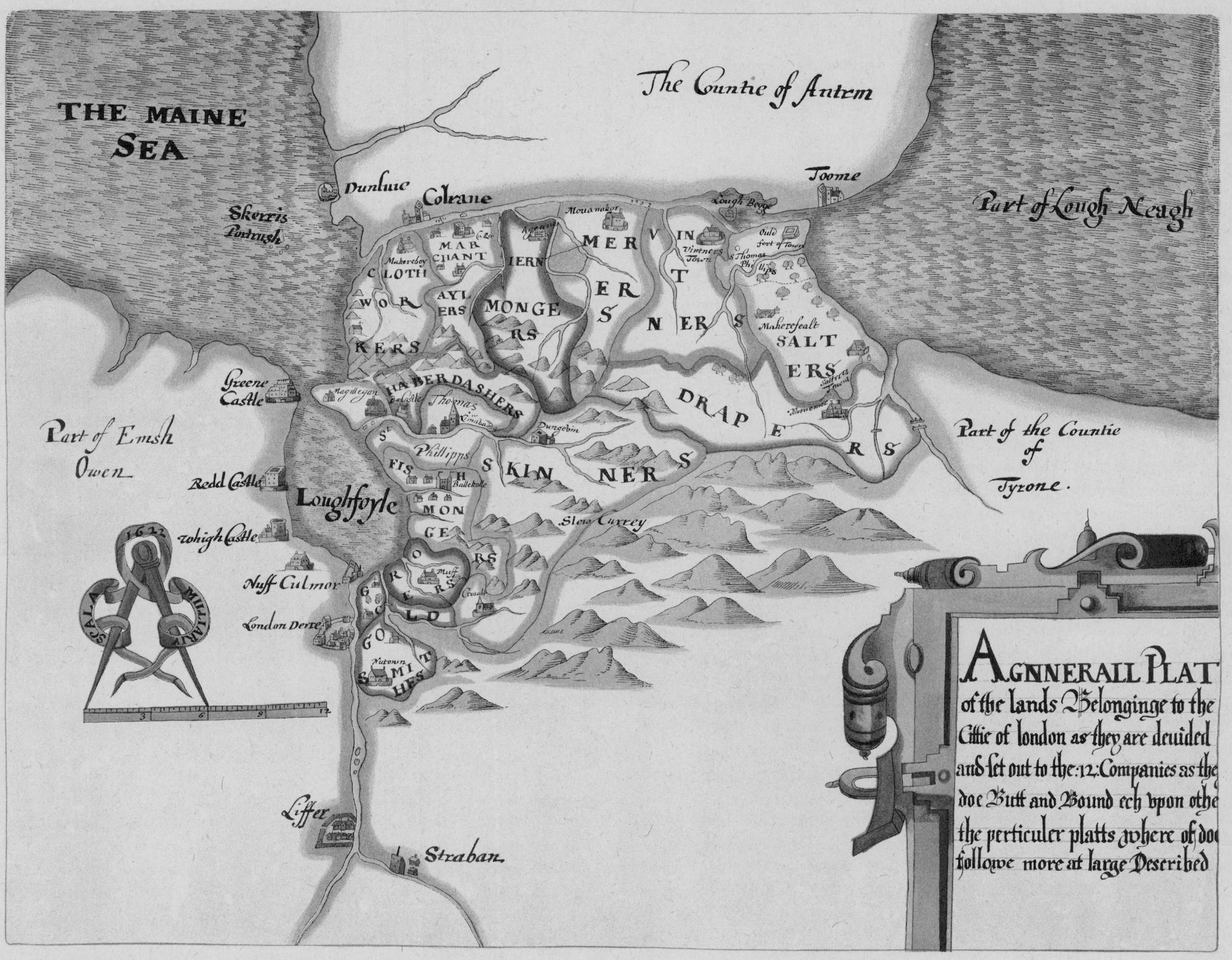

Figure 14. Map of Ulster, Northern Ireland: 1622

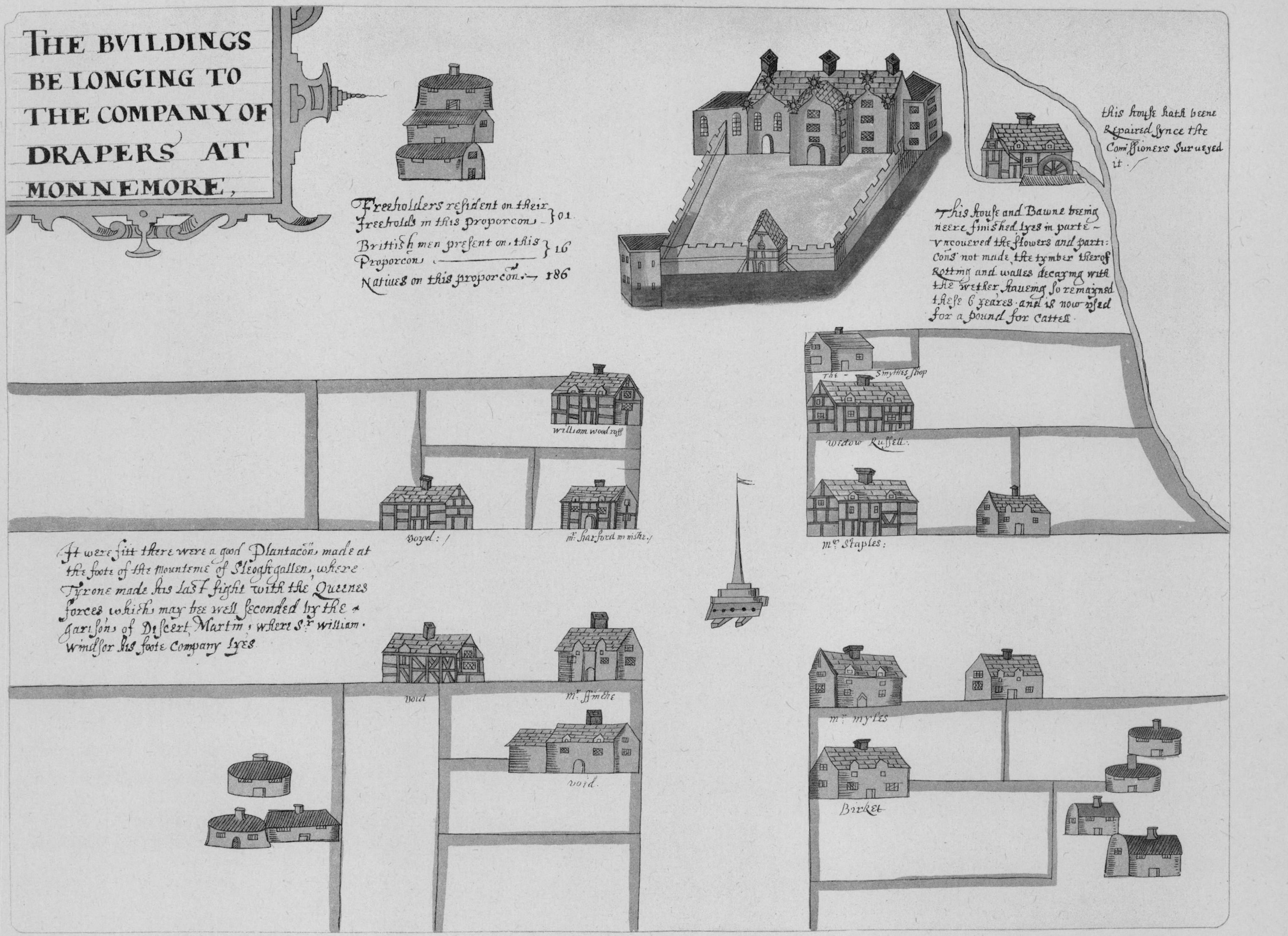
THE BVILDINGS BE LONGING TO THE COMPANY OF DRAPERS AT MONNEMORE,
Freeholders resident on their Freeholds in this proporcon } 01
Brittish men present on this Proporcon } 16
Natiues on this proporcon 186
this house hath beene Repaired synce the Commissioners Surueyed it.
This house and Bawne beeing neere finished lyes in parte vncouered the flowers and partitions not made, the tymber thereof Rotting and walles decaying with the wether haueing so remayned these 6 yeares. and is now vsed for a pound for Cattell.
The Smythes shop
william woodroff
widow Russell
Boyed
Mr harford minister
Mr Staples
It were fitt there were a good Plantacon made at the foote of the mounteine of Sleoghtgallen, where Tyrone made his last fight with the Queenes forces which may bee well seconded by the garisons of Descert Martin, where Sr william windsor his foote Company lyes
void
Mr Smethe
void
Mr myles
Birket

Figure 15. Plan of Moneymore, Northern Ireland: 1622

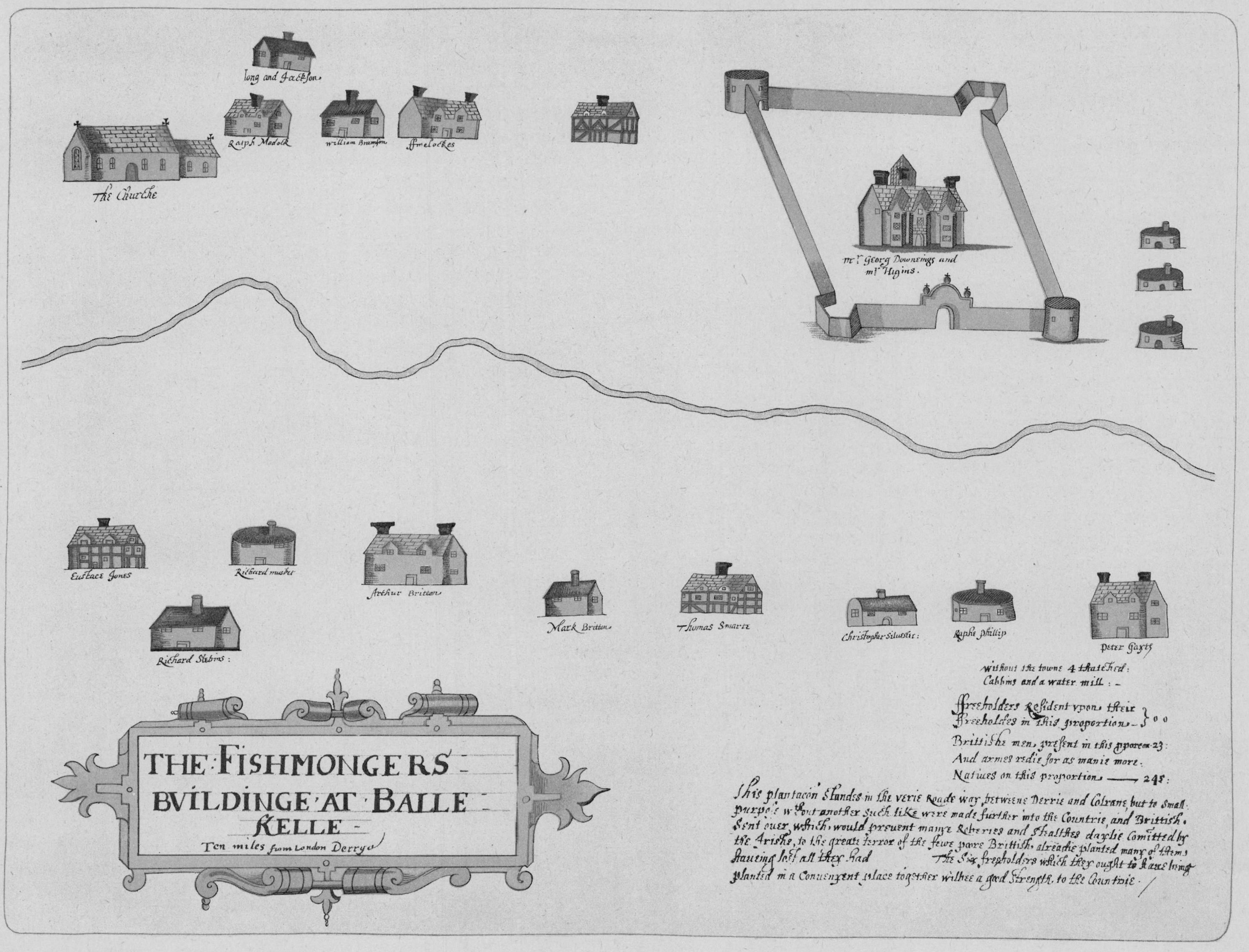

Figure 16. Plan of Ballykelly, Northern Ireland: 1622

larly in the county Londonderry where the substantial financial resources of the London companies had been enlisted. Pynnar estimated that in Ulster there were 1,974 English and Scottish families, with more than six thousand adult males capable of bearing arms. But he reported many of the English reluctant to begin large-scale husbandry because of fear of Irish raids on their cattle, and that had it not been for the more venturesome Scots the province might be faced with starvation. Much of the land was tilled by Irish tenants who, it was feared, might eventually rise against the new settlers who had seized their lands. This apprehension was ultimately justified by the rebellion of 1641.[42]

The difficulties in Irish colonization and town development were certainly real enough, though they seem minor compared to those experienced in planting the American colonies. James's dissatisfactions with the conduct of the enterprise by the joint-stock company of the Irish Society in Londonderry and private undertakers elsewhere in Ulster may have influenced his decision in 1624 to revoke the charter of the Virginia Company and to take the Virginia settlement in hand as a royal colony.

In both colonization projects the importance placed on the early establishment of towns is clear. This policy, however imperfectly executed in Ireland it may have seemed when viewed from London, proved far more difficult to carry out in Virginia and Maryland. There, geography and the dependence on tobacco as the chief agricultural product combined to thwart for many years English intentions to develop a town-based society. Conflict between the wishes and directives of colonial administrators and the response by the settlers to their natural environment is one of the great themes of tidewater history. That struggle was foreshadowed by the experience in Ulster under James I.

It is necessary in reviewing aspects of English town planning influential in the tidewater colonies to move beyond the first period of American colonization and to discuss later developments that affected the layout of certain tidewater towns. This treatment will be limited to those aspects of English town design that were echoed across the Atlantic, especially the development of the great London squares of the seventeenth and eighteenth centuries and the various plans for rebuilding the city following the disastrous fire in 1666.

The Renaissance reached England late. In town planning perhaps the first example of the new theories of urban design, aside from the plan of Londonderry, was Inigo Jones's project for Covent Garden in 1630. In many ways his design imitated continental models in Italy and France, and with some modifications it established a pattern that was to guide much of London's growth during the next two centuries. The earl of Bedford commissioned Jones to lay out a residential development on his estates, which then lay on the northern limits of the city. The plan called for the creation of a great square on which fronted imposing town houses with arcaded ground floors providing a covered walkway. On the south side of the square Jones designed St. Paul's Church in Tuscan style with extended overhanging eaves. The piazza formed by this composition was evidently meant to be covered with sand or cobbles like many of its European precedents. Soon it became a market place, and the desirability of Covent Garden as a fashionable residential area began to decline.

Its place was taken, quickly enough, by many other similar residential squares. Men of property realized that large-scale residential land development on this pattern could produce substantial income. Lincoln's Inn Fields had been regularized and laid out as a residential neighborhood by Jones as early as 1618. Leicester Fields was soon enclosed in like manner. Bloomsbury and Soho squares were planned by 1660, Red Lion Square and St. James's Square in 1684, Grosvenor Square in 1695, Hanover Square in 1712, and Cavendish Square in 1720, to name some of the more interesting of these projects. By 1746, when John Rocque's great survey of London was published, much of the west end of London had taken on a character unique among European cities. Figure 17 shows a portion of Rocque's map for which the surveys had begun in 1737. A study of this section of London makes it easy to understand the source of inspiration for Governor Francis Nicholson's proposed "Bloomsbury Square" in the plan he conceived and elaborated for the Maryland capital toward the end of the seventeenth century.

Nicholson seems to have drawn also on the different planning style that resulted from the Great Fire in 1666. This tragedy produced a spate of reconstruction plans. Three of the schemes employed rectilinear patterns, although not one of them could be termed traditional. Valentine Knight proposed to slash two dozen east-west streets across the devastated area, intersected by twelve streets more widely spaced running north and south. All of these streets were to be provided with arcades for protected foot

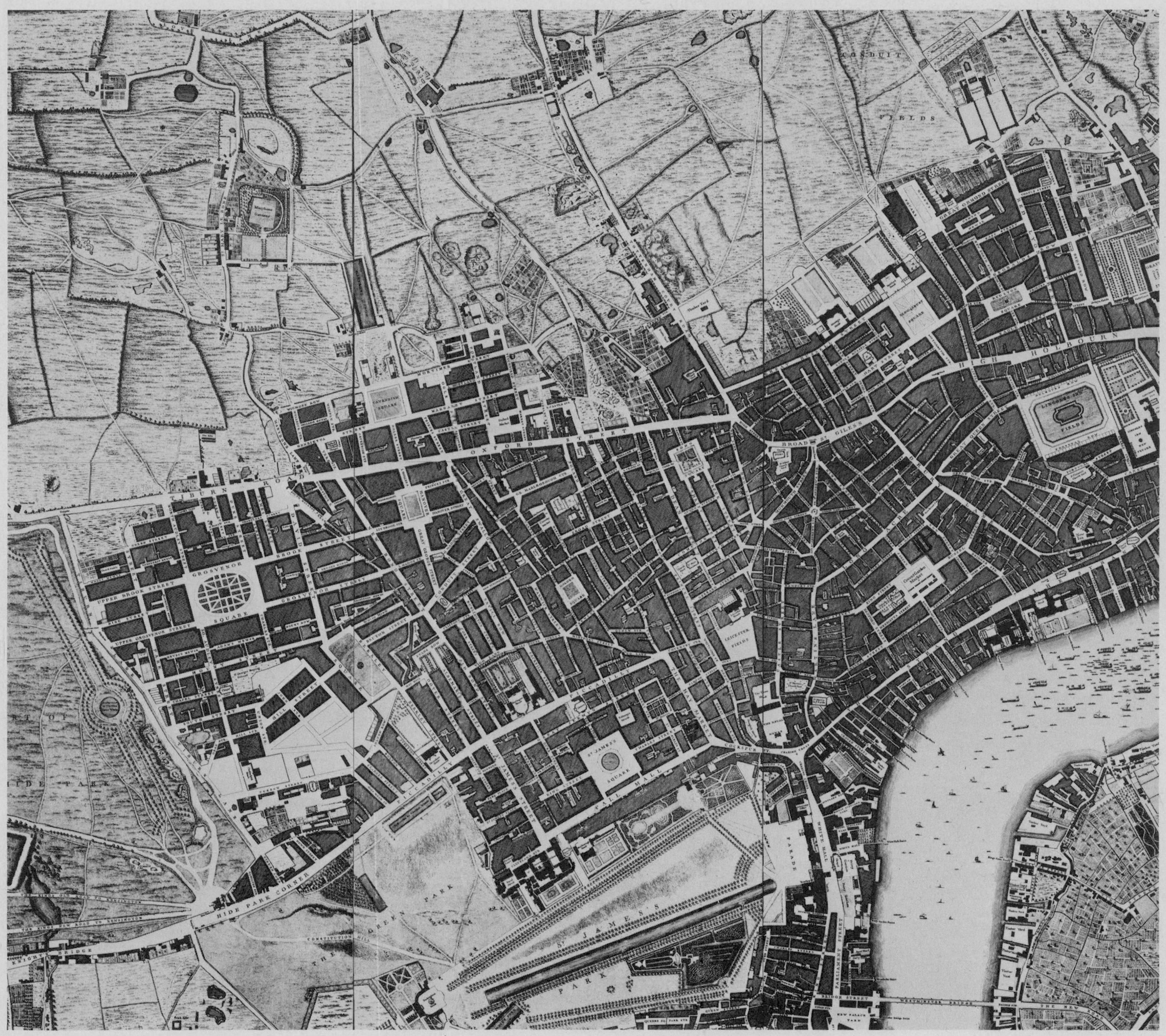

Figure 17. Plan of Portion of London, England: 1746

passage. Knight, a captain in the army, was clapped in prison for his suggestion that the king should build a canal through the city and reap a handsome profit from fines and tolls. Charles apparently objected to the suggestion that he should gain from London's calamity.

Richard Newcourt proposed two plans, the second a modification of the first. He advocated reconstructing London with a pattern of large rectangular blocks, each one containing a parish church in the center. The plan featured five large open spaces: one in the center and four others in each of the major quadrants of the city. The other gridiron plan is attributed to Robert Hooke, whose design featured a number of open squares on the Londonderry model.[43]

Plans of two other contributors are shown in figure 18. That at the top is the third and final proposal by John Evelyn. At the bottom appears the design for rebuilding London put forward by Christopher Wren. Both obviously derive from the same general school of urban design. This had gradually evolved in the continent of Europe from rather restrained statements of formality and axial planning to much more elaborate and extravagant patterns. This baroque style had already achieved large-scale application in the design of great royal gardens. In cities it had been applied mainly in the reconstruction of areas of special importance or in the expansion of certain cities beyond their original confines.

The original concept of a single great avenue leading to a square or building had been elaborated upon. Now it was deemed desirable to have a number of the major streets converging on such focal points. Where these principal and other minor axes intersected, a palace, a monumental public building, a statue or fountain, or an obelisk would be erected as a visual punctuation mark. Designers strove to create terminal vistas of this sort at the ends of many of the streets, introducing for this purpose various kinds of circles, squares, and other open spaces.

This was the new planning style. Evelyn, an amateur, produced a design that demonstrates more skill with abstract geometry than ability to use baroque design motifs sensibly. Wren's plan is masterfully done, combining as it does the radial and the gridiron systems of street layout without producing the many awkward intersections and building parcels that mar Evelyn's scheme.[44] Some of these same criticisms can be made of the plan for Annapolis that, as we shall see, was also designed by an amateur planner whose fancy had been taken by the new baroque style in civic composition.

The planning of towns in Virginia and Maryland should be seen not as a novel venture for which there were few if any precedents but as a continuation of the long tradition of English new town development. Nor, if one considers the experience in northern Ireland, did the frontier conditions of the Tidewater provide a unique setting for such activities. Moreover, both in the Irish "colony" and in those of Virginia and Maryland English officials steadfastly believed that town life would provide the essential basis for settlement.

In Ireland, where stronger forces could be mustered because of the shorter distance from the mother country and the greater resources made available by the crown, it proved easier to transplant almost intact English and European town designs to the new land. This was not to be true to the same extent in North America. The Atlantic Ocean formed a more formidable barrier than the Irish Sea. In the early years of American colonization only the most essential items could be transported to the colonial frontier. This was true not only for the material basis of existence but for concepts of urban design as well.

In comfortable London colonial officials might dream of creating not only towns but great cities in the New World. For the colonists confronted with the reality of a raw frontier existence these notions seemed completely unrealistic. The early towns of the Tidewater were therefore laid out on the simplest of patterns. It was not until after nearly a century of experience that more elaborate and sophisticated urban forms came to be introduced.

Unlike northern Ireland, where the geography and climate closely paralleled that of England, the settlers of colonial Virginia and Maryland found themselves in an environment quite different from the homeland. Geographic forces soon influenced a choice of crops and a pattern of settlement that ran directly counter to the wishes of the crown and the sponsors of these colonial ventures, who assumed that most persons would live in towns and agricultural villages much like those of Tudor England.

In the seventeenth and eighteenth centuries the conflict between colonists and colonial administrators over urban policy was to assume major proportions. At the beginning of colonization activities, however, this could not be foreseen, and it is to these initial ventures that we now turn.

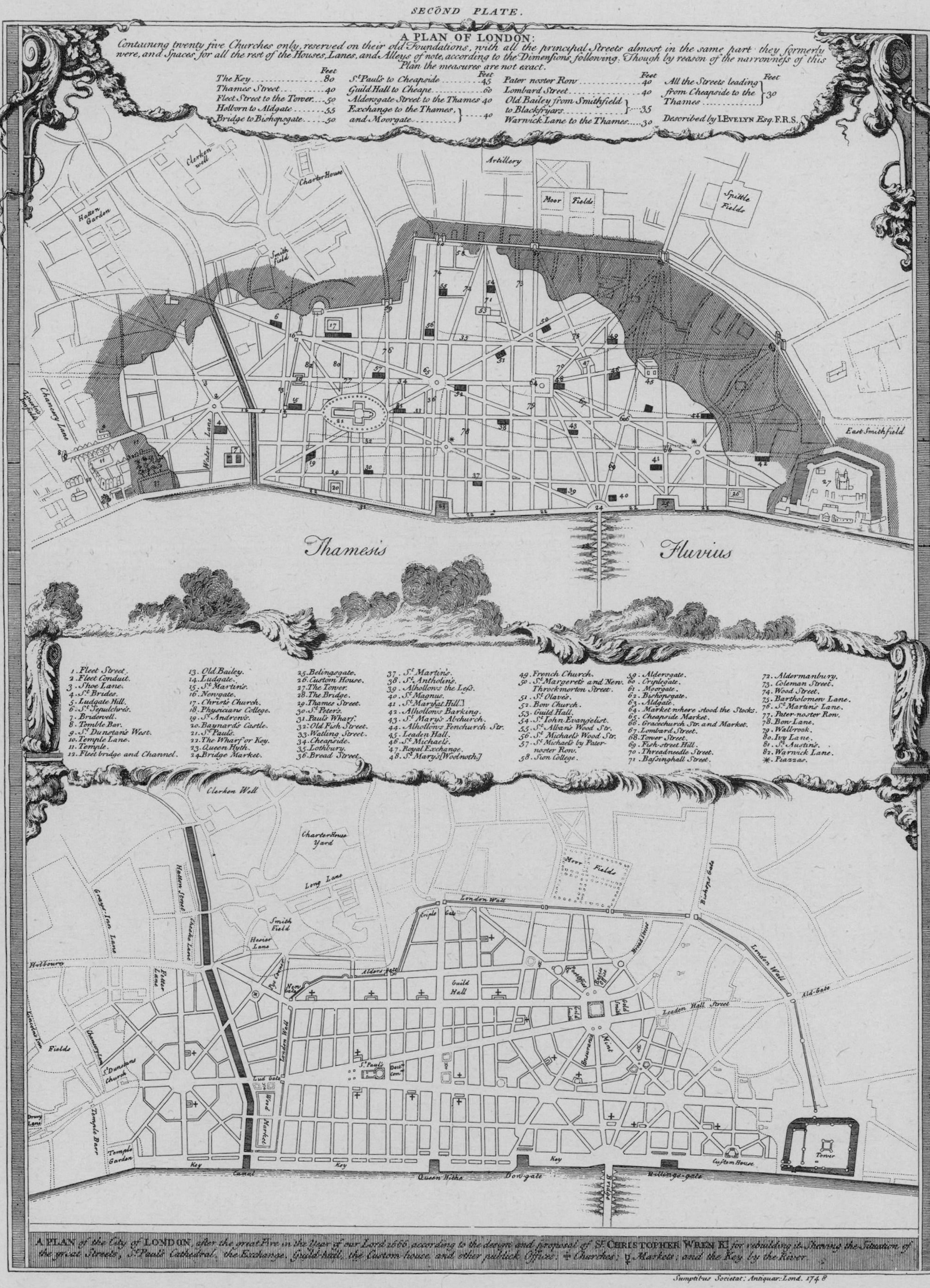

Figure 18. Plans for Rebuilding London in 1666 by John Evelyn and Christopher Wren

II. *Fort Raleigh and Jamestown: The Beginnings of English Towns in the Tidewater*

English exploration and colonization in the Western Hemisphere lagged far behind the achievements of England's great continental rival, Spain. It was nearly a century after the first voyage of Columbus that Sir Humphrey Gilbert in 1578 sailed from Plymouth to Canada in a vain attempt to establish a settlement in the New World. This enterprise of Gilbert and his half-brother, Walter Raleigh, came to an end when Gilbert lost his life in 1583 on the return voyage from Newfoundand.

Raleigh promptly obtained a new patent of exploration from Elizabeth on essentially the same terms previously granted to Gilbert.[1] Early in 1584 he dispatched Philip Amadas and Arthur Barlowe on a voyage of discovery to America to seek out a likely spot for settlement. Sailing northward from Florida, they reached North Carolina and explored the coast in some detail. After the two captains returned to England, Barlowe composed a full account of their discoveries, describing the new land in the most favorable terms.[2]

Raleigh's enthusiasm for colonization in North America led him to ask Richard Hakluyt to prepare a study of this subject. Hakluyt's statement, doubtless worked out in consultation with Raleigh, was evidently intended to convince Elizabeth and her advisors of the legality, feasibility, and desirability of immediate large-scale colonization efforts with substantial royal backing. The arguments of this remarkable essay are too long to be fully summarized, but a few points deserve emphasis.

In addition to suggesting that American colonization would undercut Spanish power and that important sources of naval stores could be developed, Hakluyt pointed out that such a policy would solve the problem of widespread unemployment at home through the movement of excess population across the Atlantic. Raleigh and Hakluyt envisaged the creation of a series of settlements "upon the mouthes of the greate navigable rivers." There forts would be built around which towns would develop. These were intended not only as centers of trade but also as places of farming and manufacture: "By makinge of shippes and by preparinge of thinges for the same, by makinge of cables and cordage, by plantinge of vines and olive trees, and by makinge of wyne and oyle, by husbandrie, and by thousandes of things there to be done, infinite nombers of the Englishe nation may be set on worke."[3] The two men clearly saw the creation of new towns as an essential part of colonization.

Elizabeth hesitated to provoke an open break with Spain over rights to colonize the lands claimed by England's powerful adversary. She approved Raleigh's request for permission to explore and settle the then ill-defined region of Virginia; she declined, however, to make this venture a crown enterprise. While under all the circumstances this policy may have been justified, its effect was to postpone permanent settlement for more than two decades.

In 1585 Raleigh assembled a fleet of seven vessels under the command of his cousin, Sir Richard Grenville. July found the fleet anchored off the outer banks of Carolina near Roanoke Island, a location previously noted by Amadas and Barlowe. As figures 19 and 20 show, the island lay between the outer banks and the mainland and was therefore protected both from

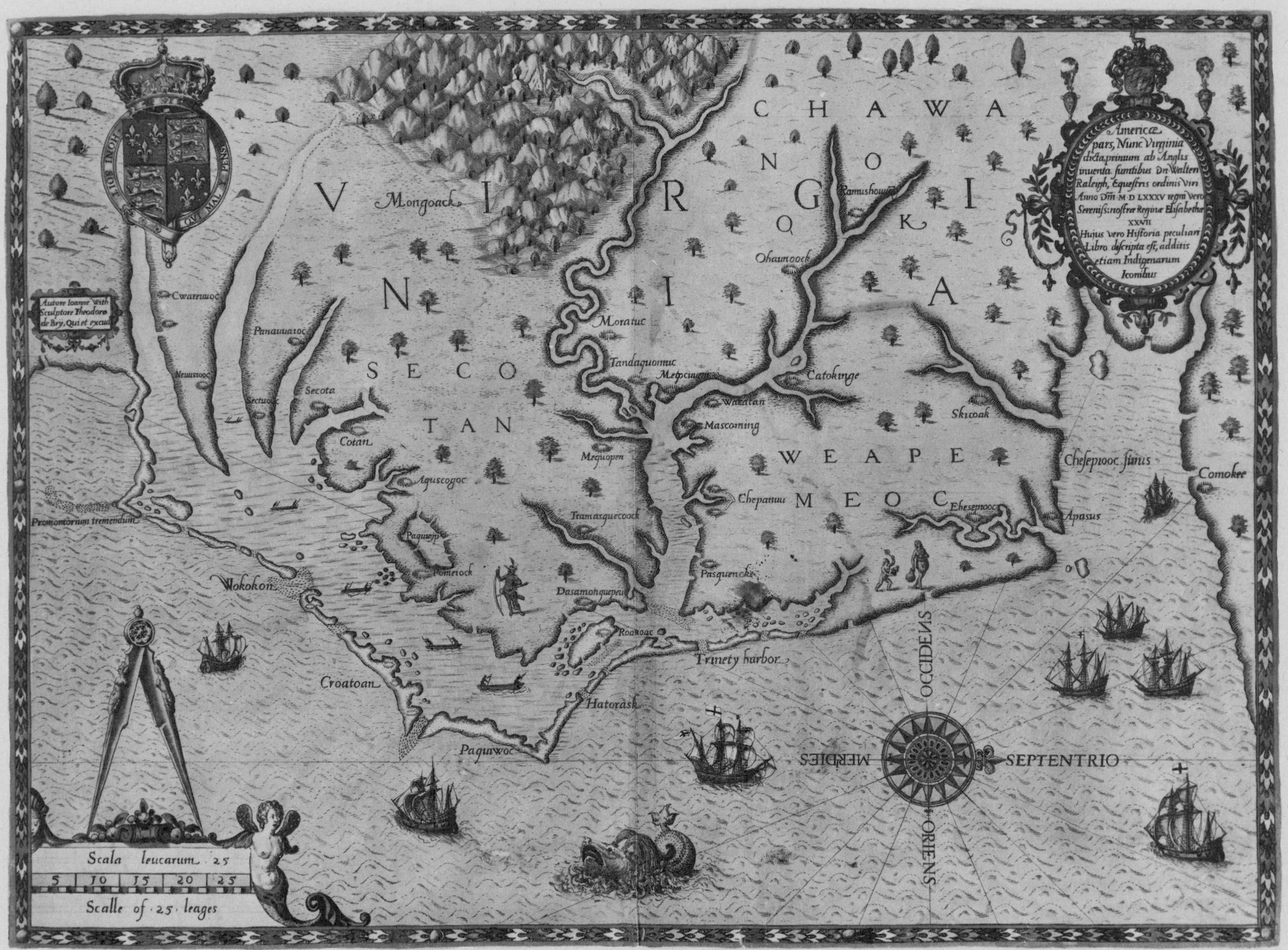

Figure 19. Map of Coastal North Carolina: 1585

Figure 20. Map of Roanoke Island, North Carolina: 1590

the sea and from the land. On the north end was a small Indian village that Barlowe's narrative indicated was inhabited by friendly natives. It was here that the leaders of the expedition decided to settle.

In determining the exact form of their settlement they may have tried to follow a suggested design described in an undated document given to Thomas Cavendish, one of the captains of a ship in the fleet, before he left England. This is written in the form of instructions bearing only the heading, "For Master Rauleys Viage." [4]

The instructions describe a five-sided enclosure with a bulwark at each corner, "with a way out of the bulwark and an other Into the Streat." The author evidently visualized the entire settlement enclosed by fortifications that included a ditch with an earthen wall, a wooden palisade fifteen feet high in the ditch, and twenty feet beyond a second wall—perhaps a wooden stockade—four feet in height. That these defensive works were to embrace more than a mere fort is suggested by the recommendation that the center was to be occupied by a market place "large, for assemblys, and to sytt in if neade be."

Of greatest interest is the proposed street pattern. The author "would have Every streat strayt to every bulwarke, and to Every gatt and to the mydst of Every Curtyne, so as standying In the market plase yow may see all the bulwarkes Curtyns and gates." What was suggested, then, was a radially symmetrical pattern with streets of the settlement leading from the central market place to each of the five bulwarks and to the midpoints of the connecting walls ("Curtyns") enclosing the town.

Although unusual, a pentagonal plan was not unknown. One such town would have been familiar to many Englishmen who had fought in the Low Countries. This was Philippeville near the southern border of modern Belgium, planned by Sebastian van Noyen for Philip II of Spain in 1555. In 1581 the third volume of Braun and Hogenberg's great *Civitates Orbis Terrarum* included an engraved plan of this town (figure 21) with one of the nearby fortified community of Marienbourg. The close correspondence of Philippeville's layout with the proposed design described in the Cavendish document strongly suggests that the intention of the expedition was to reproduce its plan on the spot selected for initial settlement. Perhaps of greater importance is this evidence that Raleigh proposed to establish not just an isolated military strong point but a true town as the first stage in large-scale colonization activities in North America.[5]

Whatever the original intention, the resources of the expedition apparently did not permit so ambitious a form of settlement. Modern archeological research has uncovered only the remains of a small fort and there is no trace whatsoever of the town referred to briefly and rather confusingly in some of the contemporary accounts of the Roanoke Island expeditions.[6]

The plan of the fort followed neither the pentagonal plan suggested in the document just described nor the more conventional quadrilateral pattern with bulwarks at each of the four corners. Instead, it appears to have been four sided but with pointed bastions at the midpoints of each side rather than at the corners. No contemporary drawing of the fort survives, but reproduced in figure 22 is a plan of a similar fortification constructed only weeks earlier on the island of Puerto Rico by Ralph Lane, second in command to Grenville and governor of the colony while at Roanoke. This drawing is the work of the talented John White, whose drawings and paintings of the natives, their villages, and the flora and fauna provide us a remarkable record of everything the English observed at the time—unfortunately and unaccountably not including a plan or view of the Roanoke settlement itself.

The plan of Fort Raleigh as determined by exhaustive site investigations appears in figure 23. The outline of its perimeter so closely follows that of Lane's Puerto Rico fort that one is justified in believing that the Roanoke Island fortification was the work of the same man. It was a small enclosure, the cleared and level area within the ramparts being an irregular rectangle less than fifty feet on each side. Its construction was simple. The material excavated from the ditch that extended around the perimeter was placed to form an angled parapet made somewhat higher by a further excavation of some of the ground within the enclosure. On the inside, a firing step provided an elevation from which soldiers could defend the fort against possible attack, and platforms at the corners allowed the placement of small cannon. Figure 24 is a conjectural view of this earthen structure.

While no trace of a separate town has been discovered, its existence is suggested by the small size of the fort and by one tantalizing reference Ralph Lane made to "them in the forte, as for us at the towne." [7] The most probable location would seem to be to the west of the fort where the ramparts are interrupted at two places to form gates or entry ways.

This settlement was soon abandoned. Grenville and his fleet returned to England in August, 1585. Those who remained on Roanoke Island

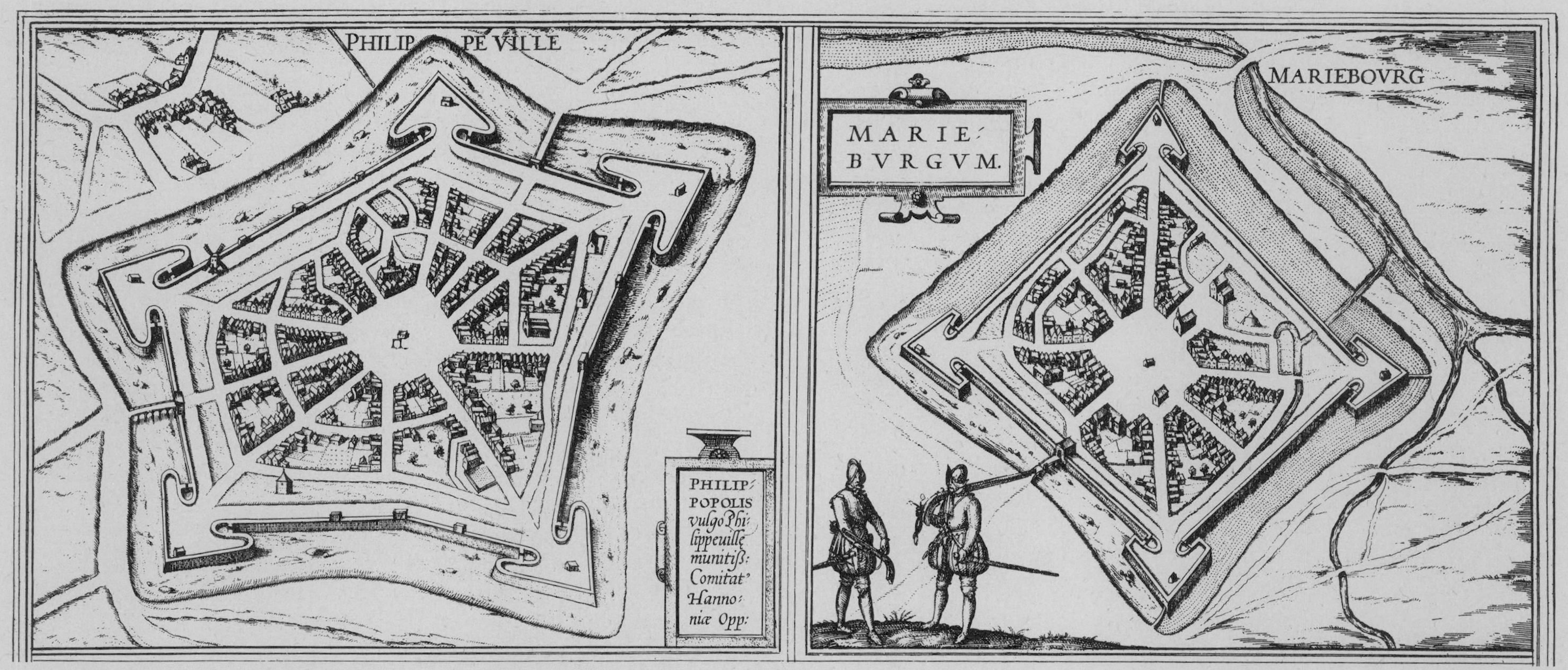

Figure 21. Plans of Philippeville and Marienbourg, Belgium: 1581

expected additional men and supplies the following spring, but by June of 1586 there was no sign of the ships promised by Raleigh or Grenville. Instead, the settlers were visited by the fleet of Sir Francis Drake on his voyage homeward following his destruction of Santo Domingo, Cartagena, and the newly established Spanish base at St. Augustine. Lane decided to accept Drake's offer to take the members of the expedition back to England, and they departed on June 18 only a few days before Raleigh's relief ship arrived to find Roanoke Island deserted. Two weeks later Grenville, with a fleet of six or seven ships and four hundred men, also reached Roanoke Island, conducted a search for the missing party, and ultimately decided to leave fifteen men at Roanoke with ample supplies and assurance that the following year a new expedition with additional colonists would be dispatched.

Even before the return of Lane with Drake's fleet, Raleigh had conceived of a second colonizing venture. This was to supplement the first and be located somewhere on Chesapeake Bay. While his first attempt had been financed largely by Raleigh himself, he now decided to enlist wider financial backing. On January 7, 1587, the corporation of the Governor and Assistants of the City of Raleigh in Virginia was created.[8] Raleigh designated the versatile John White as governor, and twelve persons were named as the "assistants." The financial details remain obscure. Thomas Hariot, mathematician and scientist, and a leading member of the colonists at

Figure 22. Plan of Ralph Lane's Fort in Puerto Rico: 1585

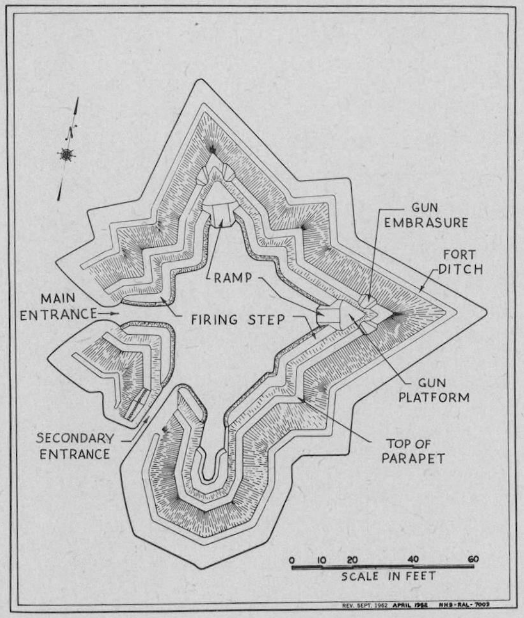

Figure 23. Conjectural Plan of Fort Raleigh, North Carolina, in 1585

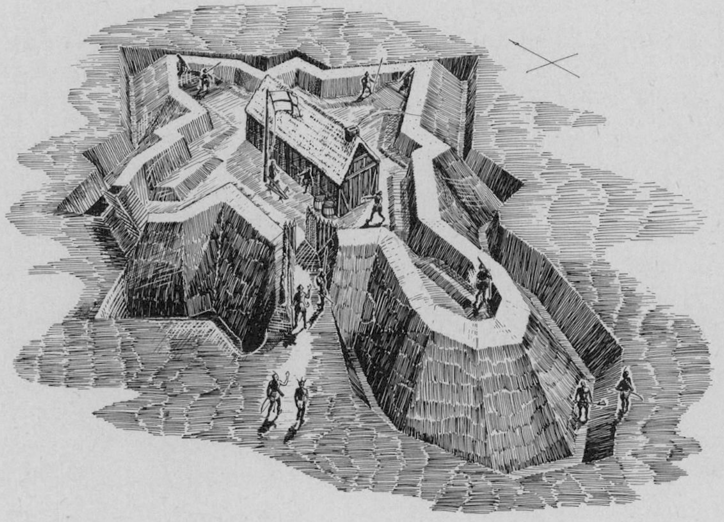

Figure 24. Conjectural View of Fort Raleigh, North Carolina, in 1585

Roanoke in 1585–1586, mentions that Raleigh in 1587 granted each settler a minimum of "five hundred acres to a man onely for the adventure of his person." [9] Doubtless individual investors in the project were to receive larger grants in proportion to their financial stake in the enterprise.

While Raleigh certainly had in mind the advantages of establishing an American base for preying on Spanish ships, he intended this new venture to create a permanent civil settlement to serve as the beginning of a new overseas empire. This belief is borne out by the composition of the group that sailed from England under White's command on May 8, 1587. The party, unlike that of the first colony, included seventeen women and nine children. Two of the women, Governor White's daughter Eleanore Dare, and Margery Harvie, were pregnant, their children being born in August of that year.

Raleigh proposed to settle on Chesapeake Bay, but a stop was to be made at Roanoke with supplies for the group of fifteen left behind by Grenville the previous year. On arrival Simon Fernandez, one of the "assistants" named in the charter and the captain of the fleet, announced that he intended to disembark the entire group of 110 persons.[10] White's protests were to no avail, and once again Roanoke Island was inhabited by Englishmen. On July 23 White,

> with divers of his companie, walked to the North end of the Island, where Master Ralfe Lane had his forte, with sundry necessarie and decent dwelling houses made by his men about it the year before, where wee hoped to finde some signes, or certaine knowledge of our fifteen men. When we came thither, wee found the forte rasd downe, but all the houses standing unhurt, saving the neather roomes of them, and also of the forte, were overgrowen with Melons of divers sortes, and Deere within them, feeding on those Mellons; so we returned to our companie, without hope of ever seeing any of the fifteene men living.[11]

Work then began on reconstructing the settlement. As White relates, "the same day order was given, that every man should be imploied for the repairing of those houses, which we found standing, and also to make other newe Cottages, for such as shoulde neede." [12] This brief reference is the only information on whatever reconstruction or additions to the original settlement took place at this time.

The Indians in the immediate vicinity began to harass the settlers. Only the Croatoans, located some distance to the south, proved friendly. With the memory of the vanished fifteen men from Grenville's party preying on their minds, the colonists requested White to return to England for reinforcements and additional supplies. Reluctantly he agreed. Before his departure on August 27 he instructed the settlers that if they should be forced to move during his absence "they should not faile to write or carve on the trees or posts of the dores the name of the place where they should be seated . . . [and] . . . if they should happen to be deistressed in any of those places, that then they should carve over the letter or name, a Crosse." [13]

With White's departure we lose further firsthand accounts of the Roanoke colony. Impending war led the Privy Council to mobilize shipping for possible naval duty, and two small vessels that Grenville managed to put at White's disposal were bested in an engagement with a French ship and forced to return to England. The Spanish Armada put an end to further supply attempts, and not until July, 1590, was White able to reach the Carolina coast.

Approaching Fort Raleigh he came across the letters CRO carved on a tree. The "secret token" of distress, a cross, was not to be seen. White then

> passed toward the place where they were left in sundry houses, but he found the houses taken downe, and the place very strongly enclosed with a high palisado of great trees, with cortynes and flankers very Fort-like, and one of the chiefe trees or postes at the right side of the entrance had the barke taken off, and 5. foote from the ground in fayre Capitall letters was graven CROATOAN without any crosse or signe of distresse.[14]

Scattered around the fort were some of the supplies of the colonists. A short distance away White had buried some of his possessions to conceal them from the Indians. He found the cache rifled and his "things spoyled and broken, and my bookes torne from the covers, the frames of some of my pictures and Mappes rotten and spoyled with rayne, and my armour almost eaten through with rust." [15]

White and his men returned to the ships intending to sail southward to the region occupied by the Croatoan Indians. Before they could take on water they were forced out to sea by a severe gale that caused some damage to their vessels. In the end the proposed search for the lost colony was abandoned before it really began. A few halfhearted attempts in later years to probe the little-known Carolina coast for information about the Roanoke settlers proved unsuccessful. The first serious and continued English effort to settle North America thus ended in failure.[16]

Raleigh's enterprise had, nevertheless, whetted English interest in the New World. Dazzling evidence of the great mineral wealth of the Spanish colonies lay before them, looted from Spanish merchant ships by English privateers. It was widely believed that similar treasure could be had in Virginia. In *Eastward Hoe,* a popular comedy written by George Chapman, Ben Jonson, and John Marston in 1605, one of the characters reflected the prevailing attitude when he described the wealth of Virginia:

> I tell thee, golde is more plentifull there than copper is with us; and for as much redde copper as I can bring Ile have thrise the waight in gold. Why, man, all their dripping-pans and their chamber-potts are pure gould; and all the prisoners they take are fetered in gold; and for rubies and diamonds they goe forth on holydayes and gather 'hem by the sea-shore to hang on their childrens coates, and sticke in their children's caps, as commonly as our children weare saffron-gilt-brooches and groates with hoales in them.[17]

English exploration of North America accelerated in the first years of the seventeenth century. Fishing fleets made regular calls off the Newfoundland and New England coasts, and several expeditions continued probing the Virginia coast and Chesapeake Bay.[18] Captain George Weymouth commanded one of these voyages to New England in 1605, and on his return joined with Sir John Zouche in a proposal for a second expedition to establish a "plantation and colonie."[19] Other and similar proposals seem to have been under discussion at this time.[20]

Ultimately two groups of influential Englishmen secured the approval of James I to embark on the establishment of two colonies in America. To the London Company, with which we shall be concerned, the king conferred colonization rights anywhere between the 34th and 41st parallels, with their grant to extend fifty miles north and south and one hundred miles inland from their first settlement. One-fifth of all the gold and silver and one-fifteenth of the copper was reserved for the crown, and the London Company was given wide discretion over the management of its domain. As was the case with the Roanoke colony, the government itself did not participate directly in the venture but placed the initiative in the hands of private individuals.[21]

In December, 1606, three ships with a hundred settlers set out from England to begin the great adventure. In April of the following year they landed at Cape Henry, across the entrance to Chesapeake Bay from Cape Charles. Then, moving westward, the colonists began their search for a suitable site on which to settle.

In this endeavor they were guided by fairly specific instructions formulated by the Council for Virginia of the London Company. That document directed them first to select some navigable river, choosing one running well into the country, preferably in a northwesterly direction, "for that way you shall soonest find the other sea."[22] This instruction was based on the assumption of the time that the Pacific Ocean lay not far to the west. The party was admonished not to be hasty in "landing your victuals and munitions" but to determine how far the river was navigable, "that you make election of the strongest, most wholesome and fertile place." The council strongly favored a location well inland,

> perchance . . . a hundred miles from the river's mouth, and the further up the better, for if you sit down near the entrance, except it be in some island that is strong by nature, an enemy that may approach you on even ground may easily pull you out, and if he be driven to seek you a hundred miles in the land in boats you shall from both sides of the river, where it is narrowest, so beate them with your muskets as they shall never be able to prevail against you.

A small garrison was to be installed at the mouth of the river with a light boat so that warning might be given quickly to the main settlement in case of impending Spanish attack. When the site had been found the entire party was to disembark and be divided into three groups. Forty men were to explore the river and surrounding countryside, half of whom were "to try if they can [to] find any minerals." Another group was to be employed "in preparing your ground and sowing your corn [wheat] and roots. The third group was instructed "to fortifie and build of which your first work must be your storehouse for victual."

The instructions were quite clear on one point. This passage urged the settlers not to "plant in a low or moist place because it will prove unhealthful," a direction the wisdom of which was to be amply demonstrated in the years to follow. Unfortunately, the site chosen by the colonists after a two-week search was exactly this kind of location. Some thirty miles from the mouth of the James River they came across a peninsula with a narrow

Figure 25. Map of Virginia: 1608

neck connecting it to the mainland on the north and with deep water lying close to the shore. Here they decided to plant the settlement to which they gave the name of Jamestown. Its location can be seen on Captain John Smith's famous map of Virginia (figure 25).

The decision on the site was not unanimous. It was made by the resident councilors who, along with the president, had been appointed by the London Company. The colonists learned the identity of those who were to govern them only after reaching Chesapeake Bay, when Captain Christopher Newport opened sealed instructions given to him in London. John Smith regarded the chosen location as "a verie fit place for the erecting of a great cittie," but he referred to "some contention . . . betwixt" Edward Wingfield, president of the councilors, and Bartholomew Gosnold, a council member.[23] This decision made, the supplies were unloaded and, as William Simmonds tells us, "Now falleth every man to worke, the Councell contrive the Fort, the rest cut downe trees to make place to pitch their Tents; some provide clapboard to relade the ships, some make gardens, some nets, &c." [24]

George Percy, who was present during those early days, wrote a valuable account of the events, recording that the three ships of the fleet, the *Susan Constant,* the *God-Speed* and the *Discovery,* could be moored to trees on the shore because the water was six fathoms deep at the selected spot. As he recalls, "we landed all our men, which were set to worke about the fortification." [25] Strangely enough the instructions from London contained nothing of any detail about the nature of these fortifications. Two paragraphs in the instructions dealt with the building of the settlement, the first establishing the priorities to be followed:

> It were necessary that all your carpenters and other such like workmen . . . do first build your storehouse and those other rooms of publick and necessary use before any house be set up for any private persons, yet let them all work together first for the company and then for private men.
>
> And seeing order is at the same price with confusion it shall be adviseably done to set your houses even and by a line, that your streets may have a good breadth, and be carried square about your market place, and every street's end opening into it, that from thence with a few field pieces you may command every street throughout, which market place you may also fortify if you think it need full.

In the relative comfort of London it was easy and logical to think of wide streets, uniform building lines, and a market place. In the lonely wilderness of Virginia these things were not so easy to accomplish. The initial form of the tiny settlement bore little resemblance to a model market town of rural England. As Percy informs us: "The fifteenth of June we had built and finished our Fort, which was triangle wise, having three Bulwarkes, at every corner, like a half Moone, and foure or five pieces of Artillerie mounted in them." [26]

A conjectural view of James Fort (figure 26) shows a palisaded triangle extending some 420 feet along the river with its other two sides measuring approximately 300 feet each. The rounded "bulwarkes" at each corner have within a platform on which the cannon were mounted. The disposition of the buildings within this enclosure as shown in the rendering may well be correct, although their size and location must remain matters of surmise. The site of James Fort cannot be investigated by archaeological techniques; long ago it was so eroded by the James River that apparently no part of the original land remains.[27]

The triangular design adopted for the fort was unusual. Standard practice called for a quadrangular perimeter with bastions at each of the corners. Except for the Blackwater fort described in the previous chapter and illustrated in figure 10, this was common in the Irish colonization venture toward the end of the sixteenth century and in the early years of the seventeenth.[28] The only similar English structure in America had been Fort Raleigh. This, too, was quadrangular, although it departed somewhat from the usual models, as we have already seen.

The idea of a triangular fortification may have come from an earlier attempt by French Huguenots under the leadership of René de Laudonnière to plant a colony on the coast of Florida near the mouth of the St. John's River. Here in the summer of 1564 they planned and constructed a triangular fort (figure 27). Just as the Roanoke expedition had its John White to record in drawings the newly discovered land, so too the Huguenots had with them Jacques Le Moyne as cartographer and artist. And just as Theodore De Bry was later to engrave and publish the White drawings of Virginia so also were the Le Moyne drawings engraved and printed by the same publisher. The account and illustrations of the French colony Fort Caroline, appeared in 1591, the year following the publication of the narrative and engravings of the Roanoke venture.

Figure 26. Conjectural View of Jamestown, Virginia, in 1607

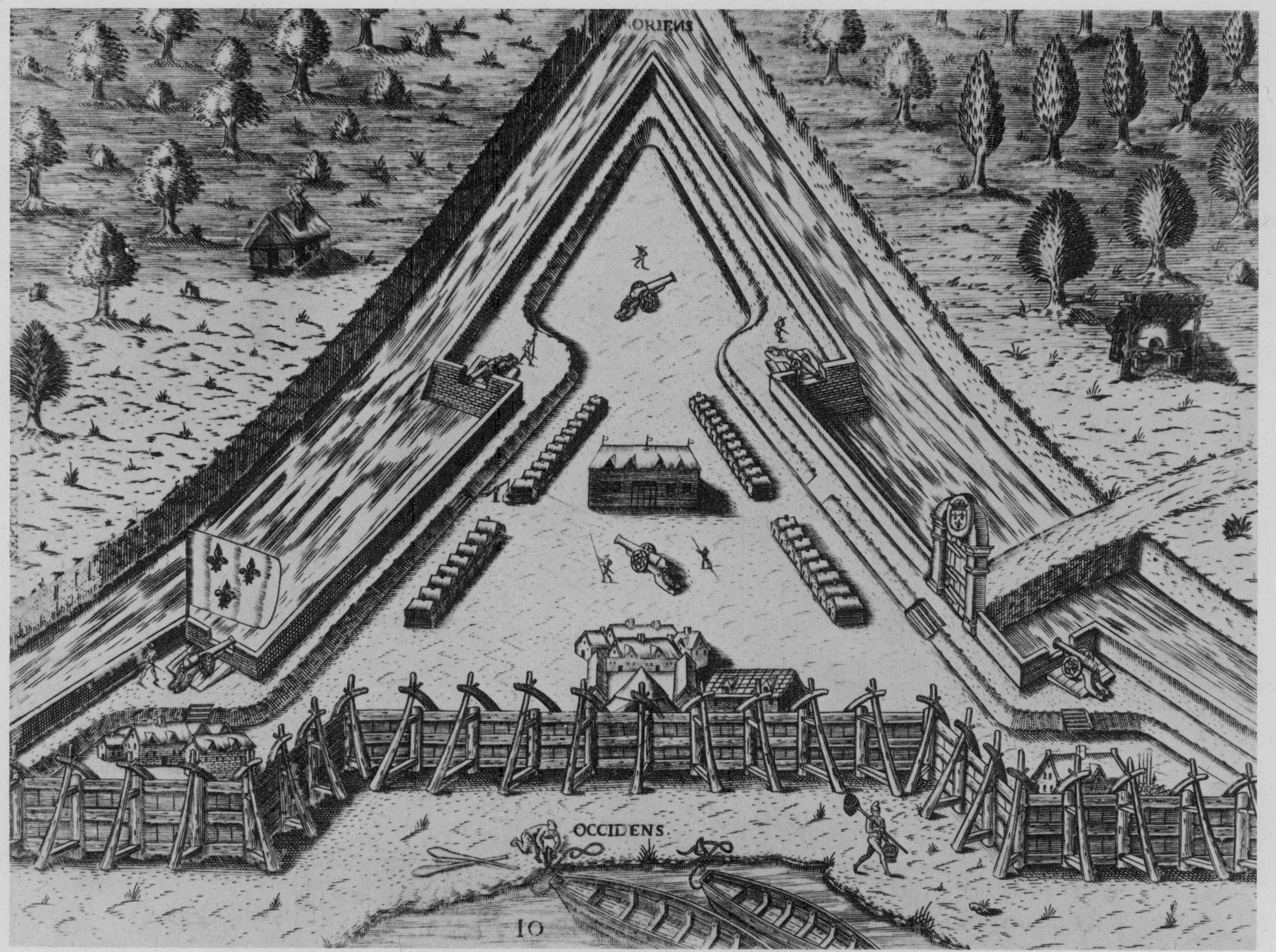

Figure 27. View of Fort Caroline, Florida: 1564

Englishmen responsible for the colonization of America were familiar with these drawings. De Bry had conferred with Richard Hakluyt about the Le Moyne drawings, which he had acquired in 1588 from the artist's widow. The English had followed with interest the Huguenot expeditions to Florida that had begun as early as 1562. They had learned with dismay of the Spanish butchery of the French Protestants at the Fort Caroline garrison in 1565. Le Moyne, one of the few survivors, had escaped to England. Raleigh and other Englishmen who fought alongside the Huguenots in France may first have heard the stories of the colony there and perhaps examined at first hand some of the original drawings. John Hawkins, one of the prominent English sea captains, had visited Fort Caroline and had left supplies to assist the French.[29]

An even earlier triangular fort had been constructed by the Spanish at St. Augustine. As copied from a Spanish manuscript plan dating from 1593, this fort and the adjacent settlement are shown in figure 28. The English had some knowledge of this settlement as well, since Drake had ample opportunity to observe St. Augustine at the time of his attack.[30] Both Fort Caroline and St. Augustine could have served as models for the triangular form adopted by the settlers of Jamestown, although this plan may have been used simply because it was the simplest and most economical method of enclosing a space by straight palisades at a period when both time and resources were limited.

On June 22, 1607, Newport sailed on the return voyage to England leaving behind about a hundred colonists and provisions for three months. By September, so Smith tells us, forty-six of the men had died, victims of disease and starvation.[31] The affairs of the colony had been ill managed. Half of the colonists were gentlemen whose talents lay in directions other than those tasks of providing the essentials for survival in an uncivilized environment. Apparently, too, Wingfield proved an inept leader. At least some of the councilors, including Smith, thought so. These and other dissensions slowed the progress of building the settlement. Smith's description of conditions in the triangular palisade reveal how little had been accomplished: "As yet we had no houses to cover us, our Tents were rotten and our Cabbins worse then nought." As to the attitude and morale of the surviving settlers,

> notwithstanding our misery, [they] little ceased their mallice, grudging, and muttering. As at this time were most of our chiefest men either sicke or discontented, the rest being in such dispaire, as they would rather starve and rot with idlenes, then be perswaded to do any thing for their owne reliefe without constraint.[32]

Many of the early settlers and probably most of the members of the London Company confidently expected to find in Virginia rich deposits of gold, silver, and precious stones. Captain Newport fed the flames of these vain hopes on his return to England. From Plymouth he wrote to Lord Salisbury an optimistic report of the country as one "very rich in gold and copper." [33] This belief in easy wealth dominated the thinking of those responsible for the direction of the enterprise in London. In their choice of supplies and their recruitment of new "adventurers" to be sent to Virginia this consideration remained paramount. It was an attitude that was to handicap the development of Jamestown.

In January of 1608, Newport returned with supplies and seventy new colonists. The boost in morale this event doubtless caused was to be brief. Four days later "there broke out . . . such a fire that, growing rapidly, it consumed all the buildings of the fort, and the storehouse of ammunition and provision." [34] Not all of the new colonists could be mustered to repair this severe damage. As Simmonds scornfully commented,

> the worst mischiefe was our gilded refiners, with their golden promises, made all men their slaves in hope of recompence. There was no talke, no hope, nor worke, but dig gold, wash gold, refine gold, load gold. Such a brute of gold, as one mad fellow desired to bee buried in the sandes, least they should by their art make gold of his bones.[35]

In May and again in September came additional supplies and colonists, the arrivals in the autumn including the first two women to reach Jamestown. During the spring of 1608 the fort was repaired, additional explorations of the region carried out, and in the fall the leadership of the colony came into the capable hands of John Smith. Under his direction, by the spring of 1609, the colonists had dug a well in the fort, "built some 20 houses; re-covered our Church . . . and . . . built a blocke house in the necke of our Ile." [36] Smith also attempted to provide a firmer agricultural base for the colony so that it would not be dependent on supplies from England or on trade with the Indians, who were becoming increasingly hostile and uncooperative. Additional land was cleared and planted in crops, and facilities were provided for raising chickens and hogs. These were wise measures, but they were insufficient to prevent a new period of starvation

Figure 28. Plan of St. Augustine, Florida: 1593

when it was discovered that most of the stored corn had spoiled or been consumed by rats.

In 1609 members of the London Company made a determined effort to place the enterprise on a sounder basis. They secured a change in the charter allowing the Council for Virginia in England to appoint a governor of the colony. This superseded the previous arrangement under which the councilors in Virginia elected their own president. Perhaps more important, the company dispatched nine ships under the command of Sir Thomas Gates and Sir George Somers with adequate supplies and five hundred additional settlers. The ship carrying Gates and Somers was wrecked during a storm off the Bermudas, but the bulk of the fleet reached Virginia in August. Although John Smith was forced to return to England for treatment of an injury suffered in an explosion, the colony appeared for the first time to be in reasonably good condition.

That winter of 1609–1610, however, proved disastrous. The food supply was exhausted. The settlers devoured their animals and, finally, household pets and even vermin. They dug in the woods for roots, they ate shoe leather, and many of them simply stumbled off into the wilderness hoping to find food at some Indian village but doubtless meeting instead with death at the hands of the natives. At the end of that dreadful winter only sixty-five shattered and broken persons were alive when Sir Thomas Gates, shipwrecked the previous year in Bermuda, arrived in May of 1610. The town itself

> appeared raither as the ruins of some auntient [for]tification, then that any people living might now in habit it: the pallisadoes he found tourne downe, the portes open, the gates from the hinges, the church ruined and unfrequented, empty howses (whose owners untimely death had taken newly from them) rent up and burnt . . . and . . . *the Indian as fast killing without as the famine and pestilence within.*[37]

The morale of the settlers was broken, and Gates could promise them little. He had managed to reach Virginia only in small ships constructed in Bermuda, and these were ill stocked with provisions. After some discussion they resolved to abandon Jamestown and Virginia altogether and to set out for England. On June 7, 1610, the ships cast off from the bank below the fort and slipped down the James. But the Roanoke experience was not to be repeated. At the mouth of the river on the following morning Gates's men saw the sails of the ships of Thomas West, Lord Delaware, the governor and captain general of Virginia who had been sent with yet another group of colonists and supplies.

It must have been with mixed feelings that the survivors of the previous winter viewed Delaware's fleet, for the governor immediately decided to reoccupy Jamestown and continue the colony. This was his first view of the town, and he found the site "a verie noysome and unholsome place, occationed much bie the mortallatie and idleness of owure people." Delaware "sett the sailors a worke to unlade shippes, and the land men some to cleanse the Town." [38]

John Smith was not a man to let pass an opportunity to boast about his own achievements. He did much to rally the colonists during his period of leadership. Yet in his history of Virginia he strongly suggests that it was Delaware who was finally able to organize the affairs of the settlers so as to ensure the success of the colony. The governor assembled all the colonists and informed them that many of their misfortunes in the past had been their own fault, "earnestly intreating them to amend these desperate follies lest hee should be compelled to draw the sword of Justice and to cut off such delinquents." [39]

Delaware accompanied his thinly veiled threat by words of encouragement. He pointed out that the provisions he had brought were sufficient to supply four hundred men for an entire year. He may have indicated also that the new colonists included many practical men who were skilled in the trades and crafts so badly needed in Virginia.[40] Delaware immediately began the reconstruction of Jamestown. It is to William Strachey, secretary to the governor, that we owe a description of the community at that time which is by far the most complete of all early accounts.

According to Strachey, the fort, which occupied "about halfe an Acre" of land

> on the North side of the River, is cast almost into the forme of a Triangle, and so Pallizadoed. The south side next the River (howbein extended in a line, or Curtaine six score foote more in length, then the other two, by reason the advantage of the ground doth so require) containes one hundred and forty yards: the West and East sides a hundred onely.[41]

Strachey repeats Percy's earlier description concerning the bulwarks at each corner within which "a peece of Ordnance or two well mounted" could be found.

Strachey's description of the arrangement of buildings within the line of fortifications is of interest:

> To every side, a proportioned distance from the Pallisado, is a settled streete of houses, that runs along, so as each line of the Angle hath his streete. In the middest is a market place, a Store house, and a Corps du guard, as likewise a pretty Chappell, . . . in length threescore foote, in breadth twenty foure. . . . [All this was enclosed within a] Pallizado of Planckes and strong Posts, foure foote deepe in the ground, of yong Oakes, Walnuts, &c. The . . . principall Gate from the Towne, through the Pallizado, opens to the River, as at each Bulwarke there is a Gate likewise to goe forth, and at every Gate a Demi-Culverin, and so in the Market Place.

We learn that in Strachey's opinion the houses of the town were "as yet in no great uniformity, either for the fashion, or beauty of the streete," but that their interiors had been made more attractive through the use of "a delicate wrought fine kinde of Mat the Indians make." This was not the only influence of native craftsmanship on the colonists, for Strachey informs us that the settlers

> have found the way to cover their houses: now (as the Indians) with barkes of Trees, as durable, and as good proofe against stormes, and winter weather, as the best Tyle defending likewise the piercing Sunbeames of Summer, and keeping the inner lodgings coole enough, which before in sultry weather would be like Stoves, whilest they were, as at first, pargetted and plaistered with Bitumen or tough Clay.

Lord Delaware was determined not only to put Jamestown in reasonable condition but to keep it that way. He revised and extended the laws and orders for the colony that Gates had proclaimed on his arrival, and these regulations included the following section dealing with sanitation at the settlement:

> There shall be no man or woman, Launderer or Launderesse, dare to wash any uncleane Linnen, driue bucks, or throw out the water or suds of fowle cloathes, in the open streete, within the Pallizadoes, or within forty foote of the same, nor rench, and make cleane, any kettle, pot, or pan, or such like vessell within twenty foote of the olde well, or new Pumpe: nor shall any one aforesaid, within lesse then a quarter of one mile from the Pallizadoes, dare to doe the necesseties of nature, since by these unmanly, slothfull, and loathsome immodesties, the whole Fort may bee choaked, and poisoned with ill aires, and so corrupt (as in all reason cannot but much infect the same) and this shall take notice of, and avoide, upon paine of whipping and further punishment, as shall be thought meete, by the censure of a martiall Court.[42]

But mere regulations, even if rigorously enforced, would not be enough for Jamestown. Strachey, like a few writers before him and many after, found the site "unwholesome and sickly." He believed, probably with good reason, that the brackish water from the James which filled their shallow well was the cause "of many diseases and sicknesses which have happened to our people, who are indeede strangely afflicted with Fluxes and Agues."[43] He could point to the fact that of several hundred persons during the previous year who had established themselves at the falls of the James, near present-day Richmond, or in the country south of the James, "there did not so much as one man miscarry, and but very few or none fall sicke."

One who did "fall sicke" at Jamestown was Lord Delaware himself, who left for England in March, 1611. On his return home he could report that while he had left the colony well provisioned they would need still more supplies and, as always, additional settlers. He also mentioned his construction of three forts. Two, east of Hampton River, were known as Fort Henry and Fort Charles. The third, at the falls of the James well above Jamestown, was called Fort West.[44] Delaware, a man of stern discipline, was matched in this characteristic by Sir Thomas Dale who in May arrived in Virginia with several ships and was reinforced later in the summer by Sir Thomas Gates with a larger force.

Dale first set about seeing that crops were planted at the several small forts near the mouth of the James. At Jamestown, despite Delaware's encouragements, admonitions, and threats of the previous year, Dale "found here likewise no corn sett, [only] some few seeds put into a private garden or Two." Although not officially abolished until a later year, the system of communal labor under which the colony had floundered along was modified by Dale who allotted to each man a private garden. He also discussed a long list of improvements to be carried out at Jamestown and started his men on these projects.[45] But Dale had an even more important mission. "According to my directions," he says, he was to "search further up [the James River] for a convenient new seat to rayse a principall

Towne." The council in London, although it could not bring itself to abandon Jamestown, had finally been persuaded to establish a second community.

In preparation for this effort Dale set his men to felling trees and preparing posts, rails, and palings for the new town. Gates, arriving at this time as governor, fully approved Dale's proposal and in September sent him off with 350 men. Ralph Hamor, who had succeeded Strachey as secretary of the colony, furnishes the details. Dale, he says, reached the site in a day and a half. Within ten days "hee had verie strongly impaled seven English Acres of ground for a Towne, which . . . hee called by the name of Henrico." By the end of four months, recalls Hamor, Dale "had made Henrico much better, and of more worth than all the worke ever since the Colony began."

Dale had selected a location where the James, in its winding course twelve to fifteen miles below Richmond, had created a peninsula with a narrow neck only two miles across. At this point Dale erected a palisade and ditch as protection against Indian attack. At the tip of the peninsula in the curve of the river he planned and built the town proper. We turn again to Hamor:

> There are in this Town three streets of well framed houses, a handsome Church & the foundation of a more stately one laid of Brick, in length an hundred foot, and fiftie foot wide, besides Store-houses, Watch-houses, and such like: there are also, as ornaments belonging to this Towne, upon the Verge of this River, five faire Block-houses, or Commanders, wherein live the honester sort of people, as in Farmes in England, and there keepe continuall centinnell for the Townes securitie.[46]

In addition to Hamor's description of the building of the new town of Henrico, we have the following account by Robert Johnson:

> The spade men fell to digging, the brick men burnt their bricks, the company cut down wood, the Carpenters fell to squaring out, the Sawyers to sawing, the Souldier to fortifying, and every man to somewhat. And to answer the first objection for holesome lodging, here they have built competent and decent houses, the first storie all of bricks, that every man may have his lodging and dwelling place apart by himselfe, with a sufficient quantitie of ground alotted thereto for his orchard and garden to plant at his pleasure and for his own use. Here they were building also an Hospitall with fourscore lodgings (and beds alreadie sent to furnish them) for the sicke and lame, with keepers to attend them for their comfort and recoverie.[47]

Against these cheerful and optimistic reports by those associated with the company must be set the following version of what was accomplished, prepared some years later by a group of settlers present at the time:

> Fortification against a foreign enemy there was none, only two or three peeces or ordenance mounted, and against a domestic noe other but a pale inclosinge the Towne to the quantitye of foure acres, within which those buildings that weare erected, coulde not in any man's judgement, neither did stande above five yeares and that not without continuall reparations; true it is that there was a Bricke Church intended to be built, but not soe much as the foundation thereof ever finished, but we contentinge our selves with a church of wood answerable to those houses. Many other workes of like nature weare by him [Dale] donne at Henrico and the precincts therof, but so slightly as before his departure hence, he himself saw the ruine and desolation of most of them.[48]

We know little more than this about the plan of Henrico and its now vanished buildings. The only graphic depiction of the settlement prepared in that era is of considerable interest as a curiosity but of little value in providing an understanding of the form of the town. In figure 29, from a German engraving dating from 1613, "Statt Henry Ville" to the east or right-hand side of the map is, of course, Henrico.[49] The representation seems to be completely stylized, probably as far away in fact from the town's actual form as is the cartography of the coastline and the James River. "Jacque Ville" is meant to be Jamestown, while the two forts apparently depict the small fortifications the colonists had erected at the mouth of the James.

At the very end of 1611 Dale established another settlement about five miles down river from Henrico. This came to be called Bermuda City. It was not, strictly speaking, a new town, for Dale simply occupied a village of the Appomattox Indians, driving off the natives who had been raiding the settlers. Doubtless the colonists who moved here and began to cultivate the nearby fields made many changes in the Indian community, but we lack any knowledge whatsoever of what they may have been.

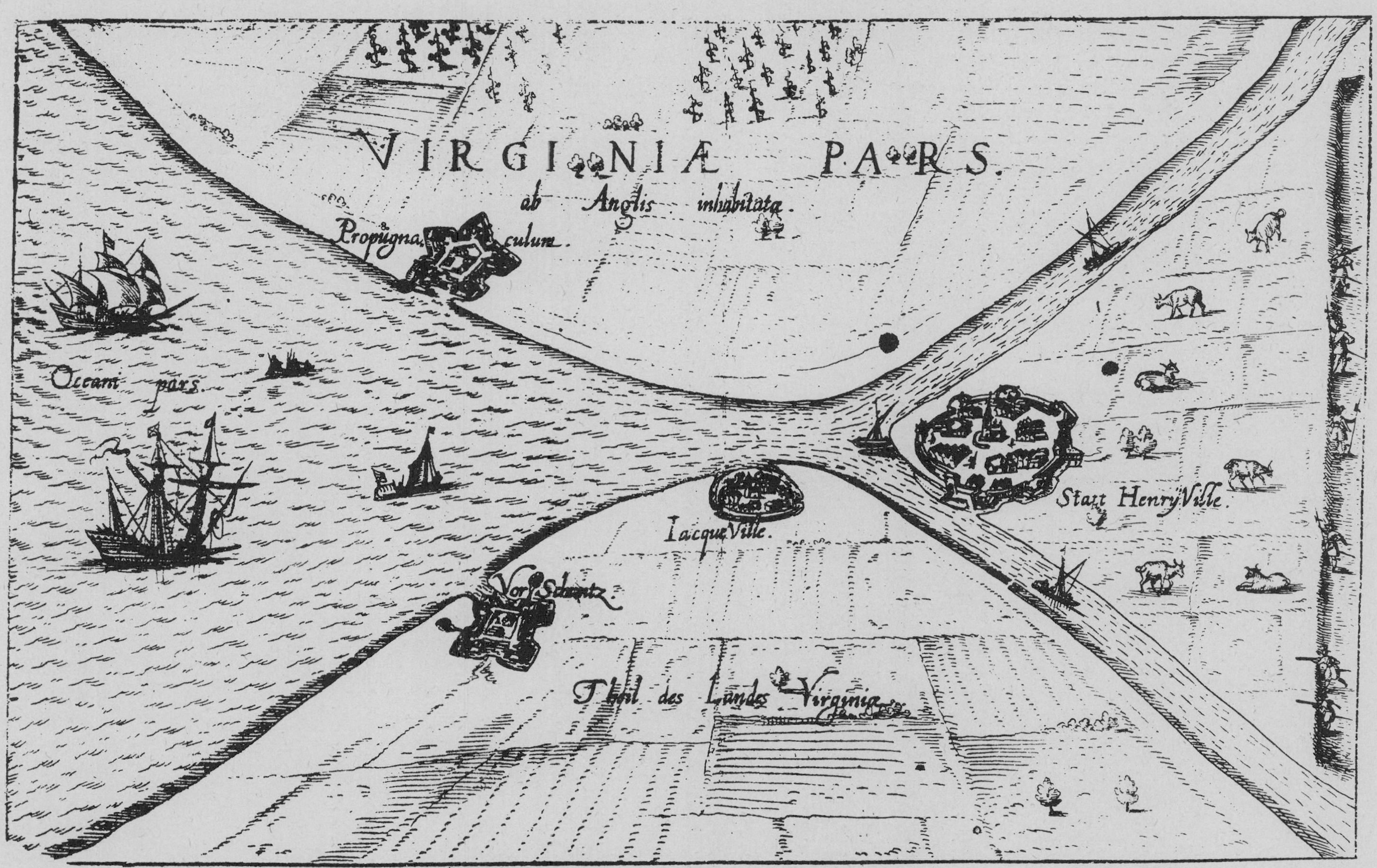

Figure 29. Map of Coastal Virginia and the James River: 1613

Figure 30. Conjectural View of Jamestown, Virginia, ca. 1614

The ambitious Dale would have gone beyond these achievements if he had possessed sufficient men and supplies. Writing to Lord Salisbury on August 17, 1611, he asked for a force of two thousand men with which he confidently expected to pacify the Indians and establish once and for all a prosperous colony, agriculturally self-sufficient and capable of yielding profitable raw materials. He would plant several new towns; one at Point Comfort in connection with one of the existing forts; a second at a site on the north bank of the York River near the town of the great Indian chief Powhatan; and a third at the falls of the James River ten miles above Henrico. He envisaged each of these three new towns, together with Jamestown and Henrico, as the centers from which the entire country could be settled: "These divisions (like Nurseries) sending out smaller Settlements . . . would affoard many excellent Seates for many a thowsand Householder."[50]

Dale never received his two thousand men, but migration of Englishmen to Virginia continued to take place. One of the new arrivals in 1612 was John Rolfe, who introduced to Virginia the variety of tobacco from the West Indies that had become so popular, first in Spain and then throughout Europe and England. He began its systematic cultivation and by this act established the economic basis for the colony. Within a decade the colonists pursued the planting and curing of tobacco with as much zeal as they had once displayed in seeking gold and silver, and the effect of this development on the planning, location, and growth of towns was to be marked.

Rolfe through his marriage with Pocahontas in the spring of 1614 contributed another gift to the colony—peace, at least temporarily, with the settlers' greatest enemy, the powerful chief Powhatan. Under these conditions life for the colonists began to ease. Of Jamestown in 1614 Hamor could write:

> The Towne . . . by the care and prouidence of Sir *Thomas Gates,* who for the most part had his chiefest residence there, is reduced into a hansome forme, and hath in it two faire rowes of howses, all of framed Timber, two stories, and an upper Garrett, or Corne loft high, besides three large, and substantiall Storehowses, joyned togeather in length some hundred and twenty feet, and in breadth forty, and this town hath been lately newly, and strongly impaled, and a faire platforme for Ornance in the west Bulworke raised: there are also without this towne in the Island, some very pleasant, and beautifull howses, two Blockhouses . . . and certain other farme howses.[51]

The Jamestown of 1614 has been depicted by a modern artist following the descriptions by Hamor and Strachey (figure 30). The "two faire rowes of howses" are shown on either side of the new street leading away from one wall of the fort. The three linked storehouses probably were at the water's edge as shown on this drawing. Beyond the paling enclosing the new addition to the community can be seen the other dwellings and farmhouses referred to by Hamor, these being guarded by the two blockhouses at the narrow entrance neck to the peninsula and on the back creek, which at that point roughly paralleled the James River. Seven years after its establishment, Jamestown was at last beginning to take form. The similarity of this primitive community to the linear villages of Ulster will at once be apparent, with James Fort serving the same function as the castle and bawn of the Irish colonial settlements.

John Rolfe has left us a valuable description of the Virginia settlements as they existed in 1616. In addition to the new town of Henrico and the original settlement at Jamestown, there were three groups of settlers in and near Bermuda City, the converted Indian village. He refers to these communities as Bermuda Nether Hundred (the Bermuda City established by Dale), and West and Shirley Hundreds, "seated on the North side the ryver lower then the Bermuda."[52] The three settlements apparently differed in form from that at Jamestown in that the houses of the settlers were not so close together. These little communities, however, were not made up of widely dispersed farmsteads since Rolfe observed that "upon anie *All-arme* they can second and succor one the other." Bermuda Nether Hundred was the largest, with 119 persons. West and Shirley Hundred numbered only 25 colonists.

Rolfe also lists settlements at "Kequoughtan," the Indian Kecoughtan, now Hampton, at the end of the peninsula formed by the James and York rivers, and at "Dales Gifte," located across Chesapeake Bay at the tip of the Eastern Shore near Cape Charles. At Kecoughtan there were 37 settlers clustered around the fort that had been erected some years earlier, and 17 colonists were located at the isolated Cape Charles community. Only 50 persons, according to Rolfe, remained at Jamestown and 38 at Henrico. The population figures for each settlement were for men only. In addition

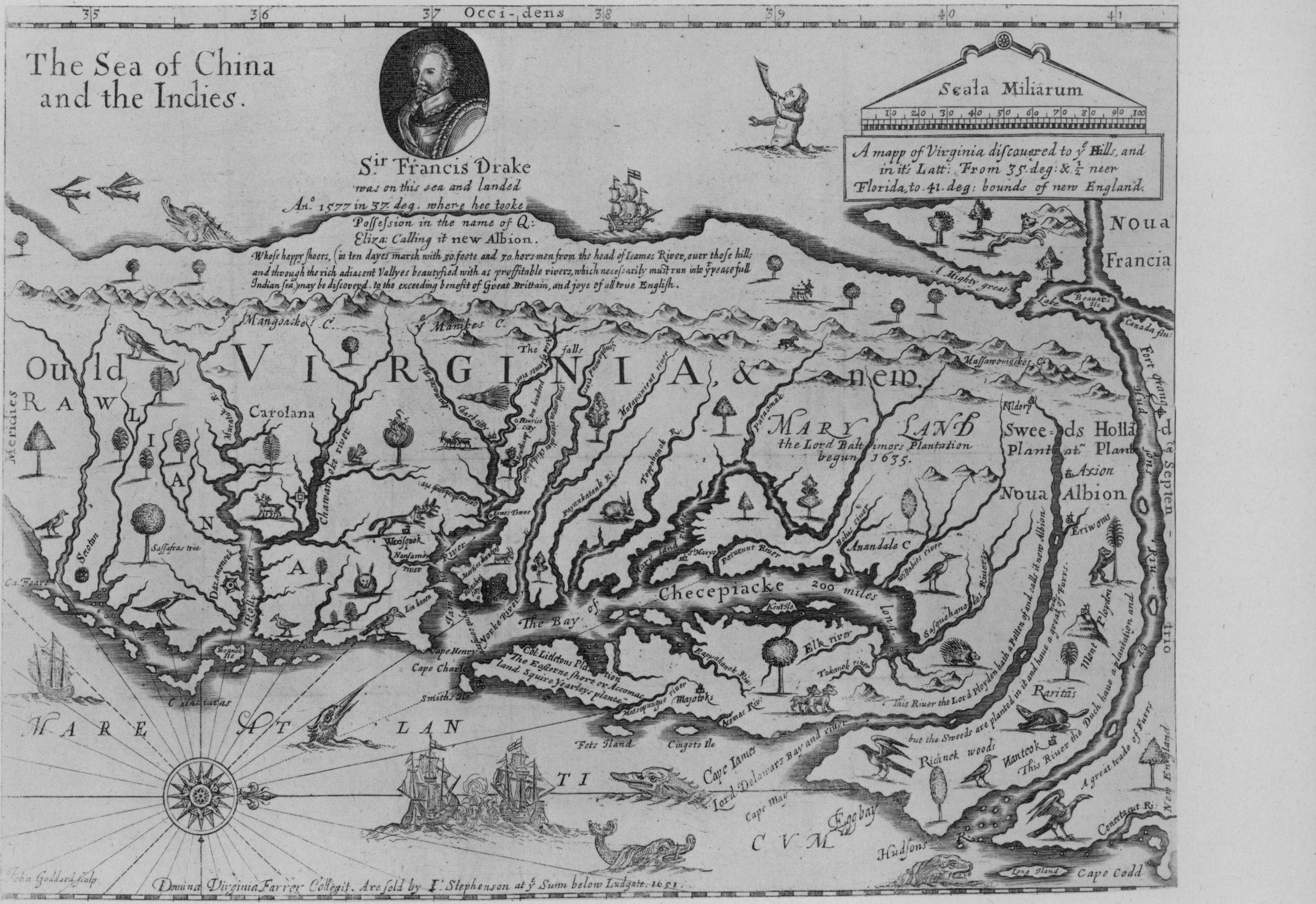

Figure 31. Map of Virginia and Maryland: 1651

Rolfe lists 65 women and children, "in every place some," making a total for all of Virginia of only 351 persons.

Dale in 1611 had begun to modify the system under which the settlers worked the land in common and received supplies from the Virginia Company. The system was officially changed in 1616, but it was not until the arrival of Governor George Yeardley in 1619 that land was formally transferred to the settlers, who then became owners of their property instead of employees in common of the Virginia Company. In that year also republican government began in Virginia. Two representatives, called burgesses, from each of the principal settlements were selected to meet with the governor and his council to frame the laws and regulations under which the colony would be governed.

The colony was divided "into four cities or Boroughs namely the chief city called James Town, Charles City [formerly Bermuda City], Henrico, and the Borough of Kiccotan." Within these areas Yeardley was directed to survey tracts of land of three thousand acres each to be used for company purposes and other tracts of fifteen hundred acres as the common land of each borough. At Jamestown three thousand acres were to be set aside for the governor's use.[53] The location of these settlements can be seen on a curious map of Virginia and Maryland (figure 31) first published in 1651. What is identifiable as Elizabeth City is the approximate location of Hampton, the oldest community of English origin in continuous existence in the New World. The map also shows Martin's Hundred, established in 1617, another loosely organized settlement halfway between Elizabeth City and Jamestown on the north bank of the James River.

One other event of that memorable year was to have a major effect on the future of the colony. In August a Dutch ship put in at Old Point Comfort near Hampton with a cargo of twenty Negroes who were traded for food and other supplies. Although these first Negroes to arrive in Virginia were apparently regarded as indentured servants, like many of the Englishmen in the colony, the status of other Negroes brought to the colony after mid-century was reduced to slavery. Through this development the basis of the later plantation economy was made possible, a change in tidewater history that was to have a profound effect on the location and growth of towns.

III. *The Growth of Settlement and the Development of Town Planning Policy*

During the years 1619–1621 several hundred additional colonists arrived in Virginia. There was also a very substantial increase in the flow of supplies and equipment sent over by the London Company.[1] It was during this period that the company began the practice of shipping to Virginia groups of unmarried women. The new husbands were expected to reimburse the company for the cost of their brides' transportation. This policy was adopted in the belief "that the Plantacon can never flourish till familes be planted, and the respect of wives and Children fix the people on the Soyle."[2]

The company still considered that towns and town life should form the basis for colonial civilization, a view summarized as follows:

> Wee think it fitt, that the houses and buildings be so contrived together, as may make if not hansome Townes, yet compact and orderly villages; that this is the most proper, and successfull maner of proceedings in new Plantacons, besides those of former ages, the example of the Spaniards in the West Indies, doth fully instance.[3]

In attempting to carry out this policy the company was to achieve only limited success. The thirst of the colonists for private land in large holdings combined with the steadily increasing market for tobacco in England frustrated the desires of the London Company to promote compact and orderly settlement in towns and agricultural villages. This conflict between the inclinations of the settlers in Virginia and the policies laid down in London was to continue throughout the seventeenth century and well into the next.

When Ralph Hamor returned to Jamestown in 1617 after a visit in England he found, according to John Smith, "the market-place, and streets, and all other spare places planted with Tobacco."[4] This plant, in the variety introduced by John Rolfe, had quickly become the staple crop of the colony. In 1619, the secretary of the colony observed, "All our riches for the present doe consiste in Tobacco, wherein one man by his owne labour hath in one yeare raised to himselfe to the value of 200£ sterling; and another by the meanes of sixe servants hath cleared at one crop a thousand pound English."[5]

Where before the settlers of Jamestown had paid little attention to the needs of the community as a whole in their vain search for gold and jewels, now it was tobacco cultivation that attracted their individual efforts and distracted them from the development of towns. John Rolfe, writing in 1617 to London, reported on the general prosperity of the colony, adding: "however in buildings, fortyficacons . . . much ruyned and greate want."[6] Jamestown, in fact, seemed perpetually on the verge of disintegration throughout its existence. Virtually every governor sent out by the Virginia Company and, later, by the crown reported back to England on the lamentable condition in which he had found the town and the efforts that would be required for its rebuilding.

The basis for Jamestown's supremacy was soon threatened. Other locations were found to be healthier. It was clearly impossible for all or most of the settlers to live in or near one community. As the Indians were subdued, dispersed settlement became possible without undue risk. The

Virginia Company itself wished to stimulate growth of other towns. Indeed, as early as 1609 it planned for the replacement of Jamestown as the seat of government in favor of a site near the falls of the James River.[7] Finally, the demand for private land on which to grow tobacco, the one activity that produced a profit, was clearly incompatible with the notion of towns as the places where most persons would live.

The Virginia Company tried to reconcile two conflicting desires: the promotion of town life and the distribution of land in fairly large parcels. The device they tried was the creation of "particular plantations." These were grants of land to groups of persons who purchased stock in the company or who, at their own expense, brought nonstockholders across the Atlantic to settle in Virginia. The instructions to Governor Yeardley in 1618 included provisions for this kind of arrangement, a system that apparently had begun two years earlier. By 1619 seven "particular plantations" had been founded. An indenture between the Virginia Company and five "adventurers" who owned a total of forty-five shares has survived and is typical of the agreements made at that time. For each share held the group was to receive a hundred acres of land. This could be claimed at any spot not already granted and at least ten miles distant from other settlements. The group agreed "to erect and built a Towne . . . to place preachers, build churches, schoolhouses and such like workes of charity." An additional fifteen hundred acres of land was to be granted to "bee imployed upon such publike uses as the said adventurers . . . shall thinke fit." For every person transported to Virginia by the group an additional fifty acres would be made available.[8]

The officials of the company may have conceived of the "Towne" to be created as essentially similar to a closely built, nucleated village of rural England. In practice, however, these "particular plantations" of Virginia took the form of very loosely knit, dispersed farming settlements strung out along the principal rivers and creeks of the tidewater area. As a device to encourage colonization this system of land grants proved successful. A census at the beginning of 1623 showed a total of 1,277 colonists living at twenty-three identified locations.[9] Towns, in the sense of compact communities like early Jamestown, did not, however, result from the policy pursued by the company in its last years or by the crown after it assumed control of the colony.[10]

This was not because no attempts were made to promote town development. If laws and proclamations could have created towns and cities, early Virginia would have been an urban civilization and Jamestown would have become a frontier metropolis. These efforts by the Virginia Company and, after 1624, by royal officials require examination in some detail.

In the spring of 1620 the Virginia Company directed each of the four "ancient boroughs," Henrico, Charles City, James City, and Kecoughtan (renamed Elizabeth City), and the several "particular plantations" to construct "a Guest house, for the lodging and entertaining of fifty persons in each, upon their first arrivall." These structures were to be 16 feet wide and 180 feet long. The company specified that while the cost of this work would fall on each locality, they were sending two heifers at company expense "for the beginning of a stocke of Cattell, for their common or Burrough Land." [11] It was not a particularly generous form of assistance, and John Pory, writing to Sir Edwin Sandys, then head of the London Company, pointed out that the colonists would almost certainly resist any order to have them construct these buildings at their own expense. He recalled that

> it is not longe agone, since the Governor made those that watched here at James Citty to contribute some labor to a bridge, and to certain platformes to mounte greate ordinance upon, beinge both for the use and defense of the same Citty, and so of themselves; yet they repyned as much as if all their goods had bene taken from them.[12]

At least one guest structure was actually constructed, although not of the size specified in the directions. Jabez Whittaker, in a letter to Sandys in May 1621, reported the completion of "a guest hous of forty foote long, and twenty foote wide to receave them at there first landing, and [I] have placed an ould woeman in it to wash their clothes and keep the house cleane and have built a little roome for the surgeon that he may be ever neere and helpfull to them." [13]

The company in London commended Whittaker in the next dispatch but included a rebuke to the governor and his council in Virginia that indicates Whittakers' guest house may have been a unique achievement: "We commend to your care especially the buildinge of Guest-houses, which we stricktly charge youe to be brought to perfeccon: we conceive that bussines would have beene effected, if half so much care and time had been taken to do it, as hath beene spent in givinge reasons to the contrary."

The guest house issue was symbolic of other efforts, partly or completely thwarted in one way or another, to promote town growth and to establish a viable economic base for the colony. The company supported the establishment of an ironworks, the results of which were negligible despite early reports that were typically overoptimistic. A party of Frenchmen skilled in grape cultivation was sent out to plant vineyards and supervise winemaking, but had produced nothing of consequence. The company endeavored to introduce silk production, sending to the colony mulberry trees and silkworms for the purpose; this effort also ended in failure. A glassworks had been constructed not far from the fort at Jamestown, and craftesmen skilled in glassblowing had been sent over. But the right kind of sand could not be found, and the manufacture of glass articles amounted to little more than a token output.[15]

Errors of judgment concerning feasible economic activities, mismanagement of resources both in London and Virginia, difficulties in obtaining relevant and accurate information about the progress of the venture, the understandable but vexing habit of the governor and council in ignoring the directions of company officials in England, and the development of factions within the company itself all added to the difficulties of the enterprise. In 1622 a disastrous new blow fell with stunning surprise. In a well-planned and efficiently executed attack, the Indians struck at the now rather widely dispersed settlers and salughtered more than 350 of them, roughly one-third of the entire population.

Jamestown was spared, but Henrico and Charles City, among other settlements, were virtually wiped out. This disaster shattered the morale of the colonists. They considered a wholesale withdrawal from the banks of the James to the eastern shore of Virginia.[16] The officials of the company, however, could not approve so drastic a step, and slowly and painstakingly the task of rebuilding was begun.

Already, in fact, work had started on the expansion of Jamestown. In 1621 the company sent William Claiborne, a land surveyor, to survey the boundaries of Virginia land grants, which until that time had not been accurately laid out.[17] Soon Claiborne found himself engaged in planning the "new town" at the capital on a tract of land located east of James Fort and beyond the area first developed outside the stockade by the "two faire rowes of howses" described in 1614 by Ralph Hamor. Between these two parts of the settlement stood the church built in 1617 by Governor Samuel Argall. A later church, dating from 1647, was eventually constructed on the foundations of its predecessor. The foundations and tower of this later structure still stand.

One of the early occupants of the "new town" was Ralph Hamor, to whom in 1624 Governor Francis Wyatt conveyed an acre and a half of land. The legal description of the property included important references to existing streets. The deed identified the lots as "lying and being about his said howse and abutting Southward upon the high way along the banke of the maine river Northward upon the backstreete Eastward upon the high way which parteth it from the ground of Georg Menefey Merchant Westward partly upon the ground of Richard Steephens Merchant."[18] At least three streets had then been laid out: one following the bank of the river; another, "the backstreete," probably roughly parallel with the first, and a third "high way" connecting the other two.

While the plan of this new section cannot be determined with complete accuracy, a conjectural reconstruction of property boundaries and street lines (figure 32) shows the general nature of this addition to the community. It evidently took the form of an elongated gridiron about one thousand feet east and west along the river. One street followed the bank of the James and was connected to a parallel street by two or three shorter streets running at right angles between the two principal thoroughfares. Although it was in this area that the growth of the town was intended to take place, other more widely dispersed dwellings and related structures were constructed elsewhere on the "island" as well as beyond the narrow neck of land connecting Jamestown with the mainland.[19]

Governor Wyatt was the last to rule Virginia under the London Company. King James found himself increasingly in conflict with its leaders on matters of domestic policy, and he was not satisfied with the company's conduct of colonial affairs. On June 16, 1624, after several years of maneuvering, the king revoked the charter of the company, and Virginia became a royal colony subject to direction from the crown.[20] From that time greater resources could be mustered for the further development of this growing overseas domain. In these efforts, the promotion of town growth and the creation of new communities were to play an important role.

The first royal governor to arrive in Virginia was Sir George Yeardley, who had already served in that capacity under the London Company. His instructions from the Privy Council under Charles I included two items of importance to us. One was an admonition not to allow new settlers "to sit down stragling, but [to be] enjoyned to live by those already planted or in sufficient number by themselves." The other specified that no ships from England should unload any of their cargo before their arrival at James-

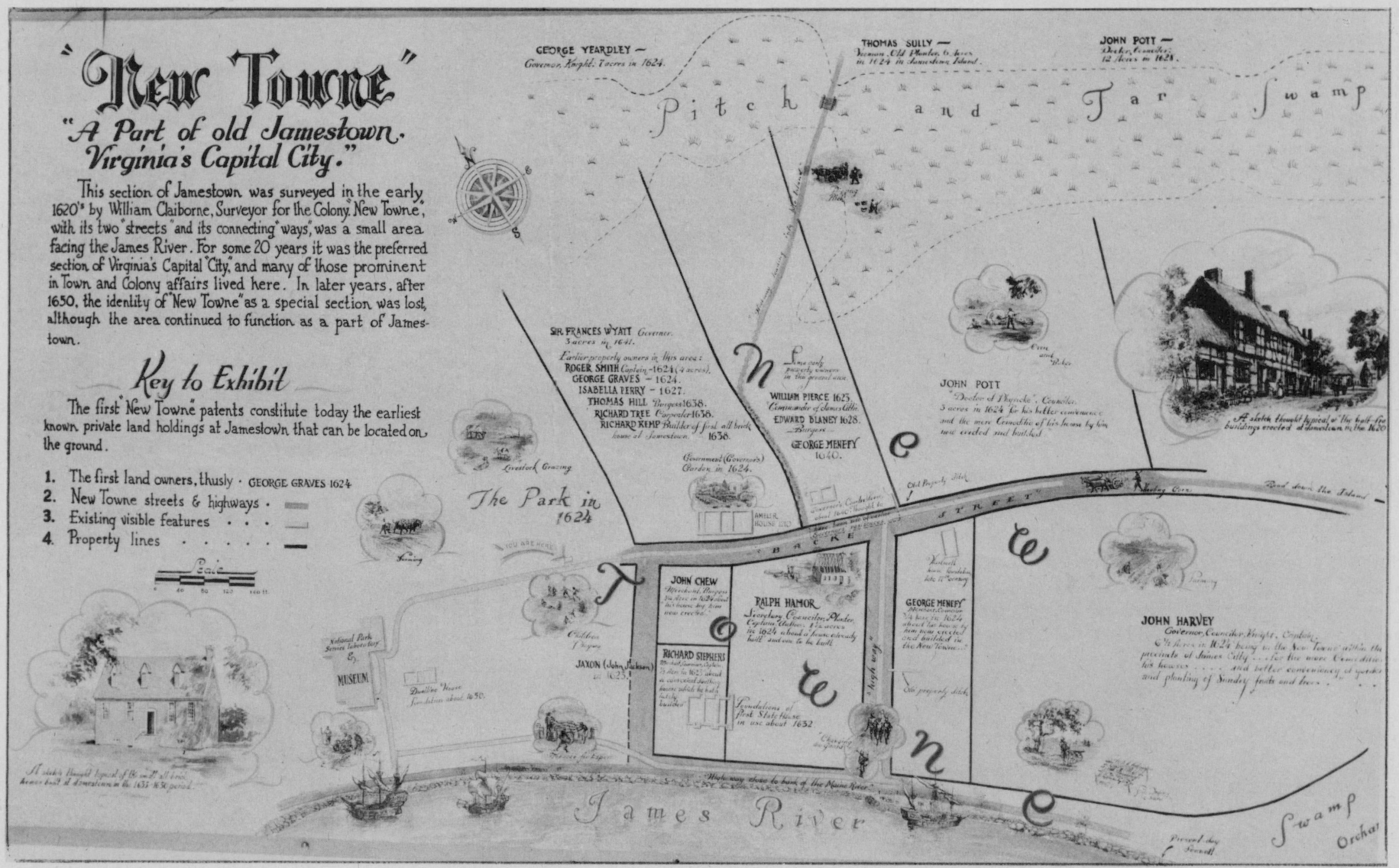

Figure 32. Conjectural Plan of a Portion of Jamestown, Virginia, ca. 1621

town.[21] This latter instruction was the first stage of what was later to become a firmly announced, if widely ignored, policy requiring shipments into and out of the colony only from designated port towns. Under Governor Sir John Harvey in 1631–1632 the Virginia General Assembly finally gave local assent to this instruction when it enacted a measure designating Jamestown as the sole port of entry. A ship's captain violating this act was to forfeit his cargo and "suffer one mounthes imprisonment.[22] The action indicates that despite a very substantial increase in population in the colony only Jamestown of all the Virginia settlements bore any resemblance to a true town. One of the purposes of this legislation was to further its growth. Governor Harvey in 1638 proudly described the results of an act of the assembly passed in the previous year that provided for grants of house and garden lots to anyone who would build in Jamestown:

> Since which order there are twelve houses and stores built in the Towne, one of brick by the Secretarye, the fairest that ever was knowen in this countrye for substance and uniformitye, by whose example others have undertaken to build framed howses to beautifye the place, consonant to his majesties Instruction that wee should not suffer men to build slight cottages as heretofore.
>
> Such hath bene our Indeavour herein that out of our owne purses wee have Largely contributed to the building of a brick church, and both masters of shipps and others of the ablest Planters have liberally by our persuasion underwritten to this work. A levye likewyse by his majesties commands is raised for the building of a State howse at James Cittie, and shall with all diligence be performed.

Then Harvey referred to an action of the Board of Trade, which had suspended the operation of the regulations providing that all goods should be unloaded at Jamestown. This had evidently come about after protests by London merchants and possibly by the planters living some distance from the official port who complained of the inconvenience suffered by them through the legislation:

> There was not one foote of ground for half a mile together by the Rivers syde in James Towne but was taken up and undertaken to be built before your Lordshipps order arrived commanding that until stores [warehouses] were built all men should be permitted to Land theire goods in such places as should be for theire owne conveniencye.
>
> Wee found the undertakers generally disheartened by this Order espetially the Report of Seamen and all others who arrived this yeare concurring that now the Ports were free, and every man might Land his goods where he pleased.[23]

The first statehouse, referred to by Governor Harvey, was soon to take form. Figure 33 is a conjectural rendering of how this building may have appeared about 1655, by which time the left-hand section had been added to the original two-unit structure.[24] Harvey located it midway along the road that followed the bank of the James River in the new town area.

Not all the buildings were this imposing. A few yards from the first statehouse to the north is the site of a modest dwelling measuring about sixteen by thirty feet. This was apparently a frame structure supported, not by a brick or stone foundation but by wooden posts and sills. Figure 34 shows the type of construction typical of the period, with heavy framing timbers and an in-filling of plaster. The only brick used was for the exterior chimney at one end.[25]

Figure 33. Conjectural View of a Building in Jamestown, Virginia

Figure 34. Conjectural View of a Building in Jamestown, Virginia

A somewhat larger house, probably dating from the first half of the seventeenth century, stood close to the river bank and a few hundred feet west of the first statehouse. Figure 35 shows how this structure, measuring about twenty by forty feet, may have appeared. The fireplace is disproportionately large, and the remnants of what may have been an oven have been discovered. This suggests that in addition to its use as a dwelling it may also have served as a bakeshop or possibly a brewery.

Tradesmen and craftsmen customarily carried out their business activities in their houses or in auxiliary structures located on the same plot of ground. Two portions of Jamestown seem to have been favored for these industries and shops. One was along the banks of the James east of the churchyard where the building depicted in figure 35 was situated. Archaeological evidence indicates that in this area there was a lime kiln, a brick kiln, some kind of furnace, and a warehouse. The other section of the town used for industrial purposes lay to the north along the edge of the Pitch and Tar Swamp, the location of which is shown in figure 32. Here there was a

large brick and tile kiln, a smelting pit, a brewhouse, and a pottery kiln.[26] While a number of new buildings had been constructed under the administration of Governor Harvey, Jamestown remained essentially a straggling village. Nevertheless, although there were tiny hamlets elsewhere in the colony at a few strategic locations, this unimposing settlement remained the only community bearing any resemblance to a true town. The absence of towns was disturbing to the king and his advisors, who believed that compact settlements were essential to colonial development. In 1642 Governor William Berkeley received new and detailed instructions to further the growth of urban centers.

He was directed to prevent tradesmen and craftsmen from becoming tobacco planters through orders that they were "to follow their severall Trades and occupations, and that ye draw you into Towns." [27] Berkeley was told to reinstate the earlier regulations preventing ships from unloading except at Jamestown. To avoid the complaints previously made by the planters that storage facilities had not been available at the port, the instructions specified "that care be taken that there be sufficient Storehouses

Figure 35. Conjectural View of a Building in Jamestown, Virginia

and Warehouses for the same and convenient laying of their goods as they shall arrive."

It was also recognized that perhaps the location of Jamestown as the chief settlement was unsatisfactory "because the buildings . . . are for the most part decayed and the place found to be unhealthy and inconvenient in many respects." Berkeley was authorized, with the consent of his council and the assembly, "to choose such other seate for your chiefe Town . . . as by them shall be judged most convenient, retaining the ancient name of James Town." Finally, Berkeley was empowered to plan other towns "to be laid out in such form and order as the Governor and Councill shall appoint." To encourage building in these new settlements he was empowered to require each person in the colony receiving a grant of five hundred acres of land to build a "convenient house of brick of 24 feet long and 16 feet broad with a cellar to it."

There is slight evidence of any significant accomplishments in town development during Berkeley's first administration. The political turmoil in England and the establishment of the Commonwealth diverted attention for a time from colonial affairs. Then in 1651 Parliament passed the Navigation Act establishing severe restrictions on colonial trade. With the restoration of the monarchy in 1660 the Virginians hoped for more favorable treatment, but the new Navigation Act of 1660 under Charles II was in many ways even more burdensome. While it provided for high duties on Spanish and Portuguese tobacco and continued the prohibition on raising tobacco in England itself, the new law limited colonial tobacco trade only to England. Further, it set a tax on tobacco imported to the home country of seven and a half pence a pound, which amounted to from 100 to 250 per cent of the value, depending on the quality of the leaf. Even with a rebate of taxes on tobacco re-exported from England, the net effect was to increase drastically the cost of marketing tobacco abroad. Together with overproduction of the product in Virginia, which tended to depress the price in any event, these enactments caused economic depression in the Virginia and Maryland colonies.

It was not, therefore, the most propitious time for a new effort at town building, particularly one that necessarily would require local taxation to be effective. Yet this is precisely what Charles II directed when he appointed Berkeley once again governor of Virginia. In his instructions to Sir William in 1662 the king was both clear and direct in stating his wishes:

> That care be taken to dispose the planters to be willing to build towns upon every River which must tend very much to their security and in time to their profit, of which they cannot have a better evidence and example than from their neighbours of New England, who obliging themselves to that order have in few years raised that Colony to great wealth and Reputation and security. We wish that there may be at least one Town upon every River and that you begin at James River, which being first seated we desire to give all countenance and to settle the Government there, and therefore as we do expect that you give good example yourself by building some houses, those which will in short time turn to your profit, so you shall in our name let the Councellors of that Colony know that we will take it very well at their hands if they will each of them build one or more houses there, and you shall give a particular account by a Letter to our self of the success of this our design, what orders are made by our assembly for the advancement thereof, and what particular persons do engage themselves to build upon this our Recommendation.[28]

It was truly remarkable that a colony with a population of perhaps forty thousand persons still had no town worthy of the name. Berkeley was determined that this should no longer be the case. The members of the assembly doubtless were unenthusiastic over the legislation that the governor insisted they pass to implement his instructions. Nevertheless, in December, 1662, *An Act for Building a Towne* emerged from their deliberations as the prototype of a series of similar enactments that were to follow in the next thirty or forty years.

This law was intended to apply the first year for the building (or, once again, the rebuilding) of Jamestown. In the following four years its provisions were then to be directed in turn to creating new towns somewhere on the York, the Rappahannock, and the Potomac rivers, and, finally, on the Eastern Shore. In fact, it appears that no effort was made to implement the provisions of this law except at Jamestown.

Each town was to consist of thirty-two brick houses forty feet long, twenty feet wide, and eighteen feet high, with roofs of slate or tile. These houses were to be "regularly placed one by another in a square or such other forme as the honorable Sir William Berkeley shall appoint most convenient."[29]

Each of the seventeen counties which had by that time been created was to be responsible for building one such house, and the act authorized them to impress skilled workmen at specified rates of compensation. The commissioners of each county court were to direct the work of building the house for which their county was responsible, and they were to be fined a thousand pounds of tobacco each if they neglected this duty. The act did not specify the uses to which these houses were to be put, but presumably they could be sold after completion. Construction of houses by individuals was also provided for. Each such private "undertaker" was allowed to build a storehouse for every dwelling he constructed, and only persons building houses were to be given the privilege of erecting such a storehouse.

In addition to this inducement, which would have given the private owners of houses a monopoly on warehouses for storing imports and exports, each undertaker and each county building a house was to receive a subsidy of ten thousand pounds of tobacco. These payments were to be obtained through a tax of thirty pounds of tobacco levied on each "poll" throughout the county. In order to expedite construction, subsidy payments were to be extended only to those completing their building within two years.

All tobacco produced in the three counties of James City, Charles City, and Surry was to be brought to Jamestown for storage in the warehouses controlled by those building the dwellings. Failure to abide by this regulation would bring a fine of a thousand pounds of tobacco. Prices for transporting tobacco to Jamestown were fixed at ten pounds of tobacco per hogshead, and the price for storage was set at six pounds. All imports or exports of merchandise destined to or originating from points above Mulberry Island (about half the way to Jamestown from the mouth of the James River) were to pass through the town, and any storage of such goods was to be at Jamestown. A violation of this provision would result in confiscation of the merchandise.

Finally, the act specified that "noe wooden houses shall hereafter be built within the limitts of the towne, nor those now standing be hereafter repaired, but brick ones to be erected in theire steads." If all this were not enough, in case that something necessary "may perhaps be omitted in this act, the redresse of such omissions is referred to the discretion of the governour and councill in the vacancie of the assembly."

As one student of this law has observed, it "might be regarded as a remarkable triumph of legislative hope over practical experience."[30] Certainly if legislation alone could have created towns in mid-seventeenth century Virginia this act would have conferred ample power for the attempt. The results, however, like many of the previous attempts to stimulate town growth, fell dismally short of Berkeley's hopes and expectations. Only at Jamestown were buildings erected, and even there the number was substantially less than the thirty-two called for by the law.

At least one county responded to the policy established by the colonial government. The records of York County show that in 1662 the county court directed Major Joseph Croshaw to supervise the construction of a house meeting the minimum requirements of the law.[31] Whether that house was ever completed and, if so, what its location was we do not know. A conjectural sketch of one Jamestown dwelling, tentatively dated as built during the period 1650–1676, is shown in figure 36. Its size, determined by archaeological remains, is slightly larger than required by the act, measuring 21½ by 48½ feet. Quite possibly this was built by some private undertaker, or its construction may have been entirely independent of the act of 1662. In either event it illustrates one type of dwelling the construction of which probably originated from this law.

Figure 36. Conjectural View of a Building in Jamestown, Virginia

Other new buildings took the form of row houses. Figure 37 suggests the possible appearance of a group of four dwellings, each twenty by forty feet built in a row with party walls separating the individual units. The foundations for this structure were discovered toward the western end of the new town area of Jamestown not quite five hundred feet from the present bank of the river. The estimated range of dates during which construction probably occurred are 1660–1700, and it is therefore possible that its erection may have resulted from the legislation of 1662.

This was not the only row house to be built in Jamestown. Figure 38 shows another similar structure. The nearest or eastern end was completed about 1666 as the new statehouse to replace the earlier building that had been destroyed by fire. In the middle are three slightly earlier row houses, supposed to be those of Philip Ludwell, while at the end is a dwelling that may have been the so-called "country house" belonging to the colony. The location of this building which is some 240 feet long is not in the "new town" area but well to the west beyond the church and the site of James Fort.

It was this building, along with the church and all of the houses, that Nathaniel Bacon put to the torch in September, 1676, during the rebellion he led to protest Governor Berkeley's failure to put down the Indians on the western frontier, as well as other policies over which there was widespread disagreement. It was ironic, in view of Bacon's destruction of

Figure 37. Conjectural View of a Building in Jamestown, Virginia

Figure 38. Conjectural View of a Building in Jamestown, Virginia

Jamestown, that one of his published complaints directed at the governor was "for not having during the long time of his Government in any measure advanced this hopefull Colony either by Fortifications, Townes or Trade." [32]

Although it was the only one of which the colony could boast, the town that Bacon burned was not very extensive. Earlier that year one witness described it as comprising only "som 16 or 18 houses . . . and in them about a dozen families (for all the howses are not inhabited) getting their liveings by keeping ordnaries, at extreordinary rates." [33] Doubtless there were a few more structures than this account mentioned, but in any event they were now destroyed. From this disaster Jamestown never really recovered, although there were further attempts to re-establish the town, and some reconstruction did occur.

The fourth and final statehouse erected in the town rose from the ruins of its predecessor. This took place only after serious consideration was given to moving the seat of government to another location. After the fire, the House of Burgesses passed a measure to move to Gloucester or Tindall's Point on the north side of the mouth of the York River. This did not receive final approval, but the days of Jamestown were numbered. Another fire, this time on October 31, 1698, consumed the rebuilt statehouse. The assembly had had enough of this ill-fated location and in the spring of the following year elected to move the capital of Virginia from the banks of the James to a site located midway between that stream and the York River. There, at what was then called Middle Plantation, the most interesting of all the tidewater towns was to be planned. Later chapters will describe the events of that episode in city development.

The creation of a new colonial venture in the tidewater area brought additional settlers to the Chesapeake Bay in 1634. The enterprise, unlike the commercial sponsorship of the Virginia colony, took the form of an individual proprietorship under the direction and virtually complete authority of Cecilius Calvert, the second Lord Baltimore. Cecilius had succeeded to the patent granted his father by Charles I to the territory between the Potomac River on the south and the fortieth parallel on the north. The Calverts were Catholic, but in their efforts to recruit prospective colonists they did not discriminate against Protestants. It was, therefore, a mixed group of some two hundred persons who sailed from England in November, 1633, under the leadership of Governor Leonard Calvert, the proprietor's twenty-five-year-old brother.

Lord Baltimore followed the precedents set by Raleigh and the London Company in furnishing instructions to his party concerning the location of their settlement and the planning of their first town. Those portions of his directive read as follows:

> That where they intend to settle the Plantacon they first make choice of a fitt place, and a competent quantity of ground for a fort within which or neere unto it a convenient house, and a church or a chappel adjacent may be built, for the seate of his Lordship or his Governor or other Commissioners for the time being in his absence, both which his Lordship would have them take care should in the first place be erected, in some proportion at least, as much as is necessary for present use though not so complete in every part as in fine afterwards they may be and to send his Lordship a Platt of it and of the scituation, by the next opportunity, if it be done by that time, if not or but part of it nevertheless to send a Platt of what they intend to do in it. That they likewise make choise of a fitt place neere unto it to seate a towne.
>
> That they cause all the Planters to build their houses in as decent and uniforme a manner as their abilities and the place will afford, and neere adjoyning one to an other, and for that purpose to cause streetes to be marked out where they intend to place the towne and to oblige every man to buyld one by an other according to that rule and that they cause divisions of Land to be made adjoyning on the back sides of their houses and to be assigned unto them for gardens and such uses according to the proportion of every ones building and adventure and as the conveniency of the place will afford which his Lordship referreth to their discretion, but is desirous to have a particular account from them what they do in it, that his Lordship may be satisfied that every man hath justice done unto him.[34]

A Virginian, Captain Henry Fleet, guided Leonard Calvert and his party to a site on which he had previously established a trading post. This was located near the tip of the peninsula formed by the Potomac and the Patuxent rivers. Leading northwards from the Potomac was St. George's River, later renamed St. Mary's. It was on its eastern bank, close to the Indian settlement of Yowaccomoco, that Calvert established St. Mary's, the first town of Maryland. The location can be seen on the map, figure 39, published the following year in London with an elaborate tract designed to promote further settlement in the new colony.

Governor Calvert purchased the Indian village and its surrounding land from the natives, who agreed to move to another site. This arrangement for immediate temporary shelter of the colonists made initial settlement much easier than in Virginia. The site was level, elevated above the river, fertile, and in general possessed all the qualities of a town location that Jamestown lacked.[35] This part of Lord Baltimore's instructions, at least, had been fully observed.

But if his directive to "send a Platt of what they intend to do" was ever followed, that drawing has either been destroyed or rests unidentified in some public archive or private collection. We lack even a contemporary description of the form the town took, although in May Leonard Calvert sent his brother a letter informing him that

> We have seated ourselves within one-half mile of the river, within a palisade of one hundred and twenty yards square, with four flanks. We have mounted one piece of ordnance and placed six murderers [small cannon] in parts most convenient, a fortification (we think)

sufficient to defend against any such weak enemies as we have reason to expect here.[36]

The fort had thus been completed within a few weeks after Calvert had taken possession of the site on March 27. Doubtless this contained the guardhouse and storehouse on which work had started immediately.[37] Since the early accounts of the settlement mention both the fort and a town, it seems safe to assume that not all the houses of the settlers were built within the confines of the palisaded enclosure. A "Water-mill for the grinding of Corne adjoyning to the Towne" was probably located on Mill Creek to the north of St. Mary's.[38] The town of St. Mary's thus likely resembled such settlements in Virginia as Bermuda Hundred more than Jamestown or Henrico. The plots of land to which most of the colonists were entitled were substantial, much of the area was already cleared for farming, and apparently there was little fear that the Indians would be hostile. The settlement pattern, therefore, was loose and rather unstructured with the houses of the colonists built at some distance from each other. Yet, as in the neighboring colony of Virginia, the system of land grants adopted in Maryland by Lord Baltimore functioned in such a way as to stifle the development of compact, nucleated communities.[39]

The exact pattern of St. Mary's is not known, although one authority has attempted a partial reconstruction based on an examination of old land records.[40] In the absence of systematic archaeological exploration of the site little more can be added to a description of the town as it existed in its initial years. The street pattern may well have followed the existing Indian paths and trails, and the first references to surveyed streets with lots one acre in size date from 1672 when Aldermanbery Street was laid out near the site of the fort. Two other short streets serving town lots may have been created in 1675 and 1678.[41] At the end of Aldermanbery Street on a point of land near the water the statehouse was constructed in 1676. Until this time the meetings of the colonial government had been held in a variety of buildings, including private houses and not always at St. Mary's. As migration to Maryland increased, other settlements sprang up. One of these was in Anne Arundel County, farther north on Chesapeake Bay. The citizens of that area in 1674 had offered to construct "a State house, Prison and Office at their own Charge," as well as a residence for the governor if the seat of government would be moved to their county.[42] The assembly rejected this offer, deciding two years later to provide proper accommodations for the government at St. Mary's.

The act passed in that year for this purpose was remarkable in that it specified in minute detail the size, form, materials, and interior arrangements of the new building down to such minutiae as the dimensions of rafters and joists. It was to be an imposing structure, "built of brick or stone . . . two stories high and to continue in length forty five foot from outside to outside with a porch in front sixteen foot long and twelve foot broad."[43] Although this building no longer exists, a modern replica has been constructed on a similar site not far away from that of the original.

By that time St. Mary's had achieved some of the qualities of a town. The governor's house, several taverns, warehouses, shops, and other buildings, along with the dwellings of the residents, composed the community four decades after its founding. Nevertheless to the eyes of Charles Calvert, the only Lord Baltimore to live at St. Mary's, the settlement appeared anything but impressive when he sent back the following description to London in 1678:

> The principal place or town is called St. Mary's where the General Assembly and provincial court are kept, and whither all ships trading there do in the first place resort; but it can hardly be called a town, it being in length by the water about five miles, and in breadth upwards towards the land not above one mile,—in all which space, excepting only my own house and buildings wherein the said courts and offices are kept, there are not above thirty houses, and those at considerable distance from each other, and the buildings (as in all other parts of the Province), very mean and little, and generally after the manner of the meanest farm-houses in England.[44]

In this same communication to the Board of Trade, Calvert mentions the lack of towns elsewhere in the colony and the inclination of planters "to have their houses near the water for convenience of trade, and their lands on each side of and behind their houses." The same forces that had been at work in Virginia created similar conditions in Maryland. Some further analysis of these factors, so important in their implications for urban development, should now be made.

George Alsop, in his fascinating record of Maryland in 1666, could also have been describing Virginia when he observed that "Tobacco is the only solid Staple Commodity of this Province."[45] The economic well-being

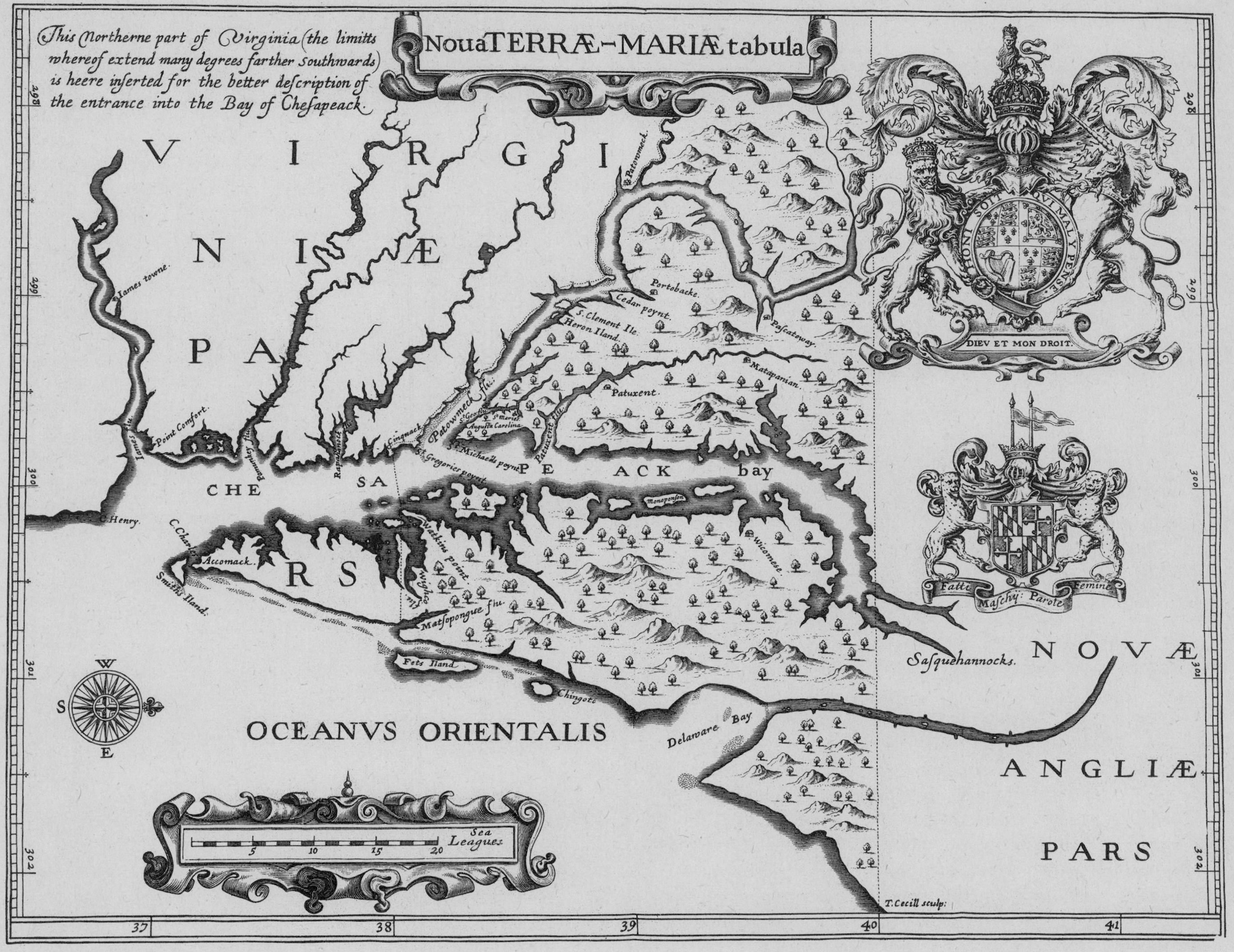

Figure 39. Map of Maryland: 1635

of both colonies depended almost entirely on the sale of the crop to English merchants. Planting began each year in March and April. Harvested in September, the tobacco leaves were then dried and cured, packed into hogsheads, and stored for shipment abroad. Although some planters shipped their tobacco to England for sale there, most of the trade took place in the colonies. Alsop describes the process:

> Between November and January there arrives in this Province Shipping to the number of twenty sail and upwards, all Merchantmen loaden with Commodities to Trafique and dispose of, trucking with the Planter for Silks, Hollands, Serges, and Broad-clothes, with other necessary Goods, priz'd at such and such rates as shall be judg'd on is fair and legal, for Tobacco at so much the pound, and advantage on both sides considered; the Planter for his work, and the Merchant for adventuring himself and his Commodity into so far a Country.

Alsop added: "Our Shops and Exchanges of Mary-Land, are the Merchants Storehouses, where with few words and protestations Goods are bought and delivered." [46]

One must not imagine this intensive trade activity occurring in some single great town in each colony. The efforts in Virginia, for example, to require all ships to load and unload only at Jamestown and, later, at several other designated points within the province, proved only mildly effective. Legislation proposed in Maryland in 1639 to create official and exclusive ports of entry failed to pass. Steadfastly the large planters resisted these governmental regulations that would have imposed additional expenses of shipping and storing their crop at points some distance from their plantations. A substantial amount of the tobacco trade, therefore, took place on the wharfs and in the warehouses of individual plantations.

The geography of the tidewater area made this possible. The rivers of Virginia and Maryland running into the Chesapeake furnished channels broad and deep enough that ocean-going shipping could penetrate the interior for many miles. The ships of the time had no difficulty in reaching almost any spot along these river estuaries. Therefore, no advantage accrued to having a single port or a limited number of ports around which, in other circumstances, towns might have been expected to develop.

John Clayton, writing in 1688, astutely identified this major geographic force as one that prevented the growth of urban centers:

> No Country in the World can be more curiously watered. But this Conveniency . . . I look on [to be] the greatest Impediment to the Advance of the Country, as it is the greatest Obstacle to Trade and Commerce. For the great Number of Rivers, and the Thinness of the Inhabitants, distract and disperse a Trade. So that all Ships in general gather each their Loading up and down an hundred Miles distant; and the best of Trade that can be driven is only a Sort of *Scotch* Pedling; for they must carry all Sorts of Truck that trade thither. . . . The Number of Rivers, is one of the chief Reasons why they have no Towns.[47]

Some years earlier, in 1657, Anthony Langston assigned three reasons for the absence of towns in Virginia. He too recognized that the configuration of the coastline and the deep indentations formed by the rivers of the tidewater region had influenced the colonists to settle "up and down by these famous Rivers (wch I think all the world cannot parallel) to seate in a stragling distracted Condition." He also suggested that the lack of manufacturing activities in the colony inhibited the growth of towns. There was little industry, according to Langston, "for want of Iron, and steele, whereby the Smiths Trade might goe forward, wch is the foundation of all other Arts."

Finally, Langston referred to the land policy that had prevailed in Virginia:

> Townes & Corporations have likewise been much hindred by our manner of seating the Country; every man having Liberty upon the right of transporting of persons to take up Land (untaken before) and there seat, build, clear, & plant without any manner of restraint from the Government . . . so that every man builds in the midst of his own Land, and therefore provides beforehand to take up so much at the first Patent, that his great Grandchild may be sure not to want Land to go forward with any great design they covet.

The conditions Langston so accurately described can be better appreciated by an inspection of Augustine Herrman's map of Maryland and Virginia in 1670. A portion of this notable cartographic achievement (figure 40), shows the lower James, York, and Rappahannock rivers. Lining the banks of these great rivers, as well as along the minor streams and creeks, are dozens of the little symbols Herrman used to indicate the major plantations.

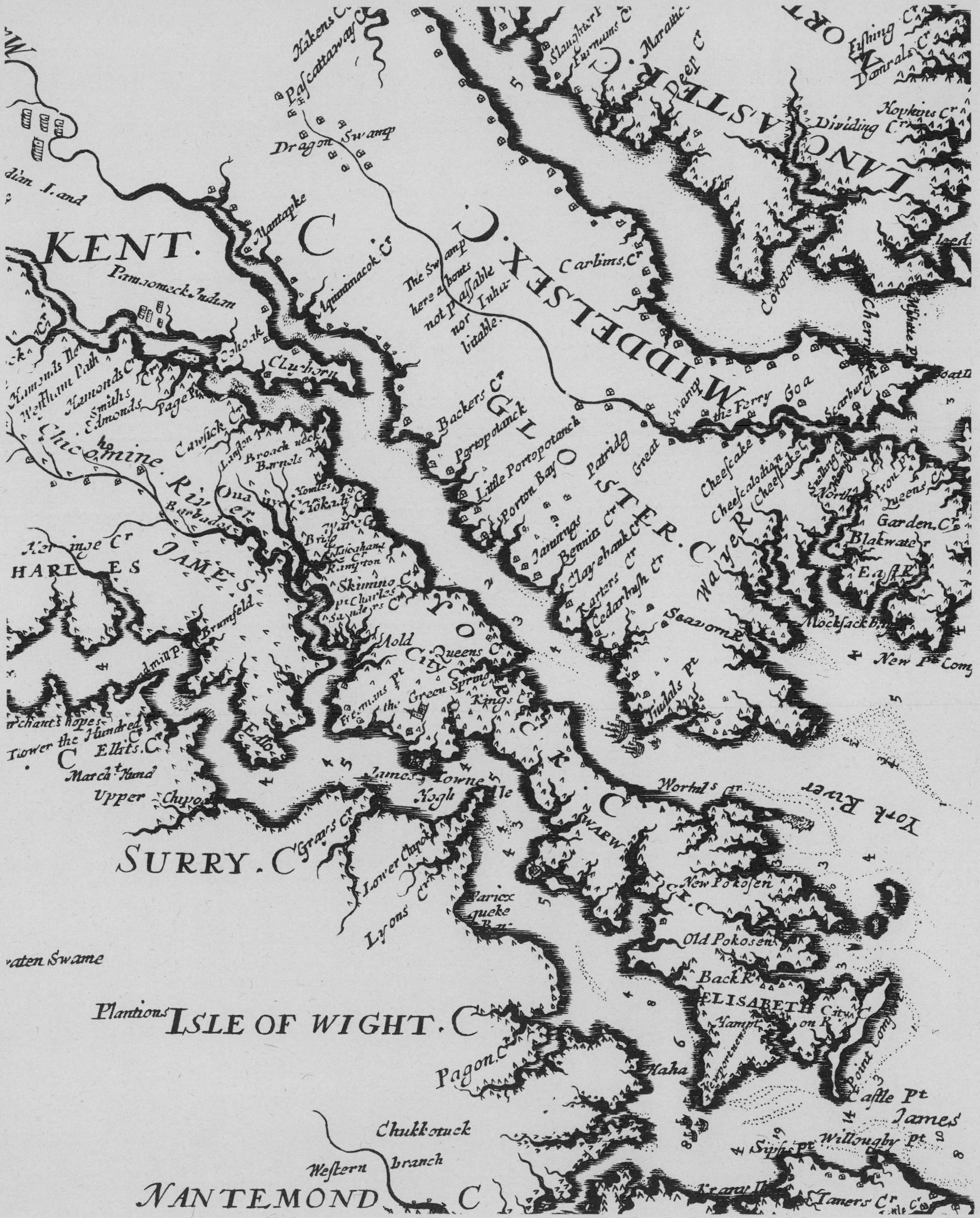

Figure 40. Map of a Portion of Virginia and Maryland: 1670

The "stragling distracted Condition" Langston had noted was a settlement pattern resulting from basic geographic forces that colonial officials seemingly could no nothing to change.

Langston proposed to remedy this situation through a program of mass immigration of tradesmen and craftsmen: "Brickmakers, Bricklayers, Carpenters, Sawyers, Joiners, Plaisterers, Coopers, Glasiers . . . Smiths, Tanners . . . Shoemakers, Millwrites . . . Hemp and Flax Dressers, Roape makers, Soape Boilers, Potash men, Felt makers, Beaver makers, & divers other Trades." [48] Even if such a program had been practical, and one is entitled to serious doubts on this score, the suggestion ran squarely counter to the mercantilist philosophy concerning the role of colonies in the English empire. Colonies should exist primarily for the production of raw materials to be processed in the home country, with finished goods being sent back to the colonies. Manufacturing in the colonies was to be restricted severely, and the two-way trade between the overseas possessions was to be carried out exclusively in ships owned and largely manned by Englishmen. In exchange for these limitations of colonial economic activities, customs duties levied on imports to England would favor raw materials produced within the empire. The Navigation Act of 1660, the Staple Act of 1663, and the Plantations Duties Act of 1673 all were in furtherance of this concept of mercantilism.[49]

English policy on towns in the tidewater colonies was thus curiously contradictory. Throughout the seventeenth and eighteenth centuries English colonial administrators continually grumbled about the lack of towns in Virginia and Maryland. Part of this dissatisfaction stemmed from an intuitive judgment that somehow no civilization could exist based almost exclusively on a rural population. Nothing appeared less natural and rational than a settlement pattern of small farmers and large plantations dispersed almost uniformly across the land. Surely this was quite un-English. The crown could and did, almost unceasingly, point to the example of New England as a prosperous colony that had properly gathered itself into nucleated settlements of at least modest size and, in the case of Boston, a community that might fairly be called a city.

Then, too, the mercantilist system required the existence of towns in the colonies as centers for administration and, above all, for the proper regulation of trade. Yet, opposed to their development stood the geographic and agricultural realities of the tidewater region. The dilemma was obvious, but London never really faced up to it. If at least port towns were necessary, then some relaxation of strict mercantile doctrine would be required to stimulate limited manufacturing there and to encourage colonial trade from those ports with other countries. Instead, directive legislation, first fully worked out in the 1662 Act for Building a Towne, was stubbornly elaborated and extended during the last decades of the seventeenth century.

The clergy joined in supporting these efforts for quite different reasons. As early as 1622 one minister of the gospel, evidently with first-hand knowledge of the emerging settlement patterns of Virginia, asserted "that Christians (if they have Liberty) ought to live together in visible united Societies, in Cities, Towns or Villages." Contrasting this model of Christian society with that of the Virginia colony, he pointed out that many persons lived at great distances from the nearest church and therefore found it easy to neglect religious duties. For this reason the colonists did not adequately support the established religion, which he characterized as "the forloren Church which is now scattered in desolate Places of that wildernesse, without any comlinesse, which should make her desired, and sought after." [50]

The solution advanced by this cleric was as simple as it was unworkable. Planters should be encouraged or directed to build houses in the nearest settlement and to live there, going out to the plantations only to oversee the work. All servants from the plantations were to be brought into town on Saturdays to the master's dwelling and were to remain overnight for the purpose of attending divine service on the Sabbath. It is true that the owners of a few of the very large plantations might have been able to delegate to a resident overseer the task of running such an enterprise. Contrary to current popular belief, however, the great bulk of the plantations were of rather modest size. In seventeenth-century Maryland only a few exceeded 250 acres.[51] These quite obviously required constant and direct supervision by their owners, who could scarcely afford to imitate the life of some great English country landlord with a London townhouse.

Moreover, to those more affluent planters of the tidewater region the tiny hamlets and straggling towns of the region would have seemed poor attractions indeed compared to life on the plantation. The larger plantations were essentially self-sufficient villages, with a variety of structures grouped around the owner's residence. Here, for example, is a description of one such plantation settlement prepared by its Virginia owner in 1686:

> The plantation where I now live contains one thousand acres at least,

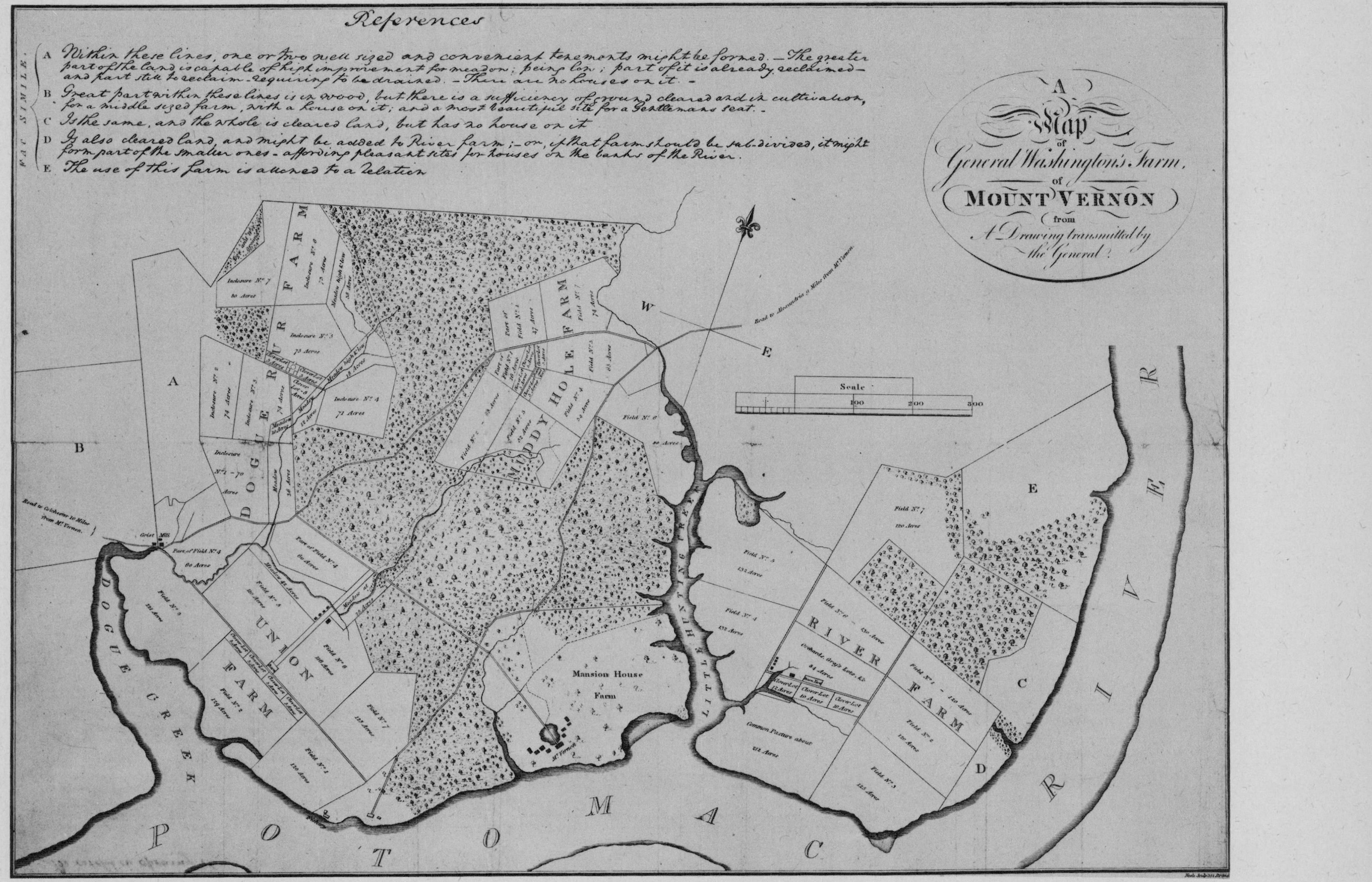

Figure 41. Map of Mount Vernon, Virginia: 1793

seven hundred acres of which are a rich thicket, the remainder good heavy plantable land without any waste either by marshes or great swamps . . . and upon it, there are three quarters well furnished with all necessary houses, grounds and fencing, together with a choice crew of negroes at each plantation . . . there being twenty-nine in all with stocks of cattle and hogs in each quarter. Upon the same land is my own dwelling house . . . and all houses for use furnished with brick chimneys, four good cellars, a dairy, dove cot, stable, barn, henhouse, kitchen and all other convenienceys. . . . About a mile and a half distant a good water grist mill, whose tole I find sufficient to find my own family with wheat and Indian corn for our necessities and occasions.[52]

It was on these large plantations rather than in towns that much of the craft industry of colonial Virginia and Maryland was carried on. In addition to the farm buildings and houses for the owner, tenants, and slaves, one could find "spinning houses, smithies, tan houses . . . ironworks, wharves for landing goods, called 'bridges,' warehouses, windmills, watermills, sawmills, glassworks, silkhouses, brick and pottery kilns, lime kilns, saltworks, and blockhouses." [53]

The complex of buildings erected to house these varied functions was often more impressive to visitors than so-called towns. Thus a Frenchman, calling at "Rosegill," Ralph Wormeley's plantation in 1686, commented that "When I reached his place" and saw some twenty buildings "I thought I was entering a rather large village, but later on was told that all of it belonged to him." [54] Two decades later John Oldmixon observed that "every Plantation is a little Town of itself, and can subsist itself with Provisions and Necessaries, every considerable Planter's Warehouse being like a Shop." [55] Toward the end of the eighteenth century a German traveler had a similar impression: "A plantation in Virginia, and also in the lower parts of Maryland, has often more the appearance of a small village, by reason of the many separate small buildings." [56]

Although it is of a later period than that now under review, the Mount Vernon of George Washington as it existed toward the end of the eighteenth century serves as an excellent and well-documented example of the plantation system. Figure 41 shows the location of the separate farms making up the plantation. Near the bottom of the drawing close to the bank of the Potomac River can be seen the cluster of structures identified

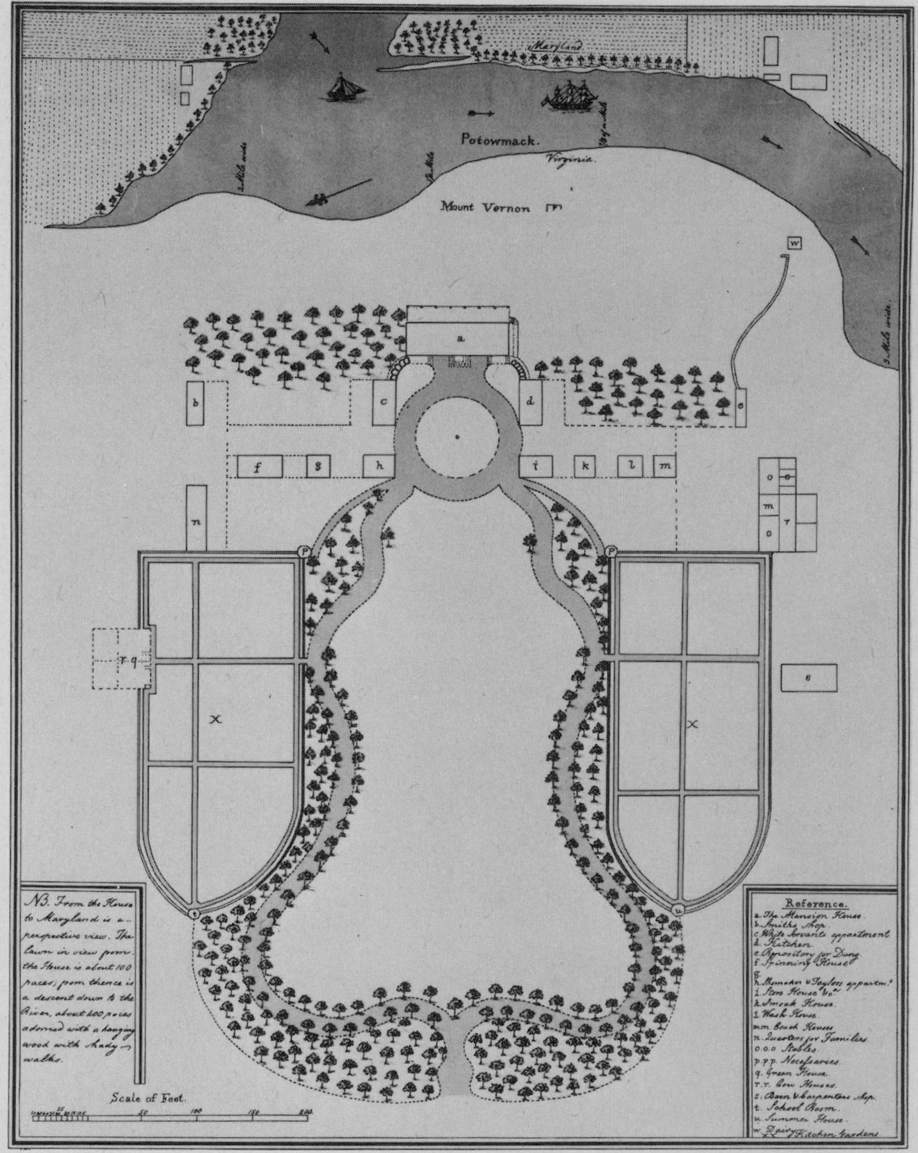

Figure 42. Plan of the Grounds of Mount Vernon, Virginia: 1784

Figure 43. View of a Southern Plantation: ca. 1825

as the Mansion House Farm. Smaller groupings of buildings are located on the outlying farms, and to the west on Dogue Creek stands the grist mill.[57] Figure 42 reveals in some detail the location and uses of the structures disposed in an orderly and formal manner near Washington's residence. Today, as restored, Mount Vernon has indeed the appearance of a hamlet or small village dominated by the mansion house of our first president.

A building strikingly similar to Mount Vernon appears in figure 43, an early nineteenth-century painting of a southern plantation. Here again we can see the various outbuildings of a village-like settlement. At the right is the mill, and in the foreground near the ship is doubtless the warehouse of the plantation owner where tobacco and other products were stored while awaiting shipment and which received the finished goods shipped from abroad. The owners of smaller plantations and farms nearby also used these facilities and arranged for such services as the plantation blacksmith, glassmaker, carpenter, and others were equipped to provide.

The attractions of towns, therefore, were meager compared to what plantation life could offer. An ambitious settler in Virginia or Maryland wishing to improve his economic position and status naturally looked to the land rather than to the town. Aside from a few craft occupations, tavern-keeping, work at the wharfs at Jamestown or St. Mary's, and the few clerical and governmental positions available, town life offered little to the tidewater colonist. Churches were often located in the open countryside serving the plantations of the region. So, too, the buildings first appointed for court use and later structures erected for that purpose could be found standing almost alone at some convenient crossroads location.

Yet, beginning in Maryland in 1668 and in Virginia in 1680, governmental authorities conducted a vigorous campaign to legislate towns into being. More than seventy-five sites in the two colonies eventually were to be designated for this purpose, a program of new town planning reminiscent of that conducted so many centuries earlier by Edward I in France, Wales, and England.

IV. *The New Town Acts of Colonial Virginia*

DURING the last third of the seventeenth century and the first few years of the one to follow, both Virginia and Maryland experimented with town planning on a large scale. These efforts to create an urban basis for colonial life in the tidewater region constitute a little-known but remarkable chapter in the story of how American town planning law and practice developed. They also are examples of the conflict between legislation and geography, as colonial officials obstinately persevered in their attempts to establish towns in the face of economic, topographic, and cultural forces that offered the strongest resistance to such endeavors. Under these circumstances successes were limited, and with few exceptions the towns that survived remained small and unimportant.

The efforts in the two colonies ran closely parallel though they differed somewhat in details. In Virginia there were fewer acts of the Assembly, the program was less ambitious both in the number of towns created and their size, and provisions governing the sites within the towns to be devoted to public uses were less precise. On the other hand, the physical results were similar. Although the town plans were far from identical, all of them employed simple gridiron patterns that reveal little skill or imagination on the part of their founders. Nevertheless, the towns that resulted from these extraordinary attempts to create almost overnight an urban culture are not without considerable interest. This chapter considers the Virginia program; the next examines the Maryland experience and evaluates the consequences in both colonies.

While it must have been evident that the act of 1662 had failed to stimulate significantly the growth of Jamestown, officials in England still hoped to create towns and ports in Virginia to serve as the centers of colonial trade and mercantile activity.[1] The instructions to the governor of Virginia drawn up in 1679 represented a new attempt to carry out this policy:

> You shall likewise endeavor all you can to dispose the planters to build towns upon every river, and especially one at least on every great river, as tending very much to their security and profit. And in order thereunto, you are to take care that after sufficient notice to provide warehouses and conveniences, no ships whatsoever be permitted to load or unload but at the said places where the towns are settled.

The force of this directive was blunted somewhat by a repetition of the older instructions to concentrate activity in Jamestown:

> And whereas we are given to understand that Jamestown is not only the most ancient but the most convenient place for the metropolis of our said colony, you are to direct all possible means to be used for the speedy rebuilding of the same, as also to take care that the chief port, the usual place of your residence, the courts of justice, and other public offices attending the government be settled and continued in that place.[2]

Accordingly, when Thomas Lord Culpeper, governor of Virginia, addressed the assembly on June 8, 1680, he recommended appropriate legislation to implement his instructions. In informing the councilors and burgesses of the king's intent, he referred to the desirability of towns "without which noe other nation ever begunne a plantacon, or any yet thrived (as it ought). . . ." Culpeper asserted his optimism, observing that while "severall difficulties will occur," he was certain "that on due examinacon, they will be remedyed." [3] He could scarcely have foreseen the problems that he and his successors would encounter in attempting to execute the king's desires. Nevertheless, he achieved his first success when the assembly responded to his urgings and shortly passed An Act for Cohabitation and Encouragement of Trade and Manufacture.[4]

The preamble to the act asserted the "greate necessity, usefulnesse and advantages of cohabitation" as a measure to help bolster trade and overcome the economic distress caused by the low prices of tobacco. As has been suggested, this appeal seemed calculated to secure the support of planters who, if not actively hostile to the idea, cared little about the creation of towns.[5] It may have been for this reason also that the assembly's act designated no less than twenty sites for new towns rather than the half dozen or so seemingly contemplated in the instructions to Culpeper. For this legislation specified that no exports from Virginia after January 1, 1681, were to be made except through one of these towns and that after September 29, 1681, all goods imported to the colony must be landed and sold at these new official ports of entry. A violation of these conditions was to result in forfeiture of the products or goods involved, with half going to the crown and the other half to the informer whose information led to the discovery of such an illegal act.

Given the dispersed pattern of population, it is quite obvious that the creation of only a few towns would have imposed a severe hardship on those whose plantations lay some distance away. John Clayton, commenting in 1688 on the legislation, harshly condemned the Virginians for their attitude when he wrote that "every one being more sollicitous for a private interest and Conveniency, than for a publick, they will either be for making forty Towns at once, that is, two in every Country [County] or none at all, which is the Country's Ruin." [6] Doubtless Clayton was correct but even with twenty towns, one in each county, many planters feared that the legislation would cause severe burdens. The act attempted some reassurance on this score. It specified the maximum cost that the owners of sloops could charge for conveying tobacco from a plantation to the nearest town: twenty pounds of tobacco for each hogshead transported up to thirty miles and not more than forty pounds of tobacco if for a longer distance. Similarly, the act established storage charges in the town warehouses. These were set at ten pounds of tobacco for each hogshead for the first month and six pounds of tobacco for each additional month. Further, for persons located at great distances from the new towns, sites for "rolling houses" were to be selected to which hogsheads of tobacco could be rolled and stored to await transportation to the nearest town. As an additional inducement to planters to make use of these facilities, any tobacco being shipped to a town or rolling house was exempted from seizure by a creditor. A similar privilege was extended to tradesmen who took up residence in the town. Provided these new residents did not grow tobacco, they were also exempt for five years from paying the normal public levies.

Town lots for dwellings, shops, and warehouses were to be made available on easy terms. Half-acre parcels were to be sold for only one hundred pounds of tobacco, with the provision that within three months from the purchase date the owner must begin construction of a dwelling and a warehouse for each lot acquired. Speculation in town lots was to be averted by the provision that if construction had not been started in the specified time the owner's title and purchase price would be declared forfeit and the lot could be sold to another person. The cost of surveying each lot and furnishing a plat to the owner was established at exactly twenty pounds of tobacco.

Each town was to be fifty acres in size. The act provided that existing owners were to be paid ten thousand pounds of tobacco for this land, which they were "to accept take and receive as a full and valueable price and consideration for the said land for ever" from the officials of the county designated to carry out its provisions. Aside from these provisions there were no specifications in the act for the plan of the town or for any public sites or spaces for civic activities. These decisions, since the law was silent concerning them, were to be made by the trustees or "feoffees"—the ancient English term—appointed by each county to acquire the site, plan the town, and dispose of the lots. Two months from the passage and publication of the act were allowed for the counties to begin this undertaking.

The locations of the twenty sites specified in the law, plus one additional site designated in a later act, are shown in figure 44. The names appearing on the map did not originate in the act but are those used in later legislation, given to the towns by county officials, or established subsequently by local use. Note that those on the James River are more numerous and

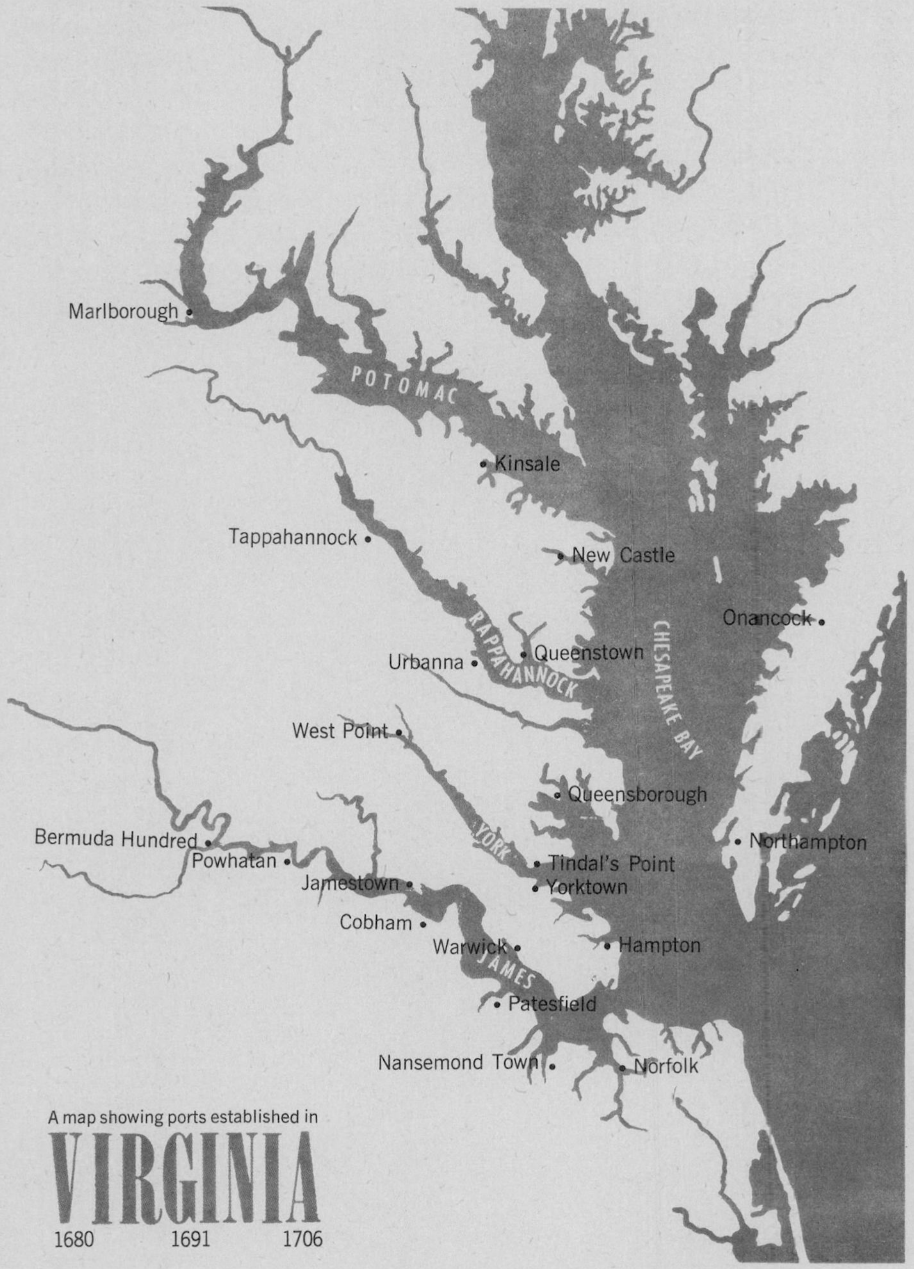

Figure 44. Map of Towns Founded in Virginia in 1680, 1690, and 1706

closely spaced than those in other parts of the colony. This distribution roughly corresponded to the density of population in Virginia at that time. Few towns, like Jamestown, were designated at locations already occupied by loosely clustered, village-like settlements. Most sites were largely vacant.

Planter reaction to this legislation must have been mixed. Colonel Nicholas Spencer expressed guarded approval of the new measure in a letter written a few days after its passage:

> We are now grown sensible that our present necessities and too much to be doubted future miseries are much heightened by our wild and Rambling way of living therefore are desirous of cohabitation. . . . And if this [act] takes effect as its hoped it may Virginia will then go forward which of late years hath made a retrograde motion.

A month later, however, he expressed some reservations:

> I much dobt it may miss its wished Effect if not totally miscarry by the multiplicity of places appointed for Towns viz one in each Country. But if all things were by His Majesties Command to ride at one place in every great River and in every of those places one town only to be erected the design would have the better prospect.[7]

Eleven years later, following the second general town-planning act containing similar provisions, William Byrd I was equally cautious in his appraisal of the probable results: "How far our New Law about Townes may Affect trade I cannot yett guess, wee must expect the confirmation of itt from England, & then I believe Some of the Ports may come in a little time to Something."[8] William Fitzhugh, a wealthy planter, was more positive in his attitude when he wrote to Captain Francis Partis in 1680: "We are also going to make towns, if you can meet with any tradesmen, that will come in & live at the Towns, they may have large privileges & immunitys."[9]

County officials soon began to exercise their new responsibilities imposed by the act of 1680. In Rappahannock County (now Essex County) the site designated "att Hobses Hole" was acquired by feoffees John Stone, William Lloyd, Henry Awbrey, and Thomas Gouldman, who named the town New Plymouth and proceeded to offer lots for sale.[10] Simultaneously the new town was designated as the county seat, and soon the community contained "the Court house, severall dwelling houses and ware houses. . . ."[11] The name New Plymouth was changed to Tappahannock in

1706, and since the division of Rappahannock County into Richmond and Essex counties in 1692 it has continued to serve as the county seat of the latter. In the two subsequent town acts this site was redesignated an official port of entry in recognition of the accomplishments under the 1680 legislation as well as for its strategic site midway between the mouth of the Rappahannock River and the upper limits of navigation.[12]

Two plans of the town have survived. The first is reproduced in figure 45 as surveyed by George Morris on October 18, 1680, and recorded seven months later. It is a curious drawing. Although Morris's notes mention that he divided the site into one hundred lots, only ninety of the little house symbols, which apparently represented the location of the individual parcels of land, appear in the drawing. The elongated open space leading from the river was doubtless intended as the principal street, but it is impossible to tell if there were to be cross streets providing double access to each tier of house lots. Even more puzzling is the absence of any location designated for the courthouse. It is possible, of course, that this drawing was prepared only as a rough diagram of the town site, the boundaries of which were described with some precision in the notes at the bottom of the drawing. At that time the surveyed plats of individual lots may have defined more accurately the pattern of streets and property lines.

The second early plan of the town appears in figure 46 as prepared by Harry Beverley in July, 1706. As lots had been sold under the acts of 1680 and 1691 this later drawing probably is a resurvey of the plan of 1680 and does not represent any substantial change in the town's design. Sixty-four lots measuring 165 by 132 feet, or exactly half an acre, are shown. The street pattern is an almost symmetrical gridiron, but the streets vary in width. The two most important, designated by the letters "A" and "B," were named Queens Street and Prince Street and platted five poles or 82½ feet wide. The two parallel streets, Duke and Marsh streets, and the principal street crossing those leading to the river, Cross Street, were four poles or 66 feet wide. Church Lane and Water Lane, the remaining cross streets, were laid out with a width of three poles or 49½ feet wide. Slightly off center and bordered by Queens, Prince, and Cross streets and Church Lane is the block of four lots designated for public use. It is on this site that the courthouse was erected and, later, a small building for the clerk and a handsome row of offices for lawyers. These and a number of eighteenth-century dwellings that have survived combine to give the

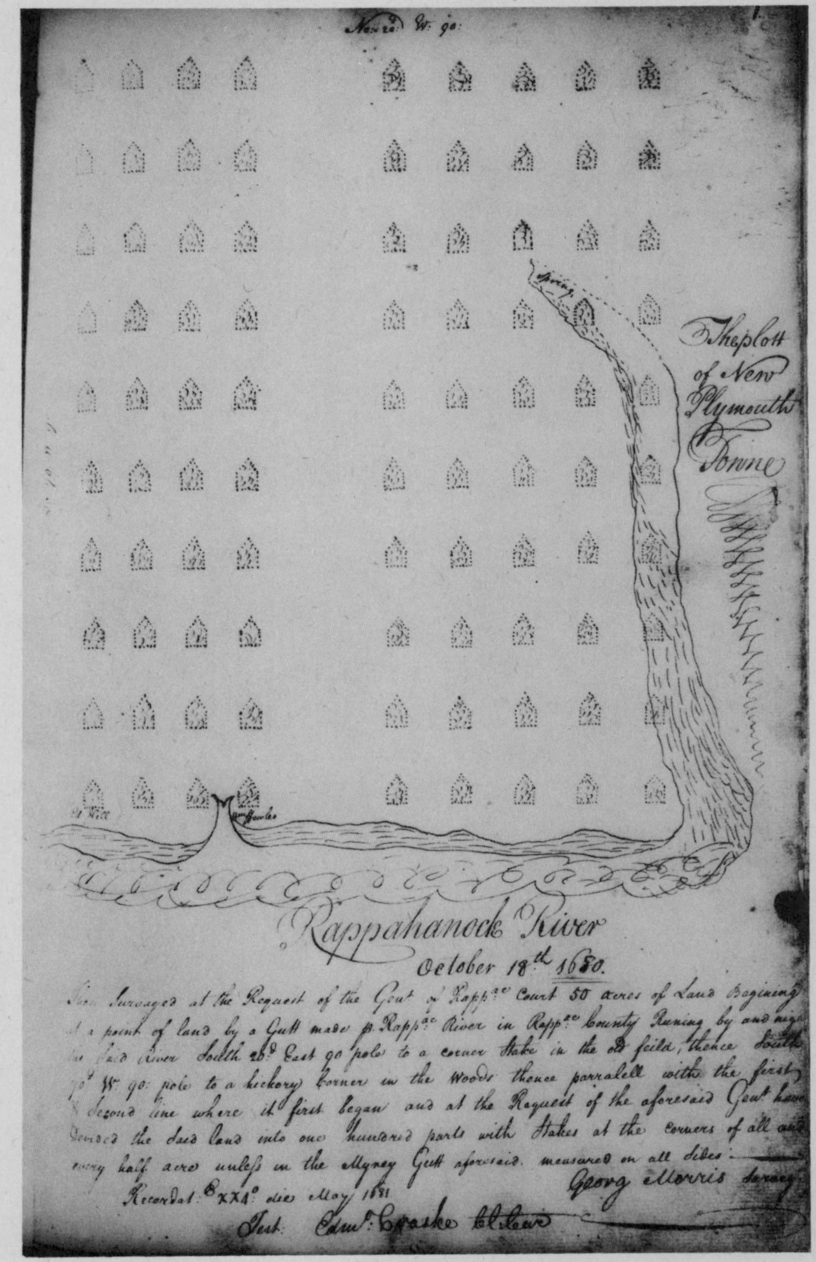

Figure 45. Plan of Tappahannock, Virginia: 1680

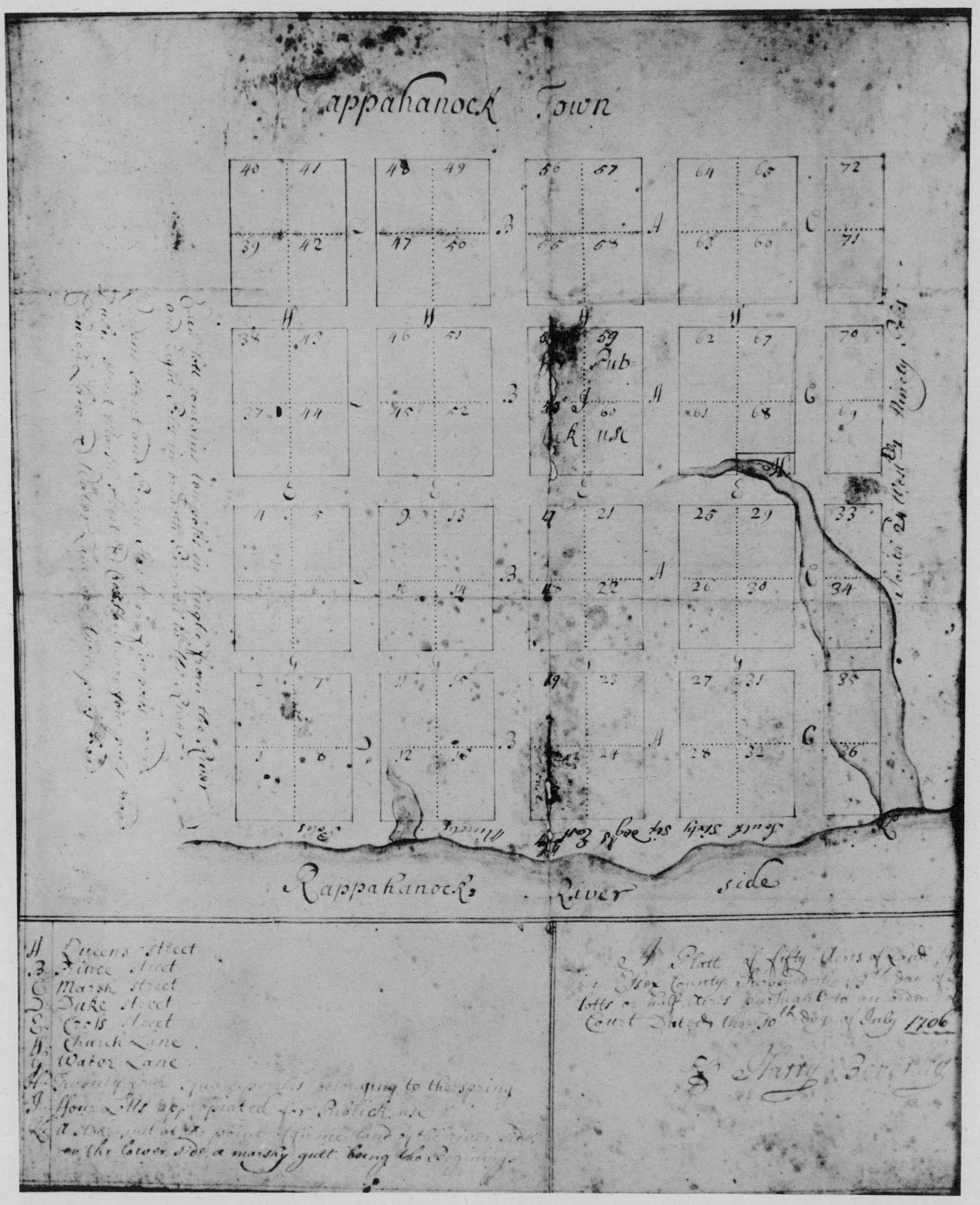

Figure 46. Plan of Tappahannock, Virginia: 1706

modern little town a graceful and spacious appearance. Its original function as a port is expressed today only by the use of its river front for recreational boating, but it once served as the shipping center for the upper half of the Rappahannock. Isaac Weld, in 1796, noted that the town then contained "about one hundred houses," but that before the Revolution it "was in a much more flourishing state than at present." [13]

Across Chesapeake Bay in Accomack County trustees John West and William Custis in 1681 acquired fifty acres of land from Charles Scarburgh for the town of Onancock. The site also was designated as the county seat, and in the next few years the courthouse was built along with "severall dwelling houses, and ware houses." [14] The plan appears in figure 47 as redrawn in 1761 from the original survey by Daniel Jenifer, who received 540 pounds of tobacco for his work.[15] On the irregular peninsula formed by the north and south branches of Onancock Creek, Jenifer laid out an elongated grid plan. Only in the middle of the town was he able to follow a pattern of rectangular lots, and those having water frontage exhibit a wide range of shapes and sizes. At the town's center, bounded by Water, King's, and Market streets and a narrow lane to the east, a market place was reserved. The location of the courthouse, which a few years later was moved to Accomac, is not known, but it may have been placed along the south side of King's Street on the second lot from Water Street. Or, together with the church, it may have occupied a portion of the market place which is the present public square.[16]

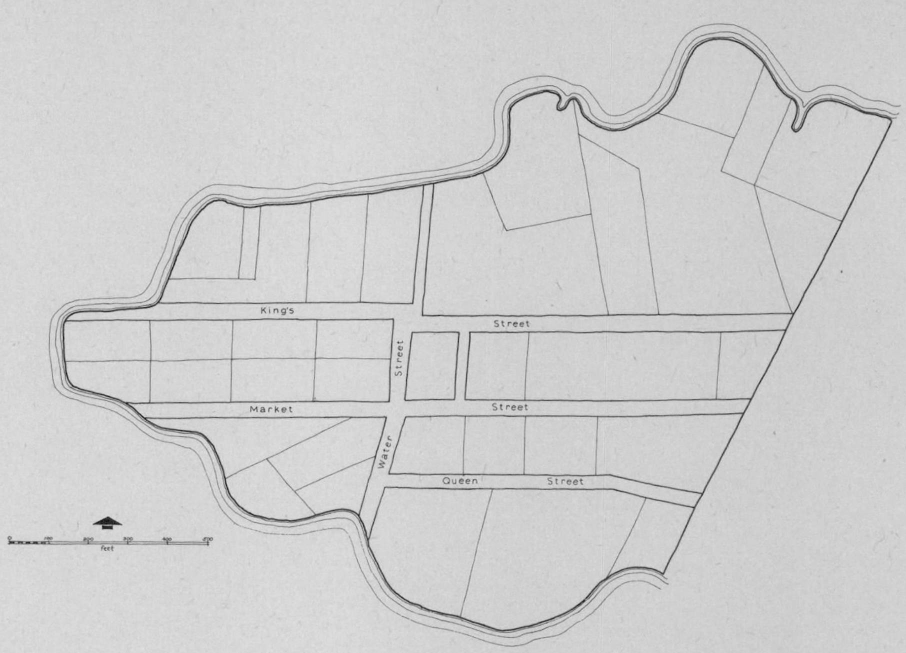

Figure 47. Plan of Onancock, Virginia: 1681

Far more advantageously located for trade and commerce were the towns near the mouths of the major rivers on the western shore of the bay. One of these, Hampton, is the oldest continually occupied English settlement in America. As Kecoughtan, this site on Hampton Creek not far from its mouth at the end of the peninsula formed by the James and York rivers, had been settled by soldiers and a few planters in 1610. Now, in 1680, it gained the status of an official port on land acquired from Thomas Jarvis. Whether the county actually proceeded to lay out a town at that time seems unlikely, for in 1691, with the second town act, we find the land being acquired again, this time from William Wilson, its new owner. In 1692 the trustees, Thomas Allamby, William Marshall, and Pascho Curle, proceeded to establish a simple street pattern. Apparently this first plan was an elementary crossroads community with King Street running northward from the water and Queen Street crossing it not quite at right angles. Half-acre lots were surveyed, and by the following year twenty-six of these had been sold.[17] When John Fontaine visited Hampton in 1716 he found it

> a place of the greatest trade in all Virginia, and all the men-of-war commonly lie before this arm of the river. It is not navigable for large ships, by reason of a bar of land, which lies between the mouth, or coming in, and the main channel, but sloops and small ships can come up to the town. This is the best outlet in all Virginia and Maryland, and when there is any fleet made, they fit out here, and can go to sea with the first start of a wind. The town contains one hundred houses, but few of them of any note, and it has no church.[18]

Fontaine, however, observed that the site was unpleasant and unhealthy because of the mud banks and marshes that surrounded it, an opinion shared by Isaac Weld in 1796 when he called the town "a dirty disagreeable place, always infested by a shocking stench from a muddy shore when the tied is out." [19]

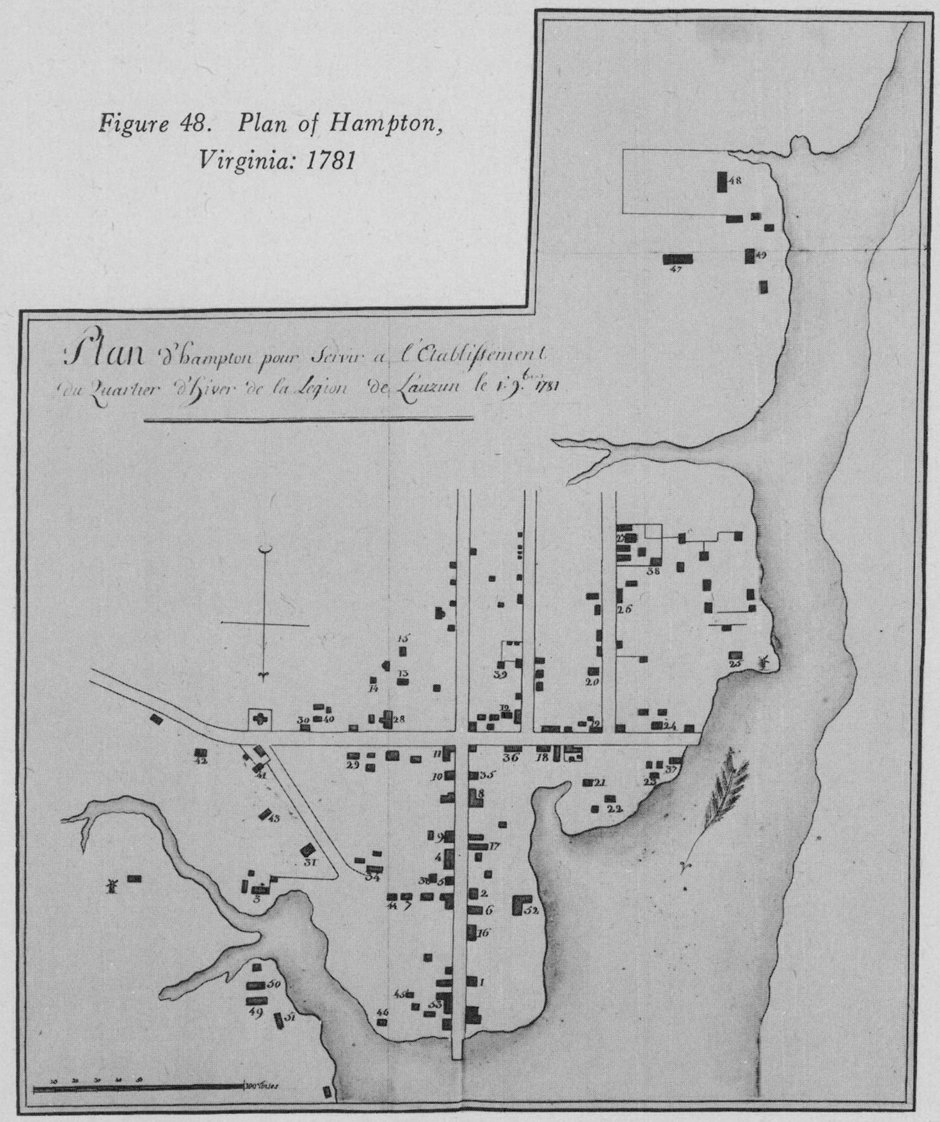
Plan d'hampton pour Servir a l'Etablissement
du Quartier d'hiver de la Legion de Lauzun le 1.9bre 1781

Figure 48. Plan of Hampton, Virginia: 1781

The town as it existed in 1781 appears in figure 48.[20] This revolutionary war map drawn by a Frenchman shows the basic street pattern of the port, whose prosperity had suffered severely though the war had bypassed the town itself. Weld, at the end of the eighteenth century, asserted that the town contained but thirty houses and a few other structures. These included St. John's Church built in 1728 and the courthouse erected in 1715 when Hampton became the county seat. Their locations and the arrangement of the original streets and their extensions can be observed more clearly on a plan of 1878 (figure 49). By that date Hampton Institute had been established on the opposite peninsula along with the National Soldier's Home. Perhaps some of the occupants of the latter institution, as well as many residents of the town, could recall the destruction of the entire town by its citizens in 1861 in an effort to prevent its occupation by Union troops. Only five houses remained standing after this conflagration, and the modern town has little except its original plan to recall its seventeenth-century origins.[21]

Not far away from Hampton, across the estuary of the James River and up the Elizabeth River, lay the site of another port town established under the act of 1680. This was Norfolk, destined to become one of the major cities of the tidewater region. A portion of the Joshua Fry and Peter Jefferson 1751 map of Virginia (figure 50) shows its location as well as the sites of other new towns planned during the period and under the legislation with which we are now concerned. These include Tappahannock and Urbanna on the Rappahannock; Delaware or West Point at the confluence of the Pamunkey and the Mattaponi; Gloucester or Tindall's Point and York across from each other near the mouth of the York; and Cobham, opposite Jamestown on the James.

Two months after the passage of the act of 1680 the county court of Lower Norfolk County ordered surveyor John Ferebee to run the town boundaries on the lands of Nicholas Wise.[22] At this wisely selected site on the north side of the Elizabeth River where it divided into its eastern and southern branches, two creeks formed a double-pointed peninsula. The following year Ferebee divided the plot into streets and lots. One street, running approximately north and south, connected the peninsula with the mainland, and Ferebee surveyed the main street of the town roughly perpendicular to the first. A short wide street led to the waterfront from a triangular market place. The original plan of Norfolk, as reconstructed from records of survey, is shown in figure 51. As at Onancock the irregularity of the site precluded lots of identical size, and the bend in the little peninsula caused two angles in the alignment of Main Street, the westernmost of which remains today. The central portion of Main Street has

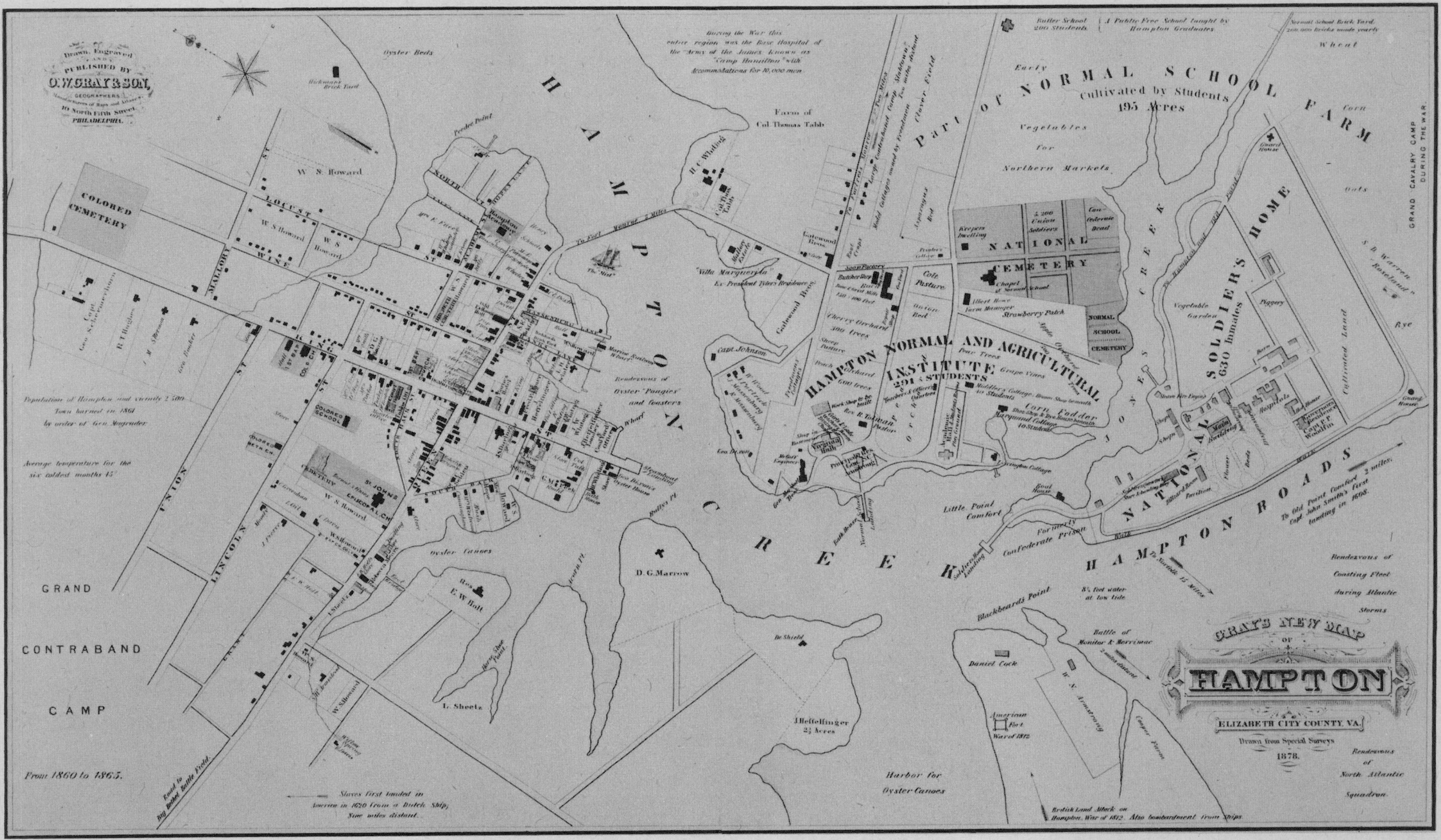

Figure 49. Plan of Hampton, Virginia: 1878

recently been eliminated in a modern urban renewal project that has changed substantially the original street pattern.

Although, as we shall see, the trading portions of the act of 1680 were suspended by the crown late in 1681 and the news must have reached Virginia within a few months, the trustees, Anthony Lawson and William Robinson, continued their town planning activities. Nicholas Wise, the son of the deceased original owner of the site, received his ten thousand pounds of tobacco in January, 1683, and the trustees made the first

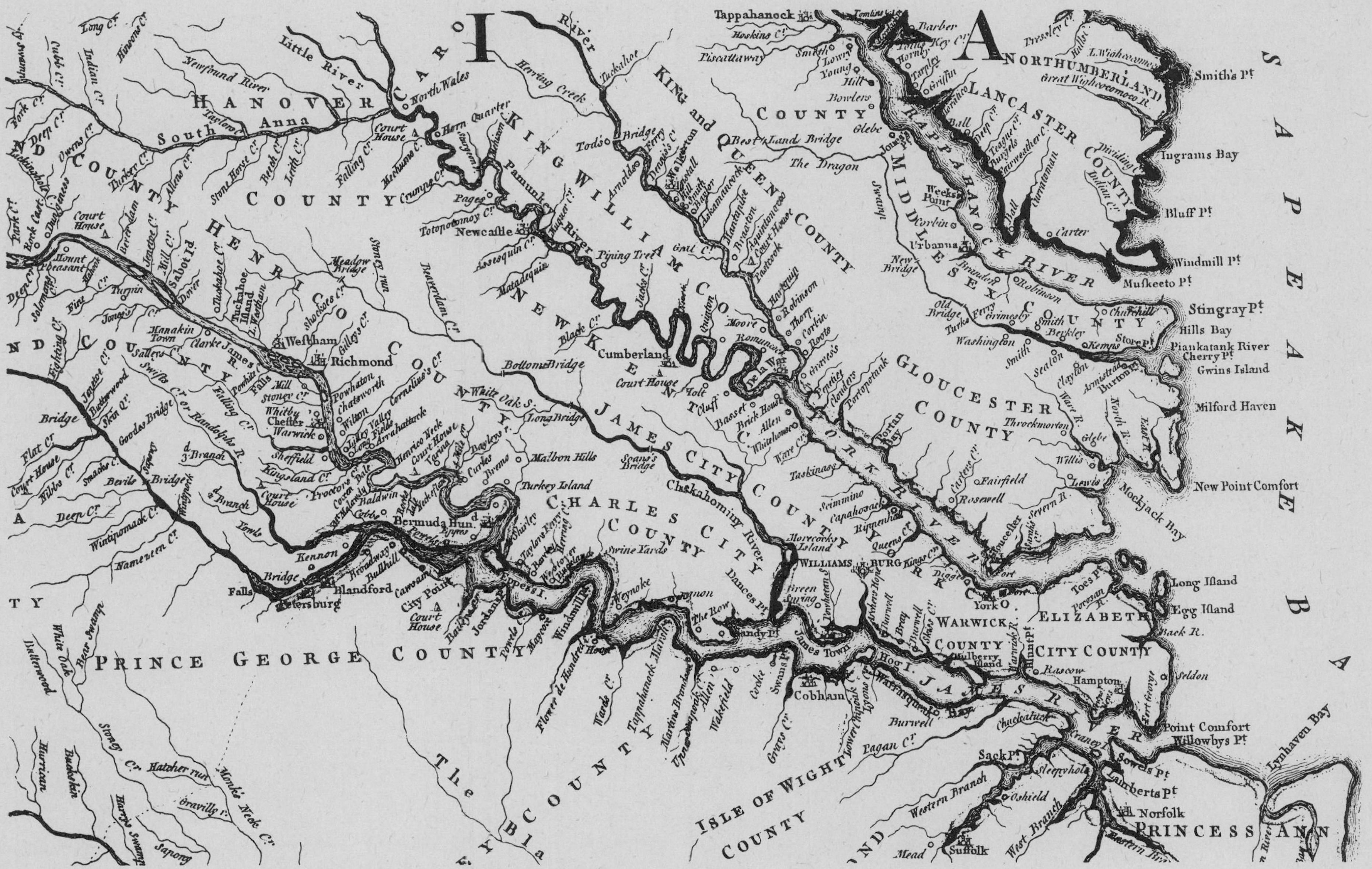

Figure 50. Map of Portion of Virginia and Maryland: 1751

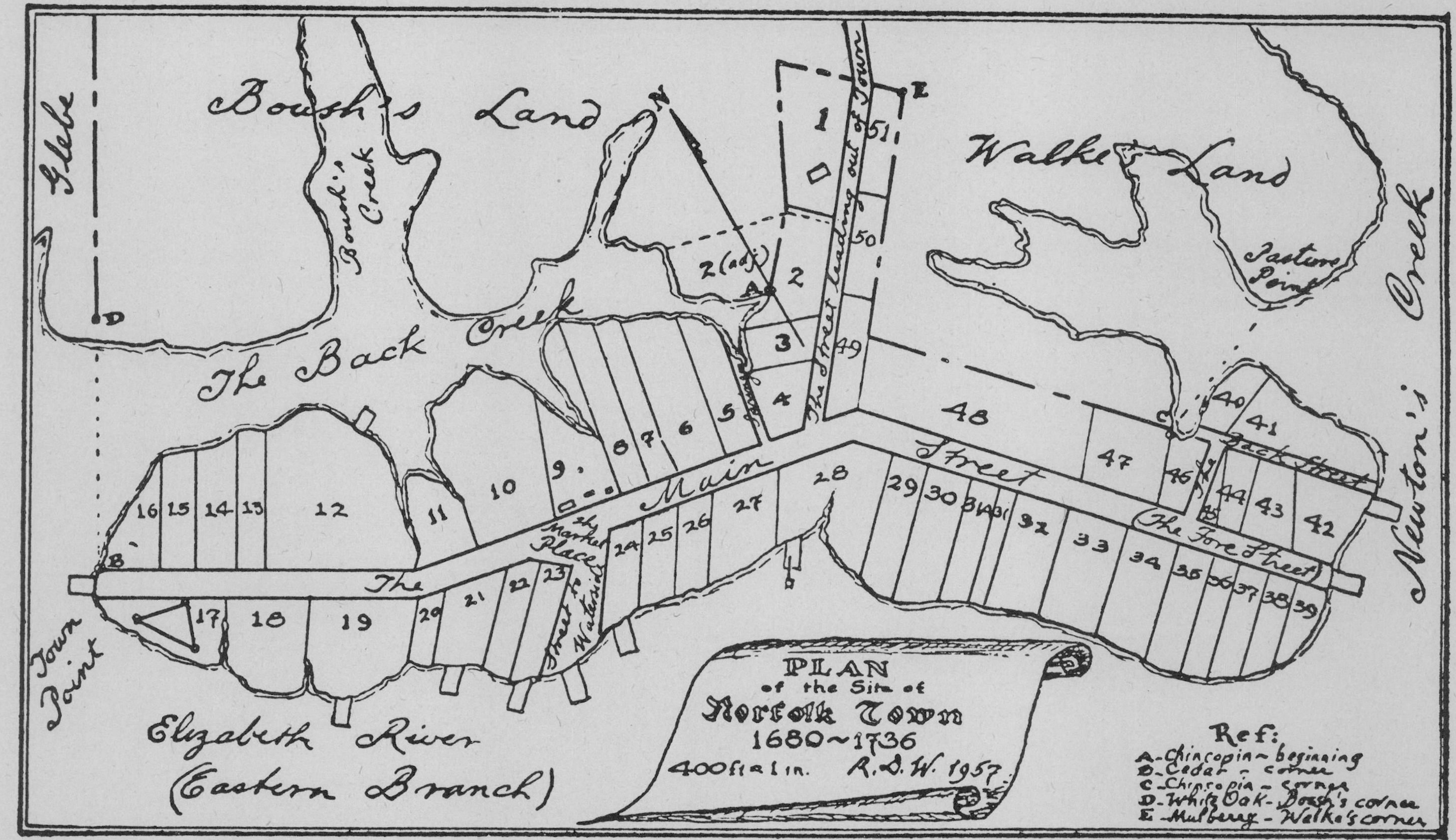

Figure 51. Plan of Norfolk, Virginia: 1680-1736

recorded sales of lots in the autumn of that year. There may well have been building activity in the new town before that time, and probably sites for a church, a school, and the courthouse had been designated as early as 1681. The churchyard was located at the northern edge of the town on the west side of the road leading to Main Street, but the first church was not constructed until 1698. Opposite the church was the school lot. The land for the courthouse stood facing the market place on the north side of Main Street. At the western tip of the peninsula was a triangular fort built in 1673.

Growth in the early years was painfully slow. By 1691 only ten lots had been sold, and three of these reverted to the county because their owners had not constructed houses within the specified period of time. Doubtless the suspension of part of the act of 1680 raised doubts in the minds of many prospective purchaser about the wisdom of investing in a new town now stripped of its exclusive port privileges; but the act for ports of 1691 again designated Norfolk as an official town and stimulated further growth. Twenty-nine additional lots were sold between that year and the spring of 1702. When in 1705 the town was also named as an official port of entry, only ten of the original fifty-one lots remained unsold, and it seems a safe assumption that most of them were occupied by dwellings, warehouses, ordinaries, or shops. The courthouse, built between 1691 and 1694, a jail, and the church all added to the developing fabric of town life.

The first extension to the town took place on the land of Colonel Samuel Boush in 1728. His property extended along the western side of the street leading northward out of the town beyond the church. By this time the town was flourishing and in that year was visited and described by that compulsive diarist and perceptive observer of the tidewater, William Byrd II. Setting off from Westover plantation late in February of 1728 to survey the boundary line between Virginia and North Carolina, Byrd and his companions reached Norfolk on March 1. This was certainly not his first visit to the busy seaport, and his long description is all the more valuable and accurate because of his familiarity with the town:

> Norfolk has most the air of a town of any in Virginia. There were then near twenty brigantines and sloopes riding at the wharves, and oftentimes they have more. It has all the advantages of situation requisite for trade and navigation. There is a secure harbor for a good number of ships of any burden. Their river divides itself into three several branches, which are all navigable. The town is so near the sea that its vessels may sail in and out in a few hours. Their trade is chiefly to the West Indies, whither they export abundance of beef, pork, flour, and lumber. The worst of it is, they contribute much toward debauching the country by importing abundance of rum, which, like gin in Great Britain, breaks the constitutions, vitiates the morals, and ruins the industry of most of the poor people of this country. This place is the mart for most of the commodities produced in the adjacent parts of North Carolina. They have a pretty deal of lumber from the borders on the Dismal, who make bold with the King's land thereabouts without the least ceremony. They not only maintain their stocks upon it but get boards, shingles, and other lumber out of it in great abundance.
>
> The town is built on a level spot of ground upon Elizabeth River, the banks whereof are neither so high as to make the landing of goods troublesome or so low as to be in danger of overflowing. The streets are straight and adorned with several good houses, which increase every day. It is not a town of ordinaries and public houses, like most others in the country, but the inhabitants consist of merchants, ship carpenters, and other useful artisans, with sailors enough to manage their navigation. With all these conveniences it lies under the two great disadvantages that most of the towns in Holland do by having neither good air nor good water. The two cardinal virtues that make a place thrive, industry and frugality, are seen here in perfection; and so long as they can banish luxury and idleness the town will remain in a happy and flourishing condition.[24]

The later development of Norfolk belongs in a subsequent chapter, for it must already be clear that of all the Virginia towns named in the act of 1680, Norfolk was destined to become the largest and most important. In the first decade or two, however, it was merely one of the eight new towns out of the twenty specified in the act on which some development had started.[25]

When the original legislation had been passed by the assembly and approved by Governor Culpeper it had been, of course, sent to England. Tobacco merchants accustomed to trading directly with plantation owners viewed the enactment with alarm. Nor did the commissioners of customs react with greater favor. In a report submitted by them to the Board of Trade the commissioners criticized the act on a number of grounds. They cited the absence of suitable wharves, warehouses, and other port facilities in the designated towns, observing:

> Trade is to be courted not forced. Where trade carries itself and where there has been reasonable accommodation for merchants, that is the place where it has been our principle to appoint a quay. But in this Act we find wharves and quays appointed where there are no warehouses or accommodation for receiving goods, nor, indeed, any inhabitants.

Then, with an eye to the interests of English traders as well as their own responsibility for collecting duties, they noted that

> on discourse with the merchants and traders to Virginia, we find them dissatisfied with this Act as burdensome to their trade and impracticable. . . . It is as certain that if this Act were enforced the traders would be aggrieved and driven to smuggling. On the whole, we recommend that the Act be by no means confirmed, but that the whole question should be referred back to the Governor of Virginia for reconsideration.[26]

The Board of Trade agreed with this suggestion and so recommended to the king. On December 21, 1681, Charles ordered the matter referred to Governor Culpeper and suspended those portions of the law requiring exports and imports to be made only through the twenty designated ports.[27] Still, the concept of creating towns as centers of trade and commerce persisted. Governor Culpeper in 1683 requested that the suspension order be lifted, but this was disapproved.[28] Yet when Lord Howard of Effingham succeeded Culpeper the following year his instructions concerning the development of towns remained unaltered from those that had given rise to the act of 1680.

Lord Howard's first opportunity to further this policy came at the assembly meeting in the spring of 1684. His speech to the assembled legislators began with a statement that the king

> is much Concern'd and thinks it strange that this Colony which hath preceded most of its Neighbours in Antiquity should bee soe late in Acting what would Conduce soe much to Its own Advantage. I meane as to the building of Towns It might very Reasonably bee Concluded that the Reputation that this Method hath given to other places should long ere this have stimulated yu to have followed their good Examples But since that hath not I hope the great security and Benefitt (which is Evident) they Enjoy by It will soe farr Encourage you, that you will bee noe longer deficient to your-selves in soe materiall a point.[29]

The assembly considered two bills, ultimately passing one entitled "An Act Appointing Portes for Preventing Frauds and Better Securing his Majesties Customes." This differed from the act of 1680 only in its title and the number of towns it would have created. The governor rejected it, doubtless reasoning correctly that if approved by him it would once again be suspended by the Privy Council.

In the 1685–1686 session of the General Assembly still another attempt was made to obtain legislation satisfactory to all parties. This, too, was to fail. The House of Burgesses passed an act and sent it to the council. Apparently the council approved the bill also, and it was perpared for the governor's signature. He, however, noted a flaw in the failure to provide fees to support the collectors of customs required for each port and declined to sign the measure on this ground.[30]

Finally, at a session begun in April, 1691, the assembly passed a new measure at the urging of Francis Nicholson, who, as lieutenant governor, had succeeded Lord Howard. The act for ports, while containing some new or modified provisions, closely resembled the earlier town legislation. Its preamble emphasized the purpose of the law as a measure to permit efficient collection of customs duties and to prevent unlawful trade, an obvious attempt to secure approval from colonial officials in England. Collectors of customs were to be appointed to supervise the provisions of the law which, as before, specified that all exports and imports were to pass through the designated ports.

The town planning provisions of the previous law were modified somewhat. Although the same amount of land was to be acquired—fifty acres—the justices of the county in which the town was located were to buy the land "at such price as . . . thought reasonable." If the owner was not willing to accept the offered sum a jury of twelve freeholders could be assembled to assess the land and compel the owner to transfer the title to trustees. The towns were to be laid out in half-acre lots which were to be sold at cost. The lot purchaser was then required to begin construction of "one good house, to containe twenty foot square at the least." Thus the arbitrary figure of ten thousand pounds of tobacco as the value of a fifty-acre site was abandoned, along with the token price for lots that in 1680 had been fixed at one hundred pounds of tobacco. The law contemplated, then, a no-subsidy and a no-profit transaction in developing each town, assuming that eventually all lots were sold.

Fifteen sites, rather than twenty, were named in the act, most of them being identical with those specified in 1680.[31] In addition five places were designated as "places for buying and selling of all manner of goods, wares, and merchantdises," but which were not created as official ports for import or export trade.[32] At these sites, too, towns were to be created. Finally, to assure those who had purchased lots and constructed buildings under the earlier legislation, the act of 1691 provided that if "any thing hath been heretofore done and acted persuant to such law, the same shall be, and is hereby deemed, held good and valid."[33]

This second town act touched off a new flurry of land acquisition, town planning, lot sales, and construction on virgin sites, and stimulated somewhat the development of those towns created under the earlier legislation. We shall select for examination only those for which some graphic evidence of their original forms has survived.

The most northerly was Marlborough in Stafford County, located on a neck of land where Potomac Creek entered the river of the same name. This was some three miles below the site at "Peace Point" previously designated for a town under the act of 1680. William Buckner prepared the town plan on August 16, 1691, under the direction of trustees John Withers and Matthew Thompson on fifty acres of land purchased from Captain Malachi Peale, who held a life lease, and from Giles Brent, a minor, who held its title.[34] Two additional acres were acquired from Brent's guardian, Francis Hammersley, for a courthouse authorized by a previous act. The total price for the land came to 13,800 pounds of tobacco, of which 3,450 went to Peale as compensation for the loss of his leasehold.

Buckner's survey as copied later by John Savage from Theodorick Bland's official plat is reproduced in figure 52. While the drawing does not identify the location of the courthouse, this structure apparently stood somewhere in the vicinity of lot 21, possibly to the west of the identation of Potomac Creek. The configuration of the two stream banks strongly influenced the patterns of streets and lots. In the upper portion of the town, the three long streets parallel the shoreline of the Potomac River. Below, "The Broad Street cross the Town" follows the direction of Potomac Creek. At that point two of the three long streets bend and lead to the creek at right angles to the cross street. In the upper portion, however, the minor cross streets were laid out parallel to the first, and the blocks and half-acre lots are angled somewhat from 90°.

These rather odd shapes did not deter prospective purchasers, and on February 11, 1692, the trustees conveyed twenty-seven lots to fifteen applicants. This promising start was halted the following year with the repeal of the act of 1691 although probably a few houses were constructed. In 1706 the third Virginia town act designated the site once again as an official port and directed it to be named Marlborough. While seven lots

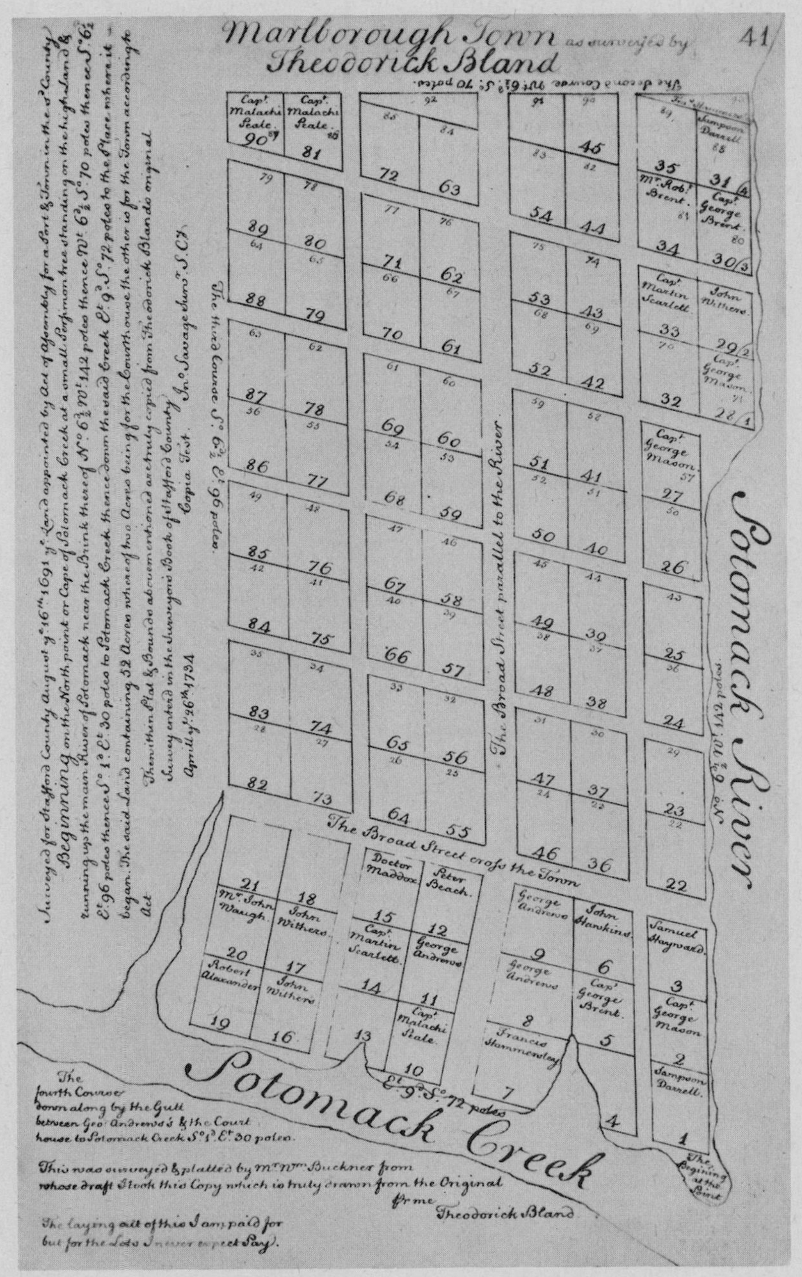

Figure 52. Plan of Marlborough, Virginia: 1691

were sold in 1708, the town failed to grow as expected. After the courthouse and several houses burned in 1718 the county seat was transferred to another location, and by 1723 the town was virtually abandoned.

Three years later John Mercer, an energetic Irish trader, settled at Marlborough and began purchasing the old town lots. Soon he had acquired almost the entire site though his title to some of this property was of questionable validity. With the consent of the Stafford county court Mercer arranged for a new survey of the town. Under Mercer's direction county surveyor John Savage modified the original plan (figure 53). Savage added a new tier of lots along the eastern edge of the town, reduced slightly the size of the remaining lots, and eliminated the angle in the streets running north and south.

Mercer attempted to revive the town. He built not only his own mansion there but constructed a mill run by water and wind, a brewery, and a glass factory. He owned a fleet of ships, which loaded and unloaded at the Mercer wharf, several warehouses, a tavern, and a racetrack where he matched his large stable of horses against those of competitors in the vicinity. When he died in 1768, however, much of the spirit of the town died with him. Although the town served as an important shipping point through the revolutionary war, it eventually faded into oblivion.[35]

Nearer Chesapeake Bay and more advantageously located for port purposes was Urbanna on a site in Middlesex County specified in the 1680 act but not planned at that time because its owner, Ralph Wormeley, stubbornly refused to transfer title to the county. There is some indication that the trustees may have surveyed the land nonetheless, and the county even directed that a courthouse be erected there in the fall of 1681.[36] Wormeley had not changed his attitude in the intervening years, and the first recorded deed for a town lot indicates that the county evidently had to resort to the condemnation procedure authorized by the act of 1691.

Robert Beverley's plan of 1747 appears redrawn in figure 54. While the lots are generally regular in size and shape, the street pattern is rather eccentric. Prince George Street (also known as Queen Street and Ferry Street) forms the spine of the town leading to the cove on the south side of the Rappahannock River. Virginia Street on the north and Watling Street, with its dog-leg alignment, also provided access to the riverfront. Virginia Street, then referred to as Main Street (and later as Princess Ann Street), was evidently the preferred location. Seven of the ten lots sold

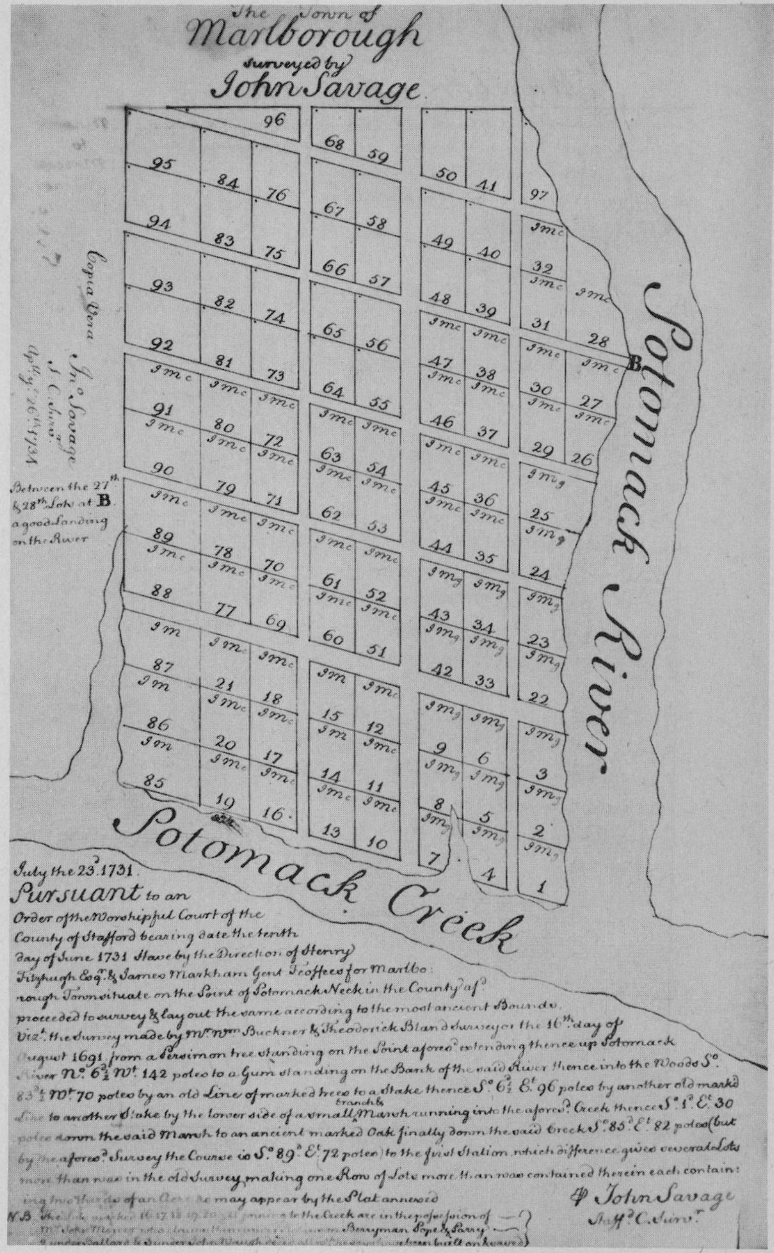

Figure 53. Plan of Marlborough, Virginia: 1731

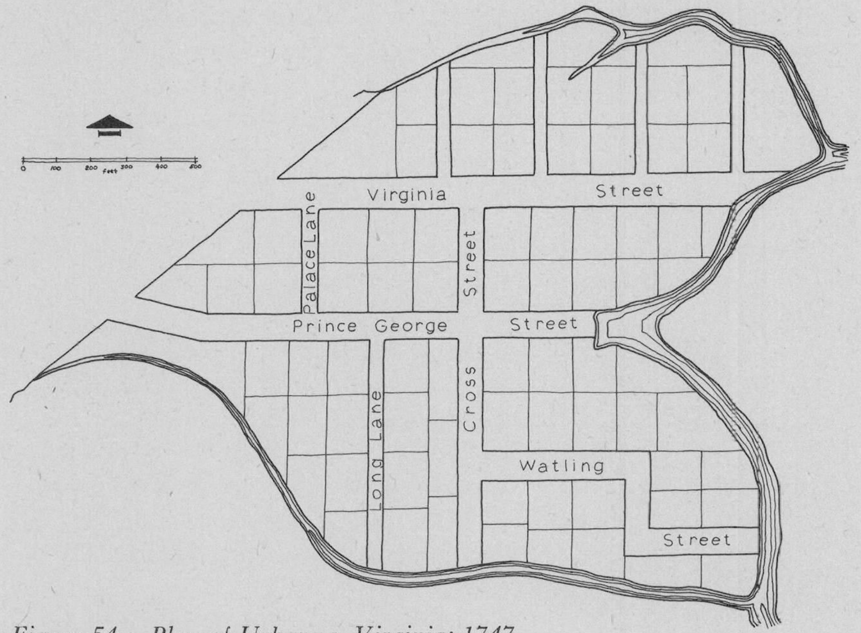

Figure 54. Plan of Urbanna, Virginia: 1747

by November, 1692, were in this area. At that time the county court authorized a levy to pay for laying out streets, the churchyard, and the market place. The courthouse and perhaps the market place occupied a site on the southwest corner of Virginia and Cross streets. The old courthouse erected there in 1745, now a club, was once converted to a church and bears little resemblance to its former appearance.

Sales of lots continued sporadically. The suspension of the act of 1691 in April, 1693, dampened enthusiasm for the project and cast a legal shadow on the transactions that had been completed. In 1699, however, the assembly confirmed all land titles that had been acquired and authorized further sales if desired. Doubtless many of the lots originally sold had become forfeit because of a failure to build a house of the prescribed size in the time specified, and these lots were once again put up for sale along with those remaining. Further impetus to sales was furnished by the third town act of 1706, which included Urbanna, and twenty-three lots were sold between 1704 and 1708. Warehouses were erected on some of the parcels, and Urbanna gradually began to serve its intended function as a port town for the plantations located along the Rappahannock.

Recently restored by the Association for the Preservation of Virginia Antiquities is a brick store built between 1763 and 1767, now occupied by the town library. This stood on the third lot from the water on the south side of Virginia Street and was used by James Mills, a Scottish merchant. Across the street is a handsome brick residence which once may have served as the customhouse for the tiny port. There must have been other structures of similar character lining the streets of the town when it was at the height of its prosperity.

Like most of the other towns created by the Virginia General Assembly during this period, however, Urbanna, was not destined to grow much. When Harry Toulmin visited there in 1793 he noted that

> Urbanna was formerly a place of some trade and importance; for as the customhouse for the Rappahannock was there, the vessels were obliged to clear at that port. But the customhouse being removed to Port Royal, it is now a deserted village and as the land in the neighborhood is engrossed by a few great proprietors there are only three or four store- or shipkeepers in the town, besides some sauntering young men, the vacuity of whose countenances unites with the grass-covered streets to give the place a most melancholy aspect. I believe there are not above a dozen houses in the town.[37]

South and slightly west of Urbanna, where the Mattaponi and the Pamunkey rivers converge to form the York River, another site must have appeared to be a strategic location for a port. There, on the neck of land bordered by the two tributaries of the York, was the location of West Point, also to be known as Delaware Town. A few streets and houses can be seen on the map (figure 55) drawn during the Revolution, and two ferries connected the town to points on the opposite shores; but it is obvious that the town was of little importance at that time. Although the land for the town was apparently acquired from its owner, John West, following the 1691 act, it is not certain when the original plan was prepared. By 1706, however, following the designation of the site as a town once again, a plan had been prepared by surveyor Harry Beverley. Thirty-two lots had been sold by June of the following year by trustees John Waller, Thomas Carr, and Philip Whitehead. Lots were priced at 480 pounds of tobacco.[38]

Beverley's plan (figure 56), redrawn from recorded sales, shows that he and the trustees planned two long streets running back from the tip of the peninsula along the higher ground roughly equidistant from the

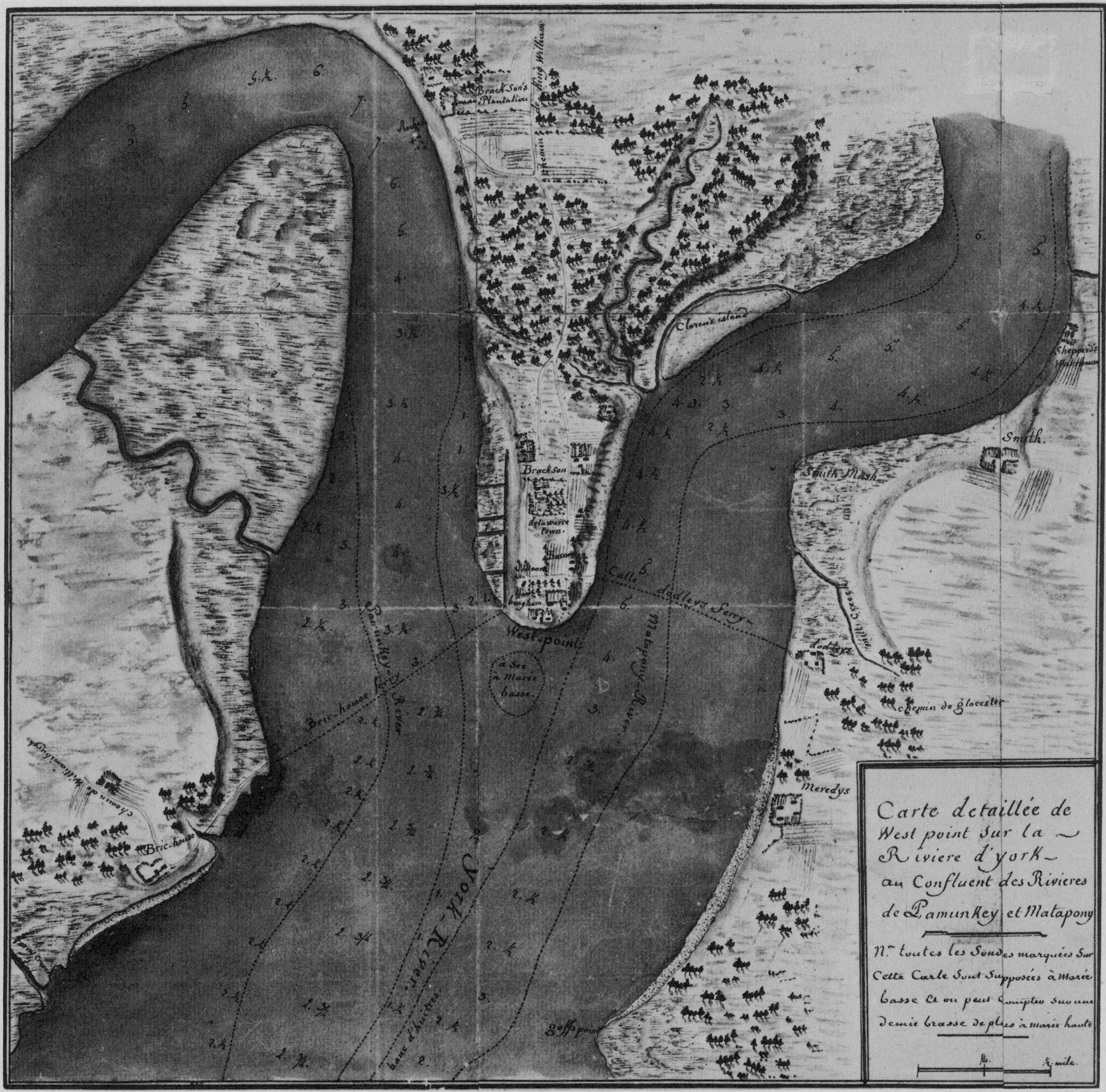

Figure 55. Map of West Point, Virginia, and Vicinity: ca. 1781

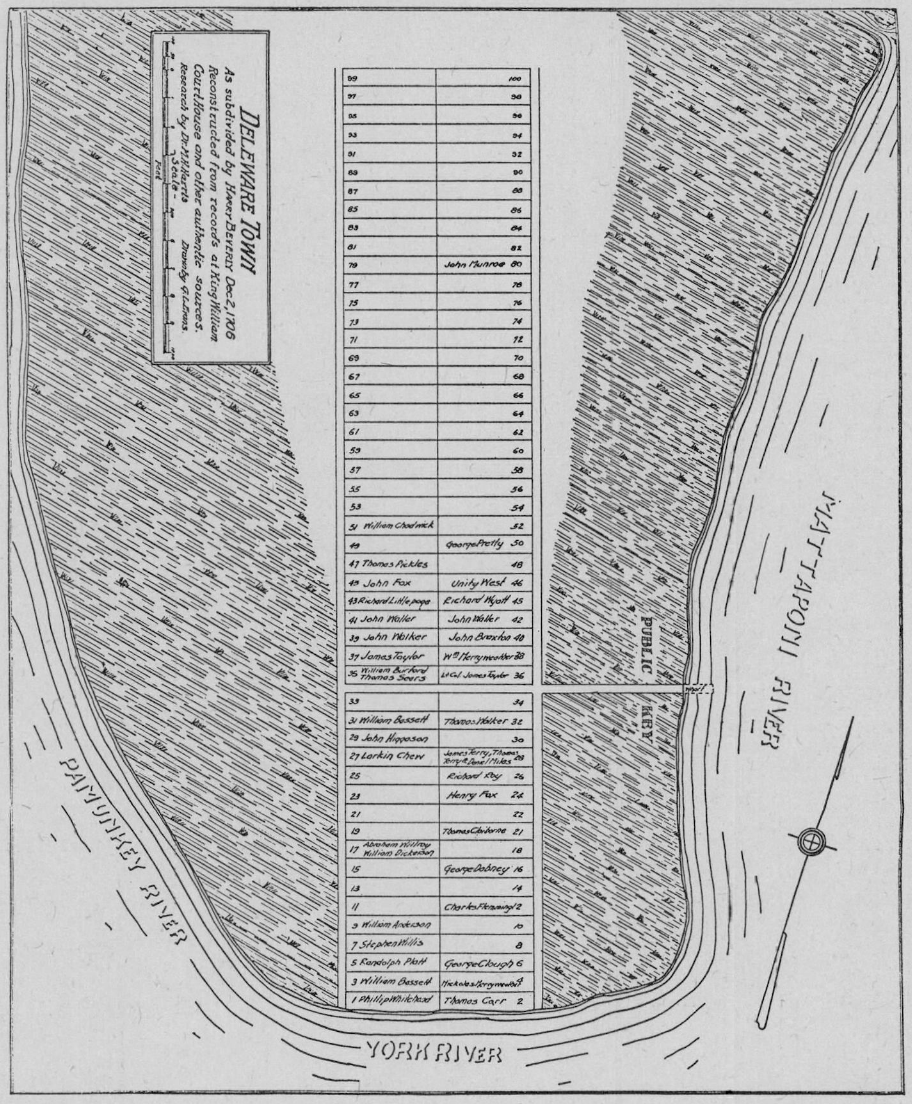

Figure 56. Plan of Delaware Town, Virginia: 1706

two rivers. The lots were twice the usual size, being 132 by 330 feet, or one acre in area. This departure from the procedure specified in the general town acts apparently was permitted under a special act designating West Point as a town in 1701, just before establishment of King William County from a part of King and Queen County. The act directed the new county to reimburse the old for the cost of the land purchased from John West.[39] The two main streets were 660 feet apart, crossed by only a single street leading to a public wharf or key on the Mattaponi River to the east. This linear gridiron plan was not long to endure, for Delaware Town failed to prosper, and most of the site reverted to plantation use. The modern West Point occupies this historic location, as well as a much greater area, but dates from the 1860s when the railroad to Richmond was completed.

The most important of the new towns begun under the act of 1691 was York—or Yorktown, to use the name that has become familiar. Although the earlier legislation had directed the development of a town in York County at the mouth of the York River, apparently the county officials ignored this mandate by the assembly. Not until July 24, 1691, did the county court take action to create a town when they

> Ordered that the court on the 29th day of this instant July meet upon Mr. Benjamin Reade's land beginning at the lower side of Smyths Creek and so running downward by the river towards the ferry being ye land appointed by Law for a Port in order to laying out of the same for a town and doeing all other things relateing thereto, and that the sheriff give notice to the surveyor of this county that he then and there give his attendance. And further this court doth hereby nominate and make choyce of Mr. Joseph Ring and Mr. Thomas Ballard to take and receive of Mr. Benjamin Reade a ffirme and authentic Deed or Conveyance of the said land as ffeoffees in trust which is accordingly by them to be confirmed to every respective pson or psons as the law directs for what shall to him or them.[40]

Colonel Lawrence Smith, the surveyor, soon was busy with his work and by August 18 he had completed the boundary survey of the town land reproduced in figure 57, a drawing recorded slightly more than a month later. Strangely enough an irregular strip of land bordering the river was not included in the land acquired from Benjamin Reade, who received ten thousand pounds of tobacco.[41] This land was later to be built on in a rather disorganized manner, quite different from the orderly layout of streets and lots in the town proper.[42] In Smith's plan for the town (figure 58) a single main street parallels the river front and a series of shorter cross streets lead inland. Eighty-three lots, each roughly half an acre in area, completed the design.

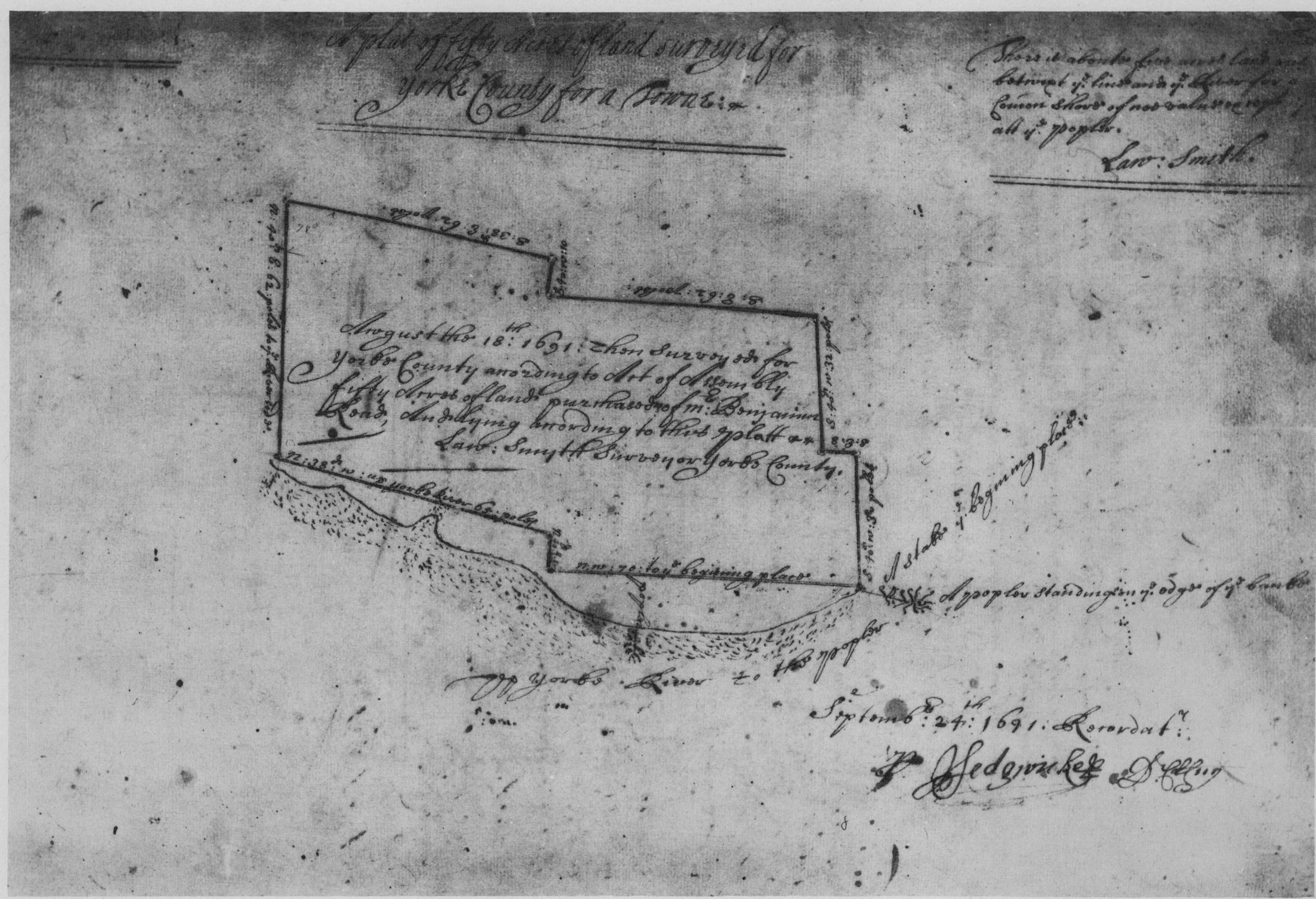

Figure 57. Map of the York, Virginia, Town Lands: 1691

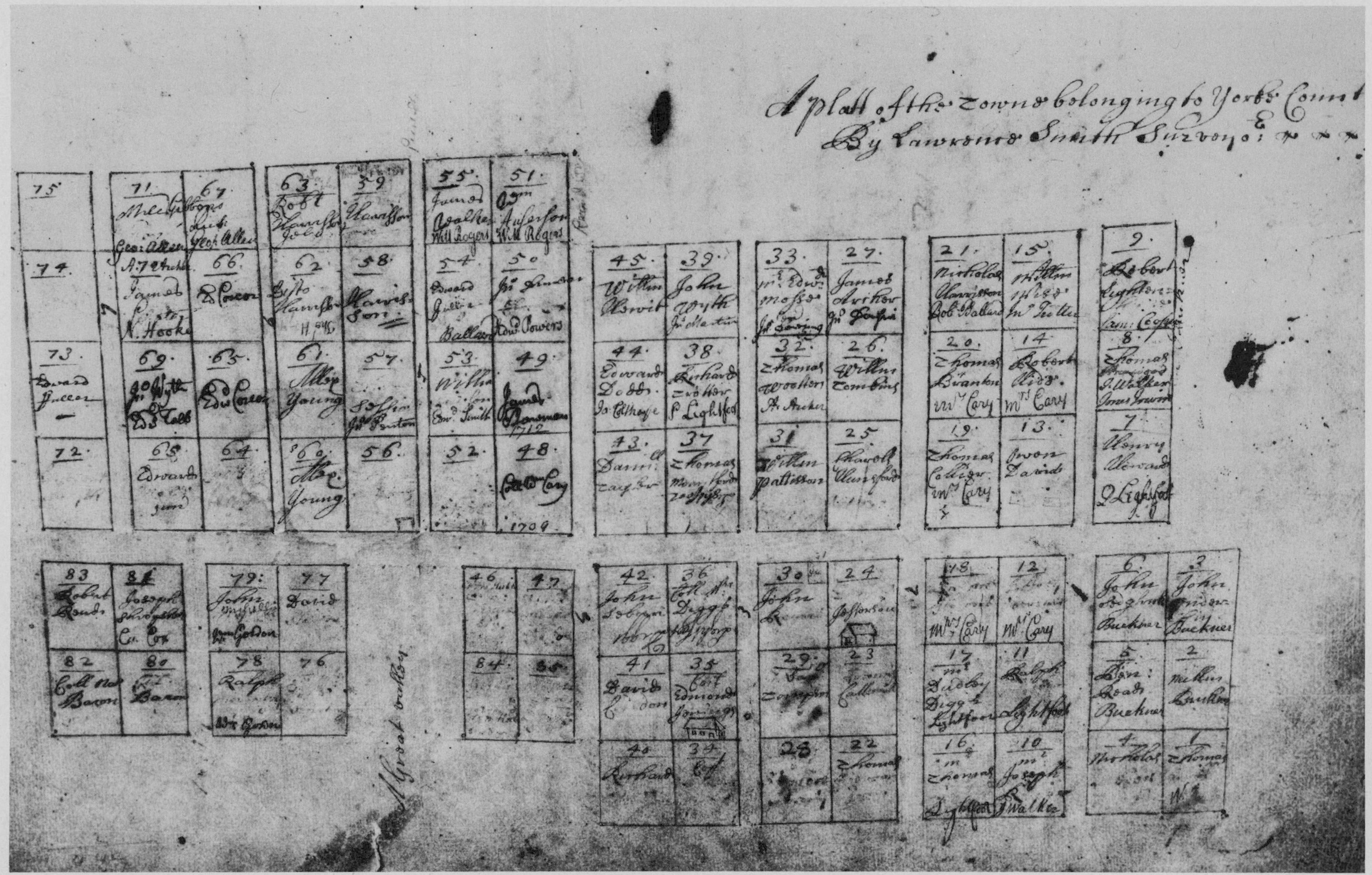

Figure 58. Plan of Yorktown, Virginia: 1691

At the time of the founding of York the court sat at the "French Ordinary," midway along the road to Williamsburg. In a rather unusual attempt to stimulate the growth of the new town the General Assembly directed that a courthouse be erected at York and imposed a penalty of fifty pounds sterling on each justice if the order were not carried out.[43] The justices promptly engaged Henry Cary of Warwick County to erect a building at a cost of thirty thousand pounds of tobacco, and on November 24, 1697, they were able to hold their first meeting at York. The location of this building can be found on Smith's plan, lot number 24, facing the main street at the corner of one of the cross streets leading toward the river. It was replaced in 1733 by a larger brick structure that served for many years, surviving considerable damage during the British occupation in the revolutionary war before succumbing to fire in 1814. On the courthouse lot also stood the first jail, completed by 1698 and replaced by a larger building in 1737.

Francis Nicholson, although then governor of Maryland, retained a deep interest in the town that had been established under the legislation he had promoted. He had offered, and presumably paid, five pounds sterling toward the completion of the courthouse. He offered in 1696 to subscribe four times this amount for the construction of a brick church if completed within two years. Soon this structure, built of marl rather than brick, took shape not far from the courthouse. During these early years of the town there must have been something of a building boom, for lot sales were brisk and York quickly developed into a thriving community.

The son of the original proprietor, perceiving the growing demand for building sites, subdivided an extensive tract of land south of the original boundaries of York. Here, too, there was much development, mainly of smaller houses for tradesmen and craftsmen.[44] In 1757 the assembly incorporated this area into the town. A visitor in 1742 was impressed by the prosperity of the community and the many larger and more imposing town and country houses erected by men of considerable wealth:

> You perceive a great Air of Opulence amongst the Inhabitants, who have some of them built themselves Houses, equal in Magnificence to many of our superb ones at St. James's; as those of Mr. Lightfoot, Nelson, &c. Almost every considerable Man Keeps an Equipage. . . . The Taverns are many here, and much frequented, and an unbounded Licentiousness seems to taint the Morals of the young Gentlemen of this Place. The Court-House is the only considerable publick Building, and is no unhandsome Structure. . . . The most considerable Houses are of Brick; some handsome ones of Wood, all built in the modern Taste; and the lessor Sort, of Plaister. There are some very pretty Garden Spots in the Town; and the Avenues leading to Williamsburgh, Norfolk, &c., are prodigiously agreeable.[45]

Some of the "unbounded Licentiousness" doubtless took place in the lower town below the bank on which the original community had been laid out. There, on what supposedly was common land, many persons had constructed warehouses, docks, shops, taverns, and other structures essential to shipping and commerce. This area had developed in a disorderly manner, as can be seen on a map showing a portion of Yorktown during the Revolution (figure 59). This rather extensive and crowded water-oriented settlement can also be seen in the unusual view of the town from the York River drawn about 1755 (figure 60). This land, like the more extensive suburb to the south of the town, had been claimed by Gwyn Read, the son of the original owner of the area. Eventually in 1738 it had to be purchased for the sum of £100, and the owners of lots in the town were assessed to meet this unexpected expense.[46] Finally, in 1788 some attempt was made to regularize land titles in the lower town when the area was surveyed, divided into lots, and sold. The irregular plots that resulted can be seen in figure 61, a manuscript drawing that survived, although damaged, in the county records.

Fire destroyed virtually all of the lower town in 1814, but York had already suffered extensive damage during the Revolution. Isaac Weld in 1796 described it as a town

> of about seventy houses, an episcopalian church, and a gaol. It is not now more than one third of the size it was before the war, and it does not appear likely soon to recover its former flourishing state. Great quantities of tobacco were formerly inspected here; very little, however, is now raised in the neighborhood. . . . The banks of the river, where the town stands, are high and inaccessible, excepting in a few places; the principal part of the town is built on the top of them; a few fishing huts and storehouses merely stand at the bottome.[47]

York's decline continued as other ports became more important in handling the trade from the west. Today the town is essentially a museum, cherished by Americans not for its place in the history of town planning but as the crucial battleground ending the Revolution.

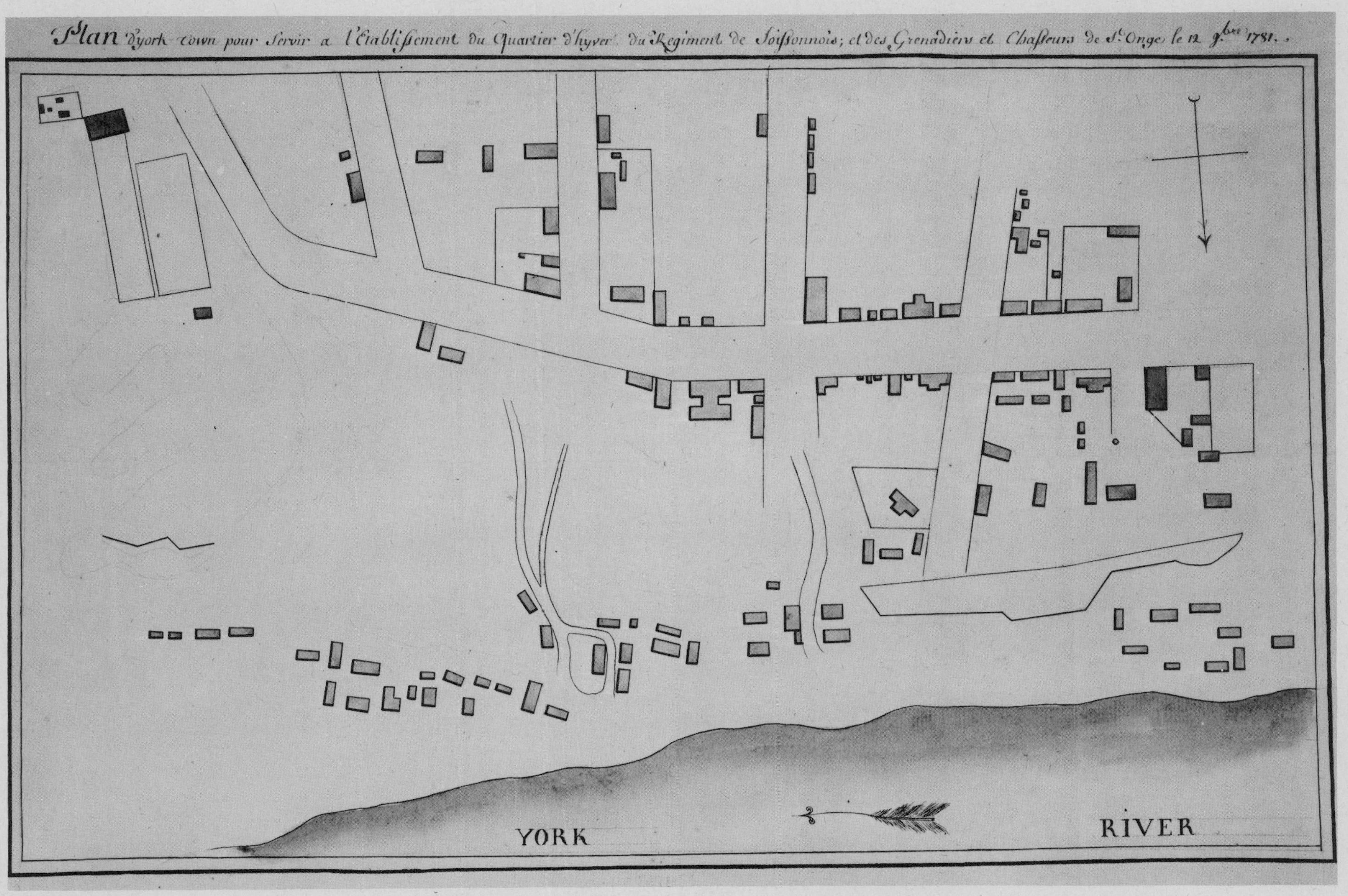

Figure 59. Plan of Yorktown, Virginia: 1781

Figure 60. View of Yorktown, Virginia: ca. 1755

The spurt in town founding stimulated by the act of 1691 did not last long. Governor Nicholson, who had supported the legislation so strongly the previous years, in 1692 campaigned for its repeal. According to a contemporary historian who attempted to account for this change in position, "He had receiv'd Directions from those *English* Merchants, who well knew that Cohabitation would lessen their consign'd Trade." [48] Whatever reasons may have been in his mind, Nicholson succeeded in obtaining from the assembly on April 1, 1693, an act suspending the 1691 port law on the grounds that William and Mary, the joint sovereigns, had not indicated their approval.[49]

Six years later the assembly partially lifted the suspension by an act that authorized the appointment of new town trustees, if necessary, permitted

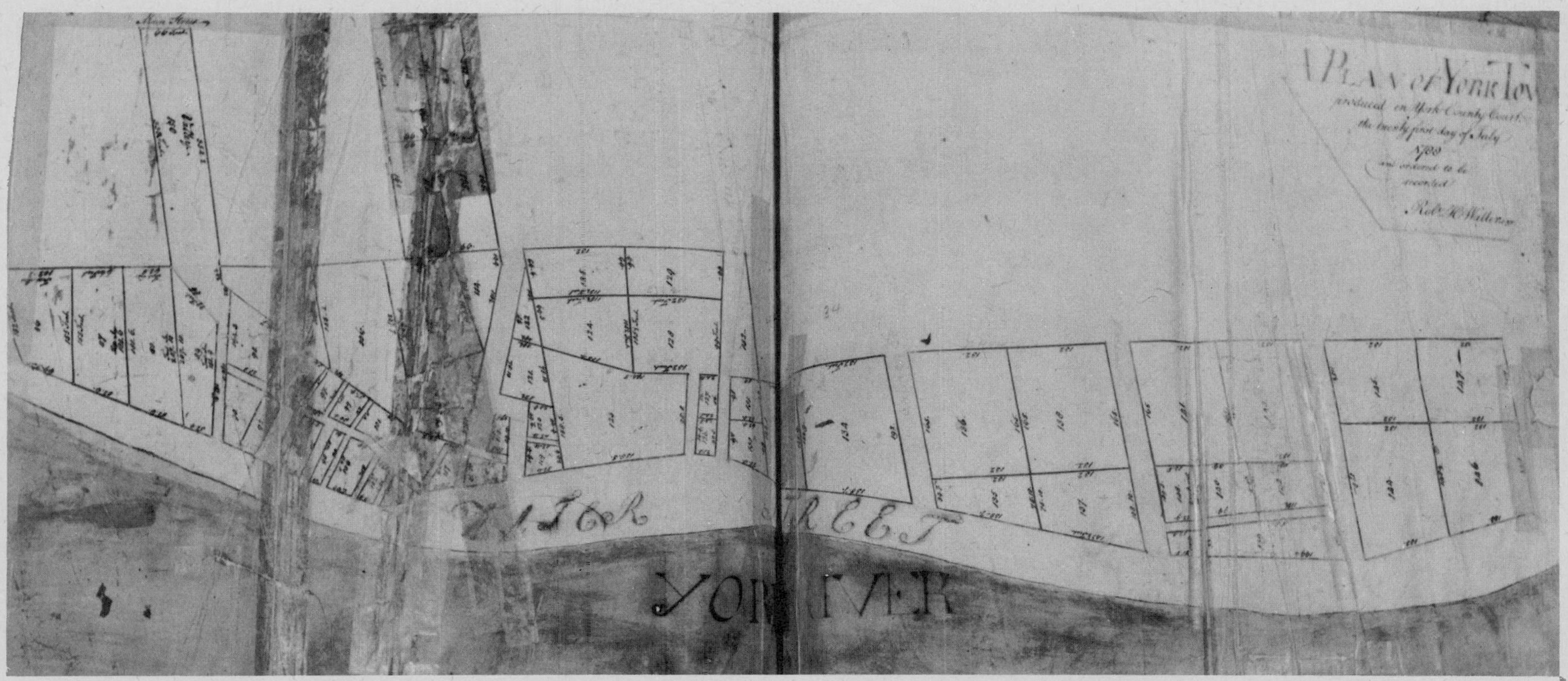

Figure 61. Plan of Portion of Yorktown, Virginia: 1788

them to sell lots in the towns, confirmed land titles acquired in previous sales, and extended to those who had ceased to build after the suspension act an additional period of twelve months to make good their title. The exclusive trading privileges of the towns, however, were not restored. This compromise position failed to satisfy colonial administrators, and once again royal instructions were sent out to the Virginia governor, Colonel Edward Nott, in 1705 directing him to secure more comprehensive legislation.[50]

The Act for Establishing Ports and Towns of 1706 resembled the previous enactments. After December 25, 1708, all imports except "servants, slaves and salt" and all exports except "coal, corn and timber" were to be cleared through one of the designated ports. No imported goods were to be bought or sold within five miles of the towns unless by persons already living within the prohibited area. The act further prohibited the licensing of an ordinary within ten miles of the towns unless at a public ferry or courthouse. These were obvious attempts to establish a monopoly of trade for the towns themselves in an effort to attract persons to their bounds. The assembly extended further benefits to town dwellers in the form of a fifteen-year exemption from all poll taxes, a reduction on duties paid by them to one-fourth the usual rate, and immunity from military service outside the town except in time of war. The act further included elaborate provisions for town government, with additional powers being made available to each town as its population increased. Each town was to be permitted markets at least twice a week as well as an annual fair. Sixteen sites were appointed for towns.[51] Land was to be acquired, surveyed, and sold as provided in the previous legislation, with a period of twelve months allowed for each purchaser to construct "one good house to contain twenty foot square at the least."[52]

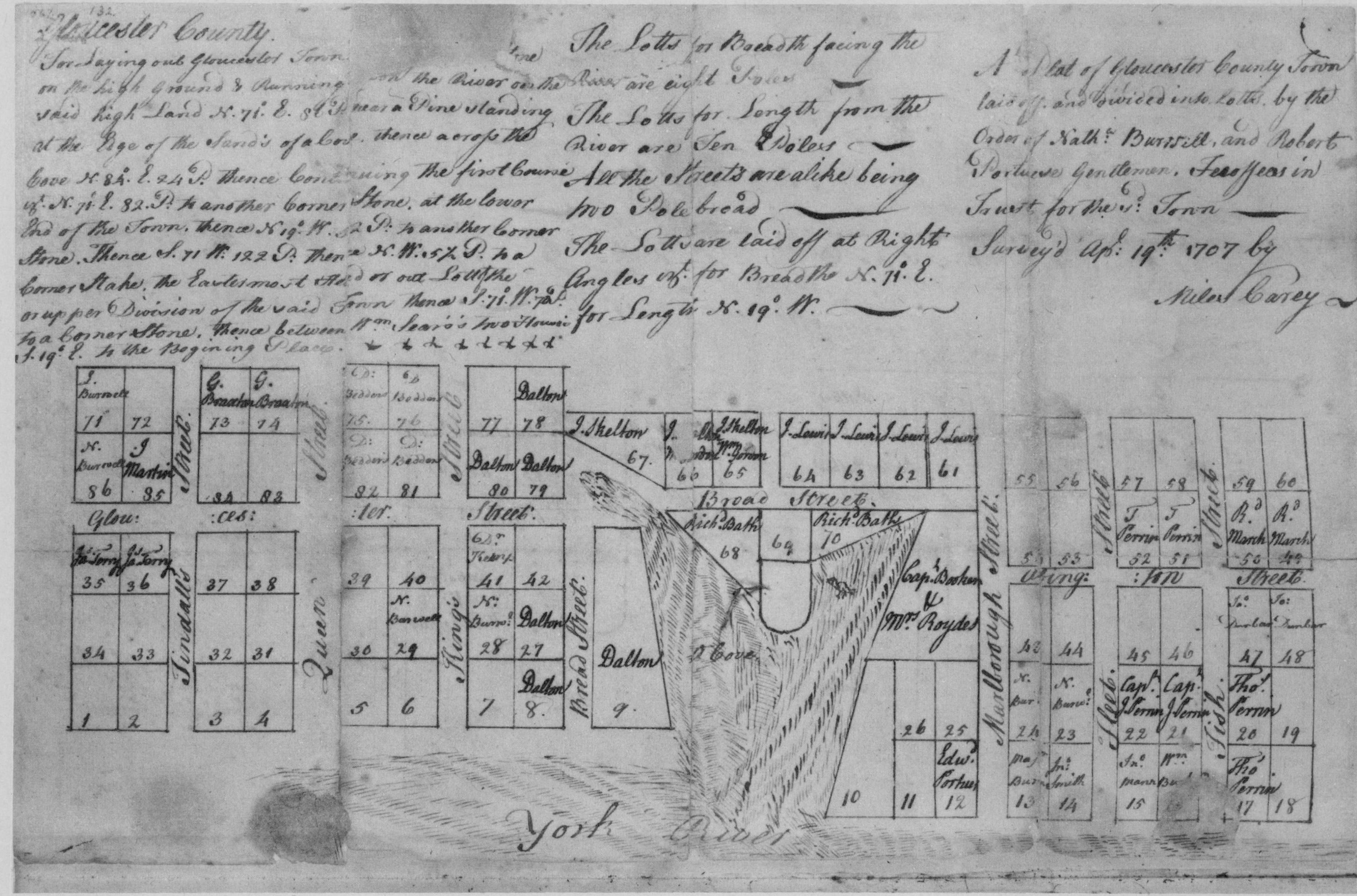

Figure 62. Plan of Gloucester Point, Virginia: 1707

Following this legislation the counties involved began new efforts at town founding or attempts to revive those ports that had remained largely paper communities. The surviving plat of Tindall's Point bears the date of 1707, although the drawing, reproduced in figure 62, may represent a resurvey of a pattern of streets and lots laid out earlier. The notes on this drawing tell us that the lots were 132 by 165 feet, exactly half an acre, though a number of parcels of irregular shape obviously departed from these measurements. Miles Carey, the surveyor who signed the plat and who presumably designed the town, made his streets only two poles, or 33 feet, wide. Interruptions in the gridiron plan were caused by the cove in the York River, and the circular projection into this harbor area was probably the site occupied by the fort ordered erected here by the Assembly in 1667. Although some development occurred, Gloucester Point never rivaled Yorktown across the river. In 1755, as the view in figure 63 reveals, its appearance was far from impressive. This place, like York, suffered during the Revolution, and Isaac Weld in 1796 found there "only ten or twelve houses."[53]

We have only fragmentary information concerning the other port towns established under the legislation enacted from 1680 to 1706. Land for Queenstown in Lancaster County near the mouth of the Rappahannock River was apparently not acquired until 1692. With young Robert Carter, later to become one of the major landowners in Virginia, as one of the trustees, the county bought for thirteen thousand pounds of tobacco the usual fifty acres from Captain William Ball. Later, in 1698, the county erected a new courthouse at the town which had evidently been surveyed into streets and lots. In 1706, Harry Beverley prepared a new survey that included a "broad street called Anne street" and another bearing the name of Prince Street.[54] The town failed to achieve its expected growth, the county abandoned the courthouse in 1771, and the little harbor on Town Creek filled up with silt. Today the site is vacant, a fate shared, among others, by a town in Northampton County surveyed once in 1681 and again in 1707.[55]

Kinsale (Kingsale in the act of 1706) in Westmoreland County still exists as a tiny gridiron settlement occupying a site on a bluff overlooking the Yeocomico River a few miles from the Potomac. Patesfield on Pagan Creek in Isle of Wight County, on the other hand, had virtually disappeared as early as 1776. In that year the assembly declared the land forfeit and authorized its disposal by county officials because the original lot

> purchasers soon finding that the said town would not answer the purpose for which it was intended, it being a remote part of the county, and very inconvenient for trade, many of them neglected to improve their lots, others who had built on them removed out of the said town, and many of the lots still remain unsold, and the said town, as such, is now entirely useless to the publick or the said county.[56]

Cobham, across the James River from Jamestown in Surry County, also failed to survive. The site was sold by Henry Hartwell for eight thousand pounds of tobacco. This was the location specified in 1691 for one of the market towns, but not an official port, described as "at the mouth of Grays Creek on the lower side thereof." Its less important status may have been caused by the failure of the county under the earlier legislation in 1680 to create a town on the first site, which lay about four miles up the creek. It is by no means certain that the county was any more successful in 1691, for the earliest survey of the town (figure 64) dates from 1738. While this design may have represented an entirely new plan, it is possible that it was merely a resurvey of the streets and lots as established under the act of 1691. Forty-nine lots are shown. Except for those fronting the river they have an area of little more than four-tenths of an acre, measuring 60 by 302½ feet. The streets were laid out 49½ feet wide, or exactly three poles. There is some evidence to indicate that this drawing represents but a portion of the town plan, since references to more than forty-nine lots appear in the land records.

This town, too, enjoyed a fleeting period of prosperity. A ferry connected it to Jamestown across the river, ships called with some frequency at the wharf, and at least one ordinary offered food, drink, and a place to gamble for the residents of the town and nearby plantation owners. Several warehouses provided places of storage for the tobacco crop, and there must have been several stores where those selling tobacco could purchase products imported from the mother country and from other American colonies. Yet today not a single structure dating from the colonial period stands on the site of this once flourishing settlement.[57]

By 1707 the very commissioners of customs who had urged the enactment of the third town act were bitterly condemning its provisions.[58] Two years later in a statement doubtless prepared for the queen they noted, in a re-

Figure 63. View of Gloucester Point, Virginia: ca. 1755

vealing summary of mercantilist policy, the reasons why the law should be suspended:

> The whole Act is designed to Encourage by great Priviledges the settling in Townships, and such settlements will encourage their going on with the Woolen and other manufactures there, And should this Act be Confirmed, the Establishing of Towns and Incorporating of the Planters as intended thereby, will put them upon further Improvements of the said manufactures, And take them off from the Planting of Tobacco, which would be of Very Ill consequence, not only in respect to the Exports of our Woolen and other Goods and Consequently to the Dependance that Colony ought to have on this

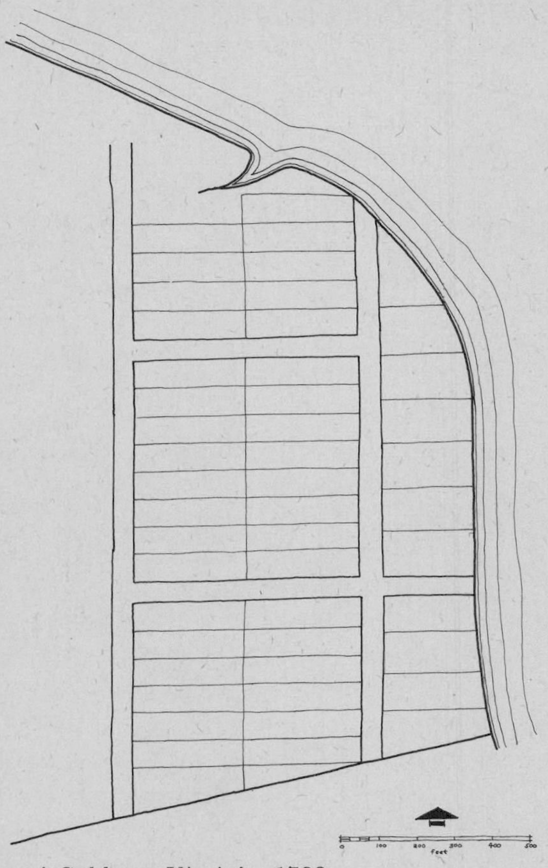

Figure 64. Plan of Cobham, Virginia: 1738

> Kingdom, but likewise in respect to the Importation of Tobacco hither for the home and Foreign Consumption, Besides a further Prejudice in relation to our shipping and navigation.[59]

The queen agreed, ordered appropriate instructions, and on August 18, 1710, Governor Spotswood could report to the Board of Trade "In Obedience to her Majesties commands, I have issued a Proclamation for repealing the act of Assembly for establishing ports and Towns. . . ."[60]

A final attempt by some members of the House of Burgesses to secure the passage of still another town act in 1711 ended in failure.[61] This marked the termination of a remarkable effort to call into being towns and ports in wholesale quantities by legislative fiat. It did not, however, signal the end of colonial town planning. Already, in 1699, the Virginia assembly had established the basis for a new capital city which was to achieve substantial success. And, throughout the eighteenth century Virginia, like Maryland, followed a new policy of establishing single towns where and when the need arose.

V. *The New Towns Program of Seventeenth-Century Maryland*

Efforts in Maryland to promote the development of towns in the seventeenth and early eighteeth centuries took a course similar to that attempted in Virginia. The legislative history is particularly complicated, beginning with several proclamations by the governor and including a series of laws and supplementary acts designating in all approximately sixty sites for new settlements. For all of this activity we have only scattered graphic evidence of the town plans, as less than a dozen early plats survive. Many of the towns named in the earliest laws also figured in later legislation, indicating that at least some of them had not succeeded in establishing themselves and suggesting also that in some cases they had not even been surveyed. A number of the drawings are of uncertain date, and even when that can be determined one cannot be sure if the drawing represents an entirely new plan on an old site or merely a resurvey of an earlier plan. In several cases, too, even the original locations are impossible to determine with confidence, for long ago in many instances all traces of the towns vanished completely.[1]

The Maryland new towns program originated with a proclamation on June 5, 1668, by Governor Charles Calvert who began with an explanation that he took the action under instructions sent by Lord Baltimore. The governor designated eleven sites for "Sea Ports Harbours creekes & places for the discharging and unlading of goods and merchandizes out of shipps & boates and other vessells."[2] Only these locations could be used for importing goods into the province, and a violation of this regulation was to be punished by imprisonment for one year without bail.

The following year the proclamation was replaced by "An Ordinance of the . . . Lord Proprietary" requiring all export as well as import trade to be channeled through twelve designated sites, most of them apparently identical with those first specified.[3] The document is of particular interest because in the description of some of the sites there is a reference to the "town land" at the location. This seems to indicate that either before the proclamation of 1668 or as a result of its adoption officials in several counties had purchased sites intended to be used for towns.[4]

Once again, this time in 1671, Governor Calvert repeated these provisions in a "declaration" listing fifteen sites as the only approved locations for the unloading of cargo.[5] Perhaps planter resistance to the ordinance of 1669 convinced Calvert that he should not require merchandise for export to pass through these ports and harbors. The descriptions of the sites resembled those in the previous executive enactment but omitted any references to "town land."

Figure 65 shows the locations of the various ports specified in this series of regulations.[6] How many towns were laid out at these sites or already existed is a matter of conjecture, for reliable information is meager. At least one town had been planned, for in 1682 some of the residents of Battle Town, later known as Calverton, petitioned the assembly to compel one William Berry to convey title to lots in the town he asked to have laid out under the ordinance of 1669.[7] John Ogilby, in his well-known work on America published in 1671, lists three towns in Calvert County and refers to others:

> There are Foundations laid of Towns, more or less in each County,

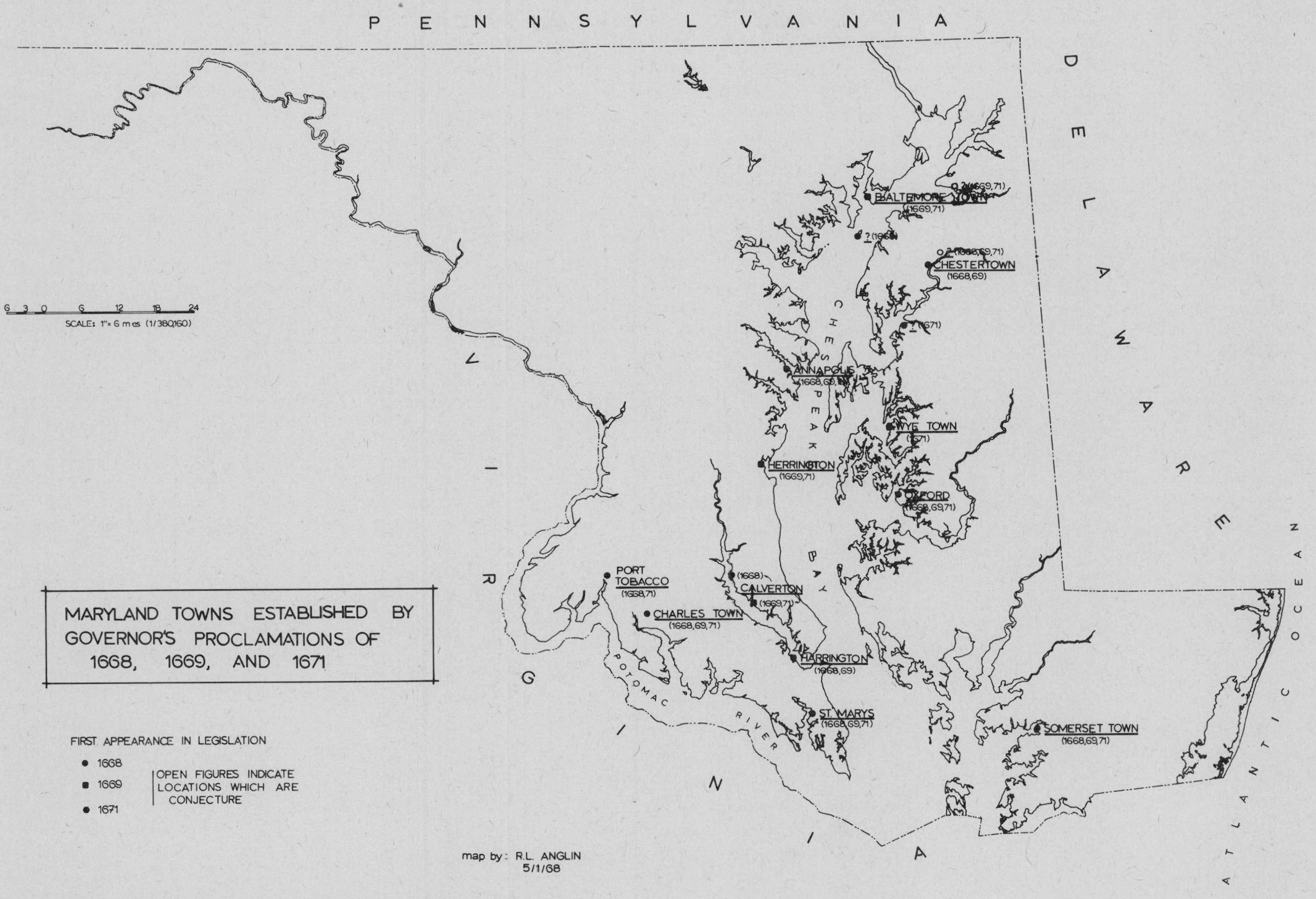

Figure 65. Map of Towns Founded in Maryland in 1668, 1669, and 1671

> according to his Lordships Proclamation, to that effect issu'd forth in the year 1668. In *Calvert County,* about the River of *Patuxent,* and the adjacent Cliffs, are the Bounds of three Towns laid out, one over against *Point Patience,* call'd *Harvington,* another in *Battel-Creek,* call'd *Calverton,* and a third upon the Cliffs, call'd *Herrington,* and Houses already built in them, all uniform, and pleasant with Streets, and Keys on the Water side.[8]

When Augustine Herrman prepared his map of Virginia and Maryland in 1670 (published in London three years later), he included a number of towns that may have had their origins in the first or second of these enactments. The relevant portion of this great cartographic work is reproduced in figure 66. Including St. Mary's, Herrman showed thirteeen places in Maryland, two of them unnamed, with the symbol he used for a town. In addition, his map included the name Oxford but without the symbol. It is possible, of course, that Herrman merely was indicating the locations specified in the executive orders we have already reviewed rather than recording actual settlement at a place surveyed into streets and lots.[9] In any event, the complete lack of town plats from that period makes it impossible to reach any conclusions concerning the forms these towns took, or if they existed at all.

During the following decade apparently little if any town development took place. Then, two years after the enactment of the first general town and port act in Virginia, Maryland prepared to take similar action. Much of the time of the upper and lower houses of the Assembly in the fall of 1682 and again in 1683 was devoted to preparing legislation for towns and ports. The governor, Charles Calvert, had then become lord proprietor. He proposed that the earlier proclamations of 1668, 1669, and 1671 designating official ports for the province be replaced by more comprehensive legislation. On October 31, 1682, the council approved a bill entitled "An Act for Advancing the Trade of Tobacco" and sent it to the burgesses for consideration.[10]

Then began a series of legislative maneuverings bewildering in their complexity and difficult to reconstruct with complete accuracy. The bill was referred to committee and eventually reported with a number of amendments. These dealt with the effective day of the measure, the right of the assembly to designate the locations of new towns and ports rather than permit the proprietor to exercise this function, the method of acquiring the necessary land and the payment of surveyors, and a number of other matters.[11]

A committee of the council was then instructed to meet with the committee of the burgesses to amend the bill. Apparently the work went smoothly, and the upper house again passed the bill with the suggested amendments. Then, however, the lower house, after twice reading the amended bill, raised a number of objections. The burgesses pointed out that nothing in the bill prevented the taking of an existing dwelling for town land, that the proposed fifty-acre sites if divided into one hundred lots would not permit any streets or if the streets were first laid out would result in lots too small to be usable. Altogether, these alleged flaws were "Enough to sett the Inhabitants together by the Eares." [12]

The lower house suggested that the whole matter be put over until the next session of the assembly, but the upper house insisted on a conference of both houses to discuss the matter. Here the speaker of the House of Burgesses raised a procedural objection: the proprietor in opening the session of the assembly, had stated that the purpose of the session was only to consider other matters; thus it was not proper to introduce this legislation.[13]

Ultimately the lower house succeeded in delaying action on the measure in 1682. From the record it appears that their objections in many cases were well founded. But one also gets the impression that opposition was directed not so much against the details of the proposed bill as at the idea of more central direction over trade and the necessity for transshipping imported and exported products between the designated port towns and the plantations. In the following year the tactics of the burgesses became more obvious, and the conflict sharpened between them and the aristocratic members of the upper house.

At the beginning of the autumn session of the assembly in 1683 the matter arose anew. Burgesses were eager to secure passage of a bill governing the method of election. This the proprietor and the council were reluctant to see enacted. Throughout the month of legislative wrangling that followed the lower house broadly hinted that the passage of one was contingent on the approval of the other.[14]

There was renewed discussion about the places to be appointed for the new towns and to what extent the burgesses would have a voice in deciding their locations. A point of contention as well was the selection of persons

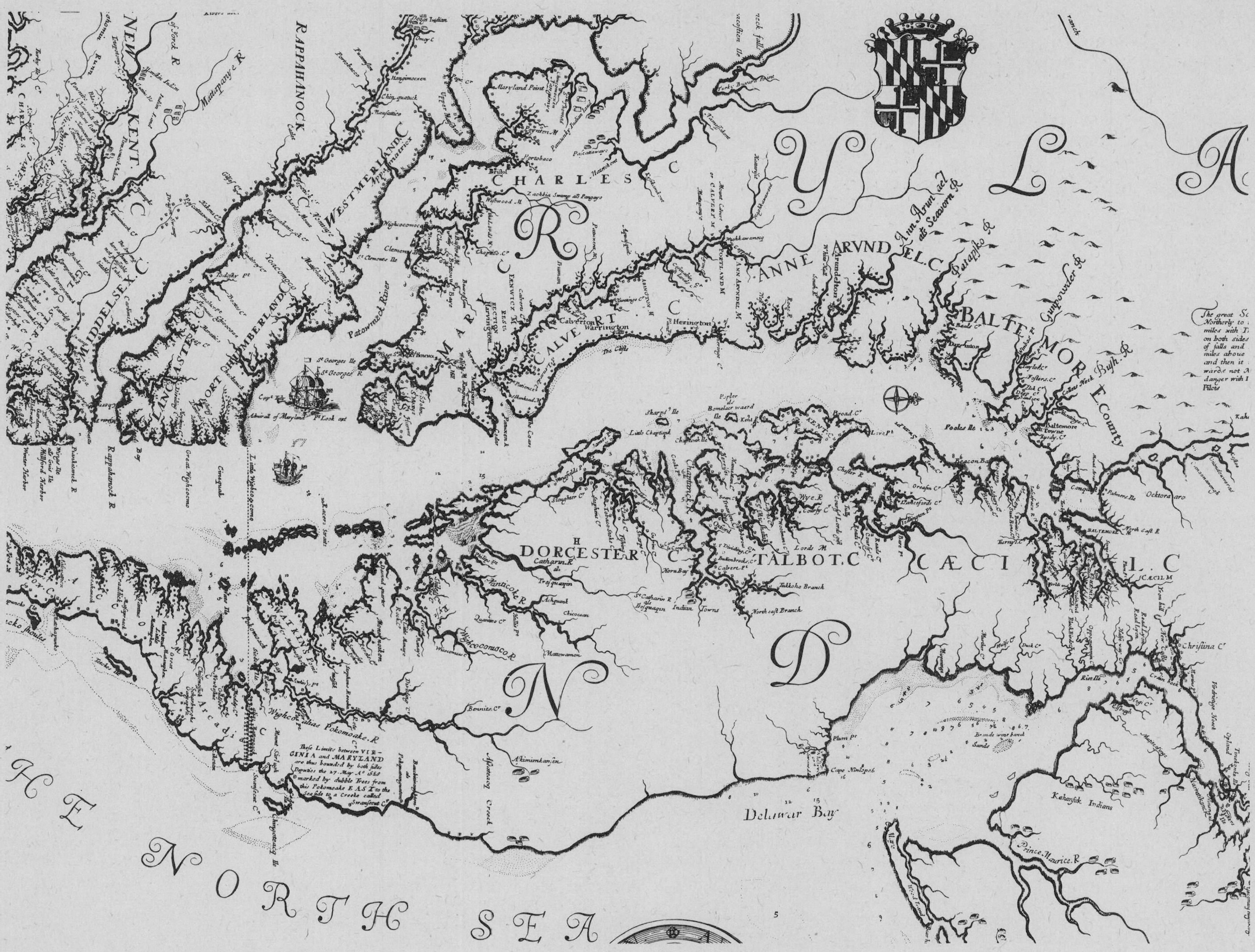

Figure 66. Map of a Portion of Maryland: 1670

who would serve as commissioners to manage the establishment of the new ports. Several lists of town locations circulated between the two houses and the proprietor, and in the course of the debates some minor changes appear to have been made.[15]

After an additional attempt by the lower house to secure the passage of two acts in which it was interested—and the election measure and another dealing with military duties—the proprietor summoned the members before him and virtually demanded passage of the port and town legislation. Eventually, and with a good deal of resentment on all sides, the burgesses reluctantly approved the bill and it received the assent of the proprietor on November 6, 1683.[16]

The law that finally emerged from the assembly closely resembled that passed in Virginia in 1680. After August 31, 1685, all imports and exports were to pass through one of the locations specified in the act. No fewer than thirty-one sites were designated for this purpose. For every county, commissioners were appointed and directed to acquire sites of one hundred acres at each of the listed spots. They were to meet sometime before March 25, 1684, to arrange for the purchase of the land required. If the owner disagreed with the value placed on his acres, the commissioners were authorized to direct the sheriff to assemble a jury for the purpose of determining a fair price.

At each of the specified sites the commissioners were to have the land surveyed and then to have it "marcked staked out and devided into Convenient streets, Laines & allies, with Open Space places to be left On which may be Erected Church or Chappell, & Marckett house, or other publick buildings, & the remaining part of the said One hundred acres of Land as near as may be into One hundred equall Lotts." The owner was to be given first choice of one lot. Sales during the first four months following March 25, 1684, were to be open only to residents of the county in which the town was located and were to be limited during this period so that no person could purchase more than a single lot. Each purchaser was obligated to build a house of at least four hundred square feet before August 31, 1685, on penalty of forfeiting his title to the land. At the end of five years if any lots remained unsold their ownership was to revert to the original owner of the site.

Severe penalties were provided for violations of the trading provisions of the law. Any goods imported to or exported from any other points in the colony were to be seized, with equal shares of the merchandise to be awarded to Lord Baltimore, to the justices of the county for purposes of furthering the growth of the new towns within their jurisdiction, and to the informer who led to the apprehension of the violator. For the protection of tobacco planters who did not maintain warehouses in the towns, the act required that the owners of such facilities accept for storage any tobacco sent to the town for that purpose, provided storage capacity was available. A maximum charge of ten pounds of tobacco annually was established for each hogshead of tobacco stored.

As an additional inducement to further the growth of these towns, the act specified that all rents due the proprietor and all public levies payable in tobacco were to be shipped to one of the towns. To reduce the costs to the residents in the formative stages of the towns the act provided that no burgesses were to be selected to represent the area in the assembly "untill such time as the said town . . . shall be actually Inhabited by such & so many familys as shall be sufficiently able to defray the Charge & expences of such Delegates . . . who shall be elected & Chosen by the freemen of each Respective towne."

It was one thing to pass such a measure; it proved quite another to arrange for its implementation. Evidently many planters opposed the legislation for the same reasons that had provoked opposition in Virginia, even though with a larger number of towns the inconveniences and expense of transportation to and from the new ports would be somewhat less than in the older colony. As the date of March 25, 1684, approached the governor and lord proprietor took notice, in a proclamation issued at the end of February, of how little had been accomplished. He referred to the fact that "little or noe progress" had been made and then issued a strict "charge and command" that

> all and singular the Commissionrs of the respective Counties . . . putt in Execution the said Act . . . by causeing the severall Ports Townes and places of Trade . . . to be forthwith layd out . . .; And that noe failure be thereof made as they will answer the Contrary at their perill, by not onely incurring our displeasure for their contempt of the said Act . . . but also running the hazard of being excluded and exempt from any future or further benefitt or advantage to be obtained of us. . . .[17]

A few days later, on March 5, the council in ordering Captain Brandt to complete his surveys for the towns and ports in Charles County took notice of opposition to the new law:

> It being credibly reported and informed to this board that severall malitious and ill affected persons to the good and wellfare of this Province have raised and spread abroad scandalous speeches and discourses concerning the Act . . . on purpose to prevent the putting forward soe good a designe as thereby is intended. It was ordered that Proclamation should issue, requireing the speedy and vigorous prosecution and putting in Execution of the said Act of Assembly and awarding punishmt on all such as shall endeavour to obstruct impede or prevent in any wise the same. . . .[18]

Two and a half years later the council used equally strong language in referring to "some evill minded persons" who were opposed to the creation of towns. They, the council states, "have noe other than covetous and sinister ends to promote their own private gain and noe way desire the publick good of this Province."[19]

One solution appeared to be the creation of additional towns so that some of the inconveniences of the act would be reduced. This step, coupled with sterner enforcement measures, was taken with the enactment of supplementary legislation passed April 26, 1684. Reciting that they had received petitions from several counties for the establishment of more official port towns, the assembly proceeded to list thirteen new sites for such purposes. Two of the previously designated towns were shifted to other sites within the same general area. That very little had been accomplished under the original act is indicated by a legislative finding that of the thirty-one towns first specified there were "very few or none layd out into Lotts And Staked out as by the said Act is Directed."[20]

The commissioners for the several counties were directed to meet some time in June, 1684, to begin their duties. An unexcused absence from this meeting was to be punished by a fine of a thousand pounds of tobacco, and a similar fine was imposed on any sheriff or surveyor who failed to carry out his duties under the act. The commissioners were authorized to divide themselves into smaller groups, each to oversee the development of the town nearest their districts. Failure to attend to these duties was also punishable by a fine of two hundred pounds of tobacco, and the same penalty was to be levied against any workman who refused to serve the commissioners in staking out the ground. Any juror who failed to carry out his obligations in setting a value on land taken for a town could be fined five hundred pounds of tobacco. The act further directed the surveyor general to "Appoint in the severall Counties . . . honest & scilfull Artists and deputy surveyours to lay out and survey the severall Towns ports And places Appointed . . . As for the want of such Artists and Deputies . . . The said Towns ports And places be not left unsurveyed and layd out." For every town not planned because of the failure of surveyors to appear the surveyor general was to be fined five thousand pounds of tobacco. All this was to be done by September 29, 1684.[21]

Despite the greater convenience of an increased number of towns and the threat of fines for failing to comply with the provisions of the act, little progress in actual town building appears to have been made. On October 3, 1685, a year after the towns were to have been planned, the council were forced to issue a proclamation extending the time for persons to perfect their lot titles and announcing that they would endeavor to persuade the proprietor to confirm such titles even though technically faulty under the basic act.[22] On November 25 of the same year they authorized ships to call first at plantations for the purpose of transporting tobacco to the towns. This action recognized the shortage in the colony of small boats that could be used for this vital purpose.

It proved impossible to please everyone. The act of 1684 had changed the location of one town in Calvert County from a site on "John Bowlings land in purtuxent River" to one identified as "Coxes Creek in the said River." In October, 1685, fifty-eight residents of the county petitioned the council to abandon the new site and allow a town to be laid out as first proposed. This the council agreed to, stating that at the next meeting of the assembly they would petition the proprietary for approval of an amending act to confirm such action.[23]

This conciliatory attitude did not last long. On September 14, 1686, the council revoked their approval of the previous year allowing ships to call at plantations and pick up cargo for the towns. From that date the trading provisions of the acts of 1683 and 1684 were to be strictly enforced "under the severest penaltyes in the said Acts mentioned."[24] The officers also announced the harshest measure of all by declaring:

> that whosoever after the Publication hereof shall presume to report or any wayes publish or declare that the Building of Townes is not for the advancement of Trade or the good of this Province or in any other

words to that effect shall be deemed as Persons ill affected to the Government and be accordingly severely punished.

The following day they adopted a set of instructions for the officers in each county appointed to enforce the trading provisions of the town acts. These required the officer to keep careful records of tobacco loaded on ships of the port and to issue certificates to the masters of the ships indicating that the cargo had been legally placed on board. The officer was required to submit information about suspected violations occurring through shipment from nearby plantations. He was further instructed to take note of any violations not only in his own area of jurisdiction but from any other place in the colony.[25]

Then late in October, 1686, the assembly passed a second supplement to the principal act of 1683. Thirteen new sites were added and four were eliminated, making a total of fifty-three in the three acts. Any five commissioners in each county were given powers to carry out the provisions of the act and were to meet before March 25, 1687. Persons buying lots in the newest of the towns, as well as those who had previously bought land but had not perfected their titles by building a house of the prescribed size within the time limit, were given until August 31, 1688, to meet these requirements of the acts. Planters shipping tobacco to the towns were required to secure a certificate from the officer appointed for that purpose. Shipment of tobacco from other points or hauling it beyond the boundaries of Maryland was made punishable by a fine of forty shillings sterling for every hogshead illegally exported or lacking a certificate. Finally, lots reverting to the original owner because of failure to sell them within five years of the effective date of the act of 1683 could, if still vacant, be purchased at twice the initial price, and the owner was required to accept this price as full value for the land.[26]

There were subsequent efforts by the council to stimulate action under these laws. They ordered the commissioners to proceed as directed with laying out towns and to provide weights and scales as required by the provisions of the act of 1686 governing the certification of tobacco shipped to the ports for export.[27] Another proclamation admonished settlers to arrange for sloops and small boats to carry tobacco from plantations to the ports.[28] The very number of these legislative acts, proclamations, regulations, and directives suggests that they were being resisted vigorously by many and complied with, when at all, only with lassitude and hesitancy. It was a period in Maryland when on a number of issues the settlers challenged the powers of the proprietary, and certainly the provisions of the town acts seemed to run counter to the wishes of most of the planters. In the mid-1680s Calvert returned to England, and there he must have felt pressures from merchants who disliked the provisions of these Maryland laws as much as they opposed those of Virginia. On July 23, 1688, from London, Calvert issued a proclamation suspending the trading provisions of the town acts.[29]

Under these circumstances it appears curious that in December of that year the assembly would pass a fourth town act that designated seven additional sites for such purposes, including one that had been dropped in the previous act. This law contained no requirements whatsoever governing trade at these places and merely stated that the seven new communities were to be created, presumably by the commissioners in the counties involved, "under such limitations & with the benifitt of such priviledges as to other Townes nominated and Appointed by the Act for Advancement of Trade & Supplimentary Acts to the same are allowed."[30] Thus, if our tabulation is correct, the assembly brought the number of new towns, at least on paper, to an even sixty.

Figure 67 shows the locations of as many of these towns as could be determined. Some of the sites are conjectural, some are not named, the names of several date from later periods, and seven of the sixty sites could not be located with any degree of confidence. The number of towns involved virtually guaranteed that few of them would be successful. Such an attempt at instant urbanization was bound to fail. In Virginia, with a greater population and fewer new towns, the results were, at best, marginal. In Maryland the percentage of success was quite obviously much lower. As we shall see later in this chapter several towns had, in fact, been started although not all were to survive. One bit of evidence indicating that sales of lots had taken place is the act of the assembly that received Governor Seymour's approval on October 3, 1704, confirming title to land granted in the towns under the general acts.[31]

By this time Maryland had become a royal colony, and Lord Baltimore's status had been reduced to that of landlord, without administrative or policy responsibilities. English colonial officials hoped to see Maryland as well as Virginia grow into the kind of colony typified by New England

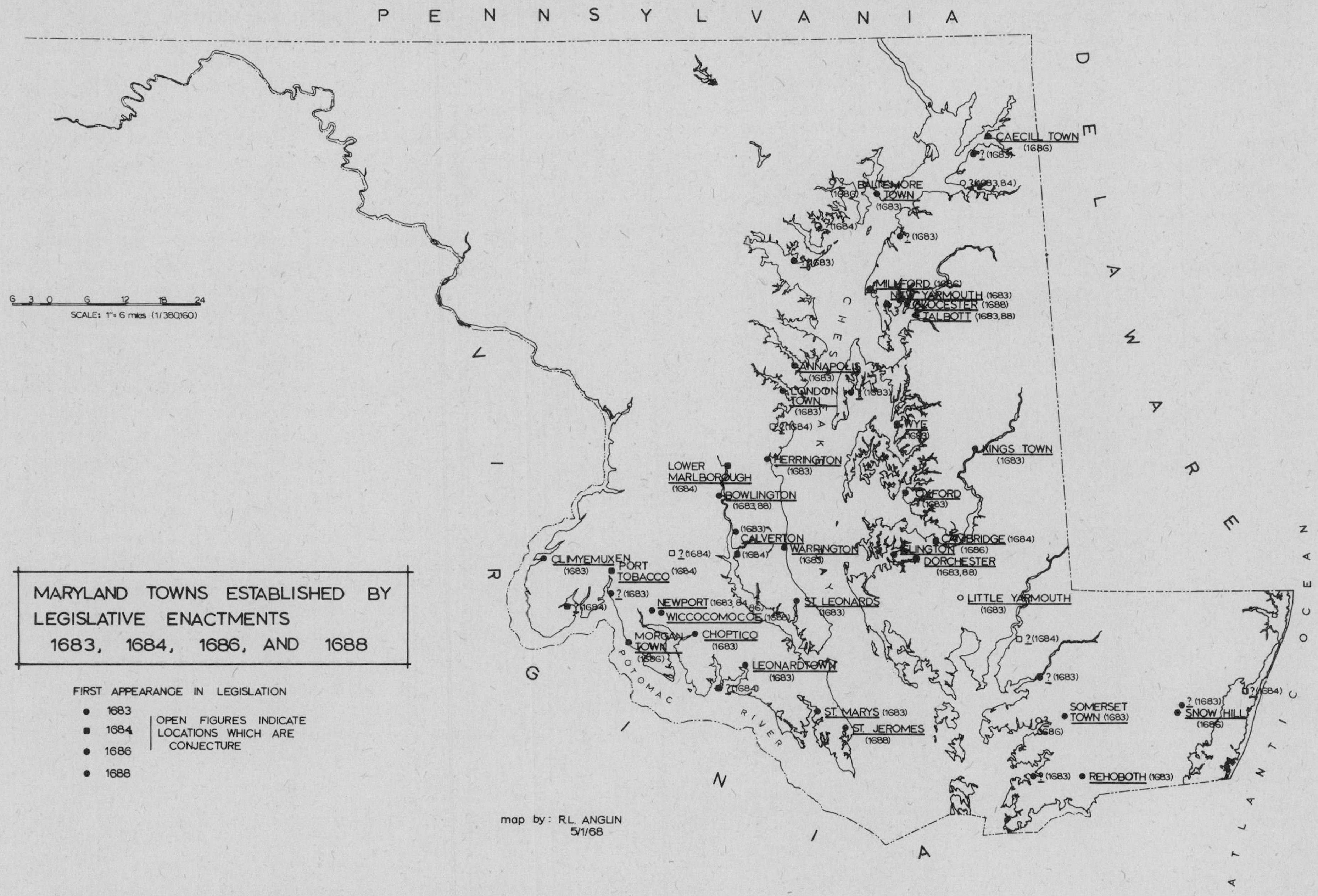

Figure 67. Map of Towns Founded in Maryland in 1683, 1684, 1686, and 1688

with a town-based culture. At the same time that the crown was sending similar instructions to the governor of Virginia, the Maryland executive received a directive "to move the assembly to pass an act for the building of towns, warehouses, wharves, and keys . . . upon the rivers of Potomac, Patuxent, and on the opposite shore in our province of Maryland." This act was to

> take in as much as possible in the several interests of the inhabitants and planters there and merchants here; in which act . . . the term of two years may be allowed from the passing thereof for the building of towns and warehouses and for the setting out and appointing of wharves and keys exclusive of any other places for the lading and unlading ships as aforesaid, the number of which towns are not to exceed three at most on each of the said rivers and two upon the opposite shore; and you are to correspond with our governor of Virginia in the carrying on of this good work in both our said colonies.[32]

The Maryland General Assembly in its tradition of multiple laws to accomplish a single purpose ultimately responded to the urgings of Governor Seymour with a new burst of town acts in 1706, 1707, and 1708. Although the governor's instructions from the crown plainly stated that no more than eight towns were to be created, the act of 1706 designated forty-two such locations. Most of the sites listed in this law had been previously identified for this purpose under one of the former acts. The provisions of the new law specifying the procedure to be followed in acquiring land, laying it out in streets, lots, and public sites, and in disposing of it were virtually identical to those first adopted in the act of 1683. Certain additional inducements to promote town development were added. Tradesmen and craftsmen were exempted from all levies during their first four years of residence; foreign merchants, tradesmen, and laborers were to become citizens after living in a town for a similar period; and male orphans under the jurisdiction of the county justices were to be put out as apprentices to the traders residing in the new towns.

The trading provisions of the law required only that all imports were to pass through one of the towns after January 1, 1707. Six of the towns received the title of ports: Annapolis, St. Mary's, Chestertown, Green Hill, Oxford, and the site on Beckwick's Island later given the name of Port St. George.[33] A supplementary act in 1707 added the significant requirement that after September 10, 1708, all merchandise for export, except "Timber pipe Staves billetts and wooden ware" were to be first brought to one of the towns that were then divided into groups as "members" of one of the six official ports.[34]

In 1707 legislation also changed a number of the town locations and reduced the size of several of them from one hundred acres to fifty. Six additional sites were designated, bringing the total to forty-eight. An extension of the time limit for perfecting title to town lots was granted, and the town commissioners in each county were empowered to acquire half-acre sites at convenient locations on the rivers and creeks as public landing places to which tobacco and other commodities could be brought and stored in rolling houses to await transportation to one of the towns.[35] Shipment of tobacco from one town to another without a permit was authorized if in a boat less than eighteen feet in length. Such shipments on larger vessels required a permit and a bond, a device enacted in an effort to curb illegal exports.

Finally, in 1708 the assembly passed a second supplemental measure that added four more towns, bringing the list to fifty-two. The legislators granted a further extension of the time specified for lot owners to build their houses and thereby confirm their land titles to November 30, 1709.[36] Thus ended the long and tedious series of legislative acts by which the governors and members of the assembly of seventeenth- and early eighteenth-century Maryland attempted to create towns along the shores of Chesapeake Bay and its tributaries. Figure 68 shows the approximate locations of forty-four of the fifty-two sites mentioned in this group of acts. The pattern of distribution closely resembled that resulting from the several laws of the 1680s, which in turn had been an outgrowth of the site selection policies followed by Governor Calvert.

For the large majority of these communities early plans are lacking. Many, perhaps most, were surveyed at one time or another. The act of 1707 contained the most specific provision on this point, as it directed the county surveyors to deliver to the commissioners appointed to supervise the work of town founding

> a fair plat of Each Town with the Course and Distance and quantity of Land Contained in every particular Lott Street Lane and Allie fairly drawn upon parchment to be kept as a record for the bounds of such Towns, and to Encourage such Surveyers fairly to draw the same and do their duty therein.[37]

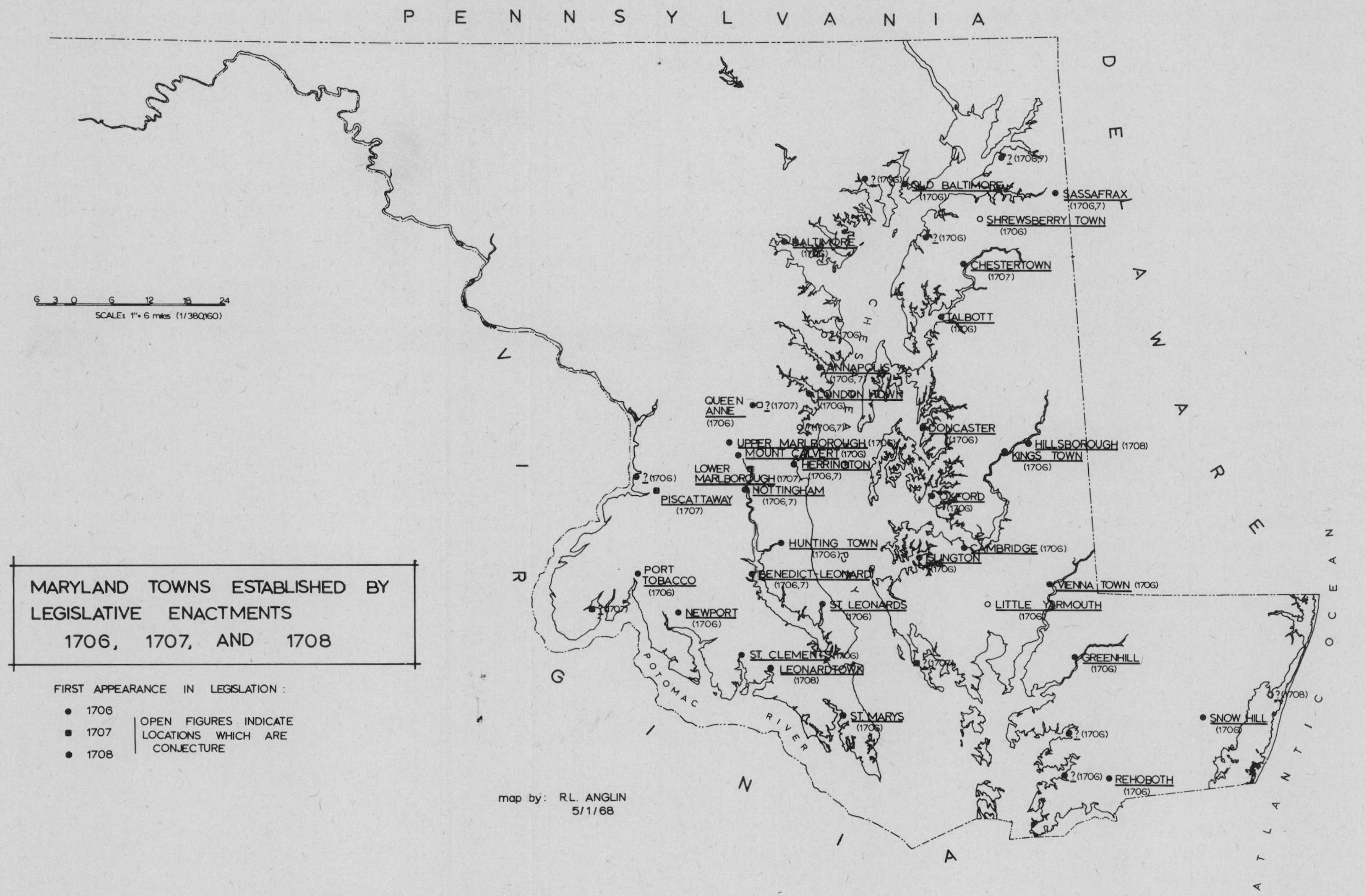

PENNSYLVANIA
DELAWARE
VIRGINIA
ATLANTIC OCEAN
POTOMAC RIVER
MARYLAND TOWNS ESTABLISHED BY LEGISLATIVE ENACTMENTS 1706, 1707, AND 1708
FIRST APPEARANCE IN LEGISLATION:
1706
1707
1708
OPEN FIGURES INDICATE LOCATIONS WHICH ARE CONJECTURE
SCALE: 1"= 6 miles (1/380,160)
6 3 0 6 12 18 24
map by: R.L. ANGLIN 5/1/68
OLD BALTIMORE (1706)
SASSAFRAX (1706,7)
SHREWSBERRY TOWN (1706)
BALTIMORE
CHESTERTOWN (1707)
TALBOTT (1706)
ANNAPOLIS (1706,7)
LONDON TOWN (1706)
QUEEN ANNE (1706)
DONCASTER (1706)
HILLSBOROUGH (1708)
KINGS TOWN (1706)
UPPER MARLBOROUGH (1706)
MOUNT CALVERT (1706)
HERRINGTON (1706,7)
LOWER MARLBOROUGH (1707)
NOTTINGHAM (1706,7)
PISCATTAWAY (1707)
OXFORD (1706)
HUNTING TOWN (1706)
CAMBRIDGE (1706)
ISLINGTON (1706)
PORT TOBACCO (1706)
BENEDICT-LEONARD (1706,7)
VIENNA TOWN (1706)
NEWPORT (1706)
ST. LEONARDS (1706)
LITTLE YARMOUTH (1706)
ST. CLEMENTS (1706)
LEONARDTOWN (1708)
GREENHILL (1706)
ST. MARYS (1706)
SNOW HILL (1706)
REHOBOTH (1706)

Figure 68. Map of Towns Founded in Maryland in 1706, 1707, and 1708

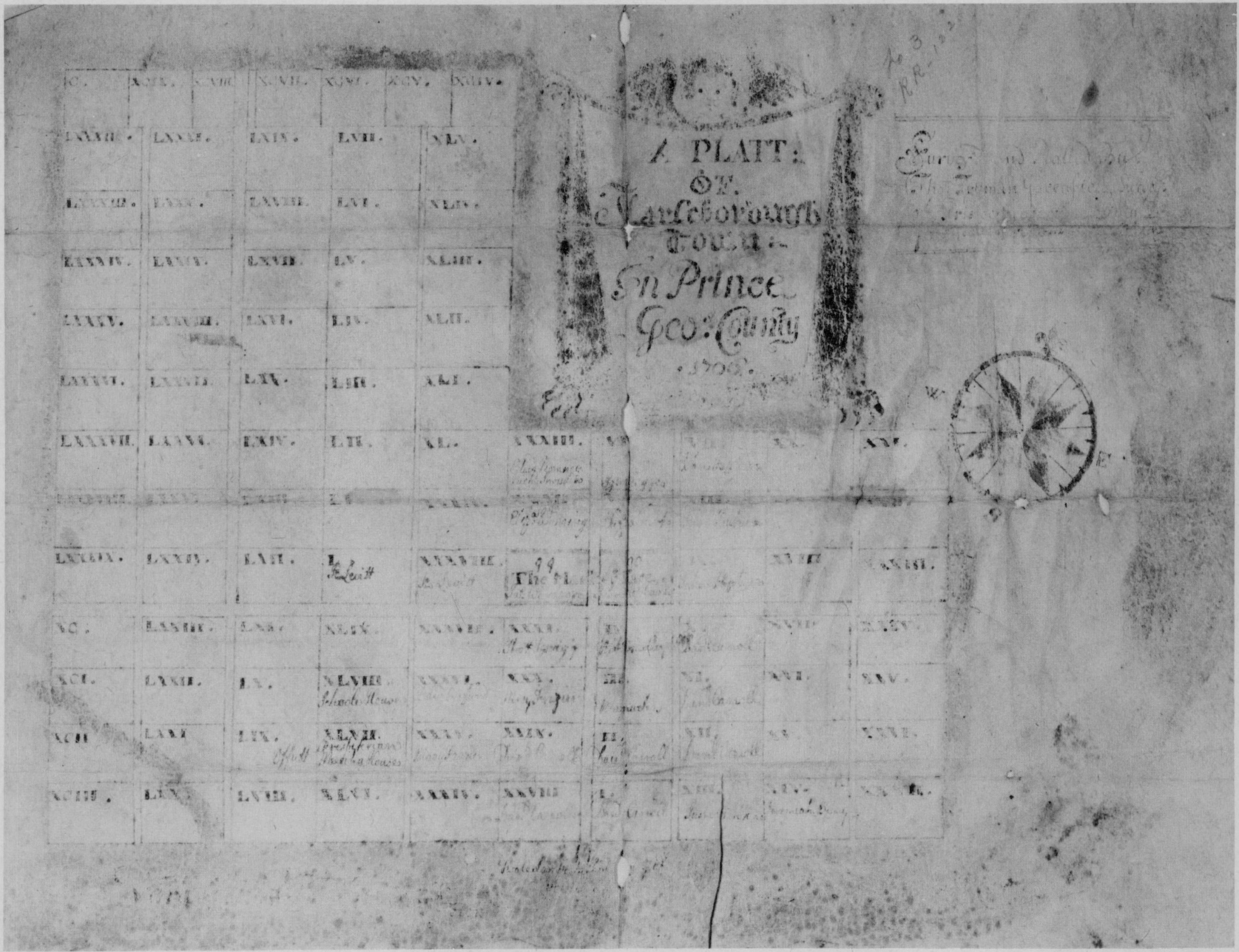

Figure 69. Plan of Marleborough Town, Maryland: 1706

It is a safe conclusion that in some cases the surveyors ignored this directive, and in others the commissioners simply failed to carry out their responsibilities despite the penalties, to which they were made subject in some of the laws, for such inaction.

We are left with only a few of these drawings from which to reach conclusions about the status of the art of town planning as practiced during this period by the officials responsible for creating new towns. One of the most regular of these towns was Upper Marlborough. Its plan as laid out and surveyed by Thomas Truman Greenfield in 1706 is reproduced in figure 69. Its rectangular plan was composed of three streets running roughly east and west crossed at right angles by two streets and four lanes forming the boundaries of the 102 lots. Two of the lots, numbered 99 and 100 in arabic numerals, where the two main streets intersect in the right-hand portion of the town, were reserved for the market place. Lot XLVII bears the inscription "Presbyterian Meeting Houses," and it seems likely that a similar site must have been set aside for the Church of England.

Many of the merchants attracted to the Chesapeake were Scots, and the identification of this site for the Presbyterian Church suggests that Upper Marlborough (called then simply Marlborough, or Marlboro) had its share of Scottish merchants or factors. The town was located in the midst of fine tobacco land and still serves as one of the major tobacco markets in Maryland. Lord Adam Gordon referred to it as "a pretty little Country Village" after he visited it in 1765.[38] Although it has grown some since that time it still retains something of its rural character. Upper Marlborough is the county seat of Prince Georges County in the rapidly urbanizing Washington metropolitan area. Its courthouse throbs with activity as modern land developers and speculators search old property records and file their subdivision plats recording new patterns of urbanization that threaten to engulf the little settlement laid out in the early years of the eighteenth century.

South of Upper Marlborough in Calvert County at the mouth of St. Leonard's Creek, which flows into the Patuxent River near its mouth on Chesapeake Bay, is St. Leonard's Town, first mentioned in the act of 1683. The plat in figure 70 may date from that period, but it is more likely the result of the redesignation in 1706 of a site in this vicinity then more specifically described as "at the head of Saint Leonards Creek on both sides of the mill branch at the mouth of the said Branch."[39] Perhaps the existence of the earlier town, surveyed but not developed nearby, explains the curious lot numbers on the plat, which begin with 38 and end with 100.

The plan itself took the form of a gridiron fitted into the irregular peninsula. Two streets, each five poles wide, led to the waterfront from the northern boundary. These were crossed by four others at right angles, with those toward the south having a width of four poles and the shorter street near the northern edge of the town being only three poles wide. Most of the lots were laid out ten by twelve poles, or exactly three-quarters of an acre in area. At the north end of the town, bisected by the narrowest street, the commissioners set aside the space of three acres as the "Publick Lotts." Although this town has managed to survive, its population has always been small.

Other new towns of the period in Calvert County included Calverton (also Calvertown and Calvert Town) on the northern shore of Battle Creek. Some time after 1650 this site had developed as a little settlement then known as Battle Town. Under the ordinance of 1669 the owner of a portion of this land, William Berry, requested that twenty acres be laid out as a town, which apparently was carried out under a warrant issued by the proprietor. It was here that the county courthouse and jail were built. This action evidently led to an increase in land values, for in 1682 a number of residents cited this in a petition to the assembly as the reason Berry "doth utterly Deny to make any Tittle or give an Assurance of the said Land . . . to the Manifest Damage of the whole County, and to the ruin of Severall Persons who have Spent their Estates in Settling themselves there."[40]

The difficulty was remedied by the act of 1683, which designated Calverton as one of the new towns; but after a brief period of growth it began to decline when the assembly moved the county seat to Prince Frederick in 1725.[41] Coxtown (now Lower Marlborough), Hunting Town, and Warrington also date from this era of wholesale town founding, but no evidence of their early plans has been discovered.

Many of the towns created under these legislative acts have disappeared altogether. Londontown, a few miles south of Annapolis on the South River, once enjoyed a considerable trade and was on its way to becoming a community of lasting importance. It served as well as the county seat of Anne Arundel County, and not even the removal of the court to the new colonial capital at Annapolis seemed to stifle its growth. But after the middle of the eighteenth century competition from Annapolis, and later from Baltimore, proved too severe and the town gradually decayed. The busy port of the early years of the century had become in 1765 only "a pleasant Village," and eventually it was to vanish.[42] The first settlement to bear the name Baltimore, on Bush River, suffered a similar fate.[43]

For the towns on the Eastern Shore we have, fortunately, several plats from the period or later resurveys that provide reasonably good evidence of their plans. One of these is of Green Hill in Somerset County, which under the act of 1706 was one of the six towns among the forty-two then established that received the title of port. Quite obviously the legislators viewed this site as one having special importance and entertained great expectations of its success as the chief town of the region. The town survey, dated 1707 and signed by the surveyor William Whittington, shows the design that he and the town commissioners adopted for the site on the Wicomico River.

Reproduced in figure 71, the plan includes three twin-turreted town gates topped by staffs and banners, a feature it seems doubtful the town itself ever possessed. The layout took the form of a modified gridiron, with its main street running roughly parallel to the river and intersected by two others leading to the upper town boundary. Several smaller lanes provided access to those lots not fronting on one of the principal thoroughfares. The lot marked "B" at the crossing of the two main streets was provided for the market, the triangular plot bearing the letter "D" is identified as "a common," while the church site, "C," appears at the upper corner of the right-hand portion of the town near the confluence of the two creeks. Here the first parish church was constructed sometime before 1723, but in 1733 a new brick church was erected on lot number 16 near the bank of the river. That structure, as later restored, is the sole surviving building in the entire town, of which otherwise virtually no trace can be found.

In Somerset County during this period, the earliest settlement would seem to have been Somerset Town, the location of which appears on the Herrman map of 1670 (figure 66). No sign of the town has survived, and even its exact site remains a matter of conjecture.[44] Of the several towns designated in this area of the colony only Snow Hill achieved any substantial size. First established by the act of 1686, Snow Hill became the county seat of Worcester County in 1742 when Somerset County was divided. The fact that in that year the town had to be resurveyed may indicate that its early years had not been particularly successful. The earliest plan of Snow Hill dates from 1793 when another survey became necessary, and it is not at all unlikely that this plan (figure 72) represents a considerable departure from the settlement pattern as first established more than a century earlier.[45]

To the north in Dorchester County are two towns that were founded in the period with which we are now concerned. For one of these—Vienna, on the Nanticoke River—unusually complete records of the town commissioners exist. These are the minutes of the meetings held by the officials appointed to acquire the necessary land, decide on the town plan, establish the price to be set for each lot, and to sell or otherwise dispose of building sites.[46] They provide a fascinating glimpse into the tedious business of founding a town as directed by the Maryland assembly under the act of 1706.

The commissioners first met on July 2, 1706, in Cambridge and appointed county clerk Jacob Lockerman to keep records of the meetings. July 9 was fixed as the day to meet at the site, then known as Emperors Landing, and the sheriff was directed to impanel a jury to fix the value of the land. On that day only five commissioners appeared, and the clerk was ordered to dispatch messages to the others requesting their presence the following day. This notice produced results, and eight commissioners met on July 10. The surveyor, Thomas Ennalls, was then directed to lay out Temb (Thames) Street three poles wide along the bank of the river with a row of lots each three-quarters of an acre in area along its west side. Broad Street, two poles wide, was also ordered laid out between lots 5 and 6.

The commissioners then called before them the owner of the land, James Anderson, who stated that he had paid "Twelve pounds currant money of this province . . . besides his own charges laid out and Expended thereon" for the one-hundred-acre site. The commissioners then offered Anderson four thousand pounds of tobacco for the land plus another thousand pounds of tobacco "for his charges and other Damages." They directed that the first fifty purchasers of lots in the town should each pay Anderson a hundred pounds of tobacco. A tenant of Anderson's, William Marrett, was to be compensated fifteen hundred pounds of tobacco for his

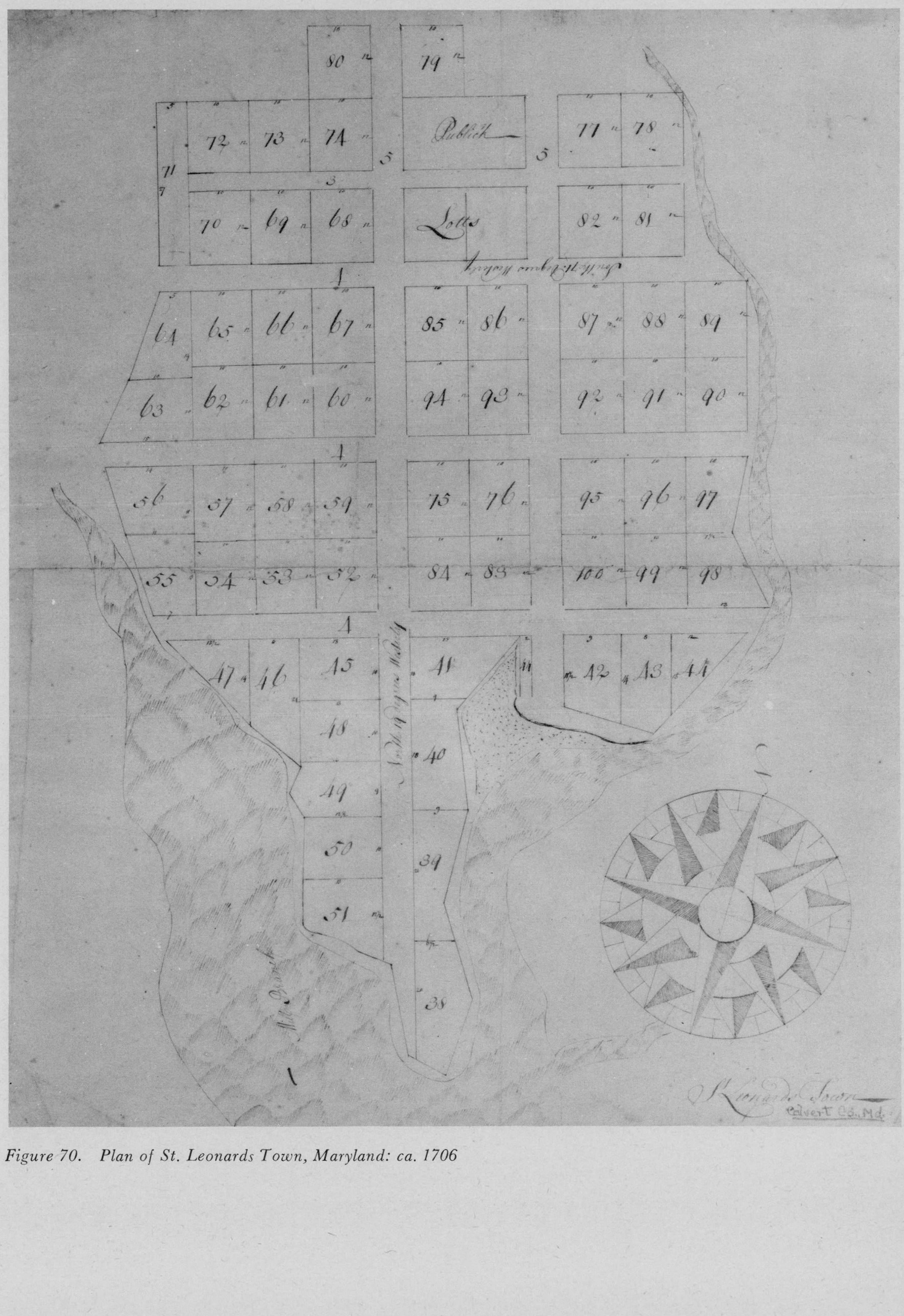

Figure 70. Plan of St. Leonards Town, Maryland: ca. 1706

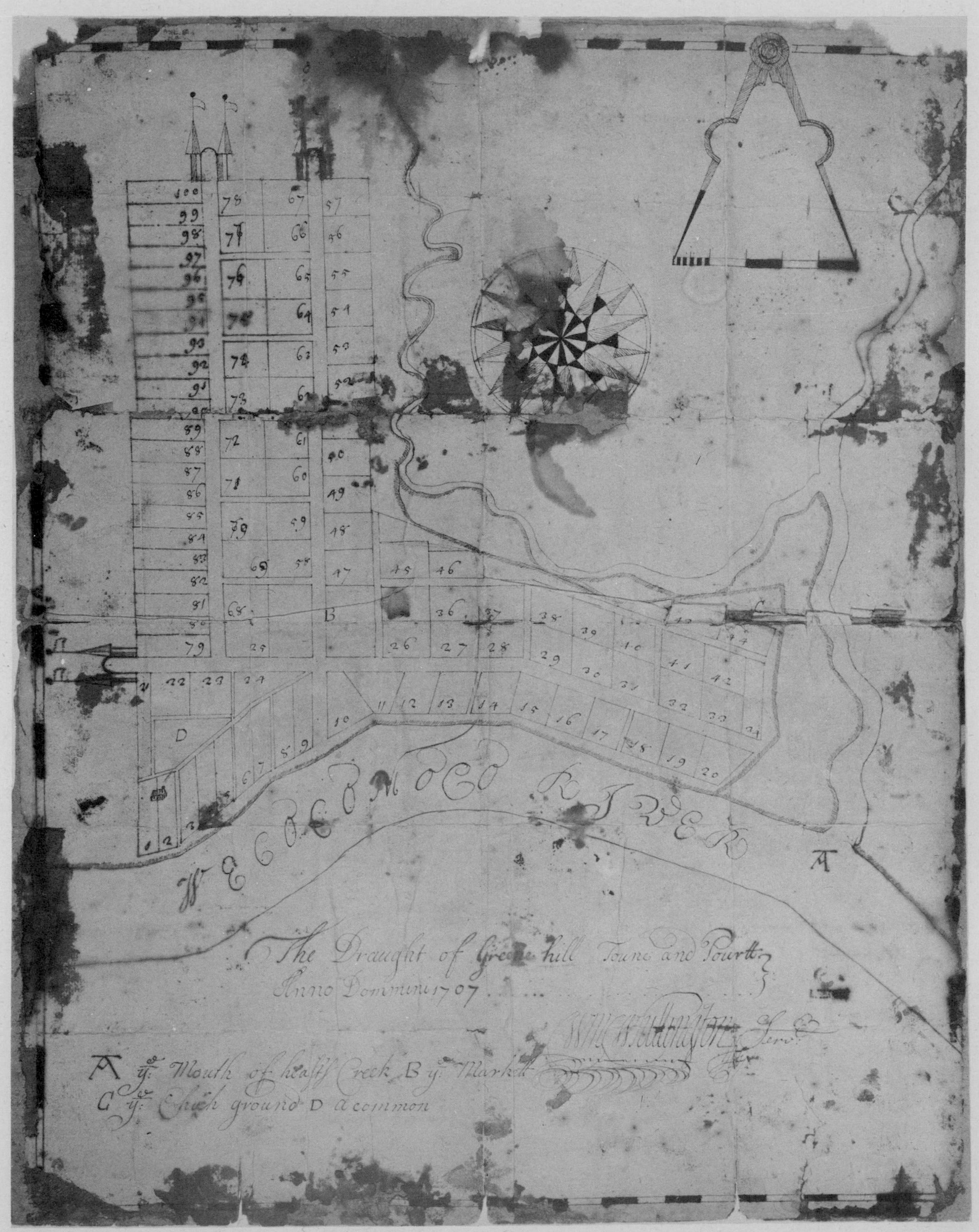

Figure 71. Plan of Greene Hill, Maryland: 1707

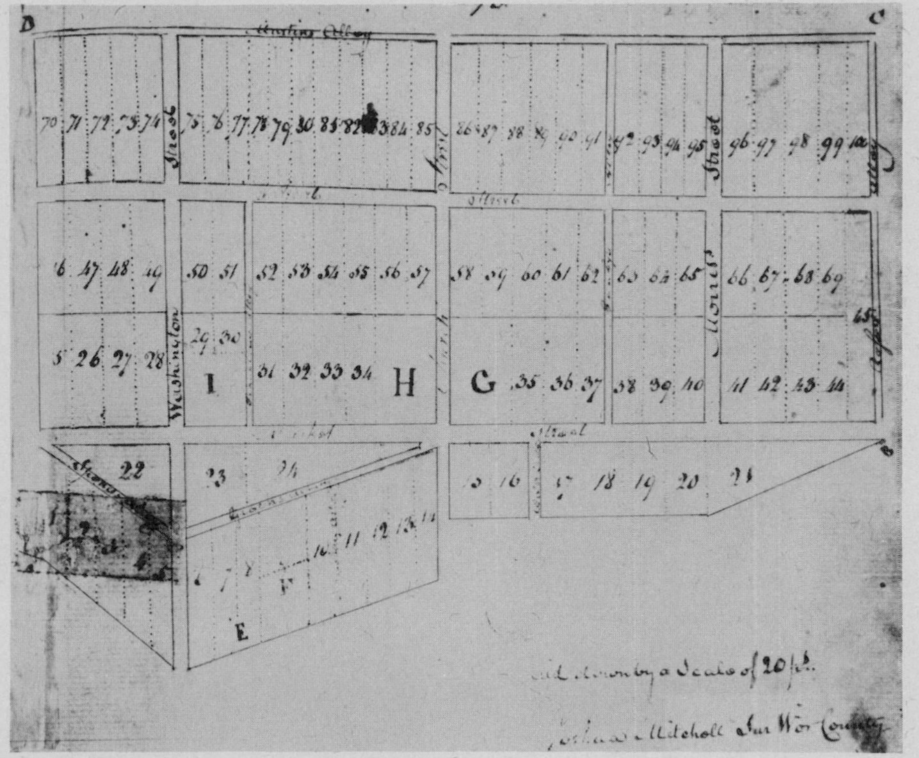

Figure 72. Plan of Snow Hill, Maryland: 1793

interest in the property by the purchasers' payment of fifteen pounds of tobacco for each of the one hundred lots. Business for that day was concluded when the commissioners ordered that one hundred stakes be prepared, doubtless to be used in identifying the lots, as required by the act.

The following day they decided to name the new community Vienna. To implement this decision they ordered "that the said name be cutt in a Board with large letters and nailed to a post and that the same bee placed in the ground on the lower Side of Broad Street and facing to Tembs Street, all which was accordingly done." Then followed a series of actions to lay out Middle Street 24 feet wide, Loe (Low) Street 30 feet wide, and other streets parallel to Thames Street each three poles or 49½ feet wide, these then being named High Street and Back Street. Each of the lots was given double frontage, and when one hundred of them were laid out the commissioners resolved "that the Residue of the said acres of Land so laid out for a town and Surveyed as aforesaid Containing by Estimation fifteen acres be Reserved and Allotted to the said Town for publick uses."

The clerk was then directed to enter into the records the purchasers of land by lot number. Twenty-nine purchasers were recorded on that day, all but one choosing one of the lots fronting on the river. The commissioners' work was done, and their meticulous record attests to the care with which they undertook this novel responsibility. It is sad to report that except for the unusually large area set aside for public uses their town plan did not match in skill or imagination their vigilance in recording their actions. The design is reproduced in figure 73, the most regular and monotonous of gridirons. The original pattern can be easily recognized by the modern visitor, and beneath modern siding, added porches, altered roof lines, and other changes, the original forms of the once handsome eighteenth-century houses fronting Thames (now Water) Street can be discerned. At the foot of Low Street stands the tiny old brick customhouse dating from the latter part of the eighteenth century and attesting to the fact that Vienna, now a sleepy village, was once a thriving port of entry important enough to be a target for English naval guns during the Revolution.[47]

Cambridge, the county seat of Dorchester County on Maryland's Eastern Shore, owes its origin to the act of 1684. The site was described as "Att Daniell Joansis plantation on the south side of Great Choptancke."[48] Two years later the assembly directed that this should also be the location of the courthouse for the county. By that time one John Kirk had acquired the land, and presumably the commissioners appointed to lay out the town arranged to purchase the hundred-acre tract from him. Probably no significant growth aside from the erection of the courthouse occurred at this time, for in the act of 1706 the assembly again listed Cambridge as one of the new towns to be established.

Early plans of Cambridge do not exist, and we are forced to rely on the survey of 1853, carried out after the second courthouse, built in 1770, was destroyed by fire in 1851.[49] That nineteenth-century plan (figure 74) also shows the design for the new court building adopted at that time. The original plat probably included only the area on either side of High Street between the mouth of Cambridge Creek and the Choptank River. Aside from the street plan, relatively few traces of colonial Cambridge remain in the present city of thirteen thousand people. The most notable

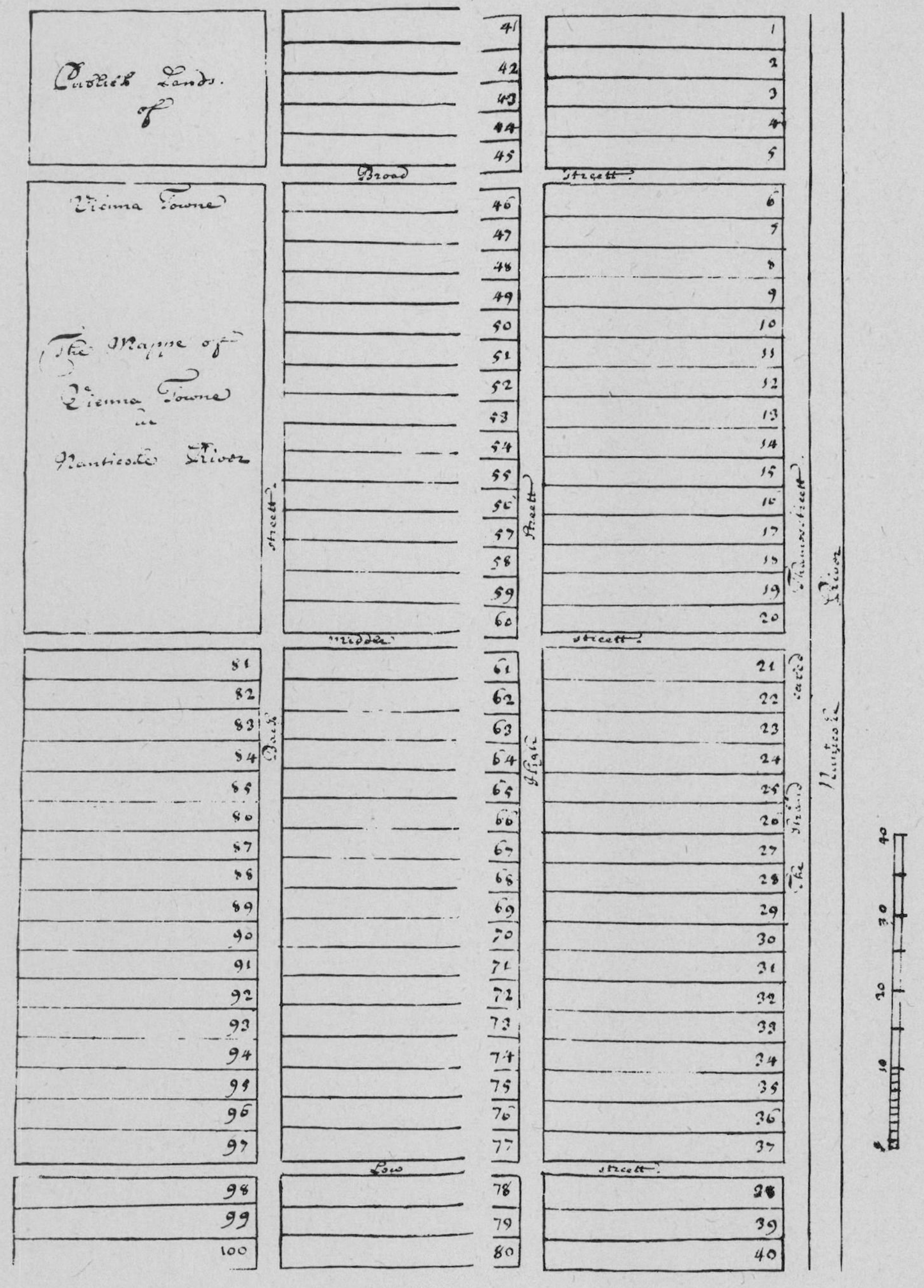

Figure 73. Plan of Vienna, Maryland: 1706

is the frame dwelling erected by Kirk about 1710 near the point of land formed by the two streams.

Across the Choptank River to the northeast, at the mouth of the Tred Avon (or Third Haven) River, lies one of the most attractive of the Eastern Shore communities. This is Oxford in Talbot County, the site of which was one of those designated in the proclamation of 1668 and again in the acts of 1683 and 1706. Oxford, along with Annapolis, was also created as an official port of entry by the assembly in an act passed at Governor Nicholson's urging in 1694.[50]

In the fall of 1668, William Stevens deeded thirty acres of land "for the settling and building of a towne in Tread-Aven Creeke in Great Choptank" to the lord proprietary.[51] Evidently some work in laying out the town began shortly thereafter, since several deeds and other records of the period 1669–1679 refer to town lots, a "store at ye town of Oxford," and the "city of Oxford" as "a fit place for an ordinary."[52] Under the act of 1683, Oxford was again designated as a town to be planned on the standard one-hundred-acre site. The commissioners met on July 29 of the following year, acquired the necessary land from William Combs, and four days later "caused the aforesaid town to be surveyed staked outt according to Act of Assembly, and the lots numbered from 1 to 100."[53] Twenty- seven lots were then sold, Mr. Combs having the first choice. Several others were sold at later dates, but not all of the lots were built on within the prescribed time, and on September 6, 1685, the records show that ten of the lots were reconveyed to new purchasers under the usual terms.

It seems doubtful that the new town was the scene of much activity, for in 1694 the assembly, in establishing Oxford and Annapolis as ports of entry, re-enacted the usual land-acquisition and planning provisions of the 1683 law. Persons who had acquired lots under the previous legislation were, however, confirmed in their title. The following year the assembly changed the name of Oxford to Williamstadt, directed that one hundred additional acres be purchased adjacent to the town "for a common or pasture for the benefit of all persons within this province that shall repair to the said town. And that the same be laid out as above expressed and that six acres of the same be reserved for public buildings."[54]

When the new commissioners met in Oxford beginning on October 19, 1694, they encountered conflicting claims of ownership of the existing town lots. The amount of land to be taken for the common was mistakenly

Figure 74. Plan of Cambridge, Maryland: 1853

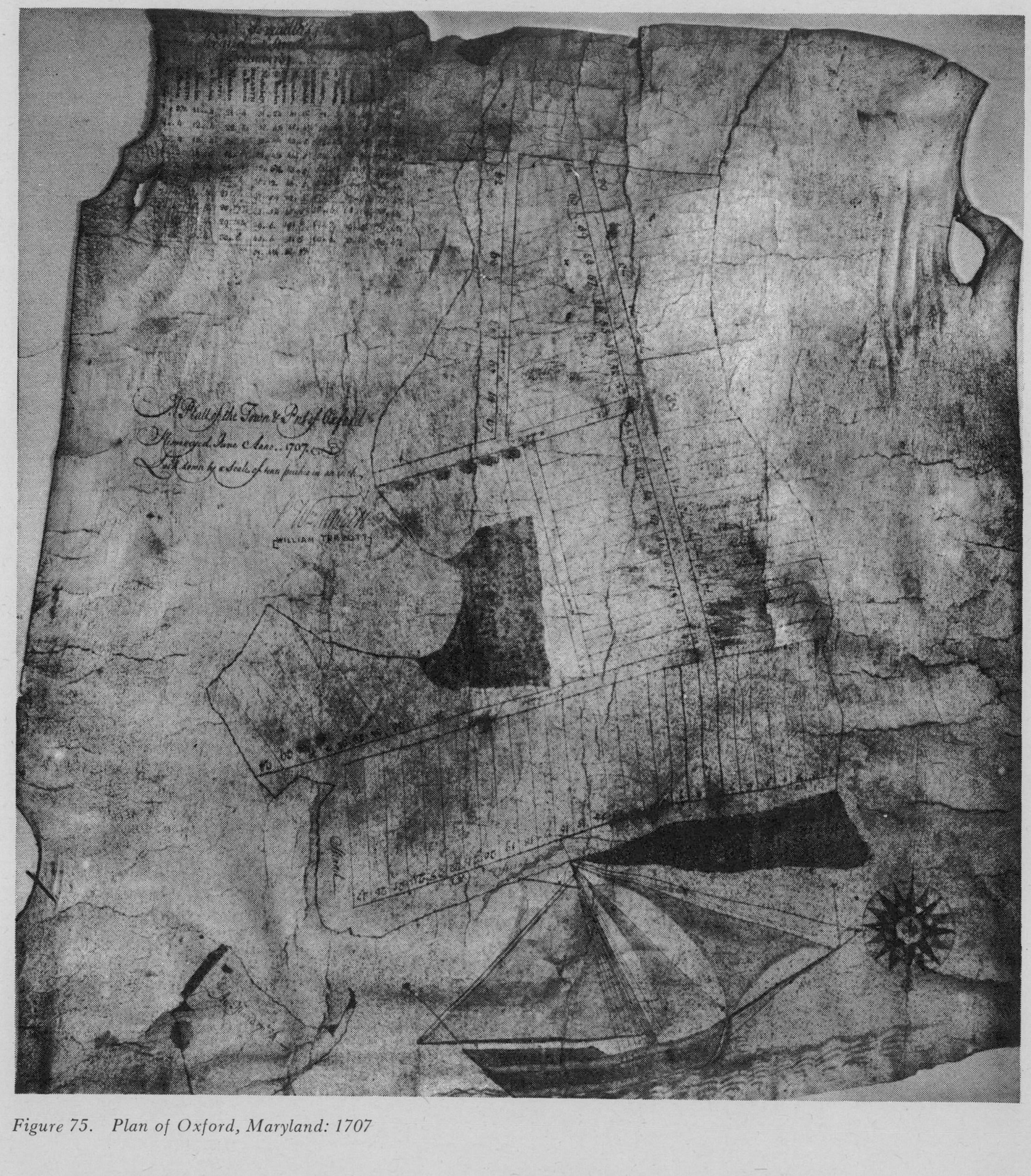

Figure 75. Plan of Oxford, Maryland: 1707

set at two hundred rather than one hundred acres, and despite the decision of a jury called to determine the value of the land, matters remained unresolved until 1696. During the intervening months the town plan had evidently been completed by Philemon Hemsley, and Governor Francis Nicholson had selected three lots in the town as provided for in the act of 1694. Then others wishing to purchase building sites determined by lot which parcels would be assigned to them. In addition to supervising these activities the commissioners found time to issue several orders for the development of the town, including the construction of a fence across the peninsula to be paid for by an assessment on all property owners. The fence was to be provided "with good substantiall gates and other conveniences for passing along the rode—the said gates to [be] hung on good substantial hinges, and to open both wayes." [55]

While Oxford was thus formally established again, much of the organizing had to be redone following the passage of the town and port act of 1706. Beginning on July 10, 1707, new commissioners met to resurvey the town and decide on the compensation the owners were to receive. The earlier plan was modified slightly, and the commissioners ruled that the then owner, Nicholas Lowe, was to receive from two hundred to one thousand pounds of tobacco for each lot sold, the amount determined "according to the goodness or conveniency" of the location.

Figure 75 is the plan of 1707 as surveyed by William Turbutt. This faded drawing shows one street leading from the waterfront on the Tred Avon River (at the bottom of the drawing near the sloop) southward along the peninsula to the edge of town. Another major street intersected the first and ran eastward (to the left) to Town Creek. Three other streets can be seen completing the irregular gridiron pattern and providing access to the eighty-two lots.

Oxford became the chief port of the Eastern Shore, as English merchants and traders established their stores and warehouses there. It had a considerable trading fleet that made regular voyages to other American ports and to the West Indies and such English maritime cities as London, Liverpool, and Bristol. The height of its prosperity appears to have been about the middle of the eighteenth century, although it still was a busy and prosperous place until the Revolution. Following the war its decline was as rapid as was the growth of its rivals Norfolk and Baltimore.

Toward the end of the nineteenth century, as can be seen in the plan of 1877 in figure 76, it had less than one hundred houses, a few stores, a small shipyard, and a packing house. This plan also identifies the marketplace, barely discernible on the previous drawing, located between the end of Market Street and the river. Sixty years ago Oxford, according to one account, had a population of less than one hundred and most of its remaining houses stood vacant.[56] Yet today Oxford has an air of quiet prosperity. No longer a major commercial port, the town has become a little resort community and an important center for pleasure boating. The old Robert Morris House at the water end of Morris Street, built in 1774, has been restored as an inn and fine restaurant, and the old market place is now a shaded park with splendid views across the river. Like a number of other towns in the tidewater region, and so many in New England, the plan gives no clue to the character of the community—which can only be experienced on the spot.

The plan of one other town in Talbot County has survived although the town has not. This is Wye on the river of the same name, designated first as a town in 1671, once more in 1683, but surveyed anew when it was established for the third time in 1706 and given the name Doncaster. In plan, as redrawn (figure 77), it is a generally symmetrical design modified slightly on its east and west sides. On the original drawing five of the lots bear the notation "improved formerly," probably indicating that this drawing by William Turbutt for the town commissioners incorporated an earlier plan. The market place was located at the corner of Landing and High streets, and it is probably here that the county justices in 1700 directed Thomas Bruff "to set up a pair of stocks and whipping post, at the town of Doncaster." [57] An almost total lack of references to Wye or Doncaster in early records or travel accounts indicates that this community, like so many of the other new towns of the period, soon faded away and was forgotten.

One of the most beautiful of the Maryland Eastern Shore communities is Chestertown, the county seat of Kent County, on the lovely Chester River. Sites here or close by had been designated in 1668 and 1669 and again in 1706. In 1707 the site was shifted slightly to a spot on the western bank of the river where the Kent County Courthouse had been constructed in 1698 on land purchased by the justices of the county for that purpose two years earlier. The new town by the act of 1706 received the title of port, and it seemed destined for instant success as the chief

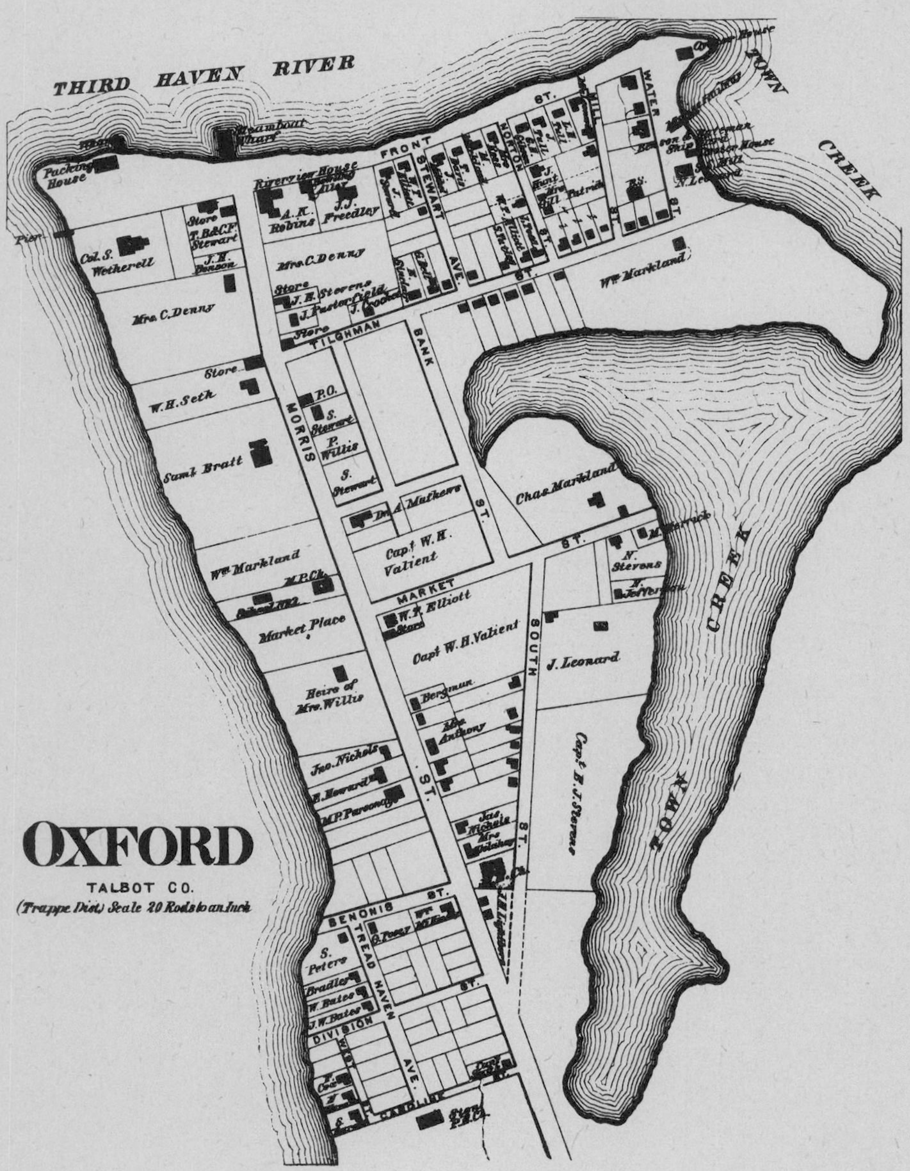

Figure 76. Plan of Oxford, Maryland: 1877

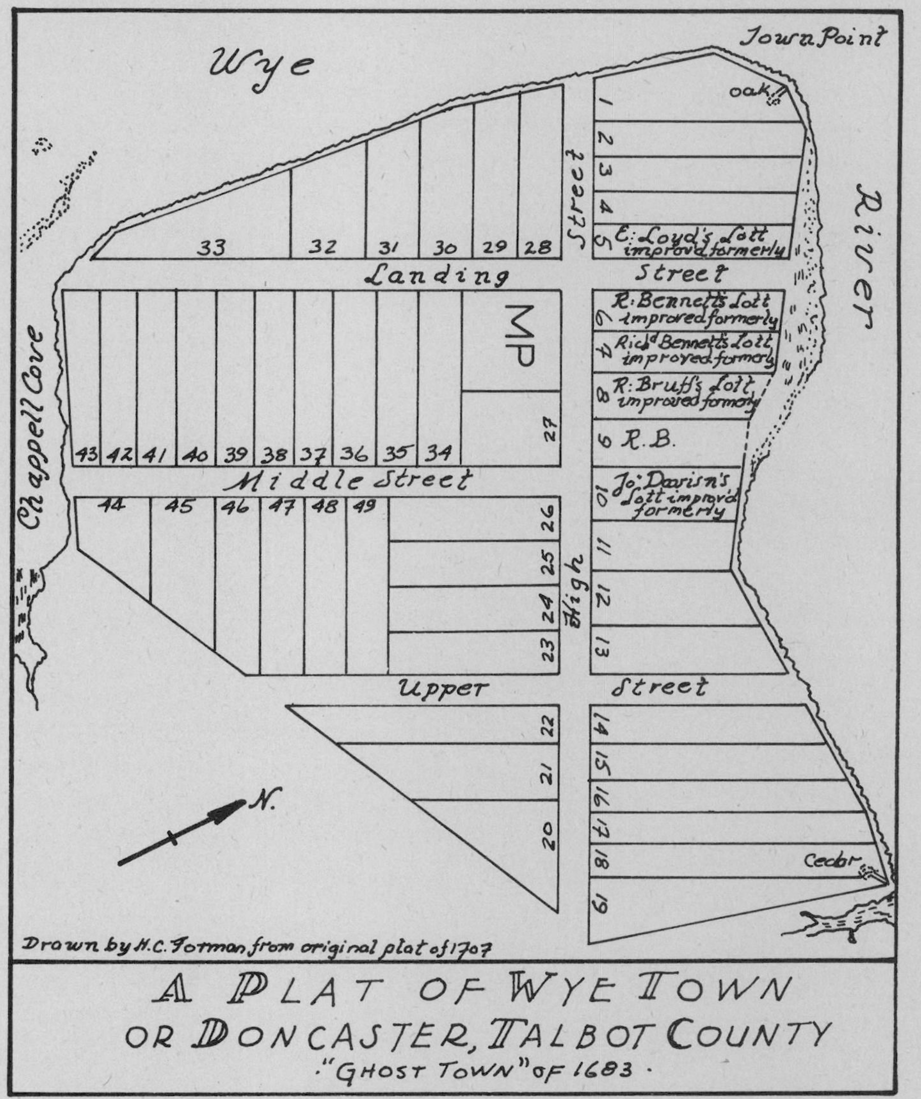

Figure 77. Plan of Wye, Maryland: 1707

town of the immediate region. The negation of the town acts, however, slowed the growth of the community, and apparently not even the subsequent legislation in 1710 confirming title to all purchasers of land proved sufficient to prevent momentary stagnation.[58]

Chestertown, in common with many of the settlements erected by the general town acts, had to be revived by a special legislative enactment. The assembly in 1730 passed such a measure "for laying out the Town a-new, commonly called Chester Town, in Kent County; and for ascertaining the Bounds thereof."[59] The act was necessary, according to the preamble, because the bounds of the town "are very uncertain, and the Improvement very much hindered, by Reason that all the Lots were not taken up and improved in Time." This law appointed new commissioners, directing them to secure a "Person skilful in surveying" and to lay out the one-hundred-acre site "as agreeable as conveniently may be to the original Plat and Survey thereof, when first laid out for a Town." Owners of unimproved lots as well as new purchasers were to be given eighteen months to build houses of at least four hundred square feet in area in order to save their titles. The assembly further directed that a sixty-foot wide strip between the river and the first tier of lots be planned as a street and that the land on "the Strand" between the street and the river be divided into lots for warehouse purposes. Cross streets were to extend across this street and the strand to the water's edge.

Two years later the assembly passed a law requiring all swine, sheep, and geese to be kept enclosed on penalty of a fine of one hundred pounds of tobacco for each violation. The reasons cited for this restriction give some idea of the problems that had been encountered:

> That divers Persons . . . do raise and keep large Quantities of Swine, Sheep, and Geese . . . whereby not only the Grass necessary for the Support of the Cows and Horses of the Inhabitants is consumed; but that also, the Ground is so rooted up, and the Streets so broke, that in Winter or wet Weather, they are almost impassable; also, that the Swine there are so numerous and ravenous, that they break into Warehouses where Grain is stored, and that several young Children have been in Danger of being devoured by them; and that the Inhabitants cannot preserve their Gardens and Inclusures from being broke down and destroyed by them."[60]

Although the original plat of the town can no longer be found, figure 78

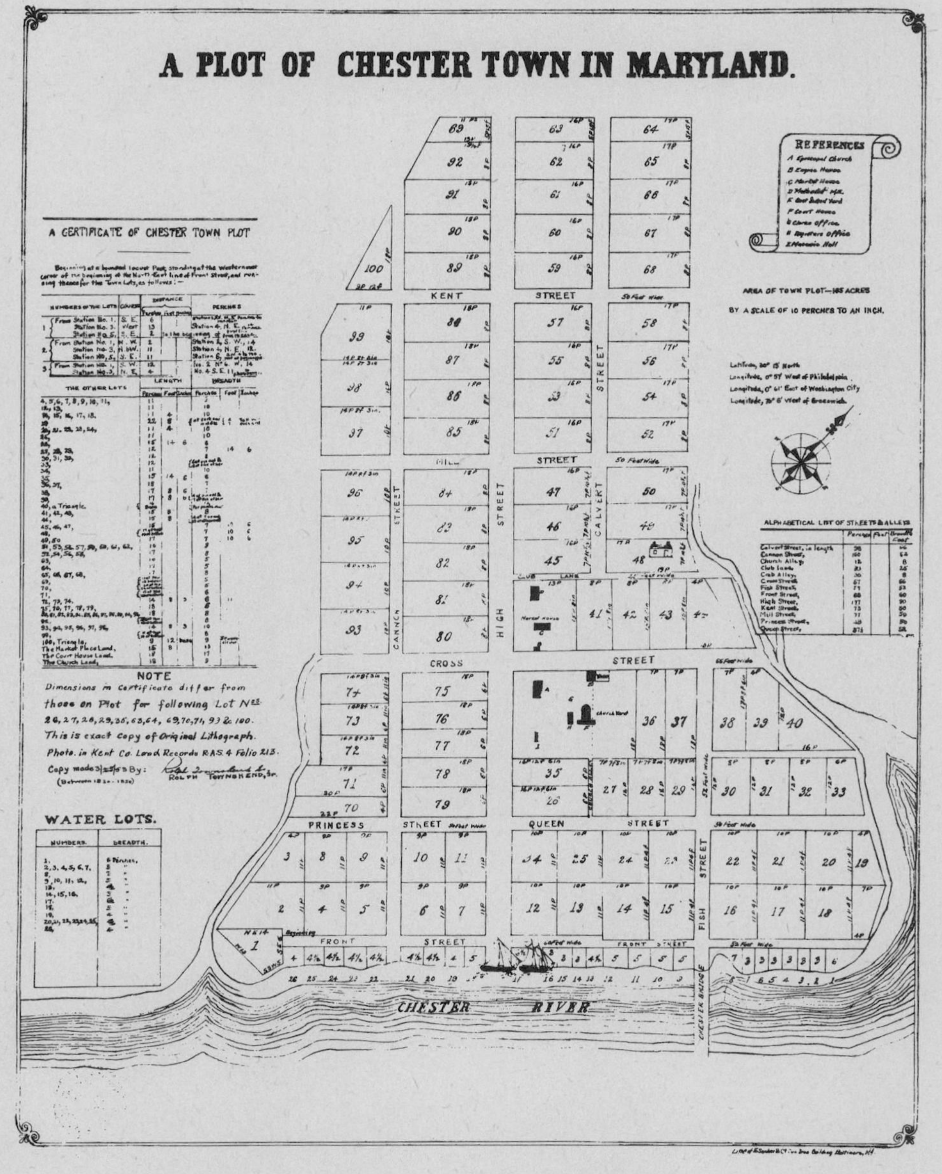

Figure 78. Plan of Chestertown, Maryland: ca. 1850

is a copy of the mid-nineteenth-century lithograph plan that recorded the pattern of streets and lots as established by the commissioners appointed under the act of 1730. To what extent this plan followed that surveyed under the first act of establishment cannot be determined, but it is likely that the two resembled each other closely. One exception, of course, was Front Street, which had not existed before 1730, and the water lots extending from it to the bank of the Chester River. The main thoroughfare, High Street, ran the length of the town from the waterfront northwesterly to the far boundary. Approximately one-third of the way from the river this broad street—platted ninety feet wide—was intersected by Cross Street with a width of sixty-six feet. Here was the land set aside for churches, market house, courthouse, and cemetery.

By the nineteenth century, as shown on the plan in figure 79 and perhaps much earlier, this area had developed into an impressive little civic center, the importance of which was emphasized by a widening of High Street on which the several buildings fronted. A group of low, closely built structures on Court Street served as law offices facing the courthouse green and the Masonic Temple, built in 1827 in late Federal style. Across High Street the business district developed with shops and inns built on the street line giving a pleasant character to the entire central composition.

Chestertown's surviving eighteenth-century houses, of which there are a great many, are equally attractive. Those on Front Street are particularly impressive and recall the prosperous days when the town was one of the most important ports of the colony; those between High and Bridge streets are especially beautiful. All were constructed of brick, either 2½ or 3 stories high, and were built in the period 1770 to 1784.[61] The old customhouse, a 3½-story brick structure, also has survived at the corner of Front and High streets near the water's edge. The remaining streets contain dozens of other houses of the period when the town flourished as a major trading center of the Eastern Shore.

Chestertown's development was far from typical. Most of the towns that the assembly attempted to create by these general acts either were never begun at all, died stillborn, remained only small hamlets, or passed away altogether. Thus, of the two towns proposed for Kent Island in Queen Annes County one site has never been conclusively located, and the other is occupied by the tiny unincorporated settlement of Stevensville.[62] Completely deserted, too, is the site of New Yarmouth, where the first Kent County courthouse was constructed and where a town had been laid out under Governor Calvert's direction in 1675. In addition to the courthouse and jail, New Yarmouth could boast of two shipyards on Gray's Inn Creek, and doubtless the town contained several houses, probably an ordinary, and other buildings. The removal of the county seat to Chestertown in 1696, however, marked the end of New Yarmouth's brief period of prosperity, and today the site can be found only with difficulty.[63]

Other towns founded by the assembly under the various acts have managed to maintain a modest existence. Benedict, located on the Patuxent River in Charles County and once bearing the more impressive name of Benedict-Leonard Town, still exhibits its simple and regular gridiron pattern. Consisting of a few hundred people, the little community survives as a minor center of fishing and yachting. Its near namesake, Leonardtown in St. Mary's County, is more imposing since it serves as the county seat. Originally called Seymour Town in honor of the governor, it was added to the list of new communities by the last general act of 1708, which also specified that it was to replace St. Mary's as the location of the county courthouse. Its original plan has unfortunately been lost, but the town contains in addition to the courthouse square a separate triangular green that may have been set aside as the market place.

We have now completed our exploration of Maryland's experience with wholesale town founding. As in Virginia, this period of half a century during which colonial officials struggled to establish a flourishing urban sector of the economy to supplement its agrarian base was one of frustration and disappointment. When the Reverend Hugh Jones published his *Present State of Virginia* in 1724, only a few years after the final series of town acts, he noted the same geographic forces working against the development of towns about which earlier observers had commented. Although his remarks were addressed to Virginia they applied with equal force to Maryland:

> No country is better watered, for the conveniency of which most houses are built near some landing-place; so that any thing may be delivered to a gentleman there from London, Bristol, etc. with less trouble and cost, than to one living five miles in the country in England; for you pay no freight for goods from London, and but little from Bristol; only the party to whom the goods belong, is in gratitude

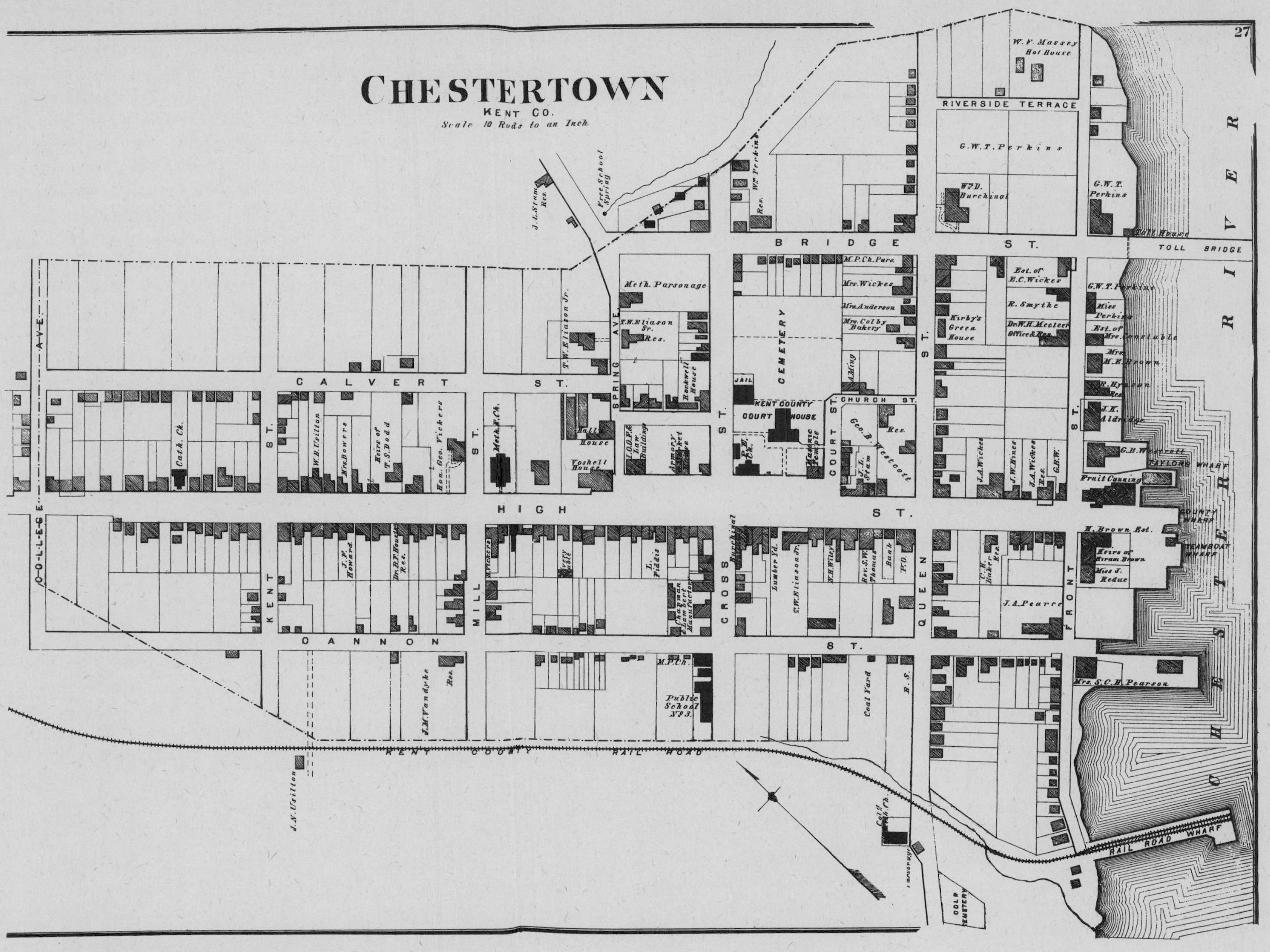

Figure 79. Plan of Chestertown, Maryland: 1877

engaged to freight tobacco upon the ship consigned to her owners in England. . . . Thus neither the interest nor inclinations of the Virginians induce them to cohabit in towns; so that they are not forward in contributing their assistance towards the making of particular places, every plantation affording the owner the provision of a little market.[64]

Writing in 1782, Thomas Jefferson echoed these observations: "Our country being much intersected with navigable waters, and trade brought generally to our doors, instead of our being obliged to go in quest of it, has probably been one of the causes why we have no towns of any consequence." Williamsburg, he noted, never exceeded a population of 1800, and Norfolk, "the most populous town we ever had, contained but 6000." Jefferson then listed "our towns, but more properly our villages or hamlets" as follows: Norfolk, Portsmouth, Hampton, Suffolk, Smithfield, Williamsburg, Petersburg, Richmond, Manchester, Charlottesville, New-London, York, Newcastle, Hanover, Urbanna, Port Royal, Fredericksburg, Falmouth, Dumfries, Colchester, Alexandria, Winchester, and Staunton.

In a succinct summary of the efforts of legislators to create towns, and the consequences of these attempts, Jefferson then observed: "There are other places at which, like some of the foregoing, the *laws* have said there shall be towns; but *nature* has said there shall not, and they remain unworthy of enumeration." As to the future, he predicted that Norfolk would maintain a pre-eminent position as the chief city of Chesapeake Bay. "Secondary to this place, are the towns at the head of the tide waters, to wit Petersburgh . . . Richmond . . . Newcastle . . . Alexandria . . . and Baltimore. From these the distribution will be to subordinate situations in the country." However, Jefferson concluded, "Accidental circumstances . . . may control the indications of nature, and in no instances do they do it more frequently than in the rise and fall of towns."[65]

During the entire era of wholesale town founding in the tidewater colonies, while the governors, councils, and houses of burgesses busied themselves so assiduously in introducing, debating, and passing legislation for towns, nature was all the while—as Jefferson suggested—exerting a quiet but effective power of veto. It is quite possible as well that the burgesses consciously set out to thwart the wishes of English colonial officials by continually increasing the number of towns recommended by the authorities in the home country and suggested by the governors in the colonies. Whether deliberate or not, these actions gave the appearance of cooperation with the appointed representatives of the crown while actually assuring that the measures would be ineffective in practice except for a few towns with particularly advantageous sites.

The town plans themselves, with few exceptions, represented no great achievements in urban design. Their simple and straightforward gridiron schemes symbolized the lack of sophistication of a frontier society, which remained unconvinced that the creation of towns would bring substantial benefits and which, even if the will had been present, lacked the necessary skills and knowledge to lay out communities on any other patterns than the most obvious. The fine urban quality of Chestertown, to take a notable example, resulted almost in spite of its plan rather than because of it.

One result of this experience, however, was to establish a tradition that in the creation of towns public officials should play a major role. In the era to follow, many of the best designed communities were created in a similar fashion by legislative acts that authorized acquisition of the site by local officials. Public landownership provided an opportunity to carry out an imaginative plan conceived by the responsible authorities as being in the public interest, rather than to leave development for the immediate speculative gain of a single private entrepreneur.

In the closing years of the seventeenth century this policy of public initiative was to result in the creation of two of the best-planned towns in colonial America. Both were the products of one man, Francis Nicholson, whose successive appointments as governor of Maryland and then of Virginia introduced a new figure to the tidewater scene. The rather dull and uninspiring quality of the town plans examined in the preceding two chapters highlights all the more the achievements of Governor Nicholson in designing his new capital cities.

VI. *The Annapolis of Francis Nicholson*

Among the early Maryland settlers on the shores of Chesapeake Bay was a group of Puritans under the leadership of Richard Bennett and William Durand, whom Governor Berkeley had expelled from Virginia. At the invitation of William Stone, a Protestant appointed governor of Maryland by Lord Baltimore in 1648, this group took up land along the western shore of the bay from the Severn to the Patuxent rivers. On the north side of the Severn near Greenberry Point they surveyed a tract of 250 acres into lots of about 15 acres and named the little community Providence.[1] Other members of the group settled across the Severn on a neck of land formed by that river and Spa Creek. This spot became known as Proctor's Landing and, after the creation in 1650 of Anne Arundel County, was sometimes referred to as Anne Arundel Town or Arundelton.[2] It was also called Severn or Proctor's, and the rather bewildering set of names may indicate the informality of its legal status and physical form. No plan of either Providence or Proctor's has survived. Hence we can only speculate about the pattern of streets and house lots at these two small settlements.

Under the governor's proclamation of 1668 this site was included among those designated for towns, being then identified as "Att Richard Actons land in Arrundell County."[3] Perhaps at this time some further surveying was carried out though no graphic record of it exists. On Augustine Herrman's 1670 map of Maryland (see figure 66 in Chapter V), Arundelton was one of the locations shown as a town. Again in 1683, with the first general town act passed by the assembly, this site was listed among those to be laid out as a town on a one-hundred-acre tract. It was then described as "the Towne Land att Proctors," which seems to indicate that some land had already been purchased for that purpose under the earlier proclamation.[4]

That session of the assembly had been held not at St. Mary's but at the house of John Larkin "at the Ridge in Anne Arrundell County," a site near the present Mt. Zion about fifteen miles south of Annapolis.[5] Governor Charles Calvert, the third Lord Baltimore, had noted the shift in the colony's center of population away from the region around St. Mary's and apparently favored a new location for the seat of government. In November, 1683, he indicated his intention of selecting a permanent location for this purpose "in South River in Ann Arundell County"[6] at a natural harbor that came to be called Londontown. Although some construction of a building or buildings seems to have been carried out here, Calvert's departure for England soon after led to the abandonment of these plans.

The days of St. Mary's as the capital, however, were numbered. Not only was it poorly located with respect to the distribution of population, but it represented the center of Catholicism in a colony that with the accession of William and Mary, had been placed under royal control with the clear purpose of securing there a dominant position for the established Church of England. The appointment of the first royal governor, Sir Lionel Copley, marked the end of Lord Baltimore's civil authority although he remained landlord of a vast territory. The ailing Copley found himself concerned with other affairs in the colony, and it was not until Francis Nicholson arrived as his successor in 1694 that the subject of a new capital site came up again.[7]

Nicholson called his first assembly meeting in September, 1694, and made the principal order of business the designation of a new location for the seat of government. Two bills were introduced to this end. Both received the governor's approval on October 18, 1694. The first followed the pattern already established by the town and port acts of previous years, although it was limited to the creation of only two such communities. It provided for the acquisition of land by purchase or eminent domain and the laying out of two ports of entry. One was Oxford in Talbot County on the Eastern Shore. The other was to be on "the Land Called the Town Land att Seavern in Ann Arundell County where the Town was formerly."[8] The last five words indicate that the site of this new town lay virtually unoccupied and that the commissioners appointed to supervise the planning would have little difficulty in following the act's instructions to "Cause the same to be marked Staked and Divided into Convenient Streets lanes and Alleys with other Spare places to be left on which may be a Church Chapell Market house or other publick building." An additional feature, applying only to Anne Arundell town, specified that the commissioners were to acquire a substantial area "adjoyning or near to the Town Land . . . to be fenced in and Called the Town Common or Pasture."

The second and more controversial measure designated "Arrundell Towne" as "the Chief place and Seat of Justice within the Province for holding of Assemblyes and Provinciall Courts."[9] While there can be little doubt that the issue of religion played an important role in this affair, the act included no reference to this factor. Instead, the preamble mentioned the inconvenience suffered by many persons because of the long journey to St. Mary's at "the Lowermost part of the westerne side" of Maryland. One consequence was said to be that many criminals escaped justice because persons were "put to so great an Inconveniency in attending Provinciall Courts in order to give their Evidence." As a justification for moving the capital to Arundelton, this argument was not entirely convincing. The site of Arundelton can be located on a map of Virginia and Maryland published in 1676 (figure 80). The town's name appears below and slightly to the right of the letter "R" in Maryland. One can see that its location toward the northern edge of settlement in the colony was almost as far from the center of population as was St. Mary's. It had, however, the best natural harbor north of the Patuxent River, and this factor probably influenced Nicholson and the assembly in choosing the site rather than one farther south on Chesapeake Bay.

Quite naturally the proposed law provoked the inhabitants of St. Mary's to vigorous denunciation of the contemplated change. Catholic and Protestant citizens alike joined in presenting a lengthy petition in defense of their community. They cited the healthy site and convenient harbor of the city as advantages not to be overlooked. They listed the improvements already undertaken for governmental purposes at St. Mary's that would be abandoned if the capital were moved. They pointed out that London was "as far from the centre of England as St. Marie's in this province; Boston, in New England; Port Royal, in Jamaica; Jamestown, in Virginia; and almost all other . . . American plantations. Their petition offered to provide

> a coach, or caravan, or both, to go at all times of public meeting of Assemblies and Provincial Courts, and so forth, every day, daily, between St. Mary's and Patuxent River, and at all other times, once a week, and also to keep constantly on hand a dozen horses at least, with suitable furniture, for any person, or persons, having occasion to ride post, or otherwise, with or without a guide, to any port of the province on the Western shore."[10]

Nicholson referred this document to the House of Burgesses, which prepared a contemptuous reply dismissing all the arguments in sarcastic language.[11]

The act as finally passed by the assembly and approved by Nicholson directed the commissioners of the town "to survey and lay out in the most comodious and convenient parte and place of the said Towne six Acres of Land intire for the Erecting a Court House and other buildings as shall be thought necessary and convenient." It specified in some detail the architectural character of the principal building to house the courts and assembly:

> [The] Court house shall be Forty six foot in length, from Inside to Inside, and Twenty two foot wide from Inside to Inside, Brickworke two story high, the lower story to be Eleaven foot in Pitch, and the upper story to be Eight foot in Pitch and plastered on the Inside with a Porch & Porch Chamber fourteen foot long & twelve foot wide of the same worke, the Roofe to be girt and hipt, to be covered with Pine or Cypress Planke and Shingled with Cypress Shingles, with convenient

Figure 80. Map of Virginia and Maryland: 1676

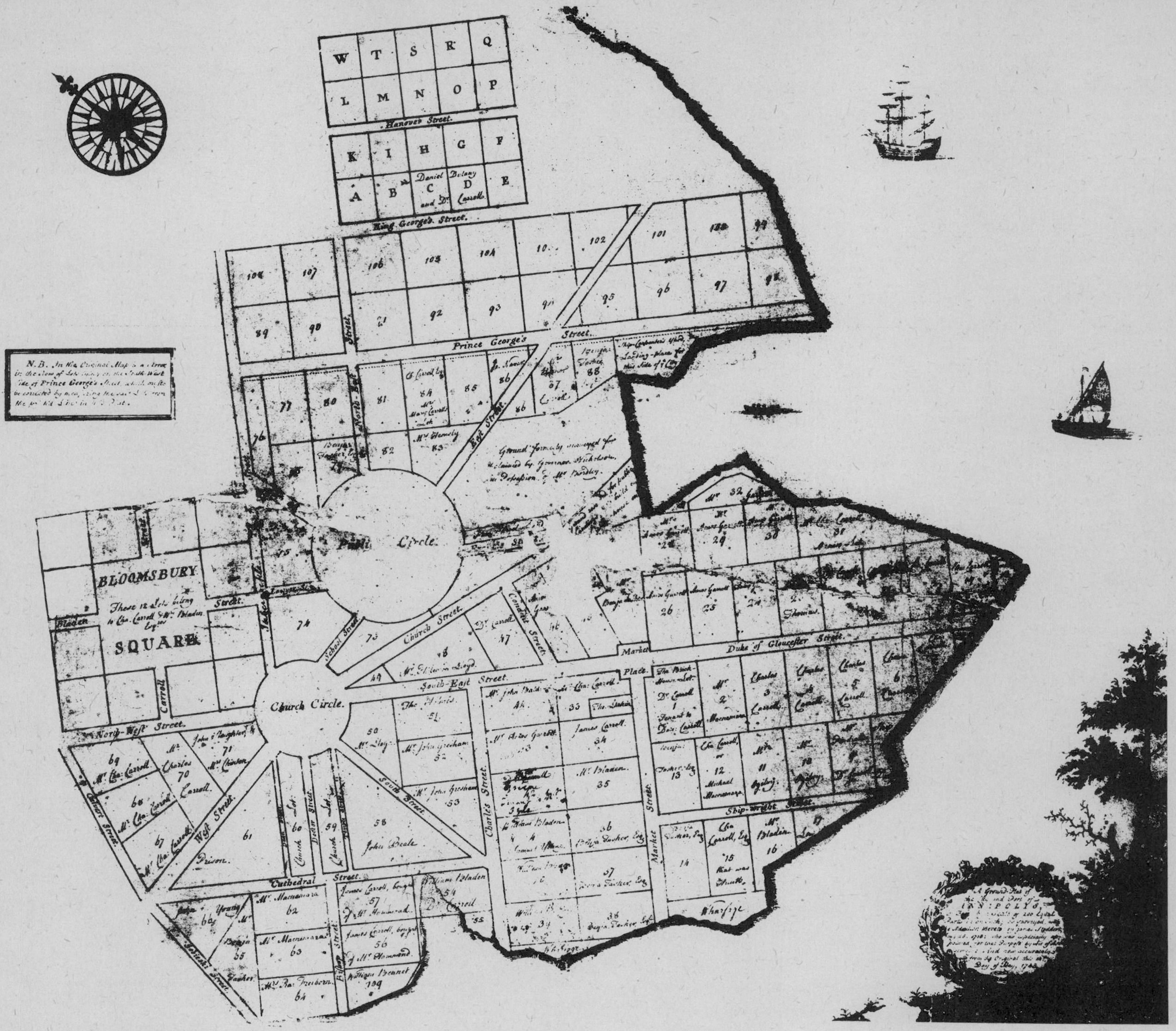

Figure 81. Plan of Annapolis, Maryland: 1718

apartments in the upper Story for one Office, and three small Roomes for Juryes, the Porch Chamber to be fitted for one other Office, at one End of the said house a Place of Judicature, in such forme as at the Stadt house now at St. Maryes is, at the other End a Chimney with a Fire place therein both belowe and above, and a Staire Case by the Syde of the said Chimney, the Staires windowes & doors uniforme or as convenient as may be, the lower floor to be laid with brick, and the upper Floors with Plancke." [12]

The following year the assembly also designated this building as the court-house for Anne Arundel County, an arrangement that continued until 1769.[13] One of the rooms in the building was also set aside for the town clerk of Annapolis, the name by which the town was officially designated in the spring of 1695.[14] But before this building could be constructed there had to be a town plan, and before tracing the gradual development of this new city we must examine its unusual design and discuss the person responsible for it.

The original drawing showing the plan of Annapolis has not survived. The burning of the statehouse in 1704 destroyed many precious records including the survey by Richard Beard "Sealed with the Great Seale of the Province att the four sides thereof and upon the backside thereof Sealed with his Excellencys Seale att Arms on a red Cross with red Tape," as described in 1696.[15] That drawing had caused Beard some difficulties. When the assembly summoned him to display his work on the first of March, 1695, he maintained "that for want of some Large Paper to draw the same on, it is not yet done." [16] The casual treatment of this important document indicates that if it had not perished in the fire it might have been destroyed anyway, for the secretary in 1697 displayed to the assembly "the said Mapp . . . spoyled in some parts by the Ratts." [17] We are forced to rely on the copy made in 1743 of a resurvey of the town drawn in 1718 by James Stoddert (figure 81). This plan apparently is a faithful copy of the first drawing prepared in 1695 with the addition of twenty lots laid out in 1718 northeast of the original town boundary.[18] Figure 82, a more recent copy of this drawing, is included for greater legibility in reading street names, dimensions, and property owners.

Perhaps Beard's problem in producing his survey lay not entirely in the difficulties in securing paper of suitable size. The plan of Annapolis differed sharply from the simple little gridiron designs that had been the standard response to the port and town legislation of previous years. Not only was it much larger, but it introduced to America for the first time a new and sophisticated urban form that must have created many technical problems for Richard Beard and doubtless baffled the provincial minds of the citizens of Maryland.

It will be recalled that Chapter I reviewed briefly the plans for rebuilding London in 1666 prepared by John Evelyn and Christopher Wren. Both of those designers employed in their reconstruction schemes the device of leading several radial or diagonal streets to an open square or circle in order to focus views on an important building or monument situated at the center or edge of the square or circle. This technique had long been employed on the continent by both landscape architects and urban planners. It had first been advocated and experimented with by Renaissance architectural theoreticians and designers charged with the embellishment of ancient towns in Italy and France or, more rarely, in the creation of entirely new settlements. By the end of the seventeenth century this and other principles of baroque design embodying formal symmetry, imposing open spaces, the closing of street vistas by important structures, and the location of major buildings on commanding sites had received widespread acceptance in Europe. If England lagged in adopting these new doctrines of garden and town planning, one could hardly wonder that they had not yet made their way across the Atlantic.

Their bearer was no architect or landscape gardener but a soldier of the crown and professional colonial administrator. How Francis Nicholson may have become interested in such matters outside his main professional concerns will be discussed later, but first his plan must be examined. At the outset it should be noted that its authorship is not established except by circumstantial evidence. Considerably stronger grounds exist for assigning to Nicholson the responsibility for the plan of Williamsburg, Virginia, only a few years later. There he was to duplicate his Maryland decision to move the capital from one site to another. The parallel accomplishments suggest strongly that in both cases he alone prepared the plans for the cities involved. Also persuasive is the completely different character of the Annapolis plan contrasted with plans for the port towns the Maryland assembly previously had labored hard to create. Everything else remained virtually the same; the new variable introduced into the Maryland scene was the personality of Francis Nicholson. No name other than his and Beard's appears con-

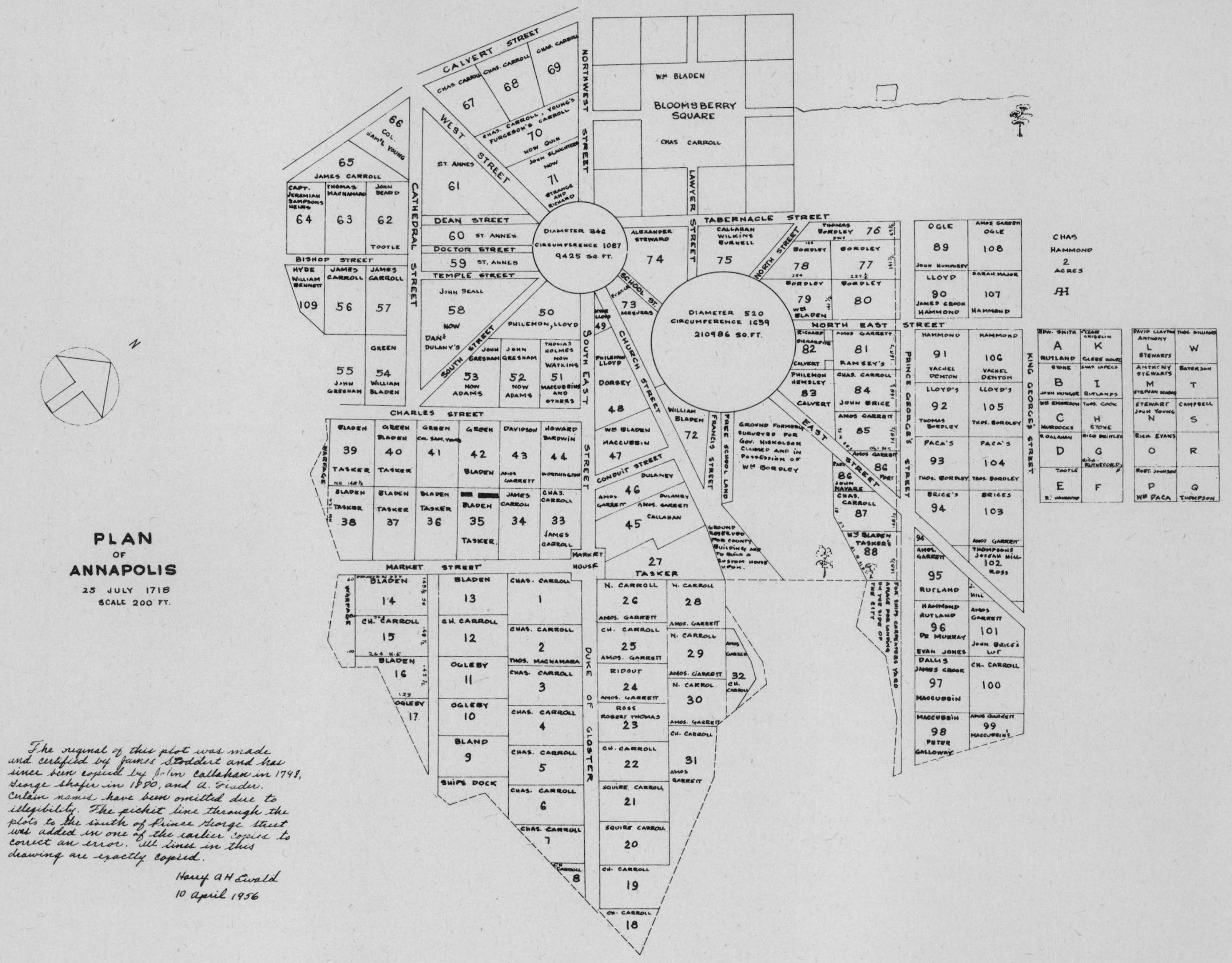

Figure 82. Plan of Annapolis, Maryland: 1718

nected with the Annapolis plan, and it is virtually impossible to believe that a frontier land surveyor suddenly received the inspiration to devise such an elaborate town pattern. So, without any evidence to the contrary, it would appear that the basic concept belonged to Nicholson, though he may have had assistance in working out some of its details.

One location within the town dominated the site. This was a knoll some 900 feet from the indentation formed by the natural harbor to the east. Nicholson selected this spot as the site for the new building in which the courts and the assembly would meet. Its grounds were defined by a circle 520 feet in diameter, not quite one acre less than the six acres specified in the act designating Annapolis as the capital. West of this knoll stood another elevation separated from Statehouse Circle by a slight dip in the ground. Here Nicholson laid out a second circle, somewhat smaller than the first, as the site for the church.

Balancing the two circular spaces were two open squares. Nicholson planned the largest on the northern edge of the town. This appears on the Stoddert drawing as Bloomsbury Square, measuring approximately 360 feet in each direction. Twelve lots form its borders, divided by four streets that enter the square at the mid-points of its sides. This is, of course, the classic pattern for an open space of this shape as worked out by Renaissance town planners. As we have seen, an early example under English jurisdiction was at Londonderry in northern Ireland near the beginning of the seventeenth century. The importance of the military in the settlement of that region suggests that Nicholson may have seen drawings of Londonderry, but it was not an uncommon form by 1695 and he may well have drawn on other examples. The derivation of the name is clear: Bloomsbury Square in London had been laid out not long before and had become a fashionable place of residence. It is apparent that Nicholson hoped for a similar development in his new town on the Severn.[19]

A second and much smaller square about 125 feet in each direction appears southeast of Church Circle midway to the town boundary. This was designated as Market Place. Although two streets—Market to the southwest and Duke of Gloucester to the southeast—lead to the water, Market Square's location is curiously isolated from the harbor area. In fact the market eventually was shifted to the edge of the harbor, a site that proved far more convenient for a town that depended so heavily on maritime trade. The new site is designated on the Stoddert drawing as

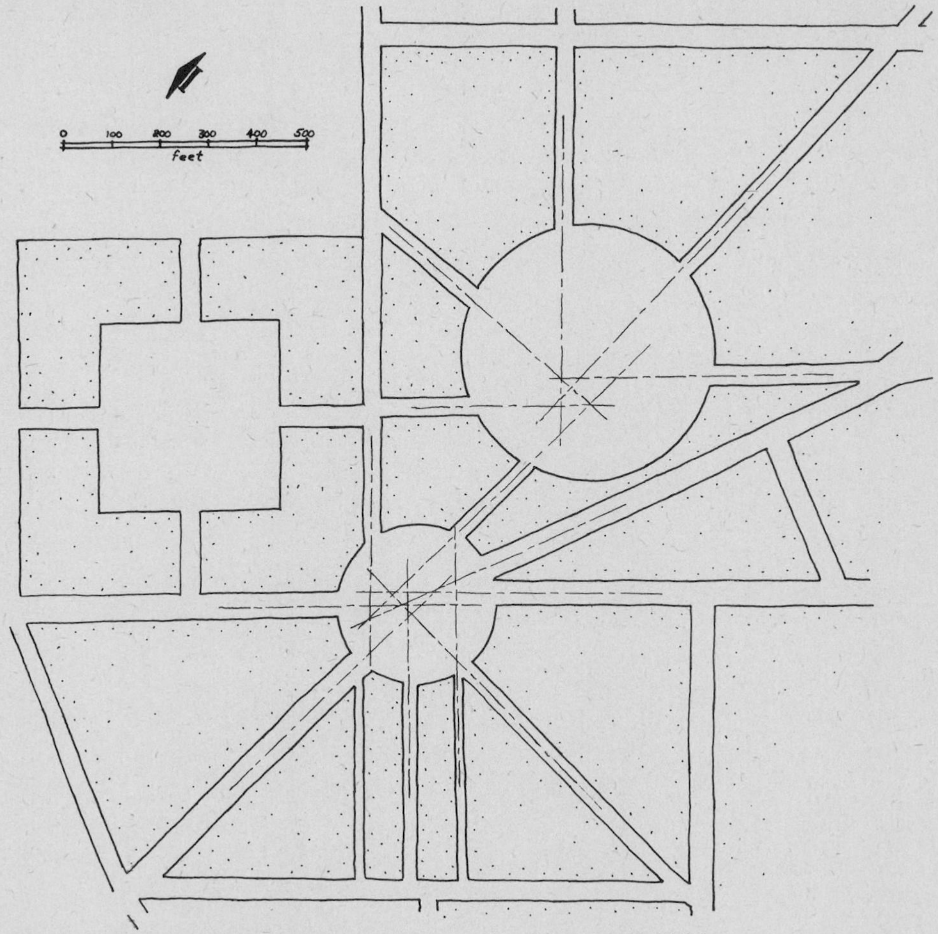

Figure 83. Plan of a Portion of Annapolis, Maryland: 1718

"Ground reserved for county building and to build a custom house upon." During the early years of the town's existence, however, the markets were held in the square southeast of Church Circle.

While the general inspiration for the system of radial streets obviously had its origins in European baroque design, the Annapolis plan includes many unusual and not fully explainable details. One feature seen rather quickly is that if the centerlines of all the streets entering the two great circles are prolonged they do not intersect at the center of the open spaces or at any other common point. The sketch in figure 83 makes this plain.

Tabernacle Street and North Street are decidedly off center. West Street, South Street, and Doctor Street, if prolonged, seem to meet at a common point, but it is not quite in the center of Church Circle. The geometry is even more confused in this respect at Statehouse Circle. It seems strange, moreover, that School Street, the short connection between the two circles, does not have quite the same bearing as East Street, which extends outward to the town boundaries from a point almost opposite. The direction of West Street is very slightly different from either of these two.

The use of radial streets by baroque designers was to focus attention from as many directions as possible on an imposing structure located at the intersection of several street axes. Why does the Annapolis plan, therefore, show so many instances where this principle is violated? It seems doubtful if surveying or drafting errors are responsible. The exceptions to this doctrine of multiaxial planning are simply too numerous and too great. It is also difficult to believe that they may have resulted from subtle adjustments to topography, though it is just conceivable that this may have been the case.

Two possibilities remain. We do not know exactly the extent to which this site had already been developed before it was designated as the capital and came under Nicholson's jurisdiction as planner. A certificate of survey by Richard Beard in March, 1684, rather vaguely described the streets he had laid out under the act of 1683. Only one would appear to have been in the area occupied by the two circles, running from a point near the market square in Nicholson's plan northwest through what became Church Circle.[20] This would not seem to account for the peculiar alignments of the several radial streets Nicholson introduced, though it is possible that some of his streets elsewhere in the city had to be reconciled with an existing pattern.

The most likely explanation is that Nicholson did not fully appreciate the objectives of baroque street design. He may, therefore, merely have adopted the most obvious features of the grand plan style—radial streets—and, doubtless with some haste, simply sketched out a plan lacking the symmetry that would have been insisted upon by someone more skilled and sophisticated in this school of urban design. The case for this explanation is strengthened by other weaknesses in the plan. There are several lots of awkward shape in the center of the composition. Perhaps the best (or worst) examples are the parcel of land bounded by School and Church streets and the adjoining lot to the south. Moreover, School Street itself seems an inadequate link between the two major sites set aside for the principal buildings of the city. In the hands of a trained designer this almost surely would have been planned much wider and more imposing. Francis Street, leading from Statehouse Circle toward the harbor, also provides a curiously weak approach to the building housing governmental activities. Here a skilled planner would have terminated that street near the waterfront at a point on the axis of both Statehouse Circle and Church Circle.

The isolated location for Market Square has already been observed. That defect might have been partially remedied by providing a street leading northeast to the harbor and customhouse site. That prominent water entry to the city would then not only have been functionally important but would have served as a strong visual orientation point from which the major components of the town could have been grasped. The potentially important intersection of East Street and Prince George's Street was also overlooked. At this point another square or open space could have been introduced into the plan as a visual focal point and to provide better shapes for the lots in that area, one of which is bisected by the East Street diagonal east of Prince George's Street.

Thus Nicholson, in his attempt to use the major elements of baroque planning without a full understanding of their implications and the difficulties of reconciling them with the gridiron system, produced something of a caricature of this style of urban design. Despite these shortcomings, however, the plan of Annapolis possessed a character distinctly superior to the dozens of little gridirons developed before this date on the shores of Chesapeake Bay and its numerous rivers. It is of considerable interest then to look briefly at the man who was responsible for introducing baroque town planning to the American scene and to speculate about how he came to be familiar with this concept.

Nicholson's first responsibility for town planning stemmed from his position as lieutenant governor and chief resident executive of Virginia at the time of the port and town act of 1691. He must have seen the plans for the towns that were laid out in the colony under that legislation, though the following year he opposed the policy that had led to their creation—the policy he himself had urged the assembly to adopt. Up to that time Nicholson's experience as a military officer would scarcely seem to have provided him with much background in the planning of towns. He doubtless knew the rudiments of fortification theory, and it seems safe to presume (though there is no direct evidence) that he would have examined at least some of the several printed atlases published by the end of the seventeenth century containing town plans of England, Europe, and parts of Africa and Asia.

In his youth as a military courier between North Africa and England he passed through such cities as Cadiz, Seville, Toledo, Madrid, Paris, and Calais. Even earlier, in the fall of 1678, Nicholson spent some time at Nieuport in Flanders, a city whose streets had been laid out with almost mathematical precision in a gridiron system.[21] It is conceivable that while passing through France he may have visited Versailles in connection with his official duties, but aside from this he does not appear to have been exposed at this stage of his career to any of the principal baroque planning achievements on the continent. Certainly from 1687 in his first American posts in New England, Nova Scotia, and New York, he had no opportunity to absorb the kind of information about town planning he was later to apply at Annapolis and, subsequently, at Williamsburg. He was briefly in London in the fall of 1689 and then came to Virginia in May of the following year to begin his first administration of that colony.

During these years Nicholson joined with the Reverend James Blair, commissary of the bishop of London, in founding the College of William and Mary, the charter for which was conferred by the monarchs on February 9, 1693. Blair was named president and Nicholson the head of its board of trustees. Nicholson, an ardent Anglican throughout his life, was deeply concerned with this infant institution, an important component of which was a divinity school. Even while in Maryland he attended meetings of its trustees.[22] And while he and Blair were eventually to become enemies, in the early years of the college's existence Nicholson spent much of his time in advancing its cause and working closely with its president.[23] Its site at Middle Plantation, halfway between Jamestown and the York River, may well have been suggested by Nicholson and was ultimately to be the location for a town planned by him as the new capital for the colony.

Given these circumstances it is almost inconceivable that Nicholson, in London from the end of 1692 until the spring of 1694, would not have spent a considerable amount of time on college affairs. In such endeavors he almost certainly would have visited the office of the surveyor-general of the King's Works, headed by the illustrious Christopher Wren, where the college's first building may have been designed.[24] Even if it was designed elsewhere, Nicholson may have sought out the noted architect for advice on its construction or appearance. Or, knowing of Wren's plan for rebuilding London, Nicholson may have discussed with him some of the problems of town planning that he had observed during his supervision of the port and town act of 1691.

There is still another possible connection between the two men. Wren, as designer of St. Paul's Cathedral and numerous other churches in London, had intimate connections with Anglican authorities. Certainly these would have included Henry Compton, bishop of London, who had been named chancellor of the College of William and Mary.[25] Nicholson must have conferred frequently with the bishop. Not only was he concerned with college affairs, but he also became closely associated with the church party in England, in which the bishop naturally played an important role.[26] Although a direct contact between Nicholson and Wren cannot be documented, it seems almost inevitable that they would have encountered each other sometime during the period of Nicholson's prolonged stay in London. If this hypothesis is correct it would explain how a Wren-like plan came to be used by the governor of far-off Maryland in 1695 when he was faced with the task of designing a new town.

While the general style of Annapolis follows that used by Wren in rebuilding London, its details more closely resemble the less skillfully prepared designs submitted at the same time by John Evelyn. A comparison of the two plans in figure 18 (Chapter I) reveals Evelyn's much less assured handling of the diagonal streets. It can be noted in Evelyn's scheme that in many cases these diagonals, if prolonged into several of the civic open spaces or major building sites, would not intersect at common points. This casual use of radial streets is, as we have already seen, an important feature of Nicholson's plan for Annapolis.

There are strong reasons for believing that Nicholson may have consulted Evelyn during his stay in England, although the latter's unusually complete diary contains no such record. Even if the two men did not come into personal contact, the evidence that Evelyn's landscape design and town planning theories influenced Nicholson in his plan for Annapolis and, later, for Williamsburg, remains compelling.

Looking again at the Annapolis plan, let us concentrate on one portion that includes a quite distinctive and decidedly unusual pattern of streets and open space. This is the area including Church Circle and the adjoining segment of the town south of North West and South East streets. Here we find two major and symmetrically located radial streets—West Street and South Street leading into Church Circle from their intersections with Cathedral Street. Three closely spaced parallel streets can be seen in the triangular space formed by Cathedral Street and the two radials. Their names—Dean, Doctor, and Temple—suggest an affiliation with the church, and on the Stoddert plan each of the two long and narrow lots between the three streets is designated as "Church Lot."

Compare this rather strange design with the illustration in figure 84. Here we find an almost exact duplicate of this uncommon pattern. It is difficult to believe that this was mere coincidence. This illustration appeared in Evelyn's translation of Jean de La Quintinie's *The Compleat Gard'ner,* published in London in May, 1693, while Nicholson was in England. This large and imposing volume could scarcely have escaped Nicholson's notice at a time when the number of books published annually in England did not exceed five hundred. It is no surprise then to find it listed among the books in his possession in a catalogue of his library compiled in the spring of 1695.[27] The bulk of his library had been acquired during the period he was in England before leaving to become governor of Maryland. There is every reason to believe, therefore, that he brought with him on that trip a copy of the recently published *Compleat Gard'ner.* Although the design in Evelyn's book showed the suggested layout for a garden rather than a city, the possibilities of using a landscape pattern for a portion of Annapolis probably occurred to Nicholson as such adaptation did to other designers of American cities.[28]

Nicholson owned another work of Evelyn's, *Sylva, Or a Discourse of Forest-Trees.* To the third edition of this work, which Nicholson possessed, Evelyn added a description of the principles of landscape design advocated by Moses Cook, whose *The Manner of Raising, Ordering, and Improving Forrest-Trees* had been published three years earlier. According to Evelyn, Cook proposed that in the planning of residential estates "Walks should not terminate abruptly, but rather in some capacious, or pretty figure, be it *Circle, Oval, Semi-Circle, Triangle,* or *Square,* especially in Parks, or where they do not lead into other Walks; and even in that case, that there may gracefully be a *Circle* to receive them." A few lines later Evelyn, in what almost could be a description of Church or Statehouse Circle, states his own preference for "the *Circle* with a *Star* of *Walks* radiating from it" as "likewise exceeding pleasant." [29]

Evelyn had, of course, employed exactly those baroque planning devices in 1666 when he prepared his various rebuilding plans for London. In a description of his proposals at that time he included a brief discussion of the desirability of variety in the design of urban open spaces and important

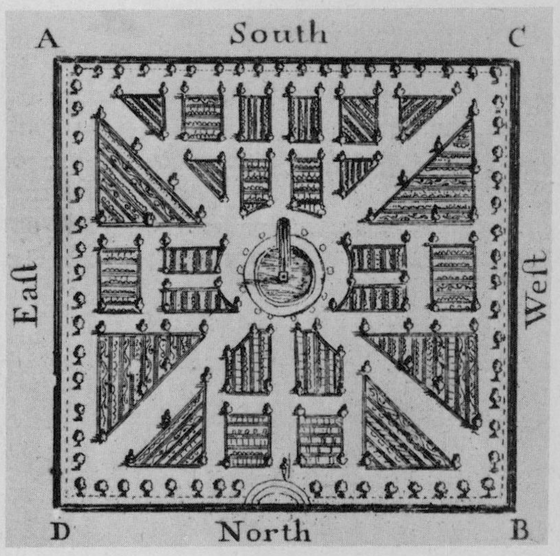

Figure 84. Plan of a Garden: 1693

building sites. He recommended that not "all of them be square, but some of them oblong, circular, and oval figures, for their better grace and capacity." Later in this same document, which was addressed to the king, he advocated the creation of separate districts some distance from town for "Brewhouses, Bakehouses, Dyers, Salt, Soap, and Sugar-boilers, Chandlers, Hatmakers, Slaughter-houses, some sort of Fish-mongers &c." [30] Both recommendations were to be followed at Annapolis under Nicholson's administration.[31]

If one examines again Evelyn's plans for London, the first version of which is reproduced in figure 85, a number of similarities between it and Nicholson's plan of Annapolis can be noticed. The London plan was, of course, for a much larger area and the spacing between its major features

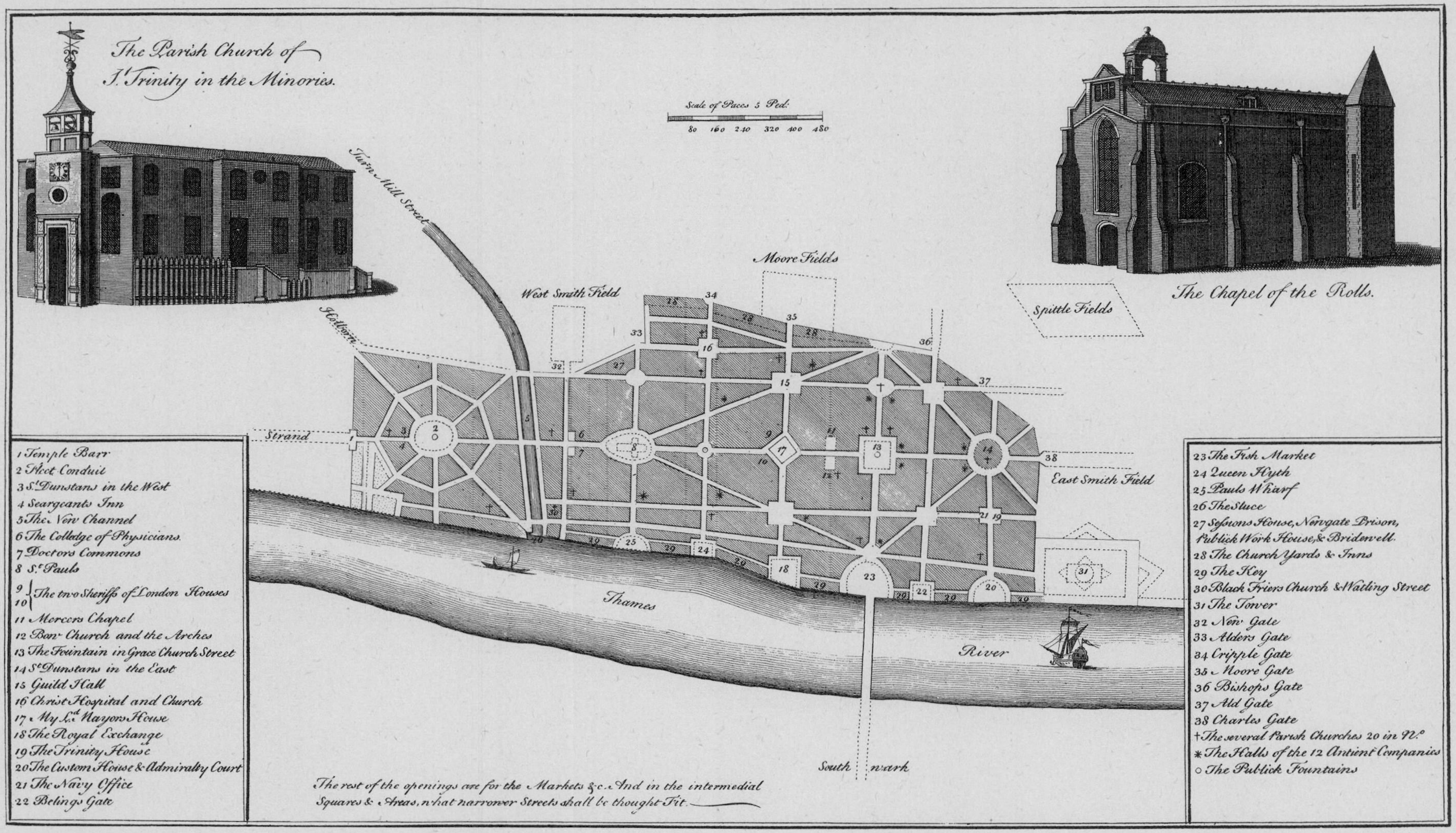

Figure 85. Plan for Rebuilding London in 1666 by John Evelyn

was correspondingly greater. It seems likely, however, that some variety of this kind of baroque plan was in Nicholson's mind when he designed the street system and the squares and circles for his new capital. We cannot be certain Nicholson actually saw Evelyn's plans for rebuilding London. No published version apparently existed before 1748, and evidently no manuscript plan has survived. Yet in December, 1666, Evelyn sent the text of his rebuilding proposals to the Royal Society in care of its secretary, Henry Oldenburg, and it seems likely one or more of his plans accompanied that document.[32] Nicholson was only later to be elected a member of the Royal Society, but it is possible he may have had access to the plan and its description through a member.

If the two men actually met in London while Nicholson was there the subject of planning would doubtless have come up. Such a meeting would have been natural. While Evelyn in 1694 was then seventy-four he enjoyed excellent health and had an active ten years of life still ahead. We know that Nicholson had an interest in gardening, for his library included several works on the subject other than the two by Evelyn; the ambitious and inquisitive colonial administrator may have sought further information on the topic from one of the few authorities in the country.

Another reason might have brought the two men together. In the spring of 1694 both Evelyn and Nicholson, then in London, independently advanced the appointment of Daniel Parke II to the Council of Virginia. Parke had been one of Nicholson's close associates in the colony. His prominent and wealthy father had been a member of the council, and in 1690 the younger Parke, then barely twenty, set in motion his plans to achieve the same office. On a visit to England with his father-in-law, Philip Ludwell, he sought out an influential kinsman—none other than John Evelyn. He became well acquainted with Evelyn and a friend of his son, to whom he wrote immediately after his return to Virginia in 1692. In that letter he asked his cousin's help in securing an appointment, adding that Governor Nicholson "has made me a Complyment & tells me he has writt home to make me one of the Councell here." [33]

The younger Evelyn asked his father to press Parke's cause with William Blathwayt, secretary to the Board of Trade. Later, in 1694, the elder Evelyn wrote on Parke's behalf to Sidney, earl of Godolphin, the first lord commissioner of the treasury. By that time Nicholson was in London where on April 4, 1694, he told Samson Sherard, Parke's brother-in-law, that he had spoken to Blathwayt about Parke's appointment to the council.

Informed of this by Sherard, Evelyn came to London from his residence at Wooton in Surrey to see Blathwayt. Failing to find him, Evelyn then wrote to this important official a warm letter of recommendation. Five weeks later Evelyn sent a letter to Parke expressing confidence that the appointment would be forthcoming. One brief passage hints that Parke had expected Nicholson and Evelyn to meet: "I have not seene Cap: *Nicholson* nor am I further knowne to him than by the Report & Character you & others give of him."

Whether the two men actually came together in the period remaining before Nicholson received his appointment as governor of Maryland we cannot be sure. At the very least these events may have first directed Nicholson's attention to Evelyn's writings, garden design theories, and plan for London in 1666 which were to influence the new governor's plans for Annapolis and, later, for Williamsburg.[34]

The hypothesis that Nicholson may have consulted Evelyn about town planning, or may have drawn on his *Sylva* or his translation of de La Quintinie's book on landscape design, is buttressed by certain similarities between Nicholson's plan for Williamsburg in 1699 and some of the features of Evelyn's plan for London as well as to a second illustration in *The Compleat Gard'ner*. This aspect of Evelyn's possible influence on American town planning is analyzed in the following chapter and should be considered along with the preceding material in evaluating the plausibility of the theory just advanced.[35]

The gradual development of Annapolis took place on the plan that by 1695 must have been staked out on the largely vacant site. By the spring of the following year construction on the statehouse was under way, although a shortage of funds and the dilatory approach to the job by the builder, Colonel Casparus Herman, combined to delay its completion.[36] It was probably ready for occupancy by the spring of 1698, only a year before it was to be damaged by a lightning bolt—an event that presaged its demolition by fire on October 17, 1704. A second building was soon begun and apparently finished within three years. This, according to one witness,

> was a very neat little brick building. An oblong square in form, the entrance a hall opposite which, two or three steps from the floor, was the judges' seat, and on each side were apartments used as jury rooms. . . . On the upper floor were three apartments, the two largest were used for the Upper and Lower House of Assembly and the other was the apartment for the mace-bearer and the other officers depending thereon.[37]

Inadequate in size and in poor condition, the building was demolished in 1770 to make way for the third and present statehouse. This imposing structure, as it appeared from the southeast on its site atop the commanding hill overlooking the town and harbor, is shown in figure 86. In typical fashion construction proceeded at a leisurely pace; not until 1780 was the building in use, though the dome may not have been finished until a still later date.[38] The octagonal building to the right in this illustration was what surely must have been the most elaborate public necessary house in the tidewater

Figure 86. View of the Statehouse in Annapolis, Maryland: 1789

Figure 87. View of Annapolis, Maryland: ca. 1800

region. This structure was completed by the end of the 1780s, echoing in its form the base of the dome atop the statehouse.[39]

The other great open space, Church Circle, also became the scene of construction activities. St. Anne's Church, probably started in 1696, was not in use until eight years later when it was still unfinished. This building, even with later additions, proved too small for the growing congregation, and the quality of its materials evidently left much to be desired. Like the second statehouse, this church too was demolished, and from 1775 until the completion of a second one in 1792 the congregation conducted services first in the theatre and later in King William School. The second church, in turn, fell victim to fire in 1858. The present structure dates from the following year and incorporates part of the walls and tower of its predecessor.[40]

An early nineteenth-century view of the second church of St. Anne's from the southwest appears in figure 87 with the third statehouse in the background.[41] Church Circle must have been far from impressive if this view accurately records the conditions then existing. Little if any grading had been done on the site, and the roadway marking the outer limits of what Nicholson obviously intended as an impressive and formal setting for one of the two major buildings of the town appears as a dusty and irregular trail. The creation of a sophisticated composition embodying advanced principles of baroque urban design had obviously encountered the realities of an America but little removed from the hardships and limited resources of a frontier culture.

Even before the establishment of Annapolis, Governor Nicholson recommended to the assembly that a school be created in Maryland, offering a personal contribution of twenty-five pounds sterling a year during his administration.[42] In 1696, King William School was founded with Francis Nicholson among its trustees, and work on its building was soon under way. This structure was located in the Statehouse Circle, probably south of the statehouse itself. It stood until the early years of the nineteenth century when it was demolished at the time the school was consolidated with St. John's College.[43]

Statehouse Circle also contained three other buildings. One was the armory or conference chamber, finished in 1718 on a site north of the statehouse. The building was used for meetings of the council and as a reception chamber for distinguished visitors. After 1769 it was designated as the county courthouse and was ultimately demolished in the nineteenth century.[44] By 1733 a building twelve by sixteen feet for the storage of public records had been erected somewhere in the circle, but the exact location cannot be determined.[45] A third building, as restored, remains. This is the treasury, situated east of the statehouse near the street marking the limits of the circle. Sometimes this has been identified as dating from Nicholson's era, but it was probably started in 1735 and completed two years later. In this modest brick structure the "Commissioners for Emitting Bills of Credit" carried out their activities as authorized by the General Assembly in 1733.[46]

Colonial Annapolis contained other public buildings located on less impressive sites in or near the town. Somewhere on the triangular lots bounded by Cathedral, West, and Dean streets stood the prison. Finished by 1707, this building replaced an earlier structure located on a site as yet unidentified. In turn, this building was abandoned for a new one begun in 1736 and located at the harbor on the irregular parcel shown on Stoddert's map as "Ship-Carpenter's Yard & Landing-place for this Side of the City." Evidently no such use had materialized and, since it was in public ownership, the site seemed advantageous for the new and larger prison.[47]

Beyond the original town boundaries stood the powder magazine, constructed by surveyor Richard Beard after the assembly approved the project in 1701. Fifteen years later this timber structure was moved to a site now occupied by St. John's College, and in 1742 a brick magazine was built in the northeast part of the town. Finally, in 1768 a third magazine was built near the statehouse, possibly within Statehouse Circle itself.[48]

While Nicholson's original plan of the town provided for a market site, apparently no market building was ever constructed there. About 1717 some kind of market building had been built near Statehouse Circle, possibly within its boundaries. We have seen how the locations of many other public buildings in Annapolis were constantly shifted, and the market proved no exception. In 1728 the assembly authorized the city to use a portion of the site set aside for the customhouse at the harbor.[49] Until 1752 this was its location. Then a third building, erected on or facing Statehouse Circle, served until 1784, when once again a location on the harbor was selected. The present market structure, much altered from the building begun in 1857, still stands on this final site.

Most of these public buildings, as well as the houses, shops, and miscellaneous other structures that were to make up colonial Annapolis, date from well after the founding of the town. Governor Nicholson did not remain in the city long enough to see more than the bare beginnings of urban growth. Of his activities in connection with Annapolis, one observer in 1699 commented:

> Governour Nicholson hath done his endeavour to make a towne. . . . There are in itt about fourty dwelling houses, of [which] seven or eight whereof cann afford good lodging and accomodations for strangers. There is alsoe a Statehouse and a free schoole built with bricke which make a great shew among a parscell of wooden houses, and the foundation of a church laid, the only bricke church in Maryland. They have two markett daies in the week, and had Governour Nicholson continued there some years longer he had brought it to some perfection.[50]

Nicholson's endeavors included securing the passage of an important measure in the fall of 1696. This "Act for keeping good Rules & Orders in the Porte of Annapolis" created the "Commissioners and Trustees for the Porte and Town of Annapolis" and conferred on them important powers.[51] It authorized them "to Purchase any Quantity or Quantitys of Land next adjacent to the Town and for Town Common and to Satisfye and pay for the same with tobacco or money that now is or hereafter shall be raised for any Lott or Lotts of Land taken up in the said Town." This portion of the act further specified that lot owners in the town would be required to pay their proportionate share of the expenses for any land so acquired or forfeit their right to use the common. The law also provided that those owners of land designated for wharf and warehouse purposes must construct these facilities within eighteen months or lose title to their property.

Perhaps the most interesting feature of the act dealt with the creation of a separate neighborhood for carrying out certain trades and industrial activities:

> That when any Baker Brewer Tanner Dyer or any such Tradsmen That by the practice of their Trade may any ways anoy or disquiett the neighbours or Inhabitants of the Town it shall and may be Lawfull for the Commissioners and Trustees aforesaid to allott and appoint to such Tradsmen such part or parcell of Land out of the present Town pasture as to the said Commissioners shall seem meet and Convenient for the Exercise of such Trade a sufficient Distance from the said Town as may not be annoyance thereto not Exceeding the quantity of one Lott or Acre of Land to any one Tradsman as aforesaid and provided the same Trade & Lotts of Land for that use may be as near together and Contiguous as the nature of the Trade will allow of without hindering or annoying one another.

Such an addition to the town was made in 1718, a project carried out at the same time as the resurvey of the city. From 1704, when the original plat of the town was destroyed in the statehouse fire, until this time no accurate map of the streets and lots existed. Evidently many disputes had arisen concerning property boundaries, and in the latter year the assembly appointed commissioners to hear and resolve such conflicts over property ownership. At the same time they directed James Stoddert to prepare an accurate survey of all property lines "and cause the Bounds thereof to be ascertained and staked out, according to the true Intent and Meaning of the original Plat or Survey of the Town."[52]

The commissioners also received directions for expanding the city. "For the better Encouragement of poor Tradesmen to come and inhabit," the commissioners were to have "Ten Acres of the Public Pasture, lying on the North Side of the said City, and to the Eastward of the Ferry Road that leads by the Hill whereon the Powder-House now stands. . . . surveyed and staked out into Twenty Lots." These parcels were to be offered at a price to be determined by the commissioners only to persons not already owning a lot in Annapolis for the first two years after they were surveyed.

This addition to the city appears on the redrawing of the Stoddert plan previously discussed as well as on another undated copy of this survey reproduced in figure 88. The new lots, designated by capital letters, are shown northeast of King George's Street. Evidently they proved attractive, for in 1725 it became necessary to further enlarge this district by a second addition that, many years later, was incorporated into the grounds of the United States Naval Academy.

The act of 1696 also authorized the commissioners to survey and convey to Governor Nicholson "A Certain parcell of Land in the publick pasture according to the Demencons thereof mentioned and layd down in the Platt of the Town for planting or makeing a Garden Vineard or Somerhouse or other use." This substantial tract ran from the harbor all the way to the eastern edge of Statehouse Circle with a frontage of about three

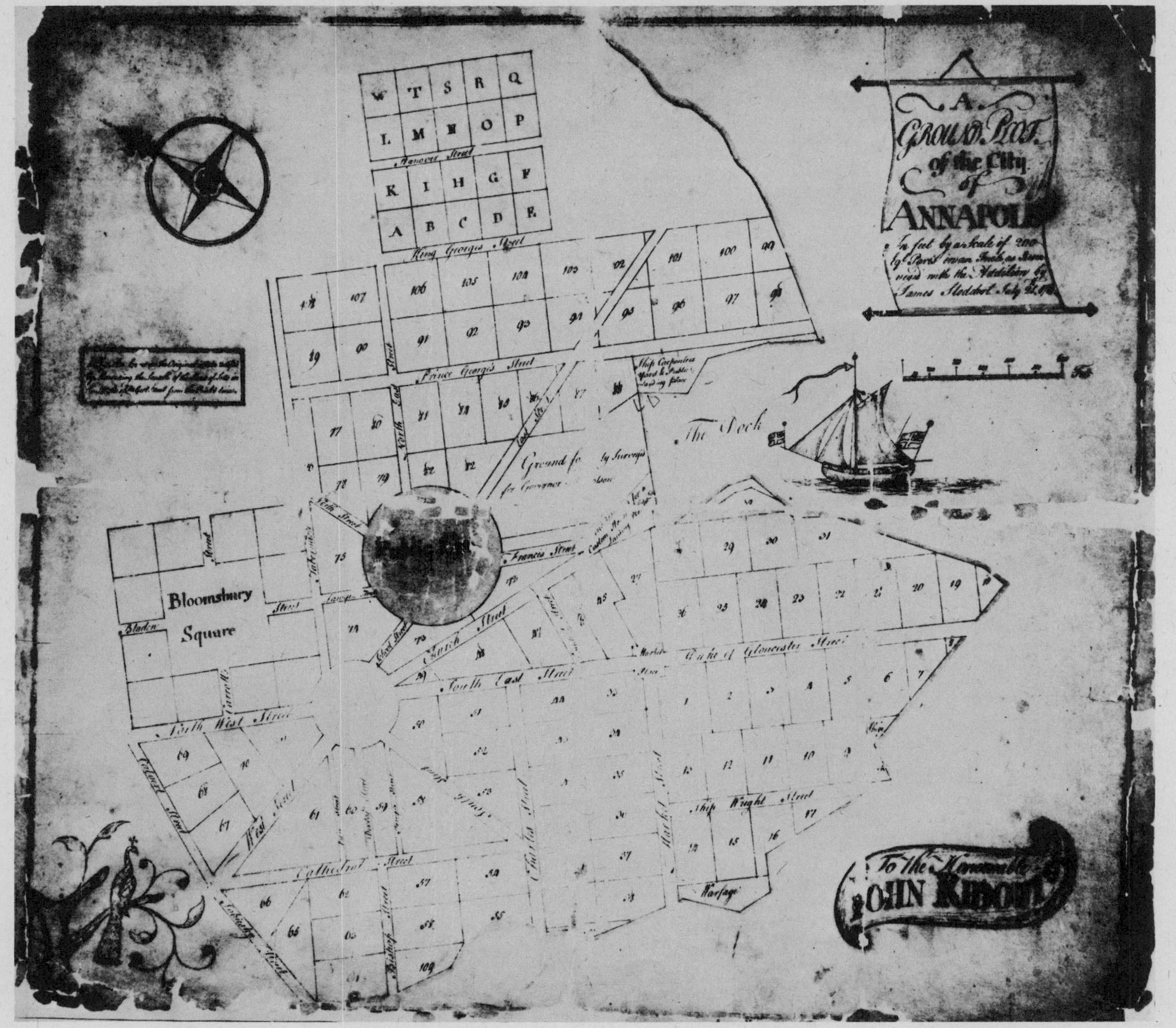

Figure 88. Plan of Annapolis, Maryland: 1718

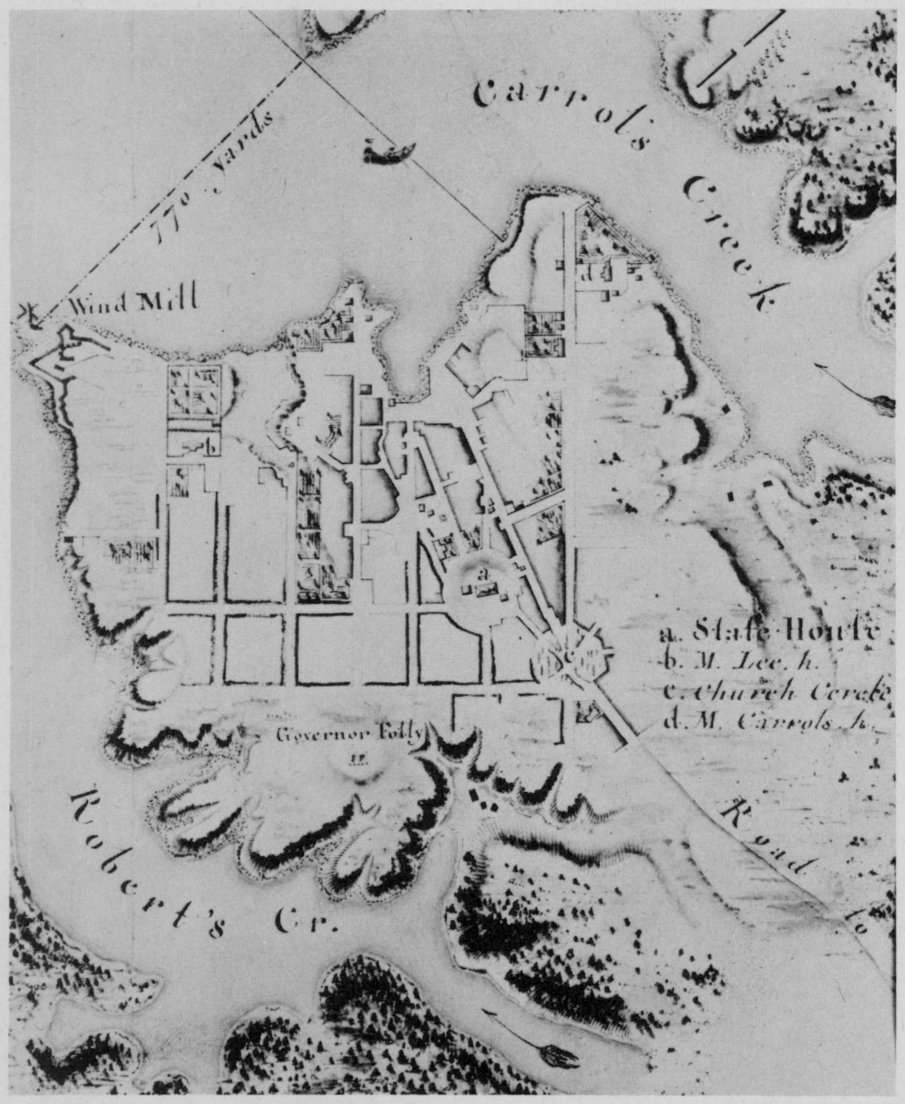

Figure 89. Plan of Annapolis, Maryland: 1781

hundred feet along East Street. It was here that Nicholson apparently began the construction of his own residence on the corner of what is now Hyde Street and Cornhill Street.[53] Cornhill Street was later cut through the Nicholson tract, perhaps following an old garden path, and in the modern city constitutes another radial thoroughfare leading toward the harbor from Statehouse Circle. Hyde Street is a narrow lane running east and west connecting Cornhill Street with Church Street, now renamed Main Street. These additional streets, as well as others added to the grid-iron section to the northeast, can be seen in a military sketch map (figure 89) of revolutionary war vintage.

That drawing shows the location of two important houses in the town. Toward the bottom of the map, between Robert's Creek and the town proper, appear the words "Governor Folly." This is now McDowell Hall of St. John's College, the grounds of which occupy that portion of the peninsula on which the town was built. This impressive structure can be seen in the distance to the left of St. Anne's Church in figure 87. It was begun by Governor Thomas Bladen, probably in 1742, but a disagreement between the governor and the legislature halted construction and the uncompleted building was allowed to deteriorate.[54] When St. John's College received its charter after the Revolution, the house and its site were conveyed to that institution, and the building was ultimately repaired and remodeled. Bladen's Folly, renamed McDowell Hall after the first president of the college, served for some years as the only building of the college. It housed both students and classrooms, and now, after its rebuilding following fires in 1909 and 1952, contains a few classrooms, administrative offices, and an assembly room.[55] A drawing of this interesting building as it appeared about 1810 is reproduced in figure 90 along with one of the statehouse by the same artist.

Near Windmill Point in figure 89 another structure, identified by the letter "b" and in the legend as "M. Lee. h," is the site of the first completed governor's house. It was built around 1740 by Edmund Jennings and was leased from him by Governor Horatio Sharpe as his official residence. Governor Robert Eden later purchased the dwelling from Jennings, only to have his property confiscated by the state. Until the house and property were conveyed to the United States government in 1866 for the naval academy it served as the residence of the governors of Maryland. When William Eddis described the building in 1769 he called it:

Figure 90. Views of the Statehouse and McDowell Hall in Annapolis, Maryland: ca. 1810

> most beautifully situated, and when the necessary alterations are completed it will be a regular, convenient, and elegant building. The garden is not extensive, but it is disposed to the utmost advantage; the centre walk is terminated by a small green mount, close to which the Severn approaches. This elevation commands an extensive view of the bay and the adjacent country. The same objects appear to equal advantage from the saloon and many apartments in the house; and perhaps I may be justified in asserting that there are but few mansions in the most rich and cultivated parts of England which are adorned with such splendid and romantic scenery.[56]

The Jennings house was by no means the only residence of imposing size and appearance in Annapolis, although the majority of the dwellings erected in the town were of more modest dimensions. The designs for a number of the great town houses in the city were obviously influenced by English architectural handbooks which chiefly illustrated mansions intended for rural locations with ample grounds. In England it would have been considered inappropriate to place such dwellings on limited town lots; in Annapolis the combination provided the Maryland capital with a most unusual and pleasant architectural heritage. For the most part these dwellings were located on or close to the street lines. Front yards where provided, were quite shallow, with the main lawns and gardens located to the rear of the dwelling for privacy and maximum use of the restricted sites.

The favorite design called for a central portion on a basement half-exposed above ground, with the main structure rising two and a half stories above. Wings customarily stood symmetrically located on each side and turned at right angles. Connecting them with the central part of the house were two lower structures whose front walls were somewhat recessed. The recently restored house built by William Paca in 1763, located on the southeast side of Prince George Street, is a superb example of this type of Annapolis town house. It is only one of several that still exist as testimony to the high level of architectural taste possessed by the aristocratic families of colonial Annapolis.

Scarcely less pleasing are the modest row houses that still line portions of many streets in the city. Invariably they were built on the front property line, either sharing party walls with the neighboring dwellings or otherwise constructed without side yards. The effect is to create a truly urban street facade with a sense of enclosure provided by the wall of buildings, unbroken except for pleasingly repetitive and well-scaled door and window openings. This tradition, begun in the colonial period, continued well into the nineteenth century. These simple row houses, together with the less numerous but more imposing town mansions and the major public buildings, have provided Annapolis with a distinctive character unmatched in America except by a handful of other cities.

Travelers who visited Annapolis in the eighteenth century had mixed impressions about the town. Certainly the most devastating description appeared in the famous satirical poem by Ebenezer Cook, *The Sot-Weed Factor,* published in 1708 and recording the unflattering views of its author about tidewater life in general. Of the newly developed Maryland capital Cook wrote:

> Up to *Annapolis* I went,
> A City Situate on a Plain,
> Where scarce a House will keep out Rain.
> The Buildings framed with Cypress rare,
> Resembles much our *Southwark* Fair:
> But Stranger here will scarcely meet
> With Market-place, Exchange, or Street;
> And if the Truth I may report,
> 'Tis not so large as *Tottenham Court.*[57]

These views were echoed by other visitors. Andrew Burnaby in 1760 referred to Annapolis as "a small, neat town," that was "tolerably well built, and has several good brick houses," but he was critical of the plan and the majority of its buildings: "The town is not laid out regularly. . . . None of the streets are paved, and the few public buildings here are not worth mentioning. The church is a very poor one, the stadt-house but indifferent, and the governor's palace is not finished." [58]

Burnaby was not the only observer who failed to grasp the unusual street pattern. William Eddis, who saw Annapolis in 1769, commented on the town's "very irregular plan." Nor was he agreeably struck by the appearance of the civic structures: "In our little metropolis, the public buildings do not impress the mind with any idea of magnificence, having been chiefly erected during the infancy of the colony, when convenience was the directing principle, without attention to the embellishment of art." Yet he noted that among the private houses "there are now several modern

Figure 91. View of Annapolis, Maryland: 1838

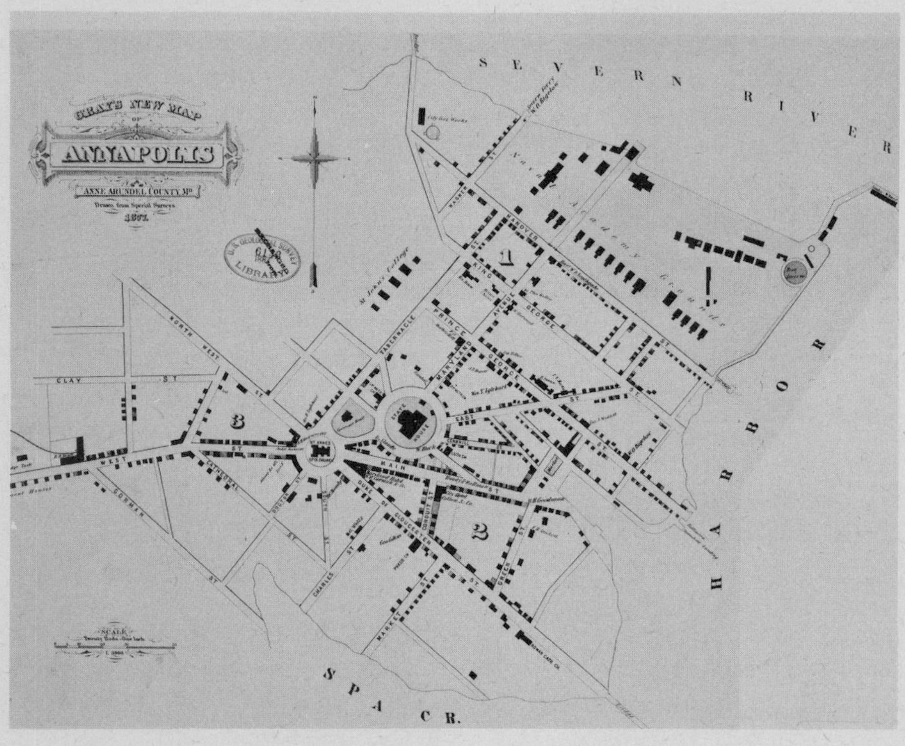

Figure 92. Plan of Annapolis, Maryland: 1877

edifices which make a good appearance. There are few habitations without gardens; some of which are planted in decent stile, and are well stocked." Eddis observed that "at present, the city has more the appearance of an agreeable village, than the metropolis of an opulent province, as it contains within its limits a number of small fields, which are intended for future erections." However, he felt that the future of the city had much in store, predicting that "in a few years, it will probably be one of the best built cities in America, as a spirit of improvements is predominant, and the situation is allowed to be equally healthy and pleasant with any on this side the Atlantic." [59]

Dr. Robert Honyman, visiting the town in 1775, also failed to understand Nicholson's baroque city plan: "They say the plan of the town is very good & regular, but it appears very confused, & the streets are extremely hilly & uneven without a bit of paving." [60] Lord Adam Gordon, on the other hand, seemed to grasp some of the essentials of the plan. While he noted that "the Town is built in an irregular form," he observed "the Streets generally running diagonally, and ending on the Town-house." [61] The unusual character of the plan also struck J. F. D. Smyth, who recorded about 1770 that "the streets are remarkable for the singular and whimsical manner of being laid out from the province-house in directions like rays from a centre." [62] It seems evident from these observations that the full impact of Nicholson's plan for the town had not been completely realized. It was not until the nineteenth century when streets were graded and paved and the vacant lots were gradually developed that the intended urban pattern began to emerge in three dimensions with greater clarity. Even then, Nicholson's rather arbitrary use of radial streets and the lack of skill with which he employed these and other baroque design principles borrowed from Europe resulted in a somewhat cramped and not completely successful expression of formal town design.

Following the Revolution, the city experienced a decline in prosperity and importance. La Rochefoucauld, who visited the town briefly during the closing years of the eighteenth century, observed what had occurred:

> Annapolis was formerly the principal city of Maryland, and there was some commerce carried on there. Since the revolution it retains the name of the metropolis of the state, and continues to be the seat of the government, but Baltimore has drawn all the commerce from it. The capitalists, or those who would become such, have quitted it to go and reside at Baltimore; and the inhabitants are in general families in easy circumstances, who have property in the neighborhood, officers of the government, and gentlemen of the law, attracted by the vicinity of the courts of justice. The population of this town diminishes every year . . . [and] . . . does not contain more than two thousand inhabitants.[63]

Under the Articles of Confederation the Congress of the United States met in Annapolis from November, 1783, until June of the following year. The city failed, however, in its bid to become the permanent seat of government for the new nation, although it was successful in fighting off the determined efforts of Baltimore to have the state capital moved to that rapidly growing community. Baltimore quickly assumed commercial dominance of the upper Chesapeake Bay and attracted most of the trade that once had supported the mercantile life of Annapolis. The water front of the

Figure 93. View of Annapolis, Maryland: ca. 1860

city, as shown in a view of 1838 (figure 91), lost much of its importance, and the harbor was used mainly for small craft and fishing vessels.

The view reveals one feature of the town that developed in postcolonial times and was to have a major impact on Annapolis. The circular structure on the shore slightly to the left of the capitol in the background is Fort Severn, erected by the United States government in 1808. This site included some eight acres of land situated northeast of the original town boundaries. It was this spot that was selected by George Bancroft, secretary of the navy in 1845, as a training site for midshipmen. While the installation was moved to Newport, Rhode Island during the Civil War, the United States Naval Academy soon returned and has been an important part of the Annapolis scene since that time.

The site occupied by the academy, as it existed in 1877, can be seen on the plan in figure 92. That drawing also records some of the changes and modifications in the original Nicholson plan that had been carried out over the years. Southwest of Church Circle two of the three parallel streets running to Cathedral Street had been eliminated. Only a portion of the land planned as part of the great Bloomsbury Square north and west of the two circles can be seen, and the open space in its center has vanished. A few new streets have been added to the south and west. The original market square has disappeared. To the north five new buildings have joined the rebuilt Governor's Folly to comprise the campus of St. John's College, which was later to extend northwest to the water's edge.

The best depiction of the city before modern growth began to blur its original outlines appears in figure 93. As drawn about 1860, this fine bird's-eye view shows at the right the buildings of the naval academy. In the background can be seen St. John's College centered around Governor Bladen's mansion. Church Circle and Statehouse Circle appear near the center, the latter site partially occupied by the second building of the Methodist church constructed in the 1820s. Most of the streets by this time had been fully built up, the later buildings harmonizing rather well with those of colonial origins in scale and design. Towering above the town was the fine statehouse dome serving, as it does today, as an orientation point in relation to which one can fix his position within the urban structure.

If not all the buildings erected in the present century have fitted easily into this little baroque composition, and many eighteenth- and early nineteenth-century structures have been needlessly demolished, much of the past still remains to be appreciated by the modern visitor. The Annapolis of Francis Nicholson stands as a precious heritage illustrating the town planning achievements of the colonial period of urbanization. Together with Williamsburg, to be discussed in the following two chapters, Annapolis deserves to be studied carefully by all who wish to understand the long tradition of American town planning and development.

VII. *Nicholson, Williamsburg, and the W and M Cipher*

THE ARRIVAL in Virginia of Francis Nicholson late in the year 1698 as captain general and governor in chief followed by only a few weeks the destruction of the Jamestown statehouse by another of those disastrous fires that had plagued the development of the settlement. Whether this event was a real cause of what was to follow or merely served as a convenient excuse is difficult to judge. One could argue that Nicholson, after his success in creating a new capital for Maryland, would have been inclined to press for similar action in Virginia even if the statehouse had remained intact. The drawbacks of Jamestown's site and its sorry appearance were well known to him from his previous residence there as lieutenant governor. He may well have become intrigued with the whole notion of new town planning as he had seen it tried in Virginia under the legislation of 1691 and under his personal direction at Annapolis. Moreover, through his active interest in establishing the College of William and Mary he would have possessed intimate knowledge of the area in the immediate vicinity of that infant institution, and he may already have formed an opinion about its desirability for further urban development. It is not unlikely either that he had considered the advantages of combining the seat of government in the colony with its center of higher education.[1]

We have already seen that the possibility of moving the site of the capital had been raised from time to time in the past. Following Bacon's Rebellion the General Assembly had met in its October, 1677, session at the house of Captain Otho Thorpe in Middle Plantation. This was the name given to the area between two palisades erected across the narrow neck of land between the James and York rivers. The first of these had been built in 1626 and ran from Martin's Hundred, identified on the map in figure 31 (Chapter II), to Kiskyacke on the York River.[2] The assembly in 1633 authorized the second palisade several miles to the west to connect Queen's Creek, which flowed into the York River, with Archer's Hope Creek, which emptied into the James.[3]

It was the "old fields" at Middle Plantation just west of the second palisade and roughly midway between the two rivers that the assembly in 1693 designated as the site for the College of William and Mary.[4] This may well have been the location that several residents of York County had in mind when, about 1677, they petitioned the king's commissioners to move the capital from Jamestown to Middle Plantation "as thought the most fitt Place being the Center of the Country as alsoe within Land most safe from any fforeigne Enemy by Shipping." [5]

The burning of the statehouse on October 31, 1698, brought the issue before the assembly once again. This time there seemed finally to be general agreement that the Jamestown site should be abandoned as the seat of government. Nicholson's active support for such a move proved conclusive, and by the middle of the following year the assembly committed the colony to a new and important step in town planning. While there may have been some competition among the various small settlements for the location of the capital, the Middle Plantation site appears to have been favored from the beginning.

With the full approval of Governor Nicholson, possibly at his suggestion, and quite likely with his help in planning the event, the faculty and students of the College of William and Mary played host to the governor, the council, the burgesses, and other notables on May 1, 1699. This May Day celebration was carefully staged. Five student orators presented discourses on the virtue of higher education, the advantages of carrying out studies in Virginia rather than England, the history of the college, and the reasons why the officials of the colony should support the institution. Between the presentations by the first two students and the pair of concluding orations came the longest speech of the day by a fifth student. He submitted to the gathering, using rather less elaborate and abstract language than his colleagues, a detailed brief for locating the seat of government at Middle Plantation and the creation there of a new town to accommodate the required facilities of governmental administration.[6]

This persuasive argument began by pointing out the advantages to the college of an urban setting. One practical need was a "good markett." Equally important was "the conveniency of good company and conversation" so that the scholars would not become mere pedants but would be "acquainted with action and business." Then, directly addressing the assembled politicians, the student presented his solution for achieving

> both these conveniencies, that is by contriving a good Town at this place, and filling it with all the selectest and best company that is to be had within the Government. Providence has put into your hands a way of compassing this without charge. I mean without any more charge than you will necessarily be at on another account, Namely the building of the statehouse, which alone will be attended with the seat of the Government, offices, marketts, good company, and all the rest.

He then took up the reasons why Middle Plantation appeared the ideal location, listing the healthy site, the excellent access provided by the James and York rivers and the two creeks running to them in opposite directions from the high ground occupied by the settlement, and the safety from enemy attack an inland location would afford. There would be mutual advantages to both town and college arising from locating the two together:

> First . . . the Colledge will help to make the Town. The chief difficulty in making a Town being in the bringing a considerable number of Inhabitants to it. . . . The very numbers of the Colledge who will be obliged to reside at this place viz the president and Masters with all their servants and attendants, the scholars with such servants as will be necessary for the kitchin, Buttery, Gardens, wooding, and all other uses will make up above 100 persons to be constantly supplyed at this markett. And these it is like will encourage Tradesmen to come and live here for their relieff and supply: Besides the Colledge being not yet finish'd will employ in builders and Labourers a very considerable number.

Likewise, the existence of a town would help attract to the college community "Tradesmen, Labourers, Shopkeepers perhaps Printers, Booksellers, Bookbinders, Mathematical instrument makers, nurses for the sick, and in short all other sort of people that can be usefull about a Colledge."

In concluding his case the student resorted to some of the arguments that had in previous years appeared in royal instructions to the Virginia governors:

> There is one thing perhaps worthy of our consideration, that is, that by this method we have an opportunity not only of making a Town, but such a Town as may equal if not outdo Boston, New York, Philadelphia, Charlestown, and Annapolis; and consequently such a Town as may retrieve the reputation of our Country, which has suffered by nothing so much as by neglecting a seat of trade, wealth and Learning, and running altogether into dispersed Country, plantations. If ever we would equal these our Rivals, we must contrive to joyn our heads and purses together, and by Companys and Societies to learn to improve our shipping and navigation, our trade and commerce, our minds and manners, and what no one man can do singly, by a friendly cohabitation and society to do jointly one with another. Whenever this is gone about it will be found to be no easy work to compass this design in such a Country as this is, where we live all dispersed in our several country plantations. And therefore, if any help presents for enlarging of the society, such as this would be of uniting the Town and the Colledge, it ought by no means to be neglected.

This eloquent statement must have had an effect on those present. Eighteen days later Benjamin Harrison, Jr., brought it officially before the House of Burgesses where it was read to the members of the lower chamber of the assembly. It was on that day too that Governor Nicholson forwarded to the burgesses the following recommendation:

> I do now cordially recomend to you the placeing Your Publick

> Building . . . somewhere at Middle Plantation nigh his Majesties Royall Colledge of *William* and *Mary* which I think will tend to Gods Glory, his Majesties Service, and the welfare and Prosperity of your Country in Generall and of the Colledge in particular.[7]

Nicholson must have been quite confident that the assembly would approve the necessary legislation, for by that date the surveyor, Theodorick Bland, was doubtless already at work running the bounds of the land adjoining the college, on which the governor had decided to plant the new town.[8] Later in May the necessary legislation was introduced and, after some amendments, it passed the assembly on June 7, 1699, and received the governor's approval the following day.[9] A new and important era of Virginia town planning was about to begin.

The site designated for the city that was to replace Jamestown as the Virginia capital, bearing the name Williamsburg, can be seen in relation to Jamestown and other Virginia settlements of the time on a chart published in 1737 (figure 94). The site was near the narrowest part of the peninsula formed by the James and York rivers. Archer's Hope Creek (shown on the map as King's Creek but named Princess Creek in the act of 1699 and later known as College Creek) and Queen's Creek were expected to provide nearby shipping facilities, but, unlike other Virginia settlements, the new capital city was essentially an inland rather than a port community.

A modern conjectural reconstruction of that portion of Middle Plantation in 1699 on which the new town was to be built appears in figure 95. Except for the college building at the left of the drawing, this part of Middle Plantation was similar in character to many of the loosely organized and dispersed settlements of tidewater Virginia. Within the churchyard near the center of the drawing can be seen the first Bruton Parish Church, a structure completed in 1683.

Connecting these two buildings and serving the scattered plantations and dwellings was a gently winding lane or horse path. It followed almost exactly the drainage divide between the James and York rivers, and its curving alignment allowed the traveler by foot or on horseback to avoid the upper reaches of the several creeks and rivulets whose headwaters extended almost to the road itself. A good part of the land was probably cleared, with some of it in cultivation and the rest available as pasture or open meadow. The few buildings on the site scarcely constituted a real community. One of the enthusiastic student orators of the famous May Day meeting could characterize the place at best only as "the beginning of a Town," with "a Church, an ordinary, several stores, two Mills, a smiths shop [and] a Grammar School." [10]

When the time came to plan the new town the buildings of both college and church served as fixed points and were influential in the town's design. Topography also played an important role. The conditions of the site almost dictated a modified linear form with the principal axis following the line of the low ridge and its natural drainage pattern. It must have been apparent that a nearly level street could be laid out running in a straight line from a point near the entrance to the college land, past the southern edge of Bruton Parish churchyard, and on to the east without encountering major difficulties with the terrain. The large area of land north and east of the church property—undivided by creek valleys—may have appeared particularly advantageous for some kind of special treatment, and it was this area that ultimately was to be the site for the market square, the governor's residence, and the long approach leading to that important building. The proposed town site contained two or three buildings that might stand in the way of development, but all other conditions were favorable for the location of a harmoniously planned town of larger size than had heretofore been established in Virginia—one whose character could reflect its intended importance as the seat of government and culture.

The act of the assembly that received Governor Nicholson's approval on June 8, 1699, was truly an unusual piece of legislation. Plainly the governor and the assembly drew on their earlier experience with town planning laws, but the act went well beyond the provisions contained in the two major laws of 1680 and 1691 for ports and towns. The gradual development of town planning legislation, which began with the efforts to stimulate the growth of Jamestown, culminated in the act that established a new capital city. The provisions of this novel law deserve detailed examination.

"An Act Directing the Building the Capitoll and the City of Williamsburgh" began with a recital of the objectives sought by the legislators. The first was defined as the planning of a building

> for the convenient Siting and Holding of the Generall Assemblyes and Courts at a healthy proper & comodius Place suitable for the Reception of a considerable Number and Concourse of People that of Necessity

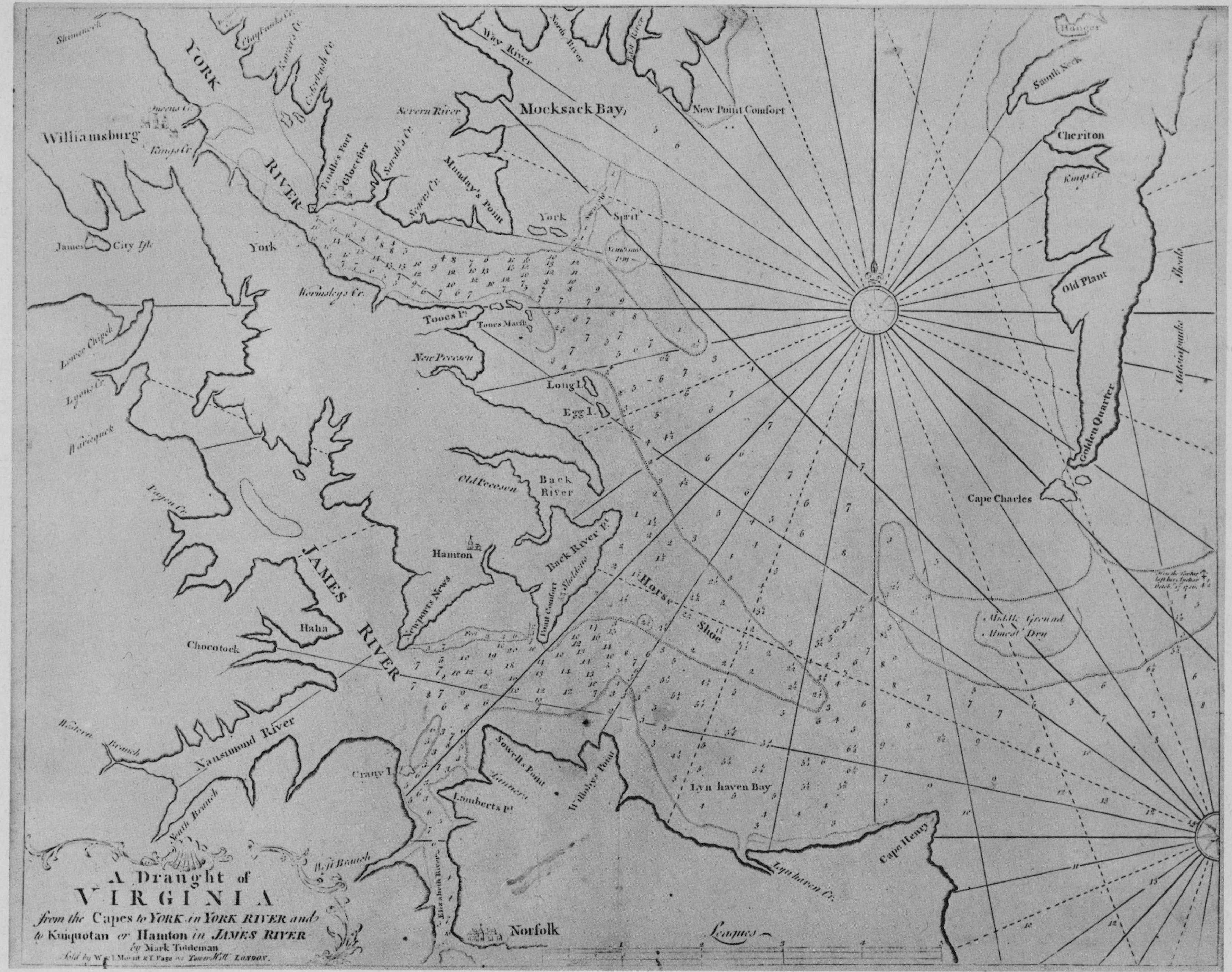

Figure 94. Map of a Portion of Chesapeake Bay and the Lower James River: 1737

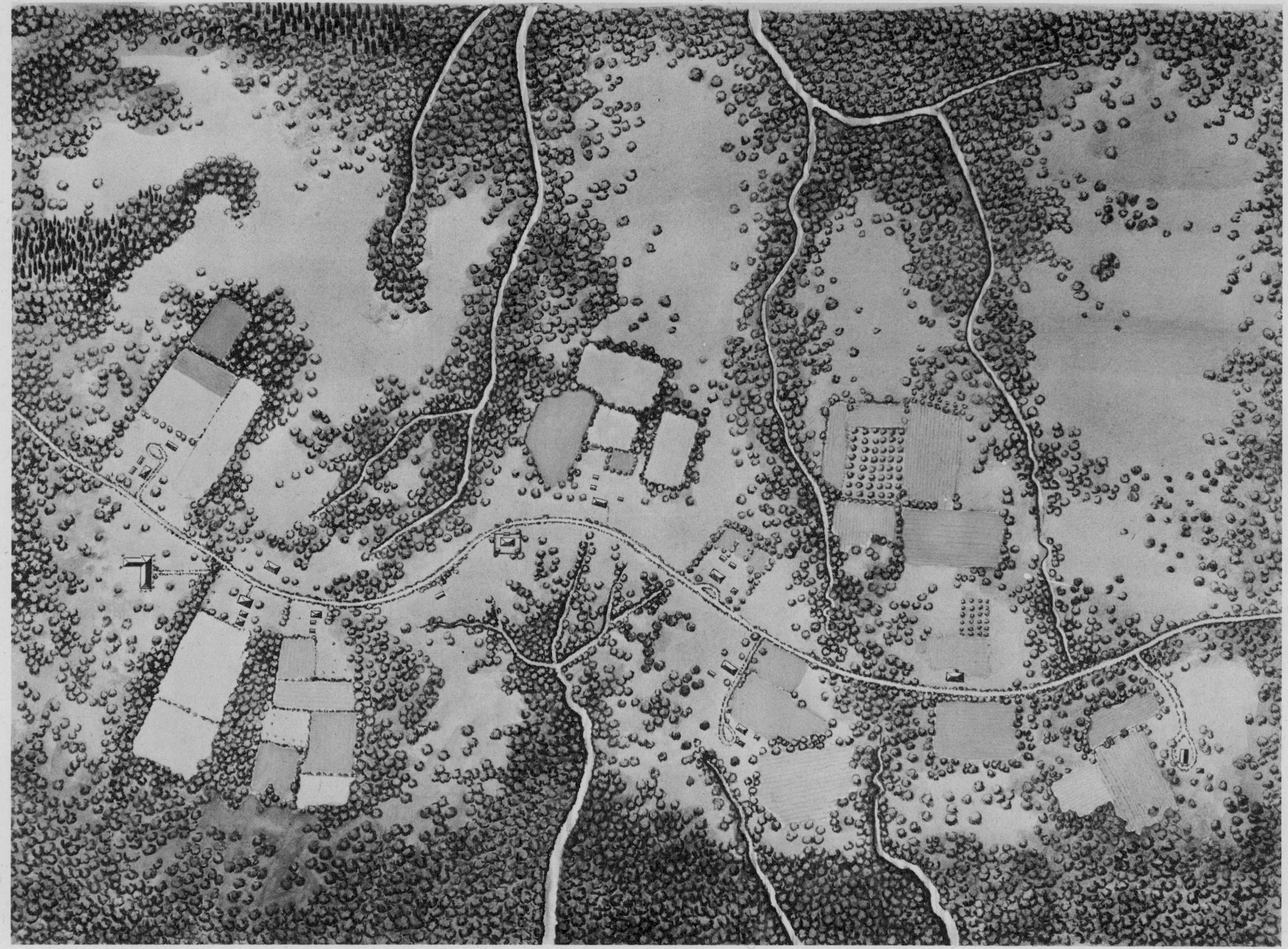

Figure 95. Conjectural Plan of a Portion of Middle Plantation, Virginia, in 1699

must resort to the Place where the Generall Assemblys will be convened and where the Councill and Supream Courts of Justice of this his Majesties Colony and Dominion will be held and kept.[11]

For this purpose the law reserved a site 475 feet square "which hath been already agreed upon by his Excelency the Governer Councill and Burgesses . . . to be taken up and surveyed as a convenient Place for such Uses." The building to be erected here was to be "caled and knowne by the Name of the *Capitoll,*" the first time this word had been applied in North America to the building housing the offices of a colonial government. The law then added that "the Space of two Hundred Foot of Ground every Way from the said Capitol shall not be built upon planted or occupied for ever but shall be wholy and solely appropriated and kept for the said Use and to no other Use or Purpose whatsoever."

The act prescribed in meticulous detail the exact size, shape, height, structural characteristics, and general architectural form of the Capitol. Its plan was peculiar. The manuscript copy of the act of 1699 reads that the building "shall be made in the Forme and Figure H," with two principal wings connected "by a cross Gallery of thirty Foot long and fifteen Foot wide each Way . . . raised upon Piazzas and built as high as the other Parts of the Building and in the Middle thereof a Cupulo to surmount the Rest of the Building which shall have a Clock placed in it. . . ." That this "Figure H" was no error in copying a capital "H" is confirmed by the enlarged portion of Bland's manuscript survey of the town site (figure 96) that shows the building. In 1701 this unusual and rather awkward plan was modified so that the building finally took the form of a simple "H" without the cross gallery.[12] Each of the two wings measuring twenty-five by seventy-five feet was to terminate at one end with a semicircular wall. The first story was to be fifteen feet high, the second ten feet, and atop this a hipped roof with dormer windows. Some of the details of the interior plan were also specified in the act along with requirements for the thickness of foundations and walls. Funds for the construction of this important building were authorized, and a committee was established to oversee its completion.

A second legislative goal was then set forth and appropriate action taken:

And forasmuch as the Generall Assembly and Generall Courts of this his Majesties Colony and Dominion cannot possibly be held and kept at the said Capitoll unless a good Towne be built and settled adjacent to the said Capitoll suitable for the Accommodation and Entertainment of a considerable Number of Persons that of Necessity must resort thither and whereas in all Probability it will prove highly advantageious and beneficiall to his Majesties Royall Colledge of William & Mary to have the Conveniences of a Towne near the same *Be it therefore enacted by the Authority aforesaid and it is hereby enacted* that two Hundred eighty three Acres thirty five Poles and a halfe of Land scituate lying and being at the *Middleplantation* in *James Citye* and *York* Countyes . . . shall be and is hereby reserved and appropriated for the onely and sole Use of a City to be there built and erected.

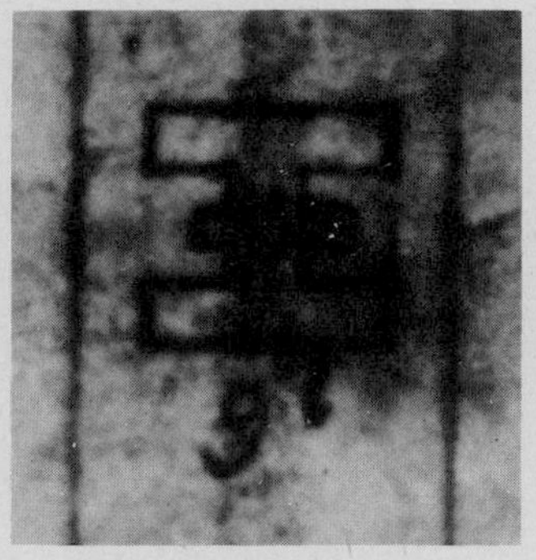

Figure 96.
Detail showing the Plan of the Capitol at Williamsburg, Virginia, from the Boundary Survey: 1699

Two hundred and twenty acres of the designated tract were then set aside for the town proper to which the name of Williamsburg was given "in Honour of our most gratious & glorious King William." The balance of the land was to be used for two ports. One was to be located on the creek running northeast to the York River. The creek was renamed Queen's Creek and its port Queen Mary's Port in honor of the late queen. Slightly more than a mile from the mouth of Archer's Hope Creek, renamed Princess Creek in the act, a second port, Princess Anne's Port, was established in honor of Princess Anne of Denmark. Included in the town lands were two roads leading to the ports, the one to the north beginning near Capitol Square and the road running south starting from a point not far from the college.

The location of these two ports in relation to the town, and the major features of the terrain, can be seen on the map in figure 97. This drawing, prepared during the revolutionary war by a French military cartographer,

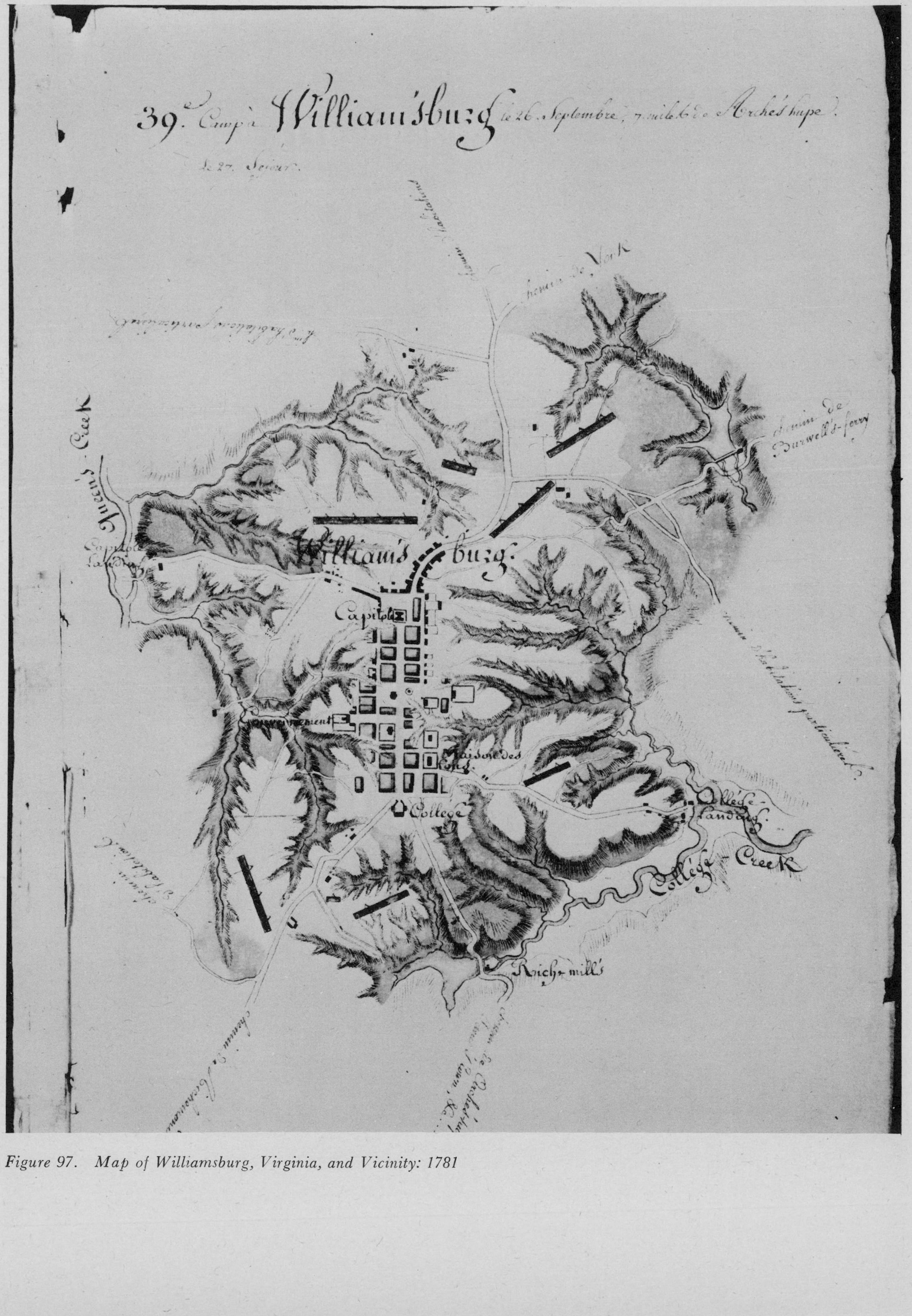

Figure 97. Map of Williamsburg, Virginia, and Vicinity: 1781

clearly shows the series of stream valleys running south to the James River at the right and north to the York River at the left. At the time this map was made the two ports had become known by names other than those specified in the act creating the town. The former Princess Anne's Port had become College Landing, while Queen Mary's Port was referred to as Capitol Landing. This map is useful also in making clear the advantageous location of the town on relatively high and flat land on the divide between two of the major rivers of the colony.

The assembly directed that the town be divided into half-acre lots. Houses fronting the chief street, named in the act the Duke of Gloucester Street, where to be built exactly six feet from the street line and were to "front a like." Those houses were to be at least twenty by thirty feet in size and of not "less than tenn Foot Pitch." Regulations for buildings on the other streets of the town were to be established by the "Directors appointed for the Settlement and Encouragement of the City of Williamsburgh." With Governor Nicholson at their head, the directors were given broad administrative discretion "to make such Rules and Orders and to give such Directions in the Building of the said City and Portes not already provided for by this Act as to them shall seem best and most convenient."

The law also specified how the land should be acquired from the owners. Twelve freeholders from James City, York, and New Kent counties were to be selected for this purpose to appraise the land. After their report of the value of each parcel the ownership of the land was to pass to six "Feofees or Trustees" who were named and appointed by the act. These trustees were then authorized to sell building sites. The proceeds from sales were to be used to repay the original landowners. Sales of lots on the Duke of Gloucester Street were to be conditional, with a requirement that construction of a house of the prescribed size was to be completed within twenty-four months of the transaction. If that condition was not met the title would become void and the lot could be offered for resale by the trustees. Similar requirements could be stipulated by the trustees for lots on other streets and made subject to the regulations established for those areas by the directors.

The lots at the two ports were not to exceed sixty feet square. It is likely that these were not intended, except incidentally, for residential purposes but as sites for warehouses and storage buildings. Not all of the land at the ports was to be sold, for the law specified "that a sufficient Quantity of Land at each Port or Landing Place shall be left in common at the Discretion of the Directors."

Although the bulk of the act dealt with the planning of the Capitol and the town, it also authorized the governor to provide at some future time for the incorporation of Williamsburg as a city with a mayor, aldermen, and common council as local officials and at that time to include a grant of privileges for holding fairs and markets. Finally, in order to provide adequate opportunity for everyone in the colony to familiarize himself with this legislation, no sales of land were to be made before October 20. It is likely also that this period was specified to allow time to work out the details of the town plan, which at the time of the act's passage had not yet been fully determined.

All the evidence points to Francis Nicholson as the author of this legislation and the designer of the plan of Williamsburg. As we shall see, two contemporary historians refer to the plan as originating with the governor. Nothing like its design had been attempted in colonial Virginia, and the one figure new to the scene was Nicholson. It was, moreover, a Nicholson fresh from his experience at Annapolis and doubtless confident of his abilities to design a town better than anyone else in the colony. The governor was not noted for his modesty, and the names of Francis and Nicholson streets bear witness to this trait. Nor was he a person inclined to defer to others in what must have appeared to him clearly a responsibility of the chief executive. Complete documentation of his authorship may be lacking, but it is almost inconceivable that the plan of Virginia's second capital stemmed from any less a personage than the royal governor.

The absence of any drawings contemporary with the first planning and early development of the city, showing details of its plan, is a distinct handicap. Later plans that have survived are in some important aspects conflicting or incomplete. And while early descriptions of the town are of considerable help, they too contain some puzzling observations difficult to reconcile with surviving graphic evidence showing the location and design of the town's streets, public buildings, and other features. Nor does an examination of early land records clarify completely the uncertainties of the original plan of Williamsburg.

Taken together, all the evidence suggests strongly that the plan of the city was modified several times and that these changes occurred almost from the beginning. It may be useful to summarize at the outset the

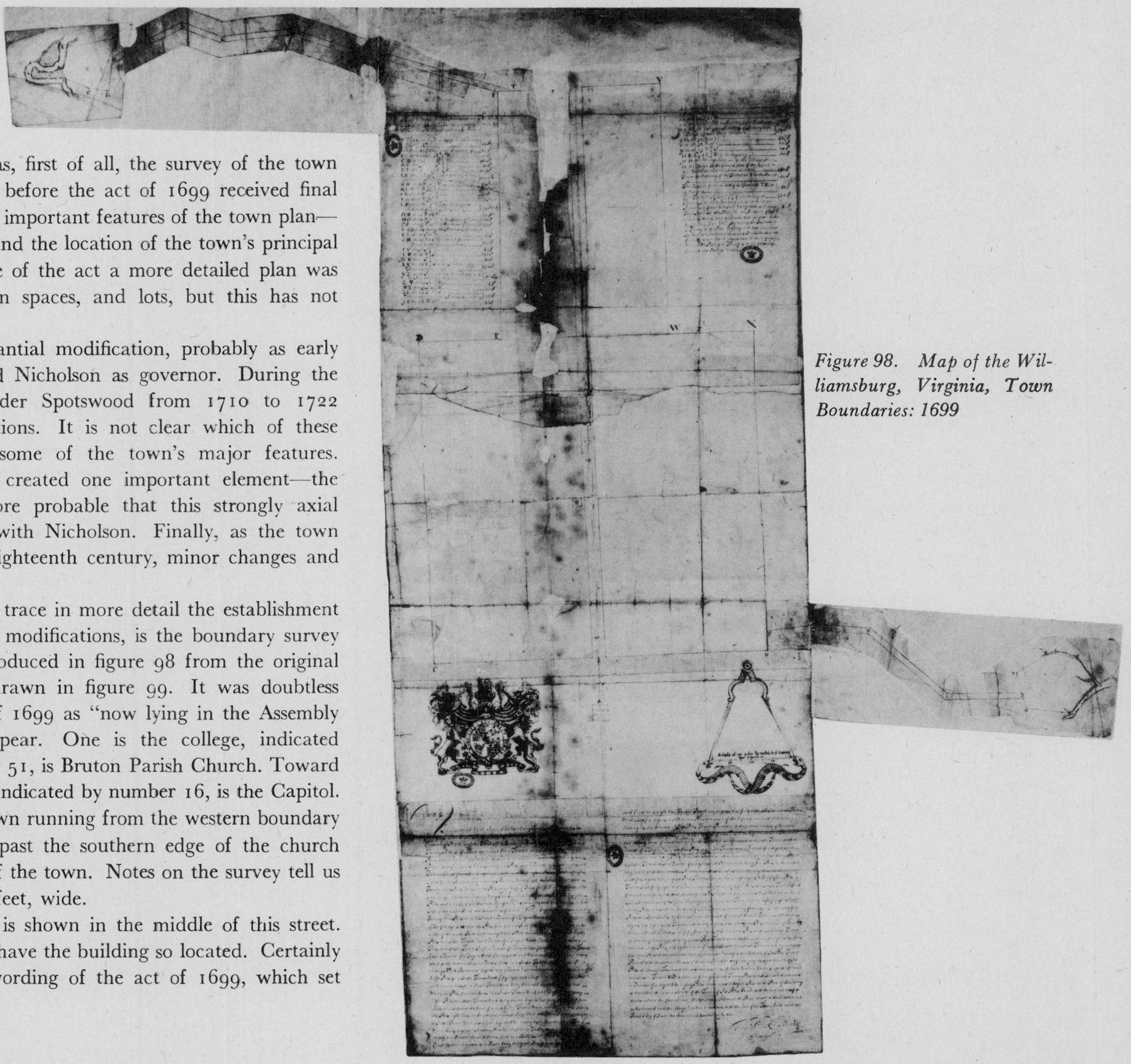

Figure 98. Map of the Williamsburg, Virginia, Town Boundaries: 1699

sequence of these changes. There was, first of all, the survey of the town boundaries that was completed even before the act of 1699 received final approval. This drawing included four important features of the town plan—the Capitol, the college, the church, and the location of the town's principal street. Immediately after the passage of the act a more detailed plan was prepared showing other streets, open spaces, and lots, but this has not survived.[13]

Nicholson's plan underwent substantial modification, probably as early as 1706 after Edward Nott replaced Nicholson as governor. During the administration of Governor Alexander Spotswood from 1710 to 1722 there were other changes and additions. It is not clear which of these administrators was responsible for some of the town's major features. Spotswood, for example, may have created one important element—the Palace Green—though it seems more probable that this strongly axial feature of Williamsburg originated with Nicholson. Finally, as the town grew during the later years of the eighteenth century, minor changes and additions were made.

The starting point for an effort to trace in more detail the establishment of the first plan of the town and its modifications, is the boundary survey prepared by Theodorick Bland, reproduced in figure 98 from the original faded and torn manuscript and redrawn in figure 99. It was doubtless the drawing referred to in the act of 1699 as "now lying in the Assembly Office." Two existing buildings appear. One is the college, indicated by the letter "A." The other, number 51, is Bruton Parish Church. Toward the eastern end of the proposed city, indicated by number 16, is the Capitol. The Duke of Gloucester Street is shown running from the western boundary of the town lands near the college past the southern edge of the church property and on to the eastern end of the town. Notes on the survey tell us that it was six poles, or ninety-nine feet, wide.

It seems strange that the Capitol is shown in the middle of this street. Perhaps the earliest intention was to have the building so located. Certainly this does not correspond with the wording of the act of 1699, which set

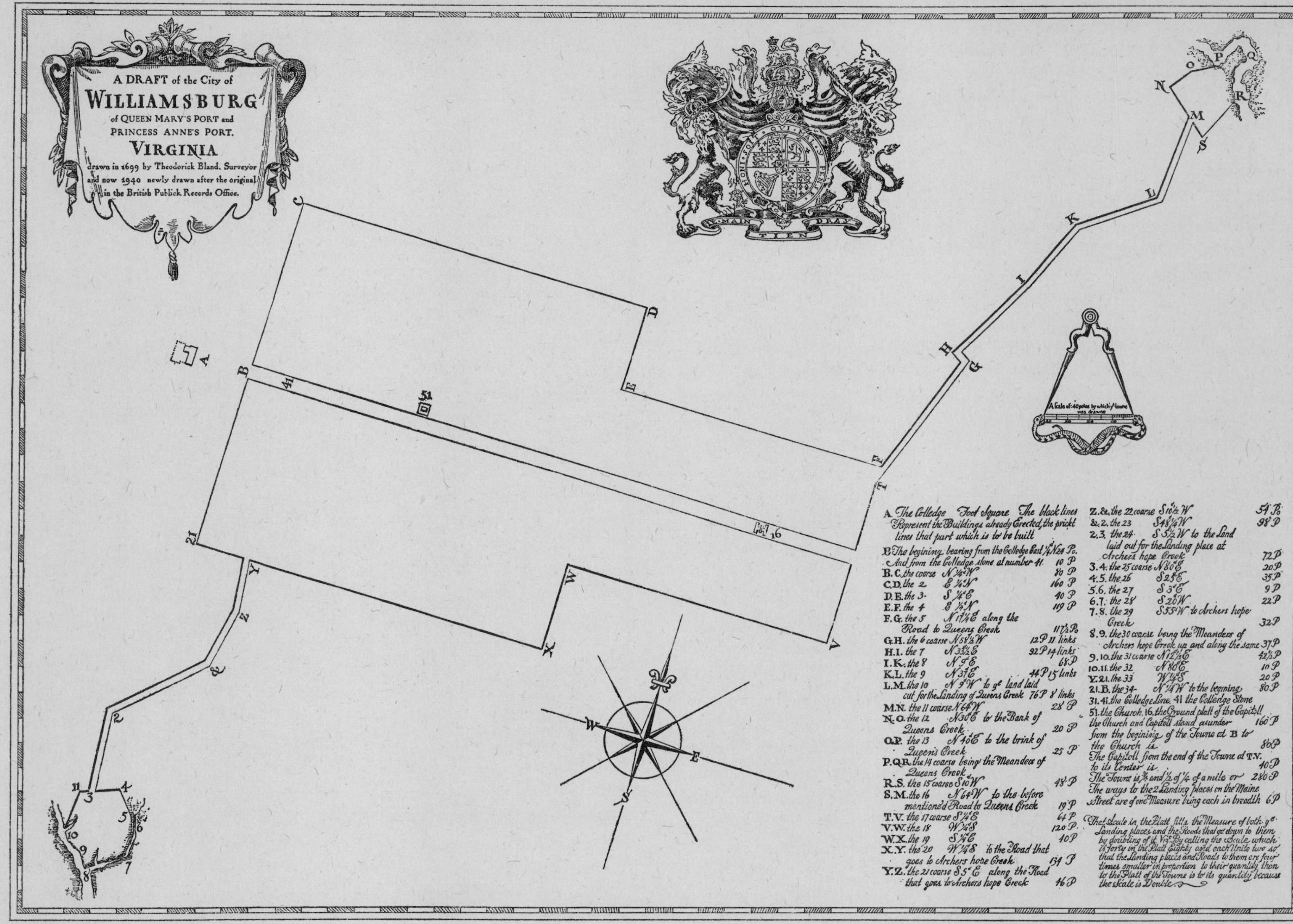

Figure 99. Map of the Williamsburg, Virginia, Town Boundaries: 1699

aside a space 475 feet on each side for the Capitol grounds. The most likely explanation of this discrepancy between the text of the act and the drawing is that the survey had already been prepared before the idea of a square for the Capitol grounds was conceived. As we shall see, this was not to be the only departure from the details shown on the Bland survey or the provisions specified in the act of 1699.

Something has already been said about the alignment of the Duke of Gloucester Street and how a straight line from the college passing to the south of the church would best fit the topography of the site. One other factor may have been important. In Bland's drawing number 41 identifies the "Colledge stone." This was a surveyor's mark, or "meare stone," which already existed in Middle Plantation and dated from 1682.[14] Approximately one and a quarter miles east of this point stood another meare stone marking the southeastern corner of the property of John Page on whose land much of the town was located. A line connecting these two stones would run through the center of the Capitol and down the center line of the Duke of Gloucester Street. That line also follows an almost exact east-west magnetic bearing, according to Bland's notes.

The geometry of the town boundary and the spacing of the important elements within it are also of considerable interest. Aside from the two ports and the roads leading to them, which were also made part of the land acquired for the town, the site encompassed 220 acres. It will be seen from Bland's drawing that the town plot is really divided into two major parts. The western portion forms a square 160 poles or half a mile on each side. The church lies at the center of this area, 80 poles from the western boundary and 80 poles from the point where the town boundaries narrow. From the center line of the Duke of Gloucester Street to the north and south boundaries of this section of the town the distance is also 80 poles in each direction. The narrower part of the town to the east is exactly half the width of the western section, measuring 80 poles north and south, or 40 poles in each direction from the center of the Duke of Gloucester Street. From the church to the proposed location of the Capitol is 160 poles. From the Capitol to the eastern boundary of the town is 40 poles. All this appears in the notes on Bland's survey.

It seems highly improbable that all this was mere coincidence. What appears likely is that Nicholson applied to the town plan a technique well known in architecture of proportioning the major elements of a design so that the component distances were in some mathematical relationship. Architects of the Renaissance had rediscovered such principles, which had been developed centuries earlier in Greece and Rome. Many of the architectural treatises written during the Renaissance and baroque periods include sections devoted to the theories of proportion applied to both plans and elevations of buildings. Nicholson somehow had encountered these ideas and used them in the design of his new colonial capital city.[15]

Another feature of the town boundaries deserves comment. The western section of the town shown on the Bland survey—the large square centering on Bruton Parish Church—contained 160 acres. The eastern section focused on the Capitol encompassed 60 acres. Nicholson probably had in mind a rough zoning scheme. The residential community with the church at its center and the church-related college at its boundary was to make up the bulk of the new town. The governmental and administrative sector lay to the east. Perhaps Nicholson intended this area to contain most of the shops, the taverns, and the inns.[16] Linking these two areas was Market Square at the eastern end of the residential district.

This possible functional division of the town helps to explain the peculiar shape of the boundaries of Williamsburg, which bears no relation to the pattern of landownership then existing. Nicholson was an ardent Anglican. His already strong interest in the established church seems to have been stimulated further during the period of his residence in England after his first administration in Virginia and before his appointment as the chief executive of Maryland. For him the logical center of the residential sector of the community would have been the church. Its existing location in 1699, approximately eighty poles or a quarter mile from the eastern boundary of the college lands, may have suggested the basic module to be used in determining the shape and size of the boundaries of the town and—repeated, divided, or multiplied—the distances between the town's major features.

The earliest surviving drawing showing the details of the Williamsburg plan, a manuscript map, bears the date 1782, eight decades after the town's founding. Its title and some of the lettering identifying streets and other features are in French. Although many English words also appear, the drawing apparently was the work of a French cartographer serving with the French army, then still in Virginia after the siege of Yorktown. The attention given to the location of individual buildings suggests that it may have been used in billeting assignments for a part of the French forces. As the reproduction in figure 100 reveals, it was not complete. Property or fence lines are omitted in several sections of the town, some of the buildings appear only in outline, and the map does not show a number of street lines that had been established well before the date it was prepared.

Compared with other town maps drawn by French cartographers during the army's march on the way to Virginia it is both larger in scale and far more detailed.[17] This could suggest that the "Frenchman's Map" (as it is now called) may have been copied, at least in part, from surveys or plans in the Williamsburg town records, though the evidence is to the contrary. The greater detail of the Frenchman's Map can be explained by the fact that French troops were quartered in the town for some time rather than merely for a day while on the march. The partial omission of fence or property lines suggests that an existing town map was not used by the cartographer. Further, there are a number of discrepancies in measurements that would not likely have occurred if its draftsman had available an accurate survey. For example, the Duke of Gloucester Street is shown as about 82½ feet wide at the Capitol end and about 75 feet wide at its termination near the college. What is identified as "Sud Street" (Francis Street) is drawn 120 feet wide compared to its surveyed width of only 82½ feet.[18]

What is even more conclusive, however, is a notation on the drawing itself just below the title. This reads "levé au pas," meaning a paced survey or one drawn by approximate measurements on foot. For the purposes of a later discussion concerning the original plan of the streets of the town as laid down by Francis Nicholson this matter becomes of critical importance. Meanwhile, the Frenchman's Map serves to explain the broad outlines of the plan of Williamsburg as it had developed during the eighteenth century.

The Duke of Gloucester Street stands as the principal axis of the city, with the views in each direction terminated by the college to the west and the Capitol to the east. The distance between these buildings is slightly greater than originally shown on the Bland survey of 1699. The site first intended for the Capitol was found to be unsuitable because of the ravine created by the small creek that can be seen on the Frenchman's Map slightly more than 200 feet to the west of the Capitol. Accordingly, the location of the building was shifted that distance eastward. Eventually this stream valley was filled where it once crossed the Duke of Gloucester Street and the street was leveled. The steep slopes of this depression, however, can still be seen in the modern city north of the street as one looks west from the Capitol. The building itself can be seen enclosed by a wall eleven by thirteen poles, or 181½ by 214½ feet. This enclosure is set within the larger square appropriated for the Capitol and related uses. The exact form of this larger square as defined by actual land sales is somewhat different from that shown on the drawing of 1782 or as it appears on other plans, a matter to be examined in due course.

Approximately midway along the Duke of Gloucester Street the plan of 1782 shows the Market Square as a central open space of considerable size. Two structures appear on the map. South of the Duke of Gloucester Street is the Magazine completed in 1716 under Governor Spotswood's administration. This took the form of an octagonal brick tower surrounded first by a wooden fence and, after 1755, by a brick wall that repeated the octagonal shape of the Magazine. It will be noted that this was placed directly on the axis of the streets entering the Market Square at the mid-points at its north and south sides. Here is one of several examples of axial planning in the design of streets and open spaces. Spotswood recognized this strong element in the plan and placed his building accordingly. Its location south of the alignment of the Duke of Gloucester Street strongly suggests that the street itself at that time ran through the square, although the Frenchman's Map does not so indicate. Nicholson's intentions may have been rather different, and that, too, will be discussed later.

North of the Magazine is the Courthouse. This was not the first building for this purpose erected at Williamsburg. About 1715 Spotswood was instrumental in moving the county seat from Jamestown to the new capital. The building to house the court occupied a lot facing Market Square at the southwest corner of Francis and England Streets. On the Frenchman's Map its location appears as the small building just below the letter "o" in the words "powder magazine."[19]

The T-shaped building identified as the "court house," nearly opposite the Magazine, dates from 1770. Its site to the west of the north-south axis of Market Square appears puzzling, but the most plausible explanation for its location is fairly simple. The Frenchman's Map shows two buildings at the eastern edge of the square on the north side of the Duke of Gloucester Street. As reconstructed in modern times this is the structure identified as Chowning's Tavern. These buildings, intruding on the original area of the square as do those across the street to the south, had the effect of

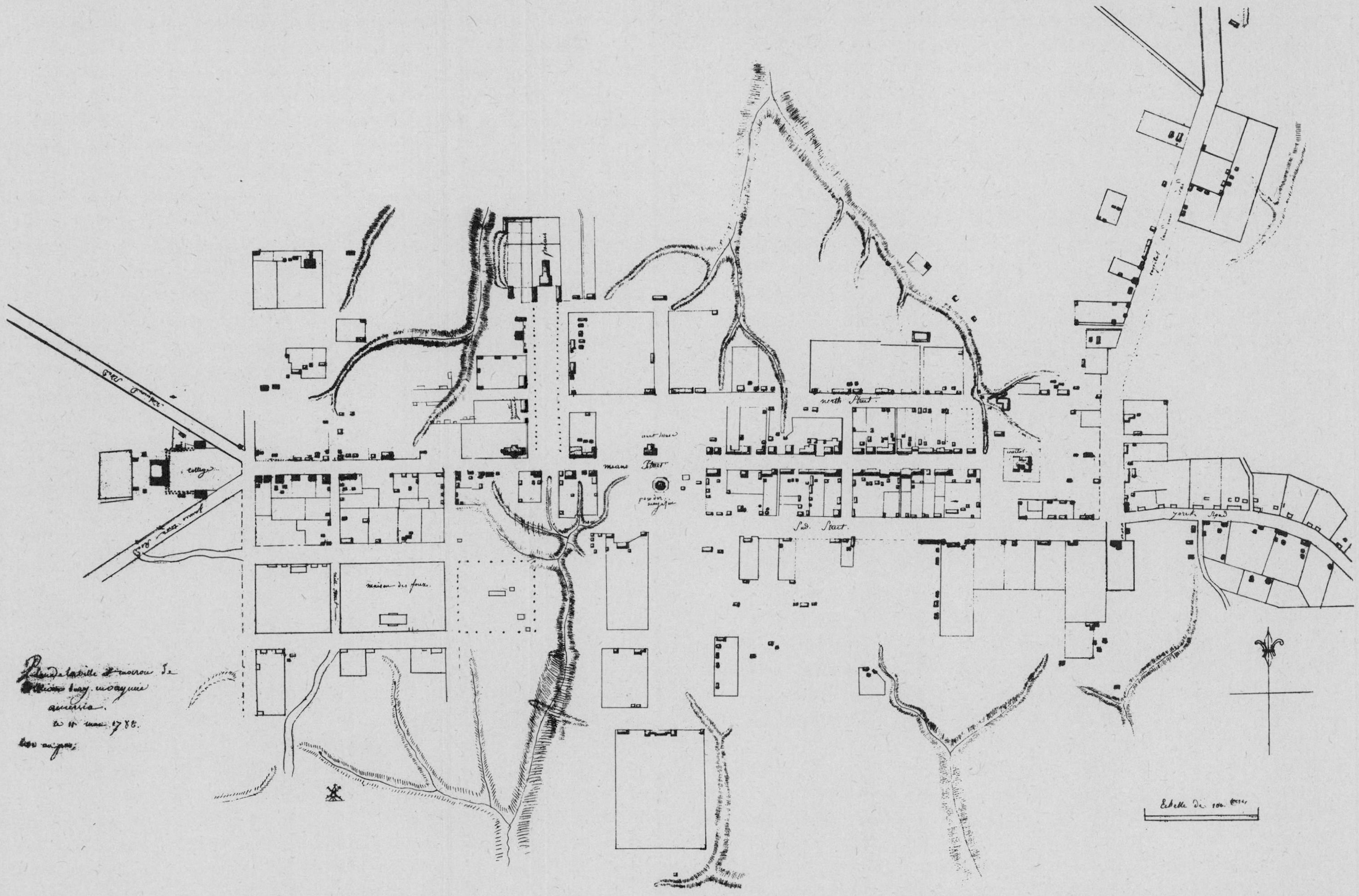

Figure 100. Plan of Williamsburg, Virginia: 1782

shifting the center of the unoccupied portion of Market Square to the west. The Courthouse was apparently sited so that it stood precisely on the new north-south axis of the open space, thus departing from the symmetry established by the original plan.

A few hundred feet westward stood Bruton Parish Church, the location of which was so important in determining the shape of the town's boundaries and in suggesting the alignment of the principal street. The Frenchman's Map shows the new church as completed in 1715 with an addition of 1751–1755 to the east and the steeple begun in 1760.[20] The new and larger building was built within the church grounds but located somewhat to the south and east of the original structure.

Bruton Parish Church clearly was an important element of the town's plan. In order to emphasize this point Nicholson introduced a major secondary axis into the plan near its location. This took the form of an elongated space running at right angles from the Duke of Gloucester Street and terminating a thousand feet to the north at the site of the Governor's Palace. Now known as Palace Green, this space was 210 feet wide between property lines. How the original designer intended it to be treated remains uncertain, but we do know something of its appearance at the close of the colonial period.

The Frenchman's Map shows a series of dots in two parallel rows running the entire distance from the Duke of Gloucester Street to the Governor's Palace. These represent catalpa trees planted there during the administration of Governor William Gooch by Philip Finch, who in 1737 was paid "the Sum of Ten pounds for laying and planting the Avenue to the Governors House."[21] Roughly contemporary with the Frenchman's Map is a drawing prepared by Thomas Jefferson showing the floor plan of the Governor's Palace. Two notes in Jefferson's hand are significant: "Palace street is 200 ft. wide," and "the rows of trees [are] 100 ft. apart, ranging with inner fronts of offices."[22]

Before 1737 it is likely that this space was not clearly divided between roadway and turf but existed simply as a wide traveled way. After that date it is possible that a single roadway led to the Palace down the middle of this area with the trees on each side. With one exception all the early maps of the town fail to indicate how this space was divided. Certainly a single roadway on the axis of the Palace entrance would have been consistent with baroque planning principles. The fact that the Frenchman's Map shows the trees on the eastern side of the street continuing right to the office building flanking the Palace and the trees on the opposite side running northward nearly as far supports the single-roadway theory.

The one drawing to show a different design appears in figure 101. This is the so-called Simcoe map, also presumed to be of revolutionary war vintage and possibly prepared by or for Lieutenant Colonel John Graves Simcoe of the English army. The drawing clearly shows a central green defined by trees on each side and two parallel roadways merging at the forecourt of the Palace. It is this design that has been followed in the modern restoration of Colonial Williamsburg. The inaccuracies of the Simcoe map are numerous and serious, and its depiction of the approach to the Palace may be unreliable.[23]

Yet the treatment of this kind of space with a central green and flanking roadways leading to an important building was also equally acceptable to baroque designers. The green strip on axis with the Palace would have provided a pleasant and unbroken vista to the south. The Frenchman's Map reveals that this view would have continued beyond the Duke of Gloucester Street, since a street opening to the south (King Street) is shown roughly opposite the termination of Palace Green. Plotted surveys reveal this to have been six poles or ninety-nine feet wide, equal to the Duke of Gloucester Street and surpassed in width only by Palace Green. It seems clear that the extra width provided for this street was the result of aesthetic considerations. On the site itself it led down a marked incline from the level of the Duke of Gloucester Street to a stream valley that ultimately drained into College Creek. Its width plainly had no utilitarian purpose and was solely to prolong the open vista from the residence of the governor.

The strong cross axis formed by Palace Green and its continuation to the south combined with the principal axis of the Duke of Gloucester Street to give Williamsburg its basic formal plan. There was a neat symmetry to the town, with the college at one end and the Capitol at the other. The Governor's Palace terminated one end of the cross axis, while the church occupied a strategic position closely related to both the major shafts of space that determined the fundamental structure of the new capital.

The first plan for the city as conceived by Governor Nicholson, while it incorporated these major elements, included a curious feature about which we have only indirect information. It has always been the most

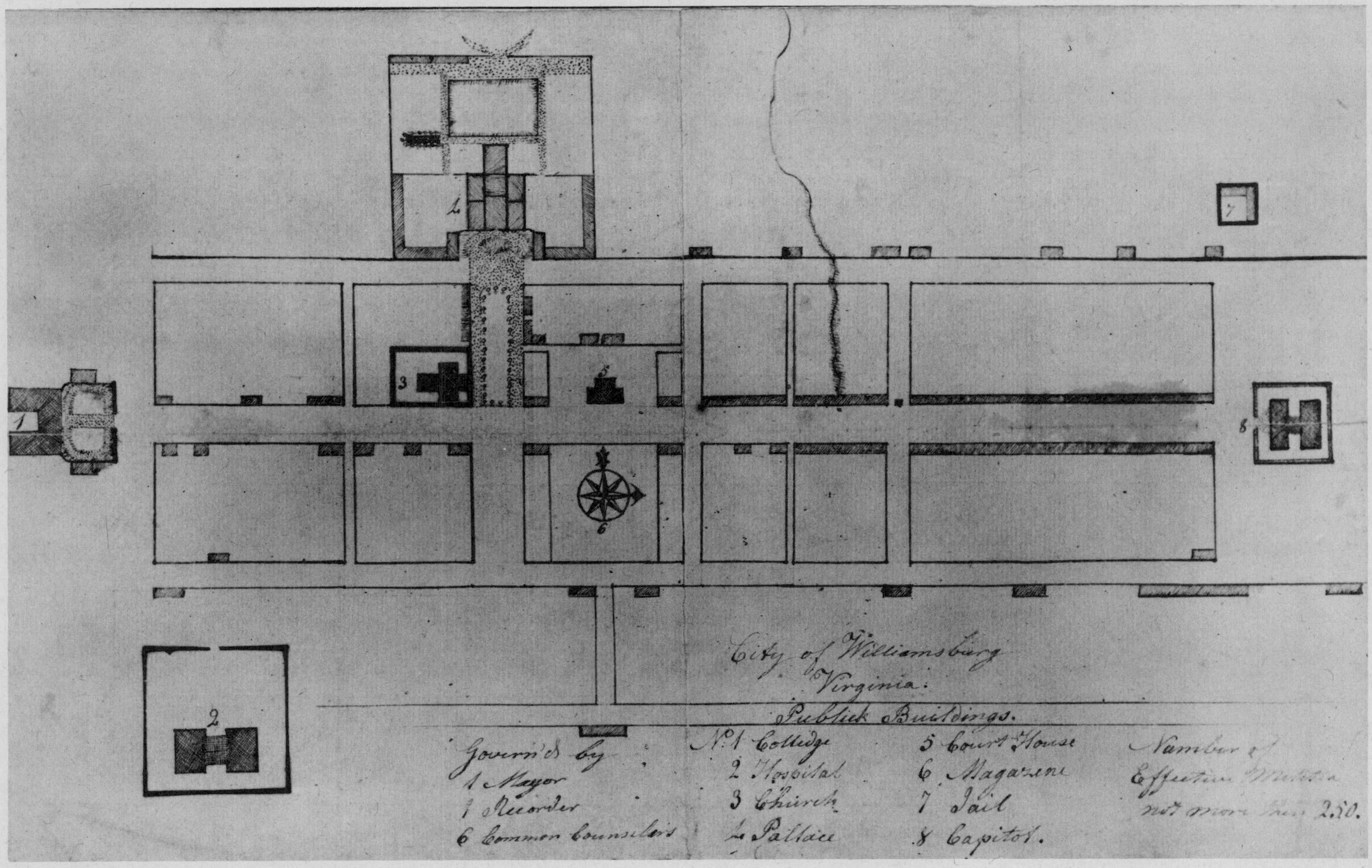

Figure 101. Plan of Williamburg, Virginia: ca. 1781

puzzling feature of the planning of Williamsburg as well as one of the most intriguing aspects of town design in American history. There are several references to it in descriptions of the town throughout the eighteenth century. The earliest appears in the writing of Robert Beverley whose *History and Present State of Virginia* was first published in 1705. The author, a Virginia plantation owner, had also served in the assembly and as clerk of the council. There can be no question of his knowledge concerning the events leading to the establishment of the new capital, since he was one of the property owners in Jamestown who opposed this action. His known dislike for Nicholson may have colored his history somewhat, but there seems no reason to question his accuracy on the subject with which we are concerned.

After describing Nicholson's successful efforts to move the seat of government to Middle Plantation, Beverley added the following: "There he flatter'd himself with the fond Imagination, of being the Founder of a new City. He mark'd out the Streets in many Places, so as that they might represent the Figure of a *W,* in Memory of his late Majesty King William, after whose Name the Town was call'd Williamsburg."[24]

The Reverend Hugh Jones, who lived in Virginia from 1716 to 1721, first as rector of the church in Jamestown and later as professor of mathematics at the College of William and Mary, contributed this information in 1724 about Nicholson and his plan: "Here he laid out the city of Williamsburg (in the form of a cypher, made of W. and M.). . . ." Jones seems to suggest that in some way the W or W and M involved the Duke of Gloucester Street and that originally it had not been carried through from the Capitol to the college as a straight line: "Fronting the College at near its whole breadth is extended a noble street mathematically streight (for the first design of the town's form is changed to a much better). . . .[25]

The change in the plan may have been carried out between 1710 and 1722, for in the second edition of his book published in 1722 Beverley added this passage in describing what had been accomplished in the city under Governor Spotswood: "In his time was also built a new Brick Church, and Brick Magazine for Arms and Ammunition: and the streets of the Town altered from the fanciful Forms of W^s^ and M^s^ to much more Conveniencies."[26] But there is also some indication that alteration of the original Nicholson plan could have taken place as early in 1706, the year after his appointment as governor of Virginia terminated.

On June 4 of that year the assembly passed an act containing several provisions suggesting that changes in Nicholson's plan were contemplated. The law appointed new directors, including Governor Edward Nott. It authorized them "to direct and order the Laying out the Lotts & Streets of the said City where the Bounds & Marks thereof are worne out," and "to lay out a convenient Space of Ground for the Churchyard." It then empowered the directors "to enlarge the Market Place and to alter any of the Streets or Lands thereof where the same are found inconvenient." After conferring power on the directors to "establish such Rules and Orders for the more regular and orderly Building of the Houses in the said City," it added the following significant clause: "Provided alway's that the main Street called Duke of Gloucester Street extending from the Capitol to the utmost Limitts of the City westward till it joyn's on the Land belonging to the College shall not hereafter be altered either in the Course or Dimensions thereof."[27]

The use of the word "hereafter" in the reference to the Duke of Gloucester Street suggests that this thoroughfare had indeed once been altered by Nicholson from the alignment shown in the Bland survey of 1699. Further, it indicates that some kind of change was contemplated as early as 1706 in the "Streets or Lands" of the market place which at the same time was to be enlarged. Finally, it will be noted that the act specified that the Duke of Gloucester Street was to run only from the Capitol to the western boundary of the town and not, as shown on the Bland survey, from the eastern boundary to and through the Capitol itself. The significance of these provisions, as well as how they lend credence to the all-too-brief description furnished by Jones, will be explained shortly.[28]

Later observers of Williamsburg, however, furnish conflicting evidence that the W or W and M pattern of the streets appeared elsewhere. John Ferdinand Dalziel Smyth, a Virginia physician, included this reference in his book on America published in 1784: "There is a whimsical circumstance attends Williamsburg; which is, a part of the town (that has been added to it since it was first built) having the streets laid out in the form of a W."[29] Johann David Schoepf, who visited Williamsburg in 1783, is more precise in locating this feature: "The straight, broad, high-street is almost a mile long; several off-streets running to the south and east, are planned in the form of the letter W."[30] None of the surviving maps of Williamsburg show this feature in either the additions to the city that were made after its founding or "to the south and east" of the Duke of Gloucester Street in the original plat.

In 1816 an anonymous observer, possibly George Tucker who had received his education at the College of William and Mary, included this comment about Nicholson and his strange street plan: "It is said also that, in a whimsical spirit of flattery, he laid out the town in the form of a W. Either however he made his letter very badly, or Time has taken the liberty to rub some part of it out; for its form cannot be very clearly traced at present.[31]

What can we make of these fragmentary and partially conflicting observations concerning the incorporation of the initials of the English monarchs into the street system of the town as established by Francis Nicholson? All previous attempts have been fruitless, and as one recent scholar remarked, "it is not too easy to see how the thing could have been done." [32] There is, however, an explanation fully consistent with all the surviving graphic evidence and which fits exactly with the contemporary observations supplied by Beverley and Jones. Before proceeding to examine it, another possibility that has been considered over the years by those who have attempted to unravel this puzzle deserves attention.

An examination of the Frenchman's Map shows two diagonal roads leading to the western end of the Duke of Gloucester Street, one on either side of the college. Their configuration suggests that they might form part of a letter W or M. If the two streets parallel to the Duke of Gloucester Street were extended to intersect these two diagonals such a letter would indeed be formed. The Frenchman's Map shows an irregular lane as a continuation of the street on the south (France Street) making just such a connection. There are, however, several reasons for rejecting this notion as an adequate solution to the problems. First, extensions of France Street and Prince George Street, the parallel street to the north of the Duke of Gloucester Street, would have been outside the boundaries of the town, and their development would therefore not have been under the jurisdiction of Nicholson and the directors.

Second, and more important, creation of a letter in such a fashion would not have affected the alignment of the Duke of Gloucester Street. It would still, using Jones's words, have been "mathematically streight," and the act of 1706 would not have needed to emphasize that its "Course or Dimensions" "shall not hereafter be altered." Of course, Nicholson could have eliminated a portion of the Duke of Gloucester Street for one or two blocks at that end to emphasize the W or M configuration of France and Prince George Street as extended, but it still would have been "mathematically streight," though short in length.

There are further objections to this theory. Here we must look closer at exactly what is implied in the Beverley and Jones observations. Beverley, it will be recalled, stated in 1705 that Nicholson "mark'd out the Streets in many Places" to form the letter W, and later, in 1722 referred to "the fanciful Forms of W^s^ and M^s^." Taken at face value, these words plainly indicate that there was more than one W or M. Equally illuminating is the statement by Jones that Nicholson "laid out the city . . . in the form of a cypher." If this is taken literally it means that Ws and Ms did not appear as isolated and single letters but were somehow linked together in the form of a monogram. Although this would appear to make the problem more difficult of solution, it actually is the key to its resolution. Certainly a single W or M formed by the diagonal roads leading into town at its western border would not jibe with the descriptions of Beverley and Jones as we have interpreted them.

Perhaps Nicholson planned something far more dramatic, possibly a series of diagonal streets through the town itself such as he had provided in his plan of Annapolis. Looking again at the Frenchman's Map we can observe that if the diagonal entering the town from the southwest is prolonged it strikes almost exactly the center of the south facade of the Governor's Palace. If the other diagonal had been similarly extended it would have reached the intersection of King Street and Ireland Street, the second street south and parallel to the Duke of Gloucester Street, on the north-south axis of the Governor's Palace. Together with the first possibility described above we would here indeed have a "cipher," formed by streets "mark'd out . . . in many Places." Figure 102 is a sketch plan showing how the letters W and M might thus have been formed.[33]

Here again, however, we cannot completely reconcile the results with Jones's observation that, after the plan had been changed, the Duke of Gloucester Street was "mathematically streight." The sketch shows that street following the alignment indicated in the Bland survey, but even its elimination west of Palace Green would not have altered the straightness of its remaining portion running east to the Capitol. Jones's words seemingly imply that the street continued to connect the college with the Capitol but that its alignment deviated from a straight line. Moreover, it seems highly unlikely that Nicholson would simply have omitted a major section of the Duke of Gloucester Street. Its absence at the college end of the town would have required a tortuous approach to the college from the east, and its removal from the plan would have been inconsistent with the strong axial design and general symmetry of the town.

Although it cannot be said categorically that this fails to explain how a W and M were originally incorporated into the street plan, the theory does seem most unlikely. Aside from the lane on the Frenchman's Map continuing France Street, and the two diagonal streets leading to Jamestown and Richmond, there is no graphic evidence to suggest that something of this kind was contemplated. Moreover, these streets lie outside the original town boundaries. Nor does it produce Ws and Ms (in the plural) as Beverley mentioned in his 1722 account. The precisely angled alignments of the Jamestown and Richmond roads as shown on the Frenchman's Map may not have represented either actual facts or surveyed lines. These roads existed as lanes or horsepaths, before the founding of Williamsburg, and it is highly unlikely they exhibited the neat symmetry of the Frenchman's Map. There is a much more tenable hypothesis of the original plan, an explanation that is based on a number of facts and, when it relies on conjecture, requires far less credulity for its support than the one just outlined.

Reproduced in figure 103 is one of four essentially similar manuscript plans of Williamsburg. It is clearly identified as a redrawing in 1867 by Robert A. Lively from the plan prepared by Benjamin Bucktrout in August, 1800. The original Bucktrout plan, now badly faded and stained, appears in figure 104. A reference to this or doubtless a similar drawing appears in a court order of 1841 directing his son, Richard M. Bucktrout, to surrender it to the court. That order recites that "in the year 1804, Benjamin Bucktrout deceased was appointed Surveyor, and directed to enquire into, and report, all the encroachments on the Streets and public lands belonging to the Corporation, and it appearing by his said report that he was in possession of the Plan of the City. . . ."[34]

Two other plans are seen in figures 105 and 106. The first is an undated and unsigned drawing, with some missing portions in the center, which will be referred to as the Unknown Draftsman's plan. Figure 106, also undated and unsigned, is clearly a copy of figure 105, as the names of owners of

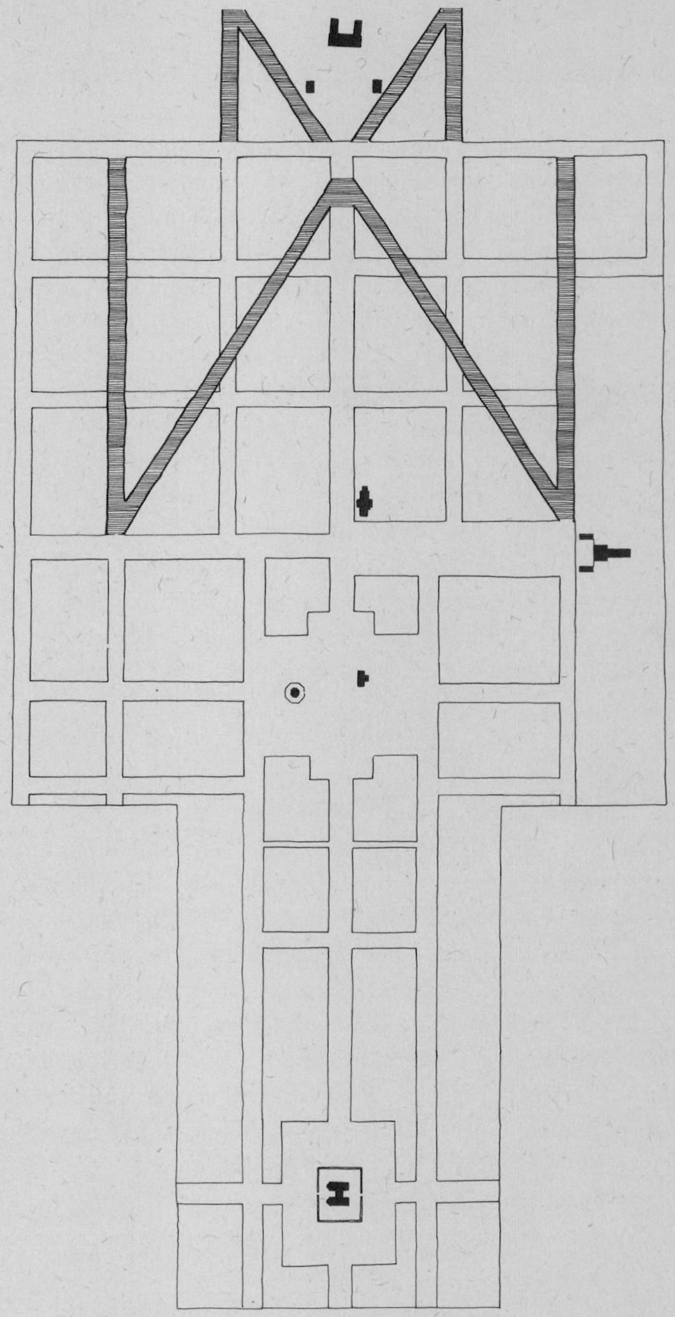

Figure 102. Conjectural Plan of Williamsburg, Virginia, in 1699

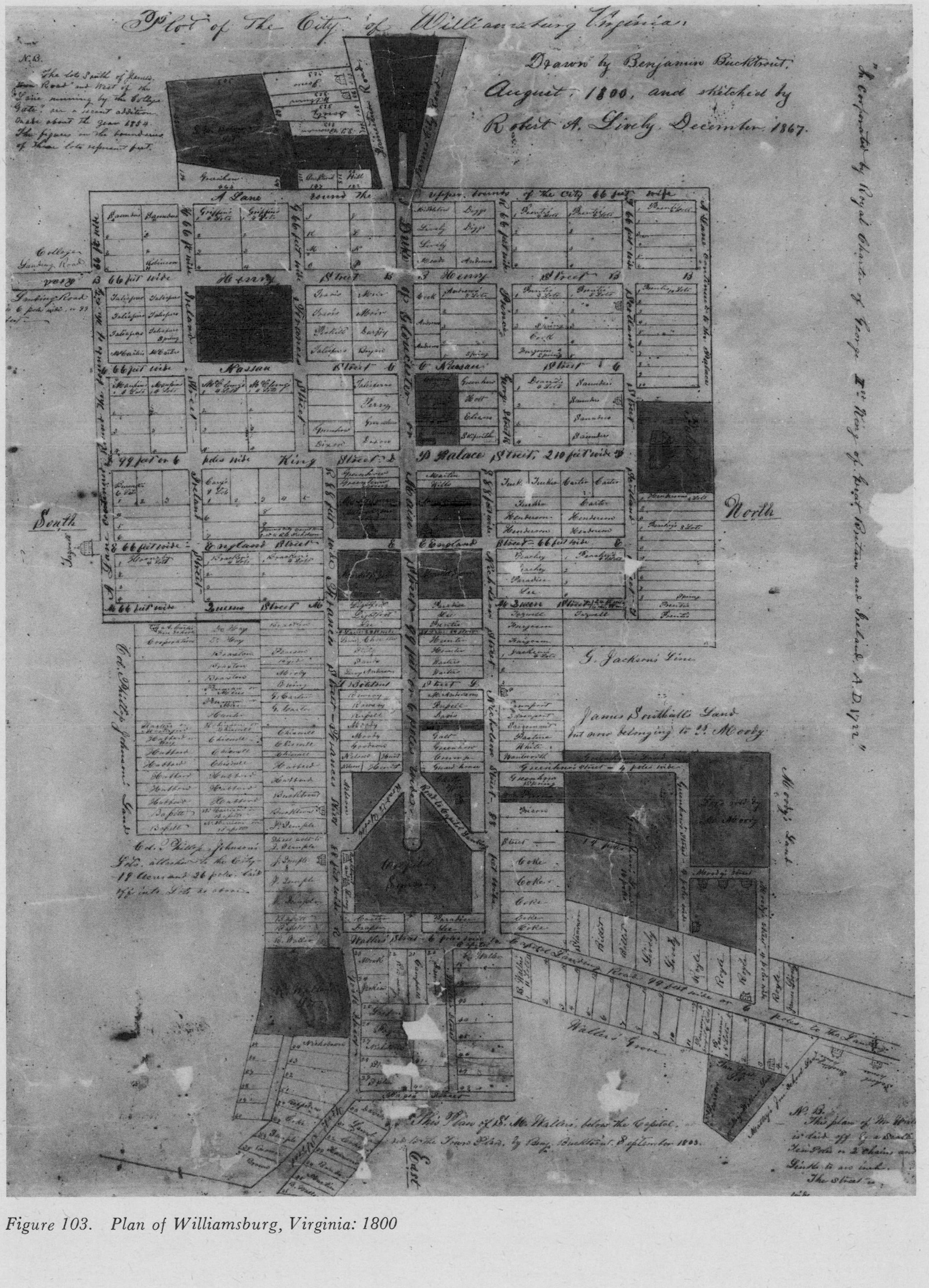

Figure 103. Plan of Williamsburg, Virginia: 1800

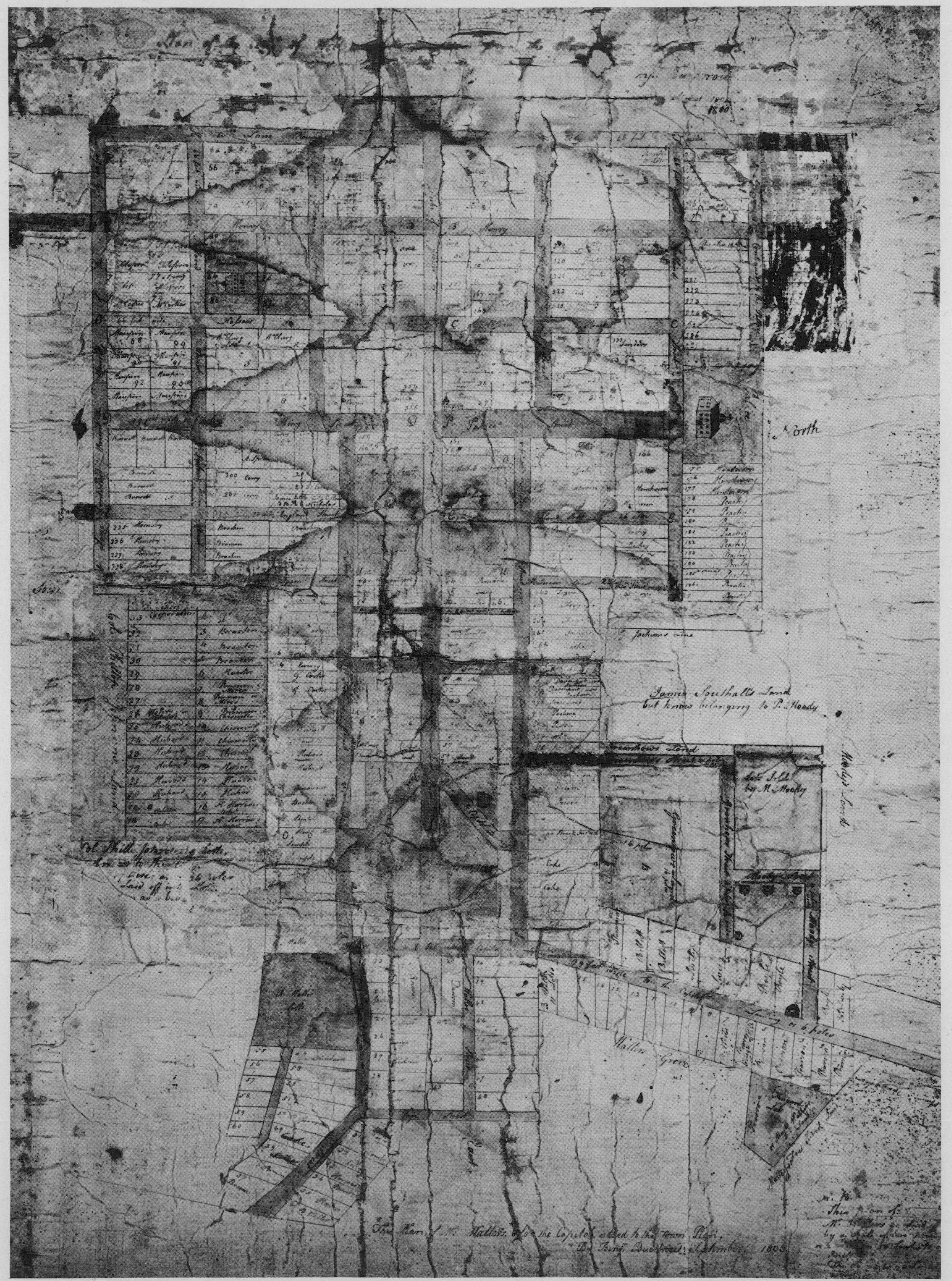

Figure 104. Plan of Williamsburg, Virginia: 1800

Figure 105. Plan of Williamsburg, Virginia: ca. 1800

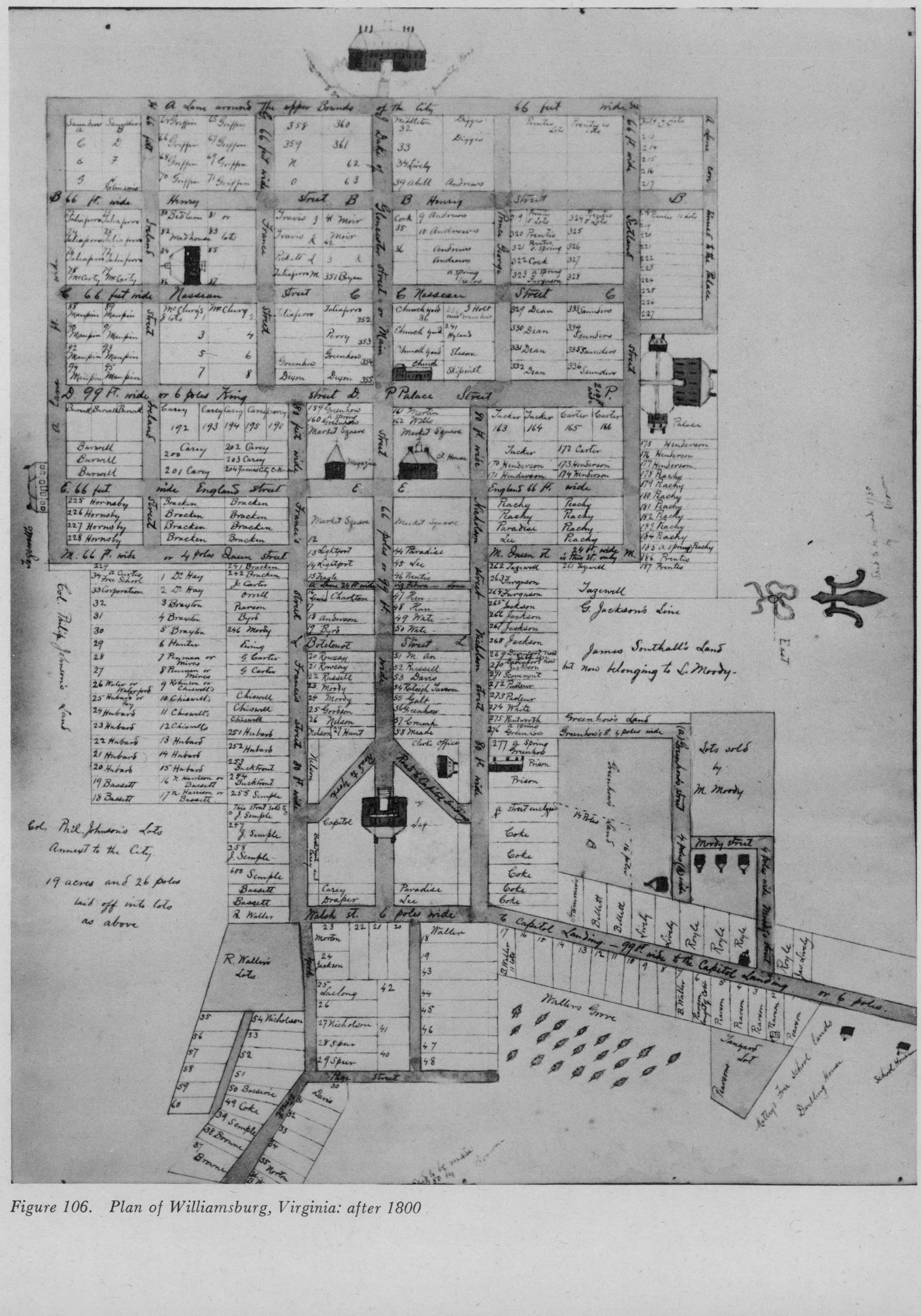

Figure 106. Plan of Williamsburg, Virginia: after 1800

the lots are incomplete on those portions of the drawing corresponding to the missing parts of the Unknown Draftsman's plan.[35]

All four of these drawings contain numerous discrepancies. The most bothersome are those arising from differences between street widths as given in notes on the plans and the dimensions obtained by scaling distances. Nor do the lot dimensions as scaled from the drawings correspond with much precision to the figures obtained from deed descriptions. Neither the Bucktrout original nor the Lively copy shows the Capitol and the outbuildings of the Palace. The Unknown Draftsman's map and its copy show the Duke of Gloucester Street at its eastern end in the same manner as the Bland survey—that is, running through Capitol Square and the Capitol itself. Which of the two "parent" drawings is the older cannot be determined. Both show names of owners known to have purchased lots at the beginning of the nineteenth century, but the written names of owners appear to be in different hands, suggesting that the drawings may be somewhat earlier and were merely brought up to date about 1800.[36]

Despite these peculiarities, which cannot be fully accounted for, it seems reasonable to conclude that both the Bucktrout and the Unknown Draftsman's plan represented attempts to show as accurately as possible the street pattern, the location of open spaces, property lines, and, in writing within the lot boundaries, the ownership of land in the city. If they were not at one time part of the official town records for tax assessment and other purposes, it seems likely they were close copies of similar maps used in this manner. The title on the Bucktrout plan, "Plot of the City of Williamsburg Virginia," and on both the parent plans the marginal annotations, the street width shown in writing, and the color wash to indicate public sites or major undivided private tracts, all indicate their intended purpose as some kind of public record.

All of the drawings show a peculiar feature in the street pattern within Capitol Square. Where the Duke of Gloucester Street enters the square from the west, two streets are shown diverging northeast and southeast to points on the north-south axis of the Capitol and then turning to intersect Francis and Nicholson streets at right angles. Viewed from the east these two short diagonals together with portions of Francis and Nicholson streets would form the letter W. As seen from the west the letter would appear as an M.

At this point we must examine another plan of the town. Reproduced in figure 107 is a redrawing of the street, block, and lot pattern of Williamsburg compiled from records of land sales and archaeological research.[37] Note the openings between the lots on the north and south sides of Capitol Square leading to Francis Street on the south and Nicholson Street on the north. Both are five poles or 82½ feet wide and are located exactly on the north-south axis of the Capitol. With the Duke of Gloucester Street entering Capitol Square at the mid-points of its east and west sides, the composition formed is the classical public square that was such a prominent feature of Renaissance town planning. The square measures twenty-eight by thirty-five poles or 462 by 575½ feet. Its form was similar to but somewhat larger than the Bloomsbury Square that Nicholson planned for Annapolis. (That earlier square, not elongated as at Williamsburg, measured approximately 360 feet on each side.)

The Bucktrout plan and its companion drawings, however, suggest the departures from established practice that Nicholson introduced in order to include the letter W or M. Further, following the lead of Jones, whose use of the word "cypher" is so suggestive, we can hypothesize that the original Nicholson plan included a mirror image of this letter on the east side of Capitol Square. Figure 108 shows how this appeared—with hatching added to emphasize how the W and M monogram would be formed.

There are two pieces of direct evidence to support the notion that the diagonal streets on the western side of Capitol Square were duplicated on the east. Figure 109 is a portion of the government topographical survey completed in the Williamsburg area in 1904. At this time the Capitol no longer existed. Note, however, the pairs of diagonal streets forming the diamond pattern around its former site at the eastern end of the city. Faint traces of irregular eastern diagonals existed as late in 1927, as the aerial photograph reproduced in figure 110 reveals. By that year the western diagonals had been pushed somewhat eastward by encroachments made on the square over the years, and they are seen here in modified form. Even greater changes had occurred in the other pair. The more southerly can be seen clearly enough, but its alignment is much different from our hypothetical sketch plan in figure 108. The remaining road is barely visible but can just be made out.[38]

Other evidence supporting the concept of two pairs of diagonals rather than one stems from the dimensions of Capitol Square and the brick wall enclosing the immediate Capitol grounds. It will be recalled that the act

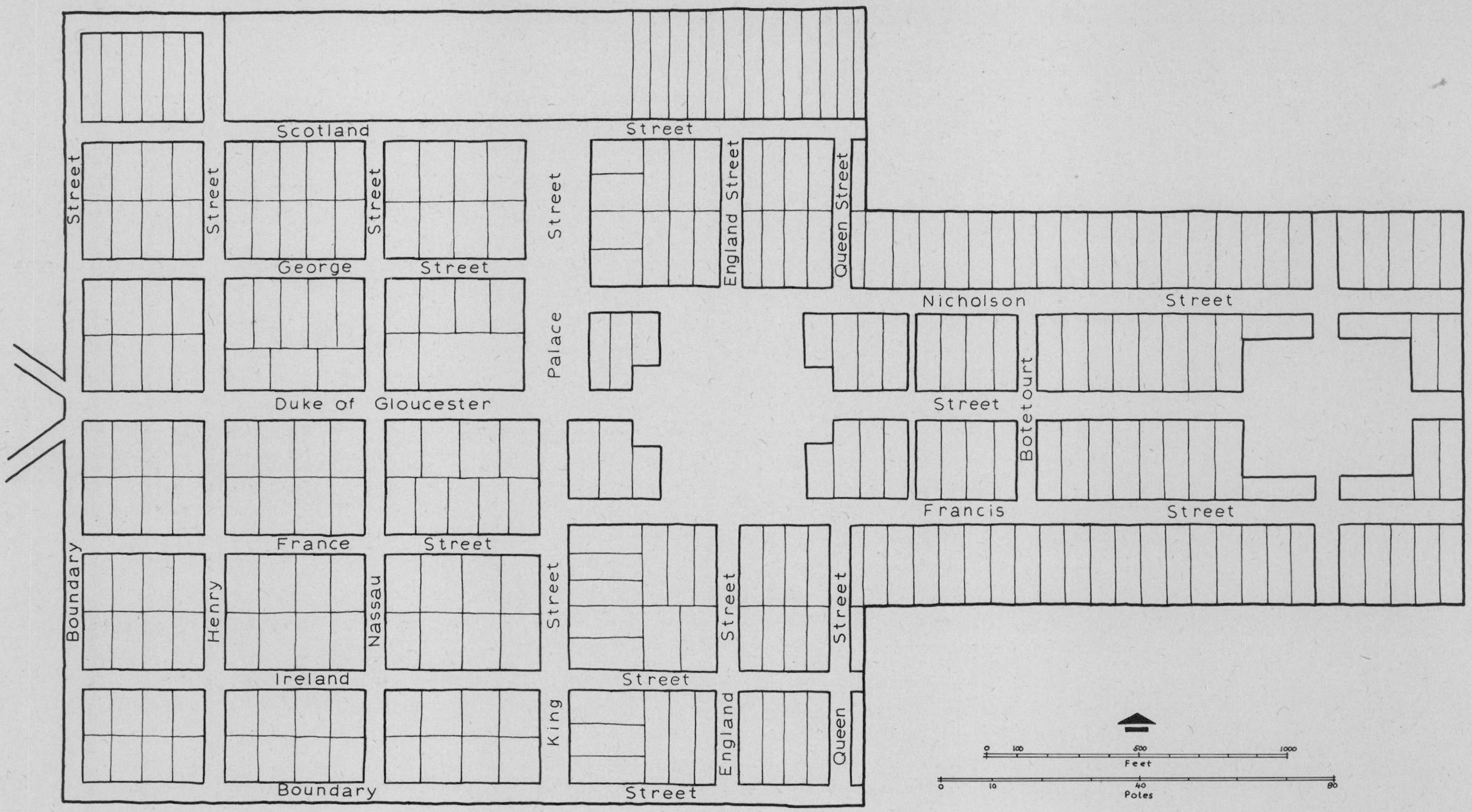

Figure 107. Plan of Williamsburg, Virginia: ca. 1750

of 1699 specified the dimensions of 475 feet on each side. As defined by land sales around its perimeter, however, the square measures twenty-eight poles north-south and thirty-five poles east-west, or 462 by 575½ feet. This alteration from the size specified in the act was certainly no surveyor's error. It may have resulted from the necessity to shift the site of the Capitol eastward because of the low ground at the location shown in Bland's survey, but if that were the case why was not the square simply moved a corresponding distance?

The reason why the square was lengthened one hundred feet in its east-west dimension may have been to allow both pairs of diagonals to be

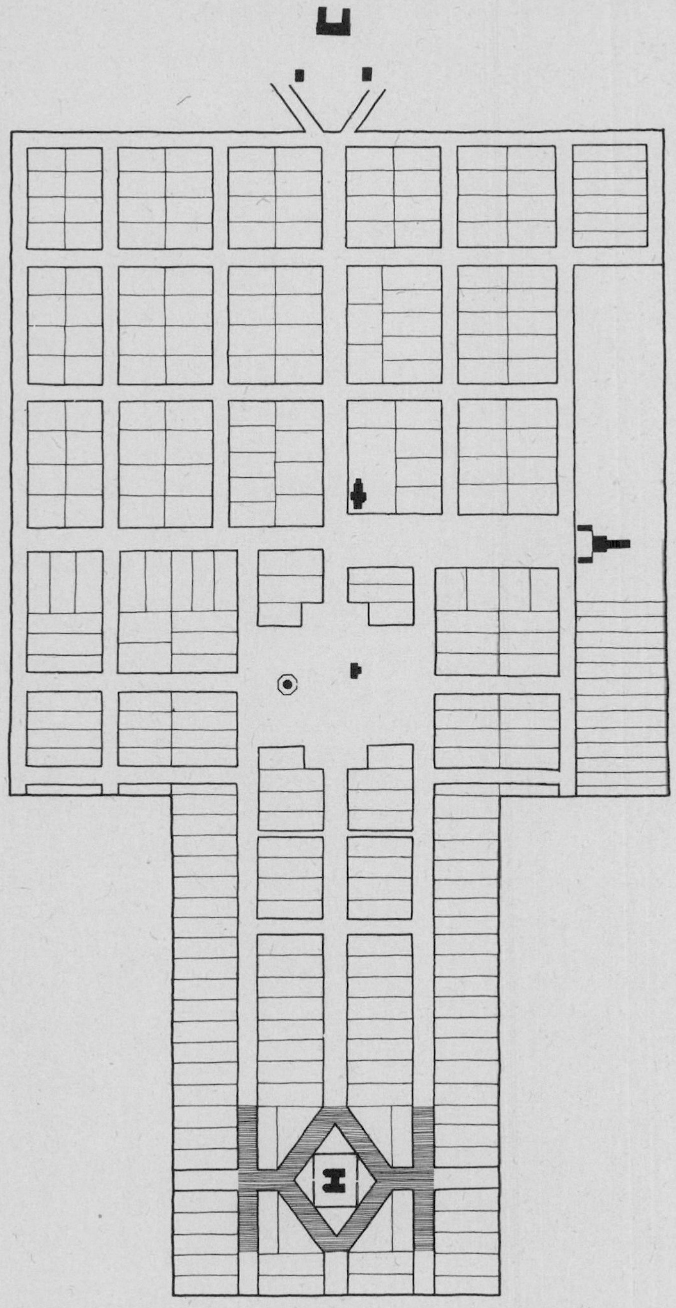

Figure 108. Conjectural Plan of Williamsburg, Virginia, in 1699

introduced into the plan without encroaching unduly on the immediate surroundings of the Capitol. On May 9, 1704, the House of Burgesses authorized the Capitol to "be inclosed with a good Brick Wall . . . distant Sixty foot from the ffronts of the East and West Buildings and ffifty foot from the North and South end of the said building with four Suitable Entrances into the same."[39] The wall as constructed measured eleven by thirteen poles or 181½ by 214½ feet. It, too, was longer in its east-west extent, but the ratio of length to width differs somewhat from that of Capitol Square.

The drawing reproduced in figure 111 shows how this smaller rectangle just fits within the diamond area enclosed by the two pairs of diagonal streets. One of two things seems to have occurred. Either the street pattern had been established first, which seems likely, and then the wall was given its dimensions to fit; or, after the wall was authorized, Nicholson realized that diagonal streets could be introduced to connect the two ends of the Duke of Gloucester Street with Francis and Nicholson streets.[40]

The fact that the early nineteenth century plans show only the western diagonals may indicate that after 1706 the other pair was officially eliminated. If so, then the streets and lanes appearing in figures 109 and 110 represent only informal traveled ways. But the curious alteration in the size and shape of Capitol Square is a strong hint that the original plan included both sets of diagonal streets laid out in such a way as to create a W and M monogram. Moreover, if one looks again at figure 96 showing the highly unusual first plan for the Capitol itself it can be seen without much imagination how the proposed cross gallery incorporated into the connection between the two main wings would have created a small monogram within the larger one formed by the streets in and surrounding the square.

If all this is true, why does the Frenchman's Map fail to show even one pair of diagonals in Capitol Square? There would seem to be two possibilities. One is that after 1706 the entire monogram was deleted from the city plan but that somehow toward the end of the eighteenth century the western pair was reintroduced. Or, the western diagonals may have existed only as paper streets on a map but were not graded or otherwise improved until sometime after 1782 when the Frenchman's Map was drawn.

The other explanation is simply that the Frenchman's Map was not a complete survey, either of recorded property lines or, in the case of streets,

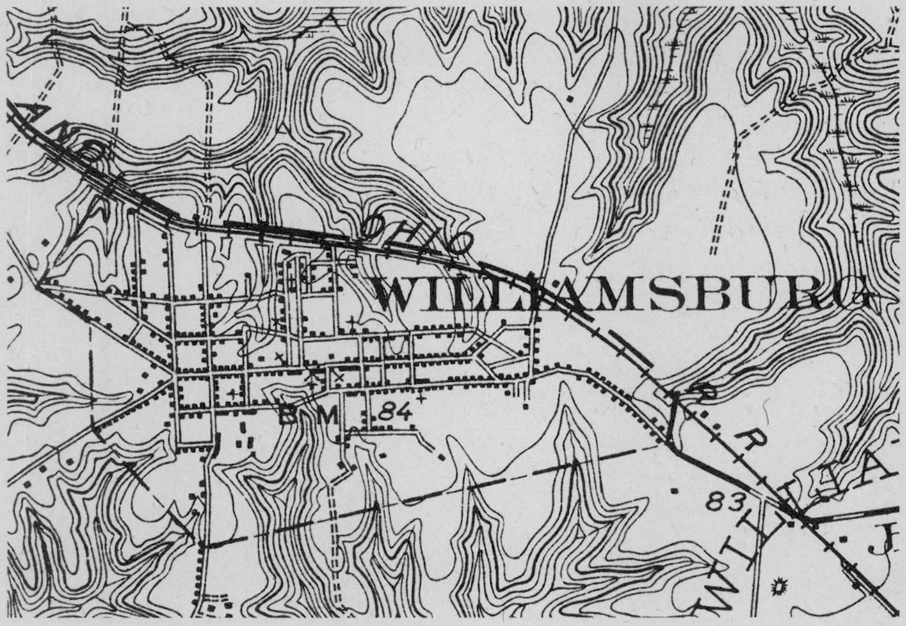

Figure 109. Map of Williamsburg, Virginia, and Vicinity: 1905

of all traveled ways. It does not, for example, show a continuation of the Duke of Gloucester Street through Market Square, yet it is almost inconceivable that there was not at that time a well-defined thoroughfare leading through this important square past the Magazine and Courthouse. The absence of the diagonal streets from a drawing done without survey instruments and bearing the notation "levé au pas," a clear warning to anyone using it that it was but a paced sketch map, is understandable and not inconsistent with the theory we have been pursuing.

There are ample grounds, therefore, for believing that we have discovered the location and form of a W and M monogram as originally planned by Nicholson. We have not, however, completely solved the problem if we accept Beverley's reference to "W^s and M^s" as accurate. Further, even if a very short portion of the Duke of Gloucester Street had been eliminated within Capitol Square and replaced by the pairs of diagonals, it is questionable whether this would have caused Jones to comment that after the plan's alteration the street was once again "mathematically streight." Indeed, this portion of the original plan may not have been changed at all. It is necessary to look for still another place where Nicholson might have located a cipher composed of a W and M. To follow up the brief but suggestive clue left by Jones, this second monogram should involve some significant change in alignment of the Duke of Gloucester Street.

Several indications point to the area of Market Square as the probable location. First, it is a space similar in size and shape to Capitol Square. Second, the act of 1706 empowered the directors "to enlarge the Market Place and to alter any of the Streets or Lands thereof where the same are found inconvenient." The most straightforward interpretation of the clause is that it referred to the streets and lands of Market Square and not to

Figure 110. Aerial Photograph of Capitol Square in Williamsburg, Virginia: 1927

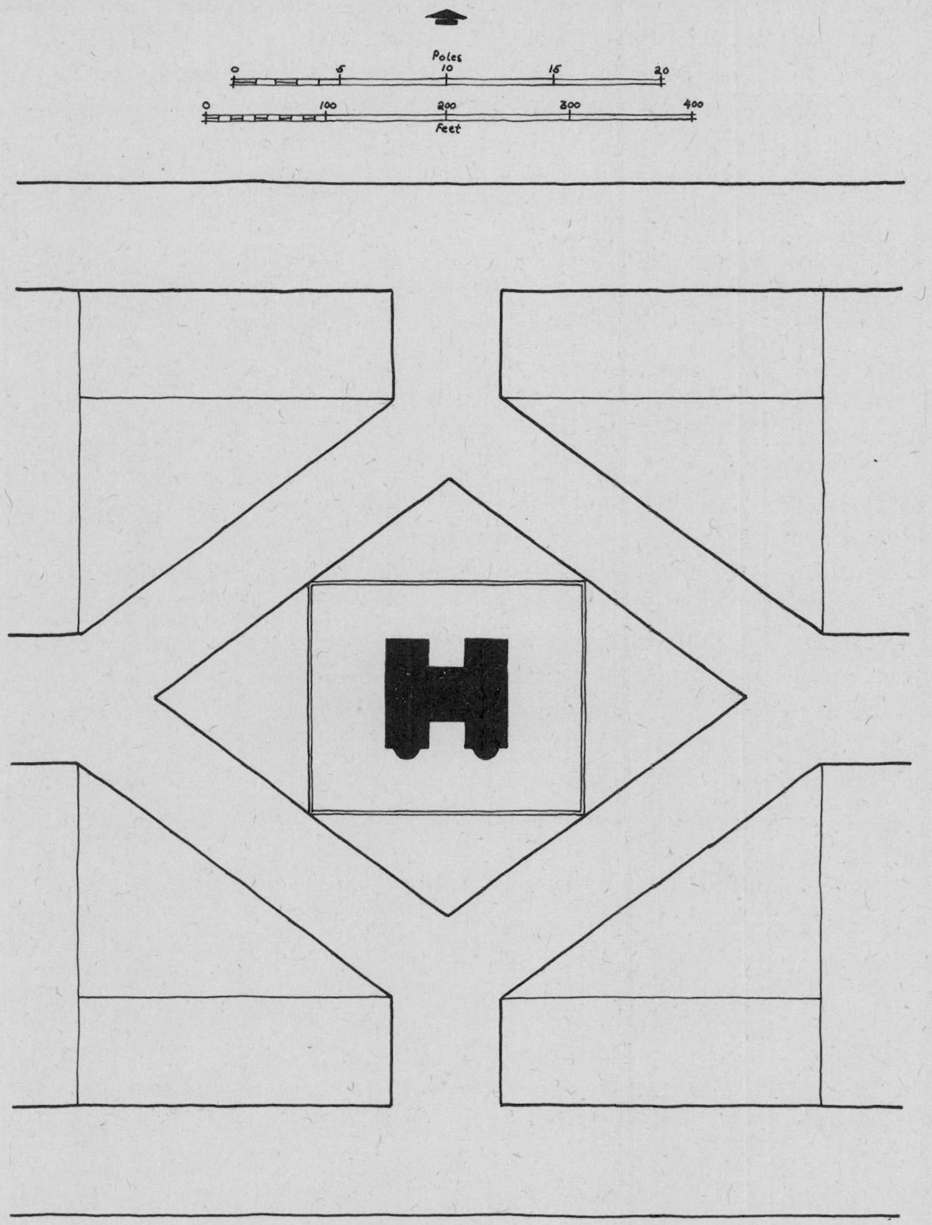

Figure 111. Conjectural Plan of Capitol Square in Williamsburg, Virginia: 1699-1704

streets and lands generally.[41] Plainly, some kind of change in the original plan was contemplated at this location.

The third bit of evidence pointing to Market Square as the site of the second monogram can be seen in the peculiar configuration of this open space as shown in figure 107. Note that Market Square is really not square at all. Where the Duke of Gloucester Street enters from the east and west the four corner lots have been reduced in length. One effect of this is to provide partial frontage on Market Square for each of the four lots adjacent to these four shallower lots.

If we draw straight lines connecting the Market Square corners of these adjacent lots and extend them diagonally toward either Francis or Nicholson streets we find that they intersect prolonged lines of North and South England streets exactly at the north and south boundaries of the square. Within the diamond-shaped space that results, other lines parallel to the first create a pattern almost exactly duplicating that produced by the hypothetical monogram we have described at Capitol Square. Figure 112 shows the street pattern that would be formed, omitting that portion of the Duke of Gloucester Street between the east and west boundaries of Market Square. Once again, hatching emphasizes the back-to-back W and M that would be formed as a cipher or monogram.

There is strong supporting documentation showing not only that this or something quite similar was once a part of the Williamsburg plan but that it had its origin as early as 1700. In September of that year the trustees conveyed to Philip Ludwell one of the four short lots on Market Square. These lots were platted only eleven poles deep rather than the sixteen poles of the other lots fronting the Duke of Gloucester Street from Capitol Square to Palace Green.[42] Ludwell's lot, purchased with two others of normal size to the east, lay at the northeast corner of Market Square. The reduced depth of this and the other lots would have made it possible to divert the Duke of Gloucester Street into two pairs of diagonal streets around the diamond in the middle of Market Square and to form the W and M monogram or cipher.

That there was such a diagonal street across this corner of Market Square is revealed by a lease granted to John Blair by the Court of Directors of Williamsburg on June 2, 1746. This represented an authorized encroachment on the market grounds west of the original Ludwell lot. The description of the parcel is confusing, since the starting point on the Duke of

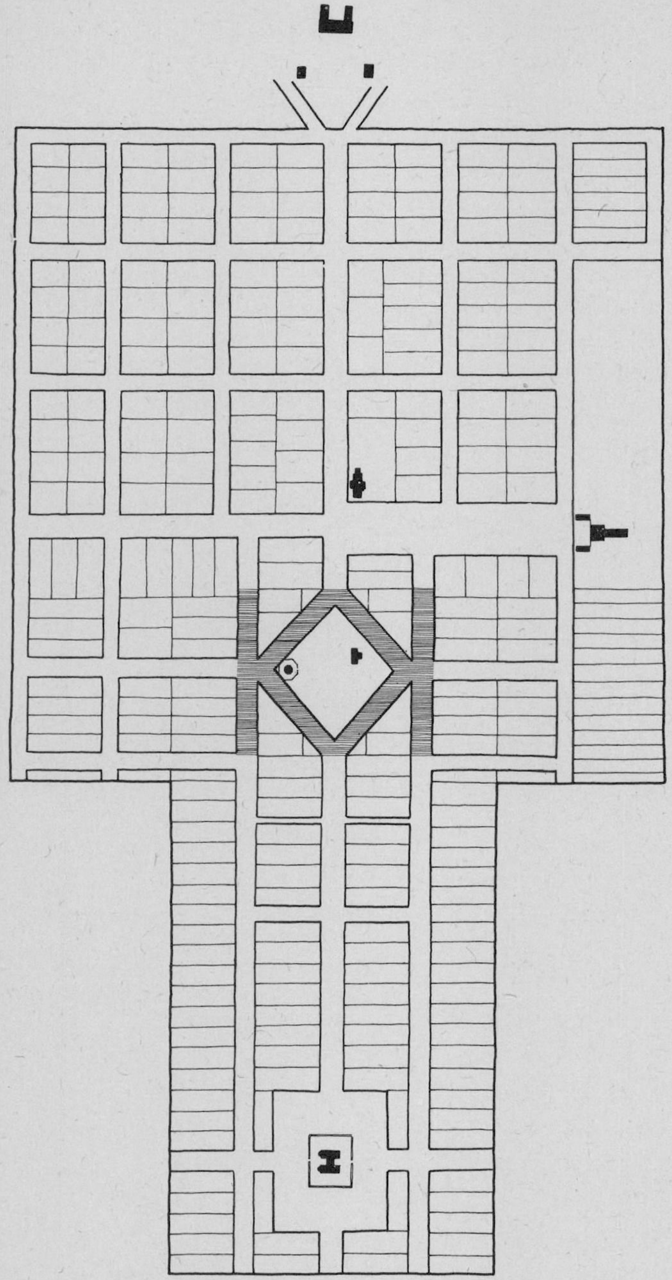

Figure 112. Conjectural Plan of Williamsburg, Virginia, in 1699

Gloucester Street within the square is not precisely located. It was to begin "at the East end of The ground leased to Mathew Moody," the occupant of another parcel still further west within the original Market Square. The bounds then ran east along the Duke of Gloucester Street forty-eight feet. The western boundary was a line north eighty feet "near a Road which lyes about S.E." Then the line apparently was to run easterly a short distance to the road, "Thence along the Road til a S. Line will hit The end of The Said 48. feet." [43]

It is, of course, this reference to a road "which lyes [runs] about S.E." that is important—a street cutting diagonally through the northeastern quadrant of Market Square connecting the Duke of Gloucester Street with Nicholson Street. By 1746 it may have been only a dusty lane, the remnant of Nicholson's monogram, but the road was still recognized in the deed as a right-of-way.

Written documentation of a similar nature is lacking for the other three lots and for the diagonal streets that doubtless touched their corners. If any such materials existed they were probably destroyed with the burning of the James City County records in Richmond during the Civil War. The Ludwell deed, fortunately, was among those preserved by York County, which at one time included part of the city.

The location of the Magazine and its enclosing wall, however, supply the missing evidence. Note in figure 112 how the inner lines of the pair of diagonal streets running through the southern half of Market Square coincide exactly with two faces of the octagonal wall around the Magazine. This suggests that at the time Spotswood erected the Magazine the two streets still existed in fact although the official plan of the town may have been changed as early as 1706. Spotswood apparently located the Magazine and its enclosure as close as possible to the apex of the two roads in order to retain most of Market Square as an open space.

If it cannot be fully proved, this hypothesis explaining the Ws and Ms taking the form of a cipher in Nicholson's original plan is at least completely consistent with all surviving maps as well as with observations and descriptions furnished by persons in Williamsburg during the first two decades of its existence.[44] External evidence also supports the theory. Nicholson employed diagonal streets as the basis for his design of Annapolis. It would seem strange indeed, when the opportunity arose within so short a time for him to lay out another town, that he would be satisfied with a

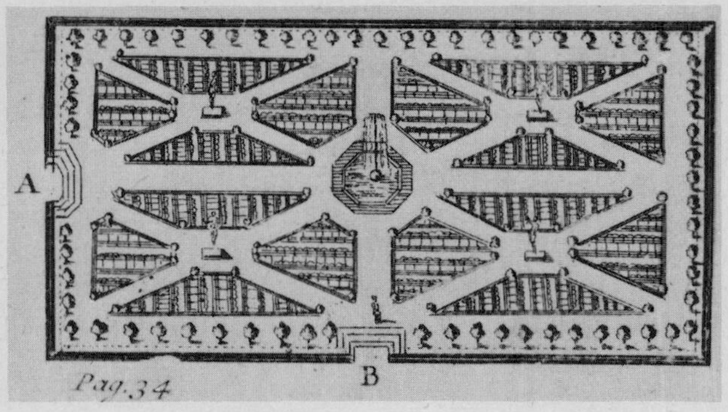

Figure 113. Plan of a Garden: 1693

plan based entirely on the gridiron system. His plan for Annapolis reveals an unconventional mind not content with usual solutions to such problems. The use of several pairs of diagonal streets to form the monograms that were certainly part of his plan for Williamsburg would not have appeared to him to be at all eccentric or unusual, however strange they might have seemed to less sophisticated Virginians at the beginning of the eighteenth century.

Nor would it have been out of character for him to have disregarded the straight alignment of the Duke of Gloucester Street as shown on the Bland survey. Nicholson recognized few if any restraints on the authority of a royal governor. His second administration in Virginia was marked by vigorous assertions of personal power and, at times, of actual threats of physical violence against those who refused to do his bidding.[45] It is not likely that he would have hesitated to interpret the act of 1699 as giving him ample authority to establish the street pattern as he saw fit.[46]

Finally, there is one other piece of evidence to consider. In Chapter VI we considered how the designs for reconstructing London in 1666, prepared by Christopher Wren and John Evelyn, may have served as possible sources for Nicholson in his plan of Annapolis. Both Wren's plan and the third and final plan by Evelyn, as reproduced in figure 18 (Chapter I) combined major diagonal avenues with a system of less important gridiron streets in an application of baroque planning principles. We have also seen the strong resemblances of one portion of Annapolis to a garden design reproduced in Evelyn's translation of Jean de La Quintinie's *The Compleat Gard'ner.*

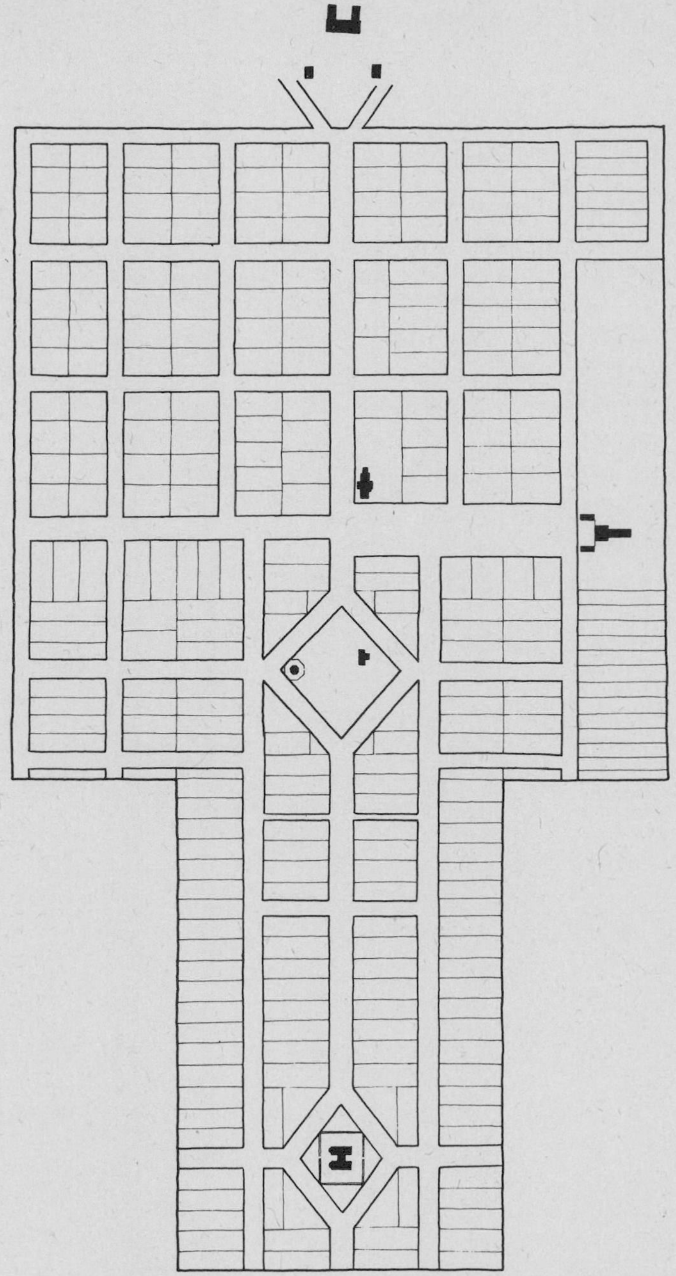

Figure 114. Conjectural Plan of Williamsburg, Virginia, in 1699

A closer look at Evelyn's proposals for rebuilding London as well as at the material in his translation of *The Compleat Gard'ner* also reveals a number of similarities with Nicholson's original plan of Williamsburg.

In figure 85 (Chapter VI), Evelyn's first plan for London as engraved for publication in 1756, it is possible to trace several Ws and Ms interlocked as monograms in the street pattern. Near the center of the plan can be seen a diamond-shaped space with the four streets entering it at its corners. This form for an urban square is exceedingly rare. Nor in exactly that form does it seem to have been used extensively in garden layout.[47] It *does* appear, however, in Evelyn's version of *The Compleat Gard'ner* which Nicholson owned. Figure 113 shows the illustration as published in 1693 for a garden design with diagonal paths leading to the corners of rectangular open spaces. Again, while it may be mere coincidence, each of the four sections of the garden forms a W and M monogram.

We have already reviewed in Chapter VI how Nicholson, before taking up his duties as governor of Maryland, might well have come into personal contact with Wren and Evelyn in London. Of the two it would seem that both at Annapolis and Williamsburg it was Evelyn who had the greater influence. It may be significant, given the width of the Duke of Gloucester Street, that Evelyn had written in his proposals for rebuilding London that "I would allow none of the principal streets less than an hundred foot in breadth."[48]

Nicholson's original plan, reconstructed according to the theories described above, is shown in figure 114. It was this city plan that was altered sometime during or after 1706 to make the Duke of Gloucester Street once again "mathematically streight." Perhaps both pairs of diagonals at Capitol Square were allowed to remain, although the case for the retention of the pair to the east is far from conclusive. The western pair may have existed for a time only as paper streets—mere lines on the official map—rather than as well-defined and fully developed thoroughfares.

In reverting to a more regular and conventional design, the directors of the town and the members of the assembly under whom they served thus obliterated the most unusual and, until now, the most baffling feature of Francis Nicholson's plan for Williamsburg. Yet the city's plan still retained a formal grace and distinctive character that shaped its pattern of growth during the eighteenth century.

VIII. *The Development of Williamsburg as the Capital of Colonial Virginia*

When Francis Louis (or Franz Ludwig) Michel, a young Swiss traver, visited Williamsburg in the spring of 1702, he saw only an embryonic town. He noted that it was "a large place" but added significantly that the location was only "where a city is intended and staked out to be built." There was not really much to be observed, for the initial pace of town development was leisurely. In addition to the buildings existing before 1699, Michel mentioned the "State House, together with the residence of the Bishop, some stores and houses of gentlemen, and also eight ordinaries or inns, together with the magazine."[1] At this stage of the town's development it must have resembled one of the many port towns of the previous century, created by legislative fiat, that rarely exceeded more than a few structures erected by adventuresome speculators on lots newly staked out by the county surveyors. As the seat of colonial government, however, Williamsburg was destined for a more promising future.

Construction of the Capitol began on August 8, 1701, with the laying of its foundation.[2] Work proceeded slowly despite the urgings of Governor Nicholson during the following years. Apparently at the time of Michel's visit the first floor alone had been completed, for only this portion, together with an outline ground plan, appear in the Swiss visitor's sketch reproduced in figure 115. The elevation shown by Michel is from the south and reveals the rounded ends of the two main wings connected by the central portion of the building. The building at the bottom of this sketch is the old Bruton Parish Church shown surrounded by a brick wall enclosing the churchyard. At the top, flanking the plan of the Capitol are crude drawings of two dwellings. That on the left is identified as the home of a merchant, and the other was intended to represent a farmer's residence.

Michel prepared a rather more detailed drawing of the College of William and Mary (figure 116). In 1702 this was easily the most imposing building in the new town and, aside from a few of the larger plantation houses in Virginia, must have far exceeded all other structures in the colony in size and elegance. This drawing is all the more valuable because it is the only record of the original appearance of the college building, gutted by fire during the night of October 29, 1705. In large part the massive walls survived not only the flames of 1705 but also a second fire in 1859 and a third in 1862, as well as the considerable alterations that accompanied each rebuilding. Thus, much of the fabric of the Wren Building today, restored in 1930 to the appearance it had from 1716 until 1859, dates from the initial construction.

The year of the first college fire marked also the completion of the Capitol, although the council had met for the first time in the partially finished building in the fall of 1703.[3] It was, therefore, only for a few months that the two major structures terminating the chief thoroughfare of the town existed for Governor Nicholson to admire their place in the plan he had devised. His recall in 1705 removed him from further supervision of the town's development and provided an opportunity for important modification in his original plan for the new capital city.

Yet in the five years of Nicholson's administration he was able to accomplish a number of projects to further the growth of the town. Payment to

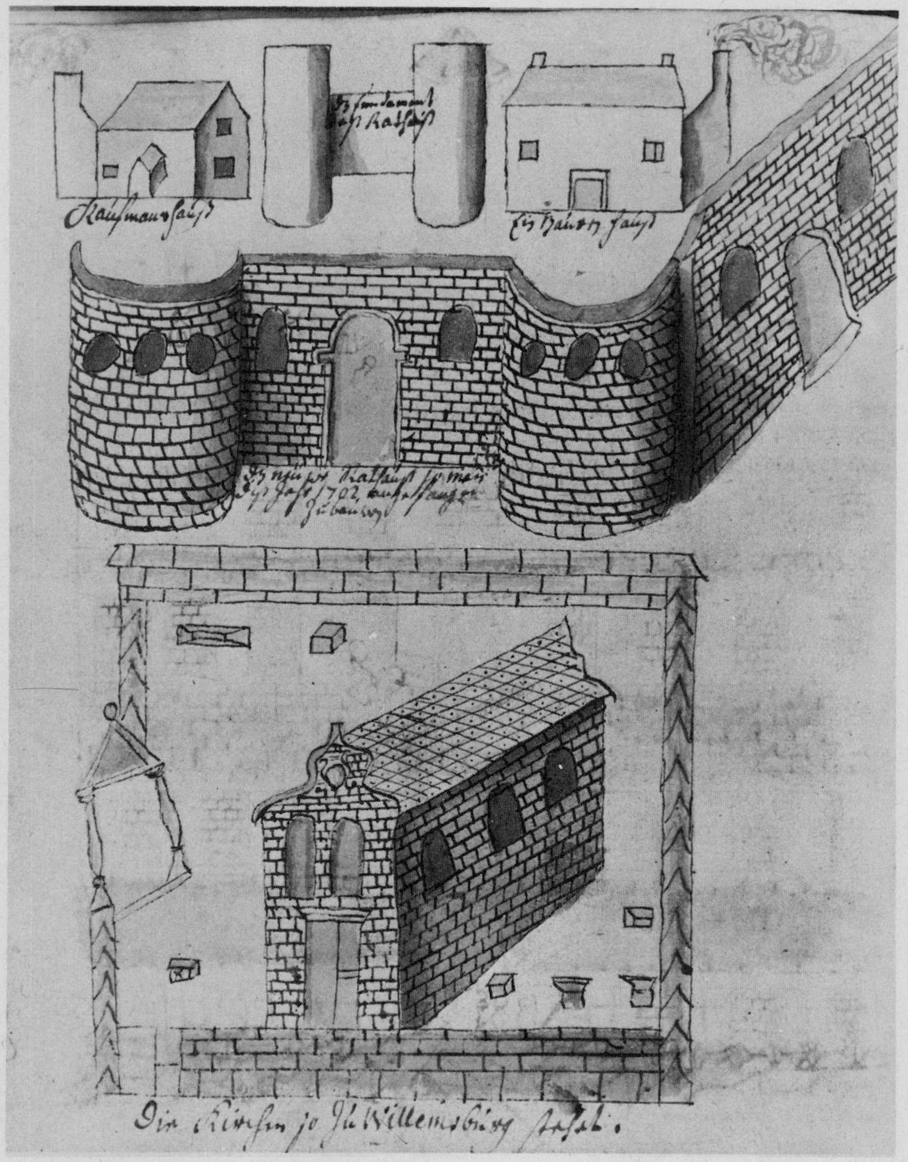

Figure 115. *Views of the Capitol and Bruton Church and a Plan of the Capitol at Williamsburg, Virginia: 1702*

Figure 116. *View of the College of William and Mary in Williamsburg, Virginia: 1702*

the original owners of the land taken for the new capital was obviously important. As lots were surveyed and sold, funds became available for this purpose. The governor and the directors on August 25, 1701, requested the House of Burgesses to approve payment for the town lands, and the following month the assembly authorized the sum of £283 5s.[4]

Some problems evidently arose over the payments, for on May 20, 1702, the council sent over to the House of Burgesses a message pointing out that some of the proprietors of the land on which the city of Williamsburg was laid out had refused to accept the money allowed them. Accordingly, the council suggested that the burgesses make sure this circumstance did not discourage anyone from taking up lots and building in the city. At the same time the council recommended that the small outbuildings belonging to Mr. John Page "standing in the street called *Gloucester* Street, leading from the College to the Capitol, be paid for, and pulled downe that so the said Street may be regularly laid out."

To Nicholson this must have seemed particularly urgent, since the Duke of Gloucester Street was such an essential element in the town plan. Yet it took two years for the removal of the Page buildings. The governor renewed the earlier recommendation in April, 1704, when he requested the burgesses to "give Directions that the old House belonging to Mr. *John Page* standing in the middle of *Gloucester* Street he pulled downe that the Prospect of the Street between the Capitol and Colledge may be cleer and that you take Care to pay what you shall judge those Houses to be worth." A week later the burgesses approved compensation of £3 to be paid to Mr. Page for "four old Houses and Oven," ordering Henry Cary, who was in charge of the construction of the Capitol, to do the demolition work. The workmen were directed to salvage the bricks from these structures and to "lay . . . [them] . . . out of the Street on the Lott of the said *John Page*."[6]

While the Capitol was under construction the General Assembly met at the college.[7] This must have been a lively place and one made more so by the colorful character and language of Nicholson. One account of 1702 describes how during a discussion of payment for work carried out on a ship which had put into a Virginia port

> the Governour flew out into such a Passion against the Commissioners of the Navy calling them all the basest Names that the Tongue of Man could express, & with such a Noise, that the People downe in the lower Roomes caime running up Stairs, & likewise Captain *Dove, Roffey* & *Midleton,* who lay in a Roome some Distance, caime running out of their Beds in their Shirts, the latter with out his wooden Leg holding himselfe by the Wall beleiveing that the Colledge had been on Fire . . . but upon Enquirey of the Ocasion, could but admire at the Folly & Passion of the Governour, saying *Bedlam* was the fittest Place for such a Man.[8]

This was not the only recorded example of the ferocity of Nicholson's temper and the searing language he employed at frequent intervals.[9] Under the best of circumstances frictions between the General Assembly and the royal governors were fairly common. With a man of Nicholson's intemperate passion serving as the chief executive, minor differences over policy could develop into substantial conflicts. This appears to have occurred over the construction of a suitable residence for the governor of Virginia. Not only was this needed as a matter of convenience, but it would serve as still another major focal point in the urban plan for the new city.

Despite frequent urging by Nicholson, the assembly resisted attempts to secure an appropriation for the purpose. One can imagine that Nicholson's comments on this matter, at least in private, were forceful if not explosive. In addition to his own desires, he was being pressed from England to carry out such a project.[10]

Nicholson had informed the assembly of his instructions on this matter when he arrived in Virginia, but no action was taken at that time. When the governor planned the city he selected a site for a future official residence. We know that it was the one eventually developed for that purpose or one very close by. In the spring of 1701 the council discussed the desirability of acquiring a tract of land outside the town boundaries to augment the area within the town designated for the residence of the governor. This was referred to as "about fifty or sixty acres adjoining to the Lotts assigned in the City of Williams Burgh for a house to be built on for the residence of the Governor, which land belongs to Henry Tyler."

Tyler's land, an area of sixty-three acres, lay immediately to the north of the lots at the end of what is now Palace Green. Nicholson repeatedly urged the burgesses to authorize construction of the residence and also to purchase the additional land. The governor maintained that the necessary funds should be supplied from tax revenues. The burgesses insisted that "This country is not in a capacity at this time to undergo the charge of building a house for the Governor," and that both this cost and the additional sum needed for the purchase of Tyler's land should "be defrayed out of H.M. Revenue appropriated for the maintenance and support of this Government and the contingent charges."[11] The best that Nicholson could accomplish was the acquisition of the sixty-three-acre tract, which on September 4, 1701, the council ordered bought from Tyler for £63. But the planner of Williamsburg retired from the scene before any work on the official residence was finally agreed to by the stubborn burgesses.

He was more successful, however, in securing the erection of a jail. In August, 1701, the assembly included in an act that provided further instructions for the erection of the Capitol a section specifying that a "Publick Prison be built near and convenient to the Siting of the Generall Court for the Reception of Criminals of both Sexes."[12] This building was to be twenty by thirty feet, the same size prescribed by the act of 1699 as the minimum size for houses on the Duke of Gloucester Street.

The jail was located to the north and almost directly opposite the Capitol. Its exact placement and orientation seem strange. The Frenchman's Map shows this structure, as subsequently enlarged from its original size, squarely in the right-of-way of Nicholson Street. Perhaps Governor Nicholson intended it to be so placed, similar to the location of the Capitol in the Duke of Gloucester Street as shown in the Bland survey. It is conceivable that when its first inmates were placed in the jail the street did continue through on each side. Governor Spotswood in 1711 and 1722 added cells for debtors and quarters for the jailer. Nicholson Street may then, as now, have been curved around the building to the south to allow greater freedom for the passage of persons, horses, and vehicles.[13]

Perhaps topography influenced the location of the jail as it had the Capitol. Branches of the same creek that had required the movement of the Capitol site some two hundred feet eastward came together west of the jail. It stood, therefore, on somewhat higher and dryer ground than if it had been placed beyond the north side of Nicholson Street. Hugh Jones referred to the structure as "a strong sweet prison for criminals" and mentioned that it also contained "on the other side of an open court another for debtors."[14] A distinguished inmate in 1779, Lieutenant Governor Henry Hamilton, who had been captured at Vincennes by George Rogers Clark, found the building strong enough but hardy "sweet," as he recorded in his *Journal:*

> We had for our domicile *a place* not ten feet square by actual measurement, the only light admitted was thro' the grating of the door which opened into the Court . . . , the light and air are nearly excluded for the bars of this grating were from three to four inches thick—In one corner of this snug mansion was fixed a kind of Throne which had been of use to such miscreants as us for 60 years past, and in certain points of wind renderd the air truly Mephytic.[15]

Possibly Nicholson's last action to promote and guide the development of the city he had planned was to draft the legislation passed late in 1705 after the governor had departed. This legislation modified somewhat the original conditions of lot ownership as first laid down in the act of 1699. The purchaser of two lots on the Duke of Gloucester Street no longer was required to construct a house of the required minimum dimensions on each of them but could retain title by building on one or both lots "one House fifty Foot long and twenty Foot broad," or "one Brick House or framed House with two Stacks of Brick Chimney's & Cellers under the whole House bricked forty Foot long & twenty Foot broad." The owner of one or two lots on the Duke of Gloucester Street and one or more lots on one of the other streets had only to construct one or more framed houses "as will make five Hundred square Feet superficiall Measure on the Ground Plat for every Lott," or, if the houses were of brick or framed with brick cellars and chimneys, "four Hundred Square Feet . . . for every Lot."

All persons owning lots on the Duke of Gloucester Street were required to "inclose the said Lotts or half Acres with a Wall Pales or Post and Rails within six Months after the Building which the Law required to be erected." Failure to meet this requirement was to be punished either by a forfeiture of title or the payment of "five Shillings a Month for every Lot or half Acre so long as the same shall remaine without a Wall Pales or Rails."[16]

When Edward Nott began his brief term as governor in 1705 he renewed Nicholson's request for a suitable residence. The assembly finally responded in June of the following year with legislation appropriating the substantial sum of £3000 for this purpose. The act specified that the site should be either on the sixty-three-acre tract purchased from Henry Tyler or on as many of the adjacent city lots as the directors of the city might decide proper. The building itself was to be an imposing structure, "built of Brick, fifty-four Foot in Length, and forty-eight Foot in Breadth, from Inside to Inside, two Story high, with convenient Cellars underneath, and one Vault, Sash Windows, of Sash Glass and a Covering of Stone Slate." Further, "A Kitchen and Stable, suitable for such an House" were also to be provided.[17] Soon Henry Cary, the builder of the Capitol, was at work on the new building, which was to play such an important role in the life of the city and provide it with one of its more attractive urban design features.

In typical fashion construction proceeded at a leisurely pace. There were delays over supplies of materials, many of which had to be purchased in England. Before long the original appropriation was exhausted. The assembly provided additional funds, but these too proved insufficient. By 1709 the basic structure had finally been completed, but the inside remained unfinished. It was left to the new governor, Alexander Spotswood, to bring the project to completion. A new act, passed at the end of 1710, appropriated money to finish the interior. Additional embellishment of the grounds was also authorized by these words:

> And be it enacted . . . That a Court-yard, of Dimentions proportionable to the said House, be laid out, levelled and encompassed with a Brick Wall four Foot high, with Ballustrades of Wood thereupon, on the said Land, and that a Garden of the Length of two Hundred fifty-four Foot and of the Breadth of one Hundred forty-four Foot from out to out, adjoining to the said House, be laid out and levelled and enclosed with a Brick Wall, four Foot high, with Ballustrades of Wood upon the said Wall, and that handsome Gates be made to the said Court-yard and Garden, and that a convenient Kitchen Garden be laid out on the said Land and be enclosed with Pailes, and that an Orchard and Pasture Ground be made on the said Land and be enclosed with a good Ditch and Fence, and also that a House of Wood for Poultry be built and finished, with a Yard thereto enclosed, on the said Land.[18]

Spotswood spent money lavishly on the building. He requested and received additional authorization from the assembly to use receipts from a duty on spirits and slaves with no limit on the total amount that might be used. Charges of waste and extravagance soon followed. At a meeting in December, 1714, the building was referred to in the records of the council as "the Palace," the first time this title had been used officially.[19] It was a word doubtless chosen deliberately and intended to be derisive.

It was not to be the end of controversy over the building, which over the years had to be extensively repaired and was later extended by the addition of a wing to the north. But at least early in its second decade, the town could boast of an official residence for the governor second to none in the English colonies. Spotswood set to work to beautify not only the Palace grounds but the approaches to it. Beyond the sixty-three-acre tract, which included the major portion of the Palace gardens, lay the land owned by John Custis. Spotswood secured permission from Custis to cut away some of the undergrowth and small bushes to provide a lengthened vista from the immediate Palace grounds.[20]

As it was in 1701 that the acquisition of the addition to the Palace grounds was first discussed, we know that the location of the governor's residence had been fixed by Nicholson. Whether his original plan included the Palace Green cannot be determined conclusively. Surviving information on sales of the lots bordering this important feature of the town reveals dates of transfer no earlier than 1716. Other deeds were prepared in 1717 and 1720. It is quite possible, then, that Spotswood may have been responsible for the exact form given to this strong secondary axis of the town, though it seems more likely that the credit must be given to Nicholson.

Spotswood's contribution to the development of Williamsburg, however, was substantial. In addition to the completion of the Palace he was responsible for the first courthouse of James City County south of Market Square and the erection and enclosure of the Powder Magazine in the southeast quadrant of that planned open space. He also enlarged the jail and prepared the design for a new and larger Bruton Parish Church, which he submitted to the parish vestry in 1711.[21]

While reconstruction of the main building of the college had begun before Spotswood's arrival, he saw that project through to completion, modifying and extending its original design. At the time his administration came to an end in 1722 plans must also have been drawn and construction may have been already under way for another major structure on the college grounds. This was the Brafferton, a substantial structure fifty-two by thirty-four feet on plan and two and a half stories high. Located south and east of the main building near the Jamestown road, it was built with funds from the Brafferton estate of Robert Boyle and was used as a school for Indian

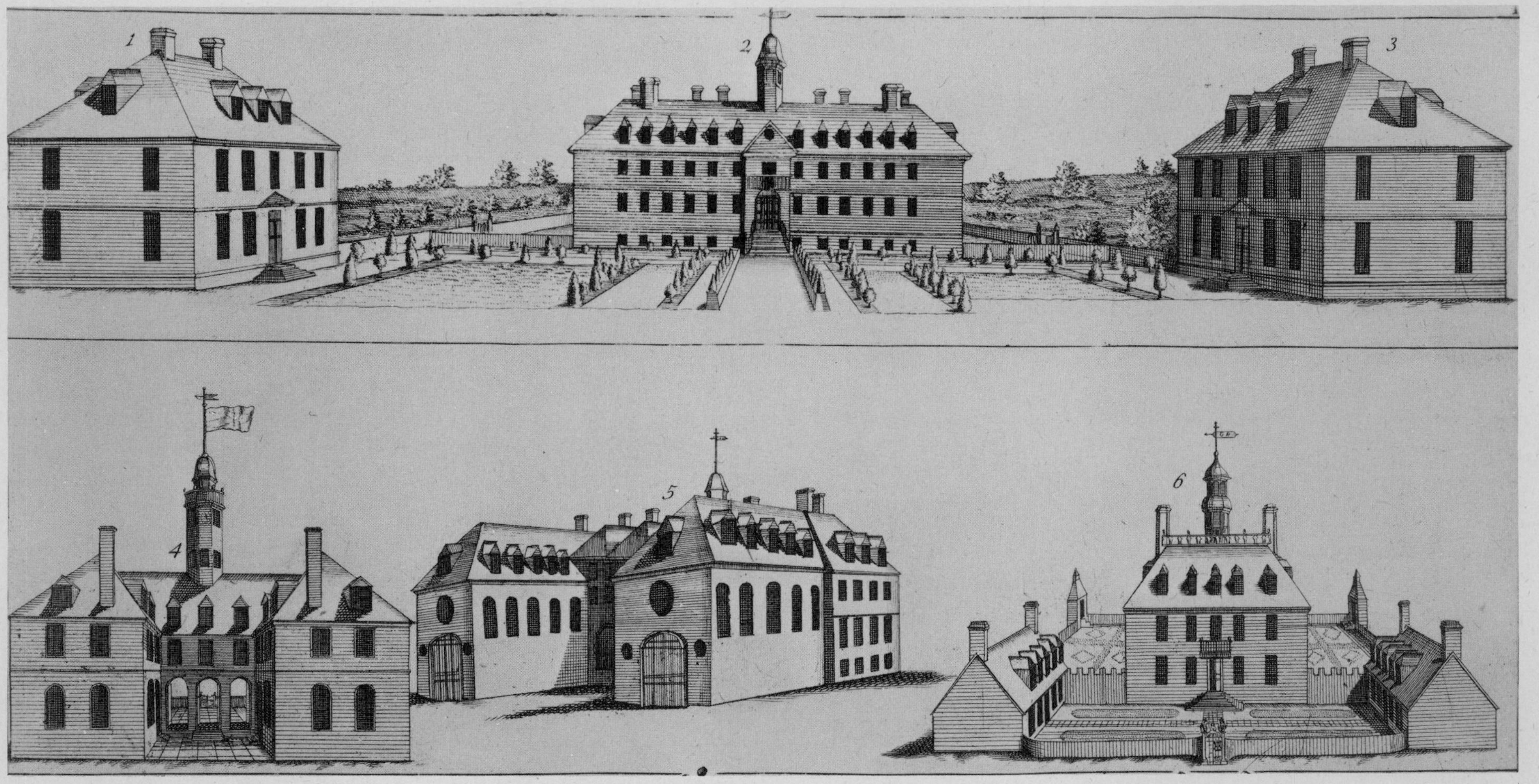

Figure 117. Views of the Principal Buildings in Williamsburg, Virginia: ca. 1737

youths. A few years later, in 1732, the foundation was laid for a nearly identical building northeast of the main structure designed as the residence for the president of the college. Together with the principal building, used for classrooms and living quarters for students and professors, these two additions to the college formed a handsome architectural composition at the western end of the Duke of Gloucester Street.

The most important buildings of the new capital city are shown in figure 117 as depicted on an engraving dating from about 1737. The three structures in the upper section show the Brafferton, the main building of the college and the President's House as viewed from the east. The rear of the main building appears in the center of the lower section as seen from the southwest. On the left is the north elevation of the Capitol with its two wings connected by the gallery. On the right is the Governor's Palace seen from above Palace Green with its imposing gate leading to the walled courtyard. It is flanked on one side by the governor's office building to the east and what may have been intended as the guardhouse on the west. The formal and symmetrical design of these important civic buildings provided a fitting architectural complement to the axial plan of the city.

As the public buildings slowly took form and as the directors sold lots and their owners erected dwellings and other structures, street improvements were also carried out. In the early years of the town's development the streets had been left ungraded. Soon it was realized that it would be necessary to provide for better drainage of surface water as the natural configuration of the land was constantly altered through these various construction activities. In November, 1720, the burgesses approved an appropriation of £150 "toward making Bridges and Causeways in the main Street" after a number of citizens had submitted a petition "complaining of the Irregularitys" in the Duke of Gloucester Street.[22]

Hugh Jones, writing of this event, described the money as a "considerable sum, which was expended in removing earth in some places, and building a bridge over a low channel; so that it is now a pleasant, long dry walk, broad, and almost level from the College to the Capitol."[23] Dry and almost level it may have been, but the sandy fill that evidently was used proved not entirely satisfactory. Several eighteenth-century visitors to Williamsburg complained, as did John Ferdinand Dalziel Smyth, that

> the street deep with sand, (not being paved) makes a singular appearance to an European; and is very disagreeable to walk in, especially in summer, when the rays of the sun are intensely hot, and not a little increased by the reflection of the white sand, wherein every step is almost above the shoe.[24]

There were not funds enough, however, to carry out all the improvements that were requested. Spotswood in 1713 asked the House of Burgesses "to Give some Assistance to this Infant Town, towards building a Market House, bettering the Landings, and Securing a few Publick Springs." The market building was still an issue seven years later when the residents petitioned the burgesses for such a structure along with their request for grading and draining the Duke of Gloucester Street. That portion of the petition, however, was not acted on.[25] Williamsburg did not have a market building until 1757, when a structure was erected and used for this purpose until 1764 on a site southeast of the Magazine on Market Square.

The legislators did authorize improvements for the public landings that, together with the roads leading to them from the town proper, were included in the original bounds of the city. At a time when water transportation played such an important role in the economic life of the colony it was clearly essential that the capital city on its inland site be made as accessible as possible by small craft. The plan of one of the two ports, Princess Anne's Port, or College Landing, has survived and is reproduced in figure 118. This survey is dated 1774 but in all probability it shows the original plan, perhaps as later extended, that was established shortly after 1699.[26] The creeks on which the two ports were located were both navigable at high tide, and development began at both locations soon after the founding of the parent town.

The drawing reveals a little gridiron of blocks formed by three straight streets running the length of the settlement, crossed by eight parallel shorter streets intersecting not quite at right angles. The lots within the blocks were much smaller than those in the city, measuring approximately sixty feet square. It is probably safe to assume that the plan of the other waterfront settlement, Queen Mary's Port (or Capitol Landing), was similar in general character although it may have differed in some details.

By 1706 ferries operated from both ports to convey persons and merchandise across the James and York rivers to landings in Surry and Gloucester counties. The roads leading from Williamsburg to the ports were constructed, including necessary bridges crossing the several creeks on the way. In 1713 the assembly authorized two public storehouses at Capitol Landing, and similar structures could be found at College Landing. Although the act of 1699 may have intended the lots at the ports to be used primarily for warehouse purposes, a number of dwellings, taverns, and ordinaries were eventually constructed along with buildings for certain industrial and mercantile activities. At College Landing alone four ordinaries received licenses from 1715 to 1728. These served not only travelers bound to or from Williamsburg but what must have been at least a modest resident population.

Several industries could be found at or near these locations. They included a brewery, a linen factory, a pottery, a tannery, and a carriage shop. The records for College Landing, for example, reveal that lots there were owned by bricklayers, carpenters, tailors, silversmiths, and other craftsmen. Doubtless they carried out their trade in portions of their dwellings. Here,

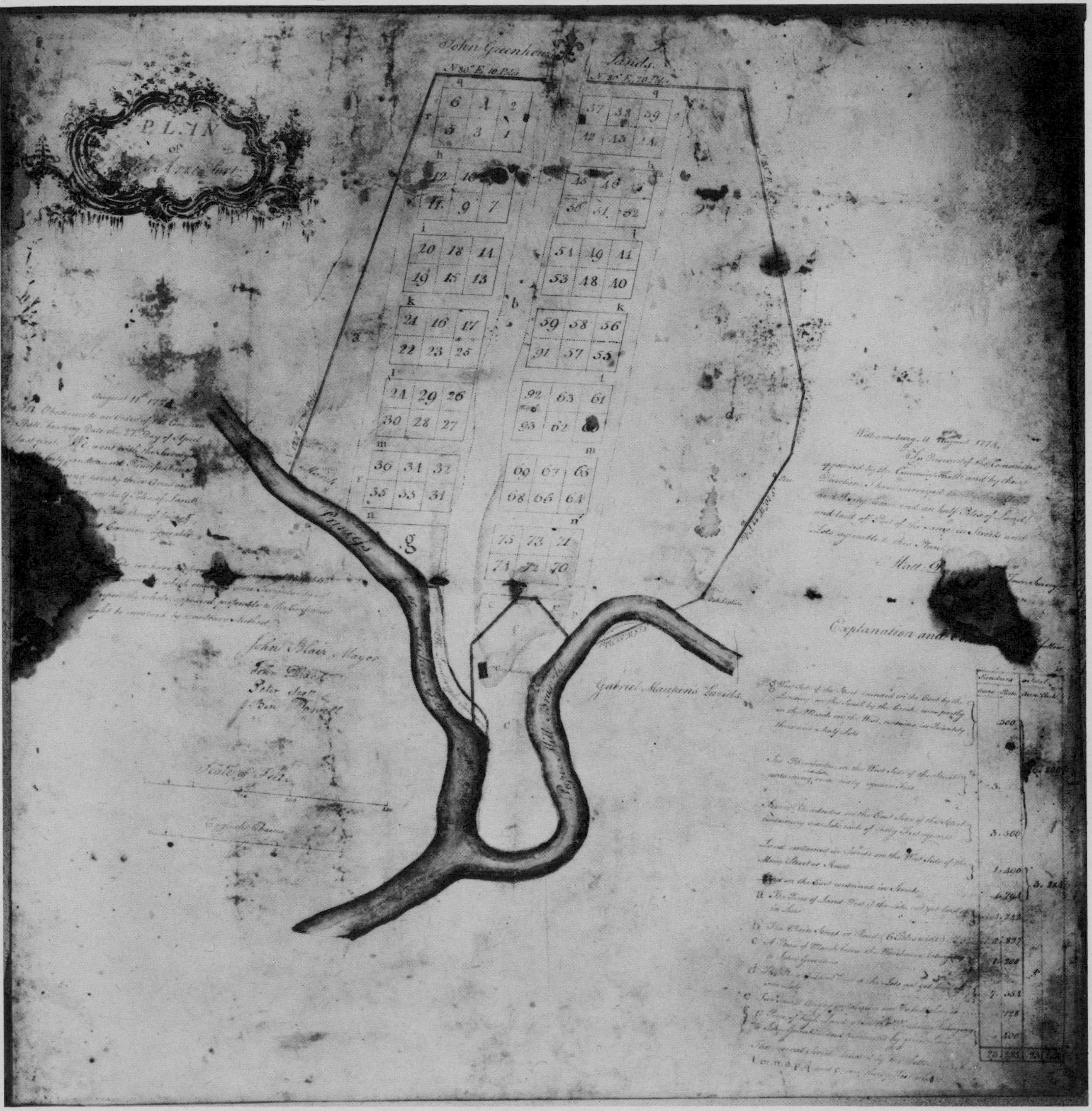

Figure 118. Plan of Princess Anne Port, Williamsburg, Virginia: 1774

too, much of the buying, selling, and inspecting of tobacco took place. Tobacco from the neighboring plantations was brought to the ports for storage in the private or public warehouses where it could be sold or exchanged for goods imported from England.

There were, of course, more extensive commercial developments in the town proper. Most of these were located along the Duke of Gloucester Street between Market Square and the Capitol. Here, too, stood most of the rooming houses, ordinaries, inns, and taverns that became such lively places during the sessions of the General Court or the assembly.[27] Many craftsmen operated shops in the town. There were blacksmiths, gunsmiths, candlemakers, tinsmiths, shoemakers, tailors, milliners, coachmakers and wheelwrights, saddlers, silversmiths and jewelers, cabinetmakers, wigmakers, and printers.[28] A windmill where meal or flour was ground stood on the north side of the town not far from the Palace. These shops and industries supplied many of the luxuries as well as virtually all of the essentials of life to both residents and visitors in the capital of a colony well beyond the stage of frontier existence.

The Market Square also served as a focal point of activity. Musters of the militia took place here, but its major function was the farmers' market held every Wednesday and Saturday. Each year on April 23, St. George's Day, and on December 12, Market Square became the site of the official town fairs. Some general merchandise, in addition to farm produce and livestock, was displayed for sale, and there were games and contests, cockfights, puppet shows, dancing and fiddling, and other country activities to attract the population from a wide section of the tidewater region. The fairs and biweekly markets had been authorized by the city charter granted in the name of George I on July 28, 1722. Although Spotswood's term of office had ended the previous month, the document bears his name and marked a fitting conclusion to the administration of the governor who had accomplished so much for the development of the town, if not always without incurring the displeasure of its citizens and the colonial legislators.[29]

Market Square was not the only outdoor center of mercantile activity. That short portion of the Duke of Gloucester running from the eastern boundaries of the town to the edge of Capitol Square became known as the "Exchange." Here, too, but without specific charter authorization, there was much buying and selling, in this case of bills of exchange. Activity at the Exchange coincided with the sessions of the General Court in April and October and the Oyer and Terminer Court in June and December. Planters throughout the colony crowded into Williamsburg at these times and augmented by many hundreds of visitors the resident population of perhaps two thousand.

If by modern standards the city of Williamsburg was small, it possessed nevertheless a distinctly urban quality. This was true particularly in the vicinity of the Capitol. That building, gutted by fire in January, 1747, and rebuilt within six years on a somewhat altered plan, dominated this section of the town by its beauty and scale. A new public building, handsome but far less imposing, stood nearby. The assembly authorized its construction, following the fire in the Capitol, as the office of the secretary of the colony and for the safekeeping of public records. It was located on Capitol Square north and west of the main building.[30]

Along the Duke of Gloucester Street one could see from the Capitol an almost solid facade of buildings all the way to Market Square. These had been constructed almost at the street line, being set back only six feet as specified in the act of 1699. They were, moreover, built close together and separated only by narrow side yards or passageways as can be seen on a detail from the Frenchman's Map in figure 119. The effect, as the modern visitor can appreciate from viewing the restored street, was of a true city with the street as an elongated but enclosed space and with the view to the east arrested by the graceful walls and cupola of the Capitol. Even on the parallel streets, Nicholson and Francis, where the density of buildings was far less and the spacing between them much greater, something of this sense of enclosure prevailed because of the fences connecting the buildings along the front property lines.[31]

The visual effect as one moved westward along the principal street was one of stimulating variety. Market Square, Palace Green, and Bruton Parish churchyard provided open spaces of contrasting shape, size, and landscape treatment. From a point at the cross axis of the town where Palace Green terminated at the Duke of Gloucester Street three other major buildings attracted attention. Close at hand loomed the church, the steeple of which, completed in 1771, added to its beauty. Terminating the view up Palace Green was the splendid Palace with its flanking outbuildings and wall forming an entrance courtyard. And to the west, like the Capitol at the other end of the Duke of Gloucester street, stood the college, punctuating the view outward from the town. As one drew closer the symmetrically placed Brafferton and President's House could be seen completing this fine architectural composition.

By 1770 still another major structure was taking form in the western portion of the town. Its location may be seen on the Frenchman's Map (figure 100) in the second block south of the Duke of Gloucester Street and an equal distance east of the college lands. This was the Public Hospital for the Insane, designed by Robert Smith of Philadelphia. The building was large, measuring thirty-two by one hundred feet with a central portion projecting somewhat beyond the width of the two main wings. Unlike the other civic buildings of Williamsburg, however, it was not placed in axial relationship to the street pattern, and some of its potential visual impact was therefore lost.[32]

Another feature of the Williamsburg plan deserves mention in this review of the qualities of urban design it encouraged. This is the difference in spacing between the streets paralleling the Duke of Gloucester Street that occurs at Palace Green and its King Street extension. The difference is easy to appreciate by a re-examination of figure 107 (Chapter VII), the drawing showing the street pattern within the original town boundaries and the division of blocks into lots. It is difficult to believe that this pattern resulted from mere accident or whim. More likely it originated with Nicholson as an attempt to create additional building sites of special visual importance.

The potential effect is obvious. Buildings located opposite the Palace Green ends of Nicholson, Francis, George, and France streets would have provided terminal vistas for these streets. In turn, from these buildings one would have long and uninterrupted views.[33] If indeed this was Nicholson's intent it was only to be partially realized. During his administration there apparently were no sales of lots on these important sites. Spotswood may not have realized the opportunity that existed, for the blocks where this effect could have been achieved were subdivided in quite a different way west of Palace Green and King Street. Lots were laid out at these strategic corners with the obvious intent of having the houses front on George or France streets.

On one important spot, however, the logic of Nicholson's plan was grasped by the owner of one of these lots. The George Wythe House, probably built about 1750 by Wythe's father-in-law, Richard Taliaferro, was constructed facing Palace Green opposite the termination of Nicholson Street. The house in effect turned away from Prince George Street, which would have been the normal frontage according to the lot pattern established under Spotswood. The view to the fine residence of one of Williamsburg's most distinguished residents is unrivaled by any other surviving dwelling. This sole example reveals the splendid opportunities that were lost at the lots terminating the streets ending at Palace Green because of a lack of understanding of this subsidiary but important feature of the original town plan.

One of those sites might appropriately have been utilized for the theatre, the first in the American colonies, that occupied a location on the east side of Palace Green as early as 1716. The building later was remodeled for use as the city hall and municipal court, and a second theatre was constructed on Waller Street near the Capitol.[34] This was not the only place of entertainment in the town. The several taverns of Williamsburg provided not only food, drink, and lodging, but they served as places for gambling, a popular activity for residents and visitors. There was a race track as well, located less than a mile southeast of the Capitol.[35]

The strongly axial design of Williamsburg suggested to several landowners that buildings might be placed to take advantage of reciprocal views. Important buildings at both ends of England Street are examples that can be observed on the Frenchman's Map. Both buildings stand exactly on the north-south axis of Market Square. The building on the south is Tazewell Hall, completed in 1762 by John Randolph and purchased by Justice John Tazewell in 1778. Although its site was just beyond the southern limits of the original town boundary, Randolph skillfully took advantage of the terminus of South England Street at his property to provide his residence with a long, uninterrupted view to Market Square and the Powder Magazine.

Opposite, at the northern end of England Street, stood another large structure, though not so imposing as Tazewell Hall. The occupant of this house could enjoy a fine view to the Market Square and, like John Randolph or John Tazewell, could take satisfaction in how his residence added to the appearance of the town when viewed from the market green.[36]

Other examples of studied building placement can be seen on the Frenchman's Map. Both ends of Botetourt Street (or Pump Street, as it was also known) terminated at structures located on the axis of this short cross street. That at the northern end no longer exists, since in the modern

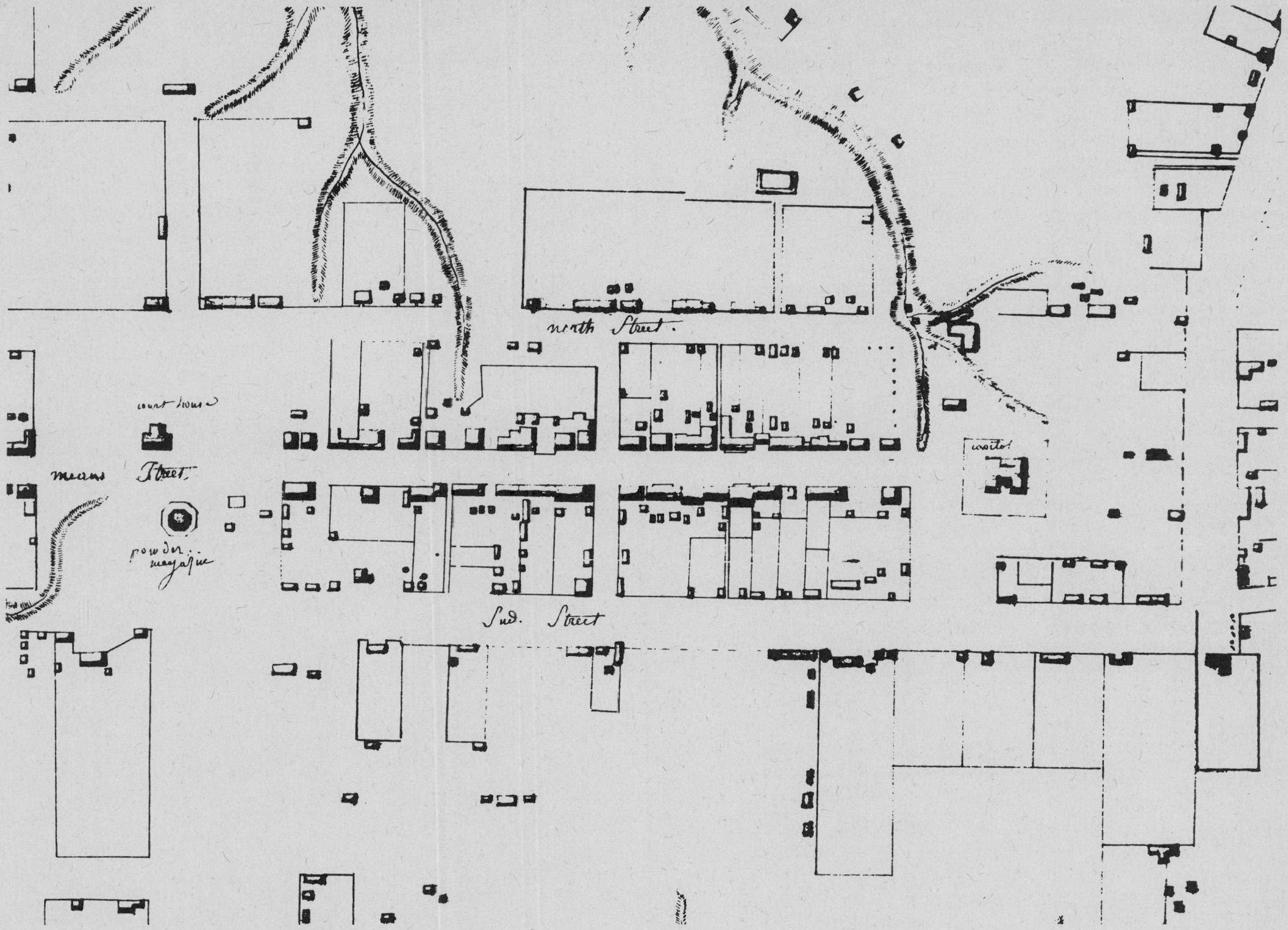

Figure 119. Plan of Portion of Williamsburg, Virginia: 1782

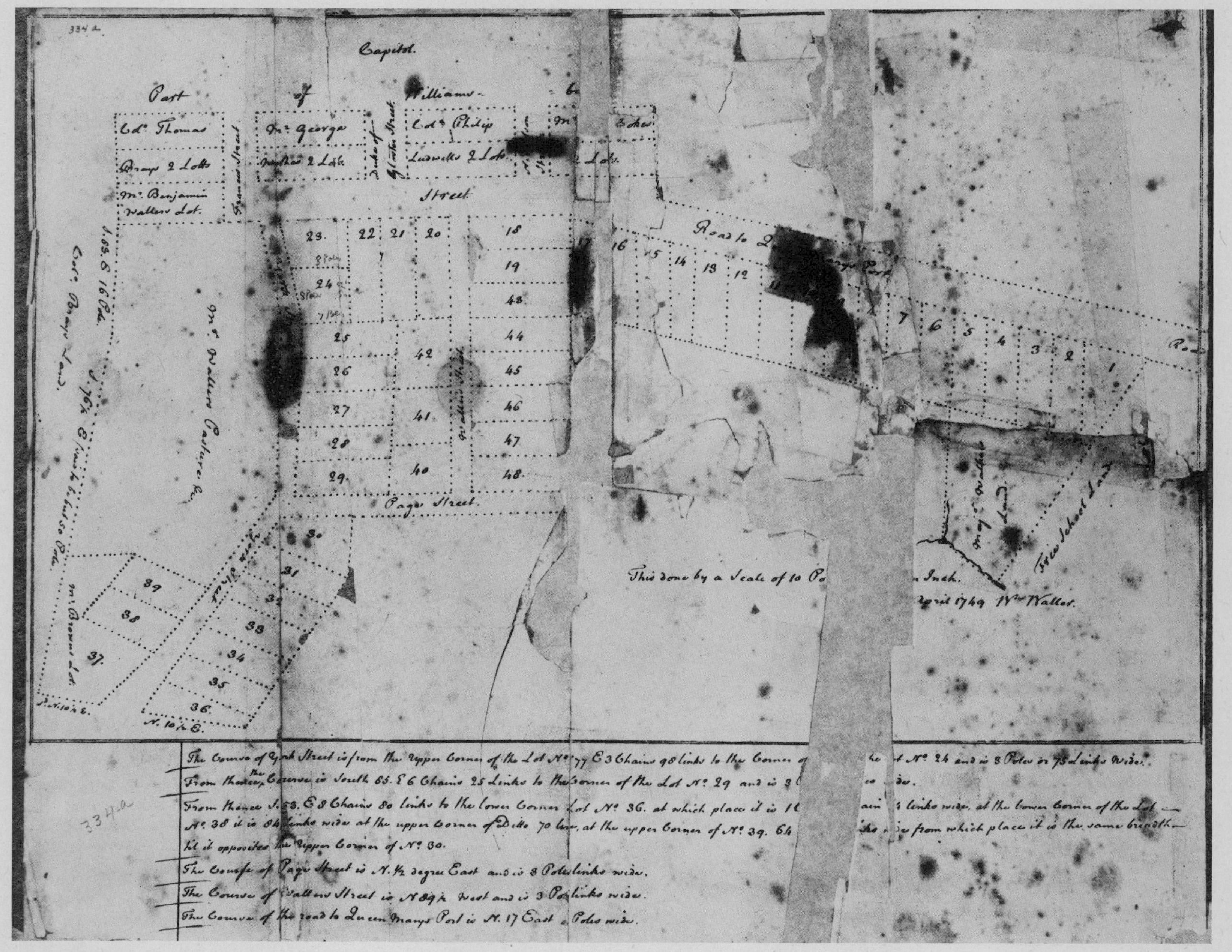

Figure 120. Plan of Portion of Williamsburg, Virginia: 1749

city Botetourt Street now extends northward beyond Nicholson Street. The view down Botetourt Street to the south, however, terminates now as it did in the eighteenth century at the house once owned by Ebenezer Ewing, a modest two-story structure that achieves added distinction from its fine location.

Obviously not all of the houses of Williamsburg were as elegant as those occupied by George Wythe or John Randolph. The majority, like the Ewing House, were smaller and less pretentious. Some of these dwellings were not occupied by year-round residents but were maintained by plantation owners living elsewhere and used by them during "Public Times" when the General Court was in session or on visits to the town during fairs or other special occasions. The first houses to be constructed were apparently located at the eastern end of the town near the Capitol, for it is in this area that the earliest sales of land are recorded. By the middle of the eighteenth century, however, the town was fairly evenly developed, though not all of the lots were occupied.

The gradual but steady growth of Williamsburg in the first part of the eighteenth century soon resulted in the subdivision by private owners of additional land lying outside the original boundaries of the town. Unfortunately, the quality of the design of these additions did not match the orderly and imposing character of the first portion of the city created under Nicholson and his successors. The plat of one such addition is shown in figure 120 as drawn in 1749 by William Waller. This land lay to the east of the original town line beyond the Capitol grounds and the road to Queen Mary's Port or Capitol Landing. The haphazard pattern of streets and lots stand in marked contrast to the straightforward and formal layout of Nicholson's little baroque design. In 1759 this subdivision, together with twelve lots laid out by Matthew Moody "on the West side of the road leading to queen Mary's port," was incorporated into the city.[37]

More regular in plan but less accessible were the thirty-four lots surveyed on the land of Colonel Phillip Johnson. These appear as the double tier of lots south of those fronting on Francis Street shown on the early nineteenth-century plans discussed in the previous chapter and reproduced in figures 103, 104, 105, and 106.

Access to this addition was indirect. The southernmost tier possibly was served by an extension of South Boundary Street. The seventeen lots to the north may have been reached by one or two narrow lanes running south from Francis Street. Figure 103 shows two narrow strips of land that may have been used for this purpose. Other lots may have been acquired by owners with houses on Francis Street and used by them as gardens or for outbuildings. The assembly in 1758 provided for incorporation of these lots into the city as soon as they were built on. Four years later John Randolph had ten acres of his estate laid off into twenty lots, and these were also annexed to the city. It was here that he constructed the residence previously described, later to be known as Tazewell Hall, which survived on the site until 1918.[38]

Figure 121, a portion of one of the revolutionary war maps of Williamsburg and its vicinity in 1781, indicates that on the lots in the Johnson addition there was only scattered development. Nor, if the map is correct, was that portion of the Waller subdivision along Capitol Landing Road completely occupied by that date. It is only fair to add, however, that not all the lots of the original city plan had been taken up and improved. Nevertheless, the map clearly reveals a town of substantial dimensions quite different in size and character from the largely unsuccessful port communities of the previous century.

Many visitors to Williamsburg in the eighteenth century came away impressed by what they saw. Although Smyth disliked the sandy streets into which his feet sank "almost above the shoe," he had little else but praise for the city:

> There is one handsome street in it, just a mile in length, where the view is terminated by a commanding object each way; the Capitol, an elegant public building, in which the assembly, or senate, and courts of judicature are held, at one end of the street; and the college of William and Mary, an old monastic structure, at the other end. About the middle between them, on the north side, a little distance retired from the street, stands the palace, the residence of the governor; a large, commodious, and handsome building.[39]

Hugh Jones had obviously been captivated by Williamsburg during his five years of residence there until 1722. He liked the inland location because it allowed the development of a town "much more commodious and healthful, than if built upon a river." The college, where he taught, he termed "beautiful and commodious, being first modelled by Sir Christopher Wren, adapted to the nature of the country by the gentlemen there; and since it was burnt down, it has been rebuilt, and nicely contrived, altered

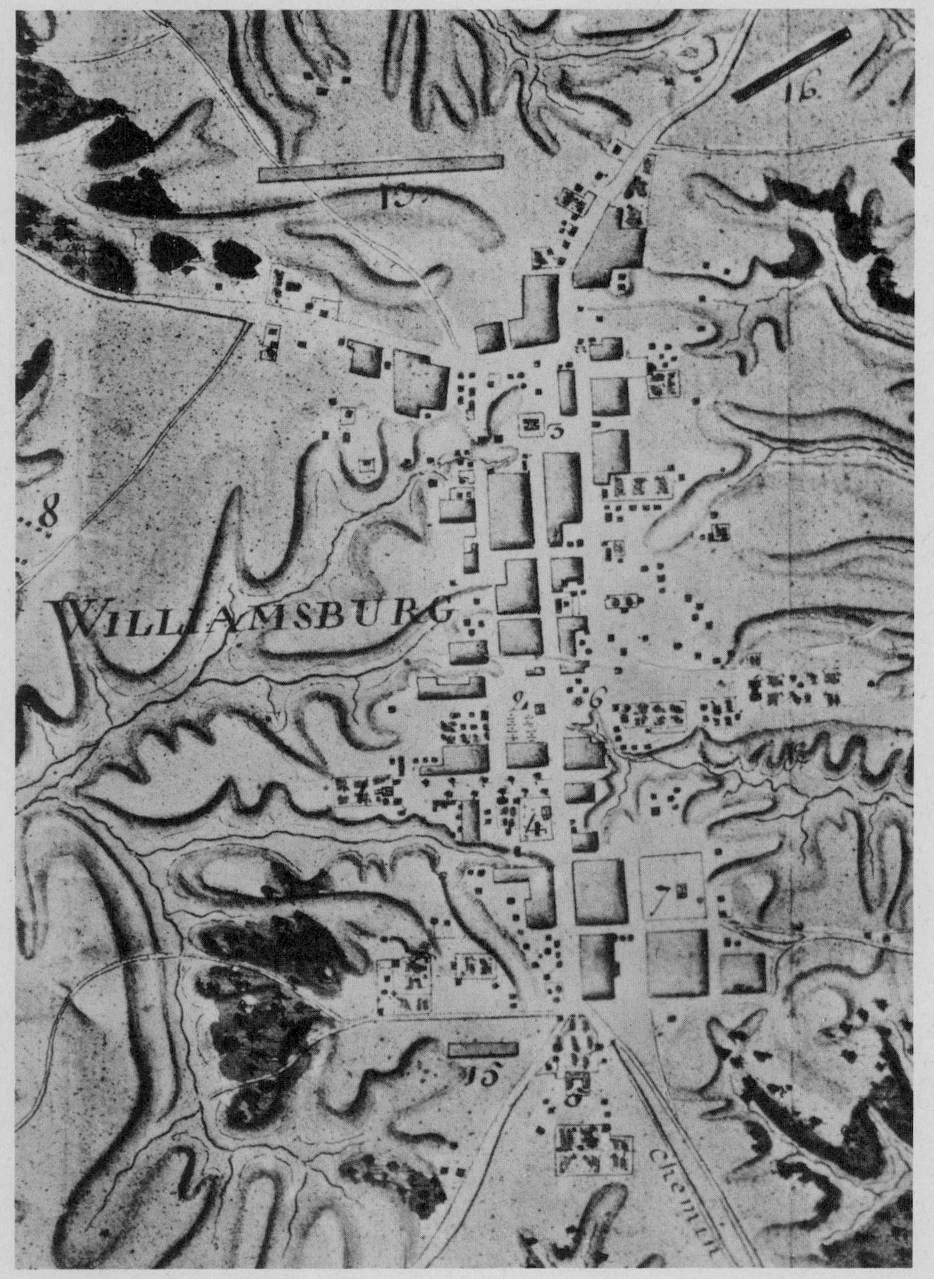

Figure 121. Map of Williamsburg, Virginia, and Vicinity: 1781

and adorned by the ingenious directions of Governor Spotswood; and is not altogether unlike Chelsea Hospital." He employed his favorite adjectives again in describing the Capitol as "a noble, beautiful, and commodious pile as any of its kind." He found Bruton Parish Church, "nicely regular and convenient, and adorned as the best churches in London." The Governor's Palace, in Jones's view was "a magnificent structure . . . finished and beautified with gates, fine gardens, offices, walks, a fine canal, orchards, etc. with a great number of the best arms nicely posited, by the ingenious contrivance of the most accomplished Colonel Spotswood." These buildings, he asserted, "are justly reputed the best in all the English America, and are exceeded by few of their kind in England."

In "this delightful, healthful, and . . . thriving city" Jones reported that the people "live in the same neat manner, dress after the same modes, and behave themselves exactly as the gentry in London; most families of any note having a coach, chariot, berlin, or chaise." Williamsburg was particularly impressive during the periods when it attracted large numbers of visitors. According to Jones:

> At the Capitol, at publick times, may be seen a great number of handsom, well-dressed, compleat gentlemen. And at the Governor's House upon birth-nights, and at balls and assemblies, I have seen as fine an appearance, as good diversion, and as splendid entertainments in Governor Spotswood's time as I have seen any where else.[40]

A half century later a French officer who saw the city in 1777 echoed these views:

> Williamsburg occupies a charming situation and is composed of a principal street, very wide and about a mile and a half long, well built up, and of two parallel streets. The main street is closed at one extremity by a very fine College, and at the other end by the Capitol which is a very beautiful building. The prospect is very agreeable. Toward the center of the city (and at about the height of the second street), is the Governor's Palace, very well built, very spacious, with a big lawn extending to the second street which forms a pretty avenue. On the opposite side is a very fine edifice which is the Insane Asylum. Beyond the Capitol, looking toward York, is a large built-up street which forms the suburb.[41]

Not everyone shared these views, however. When young Edward Kimber visited the city in 1742 he recorded his opinion that:

> *Williamsburgh* is a most wretched contriv'd Affair for the Capital of a Country, being near three Miles from the Sea, in a bad Situation. There is nothing considerable in it, but the College, the Governor's House, and one or two more, which are no bad Piles; and the prodigious Number of Coaches that croud the deep, sandy Streets of this little City. It's very surprizing to me, that this should be preferr'd to *James-Town, Hampton,* or some other Situations I could mention.[42]

The Reverend Andrew Burnaby, while conceding that the town as a whole "makes a handsome appearance," found the houses to be "but indifferently built" and "the streets . . . not paved, and . . . consequently very dusty." It was, he concluded "far from being a place of any consequence."[43]

A few years later Josiah Quincy, a young lawyer from Boston, commented that Williamsburg was "a place of no trade, and its importance depends altogether on its being the seat of government, and the place of the college." It was, he said, "inferior to my expectations. Nothing of the population of the north, or of the splendour and magnificence of the south."[44] It might be supposed that Thomas Jefferson would have appreciated the formal order and symmetry of the Williamsburg plan. Perhaps he did, but his comments about the town, generally unfavorable, were limited to critical observations of the architectural design of the principal buildings:

> The only public buildings worthy of mention are the Capitol, the Palace, the College, and the Hospital for Lunatics. . . . The Capitol is a light and airy structure, with a portico in front of two orders, the lower of which, being Doric, is tolerably just in its proportions and ornaments, save only that the intercollonnations are too large. The upper is Ionic, much too small for that on which it is mounted, its ornaments not proper to the order, nor proportioned within themselves. It is crowned with a pediment, which is too high for its span. Yet, on the whole, it is the most pleasing piece of architecture we have. The Palace is not handsome without: but it is spacious and commodious within, is prettily situated, and, with the grounds annexed to it, is capable of being made an elegant seat. The College and Hospital are rude, mis-shapen piles, which, but that they have roofs, would be taken for brick-kilns. There are no other public buildings but churches and courthouses in which no attempts are made at elegance.[45]

Despite these disparging remarks by Jefferson about the buildings and the criticisms of the town by earlier observers, the development of Williamsburg must be regarded as a significant achievement. If by modern standards it could not properly be called a great city, compared with the earlier towns founded in Virginia it provided an urban environment hitherto unknown in the colony. It represented at long last the fulfillment of a policy that had been so often urged by colonial administrators in England and pursued with frustrating results by a succession of resident governors and other officials. Considering the history of town planning efforts since the establishment of Jamestown, one would have thought that all Virginians might have viewed the results with satisfaction and pleasure. This, however, was not the case.

Within a few years after the founding of the new capital voices were raised calling for the removal of the seat of government to yet another location. Some of the arguments for this step closely resembled those used a century earlier when the abandonment of Jamestown had been advocated by those who condemned its unhealthy site and its location somewhat removed from the center of colonial settlement. The map of Virginia and Maryland in 1751, reproduced in figure 122, reveals the extent to which settlement had expanded to the north and west. While the site of Williamsburg at the time of its founding lay not far from the center of population, the westward movement of the Virginia frontier into the Piedmont and beyond had resulted in an altered pattern of settlement of which Williamsburg was no longer the heart. This had created political tensions as well. Upland farmers were less content to accept without question the policies advocated by the planter oligarchy that dominated the Tidewater. Moreover, as settlement spread to the northern portions of Virginia and westward to the mountains the site became less convenient for those seeking justice in the colonial court or traveling to the city to take their seats in the colonial legislature.

The city's inland location, viewed as an advantage by some, proved an inconvenience to many. It was not easily reached by land except for those living in the peninsula between the James and York rivers. Those making the journey to the city from the north found it necessary either to make detours around the lower reaches of the tidal estuaries or to cross these rivers by ferry. The port facilities of the new town were decidedly inconvenient and could be reached from the two rivers only by narrow, shallow, and winding creeks. The map in figure 123 shows clearly the

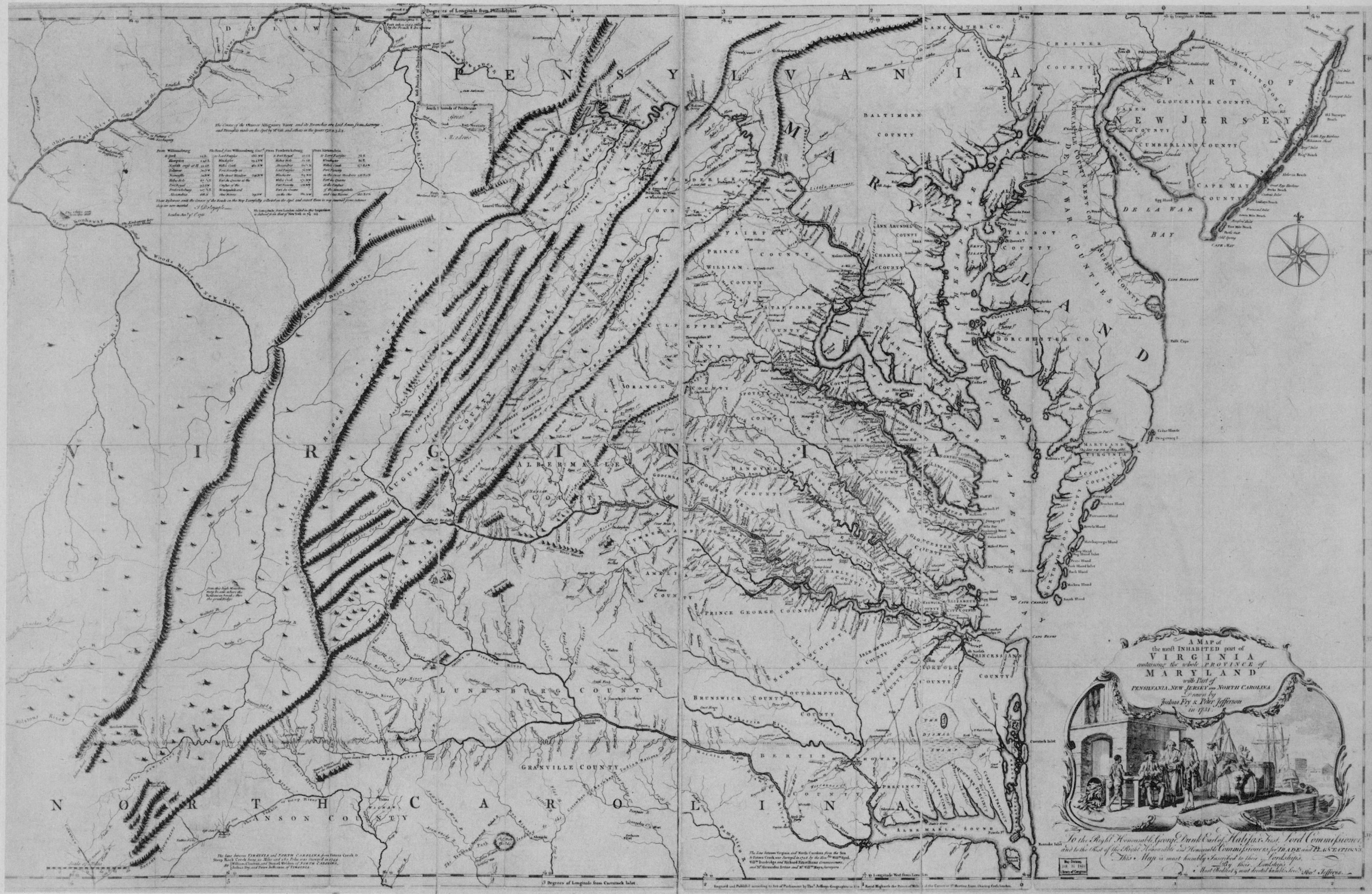

Figure 122. *Map of Virginia and Maryland: 1751*

difficult passage from the York River to Capitol Landing, which could be made only by small boats of shallow draft.

As early as 1738 the House of Burgesses had before it a motion to move the government to Bermuda Hundred on the James River or West Point on the York River.[46] This motion was defeated, but efforts to abandon Williamsburg as the capital did not end there. In 1747, following the destruction of the Capitol by fire, the burgesses considered the planning of a new capital city on the York River on the lands of William Gray and New-Year Smith. The following year they debated a proposal to locate the capital on the York River adjoining the town of Newcastle or at the land of Richard Littlepage on the Pamunkey River.[47]

In the spring of 1749 the council received from the burgesses a bill that called for the planning of a new capital city near Newscastle. Although this was rejected by the council, its supporters, who included John Robinson, Thomas Lee, and William Fairfax, advanced a strong case for passage of the measure. They argued that Williamsburg no longer stood near the center of population but was more than "two Hunded and Fifty Miles from the Frontier Inhabitants, who are continually extending the Possessions of the Crown Westward." Persons seeking justice in the highest court as well as burgesses would find the proposed site on the Pamunkey River more convenient because of its location fifty miles up country from Williamsburg. The suggested spot was located directly on a navigable river, which would provide better accessibility than the smaller creeks leading to the Williamsburg public landings.

Moreover, so it was argued, the students at the college would be benefited:

> Because the Morals of the Youth of this Colony educated at the College are greatly depraved by the evil Examples they see from the Numbers that flock to this Place at the public Meetings, the Impressions that are receiv'd at those Times being too strong for all the Care of the Masters to overcome. And we are persuaded that while the Seat of Government is continued, the Evil will increase, and our Prospect from the Corruption of the morals of the rising Generation is a very melancholy Consideration.

The proponents of change may have overstated their case in asserting to the council that:

> near fifty years Experience has convinced the Majority of the Country of the Unfitness of the present Place, and the several Attempts of the House of Burgesses to remove it to a more convenient Place, abundantly Justifies our Opinion, two thirds at least of the Country are desirous that the Seat of Government may be removed, as may be plainly evinced by the Votes of this Session.[48]

These efforts in the middle of the eighteenth century to move the seat of government away from Williamsburg were by no means the only ones. It would be needlessly tedious to trace them in any detail, but the records of the assembly contain frequent references to this issue.[49] One proposal, interestingly enough, included a provision to compensate the city of Williamsburg for the loss that would be suffered by its citizens if another city were designated as the colonial capital.

The outbreak of the Revolution brought renewed and ultimately successful attempts to move the capital. In 1776, Thomas Jefferson introduced in the House of Delegates of the newly independent state of Virginia a bill to this effect. Jefferson's reason were twofold: to reduce the danger of possible English occupation of the capital city and to provide a location more convenient for the inhabitants of the central and western portions of Virginia. The delegates rejected this measure, but in May, 1779, Jefferson was instrumental in securing the passage of essentially similar legislation. A few days later, with his election as governor by the House of Delegates, he assumed much of the responsibility of its implementation.[50]

The act designated Richmond as the new capital site, a location "more safe and central than any other town situated on navigable water." The reasons for the move were succinctly stated in the preamble:

> Great numbers of the inhabitants of this commonwealth must frequently and of necessity resort to the seat of government where general assemblies are convened, superior courts are held, and the governour and council usually transact the executive business of government; and the equal rights of all the said inhabitants require that such seat of government should be as nearly central to all as may be, having regard only to navigation, the benefits of which are necessary for promoting the growth of a town sufficient for the accommodation of those who resort thereto, and able to aid the operations of government: And it has been also found inconvenient in the course of the

Figure 123. Map of Williamsburg, Virginia, and Vicinity: 1781

> present war, where seats of government have been so situated as to be exposed to the insults and injuries of the publick enemy.[51]

The effect of this legislation, which was to become operative on May 1 of the following year, was to stimulate a new wave of urban development in Richmond (to be examined in Chapter XI). For Williamsburg, however, the act of 1779 clearly meant decline and decay. Its stunning impact was reinforced by the unhappy consequences of the war. Jefferson's fears concerning the exposed position of Williamsburg were soon justified. English forces in 1781 invaded Virginia and for ten days, beginning on June 25, occupied the city. Although one inhabitant referred to the "tyranizing" of the people, their affliction by smallpox, and "the Plagues . . . of Flies" brought with the army, there seems to have been very little deliberate destruction of property by the occupying forces under General Cornwallis.[52]

The withdrawal of the English on July 4 was followed in the fall by a new occupation, but this time by American and French troops massing for the assault on Yorktown that was to bring peace to Virginia and victory for the rebellion. Occupation in wartime even by friendly forces has never been particularly beneficial to the physical fabric of a town, and these months in the winter of 1781–1782 brought tragedy and great damage. The Governor's Palace, the Capitol, and the college buildings all were converted to hospitals. On November 23, 1781, the President's House was destroyed by fire. One month later the Palace suffered the same fate.[53] The French, who had used the President's House for their hospital, compensated the college for the damage, and the building was eventually repaired. The remains of the Palace, however, were shortly pulled down, the lands were conveyed to the college, which sold them in 1785, and the two outbuildings bordering the courtyard became private dwellings.[54]

When Bishop Francis Asbury visited Williamsburg in December 1782, he noted the sorry state of the town:

> The place has suffered and is suffering; the palace, the barracks, and some good dwelling-houses burnt. The capitol is no great building, and is going to ruin; the exterior of the college not splendid, and but few students; the Bedlamhouse is desolate, but whether because none are insane, or all are equally mad, it might, perhaps, be difficult to tell.[55]

A year later Johann David Schoepf commented on the economic consequences of the shift of the seat of government from the town:

> Williamsburg is now a poor place compared with its former splendor. With the removal of the government, merchants, advocates, and other considerable residents took their departure as well, and the town has lost half its population. The trade of this place was never great, its distance from navigable waters not being favorable to more active affairs which thus became established in smaller towns. . . . The merchants of the country round about were accustomed formerly to assemble here every year, to advise about commercal affairs and matters in the furtherance of trade. This also has come to an end. Thus, like so many older ones in Europe, do cities in this new world lament for the uncertain fate of a past glory.[56]

The citizens of Williamsburg were not content to see their town die without a struggle. They fought vainly to have the seat of government brought back from Richmond, and their efforts caused considerable concern to those attempting to stimulate growth at the new capital city. On March 18, James Madison wrote to Thomas Jefferson of his fears that a change in the construction plans for the Richmond Capitol might

> interpose a vote for its suspension, and possibly for a removal to Williamsburg. This danger is not altogether imaginary. Not a Session has passed since I became a member without . . . these attempts. At the late Session, a suspension was moved by the Williamsburg Interest, which was within a few votes of being agreed to.[57]

Some years later, in a fruitless endeavor to bring water transportation to the town, the citizens proposed the construction of a canal to link Williamsburg with the navigable streams of the Tidewater. As shown on the drawing in figure 124, the canal would have led from College Landing up to the city from the south and then would have cut diagonally through its eastern section. It is fortunate that this project was never carried through, for it inevitably would have caused demolition of many of the buildings that ultimately were to be perserved and restored.

The decline in prosperity and the disintegration of the remaining public buildings, once started, continued apace. Lack of maintenance of the former Capitol threatened its very existence. In 1793 the General Assembly authorized the city to demolish the east wing, sell the materials, and use the funds for the repairs of the remaining portion of the building.[58] At that

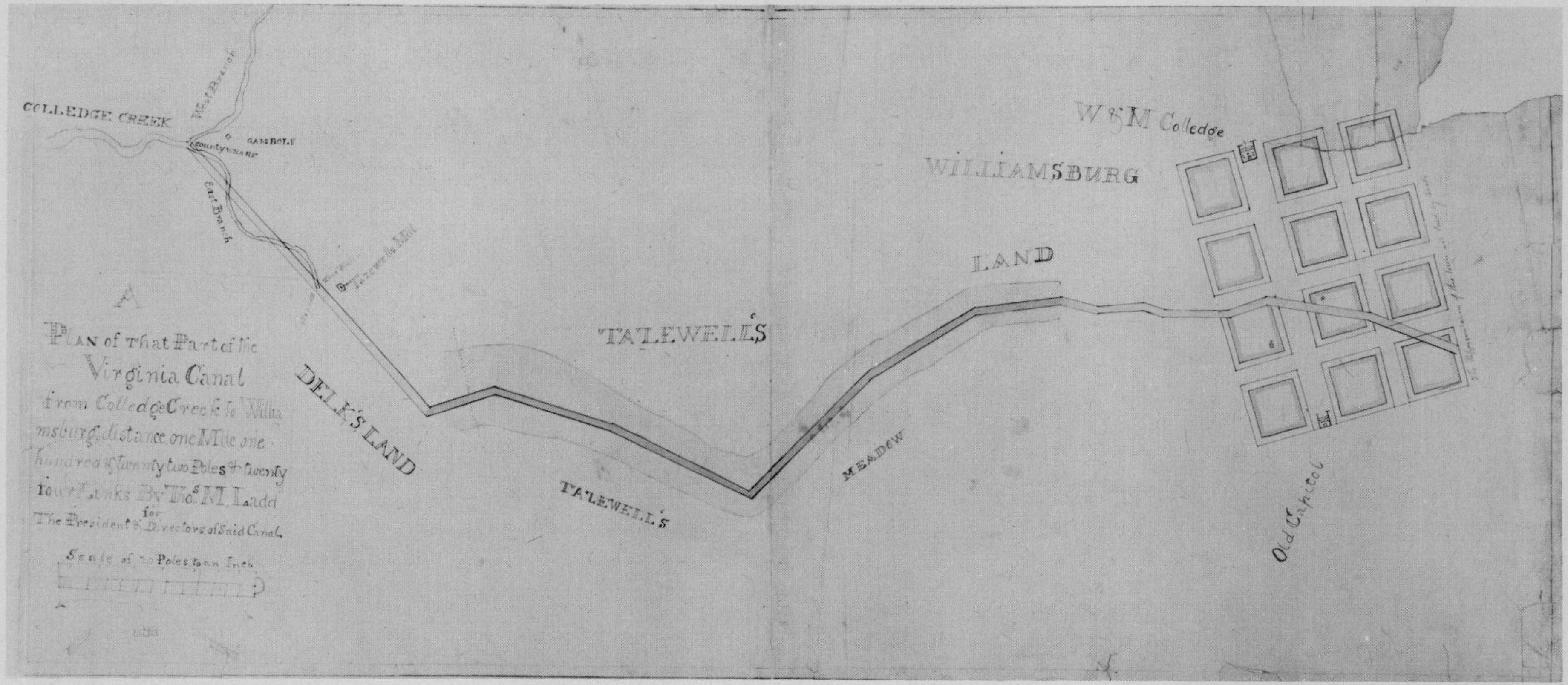

Figure 124. Map of the Proposed Canal from College Landing to Williamsburg, Virginia: 1818

time the building was in use as a grammar school, although a portion of it still served as a court. The once imposing structure, like many of its noble companions, also was consumed by fire—this unhappy event occurring in 1832.[59]

Young Charles Augustus Murray summed up the melancholy position of Williamsburg after he visited the town in 1835:

> The seat of government during the Old Dominion is now little better than a "deserted village." The center of the palace where the governor resided has long since fallen down, and even the traces of its ruins are no more to be seen. Two small wings, which formed part of the range of offices, are still standing: they have been bought and fitted up . . . in a neat cottage style. I did not scruple to enter, and ask permission to cast my eye round the apartments and adjoining garden, which was politely granted. It may be imagined with what mingled and undefinable feelings I viewed this spot, . . . the ancient capital, on the site of which I was now standing, has dwindled, in half a century, into a paltry village, without even a venerable ruin to rescue its decay from insignificance.[60]

In 1840, as shown in figure 125, the buildings of the College of William and Mary still stood at the western end of the Duke of Gloucester Street

Figure 125. View of the College of William and Mary in Williamsburg, Virginia: 1840

looking much as they did a century earlier. In 1859, however, fire damaged the main building. During the Civil War occupation of the city by Union forces, soldiers set fire to the rebuilt structure and also pulled down the buildings remaining on the former Palace grounds.[61] The bricks were used in constructing chimneys for officers' quarters at nearby Fort Magruder.[62]

The destruction of the old city was still not at an end. While Bruton Parish Church had somehow managed to survive more or less unchanged, in 1838 its interior was altered for the worse in a well-meaning but clumsy effort to "modernize" the building. Fortunately its exterior remained nearly as it had appeared during the colonial period. A second fire in 1859 destroyed the Raleigh Tavern on the north side of the Duke of Gloucester Street. This had been the largest and liveliest of the old capital's places for dining and lodging.

Elsewhere in the city private houses were demolished or remodeled, and a number of former dwellings were converted to commercial or other nonresidential uses. Toward the end of the century, however, some preliminary efforts at preservation began. In 1889 the recently organized Association for the Preservation of Virginia Antiquities purchased the old Powder Magazine as the first of many APVA efforts to save architectural remnants of an earlier day. This structure had passed through a succession of uses: market building, Baptist church, dancing school, and livery stable. The surrounding wall had been removed, and the building itself was in precarious condition. While the APVA was arranging for transfer of the title, fire destroyed the roof, and only the shell of Spotswood's octagonal building remained.

This venerable structure was restored and became a museum. Eight years later the APVA received as a gift from the Old Dominion Land Company the site and foundations of the former Capitol. When the Reverend William A. R. Goodwin accepted the rectorship of Bruton Parish in 1903, he stipulated that the interior of the church be restored to its original condition. It may have been at this time that the energetic and persuasive minister conceived of a vastly greater restoration project. As he began to develop the idea, it would consist of nothing less than the full-scale re-creation of Williamsburg as it had appeared at the height of its prosperity and glory in colonial times.

From 1908 until 1922 Dr. Goodwin was absent from the Williamsburg scene, but with his return, this time to the College of William and Mary,

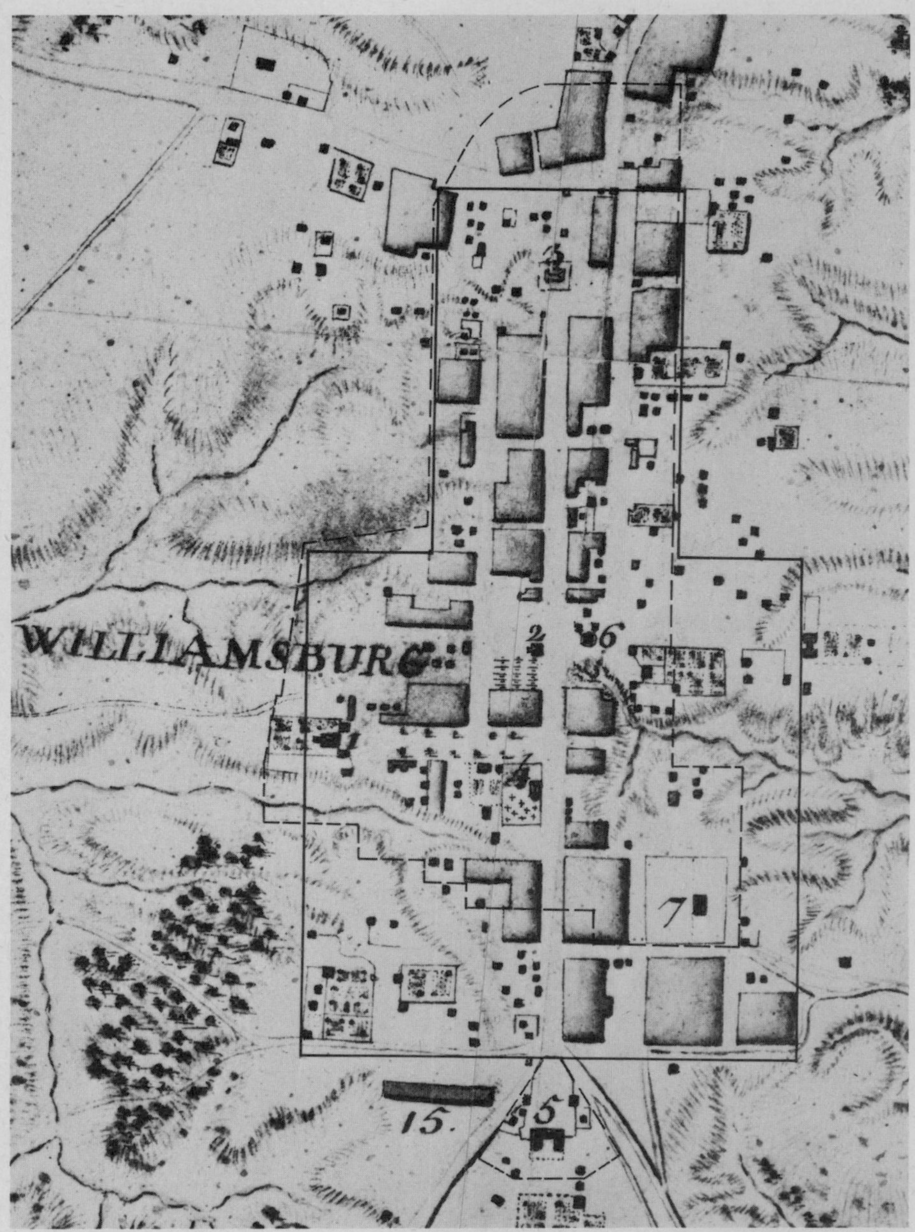

Figure 126. Map of Williamsburg, Virginia, and Vicinity in 1781 Showing the Town Boundaries in 1699 (——) and the Historic Area in 1971 (– – –)

he began to promote this seemingly wild and impractical project in earnest. The first modest success was the purchase and restoration of the George Wythe dwelling in 1926 as the parish house for Bruton Parish Church.

The indefatigable Dr. Goodwin set out to find the kind of financial support that would make possible wholesale preservation and restoration of some eighty-odd other colonial structures still standing, along with the reconstruction of many of the buildings that had been destroyed. Dr. Goodwin's address at a New York City meeting of the Phi Beta Kappa Society in 1924 provided an opportunity for him to meet John D. Rockefeller, Jr. Mr. Rockefeller accepted an invitation to visit Williamsburg two years later, at which time Dr. Goodwin "presented and explained to him the Thought which had long been in his Mind of restoring the City to its colonial Appearance, and of preserving it . . . for the Future."[63] On a second visit by Mr. Rockefeller in the same year Dr. Goodwin secured his support for a survey of the town and shortly thereafter was authorized to make secret purchases of several properties. At a public meeting, in June, 1928, Dr. Goodwin revealed the nature and scope of the intended project and the identity of the benefactor. Within a short time full-scale restoration and reconstruction activities began.

It was a project without precedent in America, and it moved forward swiftly. In December, 1935, the editors of *Architectural Record* could summarize the achievements as follows:

> Some 440 buildings of late construction have been torn down and 18 moved outside the Colonial area; 66 Colonial buildings have been repaired or restored; 84 have been reproduced upon Colonial foundations. Federal Highway 60 has been diverted to a by-pass road, and streets, open spaces and gardens have resumed their Colonial appearance, with lamp-posts, fences, brick walks, street surfaces and plantings derived from authentic records.[64]

It would be inappropriate in this book to trace the history of this project in any detail.[65] It is enough to record that once again the elegant little colonial metropolis stands much as it appeared in the eighteenth century—a living testimony and witness to the town planning skills of a previous generation of Americans.

Figure 126 shows, superimposed on a portion of one of the French military maps of 1781, the boundaries of the original town as surveyed by Theodorick Bland in 1699 and the area that in modern times has been restored by Colonial Williamsburg. It will be seen that the restored section includes most of the city as developed by the end of the colonial period. All of the essential elements of Nicholson's plan, except the abandoned diagonal streets forming the W and M monograms, lie within this area.

The merits and distinctive qualities of the Williamsburg plan have been less understood and appreciated than the other features of the town. The skillfully restored and reconstructed buildings, along with the many useful exhibitions of craftsmen, have tended to overshadow the achievements of urban design as conceived by Nicholson and developed during the eighteenth century. The plan of Virginia's second colonial capital deserves equal recognition as the basic platform on which the third dimension of architecture could take form gracefully and with full visual effect. This approach to environmental design is a great lesson Williamsburg has to teach—that only where streets, open spaces, and building sites are conceived of, not as an abstract pattern but as part of a three-dimensional concept, can cities be beautiful as well as functional. It is not the exact architectural styles or details of the buildings or the precise form of the city plan that should be imitated, but this fundamental approach to the problem of creating urban spaces defined by buildings of pleasing size, materials, and proportions. The modern generation of urban designers wrestling with the problems of great cities might ponder the lesson of Williamsburg and find much to learn from this small town of the Virginia Tidewater.

IX. *Town Planning in Eighteenth-Century Virginia*

BEFORE the end of the first decade of the eighteenth century both tidewater colonies abandoned their attempts to create new towns in wholesale numbers through general town acts. This did not by any means bring to an end efforts to establish towns. The two colonies adopted instead a policy of founding individual towns as the need for them arose. In some cases the initiative came from the colonial legislatures. In others, the legislative bodies responded favorably to petitions from groups of freeholders seeking the creation of a town in their neighborhood. The eighteenth century also saw the development of individual enterprise in town founding, as landowners saw opportunities for speculation in building sites which they created by laying out towns on advantageous locations. In these cases the private entrepreneurs usually sought legislative sanction for their activities and normally were successful in gaining legal recognition through laws incorporating the town.

The new policy evolved over a period of time. Its roots can be found in the dissatisfactions that arose over the provisions of the general town acts and the failure of those acts to produce towns of substantial size and economic viability. Writing after the passage of the first two Virginia acts and two years before the founding of Williamsburg, Hartwell, Blair, and Chilton stated that "for well built Towns . . . [Virginia] . . . is certainly . . . one of the poorest, miserablest, and worst Countries in all America." While placing some of the blame for this condition on past governors of the colony, they struck hardest at the "Obstinacy of the People" and the members of the assembly, "the major Part . . . whereof having never seen a Town . . . cannot therefore imagine the Benefit of it, and are afraid of every Innovation that will put them to a present Charge, whatever may be be the future Benefit."

The town and port acts of 1680 and 1691 had failed, in their view, because the legislators

> always appointed too many Towns, which will be still the Fault of them, if they are contriv'd by a General Assembly; for every Man desiring the Town to be as near as is possible to his own Door, and the Burgesses setting up every one of them for his own County, they have commonly contriv'd a Town for every County, which might be reasonable enough hereafter, when the Country comes to be well peopled, but at present is utterly impracticable for want of People to inhabit them, and Money to build them.

It was easier to find fault than solutions. Hartwell, Blair, and Chilton were equivocal on the policy of restricting trade only to official ports. While they pointed out that this should force traders to locate at these points, they observed that such laws had "made all People very uneasy" and that "it would be a long Time before the old Merchants, who are in the present Possession of the Trade, would be perswaded to leave their Country-Houses and Stores, to come and live at towns." [1]

Even more outspoken was the Reverend Francis Makemie who in 1705 concluded his remarkable tract on the advantages of towns for the tidewater region with these intemperate words:

> I always judged such as are averse to Towns, to be three sorts of Persons: First, Fools, who cannot, neither will see their own Interest

and Advantage in having Towns. Secondly, Knaves, who would still carry on Fraudulent Designs, and cheating Tricks, in a corner or secret Trade, afraid and ashamed of being exposed at a Publick Market. Thirdly, Sluggards, who rather than be at labour, and at any charge in transporting their Goods to Market, tho idle at home, and lose double thereby rather than do it; To which I may add a fourth, which are Sots, who may be best Cured of their Disease by a pair of Stocks in Town.

This uncomplimentary analysis could hardly have pleased the colonists though many of them doubtless could agree with the author's long and more reasoned statement listing the advantages that towns might bring to the tidewater area. But Makemie's suggestions as to how this might be achieved seemed to add little or nothing to what had already been tried:

> Give all Encouragement to Trades and Strangers, especially to such as settle in Towns; lay no uneasie Burdens upon Trade, by the Fore-runners and Patterns to your People, in complying with your own Laws . . .; And beware of over-doing at first, but make a Beginning; for by aiming to do all at once, you may do nothing at all. Let all gentlemen of Estates be expeditious in building Dwelling-houses, and stores, both for merchants Goods and Tobacco, that the Trading Part of *England* may not Complain for want of conveniences at your Towns. Let a sufficient number of craft, as Sloops and Flotts, be provided for Transportation of all Tobacco to each Town, and at moderate Prices, which will soon refund your charge.[2]

Makemie, Hartwell, Blair, and Chilton directed their attention almost entirely to towns associated with port activities. By the time Makemie published his tract in 1705, Williamsburg was already demonstrating that under certain circumstances inland locations might be satisfactory as well. As settlers pushed westward beyond the coastal plain into the Piedmont and even to the ridge and valley region of Appalachia, the Virginia assembly gave some attention to the problems of town development on this new frontier. At a session begun in December 1700, the General Assembly authorized land grants in the west of ten to thirty thousand acres to groups of settlers who would own the land in common. Two hundred acres were "to be laid out in a geomitricall square" as a town, centered on a fort, and with half-acre town lots and two-hundred-acre farm plots nearby for each settler. For every five hundred acres of land granted to these "societyes or companies of men" the group was to maintain

> one christian man between sixteen and sixty years of age perfect of limb, able and fitt for service who shall alsoe be continually provided with a well fixt musquett or fuzee, a good pistoll, sharp simeter, tomahauk and five pounds of good clean pistoll powder and twenty pounds of sizable leaded bulletts or swan or goose shott.[3]

The features of this act may well have been drawn, at least in part, from the experience earlier in 1700 with a colonization and town planning project undertaken by Governor Nicholson and the Virginia assembly on a site some twenty miles west of the falls of the James River. The settlers were a group of Huguenot refugees who had been sent from England with the intention of locating in the southern part of Virginia along the Carolina border. Disregarding the instructions from his superiors, Governor Nicholson, with the consent of the council, directed them instead to an isolated frontier site once occupied by the Monocan Indians. Apparently Nicholson was influenced in this decision by the arguments of William Byrd I, who two years earlier had unsuccessfully sought to have the Huguenots sent to this area, near his own vast holdings of land at and around the James River falls.[4]

It was Byrd who led the first party of 120 adults and children to the deserted Indian town site on the south bank of the James late in the summer of 1700. It seems likely that it was he who laid out Manakin Town, the plan of which is reproduced in figure 127.[5] Byrd's plan contains some curious and fascinating elements. Although no scale appears on the drawing, if we assume that the partially enclosed rectangles represent huts approximately 12 feet on a side the central open space would measure about 150 by 250 feet. Byrd gave the name of Nicholson Square to this area, doubtless as a compliment to the governor who had so conveniently sided with him over the location of the new community. Byrd Street, entering the square from the left would be about 50 feet wide, and the entire town would measure about 300 feet square.

The James River is indicated at the top of the drawing, with gardens between the bank and the north side of the town proper. The drawing also shows gardens between the double rows of attached dwellings on the east and west sides of the community and along its southern boundary. "Plantations" were located along the river bank east and west from the settlement. Doubtless these extended some distance in each direction, with each settler having a narrow frontage along the river and his land extending back toward the south.[6] The buildings in the four corners of Nicholson Square are identified in the drawing: the church, the hospital, the town house and school, and the laundry.

This rather charming and orderly plan suggests a pleasant community. Byrd, who had every reason to view the settlement with optimism, described it the following year, however, as consisting of "about seventy . . . hutts, being, most of them, very mean."[7] The Huguenots, arriving too late in 1700 to plant crops, had managed to survive on the supplies they had been able to bring with them and on food purchased with funds subscribed by a number of Virginians. Conditions improved in the following months, and in the spring of 1702 Michel could record that the Huguenots were

> richly provided with everything. . . . Things that are grown are there in such abundance that many Englishmen come a distance of 30 miles to get fruit, which they mostly exchange for cattle. Gardens are filled there with all kinds of fruit. . . . The cattle are fat because of the abundant pasture. The soil is not sandy, as it is generally in Virginia, but it is a heavy, rich soil.[8]

Manakin Town, like the earlier Virginia settlements, was intended as an agricultural village on European models. Its residents lived in the nucleated community around Nicholson Square and daily went to their farm fields beyond the town. As the frontier was gradually pushed westward during the eighteenth century and the danger from Indian attack was reduced and finally eliminated altogether, this pattern began to break down. Members of the colony erected farm dwellings on their outlying land, many became dissatisfied with the location and moved elsewhere, and persons not of Huguenot background bought land from the original settlers or their descendants. A large number of the Huguenots, possibly a majority, preferred to follow nonagricultural activities and migrated to one of the towns finally beginning to develop in the Piedmont and elsewhere. By the middle of the century the site had become virtually deserted and today can be located only with difficulty. This early Piedmont town experiment had ended in failure, although during its life Manakin Town served a useful function in providing a start in the new world for Huguenot refugees, who continued to settle there in dwindling numbers during the half century of its existence.

William Byrd II was to have a more successful career as town planner

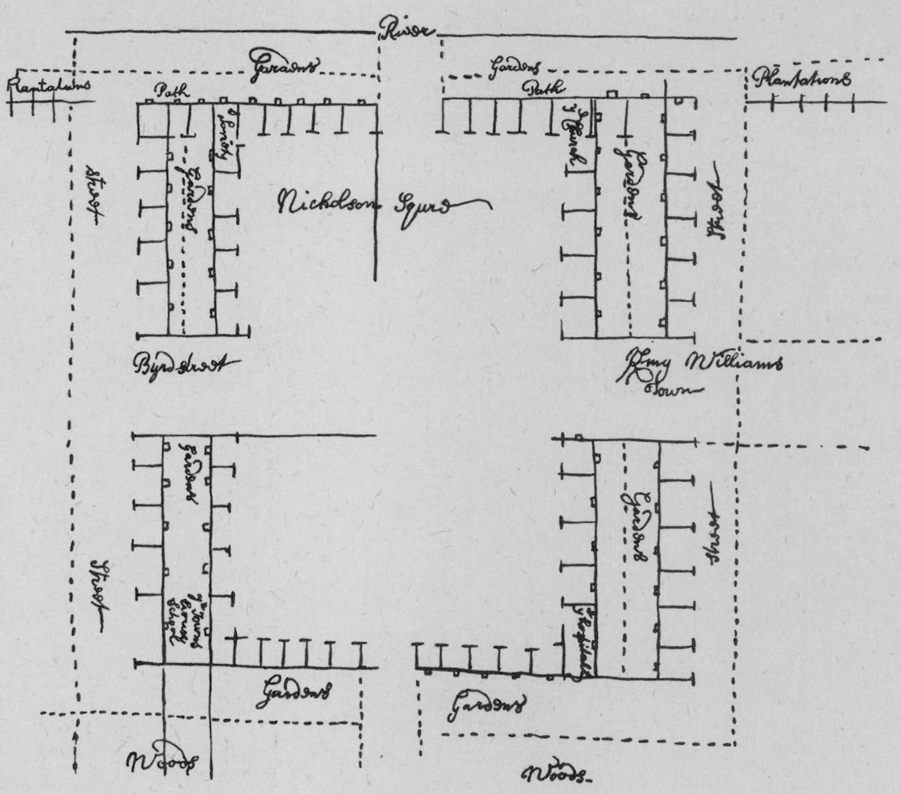

Figure 127. Plan of Manakin, Virginia: ca. 1700

than did his father, but Eden was one of his failures. In the 1730s he began a series of attempts to induce European settlement on his vast domain in the southeastern portion of Virginia. In 1736 he wrote Lord Egmont of his proposal to "plant a colony of Switzers on my land upon the Roanoke. For this good purpose, I expect to make a beginning with one hundred families at the fall of the year."[9] The area he had in mind lay on the south side of the Roanoke River (known now as the Dan) near the mouth of the Hyco River (then called the Hyco-otee) in what is the present Halifax County.

He proposed to establish a series of small communities along the river, linked by a network of roads, as shown in figure 128. This map includes in the upper left-hand corner an inset plan showing how each town would

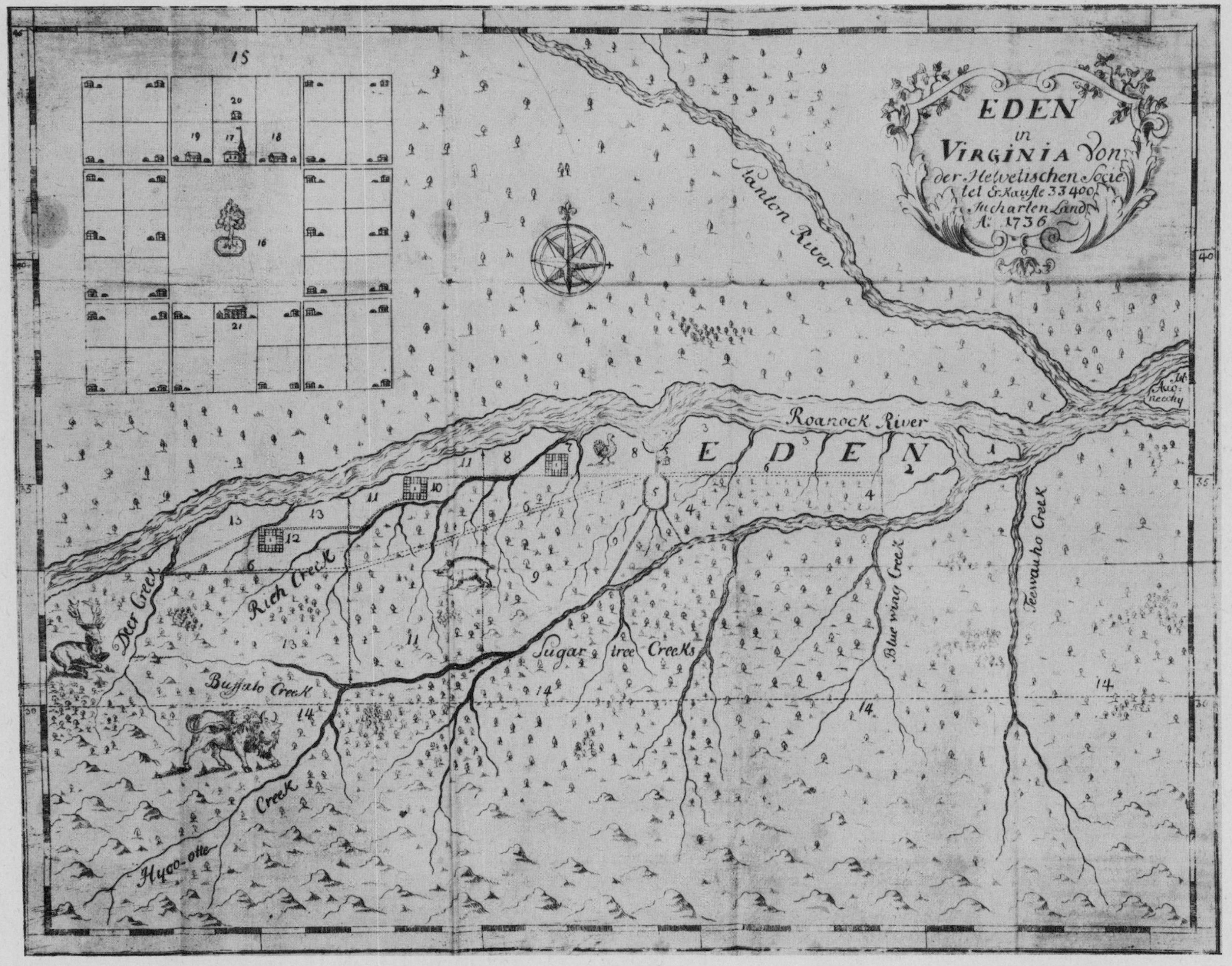

Figure 128. Map of Eden in Virginia with a Plan of One of the Proposed Towns: 1737

be laid out. The large central square, like that of Manakin Town, was plainly intended as the focus of the community, with the church and other important buildings having sites fronting this open area. House lots, probably the half-acre size that had become virtually a standard in colonial Virginia, were laid out in square plots served by a little gridiron street system. The plan closely resembled that of New Haven, Connecticut, which had been founded roughly a century earlier, although there is no evidence that Byrd knew of the design of this New England community.

The plan of Eden, engraved probably in Bern, appeared in a tract published in 1737 by the Helvetian Society as an attempt by Samuel Jenner, its American agent, to attract settlers to Byrd's land.[10] Although Jenner is recorded as paying Byrd the sum of £3,000 for 33,400 acres of land, it seems doubtful that the transaction was ever concluded. In any event the contemplated settlement never took place. The ship on which 250 Swiss colonists expected to reach America was wrecked on the coast during a violent storm, and only a few managed to escape. Despite new attempts by Byrd to interest some Scotch-Irish from Pennsylvania and new arrivals in Norfolk from Scotland in taking up residence on his estate, he was unsuccessful in his colonization efforts and on his death in 1744 the land still remained undeveloped.

Most of the eighteenth-century town planning achievements in Virginia and Maryland lacked the unusual background of Manakin Town or Eden. Nor, except in rare cases, did their plans depart from the straightforward and rather unimaginative, if serviceable, gridiron patterns that had become the almost universal form employed under the general town acts of the previous century. At least one settlement was even more primitive in its plan form, consisting solely of a few house lots arranged in linear fashion one after the other and presumably served on one side by a street or lane.[11]

Fredericksburg, strategically located near the falls of the Rappahannock River, stands as a typical example of the planning of this period, although it achieved and maintained a degree of prosperity greater than most of the new towns of the eighteenth century. The assembly created the town officially in 1727 by appointing trustees, who were to acquire fifty acres of land on the south bank of the river from John Royston and Robert Buckner and to lay out the site into streets and lots not exceeding half an acre in size. As the lots were sold, the original owners were to be compensated at the rate of forty shillings for every acre disposed of. In these provisions the act followed the precedents established earlier under the general town and port legislation.

There were some differences. The two proprietors were each to be given two lots outright, and the purchasers of building sites were to be allowed two years in which to complete a structure at least twenty feet square. More important, the act specified that certain sites were to be set aside "for a church and church-yard, a market place . . . public key, and . . . publick landings." The trustees were also authorized "if the same shall be necessary" to "direct the making and erecting of wharfs and cranes, at such public landings, for the public use."[12] The law further provided for a twin community, named Falmouth, to be planned under similar conditions on the north bank of the river opposite Fredericksburg.

The first plat of the town, figure 129, bears the date 1721 and the notation that it shows the streets and lots "as first laid off . . . by Royston & Buckner." This strongly suggests that the two proprietors had taken the initiative six years before the official creation of the town by the assembly. The trustees appointed by the act of 1727 apparently adopted this plan as their own, though it did not include any areas specifically designated for public landings. The plat does show, marked by the letters "A" and "B," the required sites for the church and the market. Royston and Buckner had provided streets of generous widths. The principal street, 82½ feet wide, ran parallel to the river. All other were four poles or 66 feet in width and comprised the little gridiron on which the town soon began to develop.

When William Byrd II visited Fredericksburg in the autumn of 1732 he recorded these observations, which indicate the limited extent to which the new town had been able to attract settlers:

> Fredericksburg . . . is pleasantly situated on the south shore of Rappahannock River, about a mile below the falls. Sloops may come up and lie close to the wharf, within thirty yards of the public warehouses, which are built in the figure of a cross. Just by the wharf is a quarry of white stone . . . . Besides that, there are several other quarries in the river bank, within the limits of the town, sufficient to build a great city. The only edifice of stone yet built is the prison.
>
> Though this be a commodious and beautiful situation for a town, with the advantages of a navigable river and wholesome air, yet the inhabitants are very few. Besides Colonel Willis, who is the top man of the place, there are only one merchant, a tailor, a smith, and an

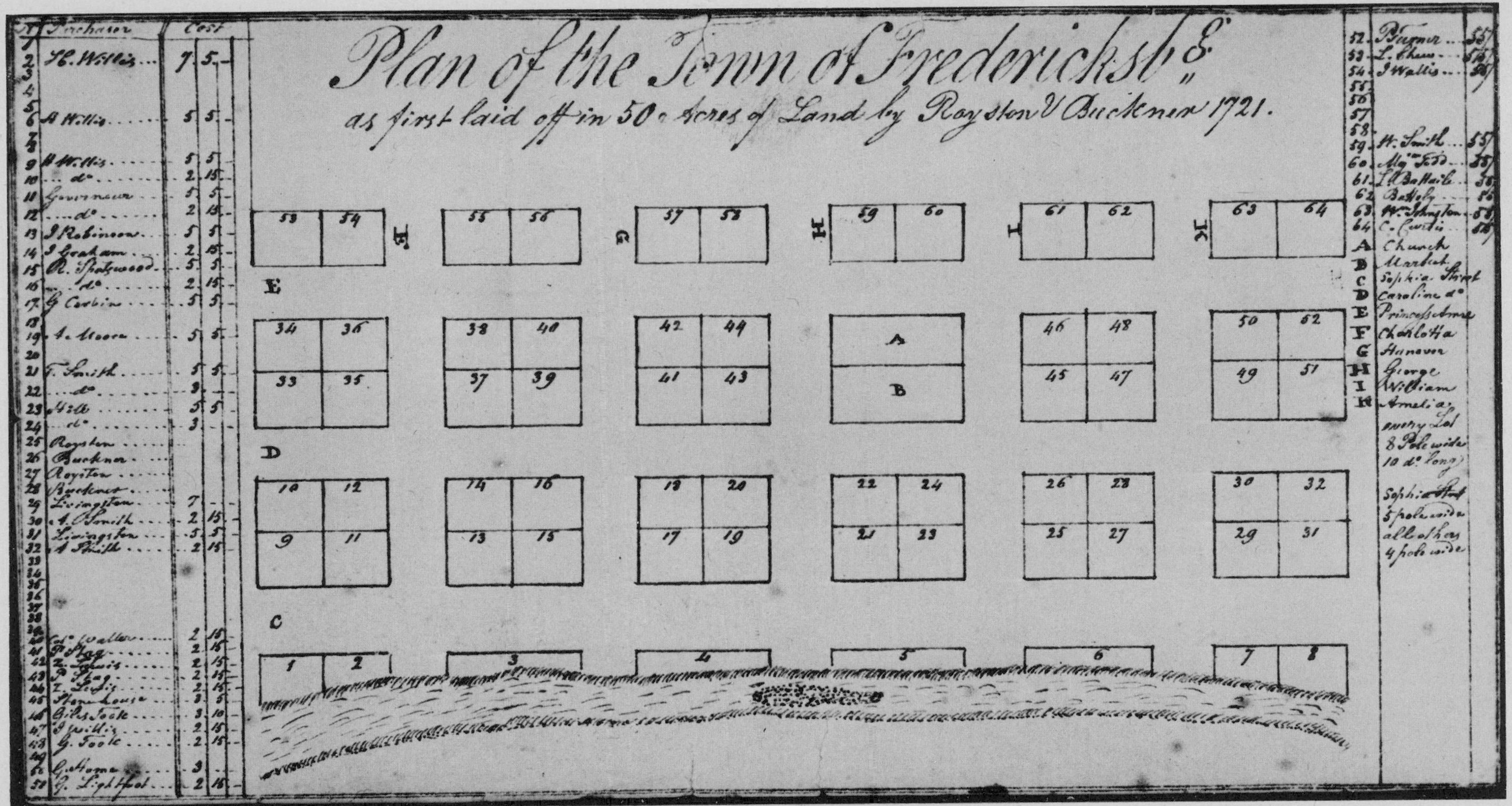

Figure 129. Plan of Fredericksburg, Virginia: 1721

> ordinary keeper. . . . 'Tis said the courthouse and the church are going to be built here, and then both religion and justice will help to enlarge the place.[13]

Byrd's optimistic views of the town's future were amply justified. At the end of the colonial period William Loughton Smith observed that Fredericksburg "appears to be thriving and carrying on a large business; there are a great many stores in it, and the houses are generally near and in good repair; it contains upwards of 300."[14]

Fredericksburg flourished as a port city, and many industries associated with shipping were located in the town. It served as well as a center of education and culture for a large region in which it was and is by far the largest urban center. Warehouses lined the banks of the river, ships of substantial size called regularly, and a great many craftsmen located in the

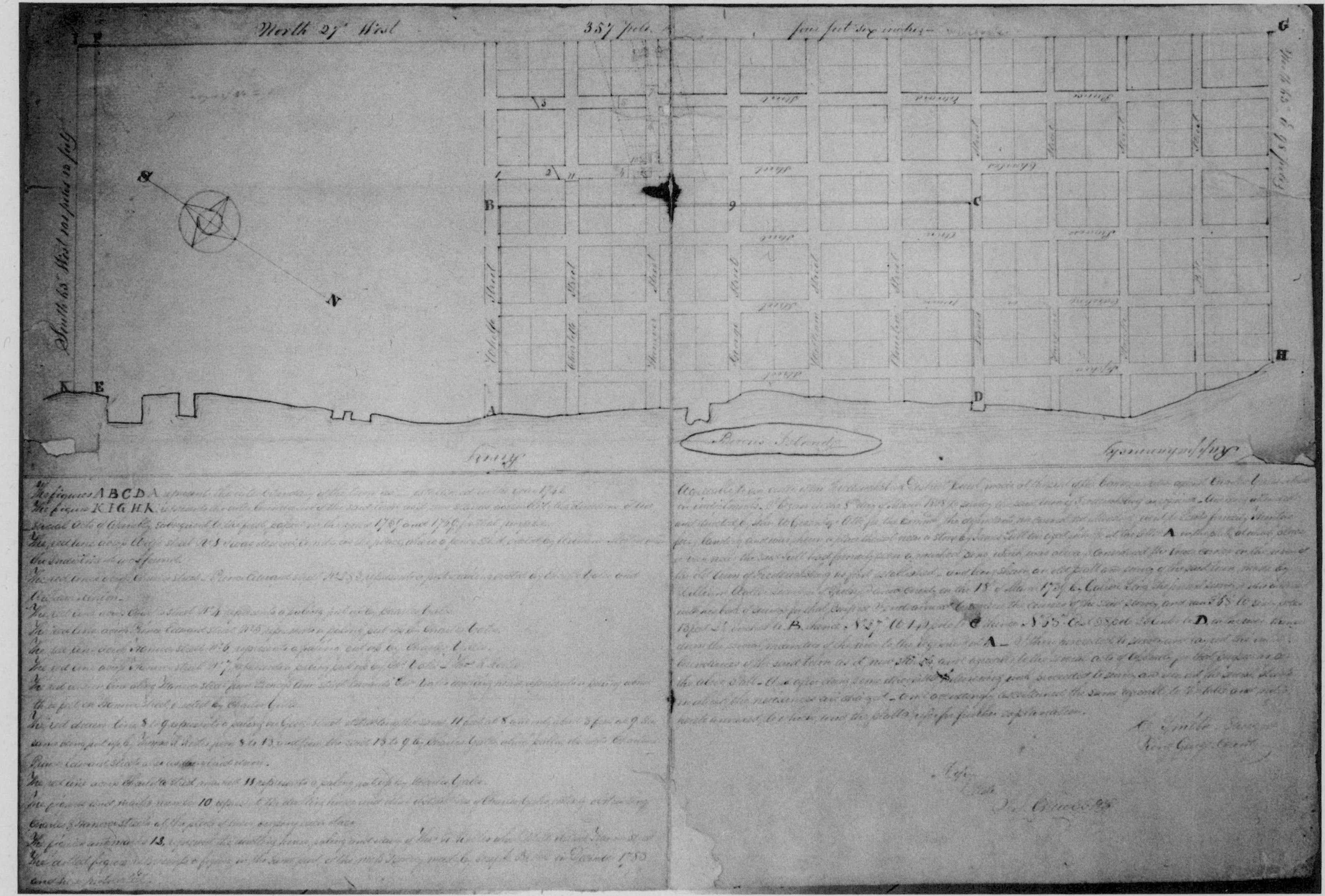

Figure 130. Plan of Fredericksburg, Virginia: 1769

town to practice their diverse trades.[15] Soon it became necessary to enlarge the town to accommodate the growing population. By 1769 the boundaries had been extended back from the river and in each direction along its banks, as shown in figure 130. The streets of the original town, the bounds of which are indicated by the line connecting the letters "A," "B," "C," and "D," were extended to enlarge the first gridiron plan, and the rectangular blocks were laid off into four lots each as had been established in the earlier design.[16]

Fredericksburg, in common with the earlier port towns created by general legislation and the towns of the eighteenth century officially erected by individual acts, received from the assembly privileges to hold fairs and markets. We find also legislative concern over matters of safety, conveniences, and sanitation in Fredericksburg reflected in directives prohibiting wooden chimneys, authorizing the trustees and directors to assess property owners for the cost of repairing streets, and "restraining the inhabitants from suffering their hogs and goats to run at large."[17] These laws affecting conditions in Fredericksburg were typical of many passed during the eighteenth century applicable to other towns and indicated a growing awareness of some of the problems connected with the rise of towns and cities.

The merchants and traders of the town erected many handsome mansions and town houses. From the countryside nearby, tobacco plantations and, later, wheat farms sent their produce to the town warehouses. On market days or when the court was in session planters and farmers from the region joined the townspeople and seamen from the port to crowd the busy streets of the thriving community. The city in the late colonial period must have resembled closely the appearance it had in 1862 when the view reproduced in figure 131 was published. And, despite a major fire in 1807 and destruction during the Civil War, many of the old buildings of Fredericksburg have survived. The original plan, as extended, serves the modern town

Figure 131. View of Fredericksburg, Virginia: 1862

reasonably well. Its population today is scarcely more than double what it was at the peak of its prosperity during the eighteenth century, and the gridiron plan of its streets is not oppressively monotonous because of its restricted size.

By the same act that created Fredericksburg, the assembly also established the town of Falmouth on a site a few miles north and on the opposite side of the Rappahannock River. Fifty acres of land belonging to William Todd were to be surveyed and planned in streets and lots not exceeding half an acre in size. Sites "for a church, church yard, market place, and public key" were to be selected, and trustees of the new town were granted the same powers conferred on those of Fredericksburg. Todd had apparently erected several structures on the site, for the act provided that he should be compensated for any buildings that lay in the right-of-way of any of the new streets. He was also to be granted four lots in the town, and "in case such houses shall fall within the bounds of any lot or lots, the the same shall be assigned him, as part of the four lots."[18]

Falmouth did not attain the size of Fredericksburg, but it was nonetheless a port and town of some importance. In 1759, according to one account, it consisted of "eighteen or twenty houses."[19] Doubtless there were also one or more tobacco warehouses, several stores, and a tavern or two. Although no early plan of the town is extant, the portion of a map of Fredericksburg and vicinity during the Civil War reproduced in figure 132 shows the traditional little checkerboard plan for the town on the bank above the river. Plainly, however, there was commerce enough at this location to support only one community of any size, and Fredericksburg's growth had dwarfed that of its sister town across the river.

South of Falmouth and across the river from Fredericksburg, nearly opposite its lower end, lies Ferry Farm, George Washington's boyhood home. Washington later sold this land to General Hugh Mercer, and either he or his son, William, attempted to duplicate the success of the planners of Fredericksburg and Falmouth by laying out the little town shown in figure 133.[20] So far as can be determined, Mercer Town failed to attract settlers, and joined many of the other paper communities of tidewater Virginia and Maryland in oblivion.

A short distance to the east and north of Fredericksburg, along the broad waters of the Potomac River, a number of towns were laid out in the eighteenth century. Dumfries, roughly halfway between Fredericksburg and Alexandria, came into existence in 1749. Its sheltered site a little distance up Quantico Creek proved to be attractive, and the town shortly developed as a minor port and trading center for the neighborhood.[22] With time, however, the creek began to silt up as the exposed and overworked tobacco fields eroded. The town dwindled in importance, and while it continued to exist, it is now little more than a village whose modern appearance gives no hint that it once served an important function in the development of its region. Two other towns in the immediate vicinity have disappeared altogether. Newport, at the mouth of Quantico Creek in Prince William County, appears in figure 134 as it was laid out in 1788. A few miles to the south, on Aquia Creek, Woodstock in Stafford County was surveyed in 1792 in a more regular gridiron on a somewhat more spacious site. Woodstock's plan, reproduced in figure 135, like that of all the eighteenth-century Virginia plans attests to the popularity, among the town planners and land surveyors of the Tidewater, of geometrically exact patterns of straight streets, right-angled intersections, and rectangular building lots.

Nowhere was this to be demonstrated more completely than in the original plan and successive extensions for the city of Alexandria. Its location a few miles below the falls of the Potomac on a gently sloping site along the west bank of the river can be seen on the portion of Joshua Fry and Peter Jefferson's map of the tidewater area in 1751 reproduced in figure 136. This map also reveals the extent to which town development had proceeded in the northeastern portion of Virginia by the middle of the eighteenth century. A number of the communities we have just examined may be noted, as well as a great many other settlements on the upper Rappahannock and Potomac rivers.

At the mouth of Hunting Creek a tobacco warehouse had been established by 1730 as a point where the crops of planters in the vicinity could be inspected and shipped and duties collected.[23] A great many such places throughout Virginia and Maryland had been so designated after the repeal of the last general town and port acts. Some of these sites were in new towns created by individual acts, while others served as more isolated facilities. Around them frequently grew up little hamlets, and apparently some development of this sort had occurred at the Hunting Creek location. Planters in the region soon began to petition the assembly for the creation of a town, and in 1749 the assembly authorized for this purpose the acquisition of sixty acres of land belonging to Philip and John Alexander

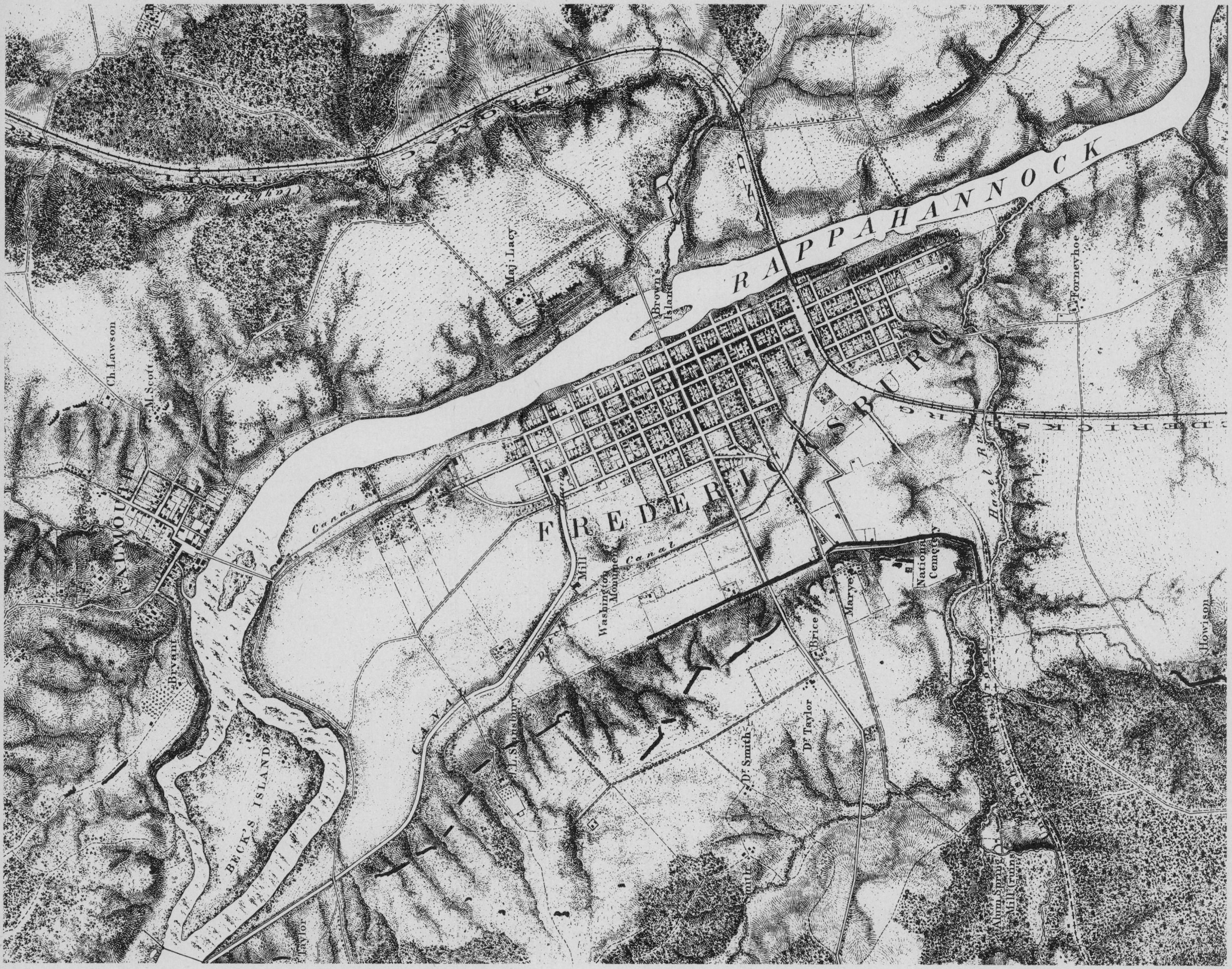

Figure 132. Map of Fredericksburg, Virginia, and Vicinity: 1867

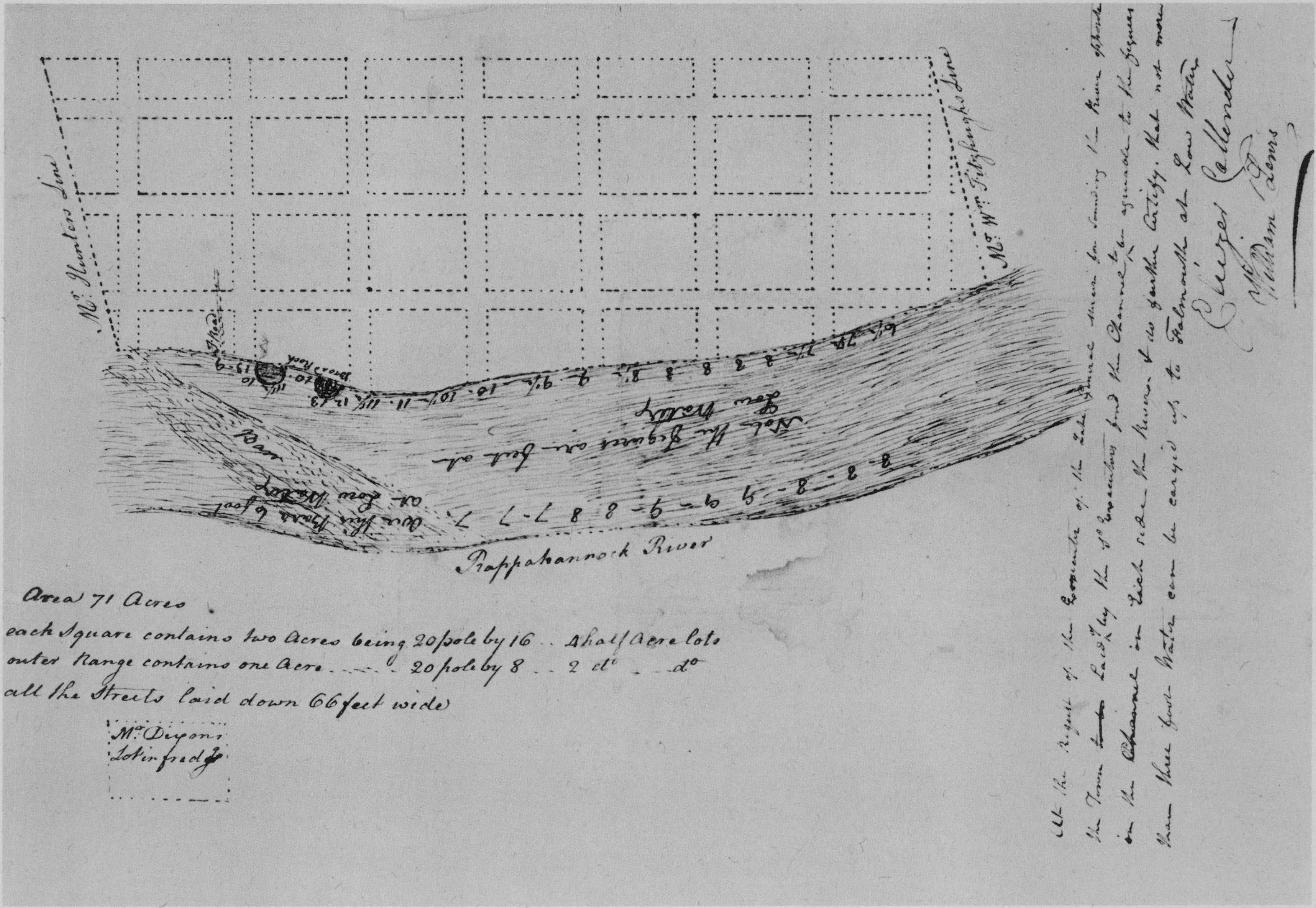

Figure 133. Plan of Mercer Town, Virginia: ca. 1785

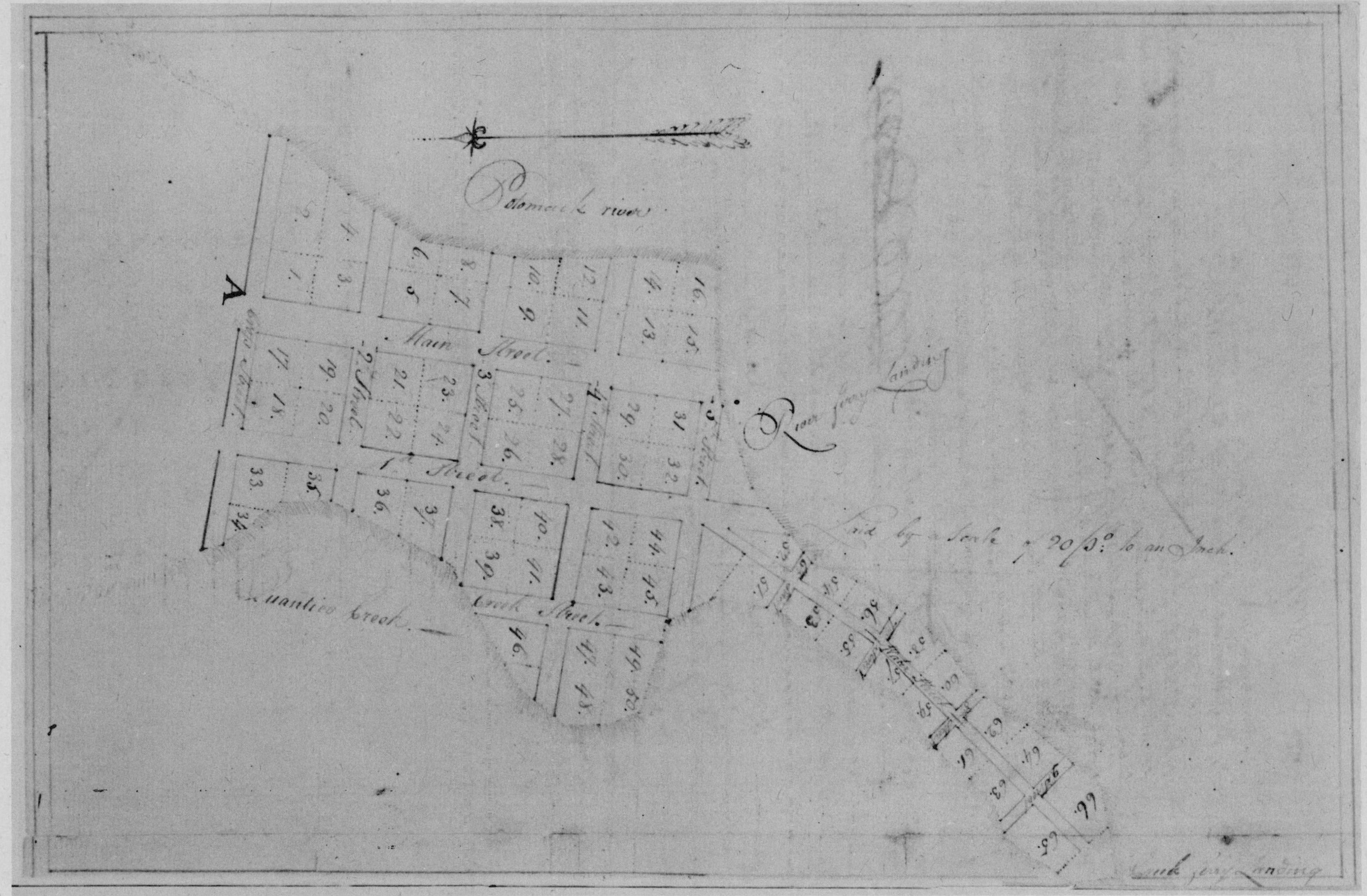

Figure 134. Plan of Newport, Virginia: 1788

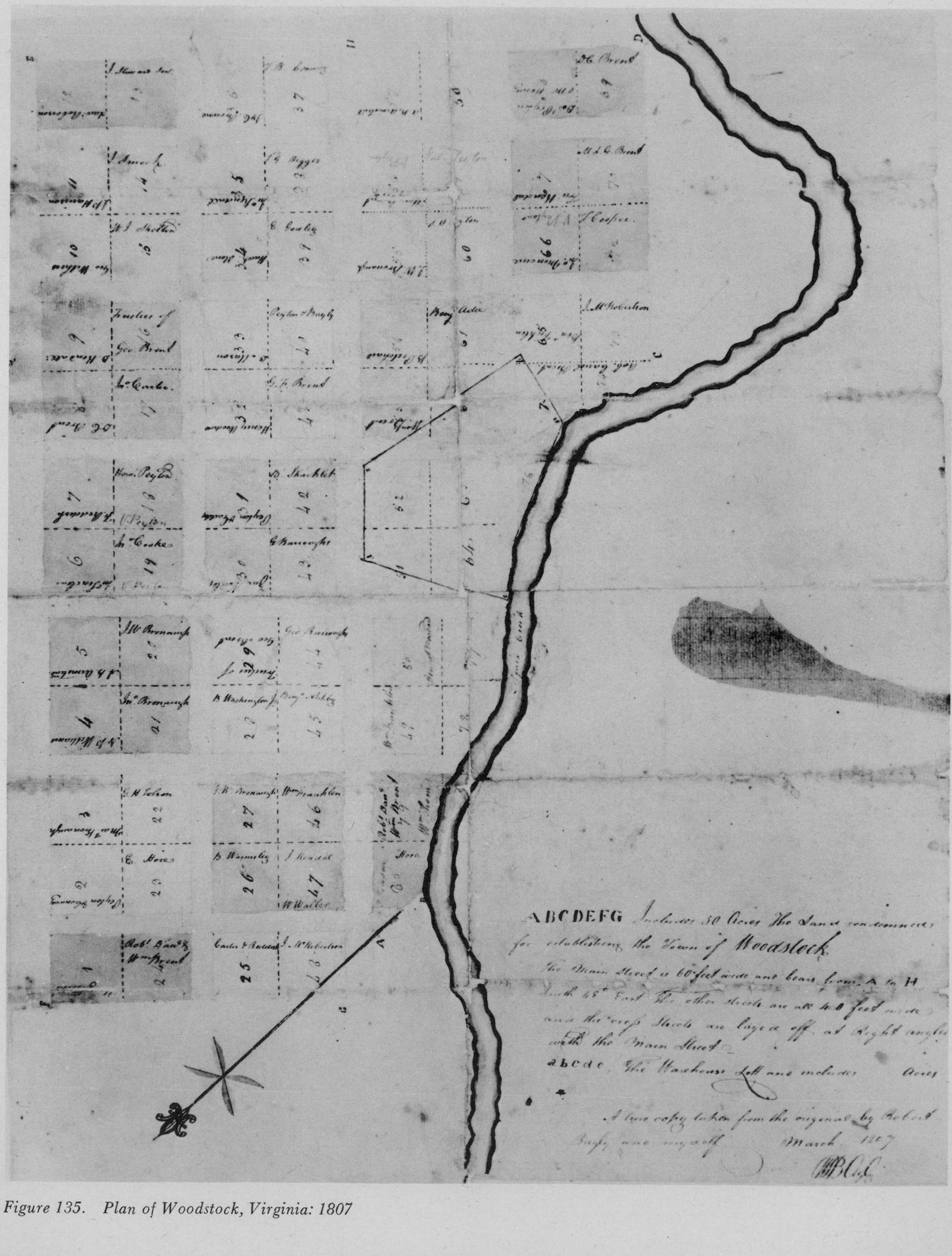

Figure 135. Plan of Woodstock, Virginia: 1807

and Hugh West. The act appointed several trustees, and in other respects was virtually identical to that establishing Fredericksburg.[24]

By the middle of July John West, the surveyor for Fairfax County, had completed his work under the direction of the trustees, who promptly arranged for a public sale of lots. Young George Washington, then studying surveying, aided West in his work. He was also an interested spectator at the sale and prepared for his half brother, Lawrence, a plat of the town with numbered lots. This drawing is reproduced in figure 137.[25] The plan, as can be seen, is a nearly regular gridiron pattern, interrupted only by the curve of the bay along the Potomac frontage. Water Street is broken by the shoreline, a curiously clumsy feature that was not to be rectified for many years when a portion of the little bay was filled in and Water and other streets extended into this reclaimed area.

There was nothing in this plan to distinguish Alexandria from dozens of other Virginia or Maryland towns, yet the city attained a size exceeded by only a few other tidewater communities and an urban character of beauty and sophistication surpassed by none. Land sales proved brisk. Twenty-four lots were sold during the first day's auction and seventeen the next.[26] By 1750, eighty of the eighty-four lots had been disposed of with two of the remaining reserved for a market and a courthouse. These two sites adjoined, with the courthouse occupying lot 43 where Cameron and Fairfax streets intersected, and with lot 44 at Royal and Cameron being set aside for the market and mustering ground for the militia.

The trustees concerned themselves with provisions to insure orderly development of the new town. Exercising their authority to adopt rules and regulations governing building, they ordered in 1752

> that all dwelling houses from this day not begun or to be built hereafter shall be built on the front and be in a line with the street as chief of the houses now are, and that no gable or end of such house be on or next to the Street, except an angle or where two streets cross, otherwise to be pulled down.[27]

Under these and other regulations pertaining to construction of streets, draining of the marsh lots, and the development of wharves and warehouses Alexandria developed into a handsome town with a prosperous economic life.

Trade provided the basis for much of the prosperity of the community.

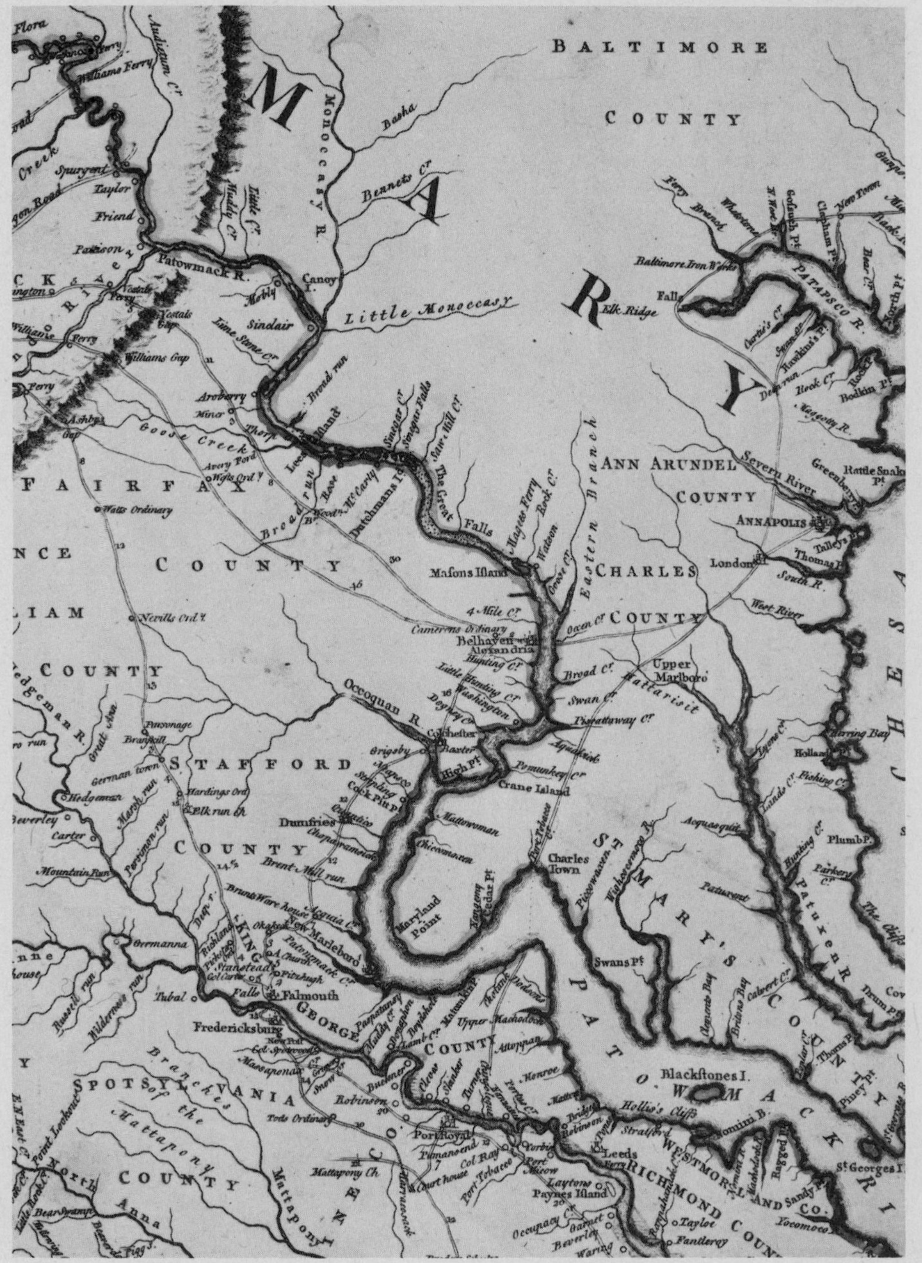

Figure 136. Map of Portion of Virginia: 1751

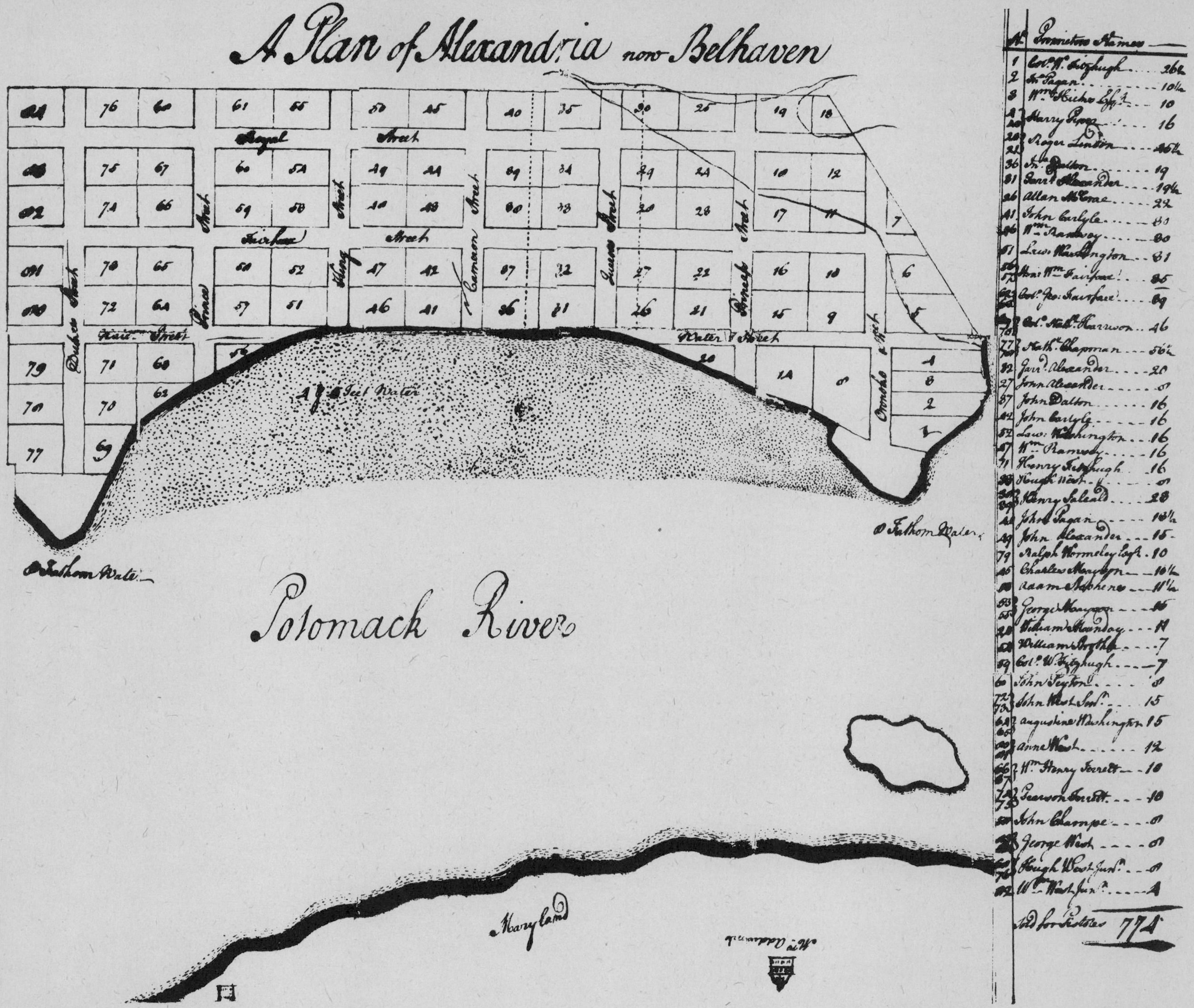

Figure 137. Plan of Alexandria, Virginia: ca. 1749

Shipbuilding and related industries soon assumed great importance. Warehouses, sail lofts, rope walks, and shipyards lined the banks of the Potomac. Shops in the town were kept busy providing foodstuffs and other supplies for provisioning ships that called at the port. Taverns and inns offered accommodations and entertainment for visiting seamen. Through this port came the numerous imports from England and elsewhere eagerly purchased by wealthy plantation owners in the vicinity as well as by the townspeople.[28] Soon the large lots surveyed in 1749 were divided into smaller plots on which were erected town houses adjacent to each other close to the street line, with gardens stretching to the rear.

Many of these handsome structures of the eighteenth century remain. Together with those built in the early nineteenth century of similar style, they provide Alexandria with a distinctive character unrivaled by any city in the Tidewater. Two blocks on Prince Street sloping down to the water from Fairfax Street have been preserved almost intact. This area provides the modern visitor an impressive view of the urban atmosphere that most of the city once possessed. Isolated structures or smaller groups of other buildings in the older part of the city stand as additional reminders of the time when Alexandria ranked with Boston, Philadelphia, and New York as a major colonial seaport.

Prosperity and population growth required extensions to the original boundaries. In 1762 the trustees requested the assembly to enlarge the town, and an act was passed conferring this authority.[29] Forty-six of the new lots were sold on May 9, 1763, others were purchased from time to time, and further extensions to the town became necessary within five years. As can be seen in the plan of the town as it existed in 1796 (figure 138), the trustees had simply expanded the original gridiron design in three directions. The sixty-six-foot street width of the first plan was retained, as well as the half-acre lot size, although in a few blocks the shapes of the lots were altered to provide narrower frontage and greater depth. In 1785 the assembly provided for further extension of the city.[30] This marked a slight change in policy as the act did not direct the city to survey the new streets but permitted existing owners to subdivide the land when they wished. In doing so, however, owners were required to follow the dimensions already established for streets and blocks, except that Washington Street was to be made one hundred feet wide. The act further permitted the city to widen to this more generous size that portion of Washington Street previously laid out. The owners of any land taken were to be compensated with funds collected for this purpose through a levy on all property within the city.

By 1798 these extensions had been carried out, as can be seen in figure 139. In addition, the bay or cove below Water Street had been filled, providing additional space for warehouses and shops, and Union Street had been added to afford access to this area.[31] Shortly before these improvements William Loughton Smith visited Alexandria and recorded these mixed impressions:

> Alexandria is a considerable place of trade, is well situated on the river which is three-fourths of a mile wide. It . . . is now thriving rapidly; the situation of the Town, a capital one, a fine eminence, plain level, and bounded by a pretty range of hills an excellent, safe, and commodious harbour, a fine back country to it, will soon make it a very important post; much business is done here; there are about 3,200 inhabitants; the houses principally of brick; the streets are not paved and being of clay after rain they are so slippery it is almost impossible to walk in them. I went to the top of Colonel Howe's house, a very lofty one, the prospect a magnificent one. The Town laid out at right angles, the harbour, river to great distance, with its windings, creeks, and island, the extensive plain contiguous to the city, all formed a fine scene.[32]

Alexandria's importance as a port, severely reduced during the Revolution, had by that time been re-established. In 1791 all but a small part of the southern portion of the city had been included in the newly created federal capital district, and its inhabitants doubtless expected to enjoy a new wave of prosperity throughout its association with the national capital a few miles up the Potomac. But this was not to be. Plagues of yellow fever in 1803 and cholera in 1832, disastrous fires in 1810 and 1824, and the trade blockade during the War of 1812 slowed the pace of growth. More important was the failure of the Potomac Canal project to link the region with the Midwest. Most of the wheat trade on which Alexandria's port activities depended was diverted to other ports, and the town's relative importance steadily declined.

It remained an attractive city nonetheless as the view of the city published in 1862 and reproduced in figure 140 reveals. Looking up King Street, in the center of the view, and the other streets leading from the

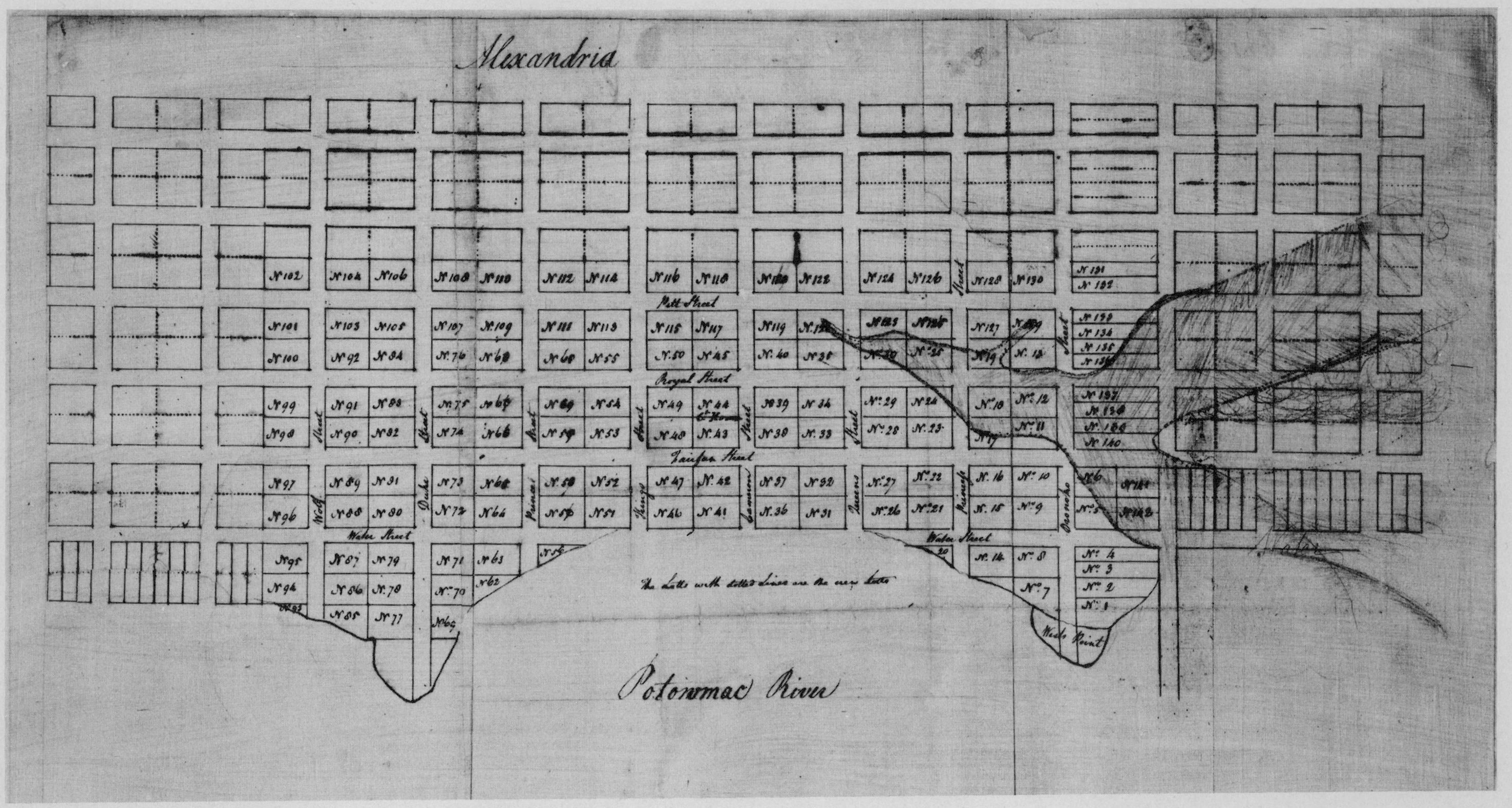

Figure 138. Plan of Alexandria, Virginia: ca. 1796

waterfront one can see the imposing town houses of the wealthy and the smaller but equally appealing dwellings of persons of more modest means. It is perhaps fortunate that Alexandria was not destined to develop as a major metropolis. If that had occurred much of the colonial city would surely have been obliterated during a period of mercantile expansion in the later nineteenth century.

The modern city, prospering now as the heart of a major residential sector of metropolitan Washington, has been moderately successful in preserving substantial portions of its colonial past. Even with modern structures clashing in scale and materials with the graceful buildings of the past, Alexandria stands as an impressive reminder of the achievements of colonial designers. The quality of the buildings surpasses the rather

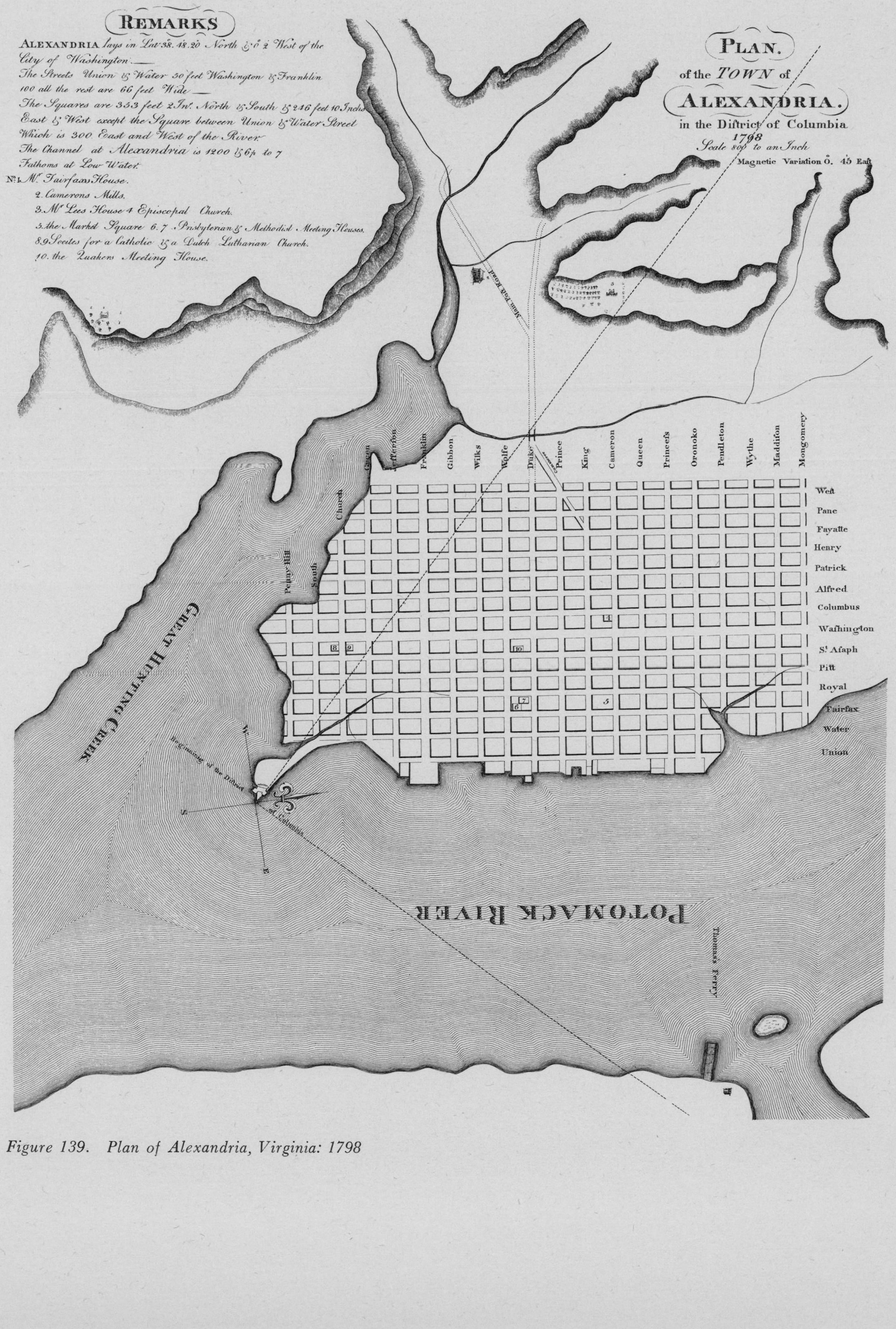

Figure 139. Plan of Alexandria, Virginia: 1798

Figure 140. View of Alexandria, Virginia: 1862

routine plan provided by John West and the distinguished trustees under whom he worked. The city would have been even more successful in its appearance if the original design had included a major focal point or a repeated pattern of public open spaces. But here, as in virtually all other tidewater towns of the eighteenth century, the lessons of civic design Francis Nicholson had sought to apply to Annapolis and Williamsburg were ignored.

Gridiron town planning was pursued in all parts of eastern Virginia with remarkable consistency. It sometimes took almost ludicrous forms, as in the case of Port Conway on the north bank of the Rappahannock River a few miles below Fredericksburg in King George County. The plan as laid out by Francis Conway in 1783 and confirmed by the assembly the following year consisted of a single street sixty feet wide, two cross streets each thirty-three feet in width, and twenty lots.[33] Figure 141 reveals the curiously elongated shape adopted by Conway and surveyed by Aaron Thornley.

Doubtless Conway hoped to attract to his property some of the trade and commerce that had developed across the river at Port Royal. There Robert Smith had directed under the terms of his will that Richard Taliaferro should lay out a town and sell lots to satisfy the debts of his estate. The assembly in 1744 passed the necessary legislation creating the town, appointing trustees, and adopting the sixty-acre plan designed by Taliaferro.[34] This, like virtually all other towns of the eighteenth-century tidewater region, took the familiar form of a gridiron of four streets leading to the water front, intersected at right angles by five others that divided the community into nearly square blocks.[35] On his visit in 1775, Dr. Robert Honyman noted that the river at this point was "A little more than a quarter of a Mile across, but deep enough to carry Vessels of great Burthen." The town then contained "20 or 30 dwelling houses, & about 6 stores, all Scotch." [36]

Smithfield in Isle of Wight County was another new town of the eighteenth century that had its beginnings in private speculation. In 1752 Arthur Smith's land along Pagan Creek, not far from its mouth on the James River, was surveyed by Jordan Thomas. Then Smith petitioned the assembly for legal recognition, and the usual act appointing trustees for regulating the town was duly passed.[37] The plan, reproduced in figure 142, took the form of a modified gridiron with a number of lots fronting on a street that followed the curve of the creek leading away from the main part of the little settlement. Evidently the town was planned to supplement the courthouse, erected three years earlier.[38] Its modern reputation as the center of a region producing the famous Smithfield hams has a long tradition, for as early as 1779 cured hams were being shipped from the town to the West Indies.

South of Smithfield lay Suffolk, established in 1742 on the edge of the great Dismal Swamp in Nansemond County. On fifty acres of land, the property of Jethro Summer, county surveyor Thomas Milner laid out the town near an earlier tobacco warehouse.[39] By 1770, according to one visitor, the town contained "about an hundred houses." They were, however, not particularly impressive, being "low . . . not more than one story high, which is indeed the ground story only." Nor were the streets, doubtless planned in the traditional gridiron, all that might be desired:

> Suffolk stands on a soil so very sandy, that in every step in the street the sand comes about your ancles, which renders it extremely disagreeable; to remedy this inconvenience in some small degree, near their doors they have emptied barrels of tar or pitch, which spreads wide, the sand incorporating with it, and forming a hard solid consistence, some kind of an apology for pavement, and thereby renders walking much more tolerable.[40]

The pitch and tar, along with turpentine, were the principal products of the pine forests that stretched across the Virginia border into North Carolina. In May, 1779, most of the town was burned by British troops, and few remains of the colonial period have survived.

The principal port towns of lower tidewater Virginia shared the wartime destruction endured by Suffolk. Among these was Norfolk, whose first founding and early development has already been examined. Here, of course, we are not dealing with the establishment of a new community but with the extension of an older one that had proved to be advantageously located and that continued to grow and develop. By 1765, according to Lord Adam Gordon, the city had become "the Port of most traffick in Virginia, it contains above four hundred houses, has depth of Water for a Forty Gun Ship, or more, and conveniences of every kind for heaving down, and fitting out large Vessels, also a very fine Rope-Walk." [41]

The Virginia asssembly in 1736 conferred on the community the status of "borough," enlarged its boundaries, established the framework for local

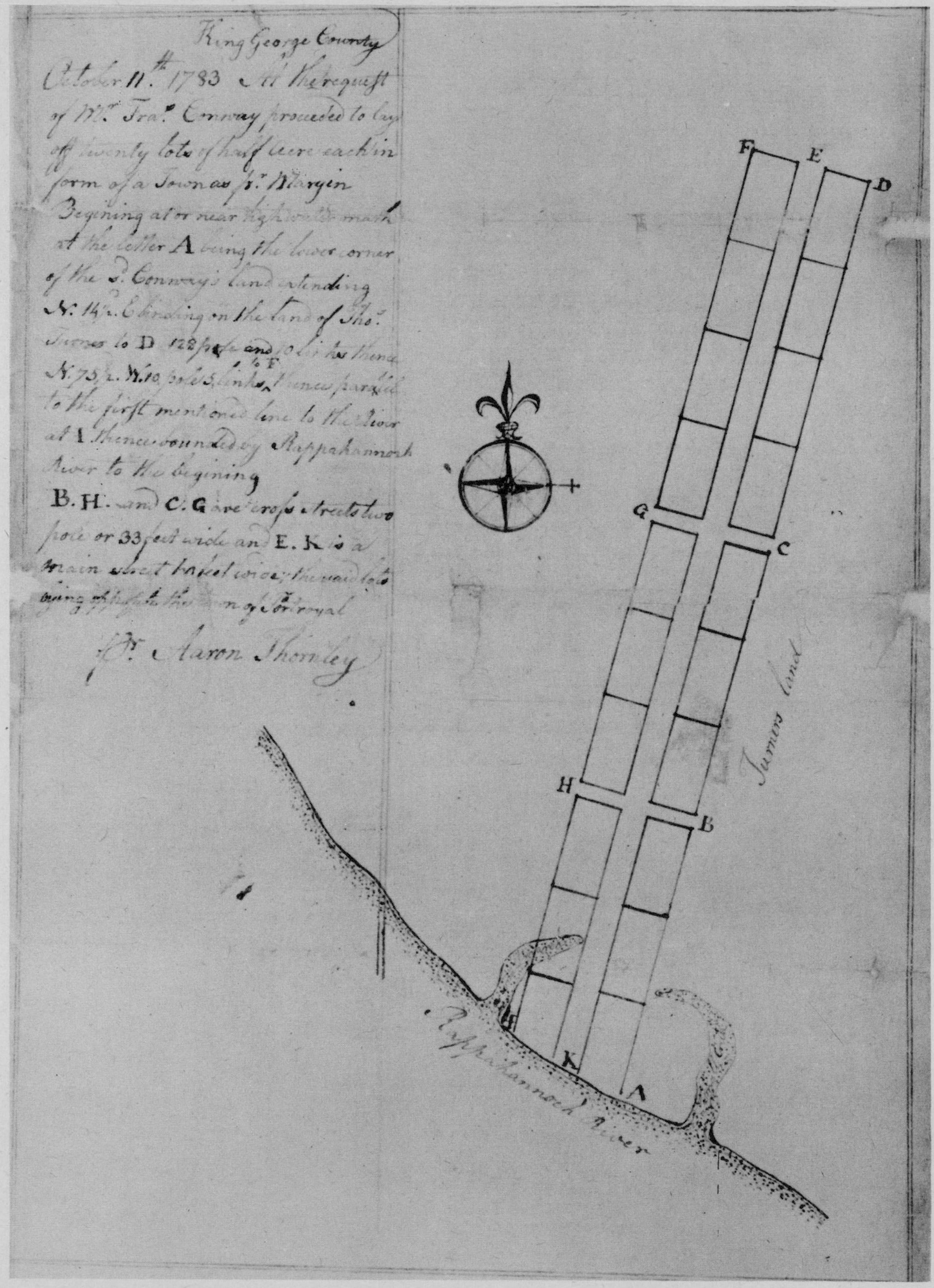

Figure 141. Plan of Port Conway, Virginia: 1783

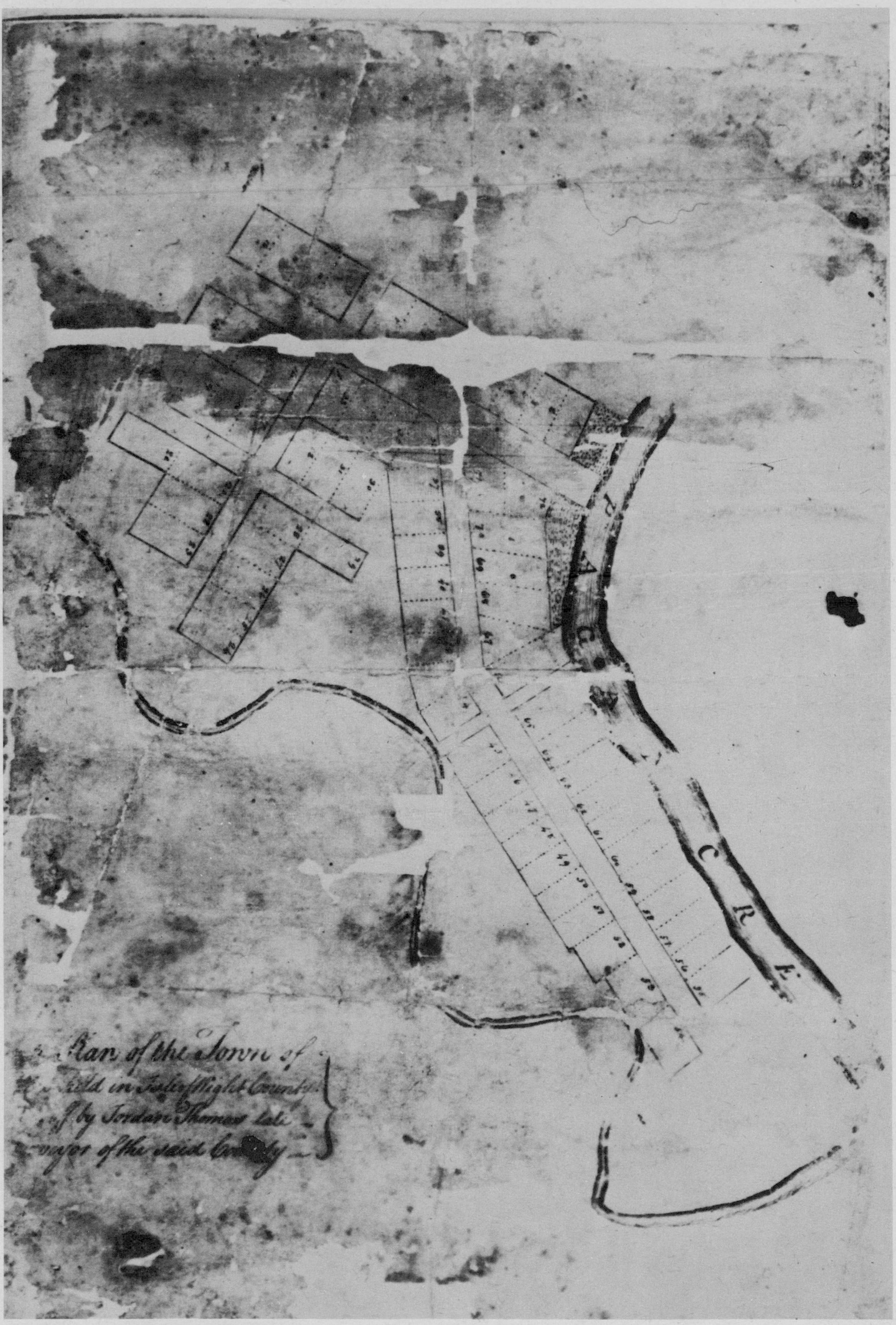

Figure 142. Plan of Smithfield, Virginia: ca. 1752

government, and conferred new privileges for holding markets and fairs.[42] The assembly found it necessary to extend the town's boundaries and municipal powers in 1757 and to enlarge the boundaries once again in 1761.[43] Although a "compleat plan" of the borough was prepared in 1753 by surveyor Gershom Nimmo, his drawing has not survived.

The earliest known plan of the entire town, dating from 1802, appears in figure 143. On flat land beyond the narrow neck that marked the outer limits of the original town, the city had expanded in an irregular grid of streets. Many of these streets which appear on the 1802 survey may well have been newly planned after 1777. The city was almost totally destroyed the previous year. Buildings that remained after intensive shelling by British forces were burned by the retreating American troops. In all, more than thirteen hundred houses were demolished, of which some four hundred were put to the torch by the revolutionary army to prevent anything of value from falling into enemy hands.[44] The General Assembly hastened to encourage rebuilding, reciting in the preamble to an act in 1777 that "the irregular manner in which the borough of Norfolk was laid off rendered the streets and lots inconvenient, and prejudicial to the health of the inhabitants . . . it is now practicable to lay out the same in a more regular and commodious manner."[45] Any land might be taken for new streets if the owners were properly compensated, and the entire expense of the replanning project was to be assessed against all proprietors of the town.

The rebuilding that eventually culminated in the pattern shown in the 1802 survey must have been sporadic. The British once again occupied Norfolk in 1780 and 1781, but it was not until the peace of 1783 that English merchant ships once again resumed substantial trade with the Chesapeake ports. Demonstrating a remarkable ability to recover from the devastation of war, Norfolk soon regained a dominant trading position in the lower Tidewater and was surpassed only on the Chesapeake Bay by the rapidly expanding city of Baltimore.

Just as William Byrd provided us with a vivid picture of Norfolk as it first evolved into a city of importance, Médéric Moreau de St. Méry sketched a striking portrait of the community in 1794 as it emerged phoenix-like from the ravages of war. Proceeding inland from the "extremely narrow" docks, he entered an "open square . . . quite deep, with shops and taverns along both sides." This was the market, one side of which was formed by "the widest and longest" street of the town. Other streets were "laid out helter-skelter," although "the sides of each street, generally speaking, are parallel."

He was not impressed by the state of improvements, noting that "none of the streets are paved, which makes them unpleasantly dusty or muddy, according to whether it is dry or rainy. The sewage ditches are open, and one crosses them on little narrow bridges made of short lengths of plank nailed on crosspieces." Norfolk then consisted of "about five hundred houses, set close together except near the upper part of the town." Almost all of the houses were of wood, most them but one story high. The courthouse, a prison, "a theatre built of brick," and an academy provided for the civic, cultural, and educational needs of the "three thousand inhabitants."

The town was then enjoying a period of rapid growth. The visiting Frenchman observed that "every day new houses spring up in the direction of Elizabeth River," and that the river front was filled with newly constructed wharves. He was critical, however, of the haphazard manner in which they had been located: "These wharves . . . are put up solely for the convenience of the owner, are built without any general plan, and inconsiderately shut off the view of the river without a thought for the future needs of the town."[46]

This is not a very flattering portrait. The irregularities of plan, the disregard by commercial interests in the town for the general welfare, and the apparent inability or disinclination of town officials to provide a firmer guide for urban growth was to characterize the town's history during the nineteenth century. Its abundant vitality and general prosperity could not mask its lack of charm and grace. Only in recent years has there been a sustained effort to plan for the city's future. Urban renewal programs have altered much of the area of the original town plan beyond recognition. Perhaps not everyone would agree that the results have always justified the efforts, but the city has at least begun the long task of rebuilding in the tradition, although not the forms, established by colonial administrators in the seventeenth century.

A rival of Norfolk for the trade and commerce of the lower Chesapeake Bay lay across the Elizabeth River to the west and south. This was Portsmouth, founded by William Craford in 1752 on his sixty-five-acre tract that fronted on the river and was bounded by Craford's Bay and Crab

Figure 143. Plan of Norfolk, Virginia: 1802

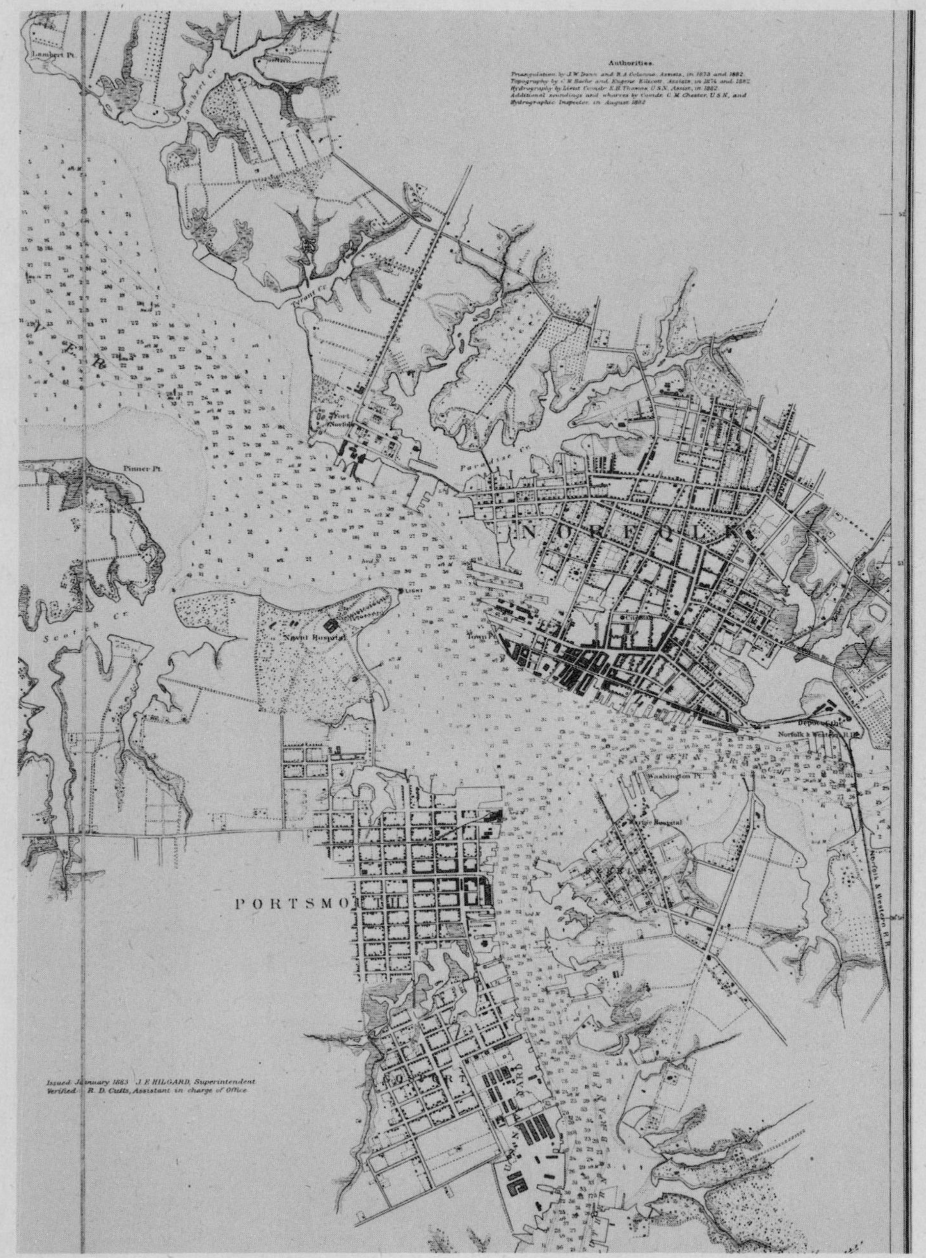

Figure 144. Map of Norfolk, Portsmouth, and Gosport, Virginia: 1882

Creek.[47] Its geographic relationship to Norfolk, as well as that town's growth to 1883, may be seen on the map in figure 144. Gershom Nimmo's plan appears in figure 145. He surveyed the two main streets each 100 feet wide, with the other streets sixty-six feet in width. Most of these lots measured just under half an acre, except for those along the water which were somewhat larger in area. Four lots at the western end of Church Street, the shorter of the two one hundred-foot thoroughfares, were set aside for a church, courthouse, jail, and market place. Shortly thereafter the assembly passed an act recognizing Portsmouth as a town and conferring on its inhabitants the usual "rights and privileges, which the freeholders of any other towns, erected by the act of Assembly, in this colony, have and enjoy."[48] In this case the assembly did not appoint trustees but simply adopted the previously surveyed plat with its 122 lots as the official plan.[49]

Portsmouth enjoyed the same locational advantages as Norfolk and became particularly important as a center of shipbuilding, which flourished there and in nearby Gosport. By the time of the Revolution the town had become completely built-up, if the plan reproduced in figure 146 is correct. This drawing shows the many wharves and docks that had been erected along the water front. Trinity Church, dating from the early 1760s, appears on the site designated in the original plan. Opposite it is the courthouse. Old Trinity Church, as rebuilt in 1829 and later remodeled, still stands, but the present courthouse dates from the middle of the last century.

The extensive fortifications of the British during the Revolution appear on the plan reproduced in figure 147. This also shows the location of Gosport beyond the "Salt Meadow" that was ultimately annexed to Portsmouth.[50] The latter city suffered through the war. Most of the buildings in the town were badly damaged or completely destroyed, and it is something of a miracle that a few eighteenth-century structures have survived to the present time. While extensive rebuilding occurrd, Portsmouth was not again to rival Norfolk. In 1790 its population was 1,700, of whom 1,039 were white, 616 slaves, and 47 free Negroes.[51] Four years later when the perceptive Médéric Moreau de St. Méry saw the place he recorded the following observations:

> Its three hundred houses do not border the streets. They are so spaced that the impression is of wide and beautiful avenues. These are

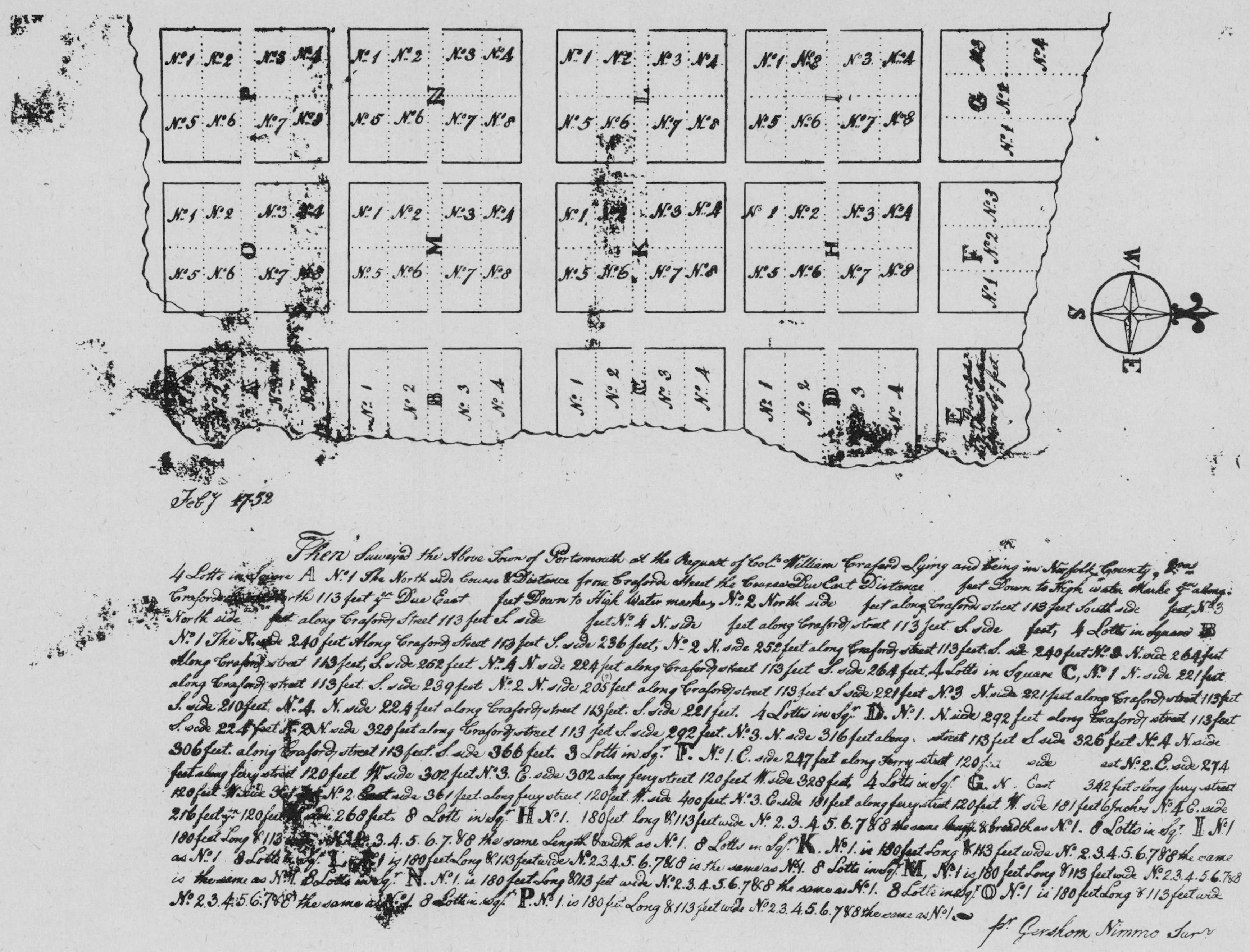

Figure 145. Plan of Portsmouth, Virginia: 1752

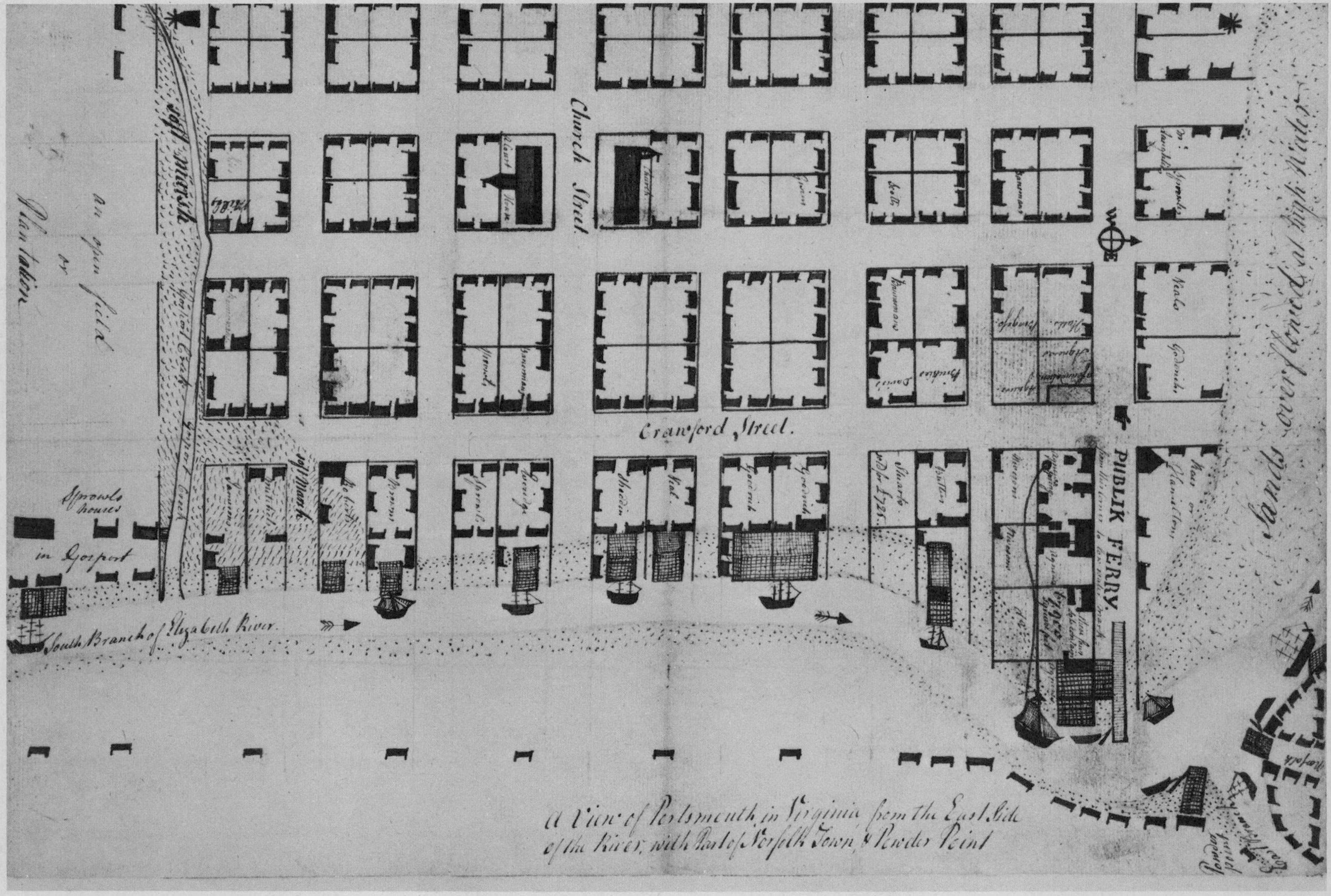

Figure 146. Plan of Portsmouth, Virginia: ca. 1780

all grass-covered, and the houses are built of wood for the most part, though a few extremely pretty ones are brick.

The Portsmouth market, also built of brick, fronts on the river. Alhough small, it is large enough for the town's needs. This market is on an open square or very wide street which runs to the outskirts of the town. On the left side of this street, going up, is the brick Anglican church, neat and well kept up. It has a rood loft, and benches throughout its entire length. Next to the door, on both sides, are two benches painted black. These are for blacks, who are not allowed to mix with the whites. . . . This place is down-at-heels because it has no commerce of its own. Vessels can come to Portsmouth as readily as to Norfolk, since the port is formed by the two banks of the Elizabeth River; but the greater age of Norfolk and the very nature of the establishments already founded there, which must necessarily determine the character of those yet to be formed, prevent Portsmouth from being a rival. . . . Portsmouth has seventeen hundred inhabitants, six hundred of whom are slaves.[52]

The later development of the town was closely associated with the fortunes of the private shipyards and, after 1801, with the United States Navy Yard at Gosport. The Dismal Swamp Canal improved communications, and the growth of lumbering in the vicinity added to manufacturing activities that already had become focused around the production of naval stores and equipment. The naval shipyard, together with the Norfolk Naval Station, constitute the largest operating naval base in the world. The Naval Shipyard Museum at the foot of old High Street on the Elizabeth River serves as a reminder, if one is needed, of Portsmouth's continued tie with the maritime world that began almost from the day of its founding.

Two other important Virginia towns owed their origins to that remarkable figure, William Byrd II. Unlike his attempt to develop the town of Eden, these efforts were to prove successful and to result in permanent communities of substantial size. On September 19, 1733, while leading a party of exploration and survey through his extensive domain in the southern portion of the colony, Byrd recorded:

> we laid the foundation of two large cities: one at Shacco's, to be called Richmond, and the other at the point of Appomattox River, to be named Petersburg. These Major Mayo offered to lay out into lots without fee or reward. The truth of it is, these two places, being

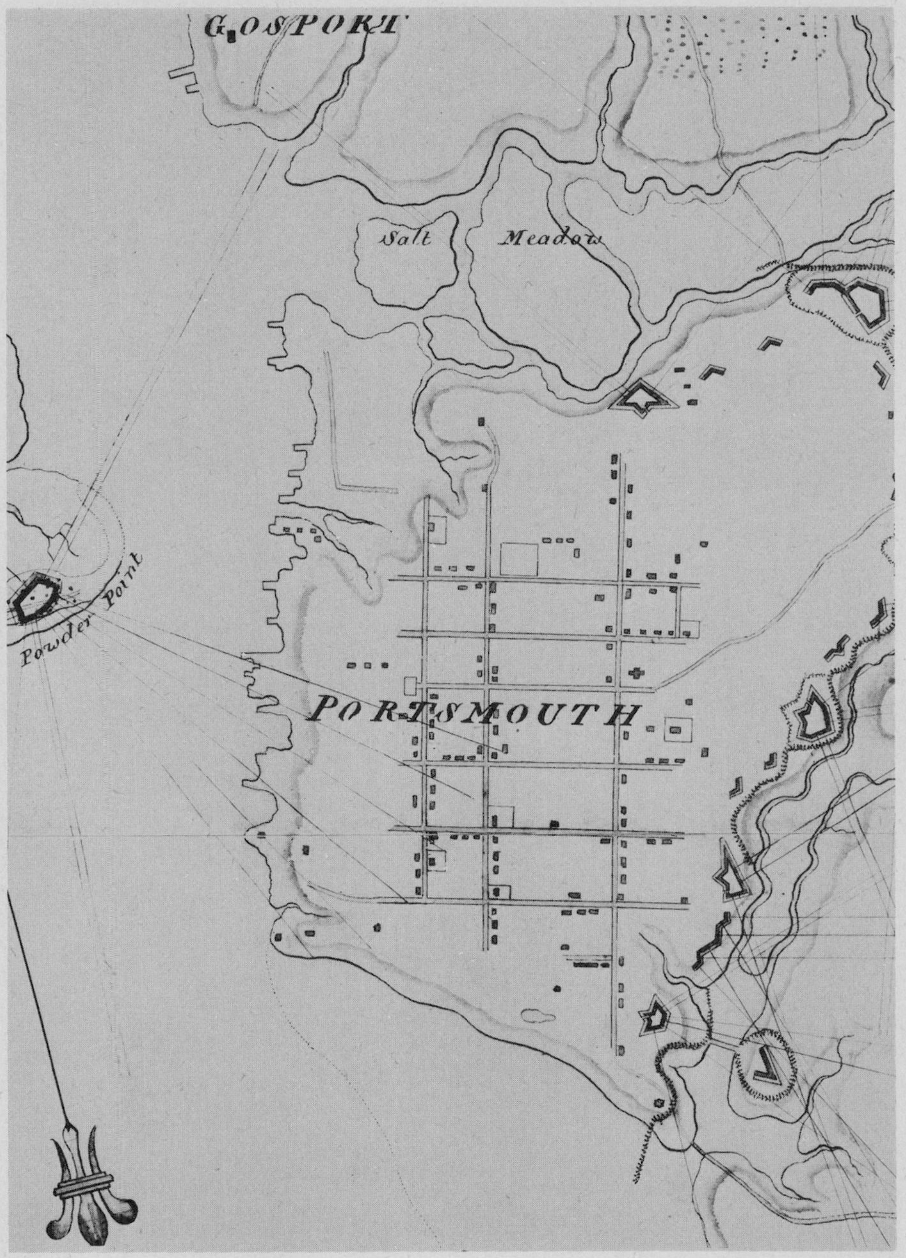

Figure 147. Map of Portsmouth, Virginia, and Vicinity: 1781

> the uppermost landing of James and Appomattox rivers, are naturally intended for marts where the traffic of the outer inhabitants must center. Thus we did not build castles only, but also cities in the air.[53]

The site of Petersburg had been recognized as one of importance as early as 1646 when the General Assembly ordered the construction of Fort Henry at the falls of the Appomattox. It was slightly more than a century later, in 1748, that the assembly incorporated not one but two towns side by side on the south bank of the river.[54] The original plat of Petersburg has apparently not survived, but its plan took the customary grid pattern. Its companion town, Blandford, shown in figure 148, was given a similar form by William Poythress. The two communities, as they appeared in 1781 to a British raiding party, are shown in figure 149. This map, while doubtless accurate in recording the main topographic features and the general location of roads and principal buildings, probably does not give a fair impression of what by that time had grown into a thriving trading community. Two years later Johann David Schoepf put the number of houses at three hundred. He noted that "Petersbourgh exports a great quantity of tobacco and other produce, supplied not only by the Virginia plantation round-about, but brought in even from North Carolina."[55]

Soon other landowners in the vicinity sought to obtain the advantages of laying their lands off into streets and town lots. Across the river Richard Witton platted a parcel of land into the standard checkerboard design, divided it into half-acre lots, and succeeded in having his initiative rewarded by an act of the assembly in 1752.[56] Although he immodestly called his new town Wittontown, the assembly gave it the name Pocahontas while confirming the details of its plan (figure 150). Pocahontas, Blandford, Petersburgh, and Ravenscroft, another adjoining town, were united and incorporated as the Town of Petersburg in 1784. This law enlarging the powers of the municipality and establishing the details of local government indicates the extent to which the community had prospered and grown.[57] At the end of the colonial era and during the early years of the nineteenth century Petersburg rivaled Richmond and was regarded by many as the likely future metropolis of that portion of Virginia. Its development, however, did not continue for long when river transportation lost much of its importance, and the city suffered severely during the Civil War. In the modern city of forty thousand there are only a few buildings of importance

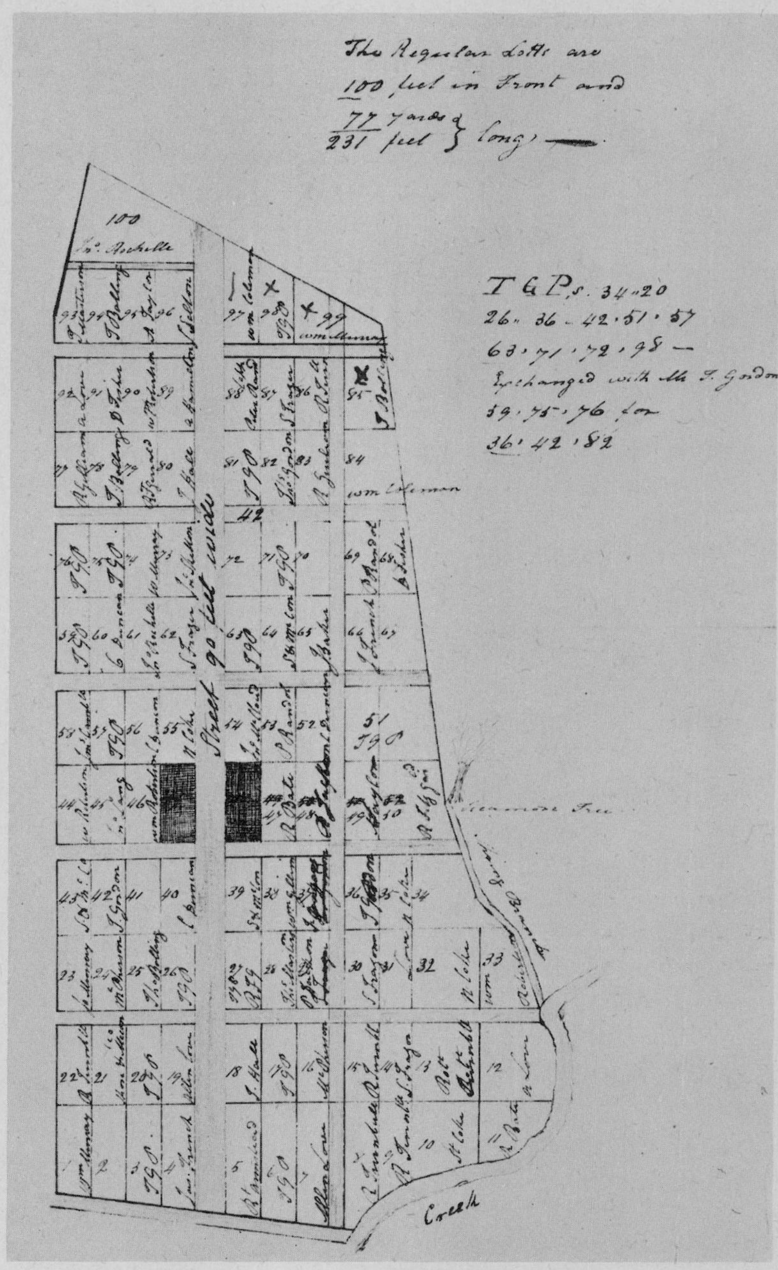

Figure 148. Plan of Blandford, Virginia: 1799

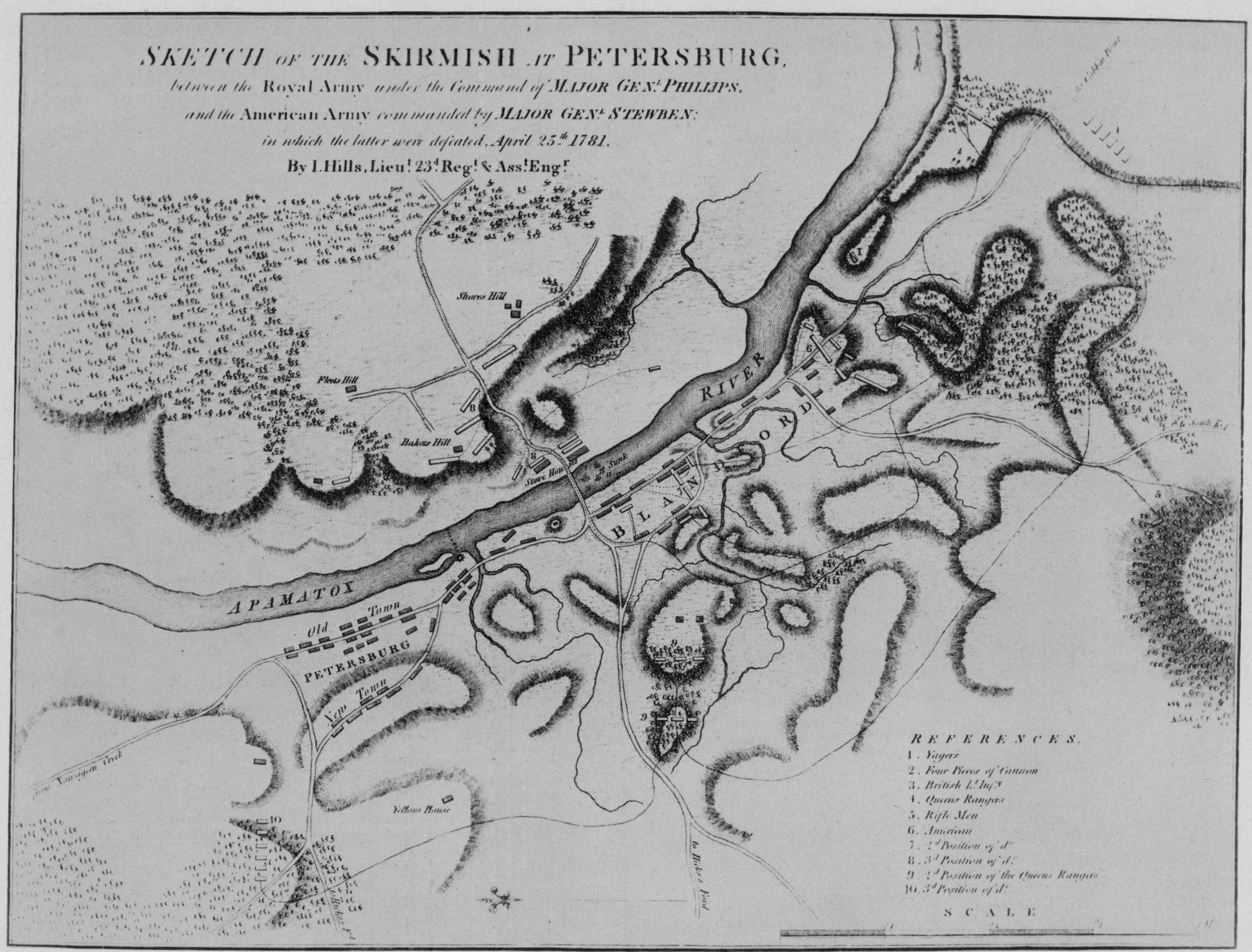
SKETCH OF THE SKIRMISH AT PETERSBURG,
between the Royal Army under the Command of MAJOR GEN.L PHILLIPS,
and the American Army commanded by MAJOR GEN.L STEWBEN:
in which the latter were defeated, April 25th 1781.
By I. Hills, Lieu.t 23d Reg.t & Ass.t Eng.r
Shores Hill
Fleets Hill
Bakers Hill
Store House
RIVER
BLANDFORD
APAMATOX
Old Town
PETERSBURG
New Town
Yellow House
REFERENCES.
1. Yagers
2. Four Pieces of Cannon
3. British L.t Inf.y
4. Queens Rangers
5. Rifle Men
6. American
7. 2d Position of d.o
8. 3d Position of d.o
9. 2d Position of the Queens Rangers
10. 3d Position of d.o
SCALE

Figure 149. Map of Petersburg, Virginia, and Vicinity: 1781

Figure 150. Plan of Wittontown, Virginia: ca. 1752

from before 1800, although the original plans of its constituent towns can still be seen comprising the core of an expanded network of streets.

Both Richmond (the development of which will be traced in detail in Chapter XI) and Petersburg were planned at the upper limits of deep water navigation on the James and Appomattox rivers. Through the early years of the eighteenth century few communities of any size were founded beyond the fall line of the major rivers leading from Chesapeake Bay to the interior. As settlers continued to press westward, however, towns became necessary in the upper Piedmont and in the ridge and valley section that lay beyond. It was only natural that the elementary gridiron pattern used so extensively in the Tidewater should also be employed in this new area of settlement.

Leesburg, in Loudoun County, the plan of which is reproduced in figure 151, is a typical example. Nicholas Minor selected its site a few miles inland from the Potomac River at the eastern entrance to a pass through the Catoctin Mountains where the new county courthouse had been erected. A year later, in 1758, the assembly recognized its existence and created the sixty-acre tract as an official town. Minor's plan was adopted, although trustees were appointed with the usual powers "to settle and establish such rules and orders for the more regular and orderly building of the houses in the said town of Leesburg as to them shall seem best and most convenient." [58] John Hough's survey shows the courthouse lots fronting on Market and King streets near the center of the town, the balance of which was laid off in streets varying in width from thirty-five to forty-five feet. These rather cramped dimensions may have resulted from a desire to make the town as compact as possible and therefore easier to defend in the event of Indian attack.[59]

An even earlier town had been created farther to the west beyond the Blue Ridge Mountains in the great valley of the Shenandoah River. Winchester began in 1744 when James Wood laid out a little community of twenty-six lots around the courthouse lot of Frederick County. He first called it Fredericktown but later gave it the name of his native city in England. It was here that George Washington came in 1748 to survey the extensive landholdings of Lord Fairfax. The building at Cork and Braddock streets, which he then used as an office and later as his headquarters during the construction of Fort Loudoun in 1756–1757, still stands and has been restored.

The assembly of 1752 passed an act conferring town status on the settlement. The original plan of twenty-six half-acre lots was recognized, but the act directed that the town be enlarged

> with fifty four other lots of half an acre each, twenty four thereof to be laid off in one or two streets, on the east side of the former lots, the street or streets to run parallel with the street already laid off, and the remaining thirty lots, to be laid off at the north end of the aforesaid twenty six, with a commodious street or streets, in such manner as the proprietor thereof, the right honourable Thomas Lord Fairfax, shall think fit.[60]

As surveyed in 1809 and with further enlargements to the street system, the plan of Winchester appears in figure 152. The courthouse square, now bounded by Loudoun, Boscawen, and Cameron streets and Rouss Avenue, served as the focus for the town. The present brick courthouse, built in 1840, replaced two earlier wooden structures that for some years were all this frontier community could afford. It was north of this location, on Loudoun Street, that Washington supervised the construction of Fort Loudoun following General Braddock's defeat in 1755 during the French and Indian War.[61]

Winchester soon developed as an important market town, not only for the rich farming area of the immediate vicinity but as a trading point for the western country. In 1793 one visitor noted the variety of mercantile activities in the community which then contained 1,660 inhabitants.

> There are saddlers, hatters, shoemakers, weavers, braziers, smiths, clockmakers, riflesmiths, cabinetmakers, a painted-chairmaker, an earthen-ware-maker, a coachmaker, a wagon-maker, buckskin breeches makers, etc. The stores, or shops, are numerous and considerable. They obtain their goods from Philadelphia, Baltimore, and Alexandria, but principally from Philadelphia, and dispose of them to people of the town, of the neighborhood, and of the back country. Multitudes of horses, sometimes bring hemp, come down every spring and return loaded with the products of Europe and the West Indies, but principally with salt and iron.[62]

An equally routine gridiron design, although somewhat larger in size than Winchester's, was the plan for Beverley, shown in figure 153. Thomas Jefferson's father, Peter Jefferson, surveyed the town in 1756 for a site on

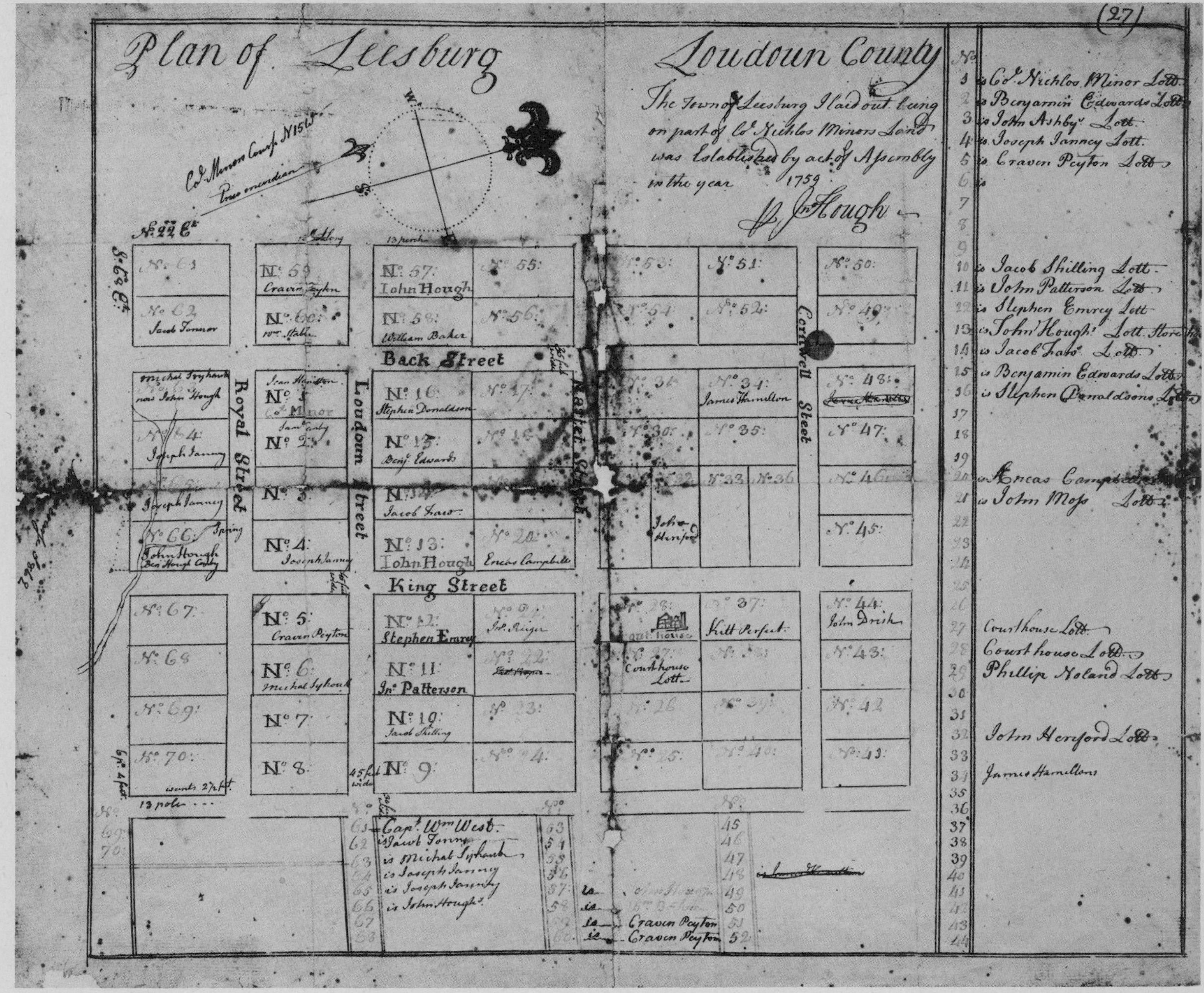

Figure 151. Plan of Leesburg, Virginia: 1759

the north bank of the James River, several miles above the falls at Richmond, using the standard half-acre lots and streets 3 poles or 49½ feet wide. Although the plat indicates numerous lot purchasers, Beverley evidently failed to attract settlers. No such name or even the indication of a settlement can be found on the detailed map of Virginia prepared in 1770 by John Henry.

In the latter part of the eighteenth and the early years of the nineteenth centuries the gridiron plan spread westward as Virginians penetrated the rugged country of Appalachia in their relentless quest for land. Lynchburg, far up the James River in Campbell County, served as a base for westward expansion while achieving considerable prosperity in the warehousing and shipping of dark tobacco. As early as 1757, John Lynch established a ferry at this point, a few dwellings were built around the ferry house, and in 1786 the place had grown sufficiently for the assembly to grant it official town recognition. As surveyed between 1787 and 1790 by Richard Stith, the plan of Lynchburg is reproduced in figure 154. Beyond the first mountain range in Botetourt County county surveyor William Preston laid out a similar plan for Fincastle on forty acres of land donated to the county by Israel Christian in 1770.[63]

In even more mountainous surroundings to the west was Newcastle, now the county seat of Craig County. As shown in figure 155, the settlement took the form of a tiny grid composed of a single street crossed at right angles by three others. Later, additional streets were added to extend the town on two sides, and the blocks thus created were divided into lots similar to those in the original plat.

Virtually the only town of this period and region to depart in any significant manner from the standardized checkerboard pattern was Bath, now known as Berkeley Springs, West Virginia. Located near the Potomac River midway between Hagerstown and Cumberland, Maryland, the place was first settled in the 1740s by persons attracted by the supposed curative properties of the mineral waters from numerous warm springs in the vicinity. Lord Fairfax successfully claimed the area when the boundaries of his vast estate were surveyed in 1745. It was then that George Washington first saw the spot. Possibly at his urging, Lord Fairfax conveyed the lands around the springs to the colony of Virginia in 1756. In doing so he stipulated that the springs were "to be forever free to the publick for the welfare of suffering humanity."[64]

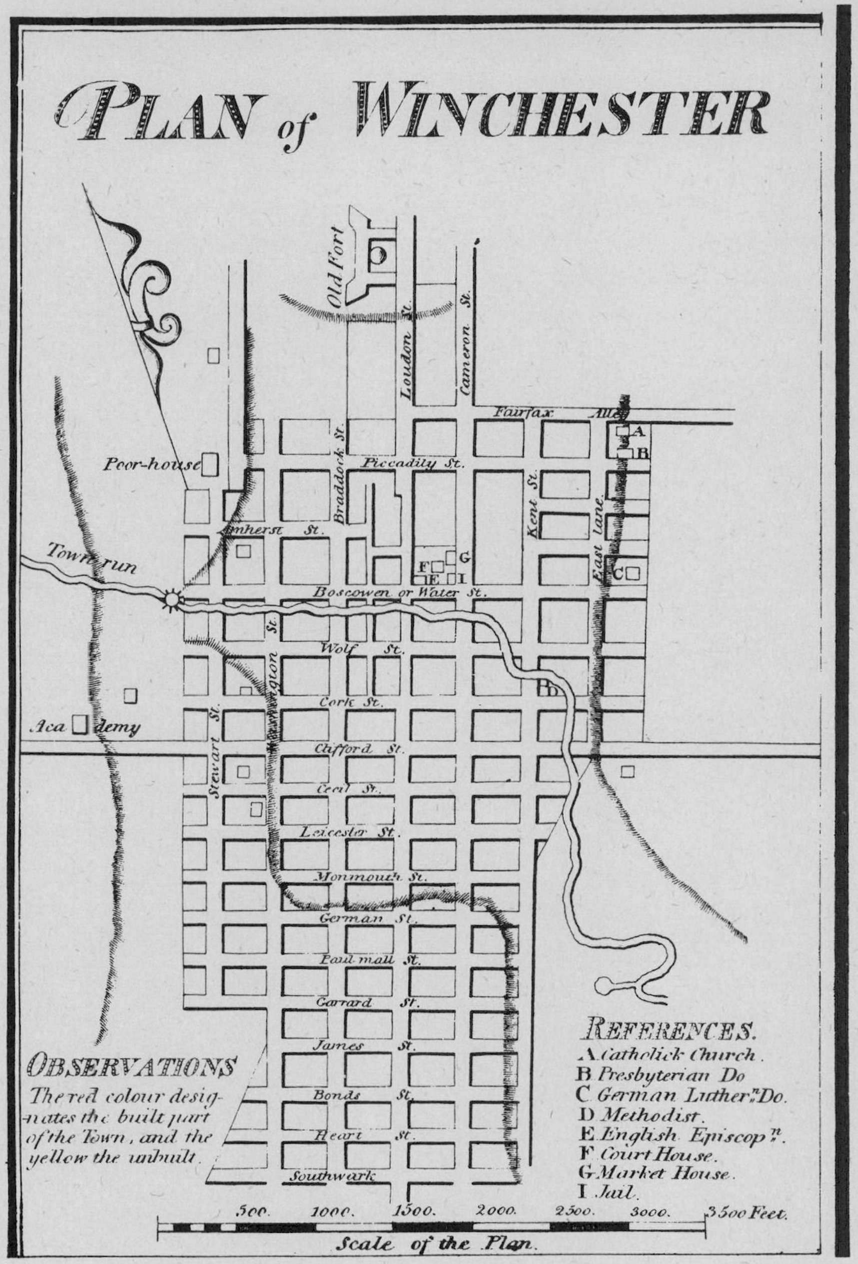

Figure 152. Plan of Winchester, Virginia: 1809

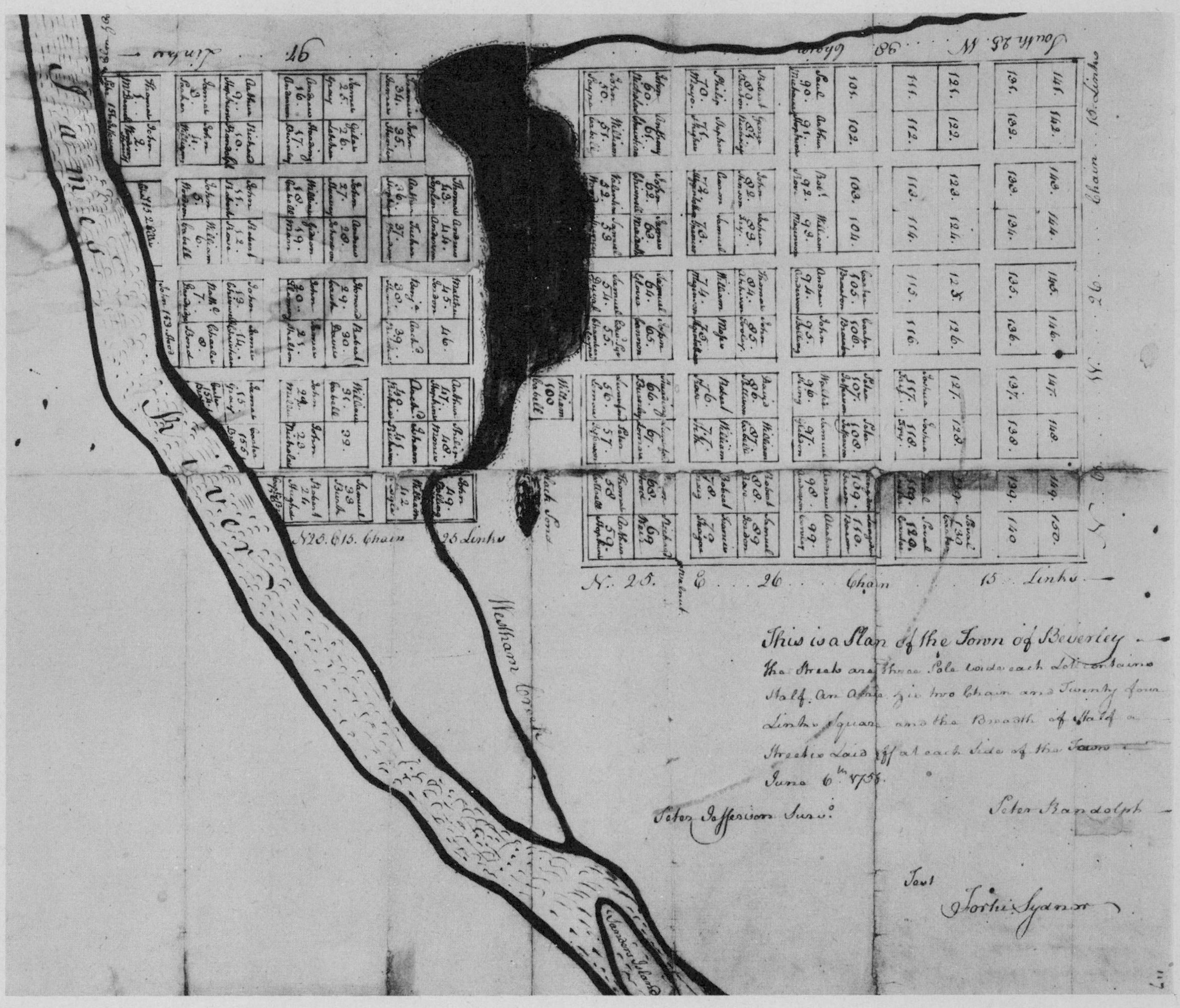

Figure 153. Plan of Beverley, Virginia: 1756

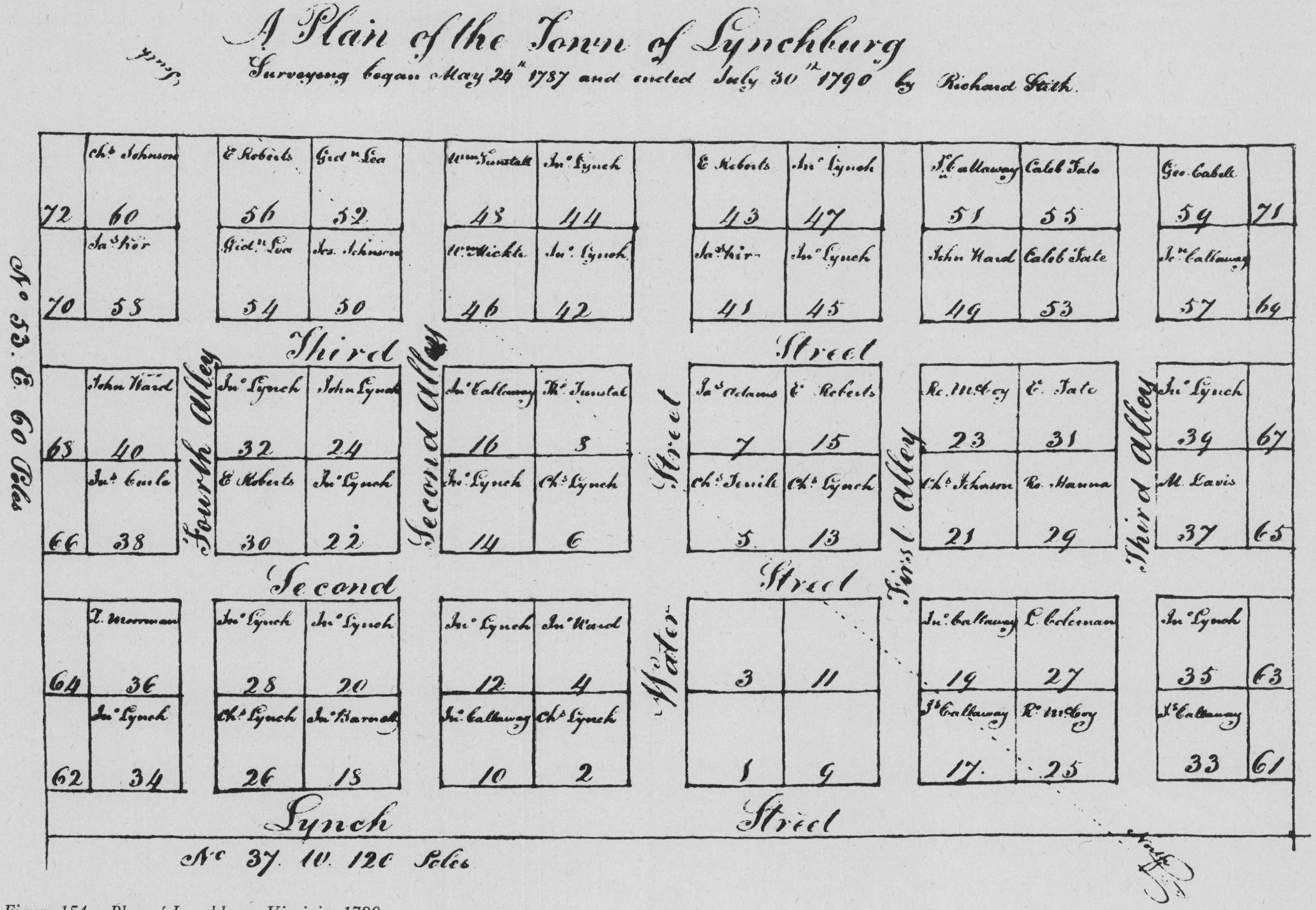

Figure 154. Plan of Lynchburg, Virginia: 1790

In 1776 the assembly acted to create the town of Bath "at the Warm Springs in the county of Berkeley."[65] The following year the town was laid out in the pattern shown in figure 156. Bath Square, four acres in area, provided a novel feature. Its creation followed the legislative directive of the assembly providing "That all the said Warm Springs, except one large and convenient spring suitable for a bath, shall be, and the same are hereby vested in the said trustees, in trust, to and for the publick use and benefit, and for no other purpose whatsoever."[66] Three streets, Liberty, Bath, and Fairfax, led into the square from the east, while two others, Wilkes and Henry, provided access from the north and south. The lots of the town, unlike almost all others in colonial Virginia, were a quarter of an acre in size, and the act establishing the town specified that dwellings on them must be at least twelve feet square and completed within twelve months of their purchase.

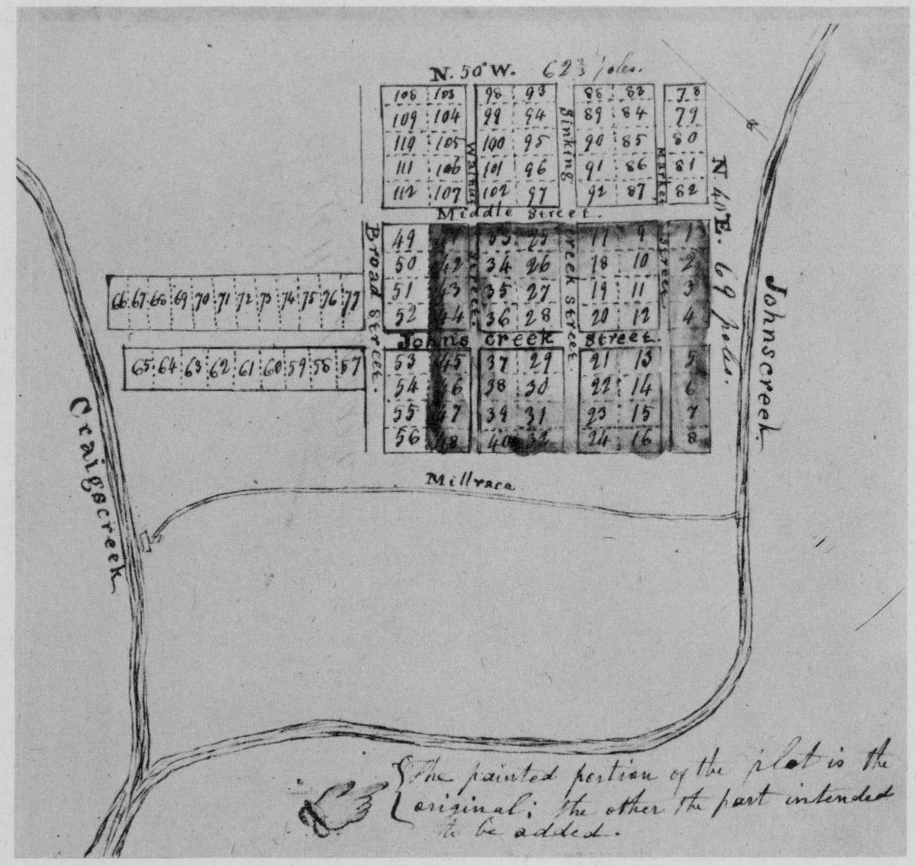

Figure 155. Plan of Newcastle, Virginia: 1834

George Washington was among those buying property in Bath. On lots 58 and 59 at the southeast corner of Fairfax and Mercer Streets he commissioned James Rumsey to construct a house, kitchen, and stable. These buildings, completed in 1784, were never occupied by the owner, and ultimately the property reverted to the town trustees after Washington and his heirs failed to pay taxes levied on it. In the first half of the nineteenth century Bath developed as a fashionable watering place and resort community. Through the generosity of Lord Fairfax and the wisdom of the assembly the springs have remained in public ownership, and their slightly sweet waters are still consumed or bathed in by many seeking relief from a variety of ailments.

It is hardly surprising to learn that in the early settlements created by Virginians beyond the Appalachian Mountains in the Ohio Valley the gridiron plan was widely employed. The best documented example of a major city is that of Louisville, Kentucky, planned by George Rogers Clark in 1779. There, too, the lots were the standard half-acre size, and those who received possession were obliged to erect a house of a required minimum size within a specified period of time.[67]

Town planners of Virginia were not alone in adopting the gridiron or checkerboard pattern for their towns. Throughout the American colonies this design, with only modest variations, had seemed the logical system to use. Only the Annapolis of Francis Nicholson and the first and partially abandoned plan of Williamsburg represented departures from the established tradition. Within a gridiron system, however, it is possible to introduce single or repeating units of open squares, to vary the dimensions and spacing of streets, or to recognize in town layout occasional strong features of topography. In Virginia this appears to have been done only rarely. In eighteenth-century Maryland these modest departures from an otherwise rigid pattern seem to have been introduced with greater frequency. And, following the Revolution, on a site within the boundaries of the state of Maryland, a major innovation in urban design was to make its appearance on the North American continent.

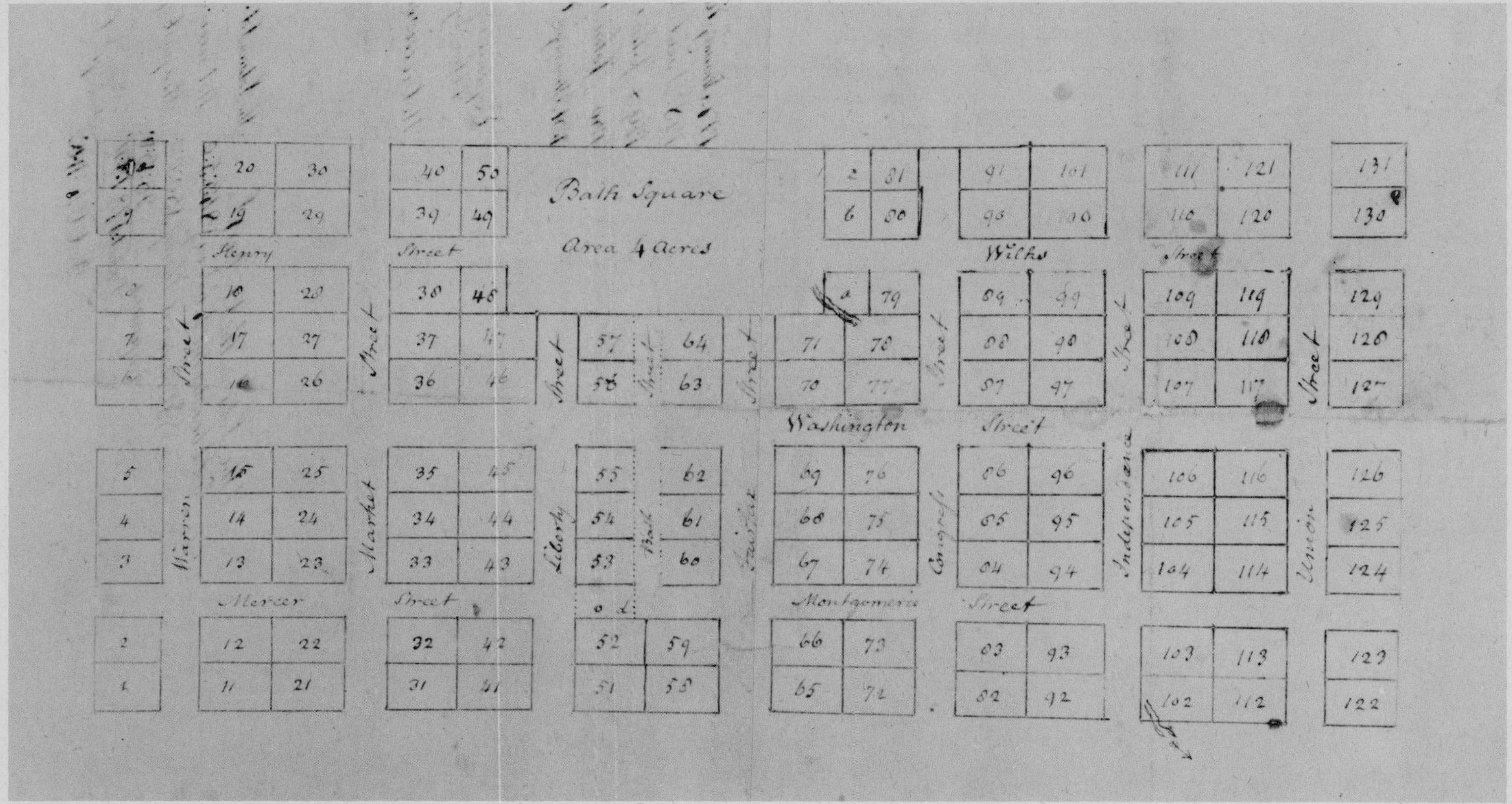

Figure 156. Plan of Berkeley Springs, West Virginia: ca. 1777

X. *Town Planning in Eighteenth-Century Maryland*

THE planning of Maryland towns in the eighteenth century, following the repeal of the last of the general port and town acts, closely resembled what occurred in Virginia. As the need arose with the steady increase in population and the demand for specialized services that only towns could conveniently provide, new communities were created on sites thought to be favorable for the purpose. Maryland's experience, however, differed from that in its sister colony in two respects. First, most of the Maryland towns seem to have resulted from the initiative of the General Assembly, either on its own motion or, quite often, in response to a petition from persons in the vicinity of the proposed town. Unlike Virginia, there seem to have been few towns first laid out by an individual on his own land and for which legislative sanction was then sought.

Second, in at least a few of the Maryland towns there were attempts to break away from the traditional and unsophisticated patterns that had been the rule during the previous era. Public or residential squares at Charlestown and St. Michaels and special treatment of the sites for public buildings at Chestertown indicate some kind of conscious attempt at civic design. True, these remained the exceptions rather than the rule, but the plans of these towns stand out all the more because of their departures from prevailing gridiron designs. As is the case with Virginia only a few contemporary drawings have survived, and it is necessary to rely on nineteenth-century surveys in some cases.

The provisions of the special town acts in Maryland were based mainly on experience gained when towns had been established by the general acts of the assembly designating many sites rather than only one. Both the similarities and differences in these two sets of legislative enactments have been summarized by one historian as follows:

> In the general town acts, twenty-four commissioners in each county were directed to lay out the several towns within their county; but each of these acts, after the first one, permitted the commissioners of each county to divide themselves into committees, and the committee composed of members living nearest to a place named for a town were authorized to superintend the laying of it out. In the particular town acts, special commissioners were directed to lay out the one town named. Squares were marked off in each town for a church, chapel, markethouse, and other public buildings. In Williamstadt, in Annapolis, and in Charles-Town on Northeast River, from one hundred to three hundred acres were purchased for the town commons. The lots were always made equal in size, usually a little less than one acre each. The general town acts directed that one hundred acres should be laid out for every town; but by the several particular acts the size of the town plots varied from twenty to five hundred acres. The general acts forbade any person to purchase more than one lot in any one town within four months from the time the town was laid out; but in the several particular acts the time during which this restriction was to continue varied from four months to three years. All acts for laying out towns required that he who took up a lot should complete the building thereon, within a specified time,—usually one year,—of a dwelling house covering at least four hundred square feet of ground, or forfeit his title to the lot. Some of the particular acts further required that the chimney of the dwelling should be built of

brick or stone. Finally, nearly all the particular acts forbade the town inhabitants to allow cattle, horses, sheep, hogs, or geese to run at large within the town.[1]

One of the earliest of the eighteenth-century Maryland towns certainly exhibited no special sensitivity to urban design on the part of its planners. This was Joppa, now in Harford county but then in Baltimore County and founded in 1724 as its county seat. The town had an earlier history, being one of more than forty designated in the act of 1706. Its site on the Gunpowder River at a place called Forster's Neck was changed the following year to a fifty-acre tract called "Taylor's Choice," and the courthouse was ordered to be erected in the town. The queen's approval of this act was not forthcoming, and in 1712 the assembly passed a further law to implement its earlier action. Then it was discovered that the land on which the courthouse had been constructed belonged to a minor who could not legally convey proper title. Until 1725 the "town" consisted only of the courthouse and jail. In that year the assembly legalized the conveyance of the courthouse lot, reduced the size of the town to twenty-one acres, designated town commissioners, and directed them to lay off the land in streets and half-acre lots, with a one-acre tract for St. John's Parish Church.[2] On April 20, 1725, the commissioners met to plan the town and shortly thereafter offered building sites for sale at £1 7s. to all those who would build a dwelling of at least four hundred square feet with a good brick or stone chimney. The proceeds were to be paid to Colonel James Maxwell, whose land the commissioners had acquired for the purpose.[3]

Figure 157 shows the survey of the town in 1725 as redrawn by a nineteenth-century historian. Two streets, Court and Church, ran east and west. They were connected along the west side of the courthouse property by Sharping Lane. Two other streets, Low and High, ran northward to the boundary of the town. The lots varied in area from the half-acre size specified by the legislature, the largest being slightly less than half an acre while the smallest measured just over one-third of an acre. Within a short time thirty of the lots had been sold, and the town became a port in the tobacco trade. Prosperity was not long to endure. With the creation of Baltimore in 1729 Joppa's population dwindled. By the end of the century there was little evidence to be seen that once a town had existed on the site. Just as Joppa had supplanted the first town called Baltimore on the Bush River to the north, it in turn gave way to the second community to bear that name located south of Joppa on the Patapsco.

In contrast to the routine gridiron of Joppa, the plan of Charlestown in Cecil County showed concern for urban splendor. Today the site on the western shore of Northeast River, at the head of navigation on Chesapeake Bay, is occupied by only a few dozen houses, and while portions of the original streets can be easily traced, Charlestown has none of the character promised by its plan or hoped for by its promoters. The assembly passed the act creating the town in 1742. Supplementary legislation in 1744 and 1745 and further laws enlarging the powers of the town commissioners and appointing an overseer of streets in 1748 and 1750 all attest to the importance this town once possessed.[4]

The town commissioners were authorized to acquire no less than five hundred acres for the project, and they directed the county surveyor, John Vesey, to lay out two hundred acres for the town proper, with the adjoining three hundred acres reserved for a town common as a source of firewood and for pasturing cattle. Plainly the intention was to create a major community on this strategic site at the head of the bay and only a few miles from the mouth of the Susquehanna River.

The first meeting of the commissioners to inspect the site and determine how to proceed with their duties was held on February 10, 1742. It was more than a year later, on April 13, 1743, that Vesey produced the plan of the town. The following month the commissioners began the public sale of lots. The records of original purchasers no longer exist, but deeds representing land sales during the next few years indicate that there were purchasers not only from Cecil and adjoining Maryland counties but from Chester and Lancaster counties in Pennsylvania and even from the city of Philadelphia.[5]

The usual conditions were attached to the deeds transferring land. If a house at least four hundred square feet in area and having a brick or stone chimney was not built on a lot within three years, the lot would be forfeited and could be disposed of again by the commissioners. The act also specified that lots be priced at a figure that would return to the commissioners a sum equal to the cost of the five hundred-acre tract, for which they ultimately paid £250 sterling. The lord proprietary's quitrent was set at two pence per lot. One unusual feature of the act was the exemption of all residents from the normal parish poll tax of forty pounds

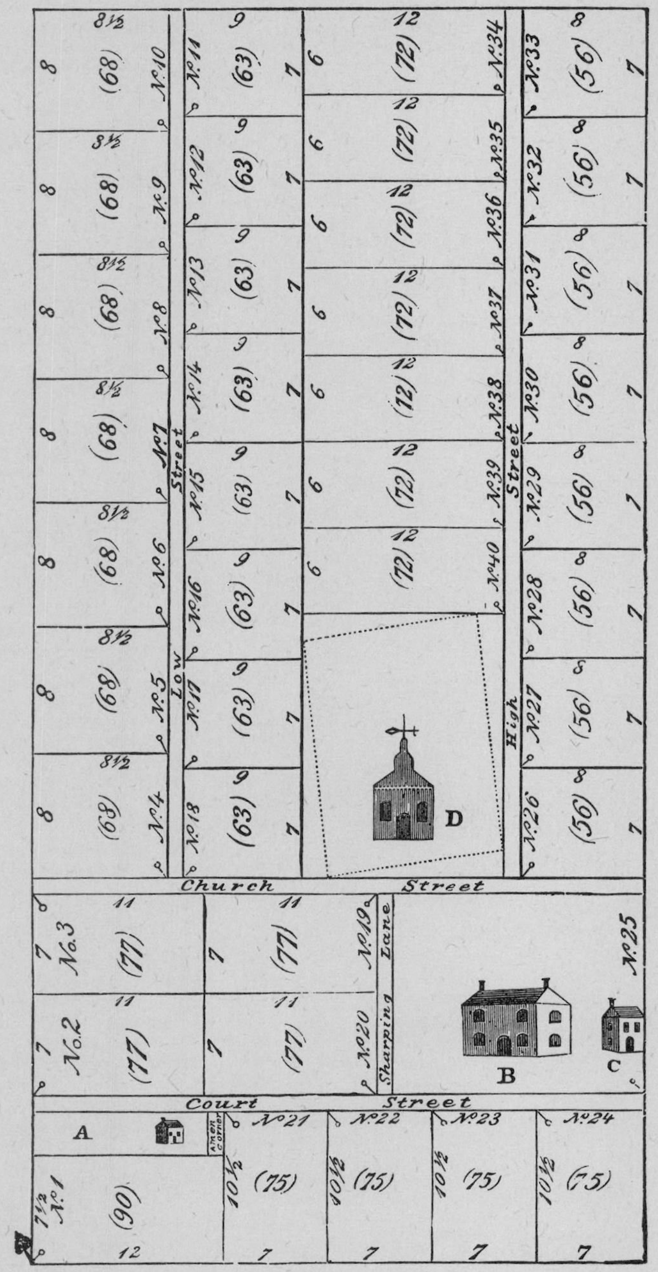

Figure 157. Plan of Joppa, Maryland: 1725

of tobacco. The law recited that this inducement was being extended with the consent of the "present Incumbent of the Parish" in order to

> encourage Persons of all Professions, Religion, Persuasions, Trades or Occupations whatsoever, to build and settle in said Town, and much conduce to the better Peopling and Seating the adjacent Lands, now uncultivated in the said Parish, to the equal benefit of the incumbents thereof.[6]

Two manuscript plans of the town and its common exist (figures 158 and 159). We are told in the text of figure 158 that all lots except for four of irregular shape measured 11½ by 9 poles, or approximately six-tenths of an acre in area. The text at the top of this drawing also describes by metes and bounds the boundaries of the common land. The other drawing more clearly depicts the town plan and identifies the public sites specified in the legislative enactment creating the town.

Four major sites were established. That marked "K" was set aside for a public wharf and warehouses. Near the center of the town the square identified by the letter "M" was designated as the marketplace. The remaining two squares of similar size and shape were to be used for "Meeting houses or other publick occasions." Four lots consolidated into one parcel, shown on the drawing with the letter "L," were for "Courthouses or other Public Use." It will be noted that these three squares were not merely normal town blocks but took the form of the typical Renaissance square with four streets entering the mid-points of their sides. The two lots on the southeast side of the market square marked "A" and "B" were reserved to the lord proprietor.

Vesey and the town commissioners used several street widths in their plan. Water and Calvert streets, running southwest-northeast parallel to the bank of Northeast River, were six poles or 99 feet wide. The three other streets paralleling them were 1 pole narrower, or 82½ feet in width. The streets crossing at right angles to these varied in width from 3 poles or 49½ feet for the two streets at either side of town to 6 poles for Conestoga Street, which led through the westernmost square to the public landing. Other streets were 4, 5, and 5½ poles wide.

The General Assembly went to extraordinary pains to provide the legislative basis for urban growth and development at Charlestown. The supplementary act passed in 1744 authorized the commissioners to construct

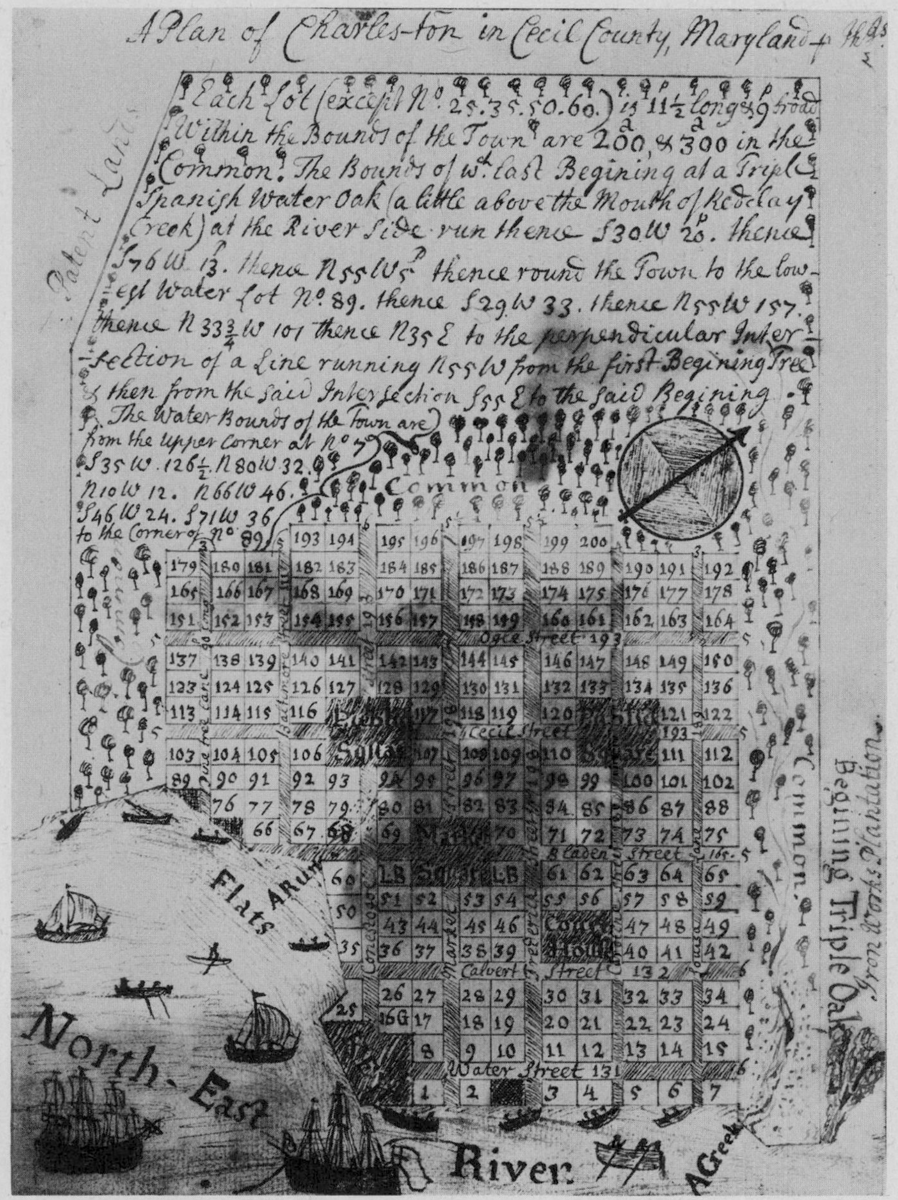

Figure 158. Plan of Charlestown, Maryland: ca. 1743

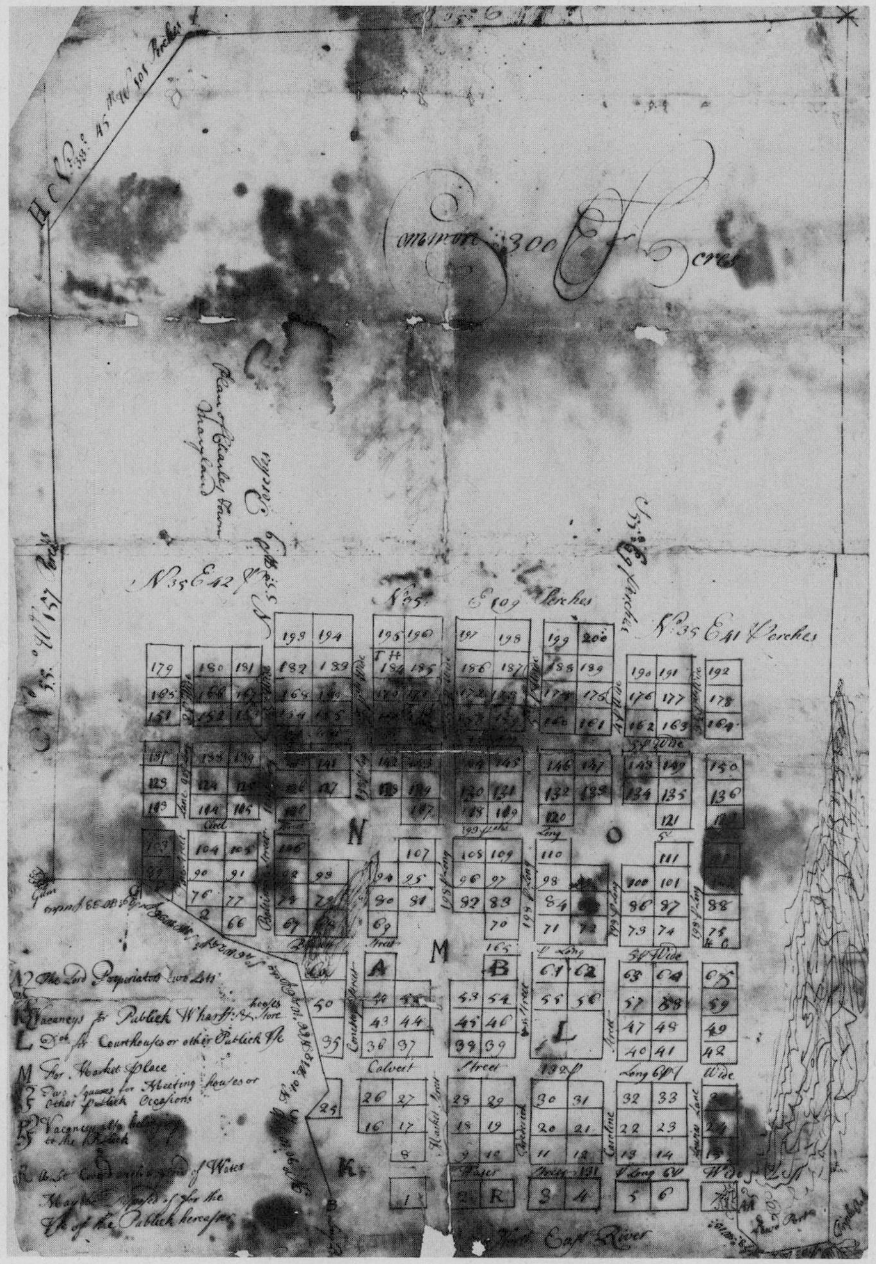

Figure 159. Plan of Charlestown, Maryland: ca. 1743

a town wharf and warehouse using the sum of £200 sterling raised by voluntary subscription of all the lot owners. When this project was completed the commissioners were to appoint "a Person of good Repute and Skill in the Goodness and Quality of Flour, Wheat, and other Grain, to be wharfinger and store-house keeper."[7] They were also authorized to appoint an inspector of flour with powers to reject, and so mark, all shipments of flour he deemed to be spoiled or otherwise unsatisfactory for export. All flour shipped from the Northeast River was to be brought first to Charlestown for such inspection. This act also conferred powers on the commissioners to authorize the use of any of the open squares for churches or "such other Public uses as to them . . . shall appear to be for the Interest, Profit, and Conveniency of the Inhabitants." The remaining portions of the public squares could then be leased for other purposes for up to twenty-one years. The act further authorized the construction of a shipyard at nearby Seneca Point and sanctioned annual spring and fall fairs.

In 1750 the assembly established the office of overseer of streets, ordered the citizens to keep their lots free of underbrush, permitted the commissioners to lease marsh areas within the town to any person who agreed to dike and drain them for meadows, directed that all foodstuffs were to be sold only in the market house, and prohibited the raising of swine, sheep, and geese in the town unless in a suitable enclosure. Three years later the assembly authorized the owners of water lots to construct wharves into the river channel as far as they wished.[8]

Charlestown attracted a substantial amount of trade in its early years and was considered as promising a community as Baltimore. Most of the export trade consisted of flour and grain from the rich wheat fields of southern Pennsylvania and northern Maryland. Merchants in Philadelphia expressed alarm that the new town might seriously compete with that city's trade and commerce. However, the initial momentum of growth could not be maintained for long. A writer in the Pennsylvania *Chronicle* scornfully commented, thirty years after its founding, "What, I beseech you, is Charlestown?—a deserted village, with a few miserable huts thinly scattered among the bushes, and daily crumbling into ruin."[9] Baltimore's more favorable position for trade with the western parts of Maryland and Pennsylvania and Philadelphia's continued dominance of the area northeast of Charlestown provided competition the new town could not meet. By 1795, as Isaac Weld noted, Charlestown consisted of "about twenty houses only . . . which are inhabited chiefly by people who carry on a herring fishery."[10] A number of owners of houses in Charlestown demolished their dwellings and shipped the materials to Baltimore to be used in erecting structures in that thriving community. Charlestown as it existed in 1799 can be seen at the bottom center of the map reproduced in figure 160 showing the northern end of Chesapeake Bay.[11] By that time the town faced the competition of Havre de Grace, which had been laid out by Robert Young some time before 1785 to intercept the trade of the Susquehanna River.

The spacious plan of Havre de Grace, shown in the inset on figure 160, represents an extension of the original settlement that received legislative recognition in 1785. The new plan was the work of C. P. Hauducoeur, whose efforts were described in a pamphlet published in 1795 as comprehending

> eight hundred and fifty acres . . . laid out in squares in imitation of the plan of Philadelphia. These squares are now divided into lots, amounting in the whole to forty-five hundred. The principal street is one hundred and thirty-two feet wide, and the others seventy.[12]

In fact, two streets were platted 132 feet in width, Union and Congress avenues which intersected near the waterfront, while Columbia Street, which met Congress Avenue at the "Exchange Square," was 100 feet wide.

Hauducoeur provided many sites for public buildings and open spaces. According to the legend on the plan these included no fewer than ten locations for churches, two of them fronting on "A public walk and Garden called Washington Square." In addition, sites were reserved for a college, a "Bettering House," a hospital, an almshouse, "Columbia Square and Theatre," a public market, a cemetery, and a courthouse and jail. While the citizens of Havre de Grace put in a determined bid in 1787 to become the county seat of Harford County, Bel Air won the election held for this purpose, and Havre de Grace failed to achieve the stature of a major city. In 1798 it contained about forty houses and some 250 inhabitants, today it numbers slightly more than 8,000. Despite its apparently advantageous location at the mouth of the Susquehanna, the hazards to navigation on this river proved too difficult to overcome, and trade was directed to Philadelphia and Baltimore from the rich farm lands of southern Pennsylvania.

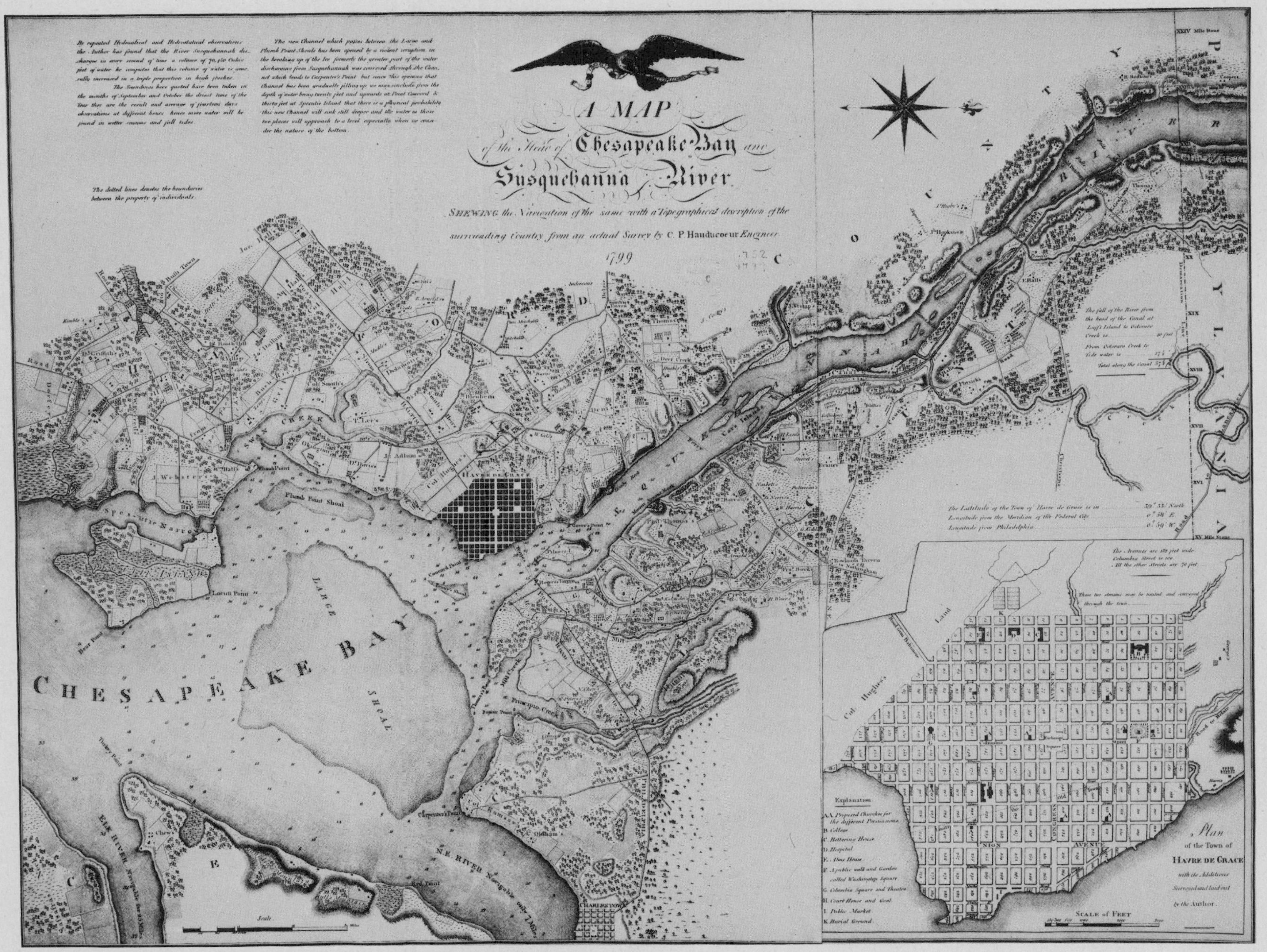

Figure 160. Map of the Northern Portion of Chesapeake Bay with a Plan of Havre de Grace, Maryland: 1799

There were other towns planned in Cecil County during the period when such high hopes were held for the future of Charlestown. In 1730 the assembly provided for the creation of Ceciltown at a place known as Broxen's Point on the Bohemia River. This or a nearby location had been designated as a town in the seventeenth century but had not been successful. The twenty-acre site was to be divided into twenty lots of equal size, the original owner was to be allowed first choice of one lot, and the remainder were to be put up for sale by the town commissioners. Within eighteen months each purchaser was obliged to complete a house with a stone or brick chimney having an area of at least four hundred feet. An unusual provision specified that "to the End, that the Houses . . . may be the more regularly placed . . . all the Houses to be erected on . . . the said Lots, shall be built on the Edge of some Street Lane, or Alley, and front the same."[13] As was common in the Maryland towns, an annual quitrent of "One Penny Current Money of Maryland" was to be paid to the lord proprietary by each lot owner.

The commissioners found themselves unable to agree on the price to be paid for the land, and in accordance with the provisions of the legislation, a jury was then convened to value the site and determine the compensation to be paid the owner. The twenty acres were finally obtained for the sum £47 10s. The plat of the town has not survived, but early records reveal that its streets were sixty feet wide. Seventeen of the lots were quickly sold, but the town itself failed to grow. In all there may have been as many as half a dozen houses. This did not fail to dampen the speculative interest in Ceciltown lots. In 1733 one of the original purchasers who had paid £2 7s. 6d. for his lot sold it for £36 to Robert Pennington, who probably regretted the transaction for the rest of his life.[14]

Ceciltown's failure did not reduce the interest of the county residents in new towns. In 1736 several persons petitioned the assembly to erect a town on the north bank of the Sassafras River. The legislature responded with the usual act authorizing the acquisition of thirty acres of land to be laid out in sixty equal lots.[15] William Rumsey, the surveyor, platted Fredericktown in three streets running east and west crossed by three others in a north-south alignment.[16]

Across the river from Fredericktown lay Georgetown, created by the assembly at the same time as if to guarantee the failure of both.[17] Perhaps the inhabitants of Kent County, who petitioned the assembly for this

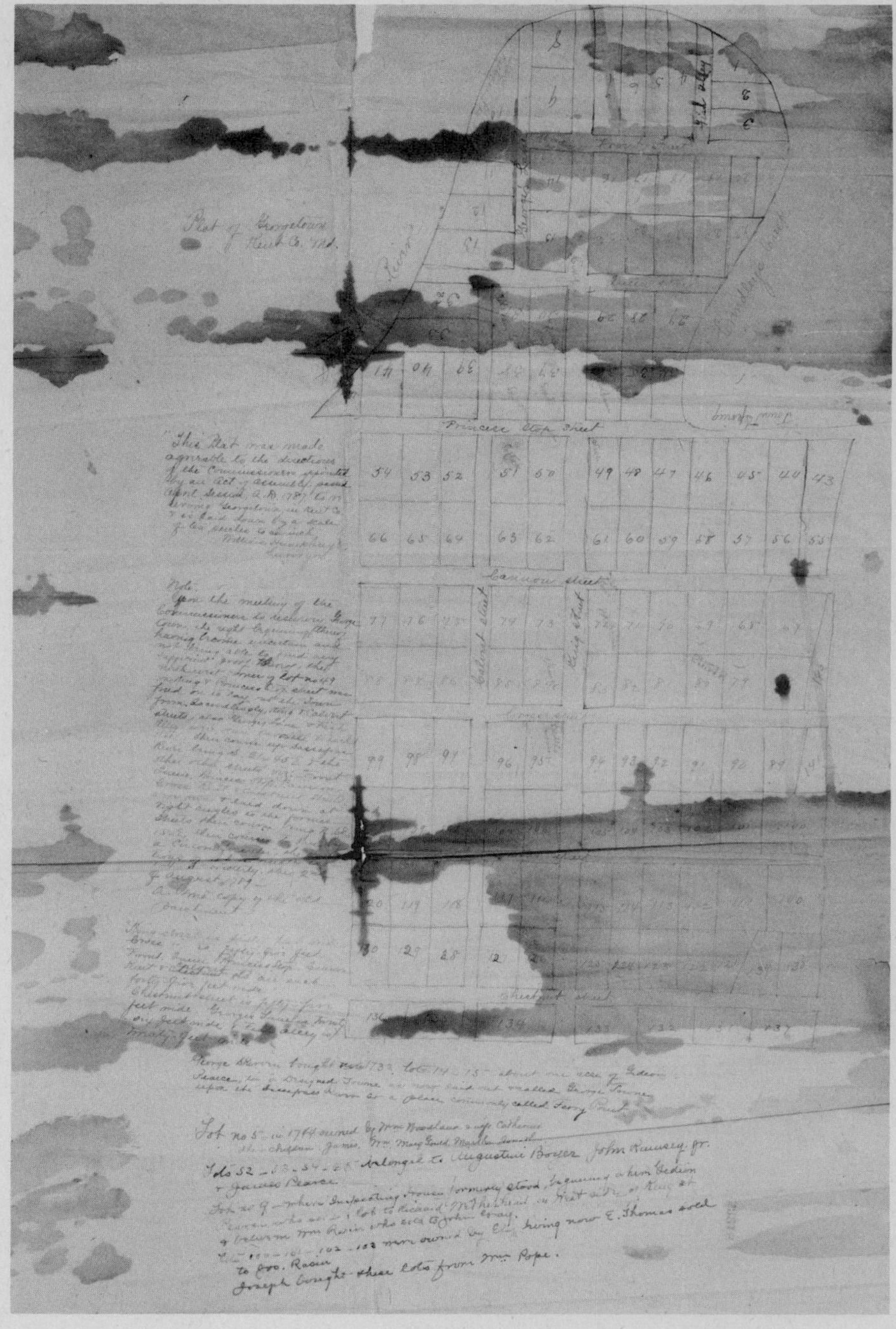

Figure 161. Plan of Georgetown, Maryland: 1787

purpose, were determined that they should not be inconvenienced by having to ship their goods through the town in the adjoining county. In any event, they were successful in obtaining their law but not much of a town. When the Reverend Andrew Burnaby passed through the area in 1760 he recorded only that "Fredericktown is a small village on the . . . Sassafras river, built for the accommodation of strangers and travellers; . . . exactly opposite to it, is another small village (Georgetown), erected for the same purpose."[18] In 1787 the assembly directed the resurvey of Georgetown. A barely legible copy of this work survives (figure 161). The notes on the drawing tell of the difficulties in re-establishing the former street lines; thus this plan may not be a completely accurate representation of the original design. It evidently includes some lots added at the time of the resurvey, for the act of 1736 specified that the town was to be divided into one hundred lots. Today the two sites are but sparsely occupied. In Fredericktown the water-front area is occupied by a marina and on the bluff above exist a few houses built on the remnants of the old grid plan. Georgetown is even smaller, and a casual traveler would not suspect that once a town of considerable size had been founded on its site.

Rather more successful was St. Michael's, one of the loveliest of the many beautiful communities on Maryland's Eastern Shore. The town is located on the east side of Miles River and on the narrow neck of an irregular peninsula that extends far into Chesapeake Bay. The area was settled in the seventeenth century, though not until 1770 was the town laid out by James Braddock, an English factor. Figure 162 is a plan of the town in 1877.[19] Braddock's town centered on St. Mary's Square in the southeastern section of the settlement shown in this illustration. It is an unusual form, with only two streets entering it on its north-south axis. Originally this functioned as a market-place, but it is now a square of residences with the exception of the town museum, an early dwelling moved to the site and modified for its present use. In addition to a number of fine houses of the late eighteenth and early nineteenth centuries, the town contains the Chesapeake Bay Maritime Museum fronting the harbor area on the northeast side of the town. During the War of 1812 the British considered the port important enough to shell it from their ships, but little damage was done.[20]

Not all of the eighteenth-century towns of the Eastern Shore had plans as interesting as those of Havre de Grace, St. Michaels, or Charlestown.

Figure 162. Plan of St. Michaels, Maryland: 1877

When Centerville was laid out in the last decade of the century as the new county seat of Queen Anne's County, a completely unimaginative grid system was used. Unlike most of the Maryland towns of this period, the plan was prepared by private landowners rather than public officials.

They and their neighbors then followed the custom widespread in Virginia of petitioning the assembly for official recognition. Although the act of 1794 conferring municipal status on the town called for the appointment of commissioners to survey the land, these officials in all probability merely adopted the existing design as their own. Figure 163 shows a dull arrangement of three streets (the present Commerce, Liberty, and Water streets) divided into thirty-seven lots with a somewhat larger tract near the middle set aside as the "Public Ground."[21]

Princess Anne in Somerset County was provided with a plan somewhat more generous though scarcely more imposing. Its creation by the assembly in 1733 stemmed from a petition of several inhabitants in the vicinity, and the usual act resulted authorizing land to be taken, appointing commissioners, specifying the details of how the lots were to be sold, and imposing a time limit for their improvement.[22] Nine years later the town was designated as the county seat of Somerset County when Worcester County was created from its eastern section, but in 1745 a second act was required to provide for laying out the town anew. Princess Anne developed as a port of some local importance, and as late as 1900 ships were able to load and unload cargo from docks on the Manokin River at the foot of Main Street.

The town plan is shown in figure 164 as it existed in 1877. The original plat included only the portion south of the river extending to Upper Alley (now Washington Street) and bounded on the east and west by Back Alley and Low Alley (now Beechwood Street and Beckford Avenue). The courthouse occupied a site facing Prince William Street, which like Main Street was given a width approximately twice that of the less important thoroughfares of the town.

Two landowners who purchased sites beyond the original town boundaries recognized the potential importance of the strong cross axis of Prince William Street. At its eastern terminus stands the large frame dwelling built about 1795 by Colonel Mathias Jones, later to be occupied by poet Ellen Dashiell. More impressive was the two-hundred-foot-long brick structure Littleton Dennis Teackle erected in 1801 at the other end of the street as extended one block beyond Low Alley to the west. The Teackle mansion, with its large central wing flanked by a long, gabled pavilion on each side, closely resembled in form the several handsome town mansions of earlier date in Annapolis. These two buildings enclose the views to

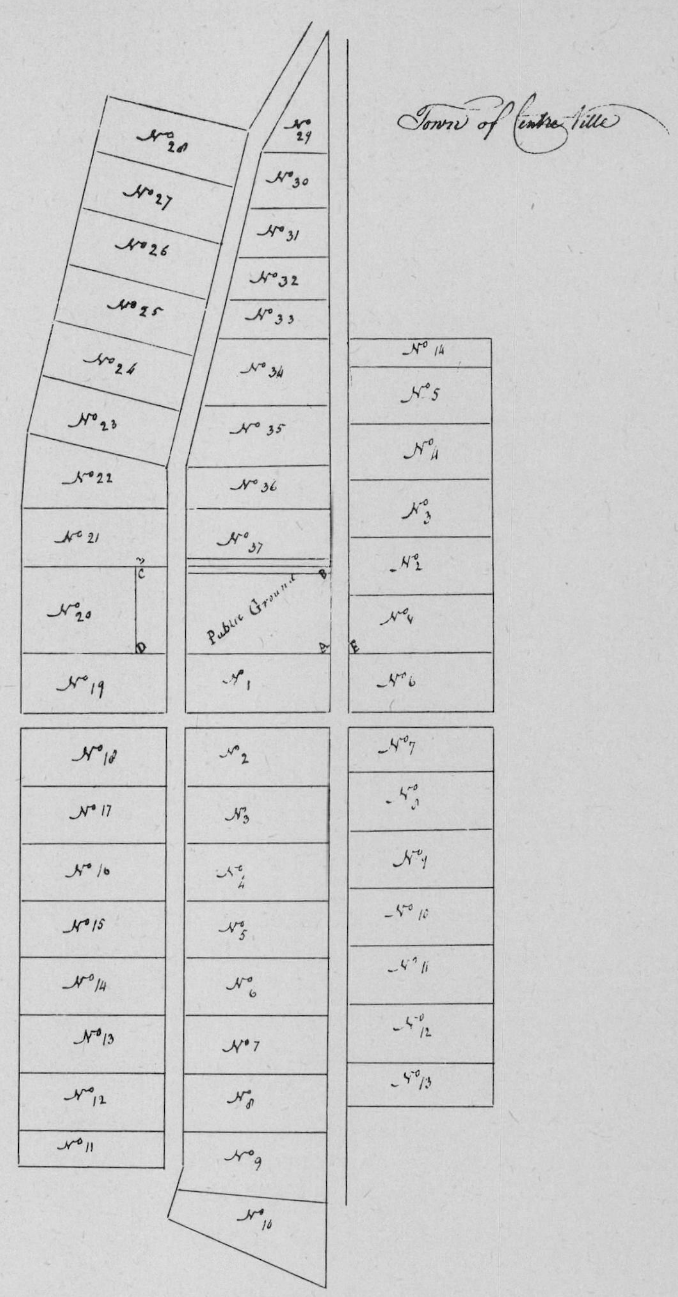

Figure 163. Plan of Centerville, Maryland: 1798

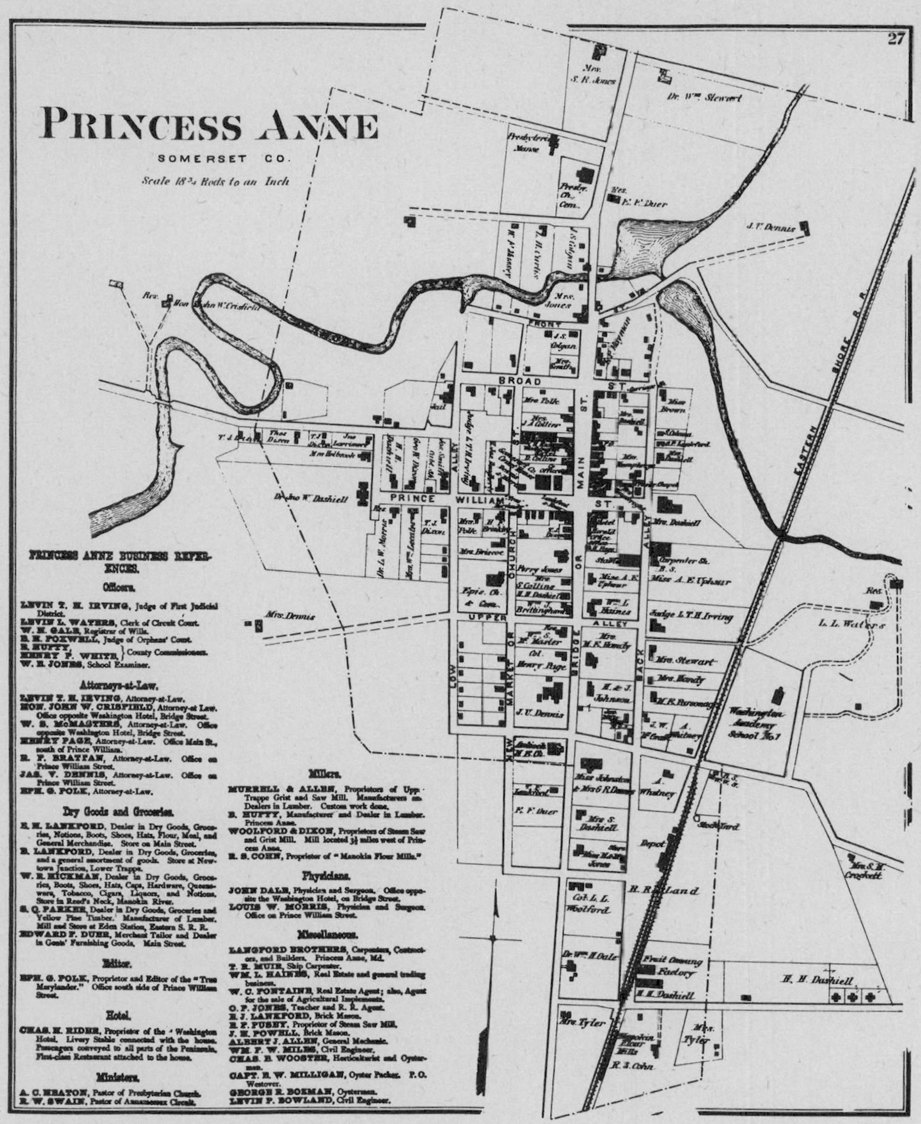

Figure 164. Plan of Princess Anne, Maryland: 1877

each end of Prince William Street and add an air of formality to this lovely town that also contains a number of other fine old houses and churches. From the plan one would not guess the splendid quality of the community that gradually took form as the town grew from its simple beginnings.

Many of the "new" towns created by the assembly during the eighteenth century represented second attempts to create communities on sites acquired for that purpose during the spate of legislation in the previous period but where no settlements of any consequence had ever developed. In many cases the original survey documents had disappeared, and the boundaries of the town as well as its internal division into streets and lots could not be ascertained. Early lot owners, discouraged because of the lack of progress in the majority of the towns created under the general acts of the seventeenth and early eighteenth centuries, drifted away and abandoned title to their land. Town commissioners died or left the area and were not replaced. In several instances, although the assembly had so ordered, county officials apparently had never actually proceeded to carry out their responsibilities. As population in the colony steadily increased and, finally, towns became necessary rather than merely desired, it was only natural that the assembly should seek to utilize the tracts of land that had been designated or purchased earlier for this purpose.

Thus, in 1728, the assembly passed a typical town act calling for the creation of Leonard Town in St. Mary's County where formerly they had sought to establish a community by the name of Seymour Town.[23] In 1732 the assembly passed another act directing the laying out into streets and lots of fifteen acres in Charles County. This site had formerly been part of a one hundred-acre tract on the Patuxent River acquired for the creation of Benedict-Leonard Town.[24]

Port Tobacco in Charles County, located on one of the broad creeks flowing into the Potomac River, also was one of the communities from an earlier period that the assembly reactivated in the eighteenth century. Apparently there had been some kind of settlement on the shore of Port Tobacco Creek by the middle of the previous century, first known as Chandlerstown, and then as Port Tobacco. During the period of wholesale town planning in the latter part of the century this spot was designated officially as a town under the name of Charlestown, though it continued to be called Port Tobacco by people in the vicinity. At first most of the settlers lived on the west side of the creek, but the east bank proved more attractive and the town gradually began to take form on the new location. A courthouse was constructed, but other information about the early extent of the town is vague.[25]

The act of the assembly in 1729 calling for the creation of a town on the site suggests that at that time the settlement was only loosely organized.[26] The law did specify, however, that "nothing in this Act shall . . . prejudice any Person or Persons . . . who have comply'd with the Requisites of the Act of Assembly, whereby Part of the said Land was actually survey'd and laid out into Lots, and then call'd Chandler Town," which indicates that some kind of town plan had been established. No early plats of the town survive, and the drawing in figure 165 shows only the extent of settlement in 1894, by which time the town had dwindled in size. Whether Port Tobacco Square, on which fronted the courthouse, the church, an inn, and several houses dates from the new plan of 1729 or from an earlier period is not known. In 1796 Isaac Weld noted that while the town "contains about eighty houses, most . . . are of wood, and very poor." Already the community, which once had been an important shipping point in the tobacco trade, was beginning to decay. Weld observed that the

> large English episcopalian church on the border of town, built of stone, which formerly was an ornament to the place . . . is now entirely out of repair; the windows are all broken, and the road is carried through the church yard, over the graves, the paling that surrounded it having been torn down.[27]

Port Tobacco suffered the fate shared by many of the early Virginia and Maryland port towns located on the smaller creeks of the Tidewater. Clearing the land for tobacco cultivation swiftly altered natural drainage conditions. With greater run-off from tilled fields and removal of the forest cover, erosion soon caused silting up of many of the streams that once had provided deep-water navigation. This factor, combined with the use of ships of deeper draft, rendered many original natural harbors unusable.[28]

Another development also caused a decline in prosperity for many of these settlements. By the eighteenth century, because of too intensive use of the tidewater lands for tobacco culture, much of the land had lost its natural fertility. The center of tobacco growing shifted to the Piedmont, and many tidewater farms were abandoned by owners who moved westward seeking more fertile soil. Weld observed the effect of these changing circumstances in the vicinity of Port Tobacco:

> From Port Tobacco to Hoe's Ferry, on the Patowmac River, the country is flat and sandy, and wears a most dreary aspects. Nothing

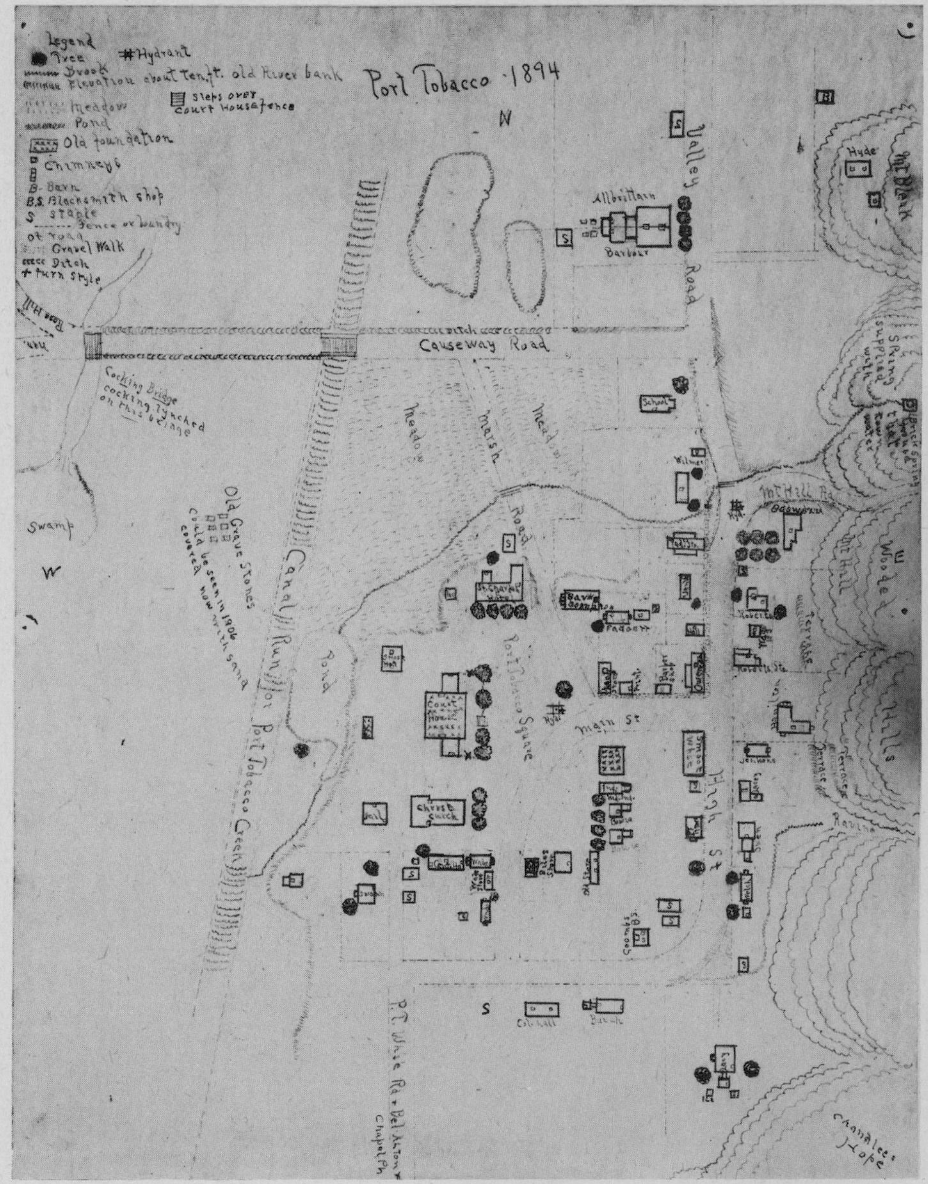

Figure 165. Plan of Port Tobacco, Maryland: 1894

> is to be seen here for miles together but extensive plains, that have been worn out by the culture of tobacco. . . . In the midst of these plains are the remains of several good houses, which shew that the country was once very different to what it is now. These . . . houses . . . have now been suffered to go to decay, as the land around them is worn out, and the people find it more to their interest to remove to another part of the country, and clear a piece of rich land, than to attempt to reclaim these exhausted plains. In consequence of this, the country in many of the lower parts of Maryland appears as if it had been deserted by one half of its inhabitants.[29]

Today the site of Port Tobacco is occupied by only a handful of houses. In 1752 it was large and prosperous enough to attract the theatrical company of Thomas Kean which had been playing at Williamsburg. There they performed *The Beggar's Opera* and probably other items in their repertoire. Several fine mansions were constructed on the hills overlooking the valley of Port Tobacco Creek. One of these estates was the property of the Jesuit order. According to Dr. Robert Honyman, who visited and was impressed by the town in 1775, it consisted of ten thousand acres and was worked by "two or three hundred" slaves. Honyman also reported witnessing a muster of "about 60 gentlemen learning the military exercise" in a field near Port Tobacco.[30] The remnants of this once important community, like so many of the lost or nearly vanished tidewater towns, whisper only the faintest echoes of these past glories.

No detailed graphic evidence survives of many other towns planned or proposed in Maryland during this era. By the time Dennis Griffith compiled his detailed map of the state in 1794 (the eastern portion of which is reproduced in figure 166), towns dotted both shores of Chesapeake Bay as well as much of the interior. Most of these had been created by acts of the assembly, but for the majority of those with colonial origins we have little but the legislative documents to inform us about the circumstances of their founding.[31]

For one group of towns in close proximity to each other we do possess both drawings and documents that make it possible to trace their founding in some detail. Their history is all the more interesting because in one way or another they became intimately related to the planning and development of a major metropolis of the region. The towns were Bladensburg, Georgetown, Carrollsburg, and Hamburg. The metropolis is, of course, the capital of the nation, Washington, D. C., and the most elaborately planned city of the tidewater area.

Bladensburg came into existence by an act the assembly passed in 1742 responding to a petition from residents of the area. At a place called Garrison Landing on the Anacostia River, or East Branch of the Potomac as it was frequently referred to, commissioners were directed to obtain sixty acres of land and lay it out into streets and sixty lots of equal area.[32] Their plan, a most curious one indeed, appears in figure 167. Two major streets, one leading north and the other east, ran from the public landing at the river. Midway along the latter thoroughfare the commissioners set aside a square parcel for a tobacco warehouse and market place surrounded by streets on its four sides. The street pattern is strangely worked out, and several of the lots appear to have had no direct access to any public way.

The early years of the town do not seem to have brought much development. Many of the lots were sold as soon as the survey had been completed, though by 1747 only twenty-eight of them had been built on and their title confirmed under the time period specified in the act. As late as 1771 only fifty-two of the lots had been legally improved, and in the intervening years there had been thirteen instances of forfeiture for failure to build, followed by resale of these parcels by the commissioners.[33]

Bladensburg's history resembles that of Port Tobacco's with a period of slow and uncertain development, an era of prosperity, and ultimate stagnation or decline. The same forces were at work to produce similar results. Tobacco became the principal item of trade, although there were two flour mills in the town, and a dozen stores, mostly operated by Scottish traders, lined its streets. The decline in importance of tobacco and the silting up of the harbor combined to reduce Bladensburg's importance. Most of the wheat and flour trade gravitated to Baltimore, where shipping facilities were superior and the waterborne approach was easier than going up the winding course of the Potomac. Alexandria's more rapid development and better harbor also overshadowed Bladensburg, and by 1800 the latter was on the wane.

Far more successful was the nearby community of Georgetown, which had similar origins as a town although a longer history as a place of settlement. At the mouth of Rock Creek on the Potomac, not far below the falls of the river, a tobacco inspection house had been established sometime after 1734 for the planters in the vicinity. Its location was slightly

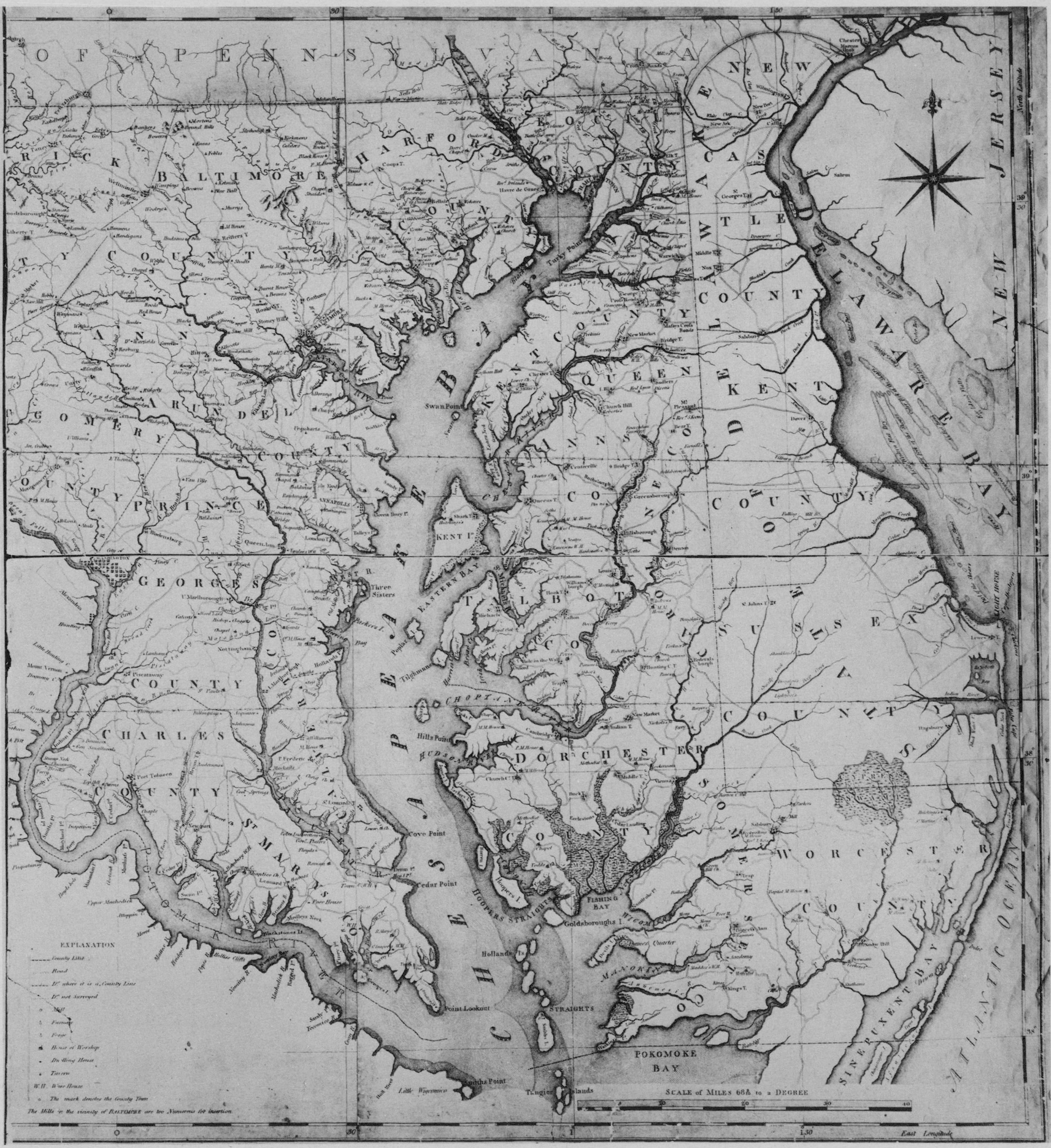

Figure 166. Map of the Eastern Portion of Maryland: 1794

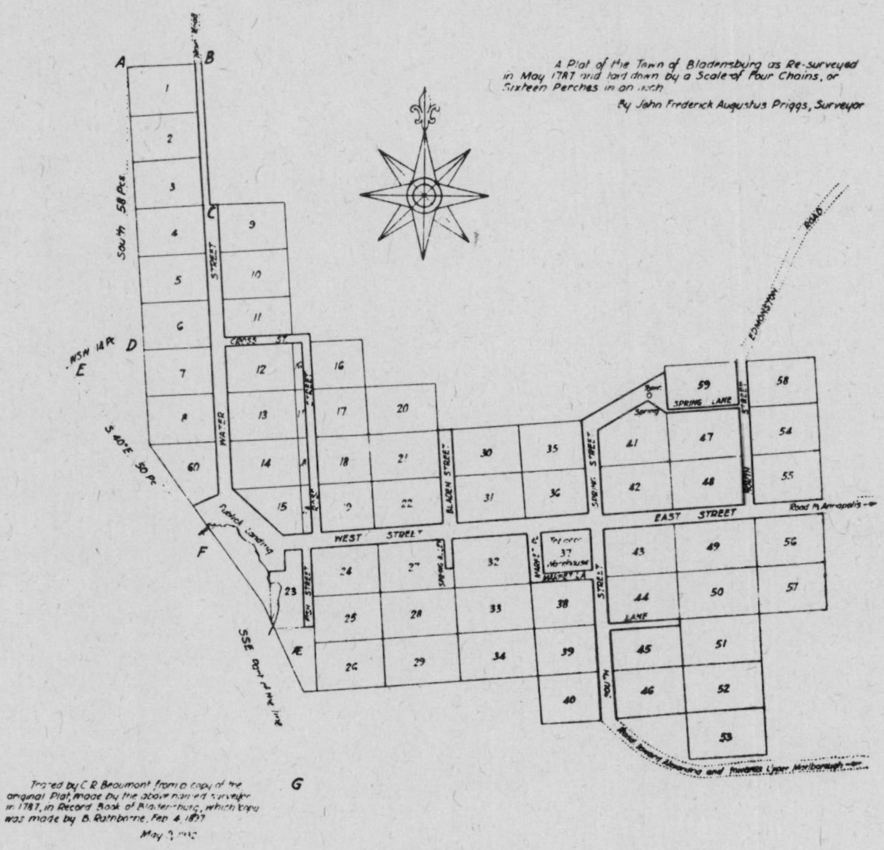

Figure 167. Plan of Bladensburg, Maryland: 1787

south of the present M Street, N.W., near what is now Wisconsin Avenue. Around this structure, constructed by George Gordon, the nucleus of a settlement began to develop. By 1751 the time seemed ripe for the creation of a town, persons in the vicinity prepared the usual petition to the legislature, and the assembly responded with a standard town act. It authorized commissioners appointed for this purpose to acquire sixty acres of land, to lay out eighty lots, and to use powers of eminent domain if the proprietors of the land declined to sell at a reasonable price.[34]

George Gordon and his neighbor, George Beall, refused to sell their land for the amount offered, and, as prescribed by the act, seventeen freeholders were convened as a condemnation jury. They awarded the two owners the substantial sum of £280. Although Gordon apparently was satisfied with his share of the compensation, Beall was not. When they were asked to select the two lots each was entitled to have under the provisions of the law, Beall at first refused. When, however, the commissioners sent him a second notice, stating that if he did not make his choice within ten days he would forfeit his rights, he reluctantly complied but angrily wrote the commissioners:

> If I must part with my property by force, I had better save a little, than be totally demolished. Rather than have none I accept . . . the lots . . . but I do hereby protest and declare that my acceptance of the said lots which is by force, shall not debar me from future redress from the Commissioners or others. If I can have the right of a British subject I ask no more. God save King George.[35]

The following day, when lots were put up for sale, interest ran high, and the commissioners were able to pay the two men £191 immediately. The land sold at that time had been surveyed under the commissioners' directions by Alexander Beall into a little gridiron settlement having lots with a variety of shapes and sizes. The plan of the town as then laid out appears in figure 168. One street followed the irregular course of the river bank and bore three names: "Wapping," "The Keys," and "West Landing." Further inland and on higher ground Beall surveyed the principal street. Its eastern portion was then called Bridge Street, a name soon extended to its entire length. In today's Georgetown this is M Street, N.W. Intersecting this on the alignment of the modern Wisconsin Avenue was Water Street, with its extension to the northern boundary of the town bearing the name of High Street. Two narrow lanes ran parallel to Water and High streets to provide additional access to the river.

Georgetown soon attained considerable prosperity, and it was not long before its citizens began to entertain optimistic thoughts that the new town might one day rival Philadelphia and New York. Merchants began to erect handsome townhouses, many of which have been preserved and restored in the present era. The Revolution brought a lull in shipping activities along the river. By the turn of the century, however, there were dozens of ships bearing Georgetown registry, and these and vessels from other ports carried on a substantial trade with Europe, the West Indies, and other maritime towns of America.[36] In addition to the usual maritime

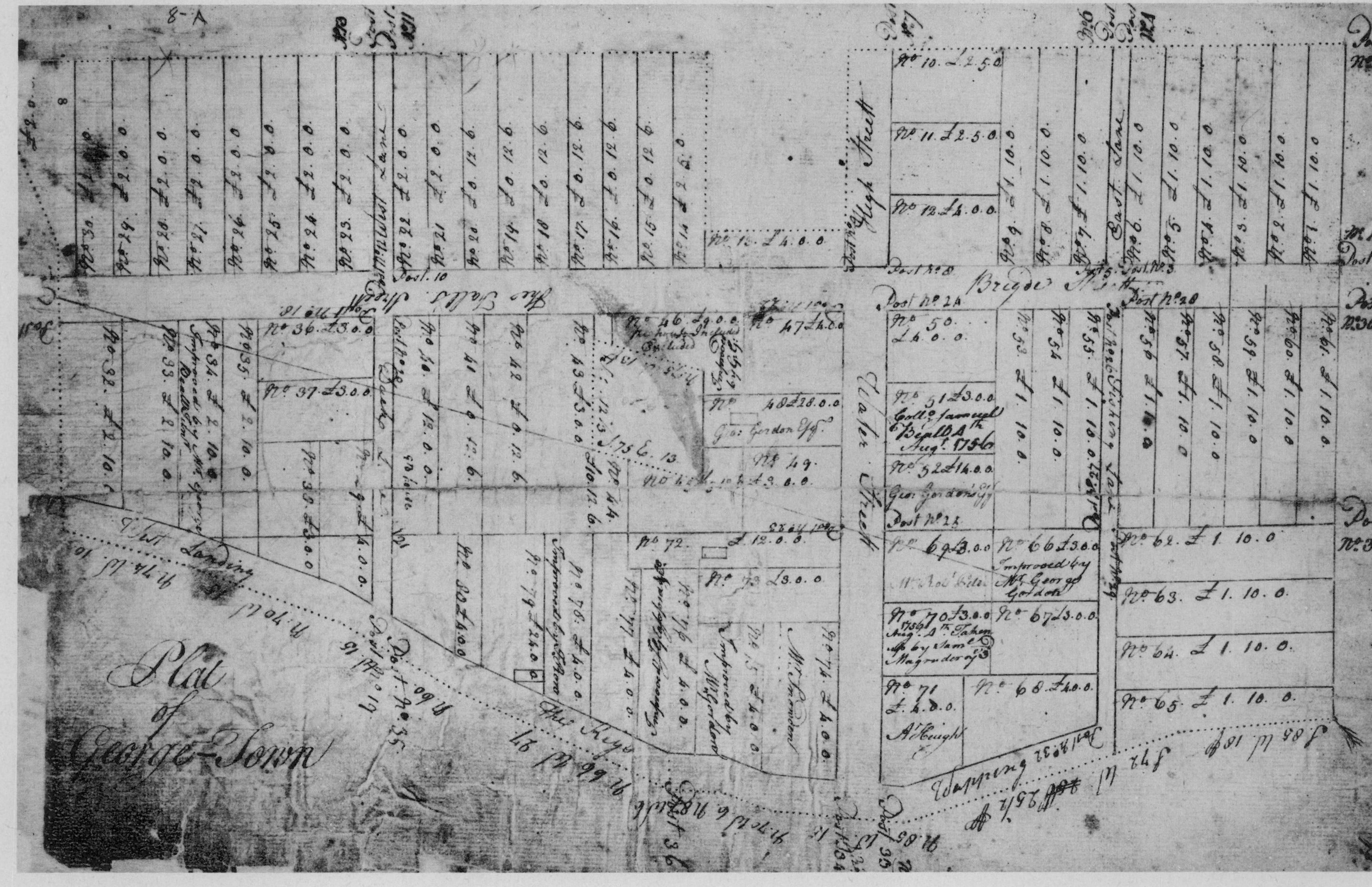

Figure 168. Plan of Georgetown, Maryland: 1751

industries the town also contained numerous shops, warehouses, a textile mill, a paper factory, and many handicraft and service establishments.[37]

Prosperity attracted population, and additional building sites were required. The plan of Georgetown in 1796, figure 169, reveals that the new area incorporated into the town far exceeded that enclosed by the original boundaries. Gridiron additions to the west and north were modified only by the angled extensions of High Street and East Lane, the latter being given the more dignified name of Congress Street. The extension plan also included a market square immediately north of the original terminus of West Lane. Nearly square in shape, this open space had a curious pattern with three access streets leading into it near its corners, and a fourth, Market Street, having as its western line a continuation of that of the square.[38]

Trade and commerce, however, were not to be the primary forces shaping the future of the growing settlement. A visitor in 1791, although impressed with the beauty of the site and the busy harbor area, was quick to note the disadvantages of the town for shipping:

> Georgetown is said to have risen to some importance in the commercial world from the same cause as Baltimore, viz., the impolitic revenue laws of Virginia, which carried her produce to Georgetown and sent the imports from Europe, which otherwise would have gone to Alexandria. The navigation is certainly not equal to that of Alexandria, for there are some rocks opposite Georgetown, the channel is narrow and bad, and no vessel can withstand the ice which comes down the Potomac, for which reasons insurance cannot be made on vessels till they have got to Eastern Branch. The situation of Georgetown is likewise inconvenient for trade, the land being very uneven, and full of steep declivities, and hollows, and lofty eminences, which though beautiful to the eye of the traveler, and afford delightful prospects, are certainly ill-calculated for trade.[39]

Georgetown seemed destined to suffer the same fate as Port Tobacco, Bladensburg, and dozens of other smaller ports of the Chesapeake and its tributaries. It was saved from this probable end by the decision, early in 1791, to locate nearby the new national capital and to include Georgetown within the borders of the federal district created for that purpose. The planning of Washington began in the federal rather than the colonial era of our history and would normally lie beyond the scope of this study, but its place among the tidewater towns is so important and the circumstances of its planning so significant that it must be included.[40]

The site ultimately selected for the national capital in 1791 had already attracted the notice of two persons as a likely spot for town development. On October 28, 1771, Jacob Funk recorded a town plat for a 130-acre site he had purchased six years earlier from one Thomas Johns.[41] A German by birth, Funk chose the name of Hamburg for his new town, though it also was known as Funkstown.[42] Funk's land was situated about a mile below Georgetown where Goose Creek (later Tiber Creek) entered the Potomac. In the present city of Washington the crossing of Virginia and New York avenues marks the approximate center of Hamburg, the plat of which is reproduced in figure 170. For the time the town was unusually large, with 287 lots. Forty of these, including one designated as "Ware house lot" were laid out along the eighty-foot wide Water Street running parallel to the bank of the Potomac on the south. Market Street, ninety feet wide, led from this intended dock and mercantile district northward to the market area, which was given an unusual shape through the reduction in depth of the 8 lots fronting on it. Entering the market from its east and west sides was Fourth or Raven Street, which had a width of eighty feet. Funk platted all the other streets sixty feet wide except for the thirty-three-foot Front Alley, which was obviously intended to serve the rear of the lots facing Water Street.

A year earlier, in 1770, Francis Deakins had surveyed a nearby tract of 160 acres for its owner, Charles Carroll. This site was located at the point of land formed by the Potomac and the Anacostia (or Eastern Branch) rivers and was bounded on the west by St. James's Creek, which divided the peninsula into two parts. Carroll's land lay immediately east of the present Fort McNair in the southern part of Washington. The plat of Carrollsburg (figure 171) bears the date of October 20, 1770, two weeks before Carroll deeded the property in trust to Henry Roxer, Daniel Carroll, and Notley Young. The purpose of this transfer was to permit a lottery to be arranged as the method of selling building sites in the town. Apparently this was held within a few weeks. The county records contain numerous deeds for Carrollsburg town lots transferred at this time, which recite that their new owners had come into rightful possession by lot as the lucky possessors of winning tickets.[43]

Carrollsburg, like Georgetown and Hamburg, was obviously intended

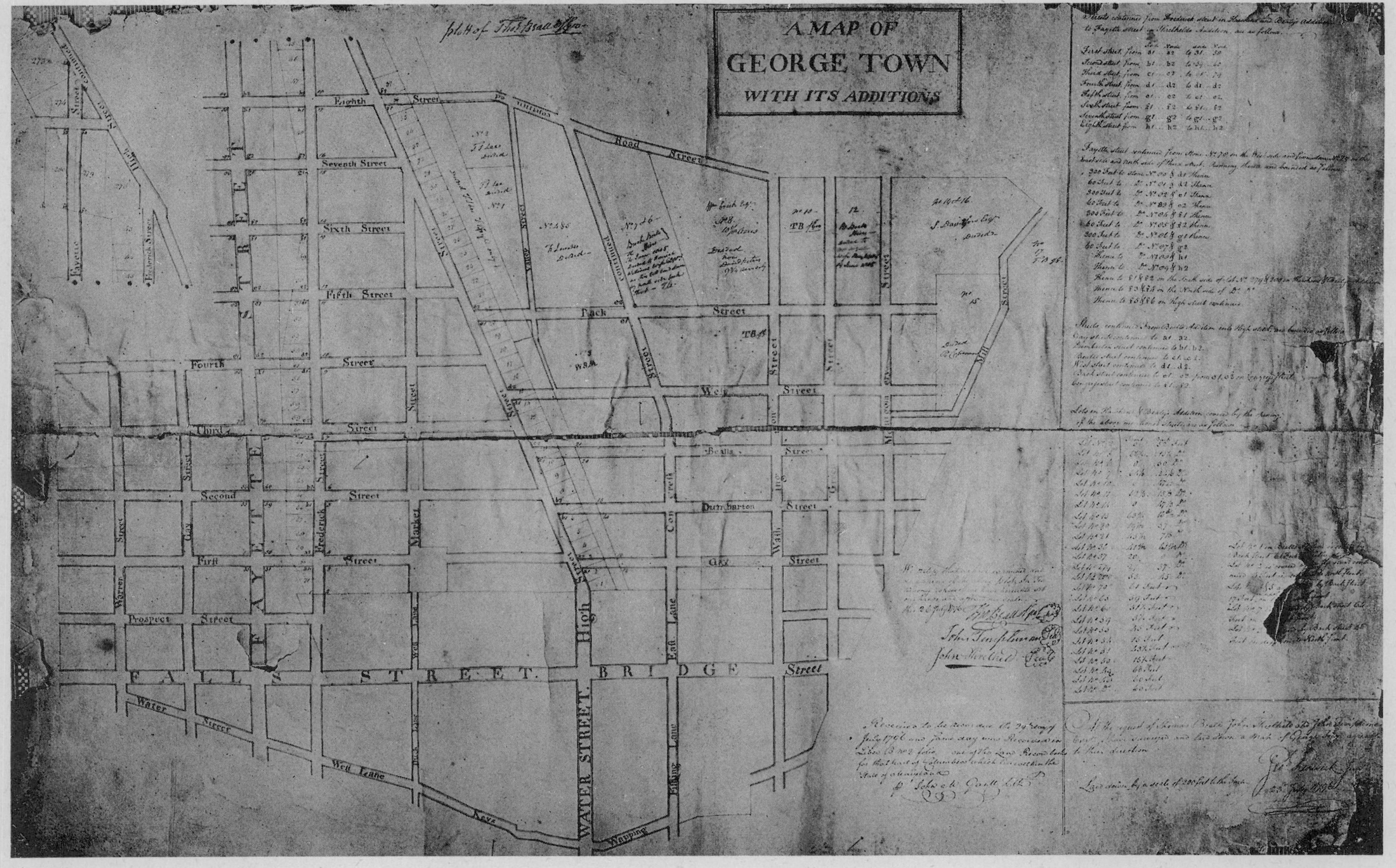

Figure 169. Plan of Georgetown in the District of Columbia: 1796

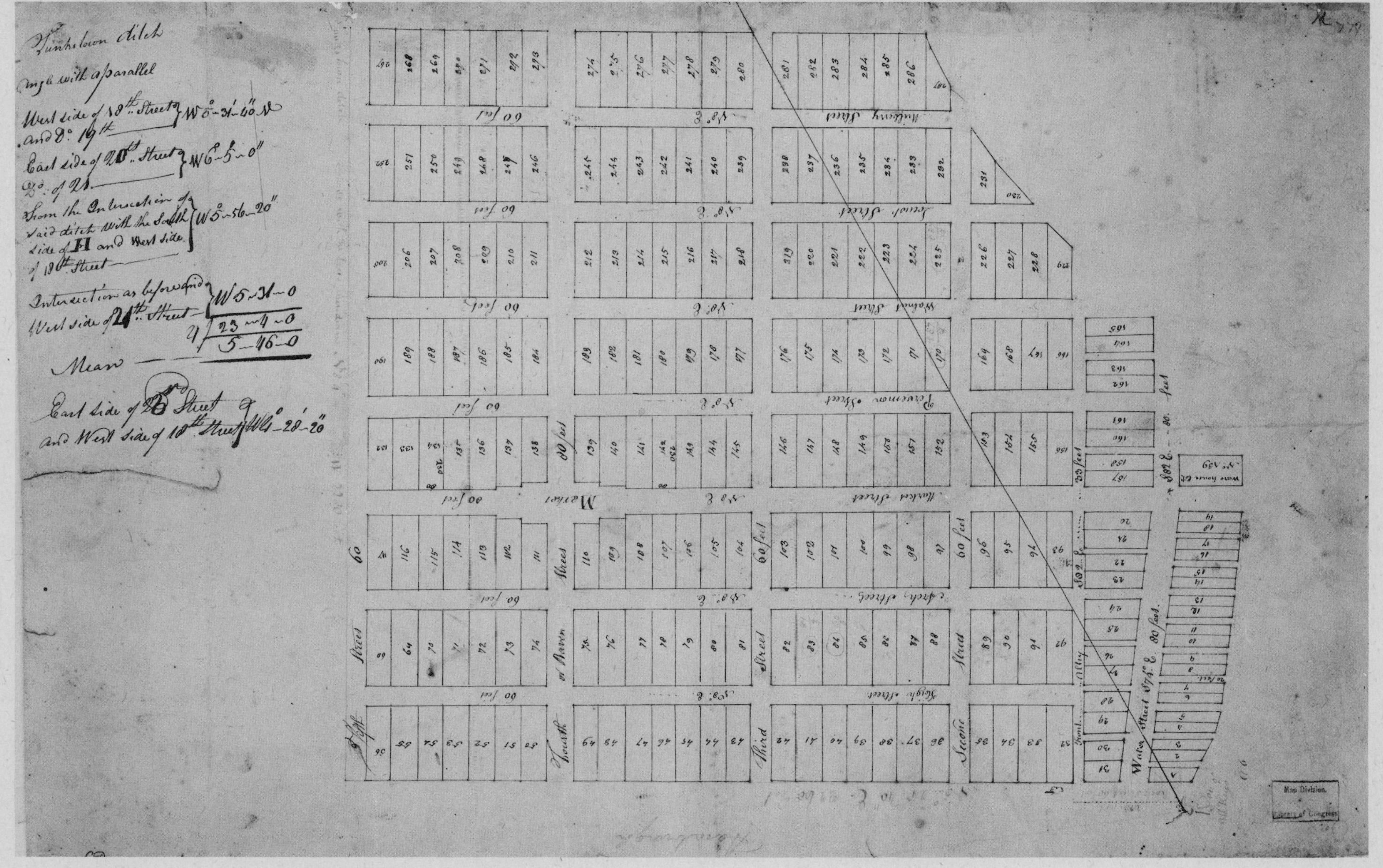

Figure 170. Plan of Hamburg, Maryland: 1768

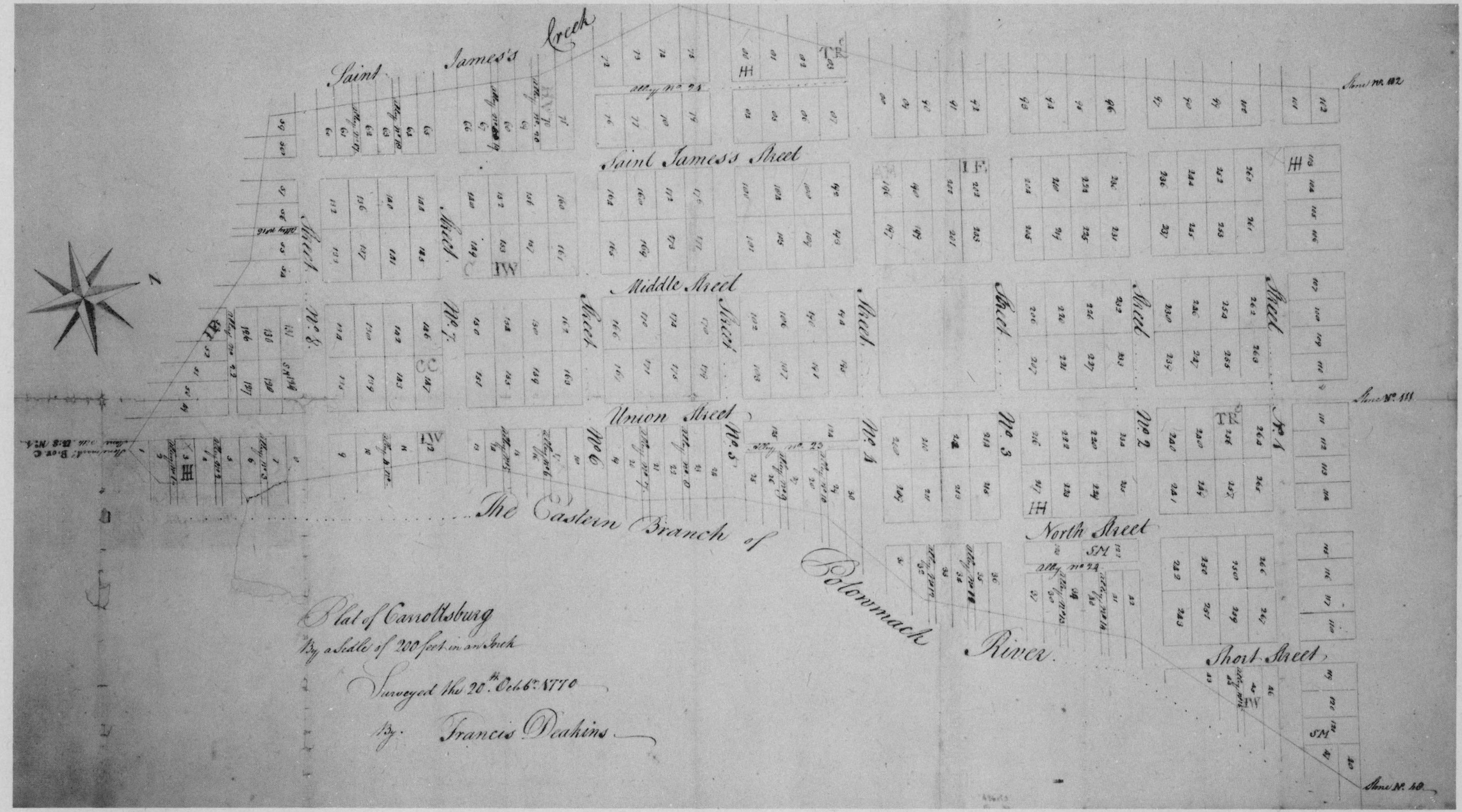

Figure 171. Plan of Carrollsburg, Maryland: 1770

as a port town. Along the deep water of the Anacostia a series of narrow lots were platted to provide sites for warehouses and other buildings that would be needed to serve shipping and manufacturing. A system of alleys between each pair of lots in this area was to provide access to these buildings and to the wharves and docks that were visualized. Although the plan itself does not so indicate, the open block bounded by 3rd and 4th and Union and Middle streets probably was set aside for a market square.

Unlike most other towns that originated through private initiative in colonial Tidewater, neither Hamburg nor Carrollsburg ever received legislative sanction from the General Assembly. One reason may have been that while a large number of lots had been sold directly by Funk and, through the device of the lottery, disposed of profitably by Carroll, most of the building sites remained vacant. The two towns faced competition from the already established and thriving communities of Georgetown and Alexandria. Soon, however, speculative interest in their future was to reach its peak.

On January 24, 1791, President Washington issued a proclamation designating a ten-mile-square district as the future site of the national capital, embracing the land occupied by Carrollsburg, Hamburg, and Georgetown as part of a much larger area in Maryland and Virginia.[44] This action culminated well over a decade of contention concerning the location of the seat of government under the Articles of Confederation and the Constitution. It followed the passage of the Residence Act of 1790 in which Congress delegated to the president authority to implement a clause in Article I of the Constitution by selecting a site of not more than one hundred square miles to be ceded by one or more states to the exclusive jurisdiction of the federal government.[45] Under the act the president was directed to choose a tract anywhere along the Potomac River between the Anacostia River and Connogochegue Creek, some eighty miles upstream. He was then to appoint three commissioners to direct the work of providing suitable accommodations for government offices by December 1800.[46]

Shortly thereafter the president assigned Andrew Ellicott the task of surveying the boundary and topography of the territory. The extent of the federal district is shown in figure 172 as mapped by Ellicott with the assistance of the talented Benjamin Banneker.[47] The ten-mile-square district as finally established included the south bank of the Anacostia River and most of Alexandria as a result of an amendment to the Residence Act requested by Washington and passed by Congress. In March, 1791, Ellicott was joined by Pierre Charles L'Enfant, whose assignment was to select sites most suitable for the public buildings. L'Enfant, trained in Paris as an artist, had come to America during the Revolution and received an officer's commission in the Corps of Engineers. After the war he was commissioned to design the medal for the Society of the Cincinnati, which Washington headed as president-general. As an architect in New York he was in charge of remodeling the city hall for its use as the temporary capitol and as the site of Washington's inauguration. In the fall of 1789 he offered his services to the president as the planner of the capital city, and it seems likely that his appointment in 1791 was the result of these prior contacts with Washington during and after the Revolution.[48]

The Residence Act provided for the acquisition within the district of "such quantity of land . . . as the President shall deem proper for the use of the United States and according to such plans as the President shall approve." It did not require the planning of a new town, although as Jefferson pointed out to the president, "no doubt it is the wish, and perhaps expectation" of Congress that this was to be accomplished.[49] He later suggested two methods by which the necessary land might be acquired. One was to offer to purchase or, if necessary, to take by eminent domain a site within the district at twice the value it "would have been had there been no thought of bringing the federal seat" to the area. The other, a variation of which was ultimately to be carried out, was to prevail upon the proprietors to "cede one half his lands to the public, to be sold to raise money."[50]

Jefferson evidently did not at first grasp the magnitude of the project. In September, 1790, he submitted to the president the sketch reproduced in figure 173 as his plan for the town on the site of Carrollsburg—a plan differing little from that paper community as already platted. Quite possibly, however, this was intended only as the first part of the city, since at the same time he suggested to Washington that one thousand five hundred acres would be required for the city and recommended also that no street be less than one hundred feet wide.[51] This view is strengthened by an examination of Jefferson's later plan of March, 1791, which he submitted to the president with a draft proclamation that would have designated the territory around Hamburg as the site of the federal city.

Jefferson's plan is shown in figure 174. Initial development was to be confined to the blocks bounded by the closely spaced dotted lines on the north bank of Tiber Creek. Surrounding that nucleus Jefferson indicated by a series of regularly spaced dots the intersections of gridiron streets in an area designated by him "to be laid off in future." Two sites, each occupying the space of three of the 600-foot-square blocks, were to be set aside for the presidential residence and the capitol. A strip of land one block wide and eight blocks long along the creek would connect them for "public walks." This latter feature may well have been the origin of the mall, as later planned by L'Enfant to connect the Capitol and the White House on his much more grandiose scale.

Figure 172. Map of the District of Columbia: 1793

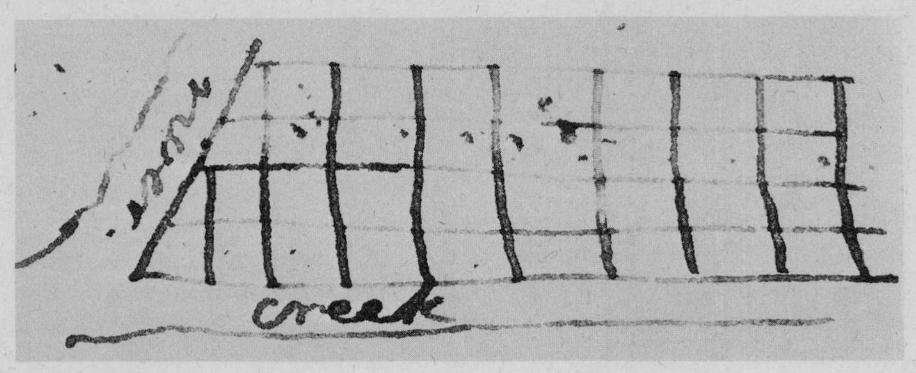

Figure 173. Plan Proposed for the National Capital: 1790

Even the greatly enlarged area shown on Jefferson's second plan was to be dwarfed by the amount of land that ultimately was to be acquired. It was Washington who worked out the necessary arrangements on a visit to Georgetown on March 28 and 29, 1791. The president had been greatly concerned over this problem and was particularly disturbed by the fact that various factions of landowners in the district were contending for the site of the city. Their actions served only to fan further the flames of speculation when it became known that the new city would be located somewhere in the area. Already Washington had written to friends in Georgetown instructing them to begin the secret purchase of land in the vicinity of that city. At the same time he saw to it that L'Enfant began his studies in the vicinity of Carrollsburg, hoping that this activity some distance away would allow his friends to purchase land near Georgetown at lower prices.[52]

On the evening of March 29, following a tour of inspection of the site with Ellicott and L'Enfant, Washington called together the two principal groups of landowners. As described in his diary, he

> represented that the contention in which they seemed to be engaged, did not in my opinion comport either with the public interest or that of their own; that while each party was aiming to obtain the public buildings, they might by placing the matter on a contracted scale, defeat the measure altogether . . . that neither the offer from George-Town or Carrollsburgh separately, was adequate to the end of insuring the object.[53]

The following day Washington again met with the proprietors who doubt-

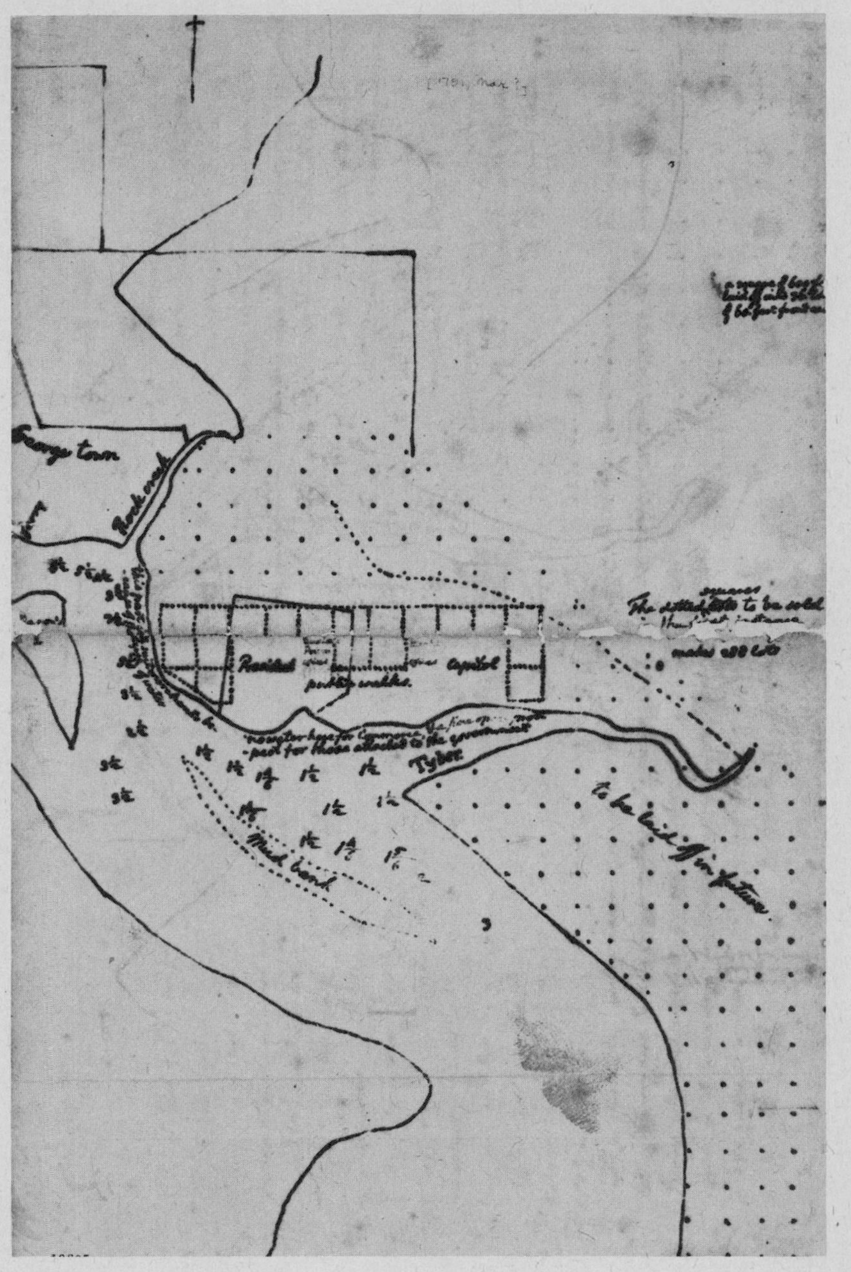

Figure 174. Plan Proposed for the National Capital: 1791

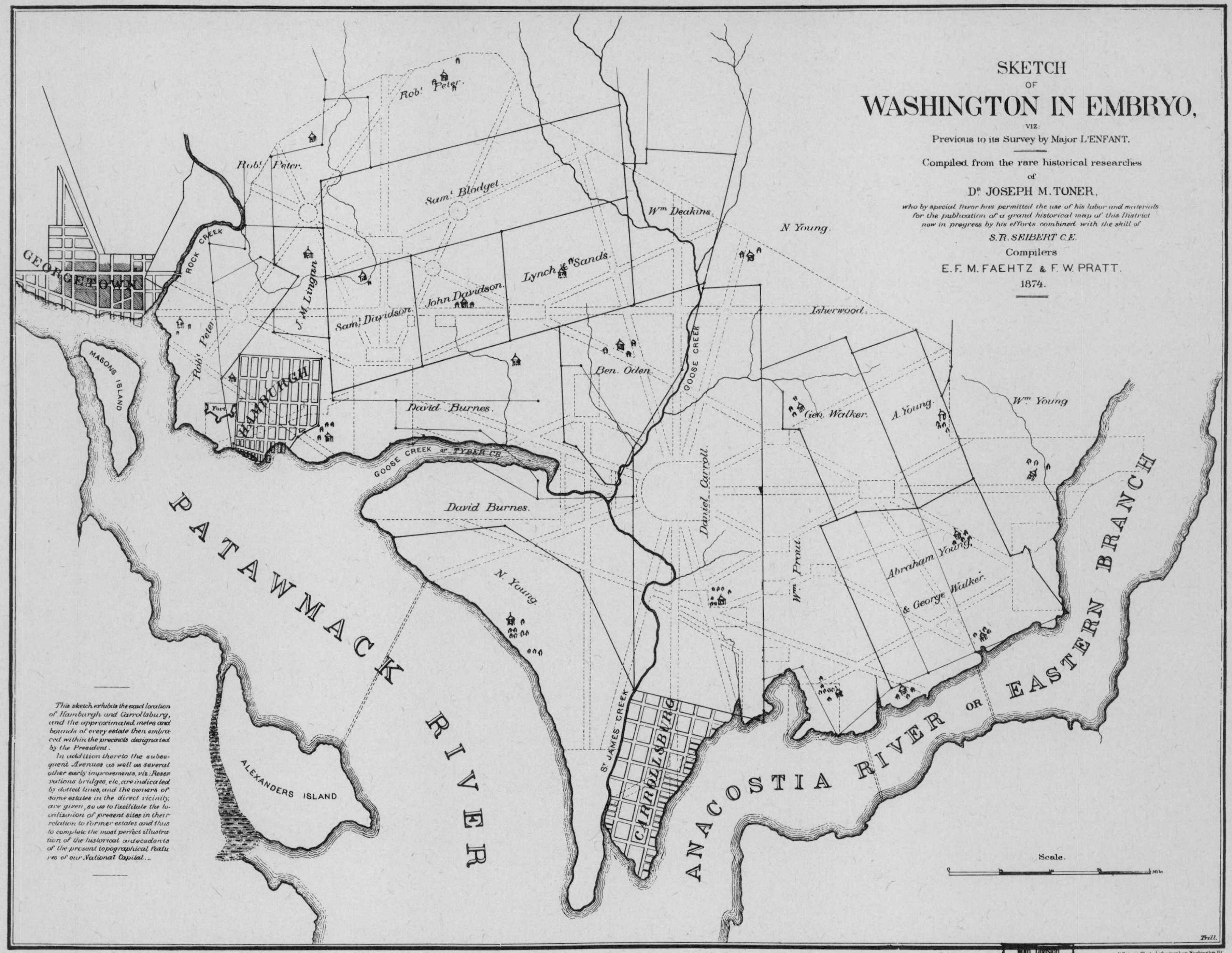

Figure 175. Map Showing the Division of Land on the site of Washington, D. C., in 1791

less had found much to discuss among themselves. On the last day of March, Washington described to Jefferson the highly favorable arrangements he had been able to work out:

> The terms . . . are That all the land from Rock-creek along the river to the eastern-branch and so upwards to or above the ferry including a breadth of about a mile and a half, the whole containing from three to five thousand acres, is ceded to the public, on condition that, when the whole shall be surveyed and laid off as a city, (which Major L'Enfant is now directed to do) the present Proprietors shall retain every other lot, and for such part of the land as may be taken for public use . . . they shall be allowed at the rate of Twenty five pounds per acre. . . . No compensation is to be made for the ground that may be occupied as streets or alleys.[54]

The generous area the president had been able to bring into temporary public ownership is shown in figure 175. The sketch also shows the boundaries of land owned by the proprietors, the paper towns of Carrollsburg and Hamburg, Georgetown, and the principal boulevards and public sites in the plan that L'Enfant was soon busily engaged in preparing. That plan, the extent of which exceeded anything yet attempted in North America and incorporating design concepts utilized only on a much smaller scale at Annapolis and Williamsburg, became possible only because of the enlightened land policy insisted upon by President Washington. To men of Washington's and Jefferson's generation there appeared nothing undemocratic in invoking governmental powers to acquire land for the planning of cities. In the latter part of the eighteenth century the city of Washington was merely the latest example of a long tradition, then firmly established in the tidewater region, of public initiative in town development. Just as Annapolis and Williamsburg represented the culmination of many years of such experience, so the new federal city marked the climax of an additional century of public efforts to create towns and cities.

L'Enfant quickly began to carry out his new assignment. Already he had noted the most prominent locations in the district and had even described for Washington his vision of a great tree-planted boulevard running from Georgetown to a bridge over the Anacostia, a street later to become Pennsylvania Avenue. He also made clear his opposition to a rigid gridiron plan as being totally unsuited to any but a perfectly flat site and "even when applyed upon the ground the best calculated to admit of it become at last tiresome and insipid."[55] On June 22, L'Enfant submitted to the president a long memorandum describing his proposals.[56] This evidently accompanied a draft plan that Washington displayed to the proprietors at a second meeting in Georgetown on June 29. Although this drawing has not survived it seems clear that by that date L'Enfant had already worked out the main elements of the plan. The president indicated to the proprietors, however, that "some deviations from it would take place—particularly in the diagonal streets or avenues, which would not be so numerous; and in the removal of the President's house more westerly for the advantage of higher ground."[57]

In his June memorandum L'Enfant described in his erratic English the basis for his proposed street plan, which combined the utilitarian grid with a system of great diagonal avenues directly connecting the chief public sites. His words are more readily understandable if they are read in connection with an outline plan of the city sent to the president on August 19 and reproduced in figure 176:

> Having determined some principal points to which I wished to make the other subordinate, I made the distribution regular with every street at right angles, North and South, east and west, and afterwards opened some in different directions, as avenues to and from every principal place, wishing thereby not merely to contract [contrast] with the general regularity, nor to afford a greater variety of seats [sites] with pleasant prospects, which will be obtained from the advantageous ground over which these avenues are chiefly directed, but principally to connect each part of the city, if I may so express it, by making the real distance less from place to place, by giving to them reciprocity of sight and by making them thus seemingly connected, promote a rapid settlement over the whole extent.

L'Enfant proposed to locate the Capitol on the highest point of land, Jenkin's Hill, a topographic feature he described as "a pedestal waiting for a superstructure." The "Presidential palace" was to be placed on another elevation toward the western end of the city with its grounds running down to the banks of the Tiber and with a view down the broad Potomac. These two sites were to be connected by one of the great avenues, all of which were to have roadways eighty feet broad bordered by addi-

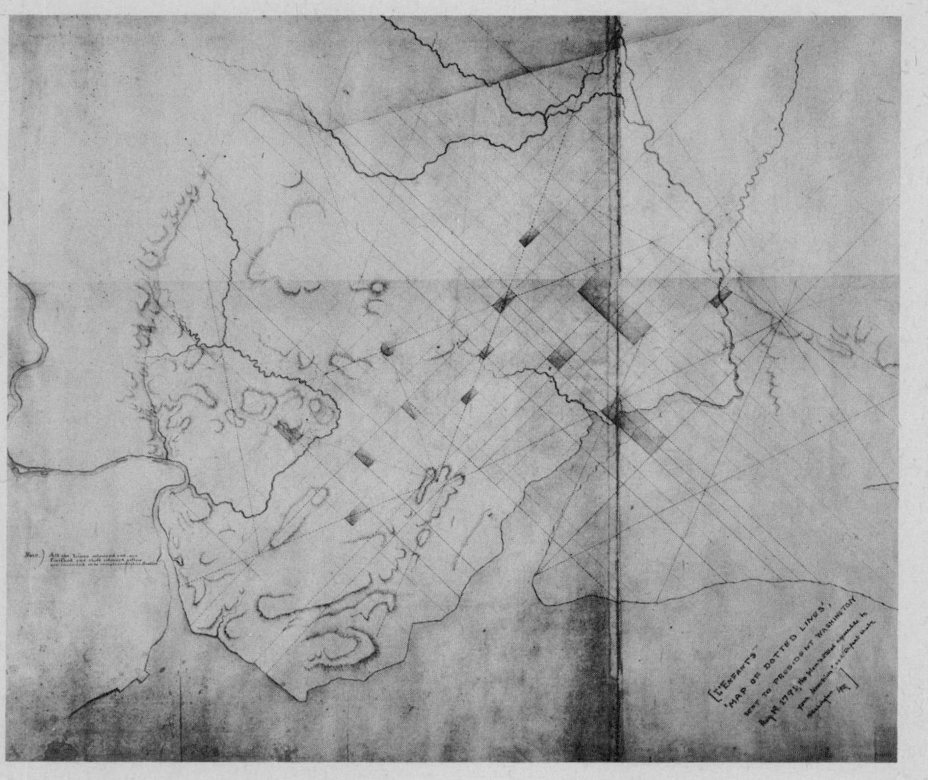

Figure 176. Plan for Washington, D. C.: 1791

tional strips thirty feet wide on either side planted in double rows of trees and flanked by ten-foot strips between the outer trees and property lines. Running along the northern bank of the Tiber between the Capitol and the presidential residence were the "public walks," the genesis of the present Mall.

In a later communication to Washington on August 19, which accompanied his final plan, L'Enfant mentioned again the principal avenue, a number of other public sites, and a proposed cascade of water that was to issue from the base of the Capitol and tumble down to a canal linking the Potomac and Anacostia rivers:

> The grand avenue connecting both the palace and the Federal House will be most magnificent and most convenient, the streets running west of the upper square of the Federal House and which terminate in an easy slope on the canal through the tiber which it will overlook for the space of about two mile will be beautifull above what may be imagined—those other streets parallel to that canal, those crossing over it and which are as many avenues to the grand walk from the water cascade under the Federal House to the President park and dependinly extending to the bank of the Potowmack, and also the several squares or area such as are intended for the Judiciary Court—the national bank—the grand church—the play house—market and exchange—all through will offer a variety of situation unparalled in points of beauties—suitable to very purpose and in every point convenient.[58]

A few days following this communication L'Enfant traveled to Philadelphia to present to Washington the final revised plan. This is shown in figure 177 as copied in 1887 from the original badly faded and partially illegible manuscript drawing. The major features previously described by L'Enfant in his communications with the president all appear along with several new elements. At many points of multiple intersections of the radial and gridiron streets the designer introduced rectangular or circular civic plazas. Fifteen of these, as he noted in the references contained along the borders of the drawing, were to be developed by the several states of the federal union and embellished with "Statues, Columns, Obelisks, or any other ornament." He also proposed the construction of "Five grand fountains intended with a constant spout of water." These are identified on the plan with the letter "E." Three major monuments appear. A "Naval itinerary Column" was to be placed on the bank of the Potomac midway between the Anacostia and the Tiber. At what is now Lincoln Park on East Capitol Street L'Enfant suggested "a mile or itinerary Column, from whose station . . . all distances of places through the continent are to be calculated."

The most important and strategically located of the three monuments was the proposed equestrian statue of President Washington to be located exactly at the intersection of the axes of the Capitol and the residence of the chief executive. Its site emphasized the strongly axial relationships toward which L'Enfant worked in his city plan. One can note how at every major public

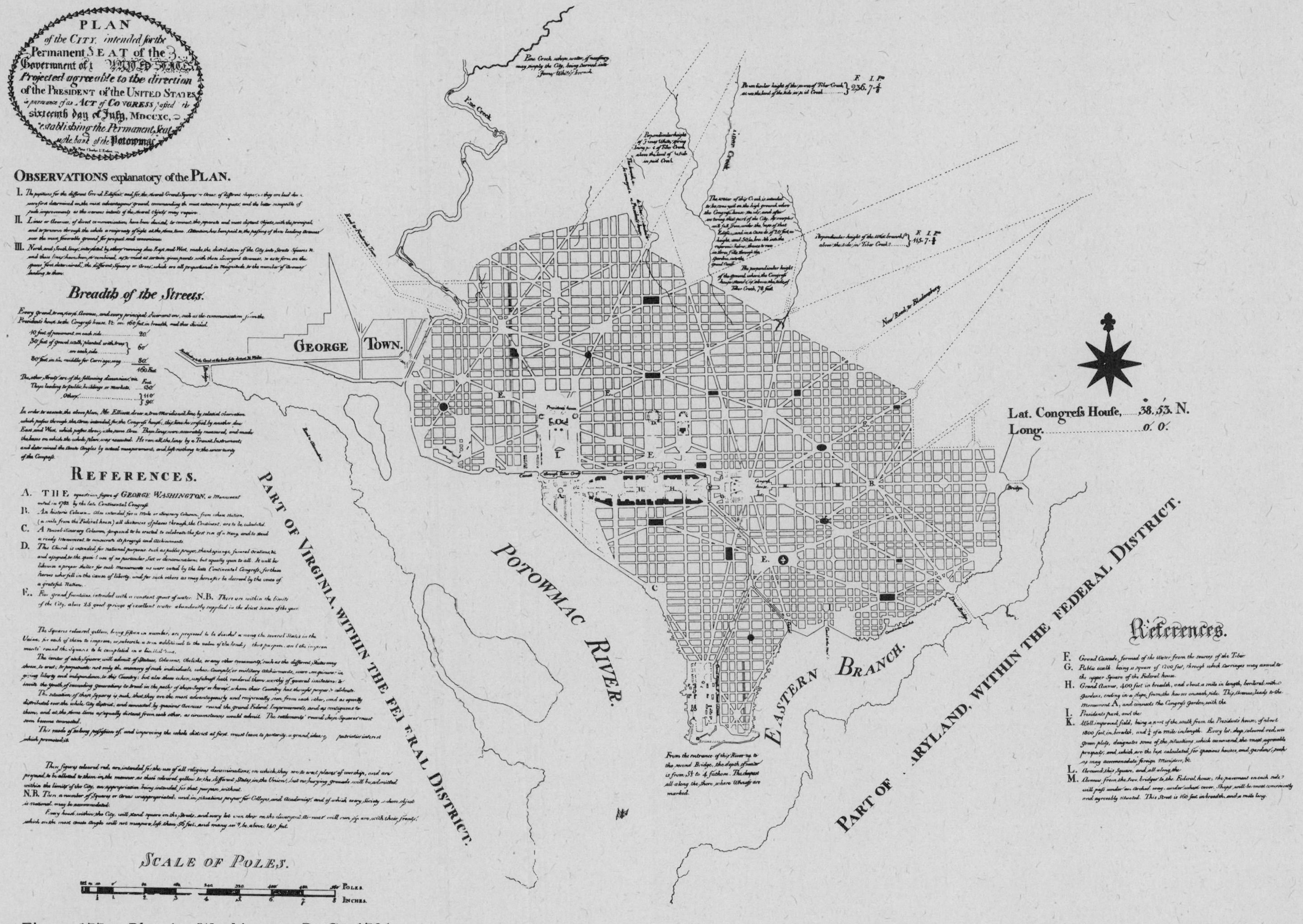

Figure 177. Plan for Washington, D. C.: 1791

site he focused a series of diagonal avenues as well as major streets of the underlying north-south grid. One of the marginal notations on L'Enfant's drawing sums up the principles of the baroque street design he employed: "Lines or Avenues of direct communication have been devised to connect the separate and most distant objects with the principal and to preserve through the whole a reciprocity of sight at the same time."

He proportioned street widths with this in mind. The main avenues were made 160 feet wide and divided as he had earlier described to the president. Streets "leading to public buildings or markets" were given a width of 130 feet. Others were to 110 and 90 feet wide. The plan featured a

> Grand Avenue, 400 feet in breadth, and about a mile in length, bordered with gardens, ending in a slope from the houses on each side. This Avenue leads to the Monument A [Washington's statue], and connects the Congress Garden with the President's park and the Well improved field, being a part of the walk from the President's house of about 1800 feet in breadth and 3/4 of a mile in length.

This feature of the central part of the city is shown on a portion of the official property map of Washington prepared by Ellicott in 1792 (figure 178). The buildings proposed along both sides of what is now the Mall were described as sites "the best calculated for spacious houses and gardens, such as may accommodate foreign Ministers, &c."

While L'Enfant continually stressed functional reasons for his system of radial avenues and hoped that the provision of direct access between major public buildings would speed development of the city, aesthetic considerations clearly influenced his design. Both in scale and general character the plan of Washington bore a close resemblance to that of the town and gardens of Versailles where L'Enfant had spent much of his youth while his father, an artist of some prominence, assisted in decorating the building housing the Ministry of War. As an art student in Paris he became intimately familiar with the monumental central axis of that city as it was developing from the Louvre, through the Tuilleries gardens to the Place de la Concorde, and up the Avenue des Champs-Élysées to what was then the beginning of the modern Place de l'Étoile. The same principles of design that Francis Nicholson had utilized in his plans for Annapolis and Williamsburg provided the sources that guided L'Enfant almost a century later in his much bolder and more sophisticated plan for the national capital.

Even this fairly detailed plan as completed by the end of August, 1791, did not exhaust L'Enfant's creative energy. Doubtless he would have continued to refine many of its features as portions of it were surveyed on the ground, and there is every reason to believe that he fully expected to make a career of translating his monumental paper plan into the reality of streets, parks, monuments, public buildings, and civic spaces. Soon, however, his inability to subordinate his temperamental personality to the administrative supervision of the three district commissioners brought about an irresolvable conflict. Ultimately, to the dismay of Washington who admired his talents and tolerated his eccentricities, L'Enfant had to be dismissed from his post.[59]

Almost from the beginning changes were made in L'Enfant's plan, although the basic design remained unaltered. L'Enfant had refused to surrender drawings in his possession when arrangements were being made to have the plan engraved so that land sales might begin. Ellicott was assigned to this task, and in preparing his drawing for this purpose he modified the original plan either intentionally or from lack of complete information. Some changes were also apparently carried out at Jefferson's direction. The most drastic was the straightening of Massachusetts Avenue, which on the L'Enfant plan had a pronounced bend toward the south from a point almost directly north of the Capitol. This modification, along with the elimination of a few of the minor radial streets, can be traced by a comparison of the L'Enfant plan with the drawing made by Robert King in 1803 reproduced in figure 179.

In June of 1800 the executive offices of the government were moved from Philadelphia to Washington, and in November the Congress held its first meeting at the Capitol. That building, designed by William Thornton as shown in an east elevation at the bottom right of King's map, consisted then only of one wing. President and Mrs. Adams found the executive mansion, shown on the King plan as designed by James Hoban, still unfinished. Only a few of the streets had been cleared, and all of them were but roughly graded. Representative John Cotton Smith of Connecticut referred to Pennsylvania Avenue as "a deep morass, covered with alder bushes."[60]

Someone once referred to Georgetown as a city of houses but not streets and to Washington as a city with streets but not houses. Benjamin Latrobe's plan of the land in the vicinity of the Capitol in 1815, reproduced in figure 180, shows how true that was for at least the newer of the two com-

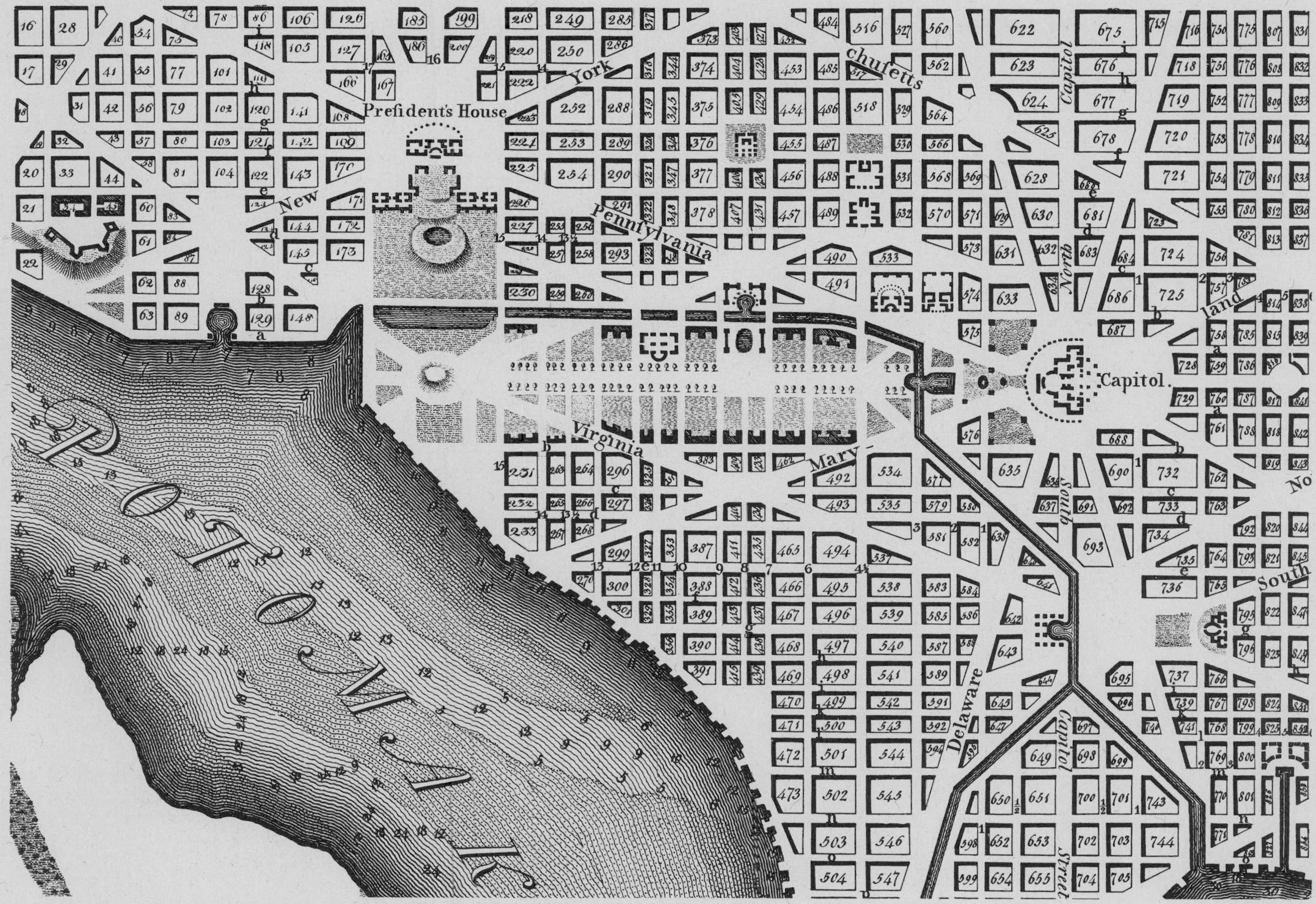

Figure 178. Plan of a Portion of Washington, D. C.: 1792

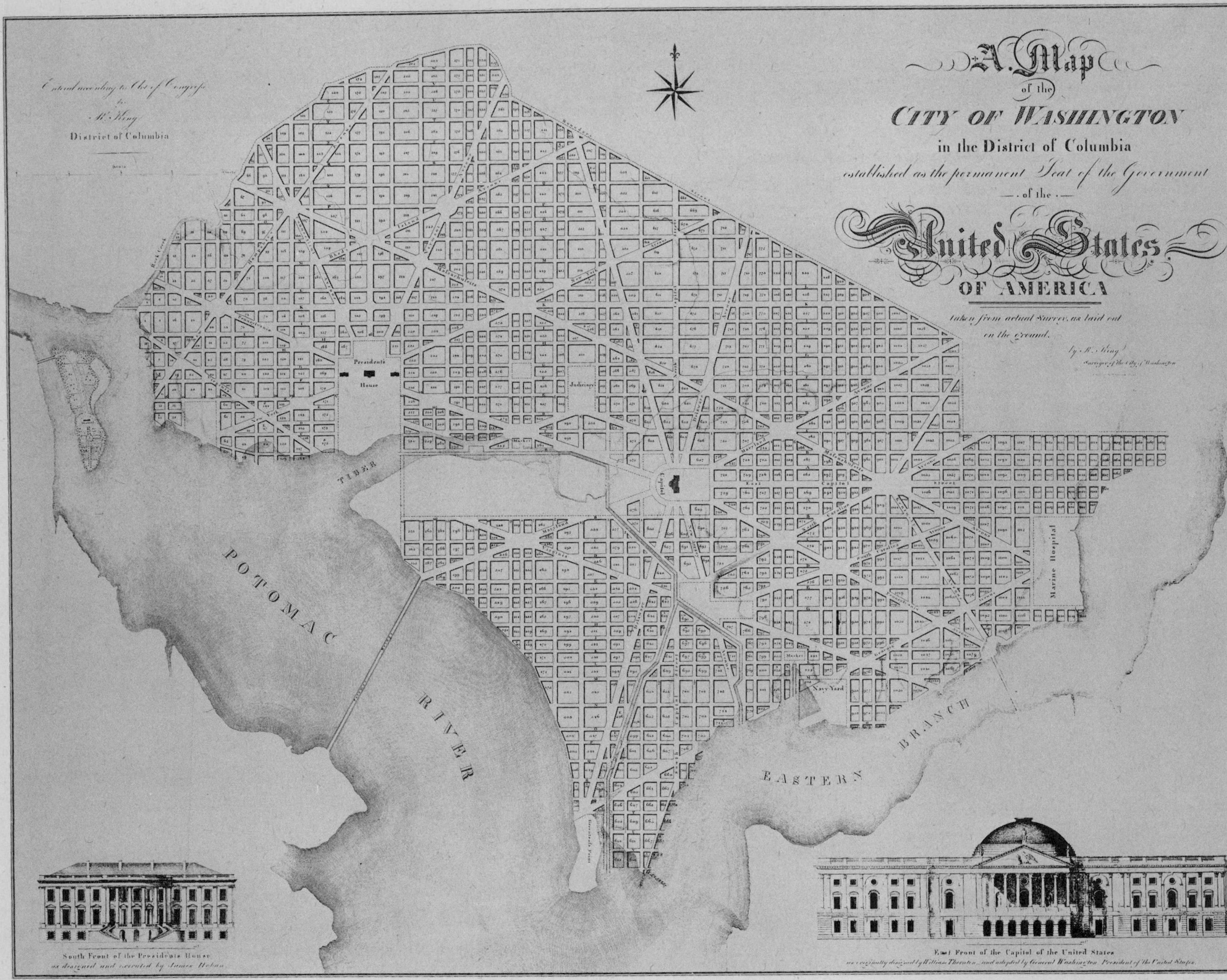

Figure 179. Plan of Washington, D. C.: 1803

munities. Although most of the buildings in Washington had been constructed in the vicinity of either the Capitol or the executive mansion, Latrobe's drawing reveals how scattered they still were in the area of Capitol Hill nearly a quarter of a century after the city had been planned. This drawing also shows the untamed character of the land on that portion of what is now the eastern end of the Mall. Its character did not change materially for many years, although eventually, after many false starts, the Washington Canal was constructed along its northern edge on an alignment shown in the drawing. And while L'Enfant had suggested that the main shops of the city should be built facing East Capitol Street along arcaded sidewalks, this street, shown at the right-hand margin of Latrobe's drawing, was then a nondescript mixture of dwellings, vacant lots, and an occasional commercial establishment like all the others.

Gradually, however, certain portions of the city began to assume some of the formal character L'Enfant had envisioned. Flanking the White House by 1820 were two pairs of red brick buildings in Federal style as shown from the north in the sketch in figure 181. These served the executive departments of State, Treasury, War, and Navy and formed an impressive composition facing Pennsylvania Avenue and Lafayette Square to the north.

By 1834, as shown in the view from the south bank of the Anacostia in figure 182, the city had begun to assume some of its present character. Dominating the skyline stood the copper-sheathed wooden dome of the capitol that many years later was replaced by the present one of cast iron. The view of 1834 shows that nothing had yet been done to implement L'Enfant's plan for the grand avenue leading from the Capitol toward the west and intersecting the axis of the White House. That portion of the city simply existed as a kind of meadow south of the canal.

The view of the city in 1862 in figure 183 shows the beginning of what was eventually to be developed as a formal park. In the foreground stands the enlarged Capitol, the extension of which had begun in 1851. The artist anticipated the completion of the dome, which was not finished until after the Civil War. In the far distance we can see another bit of artistic license. This is the Washington Monument, shown as if completed according to the original design of Robert Mills. Work on this enormous shaft had started in 1848, but because of the condition of the site at the intersection of the two major axes its site had been shifted 370 feet east of the White House axis and 123 feet south of that of the Capitol. The view shows also the building begun in 1847 for the Smithsonian Institution on a site dangerously close to the centerline of the Mall. This structure, along with the botanic garden built at the foot of Capitol Hill almost directly in front of the Capitol, threatened the realization of L'Enfant's concept of a strong axial composition running the length of the central portion of the city.

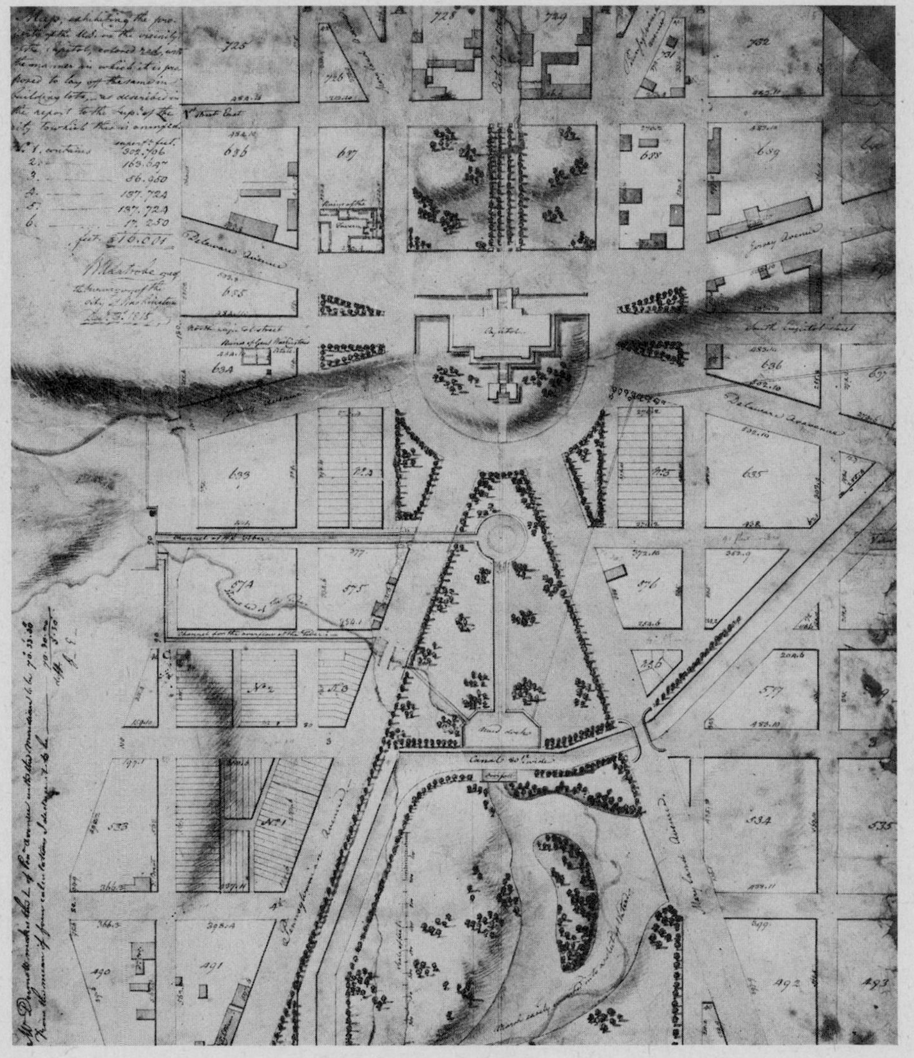

Figure 180. Plan of a Portion of Washington, D. C.: 1815

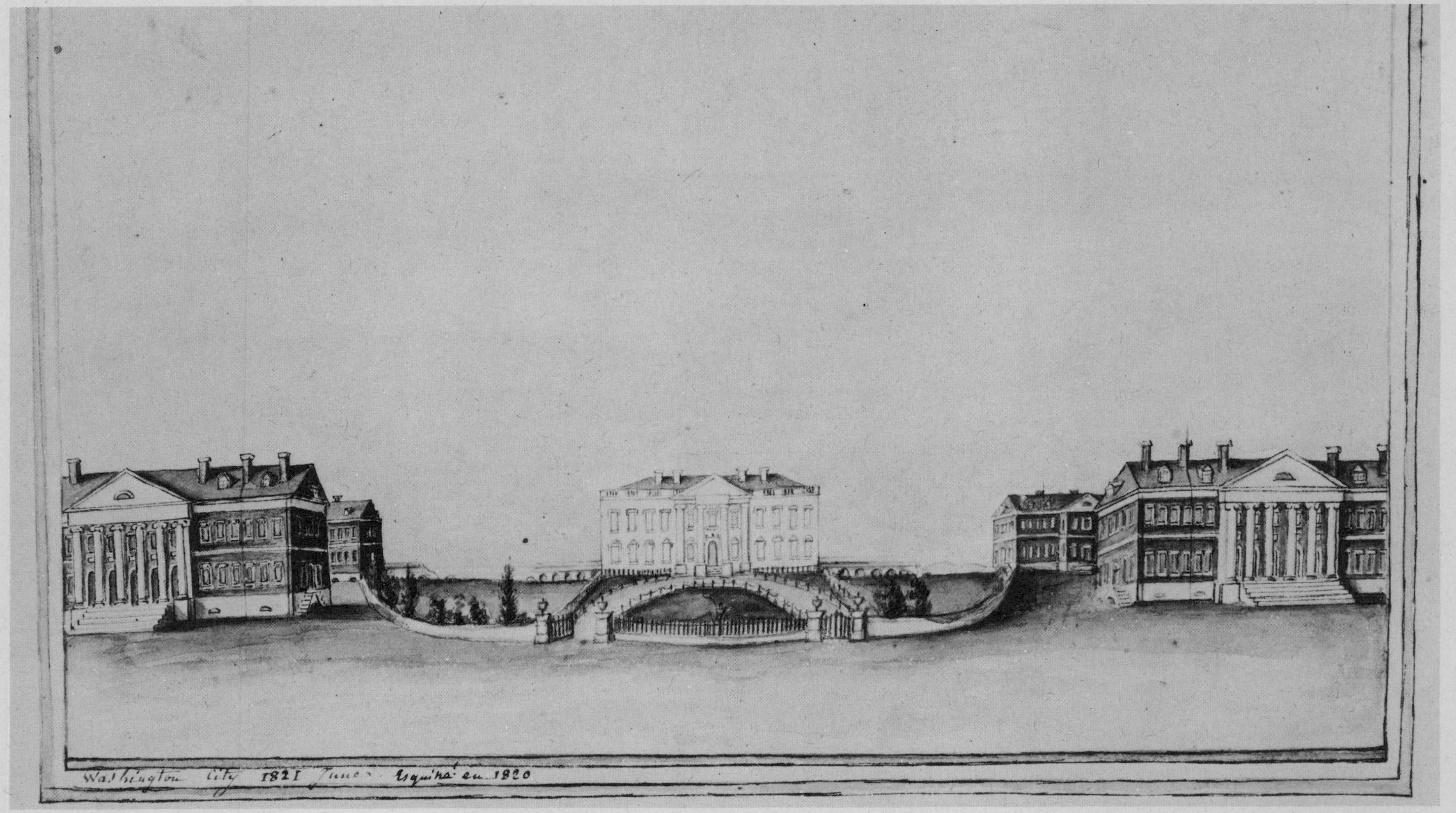

Figure 181. View of the White House, the State and Treasury Buildings, and the War and Navy Buildings in Washington, D. C.: 1821

By the middle of the nineteenth century many other public and private buildings had been constructed in Washington, and the city that had begun so slowly had now clearly become established as a major community of the Tidewater. The central section of the city in 1850 with the major buildings identified is shown in figure 184. William P. Elliott's fine Patent Office building in Greek Revival style and Robert Mills's General Post Office provided a major focus of federal activity midway between the Capitol and the White House between E and G and 7th and 9th streets. The City Hall, on the site identified in the King plan as Judiciary Square, had been built earlier on designs prepared by George Hadfield. Although

Figure 182. View of Washington, D. C.: 1834

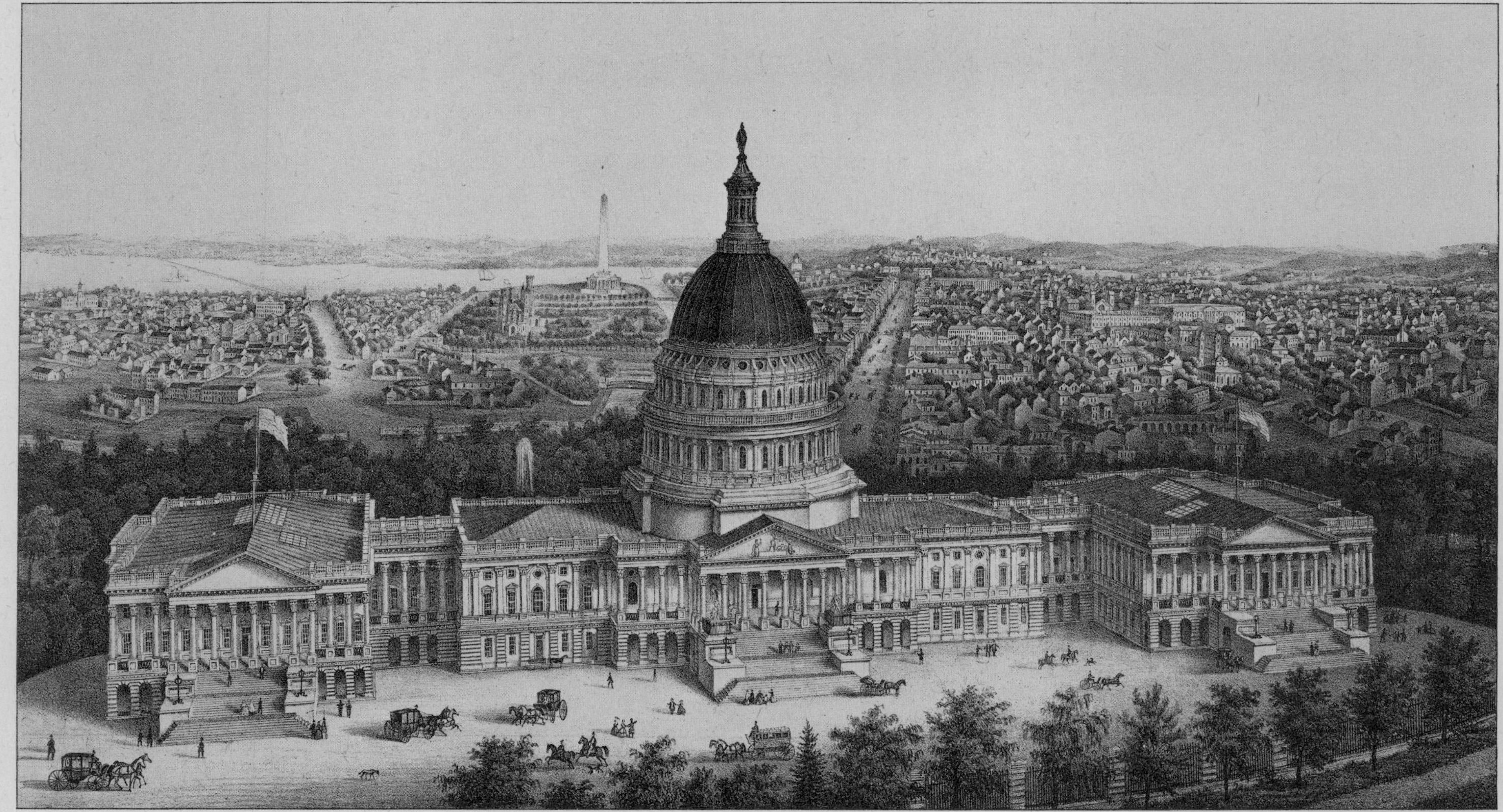

Figure 183. View of Washington, D. C.: 1862

this was and is a fine building, it apparently usurped the intended location for the Supreme Court which was not to be provided a building of its own until more than one hundred years later. These three buildings can be seen in figure 183 to the right of the Capitol dome.

The history of how the city developed following the Civil War and into the present era is well beyond the scope of this study. There were further encroachments made upon the Mall, including the construction by Congressional permission of a railroad and station and the old Agricultural building. At the turn of the century, however, a new plan was prepared for the central area of the city that recommended a course of action in harmony with, although not identical to, L'Enfant's original concept. That plan, with only relatively minor variations, has been carried out almost in its entirety and provides the national capital with a unique and powerful monumental core.[61]

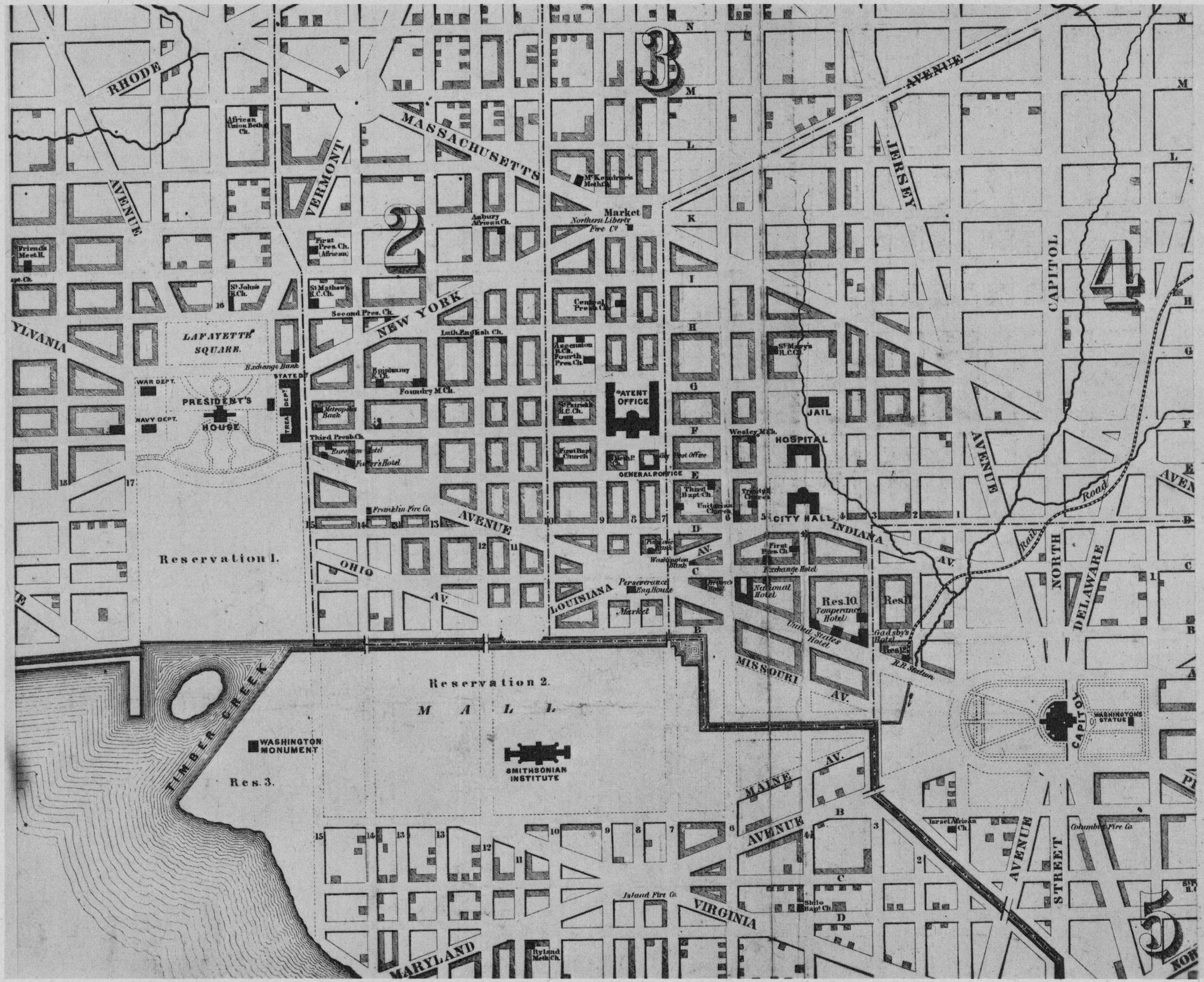

Figure 184. Plan of a Portion of Washington, D. C.: 1850

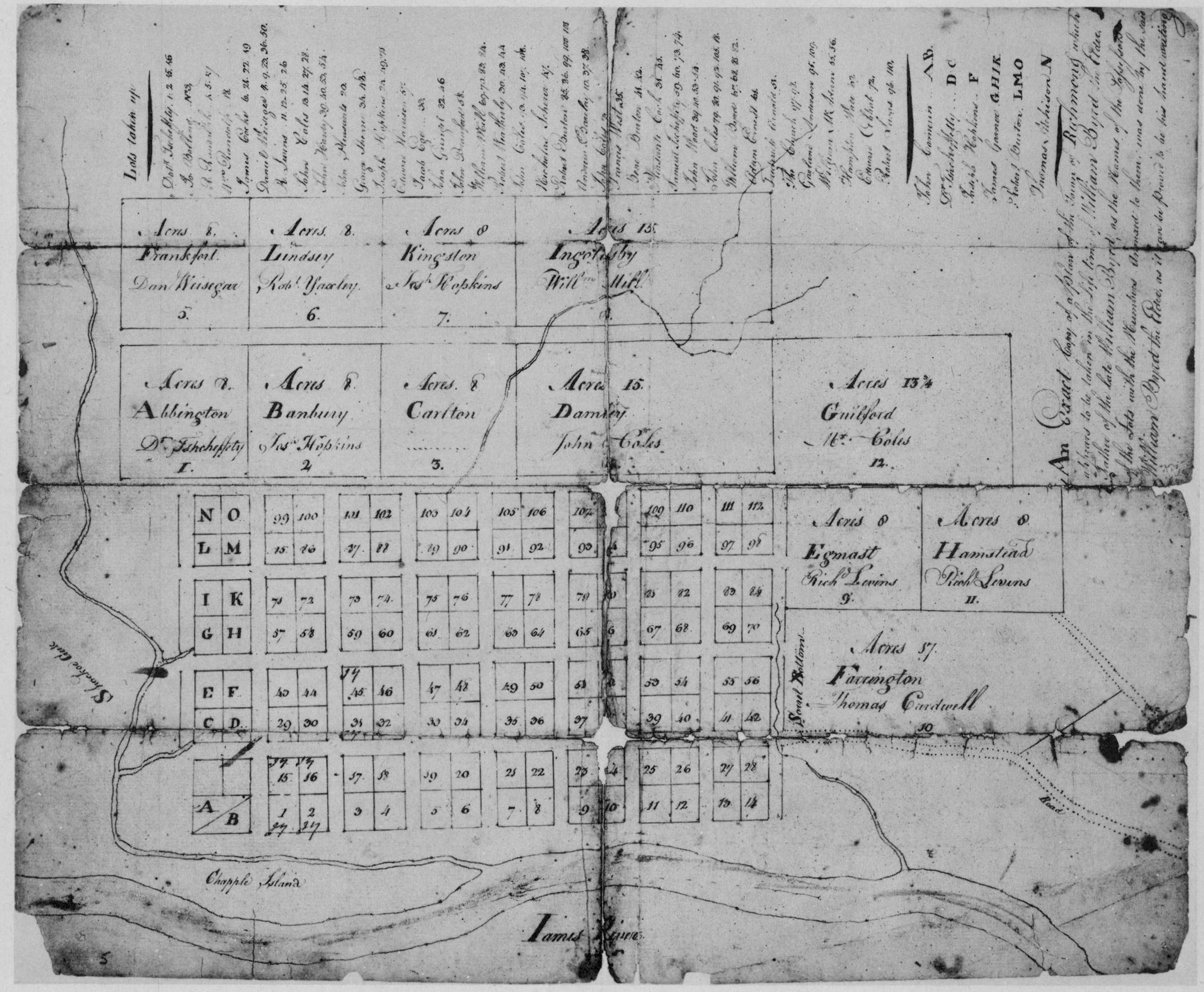

Figure 185. Plan of Richmond, Virginia: prior to 1744

XI. *Richmond and Baltimore*

THREE of the vast number of new towns founded during the colonial period in the Tidewater eventually attained major stature as important cities: Norfolk, already treated in Chapters IV and IX; Richmond, the capital of Virginia; and Baltimore, the dominant city of Maryland and the largest of all tidewater towns. Although this work is primarily concerned with an investigation of colonial town planning and development, it is desirable to trace the growth of these two cities well into the nineteenth century to observe the relationships between their original plans and their successive extensions during the period of immediate postcolonial economic and population expansion.

As already described in Chapter IX, William Byrd II selected the sites for Petersburg and Richmond. The former community developed successfully, but Richmond was destined to become far more important. Its original plan, prepared in 1737 for Byrd by his surveyor, William Mayo, certainly gave no hint of the town's great future. As shown in figure 185, the street and lot layout contained few if any features to distinguish it from the dozens of other rectangular settlements of the Virginia Tidewater.[1]

The undeviating alignment of the gridiron streets failed to reflect the steep slopes ascending northward from the James River and eastward from the valley of Shockoe Creek. This portion of present-day Richmond includes in its northern part the area known as Church Hill, one of several elevations that gave the city a natural environment of unusual beauty. Unfortunately, Byrd and those responsible for subsequent additions to the town largely ignored these topographic advantages.

Soon Byrd was advertising in the *Virginia Gazette* the sale of lots in his new community:

> This is to give notice, that on the North Side of the James River, near the Uppermost Landing, and a little below the Falls, is lately laid off by Major Mayo, a Town, called Richmond, with Streets 65 Feet wide, in a pleasant and healthy Situation, and well supply'd with Springs of good Water. It lies near the Publick Warehouse at Shoccoe's and in the midst of great Quantities of Grain and all kinds of Provisions. The Lots will be granted in Fee Simple, on Condition only of building a House in Three Years Time, of 24 by 16 Feet, fronting within 5 Feet of the Street. The Lots to be rated according to the Convenience of their Situation, and to be sold after this April General Court, by me William Byrd.[2]

In addition to the 112 numbered lots, 14 lots designated by letters and 2 without any identification made up the thirty-two blocks of the town proper. Lots numbered 97 and 98 were marked on the plan for "The Church." Byrd donated this land to the vestry of Henrico Parish, and St. John's Church was erected here in 1741. Twelve much larger plots appear outside the boundaries of the town. These vary in size from eight to seventeen acres. Each bears a name: Abbington, Banbury, Charlton, etc., and perhaps they were intended as sites for villas or mansions. Lot 18, at the southwest corner of the present 22nd and East Main Street, was deeded to William Randolph in 1750 for the courthouse of Henrico County.

Settlement appears to have been rapid, for in 1742 the assembly, in con-

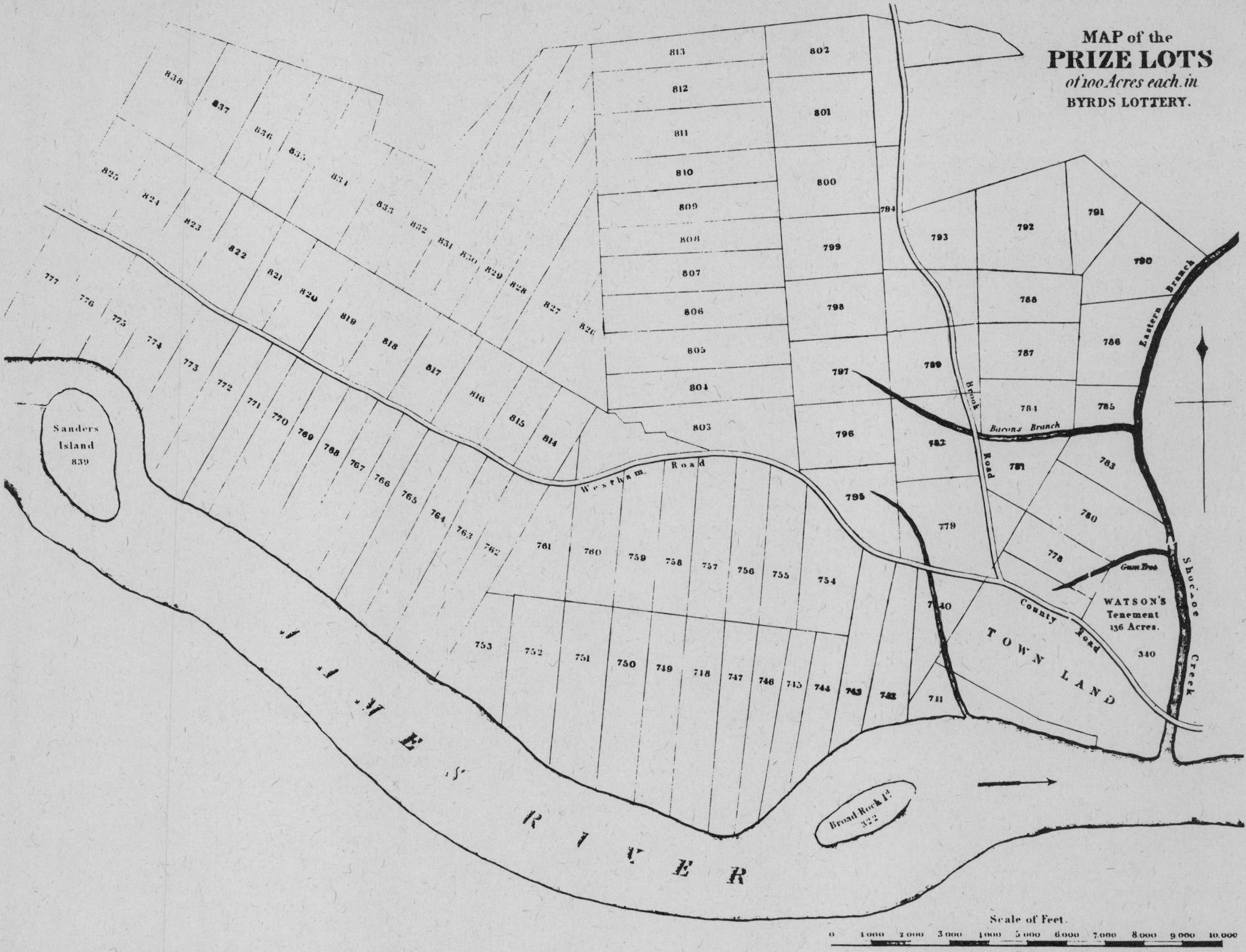

Figure 186. Map of the Prize Lots in Richmond, Virginia, in 1768

ferring town status on Richmond, recited in its act that Byrd had "made sale of most of the . . . lots, to divers persons, who have since settled and built thereon."[3] This act contained the provisions common in such situations. Byrd's plan was adopted as the official survey, two annual fairs were authorized, and persons attending these events were granted exemption from arrests and attachments for debt. The act included one unusual feature. All land between the southern boundary of the town and the James River and a smaller portion of land lying between the western boundary and Shockoe Creek was "to remain and be, as and for a common, for the use and benefit of the inhabitants of the said town, for ever."[4]

At the time of Byrd's death in 1744 the new town was apparently well under way. His son, William Byrd III, however, encountered financial difficulties and in 1756 was forced to execute a deed of trust conveying his properties in the vicinity to seven trustees to be used in settling his debts. Byrd and the trustees in 1768 hit upon the idea of a lottery to dispose of an extensive tract of land west of Shockoe Creek. This area was divided into a large number of plots of about one hundred acres each. Figure 186 shows the lots and their numbers to be used in the lottery advertised in the *Virginia Gazette* for January 14, 1768.[5] Land on the south side of the James River was also to be sold. In the following year this latter tract became the town of Manchester by an act of the assembly that also added more than three hundred acres to Richmond.[6] Manchester, as it appeared on a map published in 1835, is shown in figure 187. The 312 lots surveyed for William Byrd III by Benjamin Watkins were laid out in blocks and streets that closely resembled the earlier settlement across the river to the north. The Manchester plan shows several "tenements," land holdings evidently not belonging to Byrd at the time the town was surveyed. Six similar parcels existed within the enlarged limits of Richmond. The act permitted their owners, if they wished, to divide these lands into half-acre lots provided they continued the gridiron street pattern through the lands so subdivided. Until such time as they might avail themselves of this provision they were prohibited "to erect any house on any of the said tenements, so as to obstruct the prospect of any street which terminates at the said tenements, that may hereafter, when the same shall be laid off in lots, stop the said streets."

Initial sales of lottery tickets evidently proved disappointing. The scheduled drawing was postponed from June to November, 1768. Byrd and the trustees were forced to re-advertise and hold the drawing at Williamsburg instead of Richmond. Finally the event went off, and one of the winners was George Washington, who with Peyton Randolph and others had purchased one hundred tickets. Washington's share in this speculation came to £50, for which he received seven parcels totaling 568½ acres.[7]

As has been discussed earlier, the General Assembly in 1779 resolved to move the capital of Virginia from Williamsburg to Richmond. The act passed at the time followed closely a bill introduced in 1776 by Thomas Jefferson that would have established the capital on an unspecified site. This proposal had been rejected at its first reading, though most of its features were incorporated into the legislation of 1779 by the committee to whose membership Jefferson was appointed three days after its creation.[8] The act as finally passed contained a number of unusual features. Its provisions for public buildings read as follows:

> That six whole squares of ground surrounded each of them by four streets, and containing all the ground within such streets, situate in the said town of Richmond, and on an open and airy part thereof, shall be appropriated to the use and purpose of publick buildings: On one of the said squares shall be erected, one house for the use of the general assembly, to be called the capitol, which said capitol shall contain two apartments for the use of the senate and their clerk, two others for the use of the house of delegates and their clerk, and others for the purposes of conferences, committees and a lobby, of such forms and dimensions as shall be adopted to their respective purposes: On one other of the said squares shall be erected, another building to be called the halls of justice, which shall contain two apartments for the use of the court of appeals and its clerk, two others for the use of the high court of chancery and its clerk, two others for the use of the general court and its clerk, two others for the use of the court of admirality and its clerk, and others for the uses of grand and petty juries . . . ; and on the same square last mentioned shall be built a publick jail: One other of the said squares shall be reserved for the purpose of building thereon hereafter, a house for the several executive boards and offices to be held in: Two others with the intervening street, shall be reserved for the use of the governour of this commonwealth for the time being, and the remaining square shall be appropriated to the use of the publick market. The said houses shall be built in a handsome manner with walls of brick or stone, and porticoes where the

same may be convenient or ornamental, and with pillars and pavements of stone.[9]

Thus for the first time in an American capital city the three major branches of government were given recognition in the physical plan of the land and buildings set aside for their use. To administer the provisions of this act the assembly authorized the election "by joint ballot of both houses of assembly, five persons to be called the directors of the publick buildings." They were to acquire the necessary land, produce building plans, and supervise construction. To them also was given discretion in selecting the site to be laid out in the six blocks specified in the act. The site could be in the portion of Richmond already platted, or in a new section of the town which they were directed to lay off in "two hundred additional lots of half acres, with necessary streets . . . adjacent to such parts of the said town as to them shall seem most convenient."

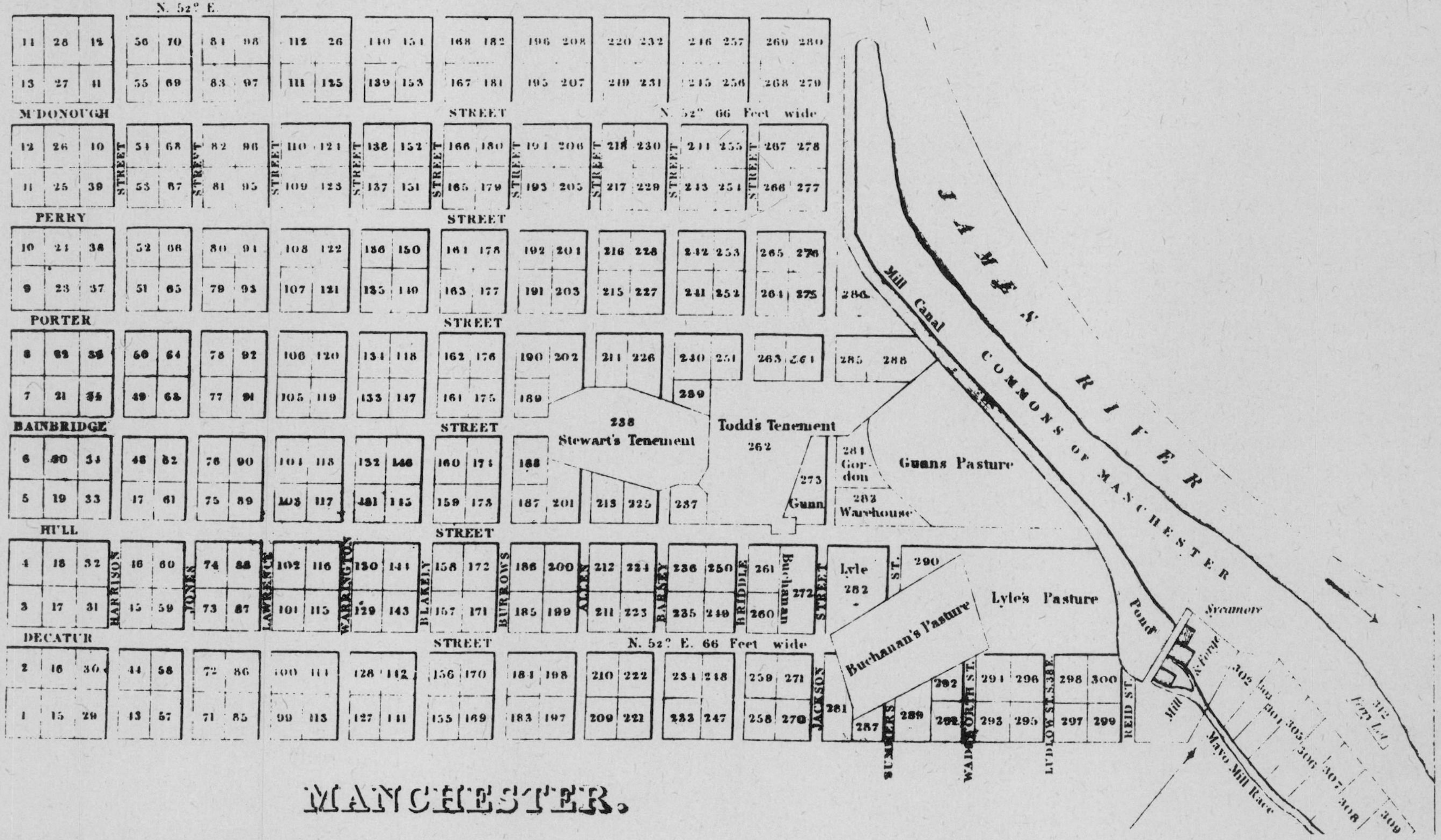

Figure 187. Plan of Manchester, Virginia: 1835

Because of the financial strain imposed by the war, "the difficulties of procuring the materials for building, and the high price for labour," the directors were ordered to provide "with all convenient speed" temporary buildings to house the offices of government. The assembly further authorized the directors to enlarge the existing Henrico County jail as a temporary expedient. The act imposed a cost ceiling of £20,000 for all these projects and further specified that the directors were not to make a final choice of the six squares, extend the city, nor enter into any building contracts until further authorization from the assembly. Finally, the act appointed the last day of April, 1780, for the transfer of the offices and records of government to the temporary facilities to be provided by the directors in Richmond.

The next year the assembly found it necessary to enact further legislation, probably as a result of reports from and recommendations by the directors. The act of 1780 designated Shockoe Hill for the site of the government buildings, specifying that the public market should be placed "below the said hill, on the same side of Shockoe creek."[10] Shockoe Hill stood some two thousand feet north of the James River. The land sloped fairly steeply up to the brow of the hill from the river as well as from the valley of Shockoe Creek to the east. The western side was also defined, though not so strongly, by a natural drainage swale. Clearly this was one of the most commanding spots in the area, rivaled only by the elevation included in the original Byrd plan on which stood St. John's Church.

Apparently some streets had been surveyed on Shockoe Hill by this time, but most of the area had not been systematically planned. Here and elsewhere within the boundaries of the town the directors were to "cause the several tenements of irregular shape and size . . . to be laid into regular squares with intervening streets at such intervals as in the other parts of the town, unless by varying the said intervals more favourable ascents may be procured up the hill." The act also directed the town officials to see that all streets of Shockoe Hill and any new streets elsewhere were to be enlarged "to a breadth, not less than eighty, or more than one hundred and twenty feet." Where existing streets had to be widened to meet these standards any houses in the right-of-way of such enlarged thoroughfares might remain for a period of twenty years.

Perhaps many, if not most, members of the assembly by this time had visited Richmond. They must have felt some concern over the difficulties of reaching the hill section from the existing community, which had largely developed on relatively flat land along the river terrace. The act addressed itself to this problem of adequate connections between the contemplated governmental center on Shockoe Hill and the mercantile settlement below. The directors were to

> lay off, in the most easy direction, whether straight or curved, so many streets for ascending and traversing with facility, the several hills in the said town as may be thought necessary in any supposed state of future increase and population, and at such intervals as shall be convenient, making them to communicate with the streets above the brow, and below the foot of each hill.

Repeated in the act were the provisions of the previous year's legislation authorizing the directors to plan new streets and blocks so as to create an additional two hundred half-acre lots. Any financial injury suffered by existing landowners through the creation of new streets was to be compensated with funds raised by an assessment on all landowners of the town. Finally, the directors were empowered to open a public subscription to secure the money necessary to clear the creek channel of sand bars so as to permit unobstructed access by water to the warehouse landing.

Legislation alone cannot create cities. The members of the legislature found no great halls of assembly when they arrived for their first meeting in Richmond. The General Assembly convened on October 16, 1780, in a large wooden structure located at the northwest corner of Pearl and Cary streets. Probably once a store and warehouse, this ungraceful building sheltered the commonwealth government until 1788.[11] Richmond in 1781, if we can accept as accurate the British-drawn revolutionary war map in figure 188, can scarcely have exhibited much charm or character. Most of the buildings of the town could be found on the east side of Shockoe Creek. On the other side were a number of other dwellings and shops and several tobacco warehouses. Manchester, on the south bank, appears as nothing more than a hamlet.[12]

The map is a valuable though perhaps not entirely accurate representation of the topography of the site. Slightly above and to the left of the center one can see St. John's Church on the edge of Church Hill. At the left, north and west of the warehouses, rises Shockoe Hill. It was on this eminence that the directors of public buildings would shortly begin their

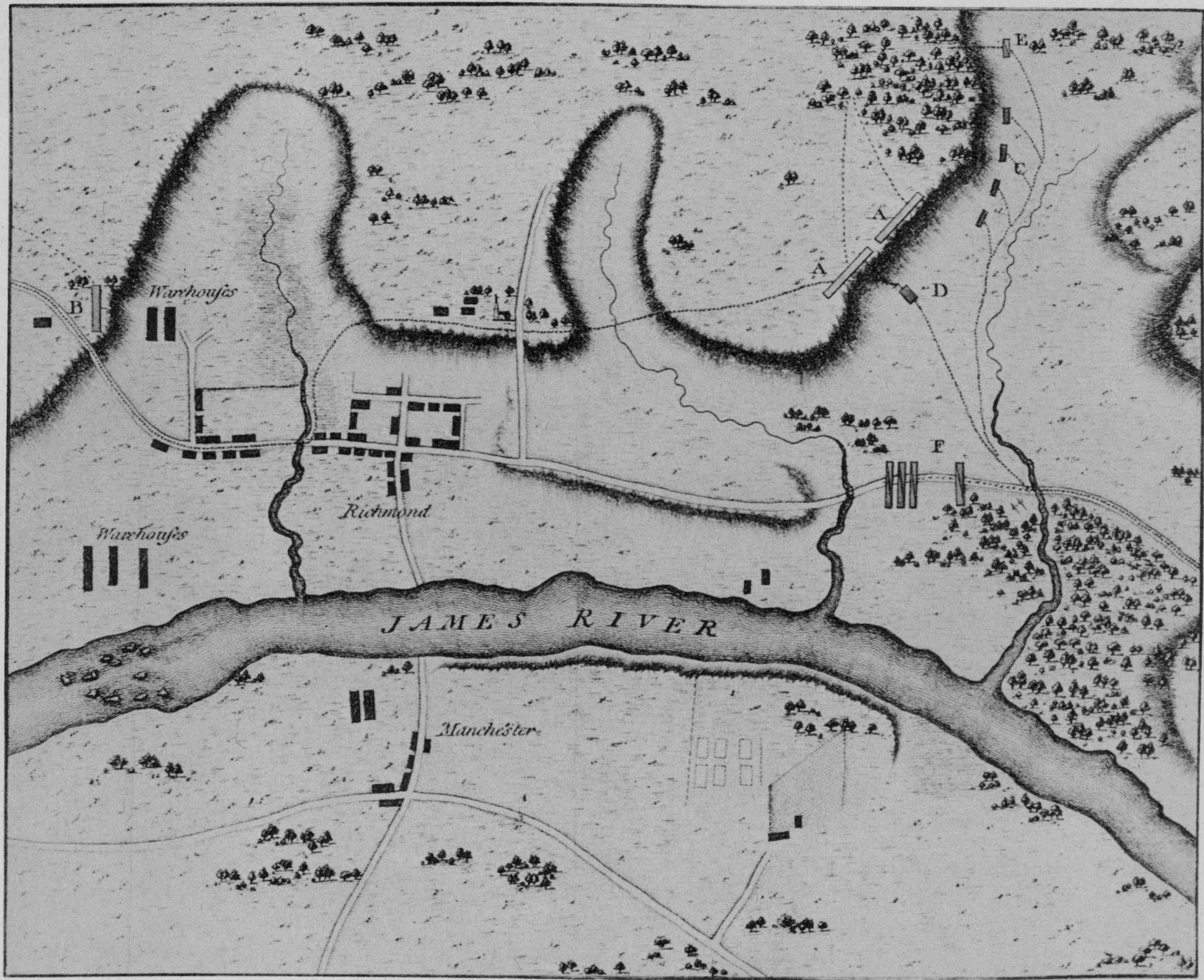

Figure 188. Plan of Richmond, Virginia: 1781

work of laying out a major addition to the town and arranging for the construction of more suitable accommodations for the offices of the Virginia government.

The act of 1780 named nine directors for carrying out the town extensions and replanning of Richmond. Listed first was Thomas Jefferson, who had been elected governor in the previous year and again for a second term on June 2, 1780.[13] Sometime in the spring of 1780, Jefferson drew a plan showing a proposed gridiron design for the Shockoe Hill area.[14] This plan, reproduced in figure 189, also showed the extension of this pattern through the irregular "tenements" then separating the platted portion of old Richmond from the new addition. Two major connecting streets running east and west were to link the two sections of the enlarged town. On the Jefferson drawing the more northerly is designated by the letter E. This is the present Main Street, with Cary Street running parallel to it on the south.

Jefferson's plan includes four hundred lots. While there is no scale, the lots appear to be the standard half-acre parcels measuring eight by ten poles or 132 by 165 feet. Using this as a guide, the streets all seem to have been planned approximately four poles, or 66 feet wide. Since this plan called for twice the number of lots specified in the act of 1780 and does not observe the requirement that no streets should be less than 80 feet in width, it may represent Jefferson's ideas of town planning prior to the enactment of that law. Nor does the drawing indicate a proposed site for the six squares to be used for the buildings of the government. Soon Jefferson set to work on this problem. His first scheme was to reserve for this purpose three blocks between F and G streets (the present Franklin and Grace streets) and 9th and 12th streets, plus the tiers of lots in the blocks north and south that fronted on F and G streets.[15] Four additional lots on the eastern end of this area completed the proposed site.[16]

As Jefferson gave more thought to the matter he evolved a second and substantially different plan. This is reproduced in figure 190. On the reverse of this drawing is the text of a resolution prepared for adoption by the directors of public buildings describing the land to be taken for this revised plan. The smaller blocks of the previous scheme were to be consolidated into three larger tracts. The portions of F and G streets running through this tract were to be relocated north and south of their original alignments, "in order that the said ground may be surrounded by streets and divided by others into three separate parcels."[17]

At a meeting of the officials responsible for these matters, at which Jefferson was present, this proposal was approved on July 17, 1780. The Jeffersonian concept of a design for a group of public buildings to reflect the three major divisions of the government seemed well on the way to realization. The need for economy intervened to thwart Jefferson's intention. In the year that he succeeded Benjamin Franklin as minister to France, the General Assembly, on the advice of the directors of public buildings, decided to erect one building to house all the branches of government.[18] In recognition of his knowledge of architecture, Jefferson was requested to secure a design for the proposed building. The directors sent to him in France a preliminary plan they felt might help the designer. With Charles Louis Clérisseau, Jefferson began work on a plan by the fall of September, 1785, which he described in a letter to James Madison:

> We took for our model what is called the Maisonquarrèe of Nismes, one of the most beautiful, if not the most beautiful and precious morsel of architecture left us by antiquity. It was built by Caius and Lucius Caesar and repaired by Louis XIV. and has the suffrage of all the judges of architecture who have seen it, as yielding to no one of the beautiful monuments of Greece, Rome, Palmyra and Balbec which late travellers have communicated to us. It is very simple, but it is noble beyond expression, and would have done honour to our country as presenting to travellers a morsel of taste in our infancy promising much for our maturer age.[19]

Jefferson added that he was "mortified with information" he had received indicating that construction was scheduled to begin on the building in Richmond before his design had been completed. It would, he said, be done within three or four weeks, and he entreated Madison to see if the work could be stopped. His eloquent argument demonstrates the depth of his feeling about the value of good architecture as an instrument for national education:

> How is a taste in this beautiful art to be formed in our countrymen, unless we avail ourselves of every occasion when public buildings are to be erected, of presenting to them models for their study and imita-

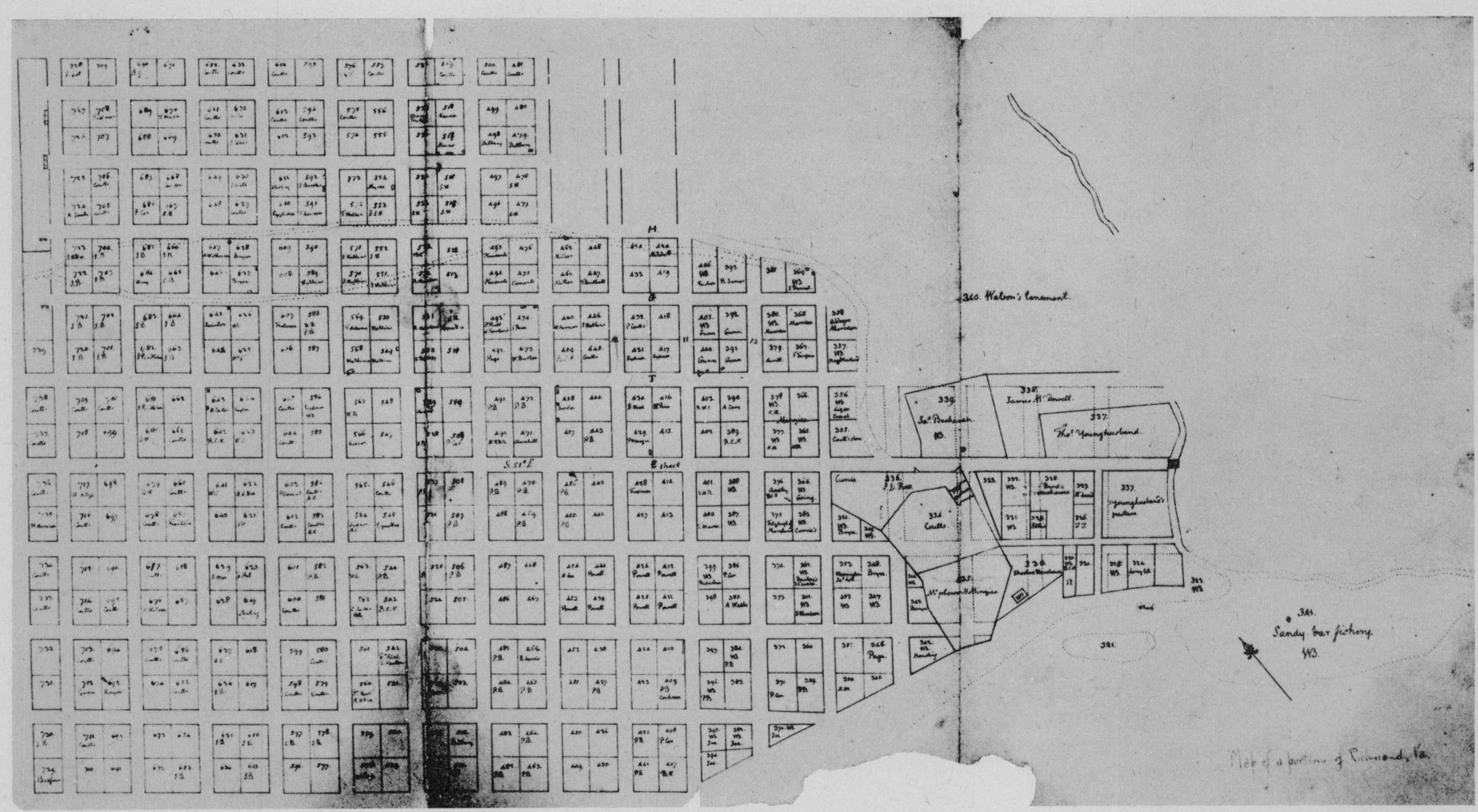

Figure 189. Plan of a Portion of Richmond, Virginia: 1780

tion? Pray try if you can effect the stopping of this work. . . . The loss will be only of the laying the bricks already laid, or a part of them. The bricks themselves will do again for the interior walls, and one side wall and one end wall may remain as they will answer equally well for our plan. This loss is not to be weighed against the saving of money which will arise, against the comfort of laying out the public money for something honourable, the satisfaction of seeing an object and proof of national good taste, and the regret and mortification of erecting a monument of our barbarism which will be loaded with execrations as long as it shall endure. . . . You see I am an enthusiast

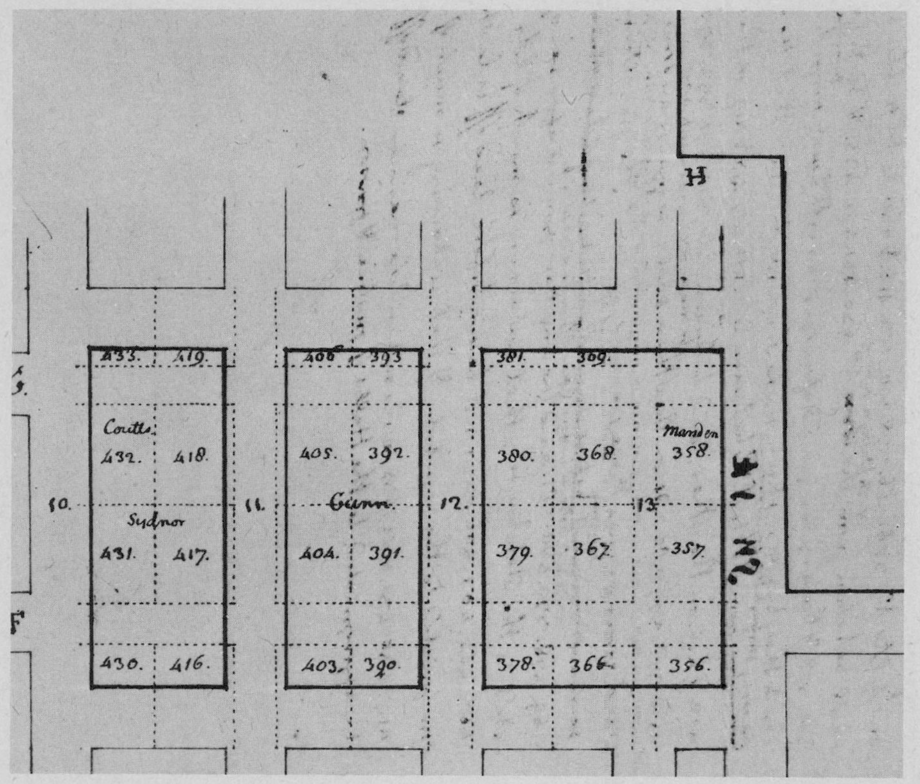

Figure 190. Plan of the Public Grounds in Richmond, Virginia: 1780

on the subject of the arts. But it is an enthusiasm of which I am not ashamed, as it's object is to improve the taste of my countrymen, to increase their reputation, to reconcile to them the respect of the world and procure them it's praise.

Ultimately it was Jefferson's design, modified in some of its details, that was to be erected. A plaster model he sent from Paris may have helped persuade the directors of public buildings and the members of the assembly of the merit of his proposal.[20] Soon Shockoe Hill was filled with workmen, and gradually the new building began to take shape. Richmond as it appeared a few years after the completion of the structure in 1792 is shown in the view in figure 191 from the south bank of the James River. Built of brick, but covered with stucco in 1798, this gleaming white Roman temple provided a distinctive element on the skyline as it loomed from its hilltop site over the buildings of the town.

William Loughton Smith was captivated by the town when he saw the place in the spring of 1791:

> The different views of Richmond, with its immense Capitol, towering above the Town on a lofty eminence, with its antique appearance, arrested my attention. . . . The Town contains about 300 houses, some of them excellent brick and well built. It carries a great deal of business and will be a flourishing place when the navigation with the county [country] is entirely opened, which will be in two or three years.
>
> The Capitol, built on the model of the Temple of Nîsmes, is an immense pile of brick work. . . . Its unfinished state gives it a heavy, singular appearance, but when complete it will be a magnificent building. The model, made at Paris . . . is a very beautiful and elegant thing. . . . The loftiness of this building, and its eminent situation render it a very striking object, and it is the first thing which strikes the traveler.[21]

As the Capitol was being constructed the town began its growth in the new area planned by Jefferson. With further enlargement of its boundaries and some additional streets and lots to the northwest, Richmond as it appeared in 1809 is shown in the plan reproduced in figure 192. It will be noted that Jefferson's proposal for the immediate grounds of the Capitol appears only in the lightly dotted lines surrounding several blocks on Shockoe Hill. Capitol and Bank streets, which were to form the northern and southern boundaries of the public reservation, existed then only as paper streets. John Tyler, who came to Richmond in 1808 when his father was elected governor, half a century later recalled the city as he first knew it:

> The population . . . did not exceed five thousand in 1808. The surface on which the city stood was untamed and broken. Almost inaccessible heights and deep ravines everywhere prevailed. The capitol Square was *ruda indigestaque moles,* and was but rudely, if at all, enclosed. The ascent to the building was painfully laborious. The two now beautiful valleys were then unsightly gullies. . . . The street west of the Square was impassable for much of the way, except by a foot-path. The governor's house, at that time called the "palace," was a building that neither aspired to architectural taste in its construction or consulted the comforts of its occupant in its interior arrangements.
>
> The brick row, now known as the Main street, which terminated at the cross street below the American, and which had its origin near

Figure 191. View of Richmond, Virginia: ca. 1804

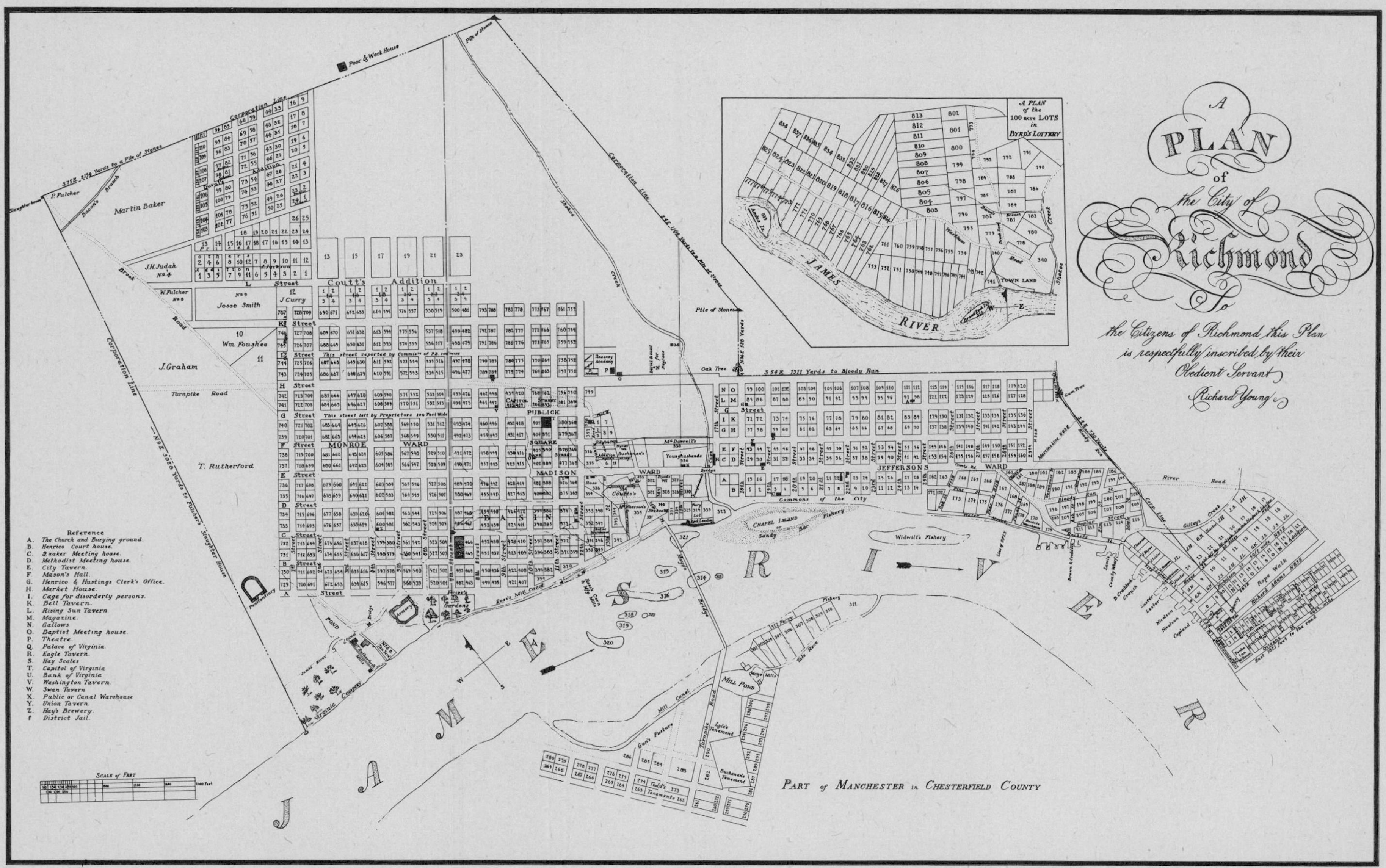

Figure 192. Plan of Richmond, Virginia: 1809

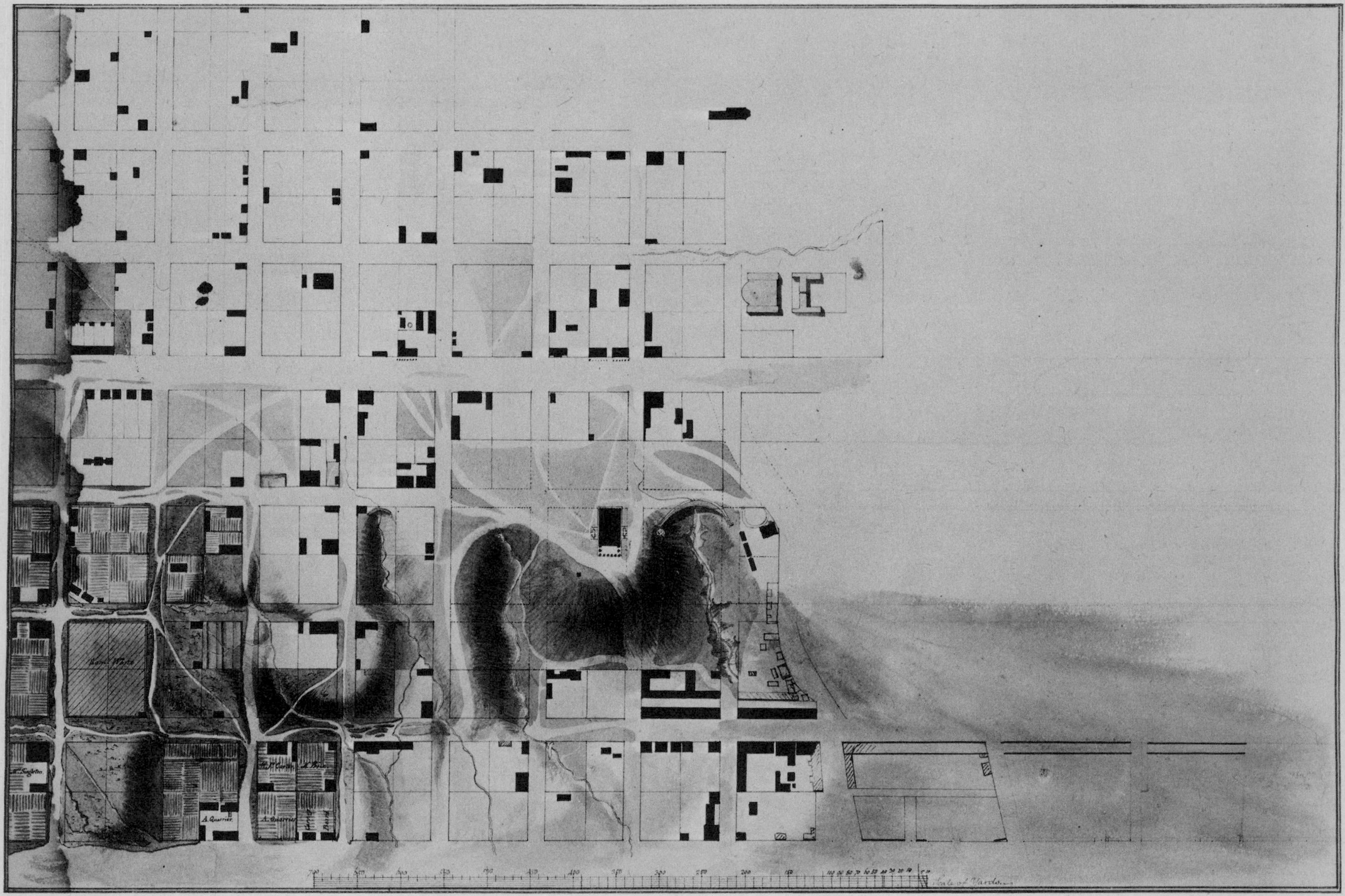

Figure 193. Plan of a Portion of Richmond, Virginia: 1798

the market place, was the chief pride of the city. The streets were unpaved, and sad was the fate of the unlucky wight who, otherwise than on horseback, undertook to pass through the lower part of the city; nor was it for many years after that the hand of the laborer went busily to work in the improvement of the city.[22]

Many of these features of Richmond described by President Tyler can be recognized in the plan of the Shockoe Hill section drawn by Benjamin Henry Latrobe in 1798. This valuable drawing (figure 193) reveals what the previous illustration does not make clear—that the streets within the area set aside for the public buildings remained only as surveyed lines and the entire reservation had been consolidated into a single large square. This drawing shows other items of interest as well. In the lower left section, the only portion of the map to be completed, one can see the irregularities of the paths and lanes not always contained within the geometric precision of the surveyed street lines. Capitol Square was crossed by several of these rambling ways produced by countless travelers seeking the easiest ascent of the steep hillside or taking the most direct diagonal route across this barren open space. Below and to the right of the Capitol on Main Street one can also see the modern business district beginning to take form.[23]

The old governor's "palace" referred to by Tyler had not yet been built at the time Latrobe drew his plan. That first official residence for the chief executive was replaced in 1813 by the present handsome two-story structure designed in early Federal style and sited north and east of the Capitol.[24] Other improvements were soon to be made in and around the public grounds of the city. By 1816 the Capitol needed extensive repairs. The act authorizing this work also provided for landscaping Capitol Square. Maximilian Godefroy secured the commission for the work and remained to design several important buildings in the city as well. Godefroy, a Frenchman exiled by Napoleon, had been a partner of Latrobe's and had worked on a number of building projects in Baltimore. With his continental background it was only natural that in landscape as well as in architectural design he followed the teachings of the French formalists.

Godefroy's plan for Capitol Square, as depicted on a plan of the city published in 1835, appears in figure 194. He adopted one feature from Jefferson's design that had not then been carried out, the development of Bank and Capitol streets to provide a clearly defined border for the square on its north and south sides. G Street was then to be carried through the square from the west to terminate on the axis of the governor's mansion. For the immediate surroundings of the Capitol he suggested a great terrace extending fifty feet from the west, north, and east sides, and stretching one hundred feet beyond the south colonnade. Below the terrace he planned two semicircular walks leading from a gate at Bank Street on the axis of the Capitol. On either side of this central composition Godefroy laid out a system of straight paths connected at the top of the hill by curves. This

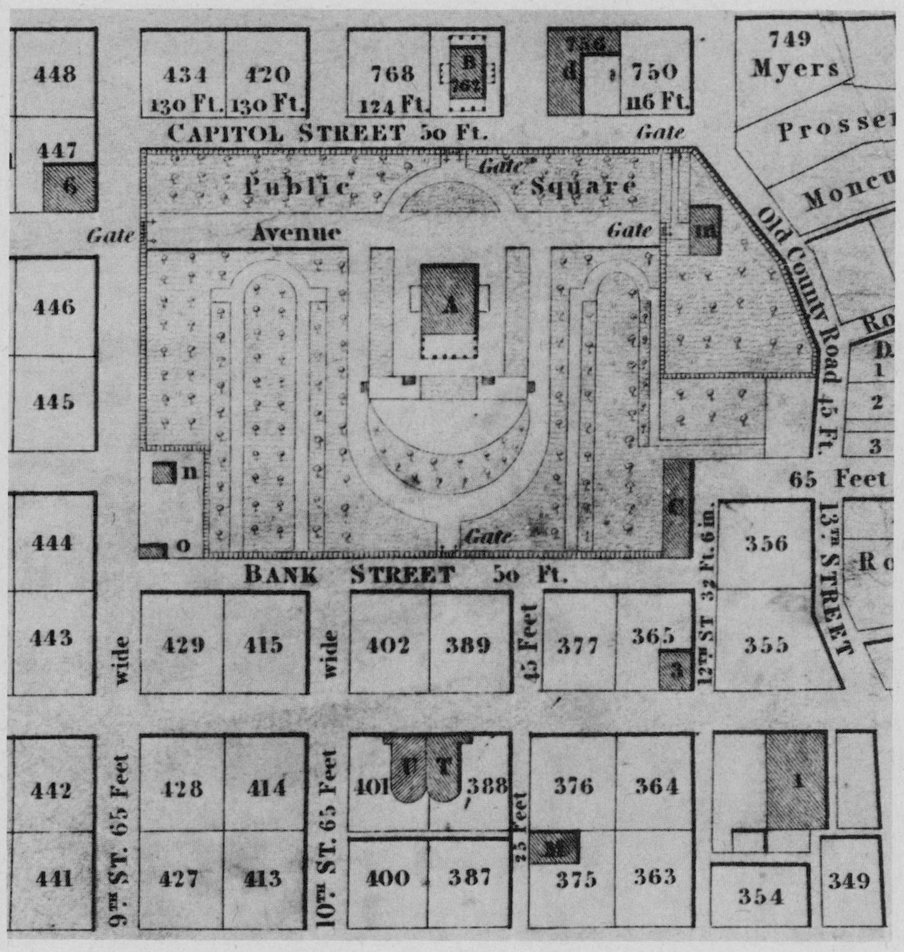

Figure 194. Plan of a Portion of Richmond, Virginia: 1835

Figure 195. View of Capitol Square in Richmond, Virginia: ca. 1850

area was to be planted in formal rows of trees. An iron fence was to enclose the entire square.[25]

Only a small portion of the plan was executed. The fence, cast in New York from designs prepared by Paul-Alexis Sabbaton, was erected in 1818, some grading within the square was completed, and several straight rows of trees were set out on each side of the Capitol. In the 1850s, following a plan prepared by John Notman, the planting of the square was altered to reflect the prevailing taste for romantic landscape design, a number of winding paths were introduced, and further grading was carried out on the mound south of the Capitol portico.[26]

Capitol Square as it appeared in the mid-nineteenth century is shown in figure 195. In the left foreground is the bell tower, constructed in 1824, which still stands. Beyond and to the right of it can be seen the monument to George Washington completed in 1858, surrounded by smaller statues of Thomas Jefferson, Patrick Henry, George Mason, Andrew Lewis, Thomas Nelson, and John Marshall. Behind the Capitol appears Godefroy's attractive and unusual domed city hall, which he designed at the time he was laying out the square and preparing plans for the reconstruction of the Capitol. This fine building and the adjacent First Presbyterian Church were pulled down in 1879 to make way for the present city hall. The Capitol itself can be seen with the odd entrance stairs on its western side. Those in our view replaced the original curving pair of entrance stairs sometime in the 1830s. It was not until 1906 that the broad steps now leading up the hill to the south portico were added. That project included the addition of a wing on each side of the original building that, while not unattractive, altered substantially the appearance of Jefferson's original design.

The city in its formative years in the first part of the nineteenth century presented an impressive appearance. The view in figure 196 from one of its western hills in 1834 is but one of many that attracted topographic artists of the period. The Capitol and, beyond it, Godefroy's city hall, dominated the landscape, along with Latrobe's penitentiary to the left, built between 1797 and 1800. Only the great public buildings of the national capital could rival this fine civic composition. The opportunity to add harmonious structures around Capitol Square as they might be needed from time to time without interfering with its fine prospect from nearly every direction was, however, ignored. Following the Civil War and throughout the present century thoughtless additions of buildings in and encroachments to Capitol Square have seriously detracted from its beauty.[27] Equally disastrous, tall office and business buildings in the lower portions of the town have now almost completely obliterated distant views of the Capitol.

Jefferson's stated intention "to improve the taste of my countrymen, to increase their reputation, to reconcile to them the respect of the world and procure them it's praise" by the construction of his noble Capitol on its splendid hilltop site proved persuasive to his contemporaries. Those who followed forgot his wise counsel and, as he feared for the Capitol itself if his design were not followed, the square and its surroundings come dangerously close to being "a monument of our barbarism which will be loaded with execrations as long as it shall endure."

Among the several dozen new towns planned in Maryland in the eighteenth century, one ultimately achieved remarkable success. In fact, Baltimore became the dominant city of the entire Chesapeake Bay, its rate of growth after the Revolution unsurpassed by any major American community. The most northerly of the southern cities and the most southerly of those of the North—a city with its own distinctive character—Baltimore by 1790 ranked as the fifth largest city in the United States. A certain historic justice attaches to the fact that it bore the name of a family so intimately associated with the settlement of the tidewater region and with the repeated attempts, so often thwarted, to achieve an urban basis of colonial life.

Its beginnings did not distinguish Baltimore from the other towns of eighteenth-century Maryland and Virginia. Around the mouth of the Patapsco River on the western side of Chesapeake Bay near its northern end a few settlers had established their plantations. In 1706 this seemed like an advantageous spot for a town, and the act of that year creating a number of such sites designated a point of land separating the two branches of the Patapsco for that purpose. The Whetstone Point settlement does not seem to have been successful, and it was not until 1729 that further efforts were made. In that year Daniel Carroll and his brother Charles, along with several other inhabitants of the area, petitioned the assembly to establish a town on the land owned by the two Carrolls.[28]

The exact site was a subject of some disagreement. An earlier proposal to place the town on land owned by John Moale on the south branch of the Patapsco was rejected following Moale's objections at Annapolis where he sat as a member of the assembly. The Carroll tract, known then as Cole's Harbor, was on the other side of the peninsula of which Whetstone Point was the tip. The water offshore here was not as deep, the area included swamps and marshes, and the site was hemmed in to the north and east by a creek that wound its way from Jones Falls upstream into the harbor area. Nevertheless, the location seemed as suitable as many chosen previously for the numerous small ports and trading communities already in existence.

The topography of the area and the site chosen for the town is clearly shown on the 1781 map in figure 197. This drawing also shows the location

Figure 196. View of Richmond, Virginia: 1834

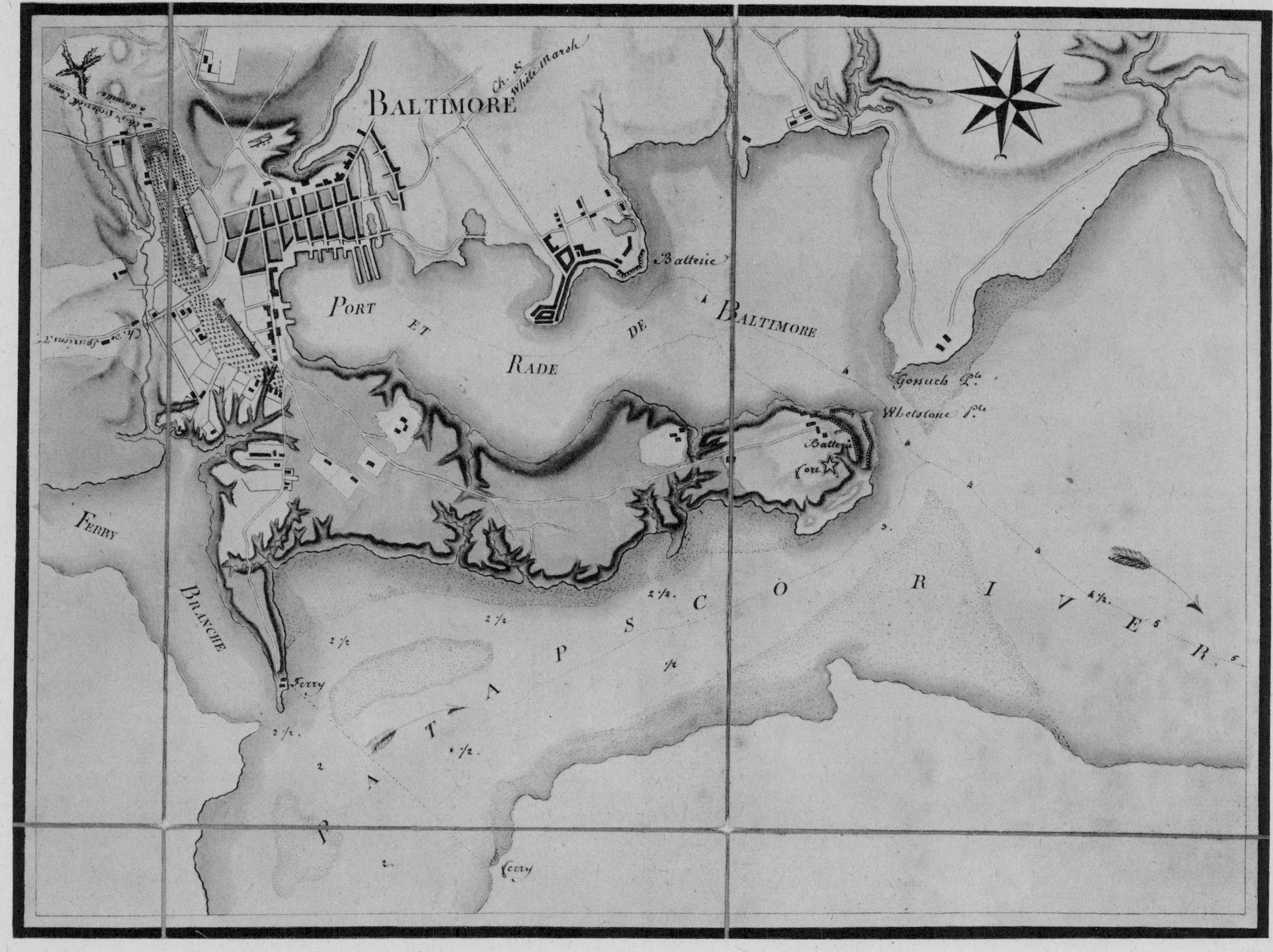

Figure 197. Map of Baltimore, Maryland, and Vicinity: 1781

of two other settlements ultimately to become part of Baltimore and to which we shall refer later. These were Jonas Town (later renamed Jones Town), immediately across Jones Falls to the east, and Fell's Point, east and south where the greater depth of water favored the development of shipping. Except for the shallow water at low tide adjacent to the land owned by the Carrolls it was a superb, sheltered site for a port community in a natural harbor leading directly to the wide waters of the Patapsco and affording excellent access to Chesapeake Bay.

The act creating the town contained the provisions customarily found in the individual port and town acts of eighteenth-century Maryland. It designated commissioners to acquire sixty acres of land and to lay out the town into streets and sixty lots of equal area. The owners of the land were to have first choice among the lots with the remainder offered for sale. During the first four months no person was to purchase more than one lot, and within eighteen months lot owners were required to construct a house of at least five hundred square feet. Any lots remaining unsold after seven years were to revert to the original owners of the land. The act also named the new community "Baltemore Town."[29]

The plan of the town was worked out by the commissioners and their surveyor, Philip Jones, in January, 1730. It is shown, as redrawn and incorrectly dated, in figure 198. The commissioners had not found it necessary to invoke the provisions of the act authorizing condemnation of the site if the owners were unwilling to sell their land, for the Carrolls accepted the offered price of forty shillings an acre, or £120 for the entire sixty acres. The rectangular lots were then offered to purchasers at the same cost. Probably most persons favored locations along the water at the southern boundary or fronting on Long Street (later Baltimore Street) which ran east and west, or on Calvert or Forest (later Charles) streets, the two major cross thoroughfares. Baltimore and Calvert streets were laid out 66 feet wide, while Charles Street was only 49½ feet in width. The several straight alleys were made 16½ feet, or one pole, wide.

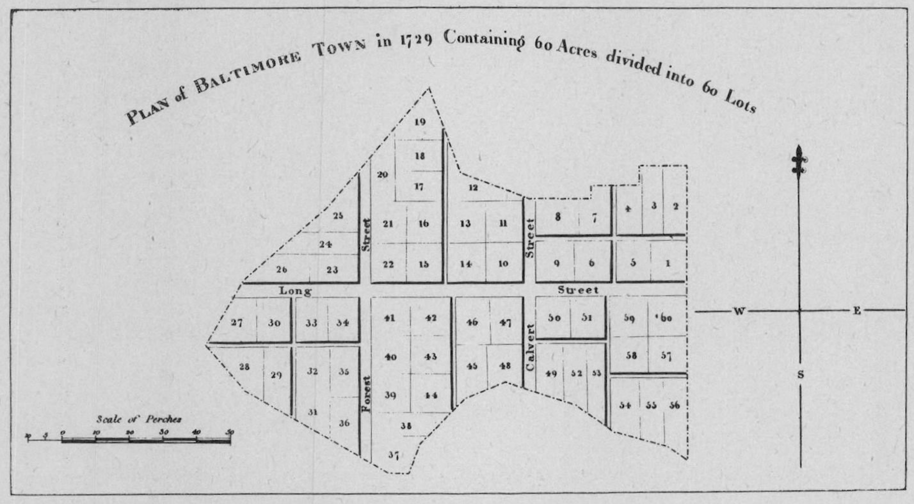

Figure 198. Plan of Baltimore, Maryland in 1730

The irregular boundaries reflected the topographic features of the site that occupied most of the high ground between the valley of Jones Falls, the harbor, a low meadow on the north, and an erosion gulley running northeast-southwest, which accounted for the diagonal boundary on that side of the original town site.[30] It was this gridiron plan that established the general pattern, width, and alignment of streets in the period of growth to follow.

Initial development, however, proved painfully slow. A little more than twenty years after its founding Baltimore consisted of perhaps twenty-five houses, a church, a brewery, a tobacco inspection house, a tavern, and a barber shop. These nonresidential uses, at least, are those identified on the view of the town in 1752 drawn by John Moale (figure 199), as published about 1815. Some of the buildings shown doubtless served as tobacco warehouses, but the single tiny wharf in the center of the view suggests that trade by water had not yet become a major activity of the settlement.

Toward the right of this view on the east bank of Jones Falls appear a few dwellings identified as "Part of Old or Jones Town up the Falls." This community attained official town status by an act of the assembly in 1732, which directed that ten acres of land should be divided into twenty lots and called Jonas Town.[31] These lots, valued at 120 pounds of tobacco each, were laid out in a linear fashion along a single street roughly paralleling the course of Jones Falls. They appear on the plan in figure 200 at the upper right numbered 1 through 20. This drawing also reveals that several extensions had been made to the original plat of Baltimore in 1747 to the east and north. Jones Town, as it soon became known, was referred to in early days as "Old Town," which may indicate that real

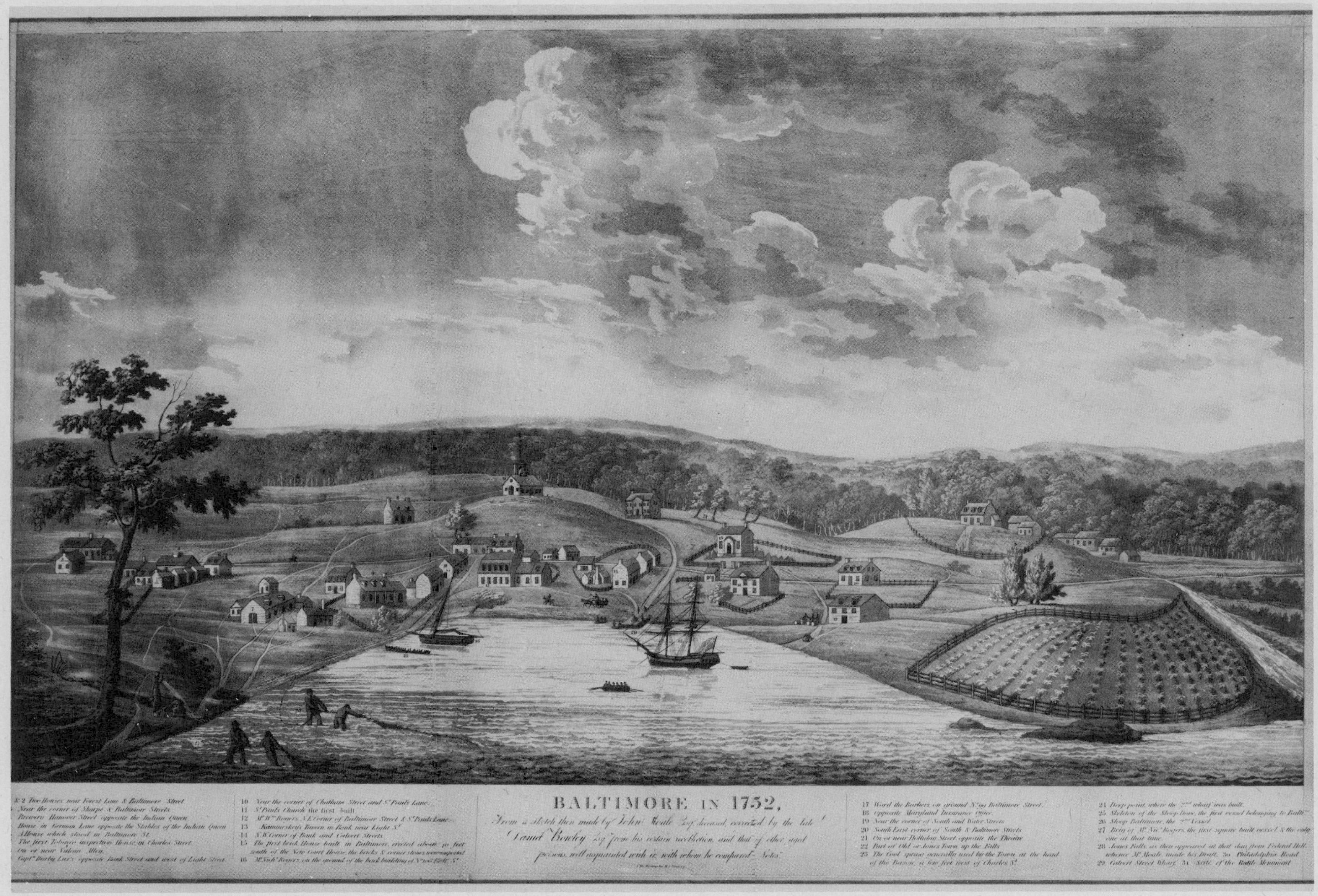

Figure 199. View of Baltimore, Maryland in 1752

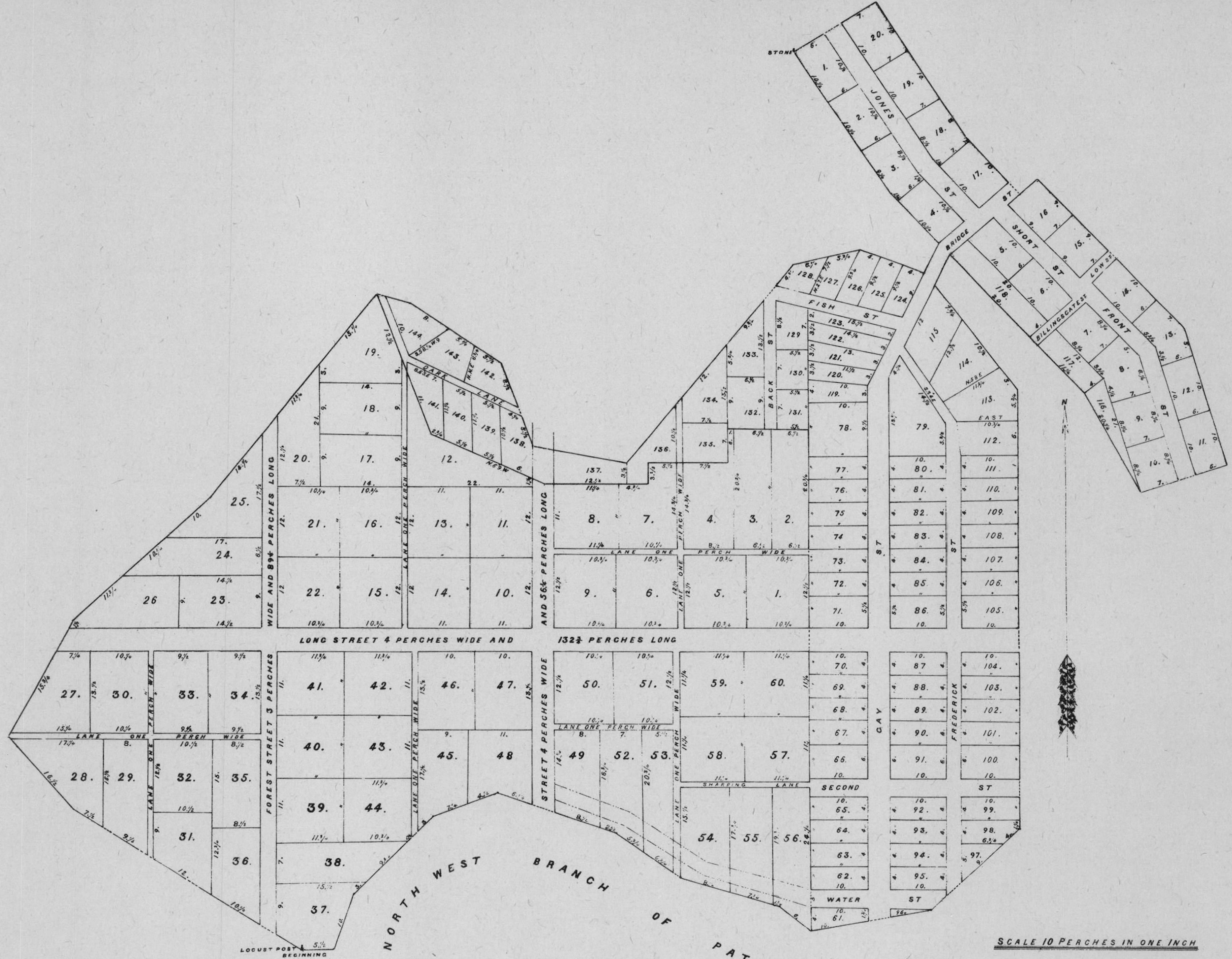

Figure 200. Plan of Baltimore, Maryland: 1747

settlement occurred here first before much development had taken place at the earlier site of Baltimore Town. A bridge connecting the two settlements was soon constructed, and in 1745 the assembly consolidated the two towns into one, retaining the older name of Baltimore for the enlarged community. That law also established the basis for future growth of the town into the shallow harbor, as one of its provisions specified that

> all improvements, of what kind soever, either wharf, houses, or other buildings, that have or shall be made out of the water, or where it usually flows, shall (as an encouragement to such improvers) be forever deemed the right, title and inheritance of such improvers, their heirs and assigns forever.[32]

While the plan in figure 200 shows the extent of the enlarged town just before 1750, it must not be imagined that all of its lots were occupied by dwellings and other structures. Many, perhaps a majority, of the building sites lay vacant, some of them forfeited by their original purchasers because of their failure to construct a house of the required size within the specified eighteen months.[33] Nor did the entire urban population of the area reside within even these extended boundaries. About 1738, William Fell began the development of his holdings at the point of land previously identified as Fell's Point, and soon this district began to compete with Baltimore. A shipyard, in operation by 1765, furnished the principal economic justification for this third community, but it must also have contained the usual complement of smaller shops, taverns, and dwellings to serve the growing population.

The older settlement, however, continued to attract settlers, and soon the boundaries of the town had to be expanded. The plan in figure 201 shows additions to the Jones Town area in 1750 and the larger areas incorporated to the west and south of old Baltimore Town in 1753 and 1765. While each increment showed some kind of internal order and design, it is plain that no overall plan existed to guide the rapid expansion of the entire city. Public improvements, however, were carried out from time to time to provide needed facilities for the growing community.

In 1748 a number of Baltimore's citizens subscribed to a fund to be used in "keeping up, repairing, and making good the fence of the said town, and supporting a person to keep it in good order."[34] When the assembly designated Baltimore as the county seat of Baltimore County in 1768, commissioners appointed for that purpose began the construction of a suitable building on a bluff overlooking Jones Falls. This site at what was then the northern end of Calvert Street blocked the extension of that important street. In 1784 a public subscription provided money to overcome this inconvenience in a novel manner. The project involved nothing less than the "underpinning and arching the said courthouse in Calvert street . . . so as large and convenient passages may be had underneath . . . to the end that new communications may be opened with the country."[35] As the steep hillside was cut away, brick piers and arches were constructed underneath the building, and soon it was suspended nineteen feet above the grade of the street. This curious structure served until 1805 when a new courthouse was constructed on the west side of Calvert Street. Then it was pulled down, its site became a kind of public square, and finally the location was chosen after the War of 1812 as the spot for Maximilian Godefroy's Battle Monument.

Earlier than the courthouse was the market building, on the northwest corner of Gay and Baltimore streets. This, too, was financed by a public subscription in 1751 and carried to completion with funds raised at a lottery in 1763.[36] The latter year also saw the construction of a new tobacco inspection house and a powder magazine. There were other improvements as well. The old bridge connecting Baltimore Town and Jones Town was rebuilt, and the streets were graded and improved. Construction of a new public wharf was aided by a public lottery in 1754, and in 1768 the assembly directed that certain fines and forfeitures were to be used by the town commissioners "in mending the Public Wharfs and Streets in the said Town."[37]

Port facilities were becoming of vital importance to the city. Although the shipment of tobacco to English markets continued to be important to Baltimore, it was the wheat trade that came to dominate the mercantile life of the port. Wheat came not only from the farms of Maryland but from Pennsylvania as well. A number of flour mills lined Jones Falls and other streams in the vicinity, and by 1800 there were no less than fifty mills within a twenty-mile radius of Baltimore.[38] To accommodate shipping many private wharves were built into the harbor, some of them a thousand feet long. In 1783 the Board of Port Wardens was created to supervise and regulate harbor improvements. The extension of private docks into the harbor toward deeper water threatened to choke the basin area so vital

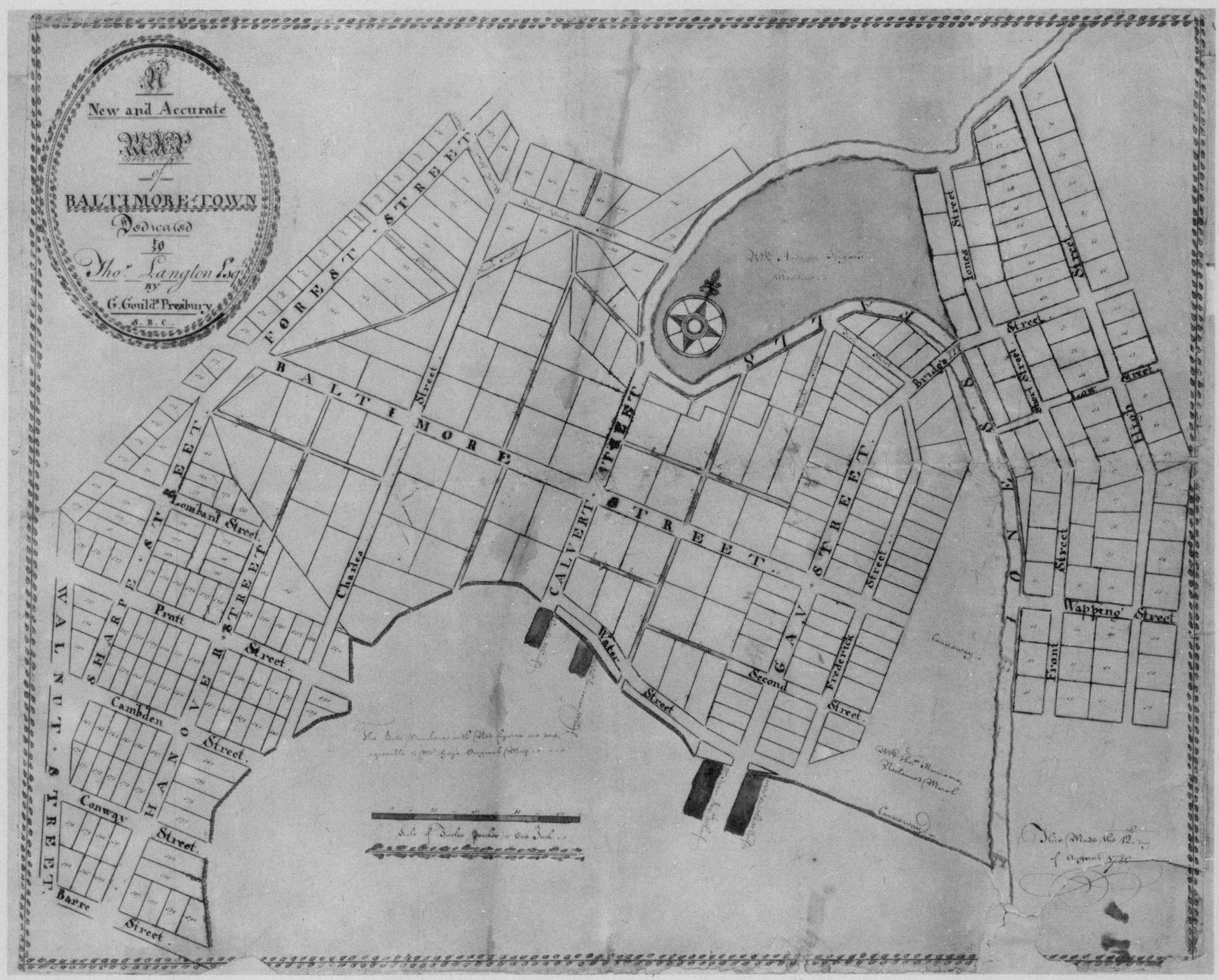

Figure 201. Plan of Baltimore, Maryland: 1780

to the economic well-being of the city. The plan of the town in 1792, reproduced in figure 202 shows the outer limits established by the port wardens for dock construction. It also reveals the extent to which owners of water-front property had already taken advantage of their right to extend piers and wharves into the original natural harbor. Ultimately most of the intervening boat slips were to be filled and built on, and the lines of the old docks can be recognized in the modern city only by the closely spaced streets running southward from the present Pratt Street.

At the time of the Revolution, Baltimore could boast of a population of nearly seven thousand persons. To Dr. Robert Honyman in 1775 it seemed "a neat, well built place," with "streets, strait & wide," although they appeared "much in need of paving."[39] By 1795, according to that meticulous observer, Médéric Moreau de St. Méry, the population had more than doubled to fifteen thousand, and there were three thousand houses, "the greater part brick and elegantly built."

Moreau de St. Méry noted with evident approval the regularity of the gridiron street system and observed that "future streets have already been staked out and even named." He listed the major buildings of the growing city: the prison, three markets, the poor house, two banks, a stock exchange, a theatre, eleven churches, and the courthouse. While he was impressed by the growth and appearance of the town as a whole, at Fell's Point he found "the buildings are much more modern than those in Baltimore, and are increasing prodigiously."

This French visitor was particularly struck by the pleasant character of the hill that rose to the north of the city. "This belongs to Colonel Howard, whose residence and out-building are situated on the front portion. The rear portion is beautified by a park. Its elevated situation; its groves of trees; the view from it, which brings back memories of European scenes: all these things together fill every true Frenchman with both pleasure and regret."[40]

The development in the Fell's Point area, annexed to Baltimore in 1773, to which this observer refers, can be seen clearly in figure 203, a plan first published in 1797 and reissued four years later. Market Street, now Broadway, was clearly the widest thoroughfare of the town, with its exceedingly generous width of ten poles or 165 feet. Crossing it and running parallel to it were the other gridiron streets of this busy commercial and residential section of the city.

The plan also shows the location of Colonel Howard's estate in the center of the engraving, splendidly situated on a hill overlooking the city and the harbor. The fashionable section of the city expanded in this direction during the nineteenth century. Growth was stimulated by the erection of the first great monument in the nation to honor George Washington. Designed by Robert Mills in 1813 for a location in the courthouse square, the monument ultimately was begun in 1815 on a portion of Howard's land directly on the axis of Charles Street. Completed in 1829, the monument dominated the city. Although Howard donated a plot of land 200 feet square for this project, he retained ownership of the surrounding area. Following his death, however, the tract was laid out as a cross-shaped open space, the two arms being named Mount Vernon Place and Washington Place. Soon handsome and imposing town houses lined its sides, and many of these still stand.

The monument and its environs were widely admired. This and other striking features of the city drew warm approval even from Mrs. Trollope who found so little in the United States to her liking. Of her visit in 1830 she wrote:

> Baltimore is, I think, one of the handsomest cities to approach in the Union. The noble column erected to the memory of Washington, and the Catholic Cathedral, with its beautiful dome, being built on a commanding eminence, are seen at a great distance. As you draw nearer, many other domes and towers become visible, and as you enter Baltimore-street, you feel that you are arrived in a handsome and populous city.... Even the private dwelling-houses have a look of magnificence, from the abundance of white marble with which many of them are adorned. The ample flights of steps, and the lofty door-frames are in most of the best houses formed of this beautiful material.[41]

The monument and its "square" appear in figure 204 as viewed looking south down Charles Street to the harbor. Four blocks to the south and fronting on Cathedral Street, a block west and parallel to Charles Street, can be seen the old Roman Catholic cathedral designed in 1804 by Benjamin H. Latrobe. Now the Basilica of the Immaculate Conception, this building's great dome and twin towers contributed a distinctive touch to the Baltimore skyline. The monument and the cathedral were not the

Figure 202. Plan of Baltimore, Maryland: 1792

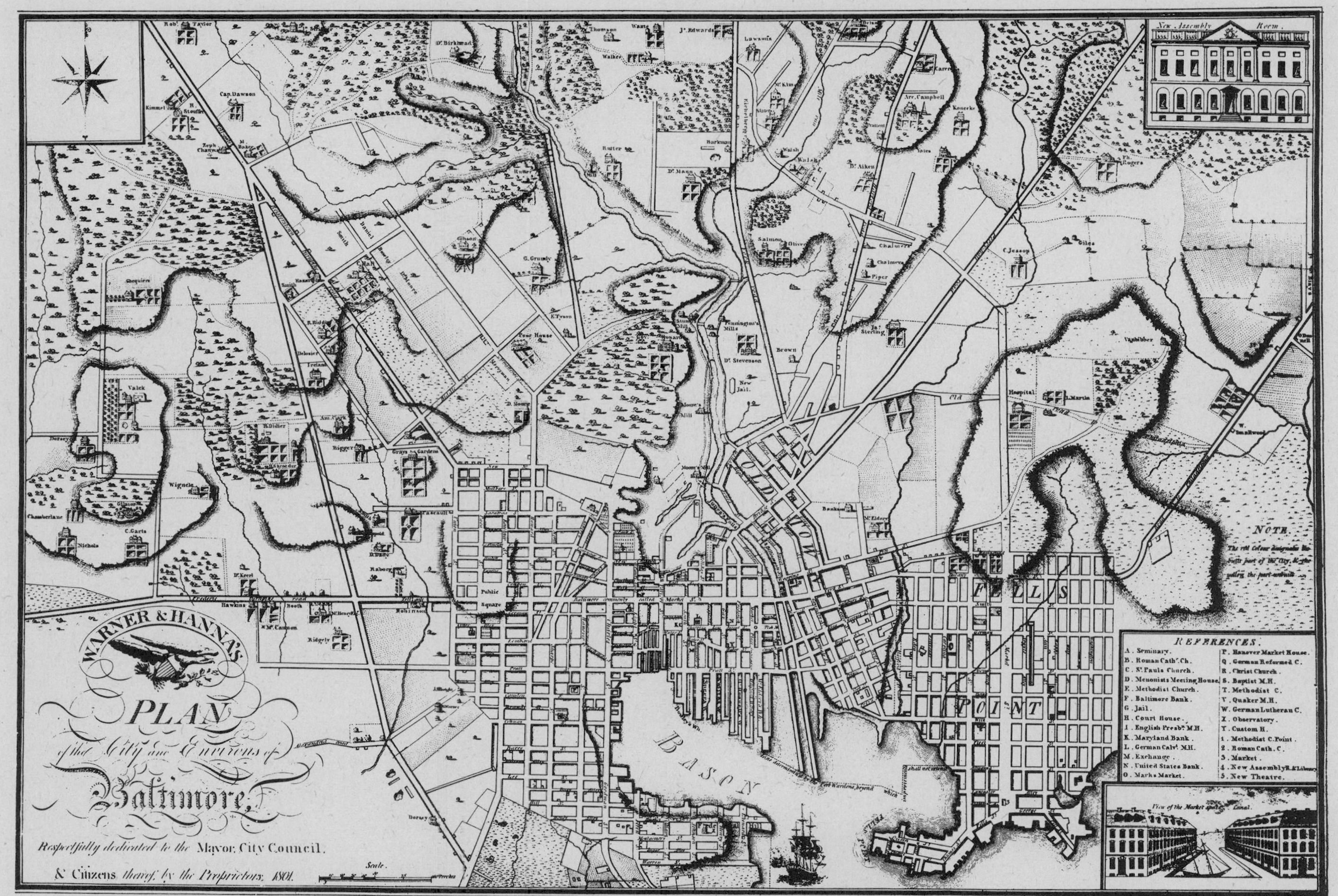

Figure 203. Plan of Baltimore, Maryland: 1797

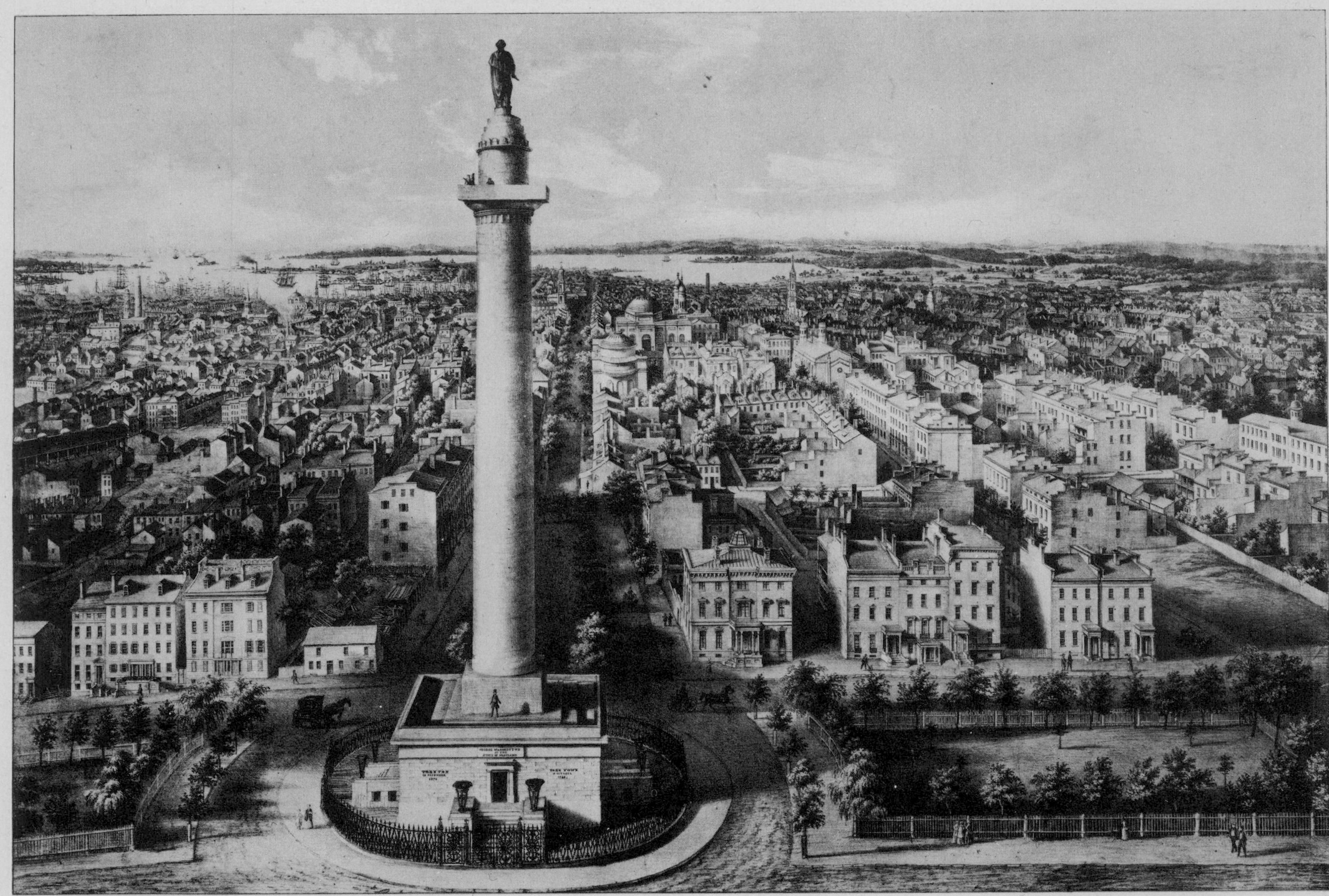

Figure 204. View of Baltimore, Maryland: 1850

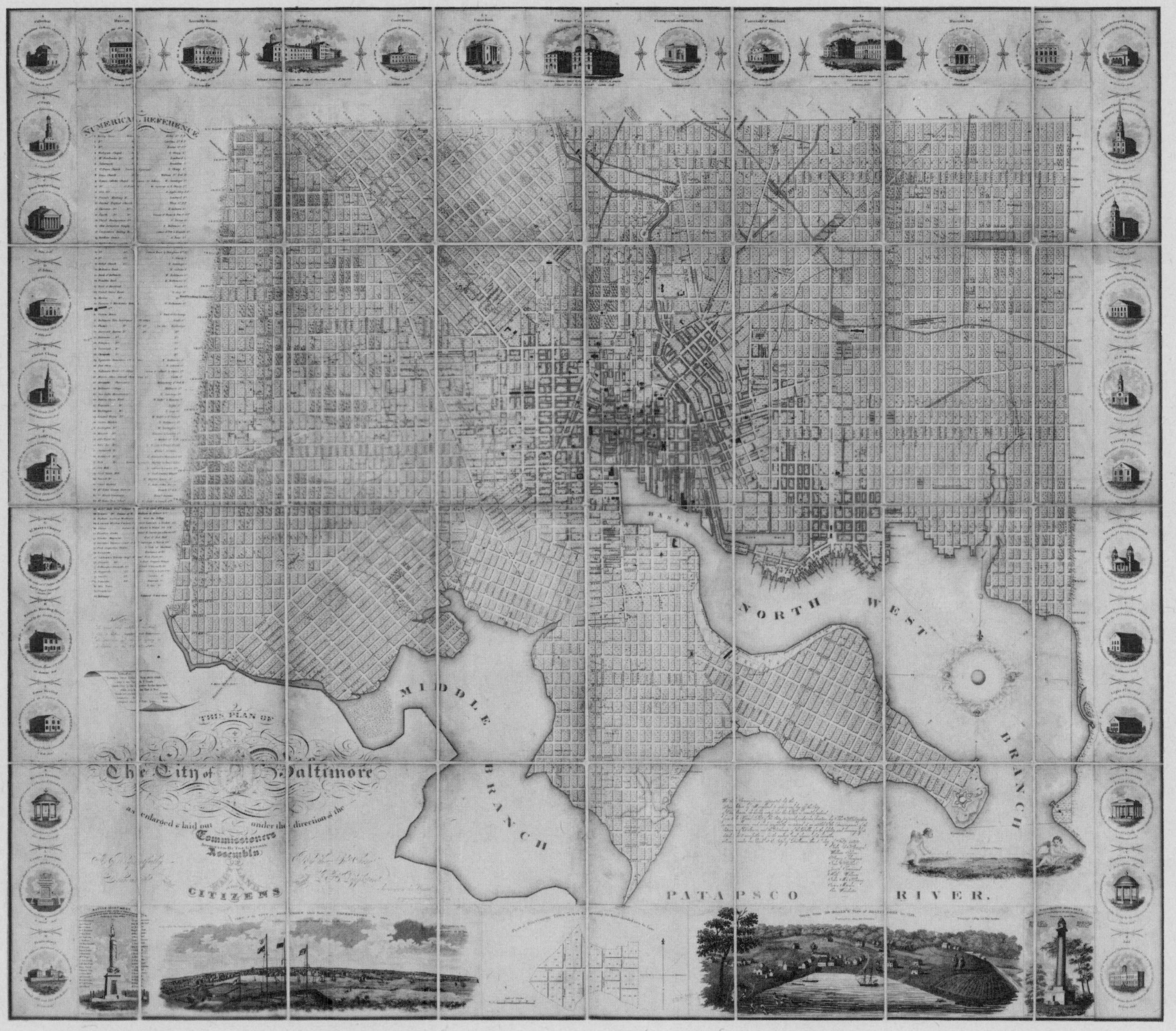

Figure 205. Plan of Baltimore, Maryland: 1823

Figure 206. View of Baltimore, Maryland: 1858

only imposing buildings to lend an air of cosmopolitan sophistication to Baltimore. By the middle of the last century the little town created by the Maryland assembly in 1729 had become a true city with a population just under 170,000. Charles Street possessed an atmosphere of domestic refinement and quiet elegance unsurpassed in any city in the country. The city's busy dock, commercial, and industrial areas throbbed with activity.[42]

It is a tragedy that the concept of great residential squares, like that of Mount Vernon Place, was not to be duplicated significantly in the period of rapid expansion in the nineteenth century as the railroad lines were developed and the era of economic prosperity continued well into the present time. The special commission appointed in 1817 to prepare a plan for the city's growth adopted an almost undeviating gridiron scheme that was to govern future development for some seventy years.

Figure 205 shows the plan approved by the special commissioners in 1818 as drawn by Thomas H. Poppleton, their surveyor, in 1823. The gridiron pattern imposed on the undeveloped land surrounding the built-up core was a mechanical extension of the module selected for the original plat in 1730. Virtually the only deviations allowed to intrude were the major highways radiating outward from the city which had been so important in the early years of its development in providing accessibility between the port and its hinterland. In that plan there was little recognition of the need to provide squares, open spaces, or other civic embellishments to afford welcome relief from the relentless grid. The need for recreation space in the growing city, as well as for focal points for architectural interest, was ignored. The desire to capture the maximum economic return on urban land, which was to characterize much of the growth of American cities in the great period of national expansion, proved a stronger force than any wishes to promote civic beauty through public action.

Figure 206 shows the city as viewed from the south shortly before the Civil War. Its expansion beyond the already built-up area that appears in this view was to be guided by the plan of 1818 for many years. Today much of the original town as laid out in 1730 is undergoing urban redevelopment. The Charles Center project represents a modern attempt to create a new image for Baltimore's core, and other planning projects have altered the pattern of the expanded street system developed over the centuries. These efforts have come too late to save many of the handsome town houses that once lined the streets leading up the hills from the harbor. Many of the survivors have been converted to other uses, not always in harmony with the original architectural form of the buildings. Mount Vernon Place, however, has retained much of its fine urban character, though there, too, unnecessarily tall buildings have threatened to overshadow the Washington Monument. Even with these intrusions, however, this splendid civic open space stands as a reminder that not all worthwhile urban planning projects date from the present century and as a testimony to the wisdom of those few persons who saw that an economically vibrant city could be beautiful in appearance as well as efficient in function.

XII. *Tidewater Town Planning in Perspective*

By the end of the eighteenth century the urban settlement pattern of the tidewater and piedmont regions of Virginia and Maryland had become well established. The long period of trial and error in the founding of towns had passed. Most of the earlier settlements surviving at that time still exist, although many have never achieved the stature of real cities, whether measured by population or by diversity of occupations and activities. Subsequent urban growth in the two states took place in and around cities and towns already existing at the beginning of the nineteenth century.

In what ways did these towns and their experience with town planning differ from towns of the other English colonies in America? To what extent did their designs merely reflect prevailing patterns and concepts widely used throughout this colonial domain? In size and in quality how did the early towns of Virginia and Maryland compare with those of other regions?

With the exceptions of Annapolis, Williamsburg, and Washington, the original plans of towns in Virginia and Maryland closely resembled those of the other English colonies. From Maine to Georgia gridiron planning predominated as it had in virtually all other periods of rapid colonization, from the time of Greek and Roman urban expansion to our own experience with internal colonization during the settlement of the American west. The plans of Boston and Dutch New York departed somewhat from rigid checkerboard patterns, but elsewhere rectilinear forms were commonly employed.

The explanations for this are not difficult to find. The gridiron plan was the easiest to devise and the least difficult to lay out on the ground. Moreover, its widespread use may well have reflected a conscious reaction against the irregularities of English cities with their narrow winding streets and lanes. Finally, the art of urban planning so well developed on the continent of Europe by the beginning of American colonization was slower to take root in England. Few persons skilled in this field existed in the home country and only rarely made their influence felt in the colonies.

Talented amateurs rather than trained professionals were responsible for the relatively few innovations in town design found in colonial America. William Penn's plan for Philadelphia in 1682 included four rectangular neighborhood parks in addition to the more common central square intended for public buildings. James Oglethorpe in 1733 devised an even more impressive system of open spaces for Savannah. He divided the town into several wards each consisting of forty house lots and four sites for public buildings grouped around an open square. Apparently he had in mind the creation of residential squares modeled after the many handsome developments of this type then existing in London's West End. It was of course another amateur, Francis Nicholson, who brought to Virginia and Maryland the most sophisticated plan forms used at Annapolis and Williamsburg.

Under these circumstances of limited professional skills, it was but natural that for the most part relatively primitive urban designs were employed in the English colonies. In this respect Virginia and Maryland differed little from the rest of Anglo-America. The dozens of tiny gridiron plans used in these two tidewater provinces were thus not peculiar to the region but symbolized the lack of sophistication in town planning characteristic of all the colonies.

Here and there, as at Philadelphia and Savannah, interesting modifications appeared in the otherwise almost ubiquitious grid. Except at Savannah these modest innovations in town layout remained features only of the original portion of the towns and were not repeated as expansion occurred. Creative efforts seem to have been focused almost entirely on the first design of settlements. Officials paid far less attention to directing wisely an ordered pattern of expansion beyond the original boundaries. Jefferson's extension plan for Richmond followed the tradition of earlier gridiron planning, but his action stands out as a rare example of public initiative in guiding urban growth at a stage well after the initial founding of the town.

Equally outstanding, as significant achievements of original design not duplicated or surpassed in interest elsewhere in the English colonies, are the little baroque plans of Annapolis and Williamsburg. And if one includes the later city of Washington with its monumental plan, splendid building sites, and sweeping vistas, the tidewater region must be assigned a preeminent rank in the creation of towns that were beautiful and visually inspiring. In quality, therefore, the colonial and early federal cities in Virginia and Maryland compare favorably with those of their sister provinces.

Nor should we scorn as unworthy of appreciation the many less-imposing gridiron plans of the tidewater region. They represent a kind of colonial norm, and if they are not of compelling interest as examples of carefully studied urban design, they at least furnish an index of the level of a frontier culture. Some, like Chestertown and Alexandria, may have lacked impressive plans but they developed nonetheless as communities of singular architectural beauty.

Justified pride in these achievements should not warp our judgment. For the most part, as compared to Europe, the state of the art of town planning during our colonial period cannot be regarded as outstanding. In this respect, as in many others, colonial life echoed but faintly the culture of the mother country. The squares of London's West End and those of Savannah were not dissimilar in plan, but it was many years after the founding of Savannah before brick town houses like those of fashionable London replaced the tiny huts of the first settlers. Similarly, Nicholson found it far easier to compose on paper his formal designs for Annapolis and Williamsburg than to create in three dimensions the buildings that were essential to give meaning to his plans for streets, open spaces, and sites for civic structures.

The early failures of attempts to create towns by legislative fiat in the two colonies has already been examined. Lack of success in such ventures was not, however, unique to Virginia and Maryland. In 1730 Governor Robert Johnson of South Carolina devised a settlement program calling for the creation of ten townships of twenty thousand acres each centered on villages of two hundred quarter-acre lots surrounded by common lands of two hundred acres. While a number of these townships eventually were surveyed, the program stimulated rural rather than urban settlement. Circumstances differed in Georgia, but the results were similar. Where Savannah survived, Old and New Ebenezer, Frederica, George Town, and numerous other early settlements failed to prosper and eventually disappeared. A closer investigation of the other colonies would doubtless reveal similar difficulties in town development.

The combination of a plantation economy—largely made possible by the institution of slavery—and the penetrations of the coastline by wide rivers and bays led, as we have seen, to a dispersed population pattern in Virginia and Maryland. Although these same factors existed in modified form in the Carolinas, it was the Chesapeake region that felt their full force. In addition to causing difficulties in town development for the reasons we have already explored, these elements encouraged the location of certain activities on relatively isolated sites—buildings and uses that in the northern colonies normally developed in towns and helped to promote urban growth.

In both Maryland and Virginia, for example, many churches stood on solitary rural sites. These were located somewhere near the centers of parishes so that they were accessible to farm and plantation families. Rural churches were by no means unknown in other English colonies, particularly the Carolinas and Georgia, but this pattern of church location differed strongly from that of Pennsylvania, New York, and New England.

Isolated courthouses were a feature particularly of the Virginia scene. These, like the rural churches, were placed so that residents of the county had equal access to their facilities. Many stood in walled enclosures that contained, in addition to the building housing the court, a jail, offices used by lawyers when the court was in session, and a caretaker's residence. Often a tavern or inn could be found nearby. In time some of these building complexes, like Gloucester Court House, became the centers of small towns as land in the vicinity was taken up for houses and other uses. Some, like King William Court House, still exist unchanged on isolated sites well away from any village or city.

The fact that such uses developed in this dispersed pattern deprived the towns of Virginia and Maryland of some of the impetus for growth enjoyed in the northern colonies where more of the churches and virtually all of the courthouses could be found in cities and towns.

If the peculiar geographic and cultural circumstances of the tidewater region are taken into account, the incidence of success in establishing towns seems remarkable. The wonder is not that there were so few urban settlements in Virginia and Maryland but that there were so many. The entire country was, after all, essentially rural. The largest city in 1810, New York, still had a population under 100,000. Boston numbered only about 33,250 inhabitants. Philadelphia remained a city of modest size with less than 54,000 people. In that year the closely grouped cities in the District of Columbia of Washington, Georgetown, and Alexandria could boast of a population of over 20,000, while Baltimore with its contiguous eastern and western precincts approached 47,000. Richmond and Norfolk, each with just under 10,000 residents exceeded Providence and Newport in population; Petersburg with nearly 7,000 persons was more populous than New Haven.

In both quality and size, therefore, the towns and cities of tidewater Virginia and Maryland compared favorably with those of other regions.

What is perhaps more important to a generation desperately seeking solutions to the vexing problems posed by modern urbanization, the planning history of the Tidewater suggests that direct governmental action in the planning of new towns is neither un-American nor ineffective. It was, after all, public ownership of the entire sites for Annapolis, Williamsburg, and Washington that made possible their unique and attractive designs. It has been urged recently and with increasing frequency that completely new cities will be needed in the United States to ease congestion in our existing communities by guiding their expansion in more socially useful patterns. When we come to face this issue, as some day we must, an examination of our past experience with the public creation of new communities may reveal unexpected lessons from the history of early town planning in the tidewater colonies.

Notes

CHAPTER I.

1. For a summary of this episode with illustrations see John W. Reps, *The Making of Urban America,* pp. 147–50.

2. [James Edward Oglethorpe?], *A New and Accurate Account of the Provinces of South Carolina and Georgia,* pp. iv–v.

3. I am not suggesting that colonial planners in America drew directly on medieval English town planning experience. My thesis agrees with that of Tout: "'Post hoc' is not necessarily 'propter hoc,' and, just as we must not affiliate the planned towns of the Middle Ages too meticulously to the planned towns of antiquity, so we must not lay excessive stress on the continuation of the mediaeval tradition in modern times. But there is this to be said for the later case of continuity, that there is a continuous history between the mediaeval and the modern town which makes us, whether we like it or not, the necessary children of the Middle Ages." T. F. Tout, *Mediaeval Town Planning,* p. 29. Tout's little book, an extension of a lecture originally delivered in 1916, was one of the earliest English attempts to investigate the subject.

4. Ibid., p. 13; Eleanor Lodge, *Gascony Under English Rule,* p. 178.

5. Professor Lavedan states that there are no discernable characteristics distinguishing English *bastides* in France from those planned by native rulers. See Pierre Lavedan, *Histoire de l'Urbanisme,* 1: 281–369 for a long and rewarding discussion of the *bastide* towns with many plans and views. A briefer summary of his findings and conclusions appears in his *Les Villes Françaises,* pp. 71–88. After visiting some fifty *bastides* of both French and English origin in July, 1951, and July, 1966, and studying the plans of these and other new towns of the region, I concur in this conclusion. Nor, as Professor Lavedan points out, does there seem to be any significant difference between towns of early origin and those founded toward the end of this era. French writing on the *bastides* is extensive. The following sources are useful: Felix de Verneilh, "Architecture Civile du Moyen Age," *Annales Archéologiques* 11 (1851): 335–46, and 12 (1852): 24–31; A. Curie-Seimbres, *Essai sur les Bastides* (Toulouse, 1880); Jean-Paul Trabut-Cussac, "Bastides ou Forteresses?," *Le Moyen Age,* 4th ser., 60, no. 9 (1954): 81–135; and Ch. Higounet, "Cisterciens et Bastides," *Le Moyen Age,* 4th ser., 56, no. 5 (1950): 69–84.

6. Caroline Shillaber, "Edward I, Builder of Towns," *Speculum* 22 (1947): 302.

7. There are many redrawn plans in the two works by Lavedan. For others with descriptive text see Cecil Stewart, *A Prospect of Cities,* pp. 80–94; and Frederick R. Hiorns, *Town-Building in History,* pp. 122–27.

8. As quoted in Tout, *Mediaeval Town Planning,* p. 27.

9. Ibid., p. 24; T. Harold Hughes and E. A. G. Lamborn, *Towns and Town-Planning, Ancient & Modern,* p. 71.

10. Hughes and Lamborn, *Towns and Town-Planning,* pp. 53–55, with a redrawn plan showing its original pattern.

11. Hughes and Lamborn, *Towns and Town-Planning,* reproduce a manuscript plan of the city ca. 1545. For a brief discussion of other examples of early English town planning before Edward I see pages 36–62 of this readable and concise summary.

12. For the planning of Salisbury see Tout, *Mediaeval Town Planning,* pp. 16–18; Hughes and Lamborn, *Towns and Town-Planning,* pp. 62–65. For an exhaustive treatment of medieval town planning emphasizing English experience see Maurice Beresford, *New Towns of the Middle Ages.* Beresford points out that in Gascony, England, and Wales nearly four hundred new towns were planned in this period.

13. For a discussion of four important Roman communities, Colchester, Lincoln, Gloucester, and York see I. A. Richmond, "The Four *Coloniae* of Roman Britain," *Archaeological Journal* 103 (1947): 57–84.

14. William Camden, *Britannia, sive Florentissimorum Regnorum Angliae, Scotiae, Hiberniae et Insularum Adjacentium ex Intima Antiquitate Chorographica Descriptio* (London, 1586).

15. For a detailed description of the Speed atlas of 1611 and the subsequent editions, see Thomas Chubb, *The Printed Maps in the Atlases of Great Britain and Ireland,* pp. 23–33. For an analysis of the Speed town plans and the sources he used, see R. A. Skelton, "Tudor Town Plans in John Speed's *Theatre,*" *Archaeological Journal* 108 (1952): 109–20.

16. For a partial listing of other English town plans printed before Speed's work, see Skelton, "Tudor Town Plans," p. 113.

17. A list of and brief biographical information concerning more than forty persons involved with both

Virginia and Irish colonization appears in Howard Mumford Jones, "Origins of the Colonial Idea in England," *Proceedings of the American Philosophical Society* 85 (1942): 463–65; see also David Beers Quinn, *The Elizabethans and the Irish,* pp. 106–22.

18. Jones, "Origins of the Colonial Idea in England," p. 454.

19. David Beers Quinn, "Sir Thomas Smith (1513–1577) and the Beginnings of English Colonial Theory," in *Proceedings of the American Philosophical Society* 89 (1945): 544.

20. An excellent account of Smith's remarkable career, including his Irish venture, is Mary Dewar, *Sir Thomas Smith.*

21. *A letter sent by J. B. Gentleman unto his very friend and master R. C. Esquire* . . . . (London, 1571). [unpaged]

22. Quoted by Quinn, "Sir Thomas Smith," p. 547. This is but one of several references in Smith's correspondence to classical models for his Irish colony. To Fitzwilliam, lord deputy of Ireland, November 8, 1572, he recalled "how England was as uncivil as Ireland until colonies of Romans brought their laws and orders, whose moulds no nation, not even the Italians and Romans, have more straitly and truly kept." Ibid., p. 546.

23. Ibid., pp. 490, 491.

24. These are summarized in Dewar, *Smith,* pp. 164–67.

25. Unfortunately, Smith's plan does not seem to have survived. It is not among Smith's papers in the Essex Record Office. Letter from Mary Dewar to the author, March 28, 1968.

26. Docwra's plan is discussed in Anthony Garvan, *Architecture and Town Planning in Colonial Connecticut* (New Haven, 1951), pp. 30–40, where the possible influence of the Ulster Plantation on town planning in Connecticut is reviewed.

27. I have relied heavily on Gilbert Camblin, *The Town in Ulster.* Camblin's valuable study includes reproductions of many manuscript and printed plans of the period and also contains a useful bibliography.

28. "Certain Considerations touching the Plantation in Ireland," in Constantia Maxwell, *Irish History from Contemporary Sources (1509–1610),* pp. 272–73. The "champion countries" mentioned by Bacon refer to those portions of England where the land was not partitioned into fields but left open and unenclosed.

29. Richard Bagwell, *Ireland Under the Stuarts and During the Interregnum,* 1: 77.

30. As quoted in Camblin, *The Town in Ulster,* p. 30. A detailed plan of the town in 1685 showing streets, lots, and buildings is reproduced opposite page 33 therein.

31. Garvan, *Colonial Connecticut,* p. 33, n. 47.

32. As quoted in John T. Gilbert, ed., *Facsimiles of National Manuscripts of Ireland* 4, no. 2 (London, 1884): lxxxviii-lxxxix. This volume of a set of annotated facsimiles printed by authority of the lords commissioners of the treasury contains several large color reproductions of manuscript maps and plans relating to the Ulster Plantation, including that of Londonderry. Other color reproductions from the same manuscripts of the plans of Londonderry and Coleraine and maps showing the distribution of land in Ulster appear in Sir Thomas Phillips, *Londonderry and the London Companies, 1609–1629.* The full text of Pynnar's report is given in Walter Harris, *Hibernica* (1747), 2d ed. (Dublin, 1770), pp. 139–241 under the title "Pynnar's Survey of Ulster."

33. A plan of Vitry-le-François is reproduced in Reps, *The Making of Urban America,* p. 7. Barret's plan appears in Garvan, *Colonial Connecticut,* p. 30.

34. Camblin, *The Town in Ulster,* p. 32.

35. Harris, *Hibernica,* pp. 224–25.

36. Camblin, *The Town in Ulster,* pp. 98–99.

37. Ibid., p. 44.

38. Harris, *Hibernica,* p. 232.

39. For a reproduction of the plan, see Camblin, *The Town in Ulster,* plate 8.

40. Their plans appear in Camblin, *The Town in Ulster,* plates 10–12. For plans of Macosquin, which had a similar design, see Garvan, *Colonial Connecticut,* figs. 8, 14.

41. Harris, *Hibernica,* p. 236.

42. For the later development of the Ulster towns see Camblin, *The Town in Ulster,* pp. 47–109. The difficulties with colonization are covered in most histories of Ireland. See, for example, Bagwell, *Ireland Under the Stuarts* and, in briefer compass, J. C. Beckett, *The Making of Modern Ireland, 1603–1923,* pp. 40–121.

43. One of Newcourt's plans is reproduced in Reps, *The Making of Urban America,* p. 164. Both appear in T. F. Reddaway, "The Rebuilding of London after the Great Fire: A Rediscovered Plan," *Town Planning Review* 18 (1939) 1: 155–61. For Hooke's plan consult *Making of Urban America,* p. 18.

44. Evelyn's first plan was much simpler and more effective. It is reproduced in fig. 85 and discussed in Chap. VI in connection with the planning of Annapolis.

CHAPTER II.

1. "Letters Patent to Walter Raleigh," David Beers Quinn, ed., *The Roanoke Voyages: 1584–1590,* 1: 82–89. Quinn's collection of the documents relating to the Roanoke colony is an indispensable source of information made even more valuable by the editor's notes and comments.

2. "Arthur Barlowe's Discourse of the First Voyage," ibid., 91–116.

3. Richard Hakluyt, *Discourse on Western Planting,* in Charles Deane, ed., *Documentary History of the State of Maine,* 2: 2.

4. The text appears in Quinn, *Roanoke Voyages,* 1: 130–39, under the title "Anonymous Notes for the Guidance of Raleigh and Cavendish."

5. Although Raleigh conceivably may have been the author of this anonymous document, it is a draft and not in his hand. The case for Raleigh as its author could only be made by supposing the manuscript to be a second draft by a clerk from an earlier one composed by Raleigh. David Quinn, in a letter to the author (February 27, 1968) suggests Sir Roger Williams as the likely source. Williams had campaigned in the Low Countries and was a military theoretician who was to publish in 1590 *A Brief Discourse on War* containing a long section on fortifications. In addition, there is evidence of his familiarity with Raleigh's proposed voyage in the form of a letter to him from Jack Roberts early in 1585. Of this Quinn's letter states that it "indicates that . . . Williams was closely in touch with the preparations being made for the 1585 Virginia voyage, as there are several joking references there to the preliminaries to the voyage which would have been unintelligible to Williams, had he not been following it closely." Quinn identifies this communication as Bodleian Library, Tanner MS 169, ff. 69*v*.–70.

6. For accounts of the archaeology of the site see Jean Carl Harrington, "Archeological Explorations at Fort Raleigh National Historic Site," *North Carolina Historical Review* 26 (1949): 127–49; J. C. Harrington,

Search for the Cittie of Ralegh; and Charles W. Porter III, *Fort Raleigh National Historic Site, North Carolina,* rev. ed. (Washington, D.C., 1956); and the sources cited by Harrington and Porter.

7. "Ralph Lane's Discourse on the First Colony," Quinn, *Roanoke Voyages,* 1: 282. Quinn comments that this passage is "the only indication that there were, apparently, sufficient cottages for them to be laid out in a street or streets. It is possible that there was even a trading-store outside the fort to which the Indians could come." p. 282, n. 5.

8. The original charter no longer exists, although an early copy of the grant of arms for the "city" and for its leaders individually is reprinted in Quinn, ibid., pp. 465–67.

9. "Thomas Hariot, *A Briefe and True Report,*" ibid., p. 385.

10. White's account of the voyage contains a number of references to disagreements between him and Fernandez over the latter's desire to engage in privateering. Fernandez obviously wished to rid himself of the colonists as soon as possible and turn his attention to more profitable attacks on Spanish merchant shipping. See "John White's Narrative of his Voyage," ibid., 2: 515–38.

11. Ibid., p. 524.

12. Ibid. As Quinn notes, "Under Lane only the principal men in the colony had houses of their own. Now, the family make-up of part of the new colony required more individual housing. White's use of the word cottages, to distinguish the new houses from those of Lane's colony, would suggest that they were smaller, single-storey erections, probably of a very temporary character." pp. 524–25, n. 6.

13. "John White's Narrative of the 1590 Voyage to Virginia," ibid., pp. 613–14.

14. Ibid., p. 614.

15. Ibid., p. 615. Could one or more of the "rotten and spoyled" maps have been a drawing of the fort and town of Roanoke? It seems inconceivable that White, a systematic recorder of all that occurred at Roanoke, would not have prepared such a drawing. It is difficult to believe, on the other hand, that he would have left this at Roanoke rather than bringing it with him to England to show to Raleigh. The history of his drawings is given by Quinn, ibid., 1: 390–464 and in Paul Hulton and David Beers Quinn, eds., *The American Drawings of John White, 1577–1590,* 2 vols., where the drawings are reproduced in color from the originals in the British Museum. See also Stefan Lorant, ed., *The New World* (New York, 1946), which contains plates made from hand-colored copies of the drawings along with reproductions of the engravings from the drawings published by Theodore De Bry in 1590.

16. White, writing in 1593 that "I would to God my wealth were answerable to my will," indicated his lingering concern over the fate of the settlers and his lack of resources to continue the search for their whereabouts. He then added that he could only commit "the reliefe of my discomfortable company the planters in Virginia, to the merciful help of the Almighty, whom I most humbly beseech to helpe & comfort them, according to his most holy will & their good desire." "John White to Richard Hakluyt," Quinn, *Roanoke Voyages,* 2: 715–16.

17. Quoted in Alexander Brown, *The Genesis of the United States,* 1: 30–31. This collection of documents on early English colonization of America is invaluable.

18. These are briefly summarized in ibid., 25–28.

19. Ibid., 33–35 provides the full text of the articles of agreement between the two parties.

20. For the text of one that may have been as early as 1605, see ibid., 36–42.

21. The full text of the letters patent appears in ibid., 52–63.

22. This and other quotations from the instructions are from the text in ibid., 79–85.

23. John Smith, *A True Relation of . . . Virginia* (London, 1608), in Lyon G. Tyler, ed., *Narratives of Early Virginia,* p. 33.

24. [William Simmonds], *The Proceedings of the English Colonies in Virginia* (London, 1612), ibid., p. 123.

25. "Observations by Master George Percy, 1607," ibid., p. 15.

26. Ibid., p. 19.

27. For a full account of attempts to discover any remains of the fort see John L. Cotter, *Archeological Excavations at Jamestown;* Samuel H. Yonge, *The Site of Old "James Towne," 1607–1698.* Henry Chandlee Forman, in his *Jamestown and St. Mary's, Buried Cities of Romance,* maintains that the site of the fort was not on the location generally accepted by other scholars. There is little evidence to support his theory.

28. For a color reproduction of "The Forte and Castel of Charlemont Built by the Lord Cawfeild, Master of the Ordnance," see John T. Gilbert, ed., *Facsimiles of National Manuscripts of Ireland,* part 4, plate 40. The lord deputy of Ireland, Charles Blount, Lord Mountjoy, erected this fort in 1602. It is four-sided with pointed bastions at each corner.

29. Lorant, *New World,* p. 16. Lorant reproduces in this volume the De Bry engravings of Florida as well as those of the Roanoke colony. For another view of Fort Caroline, based on the De Bry views, engraved by Arnoldus Montanus in 1671, see Reps, *The Making of Urban America,* p. 441.

30. It should be noted that the first published plan of St. Augustine, which depicts Drake's raid and dates from 1588, shows a six-sided fort guarding the channel that provided access from the sea to the settlement. The drawing reproduced in figure 28, despite its later date, may be that of a structure that existed before Drake's attack and that by 1586 had been replaced or modified. The plan published in 1588, later to be closely copied by Theodore De Bry in 1599, is reproduced in *The Making of Urban America,* p. 34.

31. Percy's account gives the names of the dead and the dates of death. Tyler, *Narratives,* pp. 20–21.

32. Smith, *True Relation,* ibid., p. 37.

33. Letter from Newport to Salisbury, July 29, 1607, in Brown, *Genesis,* 1: 105. It is interesting to note that Don Pedro de Zuñiga, the Spanish ambassador in England and the director of an effective intelligence network, had more accurate information which he conveyed to his king: "Of the vessels that have been to Virginia one has arrived in Plymouth. . . . I understand they do not come over well pleased; because in that country there is nothing else but good timber for masts, pitch and rosin, and some soil from which it seems to them they may obtain 'bronse'." Letter from Zuñiga to the king of Spain, August 22, 1607, ibid., 110.

34. Letter from Francis Perkins to an unknown person as transmitted by Don Pedro de Zuñiga to the king of Spain, June 16, 1608, ibid., 175. We learn from another equally brief reference to the fire that the buildings within the fort had roofs constructed of reed thatch. [Simmonds], *Proceedings,* in Tyler, *Narratives,* p. 135. See also his earlier observations about John Smith's energy and leadership in setting "some to mow, others to binde thatch, some to build houses, others to thatch them." p. 128.

35. Ibid., p. 136.

36. Ibid., p. 185.

37. Letter of the governor and Council of Virginia to the Virginia Company of London, July 7, 1610, in Brown, *Genesis,* 1: 405.

38. "The Starving Time. Letters from Lord De La Ware to the Earl of Salisbury," *Virginia Magazine of History and Biography* 14 (1907): 381.

39. John Smith, *The Generall Historie of Virginia* (London, 1624), in Tyler, *Narratives,* p. 298. This passage in Smith's history is taken from the eyewitness account by William Strachey, *A True Reportory,* in Samuel Purchas, *Purchas His Pilgrimes,* 19: 60.

40. The previous winter the London Company had made special attempts to recruit "blacksmiths, carpenters, coopers, shipwrights, turners and such as know how to plant vineyards, hunters, fishermen, and all who work in any kind of metal, men who make bricks, architects, bakers, weavers, shoemakers, sawyers and those who spin wool." Zuñiga sent to his king on February 23, 1609, a copy of a poster issued by the company holding out to such craftsmen promises of "houses to live in, vegetable-gardens and orchards, and also food and clothing at the expense of the Company . . . and besides this, they will have a share of all the products and the profits that may result from their labor, each in proportion, and they will also secure a share in the division of the land for themselves and their heirs forever more." See Brown, *Genesis,* 1: 248–49.

41. These figures conflict. The triangular area enclosed by the fort with the dimensions given by Strachey would be almost exactly one acre, double the area he indicates in the opening of the passage quoted. I think that his figures for the length of the sides of the triangle are more likely to be the correct ones. Strachey's description of Jamestown from which this and the following passages are taken appears in "A true reportory of the wracke, and redemption of Sir Thomas Gates Knight . . . his comming to Virginia, and the estate of that Colonie . . . ," in Purchas, *Pilgrimes,* 19: 55–58.

42. *For the Colony in Virginea Britannia* (London, 1612), in Peter Force, ed., *Tracts and Other Papers Relating Principally to the Origin, Settlement, and Progress of the Colonies in North America,* 3: 15.

43. Strachey, *True Reportory,* in Purchas, *Pilgrimes,* 19: 58.

44. "The Relation of the Lord De-La-Ware, 1611," in Tyler, *Narratives,* p. 212.

45. These included repairs on the church and warehouse, construction of a stable, a powder house, a new well "for the amending of the most unholsome water which the old afforded," a new blockhouse near the meadow where the cattle grazed, and a "bridge to land our goods dry and safe upon." See Dale's report to the council, May 25, 1611, in Brown, *Genesis,* 1: 491–92.

46. Ralph Hamor, "Notes of Virginian Affaires in the Government of Sir Thomas Dale and of Sir Thomas Gates till Anno 1614," in Purchas, *Pilgrimes,* 19: 99–100. For a more complete treatment of the founding of Henrico, the college proposed to be established there, and Dale's background, see Robert Hunt Land, "Henrico and its College," *William and Mary Quarterly,* 2d ser., 18 (1938): 453–98.

47. Robert Johnson, *The New Life of Virginia* (London, 1612), in Force, *Tracts,* 1: 14.

48. "A Breife Declaration of the Plantation of Virginia duringe the first twelve Yeares, when Sir Thomas Smith was Governor of the Companie, & downe to this present tyme. By the Ancient Planters nowe remaining alive in Virginia," undated, but probably 1625, in Virginia General Assembly, Joint Committee on the State Library, *Colonial Records of Virginia,* p. 75.

49. Henrico or Henricus appear to be the only names for the town used at the time of its existence. The use of the name Henricopolis has no historical basis.

50. Letter from Dale to Salisbury, August 17, 1611, in Brown, *Genesis,* 1: 504.

51. Ralph Hamor, *A True Discourse of the Present Estate of Virginia . . . till the 18 of June. 1614* (London, 1615), p. 33.

52. John Rolfe, *A True Relation of the State of Virginia,* pp. 38–39. Rolfe's account is in manuscript form, the version used here being transcribed from that in the collection of Henry C. Taylor. It was written in London when Rolfe returned to England for one year with Pocahontas in the summer of 1616.

53. "Instructions to Governor Yeardley, 1618," *Virginia Magazine of History and Biography* 2 (1894): 154–65.

CHAPTER III.

1. See "A Note of the Shipping, Men, and Provisions sent to Virginia . . . in the yeere 1619," and "A note of the shipping, men, and provisions sent and provided for Virginia . . . in the yeere 1621," in Samuel Purchas, *Purchas His Pilgrimes,* 19: 126–29 and 143–49.

2. "Virginia Company. Letter to the Governor and Council in Virginia," August 12, 1621, in Susan Myra Kingsbury, ed., *The Records of the Virginia Company of London,* 3: 493. The cost of transportation was set at 120 pounds "of the best leafe Tobbacco," an early reference to tobacco as a method of payment. This practice was to be widely used throughout the colonial period, including the payment by the government for land acquired for new towns.

3. "Treasurer and Council for Virginia. Letter to Governor and Council in Virginia," August 1, 1622, ibid., pp. 669–70.

4. John Smith, *Generall Historie of Virginia, New England and the Summer Isles* (London, 1624), in Lyon G. Tyler, *Narratives of Early Virginia, 1606-1625,* p. 330.

5. "Letter of John Pory, 1619," ibid., pp. 284–85.

6. John Rolfe to Sir Edwin Sandys, June 8, 1617, in Kingsbury, ed., *Virginia Company,* 3: 71.

7. See "Instruccons Orders and Constitucons . . . to Sir Thomas Gates," May, 1609: "We advise you to continue the Plantacon at James Towne with a Convenient nomber of men, but not as yor situacon or Citty, because the place is unwholsome and but in the Marish of Virginia, and to keepe it onely as a fitt porte for yor Shippes to ride before. . . ." This portion of the instructions of 1609 were repeated in those given Lord Delaware the following year. Ibid., p. 16.

8. "Indenture Between Sir William Throckmorton, Sir George Yardely, Richard Berkeley, and John Smyth, and the Virginia Company," February 3, 1618/19, ibid., pp. 130–34. The preparations for Virginia settlement carried out by this group and their intentions to found the town of Barkley (or Berkeley Hundred) can be traced in several documents. Ibid., 199–215. Four hundred acres were to be enclosed by "a strong pale of seaven foote and halfe highe" for the agricultural lands of this venture.

9. "Lists of the Livinge & Dead in Virginia, Feb. 16th, 1623," in Virginia General Assembly, Joint Committee on the State Library, *Colonial Records of Virginia,* pp. 37–60. By 1634 the population of the colony had increased to 4,914. "A List of the number of men, women and children Inhabitinge in the severall Counties within the Collony of Virginia. Anno Dne, 1634," ibid., p. 91.

10. Captain Nathaniel Butler, governor of Bermuda from 1619 to 1622, lived in Virginia during the winter of 1622–1623. On his return to England he prepared and submitted to the king a devastating criticism of the colony. Included in his charges was the following: "Their howses are generally the worste that ever I sawe the meanest Cottages in England beinge every way equall (if not superiour) with the moste of the best. And besides soe improvidently and scatteringlie are they seated one from an other as partly by their distance butt especially by the interposicons of Creeks and Swamps as they call them, they offer all advantages to their Sauadge enymies and are utterly depryved of all suddaine recolleccon of them selves uppon any termes whatsoever." "The Unmasked face of our Colony in Virginia as it was in the Winter of the yeare 1622," in Kingsbury, ed., *Virginia Company,* 2: 375.

11. "Treasurer, Councell, and Company for Virginia," ibid., 3: 276.

12. Letter from John Pory to Sir Edwin Sandys, June 12, 1620, ibid., p. 302.

13. Letter from Jabez Whittaker to Sir Edwin Sandys, May, 1621, ibid., p. 441. Apparently the location was somewhere on the company's property near Jamestown beyond the narrow neck that separated the peninsula from the mainland. See Henry Chandlee Forman, "The Bygone 'Subberbs of James Cittie'," *William and Mary Quarterly*, 2d ser., 20 (1940): 478.

14. "Treasurer and Company. Letter to Governor and Council in Virginia," July 25, 1621, in Kingsbury, ed., *Virginia Company*, 3: 488–89.

15. References to these activities may be found throughout the records of the London Company and the Virginia Council. They are summarized in a report to the king by the company dated April 12, 1623, "A Declaracon of the present State of Virginia humbly presented to the Kings most excellent Majesty by the Company for Virginia," ibid., 2: 348–51.

16. "Council in Virginia. Letter to Virginia Company of London," January 20, 1622/23, ibid., 4: 11–12; and "Council in Virginia. A Letter to the Virginia Company of London," April (after 20), 1622, ibid., 3: 613.

17. "Virginia Company. Instructions to the Governor and Council of State in Virginia," July 24, 1621, ibid., 477. The company also suggested to the governor and his council that with Claiborne's help "itt may be fitting and moste usefull to posteritie, to Cast an Imaginarye eye and view, where and which way the grand highwayes may bee like to strike and passe through the Dominions."

18. Land patent to Ralph Hamor in 1624, as quoted in Edward M. Riley and Charles E. Hatch, Jr., eds., *James Towne in the Words of Contemporaries*, p. 19.

19. Forman, "Bygone 'Subberbs'," 475–86.

20. Thomas J. Wertenbaker, *Virginia Under the Stuarts*, pp. 54–59.

21. "Instructions to Yeardley, 1626," *Virginia Magazine of History and Biography* 2 (1895): 394–95.

22. Act of the Virginia Assembly as quoted in Riley and Hatch, eds., *James Towne*, p. 23.

23. "Virginia Under Governor Harvey," *Virginia Magazine of History and Biography* 3 (1895): 29–30. Board of Trade, used here and hereinafter, is the commonly used designation for what at the time Governor Harvey wrote and through most of the seventeenth century was the Committee of the Privy Council for Trade and Plantations. Harvey's statement is a justification for his administration after he and the assembly had fallen into bitter conflict over his autocratic and arbitrary actions. In 1635 he had been forced to return to England to appear before the Privy Council to answer charges against him. He succeeded in obtaining a second commission as governor and was again in Virginia in 1636. In 1639 he was relieved of his office by the Privy Council. Under these circumstances we must regard with some reserve his claims of what was accomplished in Jamestown during his term of office. Harvey, like other colonial governors, was inclined to exaggerate his achievements.

24. This and other conjectural views of the buildings of Jamestown are based on archaeological findings on the site and the application of knowledge concerning seventeenth-century building practices in Virginia and England. While they doubtless convey generally accurate impressions of the appearance of the town's structures, it should be noted that there are differences of opinion among the authorities on their details and in many cases about the uses to which the various buildings were put. For an exhaustive technical account of the archaeological investigations of the Jamestown site see John L. Cotter, *Archeological Excavations at Jamestown*, and the sources cited in Cotter's bibliography. A briefer summary of some of the investigations at Jamestown appears in Ivor Noël Hume's *Here Lies Virginia*, pp. 37–73. Noël Hume's book is an informed and readable treatment of archaeology in tidewater Virginia.

25. Archaeological evidence dates this structure not earlier than 1650, but its structural details were similar to those employed at an earlier period. Cotter, *Jamestown*, p. 131.

26. Ibid., p. 67.

27. These and other quotations from the instructions to Berkeley are from "Instructions to Berkeley, 1642," *Virginia Magazine of History and Biography* 2 (1895): 281–88.

28. "Instructions to Berkeley, 1662," ibid., 3 (1895): 16–17.

29. For the text of the act from which this and other quotations are taken see William Waller Hening, ed., *The Statutes at Large . . . of Virginia,* 2: 172–76.

30. Philip Alexander Bruce, *Economic History of Virginia in the Seventeenth Century,* 2: 540. Bruce's pioneering study is still of great value, although more recent research has modified some of his findings and conclusions.

31. *Records of York County*, vol. 1657–1662: 475, as quoted in Bruce, ibid., p. 544, n.1.

32. Nathaniel Bacon, "The Declaration of the People," as quoted in Riley and Hatch, eds., *James Towne*, p. 28.

33. *A Narrative of the Indian and Civil Wars in Virginia, in the Years of 1675 and 1676*, in Peter Force, comp., *Tracts and Other Papers. . . .*, 1: 25.

34. "Instructions 13 Novem: 1633, directed by the Right Honorable Cecilius Lord Baltimore and Lord of the Provinces of Mary Land and Avalon . . .," in Clayton Colman Hall, ed., *Narratives of Early Maryland, 1633–1684*, pp. 21–22.

35. In his tract of 1635 Lord Baltimore described the site as "a very commodious situation for a Towne, in regard the land is good, the ayre wholsome and pleasant, the River affords a safe harbour for ships of any burthen, and a very bould shoare; fresh water, and wood there is in great plenty, and the place so naturally fortified, as with little difficultie, it will be defended from any enemie." Baltimore also related how the Indians agreed to make a part of their town available to the settlers immediately and to vacate the rest of it following the harvest. See *A Relation of Maryland* (London, 1635), in ibid., p. 73.

36. Letter from Leonard Calvert to Lord Baltimore,

May, 1634, in *Calvert Papers*, as quoted in Matthew Page Andrews, *History of Maryland: Province and State*, p. 32.

37. *A Relation of Maryland*, in Hall, *Narratives*, p. 74.

38. Ibid., p. 76 and n.2.

39. Andrews has summarized the policy as follows: " 'First settlers' who brought over as many as five persons were entitled to a grant of two thousand acres. When an immigrant brought over less than five, he received one hundred acres for each person over sixteen years of age, including himself and his wife, with fifty acres additional for every person under that age, the grants being subject to annual quitrents varying from twelve pence for every fifty acres in small holdings to twenty shillings for a manorial estate. These rents were to be paid to the Lord Proprietary 'in the commodities of the country.' An independent woman had like privileges as to transporting herself and other women and minors." Andrews, *Maryland*, p. 60.

40. See the map making up the back end papers of Henry Chandlee Forman, *Jamestown and St. Mary's: Buried Cities of Romance*.

41. Ibid., pp. 208–9.

42. Matthew Page Andrews, *The Founding of Maryland*, pp. 217–18.

43. The complete text of this act may be found in *Archives of Maryland* (Baltimore, 1883–), 2: 404–7. In its detail it is rivaled only by the later legislation in Virginia for the capitol at Williamsburg when that city was created in 1699 by an act to be examined in a later chapter.

44. Ibid., 5: 264–66.

45. George Alsop, *A Character of the Province of Maryland* (London, 1666), in Hall, *Narratives*, p. 363.

46. Ibid., pp. 363–64.

47. John Clayton, *A Letter . . . to the Royal Society*, May 12, 1688, in Force, *Tracts*, 3: 11.

48. "Anthony Langston on Towns, and Corporations: and on the Manufacture of Iron," *William and Mary Quarterly*, 2d ser., 1 (1921): 100–102.

49. For a brief summary of these and related policies see J. H. Parry, *Europe and a Wider World, 1415–1715*, pp. 120–26.

50. R. G., *Virginia's Cure: Or An Advisive Narrative Concerning Virginia* (London, 1622), in Force, *Tracts*, 3: 14–16.

51. The modal size of Maryland plantations was between 50 and 150 acres. V. J. Wyckoff, "The Sizes of Plantations in Seventeenth Century Maryland," *Maryland Historical Magazine* 32 (1937): 331–39.

52. Letter from William Fitzhugh to Dr. Ralph Smith, April 22, 1686, as quoted in Bruce, *Virginia*, 2: 243, n.1.

53. Henry Chandlee Forman, *Virginia Architecture in the Seventeenth Century*, p. 36.

54. Gilbert Chinard, ed. and trans., *A Huguenot Exile in Virginia* (New York, 1934), p. 142, as quoted in Hunter Dickinson Farish, ed., *Journal and Letters of Philip Vickers Fithian. . . .*, p. xxi.

55. John Oldmixon, *British Empire in America*, 2d ed. (London, 1741), 1: 339.

56. Johann David Schoepf, *Travels in the Confederation* [1783–1784], ed. and trans. Alfred J. Morrison, p. 32. A few years later Isaac Weld's travel account included an almost identical observation that every large plantation "gives the appearance of a village." Isaac Weld, *Travels Through the States of North America*, 1: 148.

57. The original manuscript by George Washington from which this engraved copy was made for publication in 1801 is in the collection of the Henry E. Huntington Library and Art Gallery, San Marino, California.

CHAPTER IV.

1. An unidentified and undated document, probably of 1678 or 1679, which may have been prepared for discussion by the king's advisers, contains this passage summarizing the recommended policy: "That there be towns built . . . on each great River if possible, And in order thereunto that after sufficient notice to provide Warehouses and other conveniences, no ships whatsoever be permitted to load or unload but at the said places where the towns are designed. . . . And in case different Interests hinder the Assembly there from agreeing [upon] the places His Majesty . . . [is] to direct them and to grant them all necessary privileges as to Trade and Markets but not to Incorporate any, or to give them any share in the Government and particularly not to choose Burgesses." "Proposals in Regard to Virginia," *Virginia Magazine of History and Biography* 25 (1917): 72.

2. Leonard Woods Labaree, ed., *Royal Instructions to British Colonial Governors, 1670–1776*, 2: 545. These instructions remained in force from 1679 to 1705.

3. "Speech of Governor Lord Culpeper. His Excellencies first Speech to the Assembly begunne at James Citty June: 8th 1680," *Virginia Magazine of History and Biography* 14 (1907): 364.

4. William Waller Hening, ed., *The Statutes at Large . . . of Virginia* 2: 471–78.

5. Edward M. Riley, "The Town Acts of Colonial Virginia," *Journal of Southern History* 16 (1950): 309–10. This valuable study emphasizes the relationship between the various town acts of Virginia and trade policy. See also Philip Alexander Bruce, *Economic History of Virginia in the Seventeenth Century*, 2: 547–61; and Edward F. Heite, "Markets and Ports," *Virginia Cavalcade* 16 (1966): 29–41.

6. John Clayton, *A Letter . . . to the Royal Society, May 12, 1688*, in Peter Force, *Tracts*, 3: 11.

7. Letters from Col. Nicholas Spencer to Mr. Secretary Coventry, July 9 and August 20, 1680, "Virginia in 1680," *Virginia Magazine of History and Biography* 25 (1917): 144, 147.

8. Letter from William Byrd I to Perry and Lane, June 3, 1691, "Letters of William Byrd, First," *Virginia Magazine of History and Biography* 28 (1920): 12.

9. Letter from William Fitzhugh to Captain Francis Partis, July 1, 1680, in Richard Beale Davis, ed., *William Fitzhugh and his Chesapeake World, 1676–1701*, p. 82. Fitzhugh strongly supported Governor Culpeper's town development policy. See his letter to Culpeper, January 8, 1683, p. 134.

10. *Records of Rappahannock County*, vol. 1680–1688, Virginia State Library, 2, as cited in Bruce, *Virginia*, 2: 552–53.

11. Hening, *Statutes*, 3: 59.

12. Tappahannock developed into a port of some consequence and became a regional trading center of importance to plantation owners in the vicinity. The diary of Colonel Landon Carter, whose great residence, Sabine Hall, lay across the river to the north in Richmond County, contains numerous references to articles purchased there, trips to the town by him or members of his family, and the activity in the port. See Jack P. Greene, ed., The *Diary of Colonel Landon Carter of Sabine Hall, 1752–1778*, 2 vols. (Charlottesville, 1965).

13. Isaac Weld, *Travels Through the States of North America . . . During the Years 1795, 1796, and 1797*, 1: 158.

14. Hening, *Statutes*, 3: 59.

15. Ralph T. Whitelaw, *Virginia's Eastern Shore* (Richmond, 1951), 2: 904.

16. Ibid., 2: 905; Nora Miller Turman, *The Eastern Shore of Virginia, 1603–1964*, p. 84.

17. Marvin W. Schlegel, "The Shire or County of Elizabeth City," in Rogers Day Whichard, *The History of Lower Tidewater Virginia*, 1: 128–29.

18. John Fontaine, "Journal of John Fontaine," in Ann Maury, ed., *Memoirs of a Huguenot Family. . . . in 1715 and 1716*, p. 293.

19. Weld, *Travels*, 1: 169.

20. On this drawing the "north point" incorrectly points south! The numbers refer to a billeting list that has not survived.

21. For the growth of Hampton during the eighteenth and nineteenth centuries see Marvin W. Schlegel, "Elizabeth City County and the Town of Hampton, 1700–1814," in Whichard, *Lower Tidewater Virginia* 1: 135–69.

22. My chief source of information about the founding and early development of Norfolk is the scholarly and exhaustive work by Whichard, *Lower Tidewater Virginia*, 1: 257–58; 325–414. I have also used this as a source in dealing with the other planned towns in the lower Tidewater. The other helpful work is Thomas J. Wertenbaker's pioneering study, *Norfolk: Historic Southern Port*, as revised and edited by Marvin W. Schlegel.

23. A plat of this land showing its division into a single, elongated tier of lots is reproduced in Whichard, *Lower Tidewater Virginia*, 1: 353.

24. William Byrd II, *The History of the Dividing Line betwixt Virginia and North Carolina, Run in the Year of Our Lord 1728*, in Louis B. Wright, ed., *The Prose Works of William Byrd of Westover*, p. 173.

25. The act of 1691, which redesignated most of the sites selected in 1680, also indicated briefly the places where some structures had been built under the previous act. In addition to Tappahannock, Onancock, Hampton, and Norfolk, these towns were: Flowerdew Hundred in Charles City County; Paitesfield in Isle of Wight County; Nansemond Town in Nansemond County; Warwick in Warwick County; and Urbanna in Middlesex County. Although the act of 1691 mentioned that in the latter place there was "a warehouse built," other evidence shows that the town had not in fact been planned before 1691. Of these eight communities begun under the 1680 legislation I have been able to locate plans only of the four discussed in the text.

26. *Calendar of State Papers, Colonial Series, America and the West Indies, 1681–85* (London, 1898), p. 152.

27. The text of the order in council can be found in Hening, *Statutes*, 2: 508.

28. Report of Lord Culpeper to the Board of Trade, September 20, 1683, *Calendar of State Papers, 1681–85*, p. 497.

29. H. R. McIlwaine, ed., *Journals of the House of Burgesses of Virginia, 1659/60–1693*, p. 251.

30. Lord Howard's explanation for his action, which caused intense ill feeling on the part of the burgesses, can be found in a letter from him to the Board of Trade, *Journals of the House of Burgesses, 1659/60–1693*, pp. 503–5.

31. Those omitted, as described in the act of 1680, were "In Henrico county att Verina where the court house is," "In Surry county att Smiths fort," "In Isle of Wight county at Pates field att the parting of Pagen Creeke," "In New Kent county att the Brick house . . .," "In Warwick county att the mouth of Deep creek on Mr. Mathews land," and "In Westmerland county att Nomenie on the land of Mr. Hardricke." The towns for the following counties as described in the 1691 act differ from the descriptions given in 1680: Gloucester, Stafford, Northampton, and Lancaster. Another new site in 1691 is described as "for the upper parts of Yorke River at West Point."

32. Three of these market towns had been created as ports in 1680: Patesfield, in Isle of Wight County; Warwick, in Warwick County; and the Westmoreland County site "att Nomenie on the land of Mr. Hardricke." The other two were described as follows in the 1691 act: "for Henrico County at Bermuda hundred poynt, on the land belonging to the wife of John Woodson," and "for Surry County at the mouth of Grays Creeke on the lower side thereof." The latter town, Cobham, was about four miles downstream from the previously designated port for the county "att Smiths fort."

33. For the complete text of this act see Hening, *Statutes*, 3: 53–69.

34. While Buckner drew the plan in August, the formal survey was delayed until October 9. C. Malcolm Watkins, *The Cultural History of Marlborough, Virginia*, pp. 7–8. Watkins's study contains not only a valuable history of the attempts at town promotion at Marlborough but a complete report of archaeological investigations on the site. Some of the information provided by Watkins is at variance with previous published accounts of Marlborough, but I have relied on this later investigation as authoritative.

35. For other accounts of Marlborough see "Petition of John Mercer," *Virginia Magazine of History and Biography* 5 (1898): 278–82; and Oscar H. Darter, "Where the West Began: Historical Sketch of Old Marleborough Town Stafford County, Virginia," *Northern Neck of Virginia Historical Magazine* 9 (1959): 801–11.

36. Wesley Newton Laing, "Urbanna's Tobacco Warehouse," Association for the Preservation of Virginia Antiquities, *Report on a Building at Urbanna, Virginia* (Richmond, 1961), is the source of this and other information about Urbanna.

37. Harry Toulmin, *The Western Country in 1793*, ed. Marion Tinling and Godfrey Davies, p. 31.

38. See Malcolm H. Harris, "'Delaware Town' and 'West Point' in King William County, Va.," *William and Mary Quarterly*, 2d ser., 14 (1934): 345–46. I have relied on this article for my information about Delaware Town and Dr. Harris's reconstruction of its original plan from early land records.

39. Hening, *Statutes*, 3: 212, 418.

40. York County Records, as quoted in "History of York County in the Seventeenth Century," *Tyler's Quarterly Historical and Genealogical Magazine* 1 (1920): 256–57. This article, presumably written by Lyon G. Tyler, is a valuable summary of the history of the county and its chief town. I have drawn freely on this source as well as from two works by Edward M. Riley: "The Colonial Courthouses of York County, Virginia," *William and Mary Quarterly*, 2d ser., 22 (1942): 399–414; and "Suburban Development of Yorktown, Virginia, During the Colonial Period," *Virginia Magazine of History and Biography* 60 (1952): 522–36.

41. As was usual, the payment was for 10,000 pounds of tobacco "and cask." The latter words meant the cost of packing the tobacco, for which an additional 800 pounds of tobacco were paid. Colonel Smith received 500 pounds of tobacco, plus 40 pounds "to caske" for his boundary survey. There was also a payment to the sheriff for his work. Altogether, to acquire

the land, have it surveyed, and laid out into streets and lots cost the county 15,216 pounds of tobacco.

42. A note in the upper right corner of Smith's boundary survey refers to this land as containing about five acres between the boundary line and the river "for a common shore of no value."

43. Hening, *Statutes*, 3: 146–47.

44. Among the trades represented by purchasers of these lots were the following: carpenter, butcher, barber, blacksmith, wheelwright, tailor, and cordwainer. York had obviously become a town of diversified occupations.

45. [Edward Kimber], "Observations in Several Voyages and Travels in America," *London Magazine*, 1745–1746, as quoted in *William and Mary Quarterly* 1st ser., 15 (1907): 222.

46. Riley, "Suburban Development of Yorktown," 527–28.

47. Isaac Weld, *Travels*, 1: 163, 165.

48. Robert Beverley, *The History of Virginia*, 2d ed. p. 89.

49. Hening, *Statutes*, 3: 108–9. The act had been considered in England by the Board of Trade, which approved in principle but believed that port facilities should be constructed first before compelling all trade to flow through the designated port towns. On June 27, 1692, the commissioners referred the matter to the General Assembly suggesting the act be amended. *Calendar of State Papers, Colonial Series, 1689–1692*, p. 611.

50. This third attempt at creating official ports apparently originated in a petition to the Board of Trade submitted on March 29, 1705, by the lord high treasurer, the commissioners of customs, and a number of English merchants. *Calendar of State Papers, Colonial Series, 1704–1705*, p. 464. The text of Queen Anne's instructions to Nott may be found in Labaree, ed., *Instructions*, 2: 545–46.

51. The sites are listed in two places in the act. The first list does not include Urbanna, apparently an oversight since it appears in the second list which gives the days authorized for markets and the annual fair. The first list also includes Tindall's Point (or Gloucester Point) as part of the town and port of York across the river. Including Tindall's Point brings the number to seventeen. With one or two possible exceptions, the sites selected had previously been designated for this purpose in either 1680 or 1691.

52. For the complete text of the act see Hening, *Statutes*, 3: 404–19.

53. Weld, *Travels*, 1: 163.

54. See the transcript of a conveyance of four lots sold by Robert Carter as feoffee to Thomas Hopper for 190 pounds of tobacco each in James Wharton, "The Lost Settlement of Queenstown," *Northern Neck of Virginia Historical Magazine* 10 (1960): 877–88.

55. Whitelaw, *Eastern Shore*, 1: 173.

56. Hening, *Statutes*, 9: 240.

57. For the history of Cobham see A. W. Bohannan, "The Old Town of Cobham," *Virginia Magazine of History and Biography* 57 (1949): 252–68. By 1777 the town had declined to such a condition that a visitor could describe it only as "a paltry shabby Village, consisting of about a dozen Houses." Fred Shelley, ed., "The Journal of Ebenezer Hazard in Virginia, 1777," *Virginia Magazine of History and Biography* 62 (1954): 411.

58. See their report in Great Britain, Board of Trade, *Journal of the Commissioners for Trade and Plantations, 1704–1708/9*, 1: 309.

59. *Calendar of Virginia State Papers* (Richmond, 1875), 1: 138.

60. R. A. Brock, ed., *The Official Letters of Alexander Spotswood*, 1: 9.

61. H. R. McIlwaine, ed., *Journals of the House of Burgesses of Virginia, 1702–1712*, 4: 321–24.

CHAPTER V.

1. One pioneer Maryland historian who wrestled with this problem summed up the difficulties: "That uncertainty exists as to the sites of some of these ancient vanished towns, is less surprising when we consider the imperfection of the topographical knowledge of the province, and the way in which they were described, which was usually 'on such a river,' or 'creek,' 'on Mr. A's land,' or 'near Mr. B's plantation.' Since then the land has passed to other owners, the stream has changed its name, perhaps its course, or disappeared altogether; the harbor has been choked up, and we cannot even conjecture the spot on which once such hopes were built." J. Thomas Scharf, *History of Maryland*, 1: 411.

2. *Archives of Maryland*, 5: 31.

3. Ibid., 47–48.

4. Those places containing such references are listed in the ordinances as follows: "in Charles County in Wicocomico River as near the Town land as Ships . . . can conveniently Ride," "in Ann Arundell afore the Town Land purchased of Richard Acton," "in Baltimore County afore the Town Land in Bush River," and "in Talbot County afore the Town Land in Chester River and afore the Town Land in Truduven in Choptank in the same County." As in the previous proclamation, St. Mary's was also listed as one of the official ports.

5. *Archives of Maryland*, 5: 92–94.

6. I am deeply indebted to Mr. Richard Anglin for preparing this and two similar maps to follow. They are the result of intensive study of old and modern maps and charts of Maryland, county histories, and the various enactments listing the sites with their usual vague descriptions. His work was carried out in 1968 as part of a graduate seminar project under my direction in the Department of City and Regional Planning at Cornell University.

7. *Archives of Maryland*, 7: 278–80.

8. John Ogilby, *America: Being the Latest, and Most Accurate Description of the New World. . .*, p. 189.

9. For a detailed listing of the place names shown on the Herrman map see J. Louis Kuethe, "A Gazetteer of Maryland, A.D. 1673," *Maryland Historical Magazine* 30 (1935): 310–25.

10. *Archives of Maryland*, 7: 343.

11. Ibid., 349–51.

12. Ibid., 368–69.

13. Ibid., 379–80.

14. One of several examples of this strategy appears in a message from the lower house on October 9, 1863, ibid., 459–61.

15. Ibid., 540–41.

16. Ibid., 609–19, for the text of the act from which subsequent quotations are taken.

17. Ibid., 17: 219–20.

18. Ibid., 358.

19. Ibid., 5: 496.

20. Ibid., 13: 114.

21. The act made it clear that already platted streets and lots within the existing "Citty of St. Maries" were not to be affected by the legislation, but that an additional one hundred acres of land adjoining the city was to be platted for the purposes of the act on land granted by Lord Baltimore. This single exemption suggests strongly that at no other of the now forty-six

sites had a town been planned prior to the act of 1683.

22. Ibid., 17: 403–4.

23. Ibid., 408–10.

24. Ibid., 5: 497.

25. Ibid., 500–2. These instructions included the names of the officers and listed the towns in each county. For some reason only thirty-five towns are named, although in the two acts a total of forty-four had been designated by the assembly.

26. Ibid., 13: 132–39.

27. Ibid., 5: 563–65.

28. Ibid., 8: 3–4.

29. Ibid., 61.

30. Ibid., 13: 219.

31. Ibid., 26: 332–33.

32. Leonard Woods Labaree, ed., *Royal Instructions to British Colonial Governors 1670–1776*, 2: 539–40.

33. *Archives of Maryland*, 26: 636–45.

34. Ibid., 27: 163–64.

35. The rolling houses were so called throughout the Tidewater because of the method used in transporting hogsheads of tobacco by land. The hogshead became in effect a wide wheel turning on short axles fixed to the two ends and was "rolled" to its destination by oxen or horses harnessed to a yoke.

36. Ibid., 346–49.

37. Ibid., 164.

38. Lord Adam Gordon, *Journal of an Officer who Travelled in America and the West Indies in 1764 and 1765*, in Newton D. Mereness, ed., *Travels in the American Colonies*, p. 409.

39. *Archives of Maryland*, 26: 636.

40. Ibid., 7: 279.

41. Ibid., 36: 581–83; Charles Francis Stein, *A History of Calvert County Maryland*, p. 96.

42. Gordon, *Journal*, p. 409. For the history of Londontown see Henry J. Berkley, "Londontown on South River, Anne Arundel County, Md.," *Maryland Historical Magazine* 19 (1924): 134–41.

43. George Armistead Leakin, "The Migrations of Baltimore Town," *Maryland Historical Magazine* 1 (1906): 45–59.

44. The possible locations of Somerset Town are discussed in Clayton Torrence, *Old Somerset on the Eastern Shore of Maryland*, pp. 410–13. This study also contains much useful material on Green Hill and the other early towns of Somerset County.

45. According to Torrence, these were not the only resurveys of the town. He indicates that county records show that "prior to June, 1728, Snow Hill Town had been 'laid out' three times." The survey of 1793 and supporting material can be found in Worcester County Records, Deed Book P, 286–93.

46. This manuscript volume in the Maryland Hall of Records is entitled "Establishment of Vienna Towne, 1706."

47. Elias Jones, *New Revised History of Dorchester County Maryland*, p. 85.

48. *Archives of Maryland*, 13: 112.

49. The only other plan of Cambridge I have been able to locate is an almost illegible manuscript drawing in the Maryland Hall of Records. It is dated 1799, and an accompanying title sheet bears the following legend: "Certificate & Plott of Cambridge Town Filed January 16th 1799 in the time of Henry Dickinson Clerk of Dorchester County Court."

50. *Archives of Maryland*, 19: 100–13.

51. Land Records of Talbot County, No. 1, 47, as quoted in Oswald Tilghman, *History of Talbot County Maryland, 1661–1861*, 2: 335. Tilghman's study, "compiled principally from the literary relics of the late Samuel Alexander Harrison," is a particularly useful local history containing much source material, adequately identified, on early towns of Talbot County.

52. See the citations of these documents in ibid., 336–37.

53. Proceedings of the commissioners, in ibid., 340.

54. *Archives of Maryland*, 19: 211.

55. Proceedings of the commissioners, as quoted in Tilghman, *Talbot County*, 348. Tilghman summarizes the difficulties of deciding on land ownership as well as other problems facing the commissioners, 344–49.

56. Recollections of Philemon Willis, as summarized in ibid., 363.

57. Ibid., 125.

58. *Archives of Maryland*, 27: 564–66.

59. Ibid., 37: 172–77.

60. Ibid., 516.

61. For dates of these and other buildings as well as for much other useful information about Chestertown I have drawn on the fine guide to the city edited by M. P. White, Jr. and Ralph U. Usilton, *A Guide to Historic Chestertown Maryland*. See also Robert L. Swain, Jr., "Chestertown as a Colonial Port, 1706–1775," *Washington College Bulletin* 14 (1936): 1–15.

62. Erich Isaac, "Kent Island, Part II: Settlement and Land Holding under the Proprietary," *Maryland Historical Magazine* 52 (1957): 217, 221–22. The much earlier settlement of Kent Island by William Claiborne in 1631 did not apparently result in the creation of any nucleated community.

63. Peregrine Wroth, "New Yarmouth," *Maryland Historical Magazine* 3 (1908): 273–76; Morris L. Radoff, *The County Courthouses and Records of Maryland. Part One: The Courthouses*, pp. 105–6.

64. Hugh Jones, *The Present State of Virginia*, ed. Richard L. Morton, p. 73.

65. Thomas Jefferson, *Notes on the State of Virginia*, pp. 152–54.

CHAPTER VI.

1. Matthew Page Andrews, *The Founding of Maryland*, pp. 226–28; Walter B. Norris, *Annapolis: Its Colonial and Naval Story*, pp. 10–13; Elihu S. Riley, *"The Ancient City"; A History of Annapolis, in Maryland, 1649–1887*, pp. 17–19; John Langford, *Refutation of Babylon's Fall* (London, 1655), in Clayton Colman Hall, ed., *Narratives of Early Maryland, 1633–1684*, pp. 254–55.

2. The county was named for Anne Arundel, the wife of the second Lord Baltimore and daughter of the earl of Arundel. When, in 1695, the town was officially designated Annapolis, it was a different Anne who inspired the name—Princess (later Queen) Anne, the daughter of James II.

3. *Archives of Maryland*, 5: 31.

4. Ibid., 7: 609.

5. Ibid., 17: 144. For this reference and much additional information concerning the events leading to the founding of Annapolis I have relied on Eugenia Calvert Holland, "Anne Arundel Takes Over from St. Mary's," *Maryland Historical Magazine* 44 (1949): 42–51.

6. *Archives of Maryland*, 7: 517.

7. A summary of Copley's administration can be found in Andrews, *Founding of Maryland*, pp. 327–34.

8. *Archives of Maryland*, 19: 110–13.

9. Ibid., 38: 23–25.

10. The complete text of the petition may be found in ibid., 19: 71–75.

11. The text of the reply dated October 11, 1694, is given in Riley, *"The Ancient City,"* pp. 61–62.

12. *Archives of Maryland*, 28: 23–25.

13. Ibid., 19: 208–9.

14. Morris L. Radoff, *Buildings of the State of Maryland at Annapolis*, p. 3; *Archives of Maryland*, 19: 211.

15. *Archives of Maryland*, 19: 502.

16. Ibid., 122.

17. Ibid., 522.

18. In the archives of St. Mary's Church in Annapolis there is another manuscript copy of the Stoddert drawing virtually identical to that in figure 81 and probably of the same age. A photocopy of this is in the Maryland Hall of Records.

19. The plan of the London Bloomsbury Square is rather different from that designed by Nicholson. See figure 17 (Chapter I) for the plan of the London counterpart in 1746.

20. In an unpublished report prepared for Historic Annapolis, Inc., Robert Kerr attempted to reconstruct the plan of 1684 from Beard's certificate of survey. Kerr's report is a valuable study of the plan and the architecture of Annapolis, and it is unfortunate that it has never been published by the organization that sponsored his work.

21. Nicholson's early career is described by Bruce T. McCully in his "From the North Riding to Morocco: The Early Years of Governor Francis Nicholson, 1655–1686," *William and Mary Quarterly*, 3d ser. 19 (1962): 534–56. A full biographical study does not exist, and only two other sources are of substantial value: Stephen Saunders Webb, "The Strange Career of Francis Nicholson," *William and Mary Quarterly*, ibid., 23 (1966): 513–48; and Charles Dalton, *George the First's Army, 1714–1727* (London, 1912), 2: 54–62.

22. Webb, "Francis Nicholson," 533.

23. Henry Hartwell, James Blair, and Edward Chilton, *The Present State of Virginia, and the College*, ed. with an introd. by Hunter Dickinson Farish, pp. 68–72. Although not published until thirty years later, this work was written in 1697.

24. The attribution of the college building to Wren has always been a matter of debate. It rests on the assertion made by Hugh Jones who came to Virginia in 1716: "The building is beautiful and commodious, being first modelled by Sir Christopher Wren, adapted to the nature of the country by the gentlemen there; and since it was burnt down, it has been rebuilt. . . ." Hugh Jones, *The Present State of Virginia*, ed. with an introd. by Richard L. Morton, p. 67. Whiffen concludes that "there remains much to be said" for the case that Wren or someone in his office designed the building, while adding that "it is as open as any such question can be." Marcus Whiffen, *The Public Buildings of Williamsburg*, pp. 32–33. Morton, in discussing Blair's activities in London on behalf of the college, observes "Blair would naturally have concerned himself with the buildings of the College when he was in London to secure a charter, and the most suitable person to consult was Sir Christopher Wren, Surveyor General of buildings for the Crown." Jones, *Virginia*, p. 185, n.65.

25. See the text of the college charter in Hartwell, Blair, and Chilton, *Present State of Virginia*, p. 84.

26. Webb, "Francis Nicholson," p. 532.

27. Nicholson's catalogue is reprinted with additional notes in John Melville Jennings, "Notes on the Original Library of the College of William and Mary in Virginia, 1693–1705," *The Papers of the Bibliographical Society of America* 41 (1947): 258–67.

28. The influence of Renaissance European garden design on town planning was substantial. I have summarized this in my *The Making of Urban America*, pp. 22–24. The most obvious, although later, connection between European landscape layout and American town planning can be seen in the plan of Washington, D.C., prepared by the Frenchman, Pierre Charles L'Enfant, in 1791. His plan resembles in scale and style the design of Versailles where L'Enfant spent part of his youth. This point is discussed briefly in Chapter X. See also Reps, *Monumental Washington*, pp. 5–8 for a fuller treatment of the Versailles plan as a source of inspiration for L'Enfant.

29. John Evelyn, *Sylva, or A Discourse of Forest-Trees, and the Propagation of Timber in His Majesties Dominions*, pp. 239, 240.

30. John Evelyn, *London Revived*, ed. E. S. de Beer, pp. 37, 47.

31. In an act of 1696 providing, among other things, for the location of certain activities beyond the town boundaries, the listing of trades closely resembles that used by Evelyn: "Baker Brewer Tanner Dyer." *Archives of Maryland*, 19: 503.

32. See de Beer's editorial notes in Evelyn, *London Revived*, p. 2.

33. The text of this letter and others quoted or referred to subsequently can be found in Ruth Bourne, "John Evelyn the Diarist, and his Cousin Daniel Parke II," *Virginia Magazine of History and Biography* 78 (1970): 3–33. Professor Bourne also summarizes the confusing genealogy of the Evelyn family and Parke's relationship to the Evelyns. Other (and conflicting) sources are: Lyon Gardiner Tyler, ed., *Encyclopedia of Virginia Biography* (New York, 1915), 1: 143–44; Annie Lash Jester, comp. and ed., *Adventures of Purse and Person: Virginia 1607–1625*, pp. 165–68; and E. S. de Beer, ed., *The Diary of John Evelyn*, 1: 1–4; 5: 574–75, n.2.

34. Parke finally achieved his ambition. He served on the council from June 11, 1695, to April 23, 1697. He was reappointed on December 9, 1698, by Governor Nicholson whose instructions so directed. *Executive Journals of the Council of Virginia*, 1. The statements in Jester, *Adventurers*, p. 167, and Tyler, *Virginia Biography*, 1: 143 that Parke was appointed to the council first in 1692 are incorrect.

35. Two other possible sources of inspiration for Nicholson's radial plan for Annapolis should be mentioned. The first is a work by the great French military engineer, Sébastien le Prestre de Vauban. The second English edition of his treatise was published in London in 1693 under the title, *A New Method of Fortification*. The previous English edition of 1691 included a plate showing a model city with radial streets leading outward to the fortifications from a central *place*. The new edition added among others, a plate of the plan of Charleroi in Belgium which had a similar street pattern. As an English officer, Nicholson almost surely saw this volume although it is not listed among the books of his library. The second source on which he may have drawn is the plan of the gardens of Hampton Court Palace near London, which at the time of Nicholson's extended visit to England were being laid out on a new design prepared by Daniel Marot. Marot, a versatile Dutch designer of Huguenot extraction, had been brought to England for this purpose by William and Mary. His new plan included several circular open spaces as well as diagonal garden paths. For a reproduction of a portion of his plan see P. Jessen, *Das Ornamentwerk des Daniel Marot* (Berlin, 1892), p. 252. Marot's plan is also reproduced, along with a view of the gardens in 1707 showing the design as executed, in Arthur Lane, "Daniel Marot: Designer of Delft Vases and of Gardens at Hampton Court," *The Connoisseur* 123 (1940): 19–24.

36. The status of construction is described and

Nicholson's recommendations for advancing the work are listed in *Archives of Maryland*, 19: 285-87.

37. A description by Mrs. Rebecca Key in 1754, as quoted in Radoff, *Buildings*, p. 15. Radoff's work is a valuable source of information on which I have relied for most of my information concerning the civic structures of the town.

38. The details of the building of the third statehouse can be traced in Radoff, *Buildings*, pp. 81–110.

39. Ibid., pp. 45–47.

40. Ibid., pp. 17–22.

41. For a detailed identification of the buildings shown in the view, see I. N. Phelps Stokes and Daniel C. Haskell, *American Historical Prints*, pp. 80–82.

42. *Archives of Maryland*, 19: 36.

43. Radoff, *Buildings*, pp. 23–31; *Archives of Maryland*, 36: 498.

44. Radoff, *Buildings*, pp. 48–54.

45. Ibid., pp. 63–65.

46. Ibid., pp. 66–70.

47. Ibid., pp. 32–40; *Archives of Maryland*, 39: 472–73. The third prison was virtually destroyed during the Revolution when it was occupied by Continental soldiers. A fourth prison was eventually built on Calvert Street near Northwest Street and later became the county jail.

48. Radoff, *Buildings*, pp. 41–44.

49. *Archives of Maryland*, 36: 282–83. This act authorized city officials to sell the market square as laid out by Nicholson and use the proceeds for the erection of the new market house on the harbor.

50. "A letter from the Reverend Mr. Hugh Jones to the Reverend Dr. Benjamin Woodroffe, F.R.S., concerning severall observables in Maryland," *Journal of Southern History* 29 (1963): 371–72. This letter, with editorial notes by Michael G. Kammen, is from one of the four clergymen with identical names who were in Virginia or Maryland in the latter part of the seventeenth and early part of the eighteenth centuries. He should not be confused with his more famous namesake who wrote *The Present State of Virginia*, and whose observations on Williamsburg are discussed in Chapter VII.

51. The complete text of this long act appears in *Archives of Maryland*, 19: 498–504, from which the subsequent quotations are taken.

52. Ibid., 33: 292.

53. Riley, "*The Ancient City*," 64. Riley, writing in 1887, states that this house, which stood "until fifteen years since . . . was of frame and of an architecture curious and ancient." It seems doubtful that Nicholson actually lived in the house. In 1695 he resided in a dwelling believed to have been constructed by Major Edward Dorsey located on Prince George Street just south of North East Street (now Maryland Avenue).

54. Lord Adam Gordon, who visited Annapolis in 1764, commented that "the timbers and Roof, tho' ready, never closed in or Shingled—and from the Weather and Moisture, is now become so much damaged, as never again to be in a condition, to be repaired or finished." Lord Adam Gordon, "Journal of an Officer who Travelled in America and the West Indies in 1764 and 1765," in Newton D. Mereness, *Travels in the American Colonies*, p. 408.

55. Radoff, *Buildings*, pp. 77–80.

56. William Eddis, *Letters from America*, p. 17. See also Radoff, *Buildings*, pp. 71–76 for the history of this building which, unhappily, was demolished in 1901. A photograph of it is reproduced by Radoff following page 47 as plate 13. A very small view of the building also appears in the legend of the view of Annapolis reproduced in figure 93. The present Governor's Mansion, as extensively remodeled in 1936, was begun in 1868 on a site between Statehouse and Church circles.

57. Ebenezer Cook, *The Sot-Weed Factor: or, A Voyage to Maryland*, pp. 24–25.

58. Rufus Rockwell Wilson, ed., *Burnaby's Travels Through North America* (New York, 1904), p. 81. Burnaby's account was first published in 1775 and reissued in enlarged form in 1798, the latter version being the one edited by Wilson.

59. Eddis, *Letters*, pp. 14–18.

60. Philip Padelford, ed., *Colonial Panorama, 1775: Dr. Robert Honyman's Journal for March and April*, p. 6.

61. Gordon, "Journal," in Mereness, *Travels*, p. 408.

62. J. F. D. Smyth, *A Tour in the United States of America*, 2: 185.

63. François Alexandre Frédéric, duc de la Rochefoucauld-Liancourt, *Travels Through the United States of North America . . .*, 2d ed. (London, 1800), 2: 579–80.

CHAPTER VII.

1. James Blair, who had been instrumental in securing Nicholson's appointment as governor of Virginia, had submitted such a recommendation the previous fall in a memorandum prepared for John Locke, who then served as an expert adviser to the Board of Trade. Writing on the absence of towns and the means by which their growth might be stimulated, Blair suggested that all of the officials of the colony should be required to reside at the chief town where the General Assembly should sit, "and if this were the same place where the Colledge is (which for health and all other Conveniences is the fittest place in the Country for such a Town) this would make one good Town at once." Michael G. Kammen ed., "Virginia at the Close of the Seventeenth Century: An Appraisal by James Blair and John Locke," *Virginia Magazine of History and Biography*, 74 (1966): 157–58. Although Nicholson and Blair were later to become enemies, at this time they were closely associated through their interest in the College of William and Mary.

2. Angus W. McDonald, Transcripts—Miscellaneous, 1619–1626 [Ms. transcripts from the British Public Record Office] Virginia State Library, 1: 297–98, as cited in Rutherfoord Goodwin, *A Brief and True Report Concerning Williamsburg in Virginia*, pp. 128–29. Goodwin's work is an invaluable and compact source of information with copious notes and quotations from early printed and manuscript sources.

3. The act directed the establishment of a "plantation of several families near the house recently built by Dr. John Pott." It offered fifty acres of land and exemption from taxes and charges to all men who would settle in this area, build houses, and secure the settlement against Indian attack. William Waller Hening, ed., *The Statutes at Large . . . of Virginia*, 1: 208–9.

4. Ibid., 3: 122.

5. F. A. Winder, Virginia Manuscripts from British Public Record Office, Virginia State Archives, 2: 84–85, as quoted in Goodwin, *Williamsburg*, p. 12. Goodwin records the scornful reply from the commissioners: "That the Town now burnt should be removed to the *Midle Plantation* which is noe other than if *Midlesex* should have desired, that *London* might have beene new built on *Highgat* Hill, and removed from the

grand River that brings them in their Trade. Ibid., p. 159.

6. The texts of all five orations are reprinted in *William and Mary Quarterly,* 2d ser. 10 (1930): 323–37, from contemporary transcripts preserved in the archives of the Society for the Propagation of the Gospel in London.

7. H. R. McIlwaine, ed., *Journals of the House of Burgesses of Virginia, 1695–1702,* [3:] 167. In submitting this recommendation Nicholson disregarded one provision of his instructions: "Whereas His Majesty is given to understand, that James Town is not only the most ancient but supposed to be the most convenient Place for the Metropolis of the Said Colony; you are to direct all possible means to be used for the speedy rebuilding, and enlargement of the same, as also to take care that the Chief Port, the usual place of your Residence, the Chief Court of Justice, and other publick offices, attending the Government, be settled and continued in that Place." Instructions for Francis Nicholson, September 13, 1698, C.O. 324/26, Grants and Warrants, 1698–1700, Public Record Office, from microfilm in research library of Colonial Williamsburg. Nicholson was conscious that his action might be invalidated. On July 1, 1699, from Jamestown he addressed a long communication to the Board of Trade. Near the end he added: "I enclose . . . a draft of the City of Williamsburgh, of Queen's Port and Princess Port, according to the Act for Building the Capitol and City of Williamsburgh. There are as many reasons against keeping the seat of government here as there are for removing it to Middle Plantation, and I hope the Act will be passed." Cecil Headlam, ed., *Calendar of State Papers, Colonial Series, America and West Indies, 1699,* 17: 314. The "draft" referred to was the survey reproduced in figure 98.

8. Bland's survey is dated June 2, 1699. This work would have required many days, perhaps several weeks, to complete. It is quite possible that Nicholson had assigned him this task even before the May 1 meeting at Middle Plantation. See "The Building of Williamsburg," *William and Mary Quarterly,* 1st ser. 10 (1901): 75–77 for the metes and bounds description of the site taken from Board of Trade Papers, Virginia, 3. Since the survey text refers to the "maine Street of the Towne of Six Poles broad" and to the location "on which the Statehouse is to be erected," it is evident that preliminary planning of some of the major elements of the new town had already been completed. Moreover, the act passed by the assembly on June 7 refers to this survey "now lying in the Assembly Office." This plat or a similar drawing was sent to England by Nicholson and referred to in his letter of July 1, 1699. *Calendar of State Papers,* . . . 17: 314.

9. *Journals of the House of Burgesses, 1695–1702,* [3:] 199, and H. R. McIlwaine, ed., *Legislative Journals of the Council of Colonial Virginia,* 1: 276.

10. *William and Mary Quarterly,* 2d ser. 10 (1930): 322.

11. This and subsequent quotations from the act are from the complete text in Goodwin, *Williamsburg,* pp. 335–49.

12. For a discussion of this feature of the first plan for the Capitol, see Marcus Whiffen, *The Public Buildings of Williamsburg,* pp. 37–39.

13. As early as 1700 lots were being conveyed by reference to lot numbers, indicating the existence of such a plan. Lots 43, 44, and 45, for example, were conveyed by the trustees to Philip Ludwell in this manner. See note 42.

14. John Page Land Patent, April 10, 1682, Virginia Land Patents, Book 7 (1680–1689), 280–81.

15. That Nicholson had some knowledge of these matters, at least in later years, is indicated by the dedication to him by Humphry Ditton of his work, *A Treatise of Perspective.* . . . (London, 1712). I am grateful to Mr. Paul Buchanan, director of architectural research, Colonial Williamsburg, for calling my attention to this fact. In addition, I am obligated to Mr. Buchanan for countless other bits of information and suggestions as well as for the use of a map compiled by him showing lot boundaries as surveyed and sold during the first half century of Williamsburg's existence. Without his help the theory advanced in the latter part of this chapter dealing with the first plan of the city could not have been formulated.

16. This belief is strengthened by the fact that the lots on the Duke of Gloucester Street from the Capitol to Palace Green, just beyond Market Square, were laid out with a double frontage, running from the main thoroughfare back to Nicholson and Francis streets. On the Duke of Gloucester Street from Palace Green to the western boundary of the town the lots were wider and shallower and butted against the rear of the lots facing the parallel streets. This latter arrangement was a more conventional treatment of residential sites.

17. Three important collections of these manuscript maps exist: the Rochambeau Collection in the Library of Congress, the Berthier Collection in Princeton University Library, and the private collection of Mr. Paul Mellon. With few exceptions, such as that in figure 47 (Chapter IV), the town plans in these collections are rather small and omit much detail.

18. Houses on the south side of Francis Street had been built with deeper front yards than elsewhere in the town, and the cartographer used the building line rather than the property line for the southern boundary of the street. Paul Buchanan has called my attention to the curious fact that for some reason two scales were used in this plan, with that employed in drawing north-south distances differing from that used in east-west dimensions.

19. Its site was on lot 204. The building was used by James City County until 1722, then jointly by the county and the city until 1745. In that year the city moved its court functions to the former theatre on Palace Street. In 1769 the city and county agreed to build a new joint structure on the northern half of Market Square facing but somewhat west of the Magazine.

20. Whiffen, *Public Buildings of Williamsburg,* pp. 75–85, 150–52.

21. H. R. McIlwaine, ed., *Executive Journals of the Council of Colonial Virginia,* 4: 413.

22. Jefferson's drawing is reproduced in Whiffen, *Public Buildings of Williamsburg,* p. 60.

23. The most obvious error of the Simcoe map is the location of the Palace itself one block south of its true site. It also fails to record the terminations of Francis and Nicholson streets, which parallel the Duke of Gloucester Street only as far as Palace Green; the buildings shown are out of scale, the jail is incorrectly located, and there are numerous minor discrepancies throughout. It was obviously neither copied from an existing accurate map nor surveyed on the spot. It probably represents an attempt by a person not very familiar with the town to reconstruct from memory its major elements. It shows but does not identify a town pump that stood at the intersection of Botetourt Street and the Duke of Gloucester Street midway between the Capitol and Market Square.

24. Robert Beverley, *The History and Present State of Virginia,* ed. with an introduction by Louis B. Wright, p. 105. John Oldmixon, who never saw the

town, doubtless drew on Beverley when he stated that Nicholson "began to build a City in honor of the King, mark'd out the Streets in the form of a W, and call'd the Town Williamsburgh," and that "*Nicholson* caused a State-house or Capital to be erected, and several Streets to be laid out in the Form of a W; but we do not find that a V, or one Angle of it is yet finished, or ever likely to be so," John Oldmixon, *The British Empire in America* 2d ed., (London, 1741), pp. 398, 407. The first edition of this work appeared in 1708.

25. Hugh Jones, *The Present State of Virginia,* ed. with an introduction by Richard L. Morton, pp. 25, 28.

26. Beverley, *The History and Present State of Virginia,* p. 250.

27. The text of the act of 1706 appears in Goodwin, *Williamsburg,* pp. 348–49 as if it were a part of an act of 1705. The 1705 law, as will be discussed in the following chapter, simply re-enacted the act of 1699 and added certain conditions governing the sale of lots. The act of 1706 amended the legislation of 1705 as I have indicated. For the act of 1706 see *Legislative Journals of the Council,* 3: 1550.

28. If these changes were not carried out in 1706 the next most likely time would seem to be in 1713 or 1714. In November, 1713, Governor Spotswood, in an address to the assembly, informed the council and burgesses "that there has been a necessity of Resurveying and marking out a new the bounds and Streets of this place." Later that month the burgesses authorized the use of funds received from sales of lots in the town "for Defraying the Charge of Resurveying and Marking out a New the Bounds and Streets of the Said City." *Journals of the House of Burgesses,* 1712–1726, [5:] 47, 60. In the process of these surveys, some of the streets in Nicholson's plan may have been altered. Beverley's categorical statement that it was Spotswood who carried through these changes should not be ignored, but it seems more likely to me that the modifications in the first plan were made shortly after the act of 1706. One other possibility remains. In November, 1720, the burgesses took note of a "Petition of the Inhabitants of the City of *Williamsburgh* complaining of the Irregularitys of their principal Street." Since the resolution of the burgesses at that time was for an appropriation to build "Bridges and Causeways in the Main street," the "Irregularitys" complained of were evidently those of vertical and not horizontal alignment. Ibid., 283.

29. John F. D. Smyth, *A Tour in the United States of America* . . . . 1, from an extract in the *Virginia Historical Register* 6 (1853): 15.

30. Johann David Schoepf, *Travels in the Confederation,* trans. and ed. Alfred J. Morrison, 2: 78.

31. *Letters from Virginia, Translated from the French* (Baltimore, 1816), as quoted in Jane Carson, *We Were There: Descriptions of Williamsburg, 1699–1859,* p. 97. Miss Carson's valuable compilation of contemporary descriptions of the city includes those quoted previously as well as two others. One is by Sir William Keith based on his observations about 1715: "Here Governor Nicholson projected a large Town, and laid out the Streets in the Form of a W, . . ." *A History of the British Plantations in America,* as quoted by Carson, p. 5. The other is from James Kirke Paulding, *Letters from the South, written during an Excursion in the Summer of 1816* (New York, 1817), 1: "The town or city of Williamsburg . . . is built in the form of a W, in compliment to King William, . . ." as quoted by Carson, p. 95.

32. Whiffen, *Public Buildings of Williamsburg,* p. 9.

33. For convenience in orienting the reader in this and the other sketch plans I have shown the principal public buildings as they existed in 1770.

34. Southall Papers, Folder 197, Earl Gregg Swem Library, College of William and Mary. For this information and for assembling much other data on the various plans of Williamsburg I am indebted to Miss Susanne Neale of the Colonial Williamsburg research department.

35. There are two other Williamsburg plans in the papers of Lyon G. Tyler, Earl Gregg Swem Library, College of William and Mary, which plainly derive from both the Bucktrout plan and the Unknown Draftsman's plan. The earliest is identified as a copy drawn in 1892. The drawing reproduced in figure 106, owned by Mrs. Mary Ware Galt Kirby, is supposed to be a copy made by a Mr. Jeffery of Richmond from one drawn by one Brown or Browne in 1780.

36. A note on the bottom of the Bucktrout plan reads "This plan of Mr. Wallers below the Capitol added to the Town Plan by Benj. Bucktrout September 1803." This addition to the city of 1749 was drawn directly on the plan, but two other additions—two blocks at the northwest corner of the town and the Johnson tract south of the lots fronting on Francis Street, laid out in 1758—were drawn on separate pieces of paper and pasted to the drawing. My belief, based on the style of drawing and general appearance, is that the Unknown Draftsman's plan is the oldest, possibly as early as 1782 with later additions to about 1800.

37. I am indebted to Mr. Paul Buchanan of Colonial Williamsburg for making available to me his drawing on which figures 107 and 108 are based. Without his valuable research, which has extended over many years, I would not have been able to reach the conclusions summarized in these pages. The lot divisions are those made up to about 1750. In figure 108 I have added the complete main building of the College of William and Mary (and its two principal subsidiary structures), the Palace, Bruton Parish Church as rebuilt on its present site, the Courthouse of 1770, and the Capitol.

38. The pattern of the W and M shown on the map of 1904 and the photograph of 1927 seem to suggest that the monogram pattern overlapped. I doubt that this was true. The Bucktrout and companion plans would seem to refute this notion, as does the plan reconstructed from land records and archaeology in figure 107. The destruction of the Capitol by fire in 1832 opened the square to indiscriminate travel, and the shortest path from the ends of Capitol Square to Francis or Nicholson streets would have led the diagonals, as modified through time, to cross rather than turning north or south to a neat intersection with the boundary streets.

39. *Journals of the House of Burgesses 1702–1712,* [4:] 75.

40. The diagonal streets on the four early nineteenth-century plans differ in one respect. Those on the Bucktrout plan and the Lively redrawing do not decrease in width slightly from the Duke of Gloucester Street end to the short entrances to Francis and Nicholson streets. Those on the Unknown Draftsman's plan and the Browne copy show a slight taper. The entrance streets were 82½ feet wide as compared to the Duke of Gloucester Street's 99 feet width. The presence or absence of a taper depends on which property corners are used to draw the connecting lines. In the sketch plan in figure 111 I have elected to follow the Bucktrout model, which also happens to meet exactly the corners of the enclosing wall.

41. The punctuation of that portion of the act is, as elsewhere, erratic. It is possible that its drafters in-

tended the word "thereof" to apply to Williamsburg generally rather than only to the market place. Even this interpretation, which in my view is rather strained, conveys the thought that in 1706 the size of Market Square was felt to be inadequate and that either here or elsewhere alterations were needed in the pattern of streets and lots because they were "inconvenient."

42. Deed from Trustees to Ludwell, September 23, 1700, recorded June 24, 1702, York County Records, Deeds II, 30–31, from the text quoted in Mary A. Stephenson, "House History of Colonial Lot 43—Block 19" (Research Report, Colonial Williamsburg, March, 1954), pp. 1–2.

43. Lease from Directors to Blair, June 2, 1746, manuscript in Colonial Williamsburg archives, as quoted in Stephenson, ibid., p. 6. After I had first formulated my theory of the W and M monograms for Capitol and Market squares and had sent the first draft of this chapter to be reviewed by members of the staff of Colonial Williamsburg with a request for information about the dates when lots were first granted, Paul Buchanan called my attention to the data available on lot 43. Following our earlier discussions concerning the W and M puzzle, he had resumed his investigation of the subject and immediately realized the significance of the deed to Ludwell and the lease to Blair as proving beyond question the existence of a diagonal street in this portion of Market Square and the early date when it had been established.

44. It is consistent as well with all but one of the later accounts. Smyth's statement that the streets in the form of a W were located in "a part of the town . . . that has been added to it since it was first built" still remains incomprehensible. Schoepf's observation in 1783 that the letter W was formed by "several off-streets, running to the south and east," may, by stretching a point only slightly, be taken to refer to the two diagonal streets in Capitol Square.

45. See Stephen Saunders Webb, "The Strange Career of Francis Nicholson," *William and Mary Quarterly,* 3d ser. 23 (1966): 513–48, especially 537–39.

46. The act of 1699 named the Duke of Gloucester Street but only indirectly indicated it was to be straight when it specified that "the said City shall be built and erected according to the Form and Manner laid downe in the said Draught or Plott," presumably that drawn by Bland. Nicholson could have asserted that the "Form and Manner" referred only to the boundaries of the town shown on the survey. We can now appreciate the full meaning of the act of 1706 when it specified "that the main Street called *Duke of Gloucester* Street extending from the Capitol to the utmost Limitts of the City westward till it joyn's on the Land belonging to the College shall not hereafter be altered either in the Course or Dimensions thereof." This was certainly intended to clear up any ambiguity of the first act.

47. Among the very large number and almost limitless variety of *parterre* designs in the great royal garden of Versailles, for example, it can be found only in a modified form with extra paths entering the diamond at the mid-points of its sides. See the detailed plan of Versailles in 1746 reproduced in Reps, *The Making of Urban America,* pp. 24–25.

48. John Evelyn, *London Revived,* ed. E. S. de Beer, p. 37.

CHAPTER VIII.

1. "Report of the Journey of Francis Louis Michel from Berne, Switzerland to Virginia, October 2, 1701–December 1, 1702," ed. and trans. William J. Hinke, *Virginia Magazine of History and Biography* 24 (1916): 26.

2. For information on the design and construction of the major buildings of Williamsburg I have relied on Marcus Whiffen, *The Public Buildings of Williamsburg.* This is both scholarly and readable. It would be redundant to cite all the sources used by Whiffen which are fully identified in the notes accompanying his text.

3. H. R. McIlwaine, ed., *Executive Journals of the Council of Colonial Virginia, 1680–1739,* 2: 339.

4. H. R. McIlwaine, ed., *Journals of the House of Burgesses of Virginia, 1695–1702,* [3:] 268, 270, 298; H. R. McIlwaine, ed., *Legislative Journals of the Council of Colonial Virginia, 1680–1776,* 1: 309, 310.

5. Cecil Headlam, ed., *Calendar of State Papers, Colonial Series, America and West Indies, Jan.–Dec. 1, 1702* (London, 1921), 20: 332–33.

6. *Journals of the House of Burgesses 1702–1712,* [4:] 55, 69.

7. "The Trustees and Governours of the Colledge of *William and Mary* in *Virginia* having made an Offer to his Excellency and the Councill of whatsoever Roomes within the said Colledge shall be wanted for the Use of the Country to hold their generall Meetings and Assemblyes till the Capitoll be built and fitted for that Purpose, it is thereupon resolved and accordingly ordered, that the present Generall Court (at the End thereof) shall be adjourned to sitt at the said Coledge in *October* next." *Executive Journals of the Council,* 2: 61.

8. Deposition in Public Record Office, London, C.O. 5/1314, as quoted in Rutherfoord Goodwin, *A Brief & True Report Concerning Williamsburg in Virginia,* p. 172.

9. See Worthington C. Ford, "A Sketch of Sir Francis Nicholson," *Magazine of American History* 29 (1893): 509–10.

10. When the content of Nicholson's instructions was being discussed in 1698 the Board of Trade included this comment in a note explaining some of the changes made in the draft: "Former instructions have ordered a convenient house to be built for the Governor, but meanwhile he receives £150 a year for house-rent. No advance, however, has been made towards that work, and we have intimated to the Governor that he must not expect a continuance of house-rent if by his neglect the house remains unbuilt." *Calendar of State Papers, . . . 27 October, 1697–31 December, 1698,* 16: 401. The council at that time was, of course, considering such a structure in Jamestown.

11. Ibid., *1701,* 19: 479, 493, 543, 547.

12. Acts of the Virginia Assembly 1662–1702, Jefferson Collection, Division of Manuscripts, Library of Congress, the text of which appears in Goodwin, *Williamsburg,* pp. 344–46.

13. I cannot account for the fact that several French maps of the town and vicinity, the Simcoe map, and the three early nineteenth-century property maps discussed in the previous chapter show Nicholson Street perfectly straight with the jail on its north side.

14. Hugh Jones, *The Present State of Virginia,* ed. with an introduction by Richard L. Morton, p. 69.

15. Henry Hamilton, *Journal,* as quoted in Jane Carson, *We Were There: Descriptions of Williamsburg, 1699–1859,* p. 46.

16. Goodwin, *Williamsburg,* pp. 347–48.

17. *Journals of the House of Burgesses,* 1702–1712, [4:] 234.

18. William Waller Hening, ed., *The Statutes at Large . . . of Virginia,* 3: 482–86.

19. *Legislative Journals of the Council,* 1: 586.

20. Letter from Custis to Philip Ludwell, April 18, 1717, Custis Mss. Virginia Historical Society, as quoted in "Custis-Maupin House, Block 13, Lot 355" (Research Report, Colonial Williamsburg, January, 1950), p. 2. Custis complained that the governor had exceeded his authority and had removed several large and valuable trees. Custis also owned at this time a town lot on the south side of the Duke of Gloucester Street opposite Bruton Parish Church. The eastern edge of this lot lay along the ninety-nine-foot wide continuation of Palace Green. It is possible, although not likely, that the governor's tree removal activities may have taken place here to provide a better view south from the Palace. The description of the land in Custis's letter as including a swamp suggests, however, that the location was on his rural holdings north of the extended Palace grounds.

21. Whiffen's account of the design and construction of this building in his *Public Buildings of Williamsburg*, pp. 77–84, is of special interest because of his analysis of the system of mathematical proportioning used by Spotswood in working out the dimensions of its plan and elevations. Spotswood used the same technique on this building that Nicholson evidently employed in his town plan.

22. *Journals of the House of Burgesses, 1712–1726,* [5:] 283.

23. Jones, *Present State of Virginia,* p. 70.

24. John Ferdinand Dalziel Smyth, *A Tour in the United States of America* (London, 1784), as quoted in Carson, *We Were There,* p. 25. One account, however, mentions that along the main street "there are some sidewalks (kept in good repair)." Jean Christophe Louis Frederick Ignace, Baron von Closen, *Revolutionary Journal,* as quoted in Carson, *We were There,* p. 49.

25. *Journals of the House of Burgesses, 1712–1726,* [5:] 48, 283. By 1795, after the abandonment of Williamsburg as the capital, the Powder Magazine on Market Square was being used as a market building. St. George Tucker, *A Letter from St. George Tucker . . . to the Reverend Jedediah Morse* (Richmond, 1795), as quoted in Carson, *We Were There,* pp. 83–84.

26. The original survey of Princess Anne's Port was lost. In 1774 the Court of Directors ordered a resurvey, directing "that the new Plan may conform, with all possible Exactness, to the Original." *Virginia Gazette* (Purdie & Dixon), May 12, 1774, as quoted in "Queen Mary's Port (Capitol Landing); Princess Anne's Port (College Landing), 1699–1800" (Research Report, Colonial Williamsburg, undated), p. 19. I have relied on this report extensively for information about the two ports of Williamsburg. See especially pp. 3, 18, and 22.

27. This portion of the town as restored in the twentieth century by the Colonial Williamsburg Foundation provides the modern visitor with a rare opportunity to recapture the feeling of the town's character in the eighteenth century.

28. James H. Soltow, "The Role of Williamsburg in the Virginia Economy," *William and Mary Quarterly,* 3d ser. 15 (1958): 469.

29. The text of the charter appears in Goodwin, *Williamsburg,* pp. 350–57. The charter conferred the title of "City" and provided for its form of government with a mayor, recorder, aldermen, and members of the Common Council.

30. The building as now existing lies partly within the lines of the diagonal street connecting the Duke of Gloucester and Nicholson streets as shown on the early nineteenth century plans discussed in the previous chapter. All these plans show this building safely outside the street right-of-way. In this respect, as well as in their depiction of the site of the jail, they appear to be curiously inaccurate.

31. A good example of this can be observed along the north side of Francis Street south of Capitol Square. The Ayscough House, the Carter-Moir House and Shop and the Draper House are all connected in this fashion by fences.

32. A drawing showing the appearance of the building about 1825 is reproduced in Whiffen, *Public Buildings of Williamsburg,* p. 165.

33. This aspect of the Williamsburg plan was first noted by Arthur A. Shurcliff in his "The Ancient Plan of Williamsburg," *Landscape Architecture* 28 (1938): 87–101.

34. Robert H. Land, "The First Williamsburg Theater," *William and Mary Quarterly* 3d ser. 5 (1948): 359–74.

35. The site of the race track is shown on a manuscript map of revolutionary war vintage. The map is No. 264 of the Clinton Papers, William L. Celements Library, Ann Arbor, Michigan. John F. D. Smyth, who visited Williamsburg about 1770, described this feature of the town as follows: "There are races at Williamsburgh twice a year; that is, every spring and fall, or autumn. Adjoining to the town is a very excellent course, for either two, three or four mile heats. Their purses are generally raised by subscription, and are gained by the horse that wins two four-mile heats out of three; they amount to an hundred pounds each for the first day's running, and fifty pounds each every day after; the races commonly continuing for a week. There are also matches and sweepstakes very often, for considerable sums." Carson, *We Were There,* p. 25.

36. This lot was conveyed by the trustees to Francis Tyler in 1717. Tyler, in 1720, sold the property to Gawin Corbin "with all houses, buildings." York County Records, Deeds, 3, 163–64, 345. Whether the building shown on the Frenchman's Map existed at that time or was a later structure built before 1782 is not known.

37. Hening, *Statutes,* 7: 316. The assembly act specified that this area was to "be added to and made part of" the city "so soon as the same shall be built upon, and saved according to the condition of the deeds of conveyance thereof."

38. The act incorporating the Johnson addition may be found in ibid., 247–48. For some reason an additional act was required three years later containing virtually identical provisions. Ibid., 452–54. For the act concerning the Randolph addition, see ibid., 598–99.

39. Smyth, *A Tour in the United States,* in Carson, *We Were There,* p. 24.

40. Jones, *Present State of Virginia,* pp. 66–71.

41. Prudhomme, Chevalier de Bore, as quoted in Carson, *We Were There,* p. 30.

42. [Edward Kimber], *Itinerant Observations in America,* as quoted in ibid., p. 14.

43. Rev. Andrew Burnaby, *Travels through the Middle Settlements in North-America, in the Years 1759 and 1760* (London, 1775), as quoted in ibid., p. 15.

44. Josiah Quincy III, *Memoir of the Life of Josiah Quincy Jun. of Massachusetts* (Boston, 1825), as quoted in ibid., p. 27.

45. Thomas Jefferson, *Notes on the State of Virginia* (London, 1787), ed. with an introd. and notes by William Peden (Chapel Hill, 1955), pp. 152–53.

46. *Journals of the House of Burgesses, 1727–1740,* [6:] 341–42.

47. Ibid., *1742–1749* [7:] 242–43, 283–84.

48. *Legislative Journals of the Council,* 2: 1037–38.

49. In 1752, for example, the burgesses approved

another bill calling for the abandonment of Williamsburg as the capital. This, too, was rejected by the council. Ibid., 1078.

50. See "Bill for the Removal of the Seat of Government of Virginia," in Thomas Jefferson, *The Papers of Thomas Jefferson,* ed. Julian P. Boyd (Princeton, 1950), 2: 271–72; *Journal of the House of Delegates of the Commonwealth of Virginia, begun . . . the third Day of May, . . . 1799* (Richmond, 1827), 29.

51. Hening, *Statutes,* 10: 85–86.

52. Letter from St. George Tucker to Frances Bland Randolph Tucker, July 11, 1781, *Magazine of American History* 7 (1881): 207–8, as quoted in Goodwin, *Williamsburg,* pp. 284–85.

53. General Washington received the following notification of the burning of the Palace: "It is with the greatest Mortification I am to acquaint your Excellency of the Accident happned on the Night of the 22 Instant, by a Fire brocke out at the Palace, where the General Hospital was keept, and the whole Building was consumed, lukely the Sick & Wounded were saved —but one—who perished by the Flames." Letter from F. Mentges to George Washington, Washington Papers, 1781, vol. 189, Library of Congress, Division of Manuscripts, as quoted in Goodwin, *Williamsburg,* p. 298. For other contemporary accounts of these two fires see "Notes About Williamsburg, 1780–1783," *William and Mary Quarterly,* 2d ser. 17 (1937): 234–38.

54. The act of 1784 conveying the Palace lands to the college may be found in Hening, *Statutes,* 11: 405–7.

55. Francis Asbury, *The Journal of the Rev. Francis Asbury,* as quoted in Carson, *We Were There,* p. 67.

56. Johann David Schoepf, *Travels in the Confederation,* as quoted in ibid., pp. 73–74.

57. Letter from James Madison to Thomas Jefferson, March 18, 1786, in Boyd, ed., *Papers of Thomas Jefferson,* 10: 332.

58. Samuel Shepherd, *The Statutes at Large of Virginia* (Richmond, 1835), 1: 273.

59. Letter from A. P. Upshur to Governor John Floyd, April 10, 1832, in H. W. Flournoy, ed., *Calendar of Virginia State Papers* (Richmond, 1892), 10: 574–75.

60. Charles Augustus Murray, *Travels in North America during the Years 1834, 1835, and 1836,* as quoted in Carson, *We Were There,* p. 107.

61. Views of the college building as reconstructed in 1859 and as rebuilt after the Civil War are reproduced in Whiffen, *Public Buildings of Williamsburg,* pp. 194, 197.

62. Ivor Noël Hume, *Here Lies Virginia,* p. 92.

63. Goodwin, *Williamsburg,* pp. 92–93.

64. *The Architectural Record* 78 (1935): 357. The entire issue was devoted to the Williamsburg restoration and is a valuable pictorial record of the accomplishments in the first years of this project. The issue also contains useful articles by Fiske Kimball, William Graves Perry, Arthur A. Shurcliff, and Susan Higginson Nash.

65. A full and documented history of the restoration would be a useful study. Brief accounts may be found, among many others, in these works previously cited: Noël Hume, *Here Lies Virginia;* Whiffen, *Public Buildings of Williamsburg;* and in A. Lawrence Kocher and Howard Dearstyne, *Colonial Williamsburg: Its Buildings and Gardens;* and Thomas Jefferson Wertenbaker, "The Restoring of Colonial Williamsburg," *North Carolina Historical Review,* 27 (1950): 218–32.

CHAPTER IX.

1. Henry Hartwell, James Blair, and Edward Chilton, *The Present State of Virginia, and the College,* ed. with an introd. by Hunter Dickinson Farish, pp. 4, 5, 12–13.

2. Francis Makemie, *A Plain & Friendly Perswasive to the Inhabitants of Virginia and Maryland for Promoting Towns & Cohabitations,* in *Virginia Magazine of History and Biography* 4 (1897): 259, 271. For Makemie's career in America see Walter L. Jones, "Francis Makemie, Disturbing Dissenter," *Virginia Cavalcade* 17 (1967): 27–31.

3. William Waller Hening, ed., *The Statutes at Large . . . of Virginia,* 3: 204–9. An even earlier act resembling this was passed in 1679. See Hening ibid., *Statutes,* 2: 448–54. This applied to the proposed settlements by Major Lawrence Smith and Captain William Byrd on the Rappahannock and the James rivers but offered similar privileges to any others who agreed to meet its specifications.

4. For the background of this project as well as a thorough treatment of its development and ultimate failure see James L. Bugg, Jr., "The French Huguenot Frontier Settlement of Manakin Town," *Virginia Magazine of History and Biography* 61 (1953): 359–94. Useful source material and documents are collected in R. A. Brock, ed., *Documents, Chiefly Unpublished, Relating to the Huguenot Emigration to Virginia and to the Settlement of Manakin-Town.* See also Robert L. Scribner, "Manakintowne in Virginia," *Virginia Cavalcade* 3 (1953): 37–41. Byrd's proposals submitted to the Board of Trade can be found in Brock, *Documents,* pp. 5–8.

5. The illustration is from a reproduction in Brock, *Documents.* Brock's work contains no word about the original drawing, and I have been unable to locate this manuscript plan. It is not among the Brock Papers in the Henry E. Huntington Library and Art Gallery.

6. Francis Louis Michel, who visited Manakin Town in April, 1702, mentions that "Each person took 50 paces in width, the length extends as far as one cares to make it or is willing to work it." "Report of the Journey of Francis Louis Michel from Berne, Switzerland to Virginia, . . ." *Virginia Magazine of History and Biography* 24 (1916): 122–23.

7. Brock, *Documents,* p. 42.

8. "Report of the Journey of Francis Louis Michel," 123.

9. As quoted by Richmond Croom Beatty and William J. Mulloy in their introduction to *William Byrd's Natural History of Virginia,* p. xix.

10. This area, despite its name, is not the better known Land of Eden described by Byrd in his famous work, *A Journey to the Land of Eden.* See William P. Cumming, *The Southeast in Early Maps,* pp. 205–6.

11. This was Germanna, in the present Orange County, founded in 1714 by Governor Spotswood for a group of German workers imported by him to mine and smelt iron at his furnaces located not far away. The earliest map to show this settlement, identified as "Germantown Teutsche Statt," is that by J. B. Homann of *Virginia, Maryland and Carolina,* published in 1714. It is reproduced in Cumming, *The Southeast in Early Maps,* plate 46. Its location also is shown on Fry and Jefferson's map of Virginia and Maryland, the relevant portion of which is reproduced in figure 136. John Fontaine described this tiny community in 1715 as consisting of "nine houses, built all in a line; and before every house, about twenty feet distant from it, they have small sheds built for their hogs and hens, so that the hog-sties and houses make a street." Ann Maury, ed., *Memoirs of a Huguenot*

Family (New York, 1853), p. 268. For a plan of the house lots based on early land records see the drawing of Woodford B. Hackley in *The Germanna Record* (Harrisonburg, Va., The Memorial Foundation of the Germanna Colonies, Inc.), April, 1962, facing p. 80.

12. Hening, *Statutes*, 4: 285.

13. William Byrd, " A Progress to the Mines in the Year 1732," in Louis B. Wright, ed., *The Prose Works of William Byrd of Westover*, pp. 367–68.

14. "Journal of William Loughton Smith, 1790–1791," Massachusetts Historical Society, *Proceedings* (1917–1918), 51: 64.

15. A list of the trades and manufacturing activities located in Fredericksburg can be found in Oscar H. Darter, *Colonial Fredericksburg and Neighborhood in Perspective*, pp. 296–98.

16. Legislative acts authorizing the town's enlargement can be found in Hening, *Statutes*, 7: 314–15, 650–52; and 8: 418–19.

17. Ibid., 7: 651–52.

18. Ibid., 4: 238–39.

19. Rufus Rockwell Wilson, ed., *Burnaby's Travels Through North America*, p. 64.

20. For the proper identification and site of the plat of Mercer Town I am indebted to Mr. George H. S. King of Fredericksburg.

21. The list of these "lost" towns is long. Among the many for which I have been unable to find the original or resurveyed plans are: Cumberland Town, in New Kent County, and Newcastle and Hanovertown, both in Hanover County. These are discussed, along with Brickhouse, one of the seventeenth-century port towns, in Malcolm H. Harris, "The Port Towns of the Pamunkey," *William and Mary Quarterly*, 2d ser. 23 (1943): 493–516. Harris provides a drawing reconstructed from early land records of a portion of Hanovertown.

22. While Dumfries in 1771 was described by a visitor first as "a very small Place, of considerable Trade," his account later states that the town "contains about 100 Houses & 600 Inhabitants." Fred Shelley, ed., "The Journal of Ebenezer Hazard in Virginia, 1777," *Virginia Magazine of History and Biography* 62 (1956): 402. Four years later Dr. Robert Honyman observed that "Dumfries contains about a dozen stores & 20 or 30 houses," perhaps a more accurate description of the town's real size. Philip Padelford, ed., *Colonial Panorama, 1775: Dr. Robert Honyman's Journal for March and April*, p. 77. The beginning of the town's decline was noted by William Loughton Smith when he observed, "a small town which has some trade, though said to be on the decline, owing to the way of navigation, as the little river on which it is placed is filling up." "Journal of William Loughton Smith, 1790–1791," p. 64.

23. Hening, *Statutes*, 4: 268.

24. Ibid., 6: 214.

25. Augustine Washington purchased two lots for his absent brother, Lawrence, who was one of the trustees of the town. In a letter dated July 19, 1749, Augustine assured Lawrence that they were favorably located "near the water upon the Main street." He added that George had sent a plan of the town by another letter, perhaps similar to that reproduced in Figure 137. See the text of the letter from Augustine Washington in Gay Montague Moore, *Seaport in Virginia: George Washington's Alexandria*, pp. 7–8. Moore's history is a valuable source of information about the early days of Alexandria, its development and trade, and its architecture.

26. Ibid. The fact that Washington's plan of the town shows fifty-eight lots sold indicates that the drawing dates from no earlier than September 20, 1749, when the next general sale of lots took place.

27. Minutes of the Trustees of Alexandria, 1749–1767, entry for July 18, 1752, as quoted in ibid., p. 9.

28. A partial but long list of such items purchased from abroad by George Washington is provided in ibid., pp. 18–20.

29. Hening, *Statutes*, 7: 604–7.

30. Ibid., 12: 205–6.

31. This plan also shows Franklin Street with a width of 100 feet, although the act of 1785, for reasons which are not known, specified that this street should be only 50 feet wide. This was the only other exception, along with Washington Street, to the uniform 66 feet required for all new additions.

32. "Journal of William Loughton Smith, 1790–1791," pp. 62–63.

33. Hening, *Statutes*, 11: 363–64.

34. Ibid., 5: 287–92.

35. Although no old plat of Port Royal has apparently survived, the town as it existed in the 1930s was carefully surveyed, and all structures then standing as well as identifiable sites of demolished buildings were located. See the four-sheet set of measured drawings by Arthur A. Shurcliff in consultation with Perry, Shaw & Hepburn, prepared for the Williamsburg Holding Corporation, in the records of the Architect's Office of Colonial Williamsburg.

36. Padelford, ed., *Colonial Panorama*, p. 1.

37. Hening, *Statutes*, 6: 274–75.

38. Floyd McKnight, "The Town of Smithfield, 1752–1957," in Rogers Dey Whichard, *The History of Lower Tidewater Virginia*, 2: 268–83.

39. McKnight, "The Town and City of Suffolk," ibid., 157–80.

40. From an extract in the *Virginia Historical Register* 6 (1853): 144–45 of John Ferdinand Dalziel Smyth, *A Tour in the United States of America*.

41. Lord Adam Gordon, "Journal of an Officer who Travelled in America and the West Indies in 1764 and 1765" in Newton D. Mereness, ed., *Travels in the American Colonies*, p. 406.

42. For the details of this act see Whichard, *Lower Tidewater Virginia*, 1: 372–74. The act may be found in Hening, *Statutes*, 4: 541.

43. Hening, *Statutes*, 7: 136–38; 433.

44. Thomas J. Wertenbaker, *Norfolk: Historic Southern Port*, ed. Marvin W. Schlegel, pp. 64–65.

45. Hening, *Statutes*, 9: 314.

46. Kenneth Roberts and Anna M. Roberts, trans. and eds., *Moreau de St. Méry's American Journey, 1793–1798*, pp. 46–51.

47. Its location can be seen on the map reproduced in Figure 50 (Chapter IV). The name does not appear, as the map was prepared from information available in 1751. Its location is directly west of the "E" in the designation of "Eastern Branch."

48. Hening, *Statutes*, 6: 266.

49. With the expansion of Portsmouth in 1763 the assembly finally designated trustees. See Floyd McKnight, "The Town of Portsmouth, 1752–1858," in Whichard, *Lower Tidewater Virginia*, 2: 2.

50. Another plan showing the fortifications, the houses of the town, and the topography of the vicinity can be found among the manuscript maps in the Clinton Collection of the William L. Clements Library at the University of Michigan. It is Clinton No. 277, drawn by James Straton, January 21, 1781.

51. McKnight, "The Town of Portsmouth," 5.

52. Roberts, *Moreau de St. Méry's American Journey*, pp. 64–67.

53. William Byrd II, "A Journey to the Land of

Eden Anno 1733," in Louis B. Wright, ed., *The Prose Works of William Byrd of Westover,* p. 388.

54. Hening, *Statutes,* 6: 211.

55. Johann David Schoepf, *Travels in the Confederation,* trans. and ed. Alfred J. Morrison, p. 72.

56. Hening, *Statutes,* 6: 276–77.

57. Ibid., 11: 382–87.

58. Ibid., 7: 236.

59. A brief but useful guide to Leesburg and its old buildings is Melvin Lee Steadman, *A Walking Tour of Leesburg, Virginia* (Leesburg, 1967).

60. Hening, *Statutes,* 6: 269.

61. A reproduction of Washington's drawing of the fort may be found in Lawrence Martin, ed., *The George Washington Atlas,* plate 13.

62. Harry Toulmin, *The Western Country in 1793,* eds. Marion Tinling and Godfrey Davies, p. 57.

63. Frances J. Niederer, *The Town of Fincastle Virginia,* p. 2. For the assembly act creating the town, see Hening, *Statutes,* 8: 616–17.

64. As quoted in U.S. Writers' Program, *West Virginia: A Guide to the Mountain State,* p. 170.

65. Hening, *Statutes,* 9: 247.

66. Ibid., 248.

67. The plan for Louisville attributed to Clark is reproduced in Reps, *The Making of Urban America,* p, 213, along with a summary of the circumstances of the town's founding and early development.

CHAPTER X.

1. Newton D. Mereness, *Maryland as a Proprietary Province,* pp. 415–16.

2. *Archives of Maryland,* 36: 573–76.

3. For the early history of Joppa see J. Thomas Scharf, *History of Maryland,* 1: 413–15 and Walter W. Preston, *History of Harford County, Maryland,* pp. 44–47.

4. These acts can be found in the *Archives of Maryland* 42: 434–40; 616–24; 44: 205; 46: 153–55 and 464–67.

5. George Johnston, *History of Cecil County, Maryland,* p. 267. Johnston's account of the founding of towns in Cecil County is unusually complete. See also Scharf, *History of Maryland,* 1: 415; 2: 63–66.

6. *Archives of Maryland,* 42: 440.

7. Ibid., 617.

8. The legislative history of Charlestown is treated at some length in Scharf, *History of Maryland,* 2: 64–67.

9. Ibid., 1: 415.

10. Isaac Weld, *Travels Through the States of North America,* 1: 39.

11. A plan of Charlestown in 1877 can be found in Lake, Griffin & Stevenson, *An Illustrated Atlas of Cecil County, Maryland,* p. 53. A portion of the market square still existed at that time although with several encroachments, but the other public open spaces had disappeared. The town then consisted of about thirty dwellings, a school, church, and two or three stores.

12. As quoted in Preston, *Harford County,* p. 250.

13. *Archives of Maryland,* 37: 168.

14. The information on land acquisition and prices in Ceciltown is from Johnston, *Cecil County,* pp. 256–59.

15. *Archives of Maryland,* 39: 490–93.

16. The original plat has disappeared, and this description of the town is derived from an account of a later copy as given in Johnston, *Cecil County,* p. 259.

17. *Archives of Maryland,* 39: 493–96. See also 40: 98.

18. Rufus Rockwell Wilson, ed., *Burnaby's Travels Through North America* (New York, 1904), p. 87.

19. A copy drawn by Thomas F. Hubbard of a resurvey of St. Michaels in 1806 is in the collection of the Maryland Historical Society.

20. A well-organized guide to the town is *A Walking Tour of St. Michaels,* available from the St. Mary's Square Museum. See also *Talbot County, Maryland: A Tourist's Guide* (Easton, 1966). Near St. Michaels is Claiborne. An unsigned and undated plan of the town in the Talbot County Land Records shows a square with some resemblance to that of St. Michaels. Streets enter at the mid-points of all four sides, and there are additional entries at two of its corners. I have not been able to discover the origins of this community. The name "Henry Clay Square" suggests that Claiborne was founded in the nineteenth century, as does its absence from the detailed map of the state drawn in 1794 by Dennis Griffith, a portion of which is reproduced in figure 166.

21. A detailed account of the founding of this town, together with a list of early landowners may be found in Frederic Emory, *Queen Anne's County, Maryland,* pp. 334–41.

22. *Archives of Maryland,* 39: 128–30.

23. Ibid., 36: 286–89. See also a supplementary act in 1730 to remove certain legal difficulties in the way of this project, 37: 164–66. Seymour Town had been named for Governor Seymour. The new name was in honor of Benedict Leonard Calvert, the fourth Lord Baltimore.

24. Ibid., 549–52. See also a supplementary act the following year, 39: 124–25.

25. Ethel Roby Hayden, "Port Tobacco, Lost Town of Maryland," *Maryland Historical Magazine* 40 (1945): 261–76. In the Charles County Land Records, vol. 5, no. 1, 1696–1698, there is an untitled manuscript plan of the courthouse lands at Port Tobacco drawn by Joseph Manning and dated September 16, 1697. There is no indication of how this property related to the town, but its location was apparently on the west side of Port Tobacco Creek and somewhat removed from the site designated in the act of 1729. See Margaret Brown Klapthor and Paul Dennis Brown, *The History of Charles County, Maryland,* p. 46. The courthouse plat is reproduced in this work following page 22 and also in Morris L. Radoff, *The County Courthouses and Records of Maryland, Part One: The Courthouses,* p. 64.

26. *Archives of Maryland,* 36: 456–59.

27. Weld, *Travels,* 1: 138. Weld's visit to Port Tobacco was in 1796.

28. For a block diagram showing original and present conditions of Port Tobacco Creek as the result of erosion and silting, see Ralph H. Brown, *Historical Geography of the United States,* p. 133.

29. Weld, *Travels,* 1: 138–39.

30. Hayden, "Port Tobacco," 267–68.

31. An exhaustive compilation of citations to the various town acts of Maryland can be found in Francis C. Sparks, comp., *Appendix to the Report of the Public Records Commission of Maryland,* pp. 202–78. Only the appendix to the report was published and was not widely distributed. A copy may be consulted in the Maryland Hall of Records. The text of the numerous town acts can be found in those volumes of the *Archives of Maryland* containing the proceedings and acts of the General Assembly. All of them contain provisions similar to those described or quoted here in the preceding pages.

32. *Archives of Maryland,* 42: 413–17.

33. Information on land disposition is from John F.

Biddle, "Bladensburg—An Early Trade Center," Columbia Historical Society, *Records,* 53–56 (1959): 310.

34. *Archives of Maryland,* 46: 630–35.

35. Letter from Beall to the Georgetown commissioners, March 7, 1752, as quoted in Harold Donaldson Eberlein and Cortlandt Van Dyke Hubbard, *Historic Houses of George-Town & Washington City,* p. 3.

36. A list of Georgetown ships is given in Hugh T. Taggart, "Old Georgetown," Columbia Historical Society, *Records,* 11 (1908): 196–201.

37. Eberlein and Hubbard, *George-Town,* pp. 4–5.

38. A recent planning and architectural survey of the old portion of Georgetown is United States Commission of Fine Arts and Office of Archeology and Historic Preservation, National Park Service, Department of the Interior, *Georgetown Historic Waterfront.*

39. "Journal of William Loughton Smith, 1790–1791," Massachusetts Historical Society, *Proceedings* (1917–1918), 51: 61.

40. Historical treatments of the planning of Washington are numerous. The most recent full-length study is my own *Monumental Washington.* The bibliography of that volume lists the principal works and sources, and the book is copiously illustrated. Chapters I and II trace the planning and development of the city up to 1900. The recently published papers of Elbert Peets contain a number of that perceptive critic's essays on the city plan and the origins of its unusual design concepts. See Paul D. Spreiregen, ed., *On the Art of Designing Cities: Selected Essays of Elbert Peets.*

41. Henry Brooke, "Origin of Carrollsburg and Hamburg," Appendix 17 in William Tindall, *Origin and Government of the District of Columbia,* pp. 113–14.

42. Maud Burr Morris, "The Lenthall Houses and Their Owners," Columbia Historical Society, *Records,* 31–32 (1930): 4.

43. Brooke, "Origin of Carrollsburg and Hamburg," p. 113. According to one historian 606 lottery tickets were sold at £2 each. George C. Henning, "The Mansion and Family of Notley Young," Columbia Historical Society, *Records,* 16 (1913): 10.

44. The text can be found in William Tindall, *Standard History of the City of Washington,* pp. 52–54.

45. *An Act for Establishing the Temporary and Permanent Seat of the Government of the United States, July 16, 1790,* 1 Stats. 130.

46. For a useful compilation of the congressional debates dealing with the site of the capital, the text of the Residence Act, the offers of cession by Maryland and Virginia, and many other relevant documents, see Tindall, *District of Columbia.* This subject is summarized in Gaillard Hunt, *The Life of James Madison,* Chap. XX, "The Struggle for the Capital." Hunt describes the political compromise between the faction led by Hamilton and that composed of southern leaders which resulted in the acceptance by northerners of a site for the new capital in the south. See also the editorial note in Julian Boyd, ed., *The Papers of Thomas Jefferson* (Princeton, 1965), 17: 452–60.

47. Ellicott's distinguished career as surveyor, engineer, and cartographer is reviewed in Catherine Van Cortlands Mathews, *Andrew Ellicott: His Life and Letters.* The March 12, 1791 Georgetown *Weekly Record* noted that Banneker was "an Ethiopian, whose abilities as a surveyor and astronomer clearly prove that Mr. Jefferson's concluding that race of men were void of mental endowments was without foundation." Quoted by Taggart, "Old Georgetown," 212. The *Weekly Record's* assessment of Jefferson's views was misleading. Later in 1791, Jefferson, after receiving from Banneker an almanac the latter had compiled, wrote to him the following: "Nobody wishes more than I do to see such proofs as you exhibit, that nature has given to our black brethren, talents equal to those of the other colors of men, and that the appearance of a want of them is owing merely to the degraded condition of their existence, both in Africa and America. I can add with truth, that nobody wishes more ardently to see a good system commenced for raising the condition both of their body and mind to what it ought to be." H. A. Washington, ed., *The Writings of Thomas Jefferson* (Philadelphia, 1871), 3: 291.

48. The only full-length biography of L'Enfant is H. Paul Caemmerer's *The Life of Pierre Charles L'Enfant.* A summary of his career and the sources on which he drew in planning the city can be found in Reps, *Monumental Washington,* pp. 5–9.

49. "Jefferson's Draft of Agenda for the Seat of Government," August 29, 1790, in Boyd, *Papers of Thomas Jefferson,* 17: 460.

50. "Jefferson's Report to Washington on Meeting Held at Georgetown," September 14, 1790. Ibid., 17: 462.

51. Jefferson's recommendations to Washington appear in two documents of August 29 and September 14, 1790. The two are erroneously given as one and dated November 29, 1790, in Saul K. Padover, ed., *Thomas Jefferson and the National Capital* (Washington, 1946), pp. 30–35, and are so identified in my *Monumental Washington.* They are correctly presented by Boyd to whom I am indebted for calling my attention to this mistake.

52. Letter from Washington to Benjamin Stoddert and Will Deakins, Jr., February 3, 1791, in Tindall, *Standard History of Washington,* pp. 62–63. Letter from Jefferson to L'Enfant, March 17, 1791, in Padover, *Jefferson and the National Capital,* p. 51. A number of the landowners in the vicinity of Georgetown had submitted a proposal in October, 1790, urging that the federal buildings be constructed adjacent to that city. "Proposals by Georgetown Landowners," October 13, 1790, in Boyd, *Papers of Thomas Jefferson,* 17: 469–71.

53. Washington diary entry for March 29, 1791, as quoted in Tindall, *Standard History of Washington,* pp. 75–76.

54. Letter from Washington to Jefferson, March 31, 1791, in Padover, *Jefferson and the National Capital,* p. 54. The text of the agreement is given in H. Paul Caemmerer, *Washington: The National Capital,* pp. 19–21; and in Tindall, *Standard History of Washington,* pp. 76–78.

55. Undated note by L'Enfant, probably given to Washington before or during the meeting in Georgetown the end of March. The text appears in Elizabeth S. Kite, *L'Enfant and Washington,* pp. 43–48.

56. Undated memorandum from L'Enfant to Washington, probably June 22, 1791, in Kite, *L'Enfant,* pp. 52–58.

57. Washington diary entry for June 29, 1791, Joseph A. Hoskins, ed., *President Washington's Diaries, 1791 to 1799,* p. 52.

58. Letter from L'Enfant to Washington, August 19, 1791, the complete text of which is in the Columbia Historical Society, *Records,* 2: (1899), 38–48.

59. For the series of incidents that led to L'Enfant's downfall see Caemmerer, *L'Enfant,* pp. 169–215. Washington's attitude toward L'Enfant is described at length in his letter to the commissioners, November 20, 1791, in Tindall, *Standard History of Washington,* pp. 125–29.

60. As quoted in John B. Ellis, *The Sights and Secrets of the National Capital*, p. 42.

61. See Reps, *Monumental Washington*, Chaps. 3–7 and sources cited therein for the background of this plan, its recommendations, and its implementation.

CHAPTER XI.

1. A nearly identical manuscript plan, although not so legible, is in the collection of the Virginia State Library. It is entitled "A Plan of Richmond." On the reverse is the following note: "The plan of Richmond Town laid off by Colo. Wm. Mayo & James Wood in the year 1736 February ye 12." The Virginia State Library collection also includes a manuscript plan of Richmond drawn in 1787 that closely resembles that in figure 185. It bears the following title: "An exact copy of a plan of the town of Richmond which appears to be taken in the lifetime of William Byrd the elder. . . ." On the reverse is this note: "We do certify that the within is a true copy of the plan referred to in Edmd. Pendleton Esqr's disposition. Robt. Boyd. A Roberts 5 Nov 1787."

2. As quoted in Alexander Wilbourne Weddell, *Richmond Virginia in Old Prints, 1737–1887*, p. 3.

3. William Waller Hening, ed., *The Statutes at Large . . . of Virginia*, 5: 191.

4. Ibid., 6: 281–82.

5. A facsimile of the advertisement appears in Weddell, *Richmond*, p. 9.

6. Hening, *Statutes*, 8: 421–24.

7. Weddell, *Richmond*, p. 7.

8. For the details of these events, the changes in the bill during committee stages and in the assembly, and for a comparison of the features of the 1779 legislation with Jefferson's bill in 1776, see the editorial note in Julian P. Boyd, ed., *The Papers of Thomas Jefferson* (Princeton, 1950), 2: 271–72.

9. Hening, *Statutes*, 10: 86.

10. Ibid., 317–18.

11. Weddell, *Richmond*, pp. 22–23. See also Samuel Mordecai, *Richmond in By-Gone Days* (Richmond, 1860), pp. 54–55.

12. This engraving, which has an appearance of accuracy, may be misleading. It was prepared from a manuscript map drawn shortly after Richmond was occupied by British troops for one day. The engraving is a faithful copy of the manuscript, which is among the Simcoe Papers in the collection of Colonial Williamsburg. That collection, however, also includes the field sketch from which the manuscript map was prepared. The sketch shows streets and topographic features but no buildings. Buildings may have been added by the cartographer from verbal descriptions or may simply have been drawn arbitrarily to provide a diagramatic representation of the town.

13. Other directors were Archibald Cary, Robert Carter Nicholas, Richard Adams, Edmund Randolph, Turner Southall, Robert Goode, James Buchanan, and Samuel Du-Vall.

14. In his great work on Jefferson's architectural drawings Fiske Kimball originally assigned a date of 1782–1785 to this drawing on the basis of the paper used. See his *Thomas Jefferson, Architect*, p. 139. His later studies led him to revise this on the basis of other evidence and to conclude that it "must have been drawn not later than the spring of 1780." Fiske Kimball, "Jefferson and the Public Buildings of Virginia. II. Richmond, 1779–1780." *Huntington Library Quarterly* 12: (1949): 305.

15. On the Jefferson plan reproduced in figure 189 and his other drawings of the time the numbers assigned to the north-south streets are each one higher than those finally adopted and still used today. Thus, the blocks as shown on his drawing were bounded by streets to which he gave the numbers 10 and 13.

16. A reproduction of this plan from the manuscript in the Coolidge Collection of the Massachusetts Historical Society appears in Kimball, *Thomas Jefferson, Architect*, figure 103.

17. As quoted from the text on the reverse of the drawing in Kimball, "Jefferson and the Public Buildings of Virginia," p. 305.

18. Jefferson was informed of this action in Paris by James Buchanan and William Hay in a letter from Richmond dated March 20, 1785. Boyd, *Papers of Thomas Jefferson*, 8: 48–49.

19. Thomas Jefferson to James Madison, Paris, September 20, 1785, in ibid., 534–35.

20. This model has survived and may be seen in the Capitol. Jefferson had already sent it to Richmond when he received a reassuring note from two of the directors, James Buchanan and William Hay, on January 19, 1786, that his design would be followed if possible. See their letter dated from Richmond, October 18, 1785, in ibid., 648.

21. "Journal of William Loughton Smith, 1790–1791," Massachusetts Historical Society, *Proceedings* (1917–1918) 51: 65–66.

22. John Tyler, "Richmond and its Memories," an address delivered at the Richmond Mechanics Institute in November, 1858, as quoted in Weddell, *Richmond*, p. 31.

23. Latrobe's plan was prepared to show the location of a proposed theatre, which he designed to replace the one burned on January 23, 1798. Its site is shown in the upper right portion of the plan. A brief account of this project, a reproduction of figure 193 in color, and views and plans of other buildings in Richmond designed by Latrobe and Robert Mills can be found in "An Architect Looks at Richmond," *Virginia Cavalcade* 16 (1967): 22–29.

24. The small building immediately to the right of the Capitol in figure 196 is the governor's residence.

25. For a description of Godefroy's proposals and an account of the buildings he designed in Richmond see Robert L. Alexander, "Maximilian Godefroy in Virginia: A French Interlude in Richmond's Architecture," *Virginia Magazine of History and Biography* 69: (1961): 418–31.

26. Mary Wingfield Scott and Louise F. Catterall, *Virginia's Capitol Square: Its Buildings & Its Monuments*, pp. 5–6.

27. These are summarized in ibid., pp. 6–7, 11–13, 34.

28. *Archives of Maryland*, 36: 315. For the progress of the bill introduced shortly thereafter see 331, 334, 351, 388, 396, 397, 411, 415, 418, 425, 428, and 429. The text of the act as passed is given on 464–66.

29. Ibid., 464–66. This was not the first town in Maryland to be given this distinguished name. The Herrman Map, drawn in 1670 and published three years later, shows a settlement with this name at the mouth of Bush River, about halfway between the present Baltimore and the mouth of the Susquehanna. It is doubtful if this town ever was developed, although its location appeared on several subsequent maps, including those of the early eighteenth century by John Senex and J. B. Homann. Even the detailed map of Virginia and Maryland prepared in 1751 by Joshua Fry and Peter Jefferson showed the old Baltimore Town and not the new. For a review of the use of Baltimore as a

place name for Maryland towns, see George Armistead Leakin, "The Migrations of Baltimore Town," *Maryland Historical Magazine* 1 (1906): 45–59.

30. For this information on the characteristics of the site of Baltimore as well as for much other useful material I am indebted to Mr. Wilbur H. Hunter, director of the Peale Museum in Baltimore, who allowed me to draw on a portion of his unpublished manuscript tracing the founding and development of the city. Hunter's work also formed the basis for a graduate seminar paper prepared under my direction in the spring of 1968 by Mr. Lawrence E. Parker, a student at Cornell University. Parker used a series of plans of the city in tracing in detail its gradual physical expansion throughout the colonial period. This proved of great value in preparing this section of the present chapter. I have also found useful the works of J. Thomas Scharf. See his *Chronicles of Baltimore;* and *History of Maryland from the Earliest Period to the Present Day.*

31. *Archives of Maryland,* 37: 533–36.

32. Scharf, *Chronicles of Baltimore,* pp. 35–36.

33. J. H. Hollander, *The Financial History of Baltimore,* p. 7.

34. As quoted in Scharf, *Chronicles of Baltimore,* p. 39.

35. The complete text of this announcement and a list of subscribers and their contributions are in ibid., pp. 63–64.

36. The text of the announcements of the public subscription and the lottery are given in ibid., pp. 47, 56.

37. Hollander, *Financial History of Baltimore,* p. 12, and Chapter 35 of the Laws of Maryland, 1765, as quoted by Hollander, p. 14.

38. Hunter, unpublished manuscript history of the development of Baltimore, p. 14.

39. Philip Padelford, ed., *Colonial, Panorama, 1775: Dr. Robert Honyman's Journal for March and April,* p. 75.

40. Kenneth and Anna M. Roberts, trans. and eds., *Moreau de St. Méry's American Journey, 1793–1798,* pp. 76–80.

41. Frances Trollope, *Domestic Manners of The Americans* 1: 289–90.

42. Baltimore after the Revolution favorably impressed nearly every visitor. For a valuable and informative collection of the accounts of these travelers see Raphael Semmes, *Baltimore as Seen by Visitors, 1783–1860.*

Bibliography

Acts of the General Assembly of Virginia, Relative to the Jurisdiction and Powers of the Town of Petersburg. Petersburgh: Edward Pescud, 1824.

Alexander, Robert L. "Maximilian Godefroy in Virginia: A French Interlude in Richmond's Architecture." *Virginia Magazine of History and Biography,* 69 (October 1961), 420–31.

Ames, Susie May. *Studies of the Virginia Eastern Shore in the Seventeenth Century.* Richmond: Dietz, 1940.

"An Architect Looks at Richmond." *Virginia Cavalcade,* 16 (Winter 1967), 22–29.

A Narrative of the Indian and Civil Wars in Virginia, in the Years 1675 and 1676. Boston: John Eliot, 1814.

Andrews, Matthew Page. *History of Maryland: Province and State.* Garden City: Doubleday, Doran, 1929.

———. *The Founding of Maryland.* Baltimore: Williams & Wilkins, 1933.

Anglin, Richard L., Jr. *Maryland New Towns: 1668–1708.* Unpublished seminar paper, Department of City and Regional Planning, Cornell University, July 22, 1968.

"Anthony Langston on Towns, and Corporations; and on the Manufacture of Iron." *William and Mary Quarterly,* 2nd ser., 1 (April 1921), 101–6.

Architectural Record, 78 (December 1935), 359–458.

Archives of Maryland. 70 vols. Baltimore: Maryland Historical Society, 1883–1964.

Bacon, Edmund N. *Design of Cities.* New York: Viking, 1967.

Baer, Elizabeth. *Seventeenth Century Maryland: A Bibliography.* Baltimore: John Work Garrett Library, 1949.

Bagwell, Richard. *Ireland Under the Stuarts and During the Interregnum.* 3 vols. London: Holland, 1963.

Barker, Charles Albro. *The Background of the Revolution in Maryland.* New Haven: Yale University Press, 1940.

Bassett, John Spencer. "The Relation Between the Virginia Planter and the London Merchant." American Historical Association, *Annual Report for 1901,* 1 (1902), 551–75.

Beardslee, William A. "The First Attempt to Found an American College." *Magazine of American History,* 29 (May–June 1893), 367–70.

Beckett, J. C. *The Making of Modern Ireland, 1603–1923.* London: Faber & Faber, 1966.

Beirne, Francis F. *Baltimore: A Pictorial History, 1858–1968.* Baltimore: Bodine, 1968.

Beresford, Maurice. *New Towns of the Middle Ages: Town Plantation in England, Wales, and Gascony.* London: Lutterworth, 1967.

Berkley, Henry J. "Extinct River Towns of the Chesapeake Bay Region." *Maryland Historical Magazine,* 19 (June 1924), 125–41.

———. "The Port of Dumfries." *William and Mary Quarterly,* 2nd ser., 4 (April 1924), 99–116.

Bertelson, David. *The Lazy South.* New York: Oxford University Press, 1967.

Beverley, Robert. *The History and Present State of Virginia* (London, 1705). Edited, with an introduction by Louis B. Wright. Chapel Hill: University of North Carolina Press, 1947.

———. *The History of Virginia.* 2nd ed. London: B. and S. Tooke, 1722.

Biddle, John F. "Bladenburg—An Early Trade Center." Columbia Historical Society, *Records,* 53–56 (Washington 1959), 309–26.

Bidwell, Percy W., and Falconer, John I. *History of Agriculture in the Northern United States, 1820–1860.* Washington, D.C.: Carnegie Institution, 1925.

Bohannan, A. W. "The Old Town of Cobham." *Virginia Magazine of History and Biography,* 57 (July 1949), 252–68.

Bolton, Herbert Eugene, and Marshall, Thomas Maitland. *The Colonization of North America, 1492–1783.* New York: Macmillan, 1925.

Bourne, Ruth. "John Evelyn the Diarist, and his Cousin Daniel Parke II." *Virginia Magazine of History and Biography,* 78 (January 1970), 3–33.

Branch, Melville C. "Rome and Richmond: A Case Study in Topographic Determinism." *Journal of the American Institute of Planners,* 28 (February 1962), 1–9.

Brewington, M. V. *Chesapeake Bay: A Pictorial Maritime History.* Cambridge, Maryland: Cornell Maritime Press, 1953.

Brock, R. A., ed. *Documents, Chiefly Unpublished, Relating to the Huguenot Emigration to Virginia and to the Settlement at Manakin-Town.* Richmond: Virginia Historical Society, 1886.

———. *The Official Letters of Alexander Spotswood.* Richmond: Virginia Historical Society, 1882.

Brown, Alexander. *The Genesis of the United States.* 2 vols. Boston: Houghton Mifflin, 1890.

Brown, Ralph H. *Historical Geography of the United States.* New York: Harcourt, Brace, 1948.

———. *Mirror for Americans: Likeness of the Eastern Seaboard, 1810.* New York: American Geographical Society, 1943.

Browne, C. A. "Reverend Dr. John Clayton and His Early Map of Jamestown, Virginia." *William and Mary Quarterly,* 2nd ser., 19 (January 1939), 1–7.

Bruce, Philip Alexander. *Economic History of Virginia in the Seventeenth Century.* 2 vols. New York: Macmillan, 1896.

Brydon, G. MacLaren. "The Huguenots of Manakin Town and Their Times." *Virginia Magazine of History and Biography,* 42 (October 1934), 325–35.

Bugg, James L., Jr. "The French Huguenot Frontier Settlement of Manakin Town." *Virginia Magazine of History and Biography,* 61 (October 1953), 359–94.

Butt, Marshall W. *Portsmouth Under Four Flags, 1752–1961.* Portsmouth: Portsmouth Historical Association, 1961.

Byrd, William (I). "Letters of William Byrd, First." *Virginia Magazine of History and Biography,* 38 (January 1920), 11–25.

Byrd, William (II). *William Byrd's Natural History of Virginia or The Newly Discovered Eden.* Edited and translated from a German version by Richmond Croom Beatty and William J. Mulloy. Richmond: Dietz, 1940.

Camblin, Gilbert. *The Town in Ulster.* Belfast: William Mullan, 1951.

Caemmerer, H. Paul. *The Life of Pierre Charles L'Enfant, Planner of the City Beautiful, The City of Washington.* Washington, D.C.: National Republic, 1950.

———. *Washington: The National Capital.* Washington, D.C.: Government Printing Office, 1932.

Campbell, Charles, ed. *The Bland Papers, Being a Selection from the Manuscripts of Colonel Theodorick Bland, Jr., of Prince George County, Virginia.* 2 vols. Petersburg: E. and J. C. Ruffin, 1839–1843.

Cappon, Lester J., and Duff, Stella F., comp. *Virginia Gazette Index 1736–1780.* 2 vols. Williamsburg: Institute of Early American History and Culture, 1950.

Carson, Jane. *Travelers in Tidewater Virginia, 1700–1800: A Bibliography.* Williamsburg: Colonial Williamsburg, 1965.

———. *We Were There: Descriptions of Williamsburg, 1699–1859.* Williamsburg: Colonial Williamsburg, 1965.

Chubb, Thomas. *The Printed Maps in the Atlases of Great Britain and Ireland: A Bibliography, 1579–1870.* London: Homeland Association, 1927.

Colonial Williamsburg, Department of Research and Education. "Notes About Williamsburg, 1780–1783." *William and Mary Quarterly,* 2nd ser., 17 (April 1937), 234–38.

Cook, Ebenezer. *The Sot-Weed Factor: or, A Voyage to Maryland.* London: D. Bragg, 1708.

Cotter, John L. *Archeological Excavations at Jamestown Colonial National Historical Park and Jamestown National Historic Site, Virginia.* Archeological Research Series, no. 4, National Park Service, U.S. Department of the Interior. Washington, D.C.: Government Printing Office, 1958.

Cresswell, Nicholas. *The Journal of Nicholas Cresswell, 1774–1777.* New York: Dial, 1924.

Culliford, S. G. *William Strachey, 1572–1621.* Charlottesville: University Press of Virginia, 1965.

Cumming, William P. *North Carolina in Maps.* Raleigh: North Carolina State Department of Archives and History, 1966.

———. "The Identity of John White, Governor of Roanoke, and John White, the Artist." *North Carolina Historical Review,* 15 (July 1938), 197–203.

———. *The Southeast in Early Maps.* 2nd ed. Chapel Hill: University of North Carolina Press, 1962.

Daniel, J. R. V., comp. and ed. *A Hornbook of Virginia History.* Richmond: Division of History, Virginia Department of Conservation and Development, 1949.

Darter, Oscar H. *Colonial Fredericksburg and Neighborhood in Perspective.* New York: Twayne, 1957.

——. "Where the West Began: Historical Sketch of Old Marleborough Town Stafford County, Virginia." *Northern Neck of Virginia Historical Magazine,* 9 (December 1959), 801–11.

Davis, Edward G. "Raleigh's 'New Fort in Virginia'—1585," *Magazine of American History,* 29 (May–June 1893), 459–70.

Davis, Richard Beale, ed. *William Fitzhugh and His Chesapeake World, 1676–1701.* Chapel Hill: University of North Carolina Press, 1963.

de Beer, E. S., ed. *The Diary of John Evelyn.* 6 vols. Oxford: Clarendon, 1955.

Dewar, Mary. *Sir Thomas Smith: A Tudor Intellectual in Office.* London: Athlone, 1964.

Dodson, Leonidas. *Alexander Spotswood: Governor of Colonial Virginia, 1710–1722.* Philadelphia: University of Pennsylvania Press, 1932.

Dulaney, Paul. *The Architecture of Historic Richmond.* Charlottesville: University Press of Virginia, 1968.

Dunlop, Robert. "Sixteenth Century Schemes for the Plantation of Ulster." *Scottish Historical Review,* 32 (October 1924), 51–60; (January 1925), 115–26; (April 1925), 199–212.

Eberlein, Harold Donaldson, and Hubbard, Cortlandt Van Dyke. *Historic Houses of George-Town and Washington City.* Richmond: Dietz, 1958.

Eddis, William. *Letters from America.* London: The Author, 1792.

Ellis, John B. *The Sights and Secrets of the National Capital.* New York: United States Publishing Company, 1869.

Emory, Frederick. *Queen Anne's County Maryland.* Baltimore: Maryland Historical Society, 1950.

Evelyn, John. *London Revived.* Edited by E. S. de Beer. Oxford: Clarendon, 1938.

———. *Sylva, or A Discourse of Forest-Trees, and the Propagation of Timber in His Majesties Dominions.* 3rd ed. London: John Martyn, 1679.

"Extracts from the Proceedings of the Council, Relating to the Building of the Capitol in Williamsburg, 1702–1704," *William and Mary Quarterly,* 10, 1st ser. (January 1902), 158–66.

Fithian, Philip Vickers. *Journal and Letters of Philip Vickers Fithian, 1773–1774; A Plantation Tutor of the Old Dominion.* Edited by Hunter Dickinson Farish. Williamsburg: Colonial Williamsburg, 1957.

Fontaine, John. "Journal." In *Memoirs of a Huguenot Family: Translated and Compiled from the Original Autobiography of the Rev. James Fontaine, and Other Family Manuscripts. . . .* Edited by Ann Maury. New York: Putnam, 1853.

Footner, Hulbert. *Maryland Main and the Eastern Shore.* Hatboro, Pennsylvania: Tradition Press, 1967.

Force, Peter, comp. *Tracts and Other Papers Relating Principally to the Origin, Settlement, and Progress of the Colonies in North America.* 4 vols. Washington, D.C.: P. Force, 1836–1846.

Ford, Worthington C. "A Sketch of Sir Francis Nichol-
1893), 500–13.
son." *Magazine of American History,* 29 (May–June

———. "Early Maps of Carolina." *Geographical Review,* 16 (April 1926), 264–73.

Forman, Henry Chandlee. *Jamestown and St. Mary's, Buried Cities of Romance.* Baltimore: Johns Hopkins Press, 1938.

———. "The Bygone 'Subberbs of James Cittie.'"

William and Mary Quarterly, 2nd ser., 20 (October 1940), 475–86.

———. "The St. Mary's City 'Castle,' Predecessor of The Williamsburg 'Palace.'" *William and Mary Quarterly,* 2nd ser., 22 (April 1942), 136–43.

———. *Tidewater Maryland Architecture and Gardens.* New York: Architectural Book Publishing Company, 1956.

———. *Virginia Architecture in the Seventeenth Century.* Williamsburg: Virginia 350th Anniversary Celebration Corporation, 1957.

For the Colony in Virginia Britannia. Lawes Divine, Morall and Martiall &c. London: Walter Burre, 1612.

Friis, Herman H. *A Series of Population Maps of the Colonies and the United States.* New York: American Geographical Society, 1940.

Gilbert, John T., ed. *Facsimiles of National Manuscripts of Ireland.* 5 vols. Dublin and London: Public Record Office of Ireland, 1874–1884.

Goodwin, Rutherfoord. *A Brief and True Report Concerning Williamsburg in Virginia.* 3rd ed. Williamsburg: Colonial Williamsburg, 1940.

Goolrick, John Taquette. *Fredericksburg and the Cavalier Country.* Richmond: Garrett and Massie, 1935.

Gordon, Lord Adam. "Journal of an Officer who Travelled in America and the West Indies in 1764 1765." In *Travels in the American Colonies.* Edited by Newton D. Mereness. New York: Macmillan, 1916.

Gottschalk, L. C. "Effects of Soil Erosion on Navigation in Upper Chesapeake Bay." *Geographical Review,* 35 (April 1945), 219–38.

Great Britain, Public Record Office. *Calendar of State Papers, Colonial Series, America and West Indies.* 43 vols. London: 1860–1963.

Griffin, Cornelia. *The Land at the Falls.* Unpublished seminar paper, Department of City and Regional Planning, Cornell University, Spring 1968.

Gutkind, Erwin A. *Urban Development in Southern Europe: Spain and Portugal.* New York: Free Press of Glencoe, 1967.

Hakluyt, Richard. "Discourse on Western Planting." In *Documentary History of the State of Maine,* vol. 2. Edited by Charles Deane. Cambridge: John Wilson, 1877.

Hall, Clayton Colman, ed. *Narratives of Early Maryland, 1633–1684.* New York: Scribner's, 1910.

Hamor, Ralph. *A True Discourse of the Present Estate of Virginia . . .* (London 1615). Introduction by A. L. Rowse. Richmond: Virginia State Library, 1957.

Harrington, J. C. "Archeological Explorations at Fort Raleigh National Historic Site." *North Carolina Historical Review,* 26 (April 1949), 127–49.

———. *Search for the Cittie of Ralegh: Archeological Excavations at Fort Raleigh National Historic Site, North Carolina.* Washington, D.C.: Government Printing Office, 1962.

Harris, Malcolm. "'Delaware Town' and 'West Point' in King William County, Virginia." *William and Mary Quarterly,* 2nd ser., 14 (October 1934), 342–51.

———. "The Port Towns of the Pamunkey." *William and Mary Quarterly,* 2nd ser., 23 (October 1943), 493–516.

Harris, Walter. *Hibernica.* 2nd ed. Dublin: J. Milliken, 1770.

Harrison, Fairfax. *Landmarks of Old Prince William.* Berryville, Virginia: Chesapeake Book Company, 1964.

Hartwell, Henry; Blair, James; and Chilton, Edward. *The Present State of Virginia, and the College* (London 1727). Edited with an introduction by Hunter Dickinson Farish. Williamsburg Restoration Historical Studies, No. 1. Williamsburg: Colonial Williamsburg, 1940.

Hatch, Charles E. *Jamestown, Virginia: The Townsite and Its Story.* Rev. ed. Washington, D.C.: Government Printing Office, 1957.

Hayden, Ethel Roby. "Port Tobacco, Lost Town of Maryland." *Maryland Historical Magazine,* 40 (December 1945), 261–76.

Heinton, Louise Joyner. "Charles Town, Prince George's First County Seat." *Maryland Historical Magazine,* 63 (December 1968), 401–11.

Heite, Edward F. "Markets and Ports." *Virginia Cavalcade,* 16 (Autumn 1966), 29–41.

Hening, William Walter, ed. *The Statutes at Large . . . of Virginia.* 13 vols. Richmond: Samuel Pleasants, 1809–23.

Henning, George C. "The Mansion and Family of Notley Young," Columbia Historical Society, *Records,* XVI (1913), 1–24.

Higounet, Ch. "Cisterciens et Bastides." *Moyen Age,* 56 (4th ser., 5), (1950), 69–84.

Hiorns, Frederick R. *Town-Building in History.* London: Harrap, 1956.

"History of York County in the Seventeenth Century." *Tyler's Quarterly Historical and Genealogical Magazine,* 1 (April 1920), 231–75.

Holland, Eugenia Calvert. "Anne Arundel Takes Over from St. Mary's." *Maryland Historical Magazine,* 44 (March 1949), 42–51.

Hollander, J. H. *The Financial History of Baltimore.* Baltimore: Johns Hopkins Press, 1899.

Hoskins, Joseph A., ed. *President Washington's Diaries, 1791 to 1799.* Summerfield, North Carolina: n.p., 1921.

Howard, George W. *The Monumental City.* Baltimore: J. D. Ehlers, 1873.

Howland, Richard Hubbard. *The Architecture of Baltimore: A Pictorial History.* Baltimore: Johns Hopkins Press, 1953.

Hughes, T. Harold, and Lamborn, E. A. G. *Towns and Town-Planning, Ancient and Modern.* Oxford: Clarendon, 1923.

Hulton, Paul, and Quinn, David Beers, eds. *The American Drawings of John White, 1577–1590.* 2 vols. London: British Museum, 1964.

Hunt, Gaillard. *The Life of James Madison.* New York: Doubleday, Page, 1902.

Hunter, Wilbur H. "The Mercantile Age." Chapter I of an unpublished book manuscript, August 31, 1962.

"Instructions to Governor Yeardley, 1618." *Virginia Magazine of History and Biography,* 2 (October 1894), 154–65.

"Instructions to Lord Culpeper," *Virginia Magazine of History and Biography,* 38 (January 1920), 41–53.

"Instructions to Our Trusty and Well Beloved Servant Sir William Berkeley, Knight, Our Governor of Our Colony of Virginia." *Virginia Magazine of History and Biography,* 3 (July 1895), 15–20.

"Instructions to Sir William Berkeley, Knight, One of the Gentlemen of Our Privy Chamber, Governor of Virginia, and to the Council of State There." *Virginia Magazine of History and Biography,* 2 (January 1895), 281–88.

Isaac, Erich. "Kent Island." *Maryland Historical Magazine,* 52 (June 1957), 93–119; (September 1957), 210–32.

Jefferson, Thomas. *Notes on the State of Virginia.* 2nd American ed. Philadelphia: Mathew Carey, 1794.

Jennings, John Melville. "Notes on the Original Library of the College of William and Mary in Virginia, 1693–1705." *Papers of the Bibliographical Society of*

America, 41 (Third Quarter 1947), 239–67.

Jester, Annie Lash, comp. and ed. *Adventurers of Purse and Person: Virginia, 1607–1625.* Princeton: n.p., 1956.

[Johnson, Robert]. *Nova Britannia.* London: Samuel Macham, 1609.

———. *The New Life of Virginea: Declaring the Former Successe and Present Estate of that Plantation, Being the Second Part of Nova Britannia.* London: William Welby, 1612.

Johnston, George. *History of Cecil County, Maryland.* Elkton, Maryland: The Author, 1881.

Jones, Elias. *New Revised History of Dorchester County, Maryland.* Cambridge, Maryland: Tidewater Publishers, 1966.

Jones, Howard Mumford. "Origins of the Colonial Idea in England." American Philosophical Society, *Proceedings,* 85 (September 1942), 448–65.

Jones, Hugh. "Part of a Letter from the Reverend Mr. Hugh Jones . . . Concerning Several Observables in Maryland." Royal Society of London, *Philosophical Transactions,* London, 21, no. 259 (1700), 436–42.

———. *The Present State of Virginia* (London 1724). Edited with an introduction by Richard L. Morton. Chapel Hill: University of North Carolina Press, 1956.

Jones, Walter L. "Francis Makemie, Disturbing Dissenter." *Virginia Cavalcade,* 27 (Summer 1967); 27–31.

Karimen, Arthur. "Maryland Population: 1631–1730: Numerical and Distributional Aspects." *Maryland Historical Magazine,* 54 (December 1959), 365–407.

———. "Numerical and Distributional Aspects of Maryland Population 1631–1840. Part II. Distributional Characteristics 1631–1730." *Maryland Historical Magazine,* 60 (June 1965), 139–59.

Keith, Sir William. *The History of the British Plantations in America.* London: S. Richardson, 1738.

Kelbaugh, Paul R. "Tobacco Trade in Maryland, 1700–1725." *Maryland Historical Magazine,* 26 (March 1931), 1–33.

Kerr, Robert J., II. Unpublished and undated report prepared for Historic Annapolis, Inc.

Kimball, Fiske. "Jefferson and the Public Buildings of Virginia." *Huntington Library Quarterly,* 12 (February 1949), 115–20; (May 1949), 303–10.

———. *Thomas Jefferson: Architect.* Boston: Riverside, 1916.

[Kimber, Edward]. "Observations in Several Voyages and Travels in America." (*London Magazine,* 1745–1746), *William and Mary Quarterly,* 1st ser., 15 (January 1907), 143–59; (April 1907), 215–24.

Kingsbury, Susan Myra, ed. *The Records of the Virginia Company of London.* 4 vols. Washington, D.C.: Government Printing Office, 1906–1935.

Kirkland, Edward C. *History of American Economic Life.* New York: Crofts, 1932.

Kite, Elizabeth S. *L'Enfant and Washington, 1791–1792.* Baltimore: Johns Hopkins Press, 1929.

Klapthor, Margaret Brown, and Brown, Paul Dennis. *The History of Charles County, Maryland.* La Plata, Maryland: Charles County Tercentenary, 1958.

Kocher, A. Lawrence, and Dearstyne, Howard. *Colonial Williamsburg: Its Buildings and Gardens.* Williamsburg: Colonial Williamsburg, 1949.

Kuethe, J. Louis. "A Gazetteer of Maryland, A.D. 1673." *Maryland Historical Magazine,* 30 (December 1935), 310–25.

Labaree, Leonard Woods, ed. *Royal Instructions to British Colonial Governors, 1670–1776.* 2 vols. New York: Appleton-Century, 1935.

Lake, Griffing and Stevenson. *An Illustrated Atlas of Cecil County, Maryland.* Philadelphia: Lake, Griffing and Stevenson, 1877.

———. *An Illustrated Atlas of Kent and Queen Annes Counties, Maryland.* Philadelphia: Lake, Griffing and Stevenson, 1877.

———. *An Illustrated Atlas of Talbot and Dorchester Counties, Maryland.* Philadelphia: Lake, Griffing and Stevenson, 1877.

———. *Atlas of Wicomico, Somerset and Worcester Counties, Maryland.* Philadelphia: Lake, Griffing and Stevenson, 1877.

Land, Robert Hunt. "Henrico and Its College." *William and Mary Quarterly, 2nd ser.,* 18 (October 1938), 453–98.

———. "The First Williamsburg Theater." *William and Mary Quarterly,* 3rd ser., 5 (July 1948), 359–74.

Lane, Arthur. "Daniel Marot: Designer of Delft Vases and of Gardens at Hampton Court." *Connoisseur,* 123 (January 1949), 19–24.

Latrobe, John H. B. "Construction of the Public Buildings in Washington." *Maryland Historical Magazine,* 4 (September 1909), 221–28.

Lavedan, Pierre. *Histoire de l'Urbanisme.* Paris: Laurens, 1926.

———. *Les Villes Françaises.* Paris: Vincent, Fréal, 1960.

Leakin, George Armistead. "The Migrations of Baltimore Town." *Maryland Historical Magazine,* 1 (March 1906), 45–59.

Lefler, Hugh Talmage, and Newsome, Albert Ray. *North Carolina.* Rev. ed. Chapel Hill: University of North Carolina Press, 1963.

Lodge, Eleanor C. *Gascony Under English Rule.* London: Methuen, 1926.

McCully, Bruce T. "From the North Riding to Morocco: The Early Years of Governor Francis Nicholson, 1655–1686." *William and Mary Quarterly,* 3rd ser., 19 (October 1962), 534–56.

McIlwaine, H. R., ed. *Executive Journals of the Council of Colonial Virginia, 1680–1739.* 4 vols. Richmond: Virginia State Library, 1925–1930.

———. *Journals of the Council of the State of Virginia, 1776–1781.* 2 vols. Richmond: Virginia State Library, 1931.

———. *Legislative Journals of the Council of Colonial Virginia, 1680–1776.* 3 vols. Richmond: Virginia State Library, 1918, 1919.

McIlwaine, H. R., and Kennedy, J. P., eds. *Journals of the House of Burgesses of Virginia, 1619–1777.* 13 vols. Richmond: Virginia State Library, 1905–1915.

Mackall, Sally Somervell. "Mackall Square." Columbia Historical Society, *Records,* 18 (1915), 92–4.

Makemie, Francis. "A Plain and Friendly Perswasive to the Inhabitants of Virginia and Maryland for Promoting Towns and Cohabitation" (London 1705). *Virginia Magazine of History and Biography,* 4 (January 1897), 255–71.

Martin, Lawrence, ed. *The George Washington Atlas.* Washington, D.C.: United States George Washington Bicentennial Commission, 1932.

Mathews, Catherine Van Cortlands. *Andrew Ellicott: His Life and Letters.* New York: Grafton, 1908.

Mathews, Edward B., comp. *Bibliography and Cartography of Maryland.* Baltimore: Johns Hopkins Press, 1897.

———. "The Maps and Map-Makers of Maryland." *Maryland Geological Survey Report,* 2, 337–488. Baltimore: Johns Hopkins Press, 1898.

Maxwell, Constantia. *Irish History from Contemporary Sources (1509–1610).* London: Allen and Unwin, 1923.

Mayer-Rotermund, Gerda. *Alte Gerichtsbegaude in Virginia.* Unpublished Dr. Ing. Dissertation, Technischen Hochschule. Braunschweig, 1958.

Mereness, Newton D. *Maryland as a Proprietary Province.* New York: Macmillan, 1901.

Merrens, Harry Roy. "Historical Geography and Early American History." *William and Mary Quarterly,* 3rd ser., 22 (October 1965), 529–48.

Michel, Francis Louis. "Report of the Journey of Francis Louis Michel from Berne, Switzerland, to Virginia, October 2, 1701–December 1, 1702," Translated and edited by William J. Hinke, *Virginia Magazine of History and Biography,* 24 (January 1916), 1–43; (April 1916), 113–41; (June 1916), 275–88.

Middleton, Arthur Pierce. *Tobacco Coast: A Maritime History of Chesapeake Bay in the Colonial Era.* Newport News: Mariners Museum, 1953.

Moore, Gay Montague. *Seaport in Virginia: George Washington's Alexandria.* Richmond: Garrett and Massie, 1949.

Moorehead, Singleton P. "An Exemplar of Early Building in the Virginia Manner." *Southern Literary Messenger,* 1 (January 1939), 34–38; (May 1939), 314–18.

Moreau de St. Méry, Médéric. *Moreau de St. Méry's American Journey, 1793–1798.* Translated and edited by Kenneth Roberts and Anna M. Roberts. Garden City: Doubleday, 1947.

Morris, Maud Burr. "The Lenthall Houses and Their Owners." Columbia Historical Society, *Records,* 31–32, 1–35. Washington, D.C.: Columbia Historical Society, 1930.

Morton, Richard L. *Colonial Virginia.* 2 vols. Chapel Hill: University of North Carolina Press, 1960.

Niederer, Frances J. *The Town of Fincastle, Virginia.*

Noël Hume, Ivor. *Here Lies Virginia.* New York: Knopf, 1963.
Charlottesville: University Press of Virginia, 1965.

Norris, Walter B. *Annapolis: Its Colonial and Naval Story.* New York: Crowell, 1925.

Ogilby, John. *America: Being the Latest, and Most Accurate Description of the New World. . . .* London: John Ogilby, 1671.

Oglethorpe, James Edward (attributed). *A New and Accurate Account of the Provinces of South Carolina and Georgia.* London: J. Worrall, 1732.

Oldmixon, John. *The British Empire in America.* 2 vols. London: J. Nicholson, B. Tooke, 1708.

O'Neal, William B. *Architecture in Virginia.* New York: Walker, 1968.

Padelford, Philip, ed. *Colonial Panorama, 1775: Dr. Robert Honyman's Journal for March and April.* San Marino: Huntington Library, 1939.

Palmer, William P., ed. *Calendar of Virginia State Papers and Other Manuscripts, 1652–1781.* 4 vols. Richmond: Superintendent of Public Printing, 1875–1884.

Parker, Lawrence E. *The Growth of the Plan of Baltimore, 1729–1797.* Unpublished seminar paper, Department of City and Regional Planning, Cornell University, May, 1968.

Parry, J. H. *Europe and a Wider World, 1415–1715.* 3rd ed. London: Hutchinson University Library, 1966.

———.*The Age of Reconnaissance,* Cleveland: World, 1963.

"Petition of John Mercer." *Virginia Magazine of History and Biography,* 5 (January 1898), 278–82.

Phillips, Cabell. "The Town That Stopped the Clock." *American Heritage,* 11 (February 1960), 22–25, 80–81.

Phillips, P. Lee. "Some Early Maps of Virginia and the Makers, Including Plates Relating to the First Settlement of Jamestown." *Virginia Magazine of History and Biography,* 15 (July 1907), 71–81.

———. *The Rare Map of Virginia and Maryland by Augustine Herrman, First Lord of Bohemia Manor, Maryland.* Washington, D.C.: Lowdermilk, 1911.

———. "Virginia Cartography, a Bibliographical Description." In *Smithsonian Miscellaneous Collections,* 37, no. 1039. Washington, D.C.: Smithsonian Institution, 1896.

Phillips, Sir Thomas. *Londonderry and the London Companies, 1609–1629* Edited by D. A. Chart. Belfast: H. M. Stationery Office, 1928.

Porter, Charles W., III. "Fort Raleigh National Historic Site, North Carolina: Part of the Settlement Sites of Sir Walter Raleigh's Colonies of 1585–1586 and 1587." *North Carolina Historical Review,* 20 (January 1943), 22–42.

Preston, Walter W. *History of Harford County, Maryland.* Baltimore: Press of Sun Book Office, 1901.

"Proposals in Regard to Virginia." *Virginia Magazine of History and Biography,* 25 (January 1917), 71–74.

Purchas, Samuel. *Hakluytus Posthumus or Purchas His Pilgrimes.* 20 vols. Glasgow: MacLehose, 1905–1907.

Quinn, David Beers. "Sir Thomas Smith (1513–1577) and the Beginning of English Colonial Theory." American Philosophical Society, *Proceedings,* 89 (December 1945), 543–60. Philadelphia: American Philosophical Society, 1945.

———. *The Elizabethans and the Irish.* Ithaca: Cornell University Press, 1966.

———, ed. *The Roanoke Voyages, 1584–1590.* 2 vols. London: Hakluyt Society, 1955.

de La Quintinie, Jean. *The Compleat Gard'ner . . . .* Translated into English by John Evelyn. London: Matthew Gillyflower and James Partridge, 1693.

Radoff, Morris L. *Buildings of the State of Maryland at Annapolis.* Annapolis: Hall of Records Commission, State of Maryland, 1954.

———. *The County Courthouses and Records of Maryland. Part One: The Courthouses.* Annapolis: Hall of Records Commission, State of Maryland, 1960.

——; Skordas, Gust; and Jacobsen, Phebe R. *The County Courthouses and Records of Maryland. Part Two: The Records.* Annapolis: Hall of Records Commision, State of Maryland, 1963.

——— ,ed. *The Old Line State: A History of Maryland.* Hopkinsville, Kentucky: Historical Records Association, 1956.

Rainbolt, John C., "The Absence of Towns in Seventeenth-Century Virginia." *Journal of Southern History* 35 (August 1969), 343–360.

"Reasons for Repealing the Acts passed in Virginia and Maryland Relating to Ports and Towns." *Calendar of Virginia State Papers,* 1, 137–38. Richmond: Superintendent of Public Printing, 1875.

Reddaway, T. F. *The Rebuilding of London After the Great Fire.* London: Jonathan Cape, 1940.

———. "The Rebuilding of London After the Great Fire: A Rediscovered Plan." *Town Planning Review,* 18 (July 1939), 155–61.

Reps, John W. *Monumental Washington: The Planning and Development of the Capital Center.* Princeton: Princeton University Press, 1967.

———. *The Making of Urban America: A History of City Planning in the United States.* Princeton: Princeton University Press, 1965.

———. *Town Planning in Frontier America.* Princeton: Princeton University Press, 1969.

R. G. *Virginia's Cure: Or an Advisive Narrative Con-*

cerning Virginia. London: Henry Brome, 1662.
Richmond, I. A. "The Four *Coloniae* of Roman Britain." *Archaeological Journal,* 103 (1947), 57–84.
Riley, Edward M. "Suburban Development of Yorktown, Virginia, During the Colonial Period." *Virginia Magazine of History and Biography,* 60 (October 1952), 522–36.
———. "The Colonial Courthouses of York County, Virginia." *William and Mary Quarterly,* 2nd ser., 22 (October 1942), 399–414.
———. "The Town Acts of Colonial Virginia." *Journal of Southern History,* 16 (August 1950), 306–23.
———, and Hatch, Charles E., Jr., eds. *James Towne in the Words of Contemporaries.* National Park Service, Source Book Series no. 5. Washington, D.C.: Government Printing Office, 1955.
Riley, Elihu S. *"The Ancient City": A History of Annapolis, in Maryland, 1649–1887.* Annapolis: Record Printing Office, 1887.
Robert, Joseph C. *The Story of Tobacco in America.* New York: Knopf, 1949.
Rolfe, John. *A True Relation of the State of Virginia Lefte by Sir Thomas Dale Knight in May last 1616.* Edited with notes by Henry C. Taylor, John Cook Wyllie, John Melville Jennings, and Francis L. Berkeley, Jr. New Haven: Yale University Press, 1951.
Rose, Alexander. "Alexander Rose to Robert Grant, Tillyfour, Scotland." *Virginia Magazine of History and Biography,* 33 (January 1925), 82–4.
Roth, Lawrence V. "The Growth of American Cities." *Geographical Review,* 5 (May 1918), 384–98.
Rowse, A. L. "Of Raleigh and the First Plantation." *American Heritage,* 10 (June 1959), 4–19, 105–11.
Scharf, J. Thomas. *History of Maryland from the Earliest Period to the Present Day* (Baltimore, 1879). 3 vols. Hatboro, Pennsylvania: Tradition Press, 1967.
———. *The Chronicles of Baltimore.* Baltimore: Turnbull, 1874.
Schoepf, Johann David. *Travels in the Confederation, 1783–1784.* Translated and edited by Alfred J. Morrison. Philadelphia: Campbell, 1911.
Sisco, Louis Dow. "A Site for the 'Federal City': The Original Proprietors and Their Negotiations with Washington." Columbia Historical Society, *Records,* 57–59 (1961), 123–47.
Scott, Mary Wingfield, and Catterall, Louise F. *Virginia's Capitol Square: Its Buildings and Its Monuments.* Richmond: Valentine Museum, 1957.
Scribner, Robert L. "Manakintowne in Virginia." *Virginia Cavalcade,* 3 (Winter 1953), 37–41.
Semmes, Raphael. *Baltimore as Seen by Visitors.* Baltimore: Maryland Historical Society, 1953.
Shelley, Fred, ed. "The Journal of Ebenezer Hazard in Virginia." *Virginia Magazine of History and Biography,* 62 (October 1954), 400–23.
Sherman, Richard P. *Robert Johnson: Proprietary and Royal Governor of South Carolina.* Columbia: University of South Carolina Press, 1966.
Shillaber, Caroline. "Edward I, Builder of Towns." *Speculum,* 22 (July 1947), 297–309.
Shurcliff, Arthur A. "The Ancient Plan of Williamsburg." *Landscape Architecture,* 28 (January 1938), 87–101.
Skelton, R. A. "Tudor Town Plans in John Speed's Theatre." *Archaeological Journal,* 108 (1952), 109–20.
[Smith, Thomas] *A Letter sent by J. B. Gentleman unto his very Friend and Master R. C. Esquire.* London: 1571.
Smith, William Loughton. "Journal of William Loughton Smith, 1790–1791," Massachusetts Historical Society, *Proceedings,* 51 (October 1917–June 1918), 20–88. Boston: Massachusetts Historical Society, 1918.
Smyth, John Ferdinand Dalziel. *A Tour in the United States of America.* 2 vols. London: G. Robinson, 1784.
Soltow, James H. "The Role of Williamsburg in the Virginia Economy." *William and Mary Quarterly,* 3rd ser., 15 (October 1958), 467–82.
"Some Early Maps of Virginia and the Makers." *Virginia Magazine of History and Biography,* 15 (July 1907), 71–81.
Sommerville, Charles William. "Early Career of Governor Francis Nicholson." *Maryland Historical Magazine,* 4 (June 1909), 101–14; (September 1909), 201–20.
Sparks, Francis C. *Appendix,* Report of Public Records Commission of Maryland. Baltimore: 1904.
"Speech of Governor Lord Culpeper. His Excellencies first Speech to the Assembly begunne at James Citty June: 8th 1680." *Virginia Magazine of History and Biography,* 14 (April 1907), 362–66.
"Speeches of Students of the College of William and Mary Delivered May 1, 1699." *William and Mary Quarterly,* 2nd ser., 10 (October 1930), 323–37.
Spreiregen, Paul D., ed. *On the Art of Designing Cities: Selected Essays of Elbert Peets.* Cambridge: M.I.T. Press, 1968.
Sprunt, James. *Chronicles of the Cape Fear River, 1660–1919.* 2nd ed. Raleigh: Edwards and Broughton Printing Company, 1916.
Stanard, Mary Newton. *Richmond: Its People and Its Story.* Philadelphia: Lippincott, 1923.
Stearns, Raymond Phineas. "Colonial Fellows of the Royal Society of London, 1661–1788." *William and Mary Quarterly,* 3rd ser., 3 (April 1946), 208–68.
Stein, Charles F. *A History of Calvert County, Maryland.* 2nd ed. Baltimore: Published by the author in cooperation with the Calvert County Historical Society, 1960.
Stewart, Cecil. *A Prospect of Cities.* London: Longmans, Green, 1952.
Stith, William. *The History of the First Discovery and Settlement of Virginia* (Williamsburg, 1747). Spartanburg, South Carolina: The Reprint Company, 1965.
Stokes, I. N. Phelps, and Haskell, Daniel C. *American Historical Prints.* New York: New York Public Library, 1932.
Strachey, William. *The Historie of Travell into Virginia Britania* (1612). Edited by Louis B. Wright and Virginia Freund. London: Hakluyt Society, 1953.
Summerson, John N. *Georgian London.* New York: Scribner's, 1946.
Sutherland, Stella H. *Population Distribution in Colonial America.* New York: Columbia University Press, 1936.
Swain, Robert L., Jr. "Chestertown as a Colonial Port 1706–1775." *Washington College Bulletin,* 14 (July 1936).
Swem, Earl G., comp. "Maps Relating to Virginia in the Virginia State Library and Other Departments of the Commonwealth with the 17th and 18th Century Atlas-Maps in the Library of Congress." In Virginia State Library, *Bulletin,* 7 (April–July 1914), 33–263.
———. *Virginia Historical Index.* 2 vols. Roanoke: Stone Printing Company, 1934–36.
Taggart, Hugh T. "Old Georgetown." Columbia Historical Society, *Records,* 11 (1908), 120–224.

Taylor, Donald Ransome. *Out of the Past—The Future.* Hampton, Virginia: Prestige Press, 1960.

"The Building of Williamsburg." *William and Mary Quarterly,* 1st ser., 10 (October 1901), 73–92.

"The Starving Time. Letters from Lord De La Ware to the Earl of Salisbury." *Virginia Magazine of History and Biography,* 14 (April 1907), 378–83.

Thompson, Edward. *Sir Walter Ralegh.* New Haven: Yale University Press, 1936.

Thornton, Mary L., comp. *A Bibliography of North Carolina, 1589–1956.* Chapel Hill: University of North Carolina Press, 1958.

Tilghman, Oswald. *History of Talbot County Maryland, 1661–1861, Compiled Principally from the Literary Relics of the Late Samuel Alexander Harrison, A.M., M.D.* (Easton, 1915). 2 vols. Baltimore: Regional Publishing Company, 1967.

Tindall, William. *Origin and Government of the District of Columbia.* Washington, D.C.: Government Printing Office, 1908.

———. *Standard History of the City of Washington.* Knoxville: H. W. Crew, 1914.

Torrence, Clayton. *Old Somerset on the Eastern Shore of Maryland.* Baltimore: Regional Publishing Company, 1966.

Toulmin, Harry. *The Western Country in 1793.* Edited by Marion Tinling and Godfrey Davies. San Marino: Huntington Library, 1948.

Tout, Thomas Frederick. *Mediaeval Town Planning.* Manchester: Manchester University Press, 1948.

Trabut-Cussac, Jean-Paul. "Bastides ou Forteresses? Les Bastides de l'Aquitaine Anglaise et les Intentions de leurs Foudateurs." *Moyen Age,* 60 (4th ser., 9), (1954), 81–135.

Trewartha, Glenn T. "Types of Rural Settlement in Colonial America." *Geographical Review,* 36 (October 1946), 568–96.

Trollope, Frances. *Domestic Manners of the Americans* (London, 1832) 2 vols. New York: Dodd, Mead, 1894.

Troubetzkoy, Ulrich. "George Washington, Surveyor." *Virginia Cavalcade,* 10 (Winter, 1960–61), 5–10.

Turman, Nora Miller. *The Eastern Shore of Virginia, 1603–1964.* Onancock, Virginia: Eastern Shore News, 1964.

Tyler, Lyon G. "Bruton Church." *William and Mary Quarterly,* 1st ser., 3 (January 1895), 169–80.

———. ed. *Narratives of Early Virginia, 1606–1625.* New York: Scribner's, 1907.

———. "History of York County in the Seventeenth Century." *Tyler's Quarterly Historical and Genealogical Magazine* 1 (July 1919–April 1920), 231–75.

———. *The Cradle of the Republic: Jamestown and James River.* 2nd ed. Richmond: Hermitage Press, 1906.

———. "Williamsburg—The Old Colonial Capital." *William and Mary Quarterly,* 1st ser., 16 (July 1907), 1–65.

U. S. Bureau of the Census. *A Century of Population Growth.* Washington, D.C.: Government Printing Office, 1909.

———. *Aggregate Amount of Each Description of Persons within the United States of America . . . in the Year 1810.* Washington, D.C.: Government Printing Office, 1811.

U. S. Commission of Fine Art and Office of Archeology and Historic Preservation, National Park Service, Department of the Interior. *Georgetown Historic Waterfront.* Washington, D.C.: Government Printing Office, 1968.

U. S. Writers' Project. *Alexandria.* Alexandria: Williams Printing Company, 1939.

———. *Maryland: A Guide to the Old Line State.* New York: Oxford University Press, 1940.

———. *Prince William, The Story of Its People and Its Places.* Richmond: Whittet and Shepperson, 1941.

———. *Sussex County: A Tale of Three Centuries.* Richmond: Whittet and Shepperson, 1942.

———. *Virginia: A Guide to the Old Dominion.* New York: Oxford University Press, 1940.

———. *West Virginia: A Guide to the Mountain State.* New York: Oxford University Press, 1941.

Verner, Coolie. "The First Maps of Virginia, 1590–1673." *Virginia Magazine of History and Biography,* 58 (January 1950), 3–15.

[Virginia General Assembly, Joint Committee on the State Library] *Colonial Records of Virginia.* Richmond: R. F. Walker, Superintendent Public Printing, 1874.

"Virginia in 1680." *Virginia Magazine of History and Biography,* 25 (April 1917), 139–48.

"Virginia Under Governor Harvey." *Virginia Magazine of History and Biography,* 3 (July 1895), 21–34.

Watkins, C. Malcolm. *The Cultural History of Marlborough, Virginia: An Archeological and Historical Investigation of the Port Town for Stafford County and the Plantation of John Mercer. . . .* Washington, D.C.: Smithsonian Institution Press, 1968.

Webb, Stephen S. "The Strange Career of Francis Nicholson." *William and Mary Quarterly,* 3rd ser., 23 (October 1966), 513–48.

Weddell, Alexander Wilbourne. *Richmond Virginia in Old Prints, 1737–1887.* John Lee McElroy, associate editor; foreword by Douglas S. Freeman. Richmond: Richmond Academy of Arts, 1932.

Weld, Isaac. *Travels through the States of North America and the Provinces of Upper and Lower 1797.* 2 *Canada, during the Years 1795, 1796, and* vols. 4th ed. London: J. Stockdale, 1807.

Wertenbaker, Thomas J. *Norfolk: Historic Southern Port.* 2nd ed. Edited by Marvin W. Schlegel. Durham: Duke University Press, 1962.

———. "The Restoring of Colonial Williamsburg." *North Carolina Historical Review,* 27 (April 1950), 218–32.

———. *Virginia Under the Stuarts.* Princeton: Princeton University Press, 1914.

Wharton, James. "The Lost Settlement of Queenstown." *Northern Neck of Virginia Historical Magazine,* 10 (December 1960), 875–79.

Whichard, Rogers Dey. *The History of Lower Tidewater Virginia.* 3 vols. New York: Lewis Historical Publishing Company, 1959.

Whiffen, Marcus. "The Early County Courthouses of Virginia." *Journal of the Society of Architectural Historians,* 18 (March 1959), 2–10.

———. *The Eighteenth Century Houses of Williamsburg.* Williamsburg: Colonial Williamsburg, 1960.

———. *The Public Buildings of Williamsburg.* Williamsburg: Colonial Williamsburg, 1958.

White, M. P., Jr., and Usilton, Ralph H. *A Guide to Historic Chestertown Maryland.* Chestertown: Kent Publishing Company, 1967.

Whitehill, Walter Muir. *Boston: A Topographical History.* Cambridge: Belknap Press of Harvard University Press, 1959.

Williams, Neville. "England's Tobacco Trade in the Reign of Charles I." *Virginia Magazine of History and Biography,* 65 (October 1957), 403–21.

Willison, George F. *Behold Virginia!* New York: Harcourt, Brace 1951.

Wilson, Rufus Rockwell, ed. *Burnaby's Travels Through North America.* 3rd ed. London: T. Payne, 1798.

Wilstach, Paul. *Potomac Landings.* Indianapolis: Bobbs-Merrill, 1920.

———. *Tidewater Virginia.* Indianapolis: Bobbs-Merrill, 1929.

Wright, Louis B., ed. *The Prose Works of William Byrd of Westover.* Cambridge: Harvard University Press, 1966.

Wroth, Peregrine. "New Yarmouth." *Maryland Historical Magazine,* 3 (September 1908), 273–76.

Wyckoff, V. J. "The Sizes of Plantations in Seventeenth Century Maryland." *Maryland Historical Magazine,* 32 (December 1937), 331–39.

Wyckoff, Vertrees J. *Tobacco Regulation in Colonial Maryland.* Baltimore: John Hopkins Press, 1936.

Yonge, Samuel H. *The Site of Old "James Towne," 1607–1698.* Richmond: Association for the Preservation of Virginia Antiquities, 1904.

Notes on the Illustrations

This list contains bibliographic information about the illustrations reproduced in this work. The following symbols indicate the source of these materials:

A	Author's collection
APSL	American Philosophical Society Library, Philadelphia, Pennsylvania
BB	Burgerbibliothek, Bern, Switzerland
BCW	Bruton Parish Church, Williamsburg, Virginia
BM-M	British Museum, Map Room, London, England
BM-MS	British Museum, Department of Manuscripts
BM-PD	British Museum, Department of Prints and Drawings
CNHP	Colonial National Historical Park, Yorktown, Virginia
CU-FA	Cornell University, Fine Arts Library, Ithaca, New York
CU-O	Cornell University, Olin Library
CW	Colonial Williamsburg, Williamsburg, Virginia
CWMS	College of William and Mary, Swem Memorial Library, Williamsburg, Virginia
FCL	Filson Club Library, Louisville, Kentucky
FCPR	Fredericksburg Courthouse Public Records, Fredericksburg, Virginia
HEHL	Henry E. Huntington Library and Art Gallery, San Marino, California
HSP	Historical Society of Pennsylvania, Philadelphia, Pennsylvania
JCB	John Carter Brown Library, Brown University, Providence, Rhode Island
LC-M	Library of Congress, Division of Geography and Maps, Washington, D.C.
LC-MS	Library of Congress, Division of Manuscripts
LC-P	Library of Congress, Division of Prints and Photographs
MDHS	Maryland Historical Society, Baltimore, Maryland
MHR	Maryland Hall of Records, Annapolis, Maryland
MMA	Metropolitan Museum of Art, New York, New York
MMNN	Mariners Museum, Newport News, Virginia
MWGK	Private collection of Mrs. Mary Ware Galt Kirby, Williamsburg, Virginia
NBL	Newberry Library, Chicago, Illinois
NLI	National Library of Ireland, Dublin, Ireland
NY-R	New York Public Library, Rare Books Division, New York, New York
NY-S	New York Public Library, Stokes Collection
PM-G	Peale Museum, General Collection, Baltimore, Maryland
PM-H	Peale Museum, Hambleton Collection
PNSM	Portsmouth Naval Shipyard Museum, Portsmouth, Virginia
PRO	Public Record Office, London, England
PU-R	Princeton University Library, Rare Books Department, Princeton, New Jersey
RDPW	Richmond Department of Public Works, Richmond, Virginia
RGS	Royal Geographical Society, London, England
UVMcL	University of Virginia, McGregor Library, Charlottesville, Virginia
VHS	Virginia Historical Society, Richmond, Virginia
VSL	Virginia State Library, Richmond, Virginia
WLC	William L. Clements Library, Ann Arbor, Michigan
YCRY	York County Records, Yorktown, Virginia

FIGURE 1. *Plan Général de Montpazier* (Dordogne). Plan of Monpazier, France, in 1284; drawn by F. de Verneilh, engraved by Th. Olivier; published in Victor Didron, ed., *Annales Archéologiques*, 12 (Paris, 1852). CU-FA

FIGURE 2. *Plan Partiel de la Ville de Beaumont en Périgord (Dordogne)*, Plan of Beaumont en Périgord, France, in 1272; drawn by F. de Verneilh, engraved by T. Olivier; published in Victor Didron, ed., *Annales Archéologiques*, 6 (Paris, 1847). CU-FA

FIGURE 3. *Flint.* Inset plan of Flint, Wales, on a map of Flintshire; drawn by John Speed, engraved by Jodocus Hondius in 1610; from John Speed, *Theatre of the Empire of Great Britaine* (London, 1611). BM-M

FIGURE 4. *Caernarvon.* Inset plan of Carnarvon, Wales, on a map of Carnarvonshire; drawn by John Speed in 1610; from John Speed, *Theatre of the Empire of Great Britaine* (London, 1611). BM-M

FIGURE 5. *Hull.* Inset plan of Hull, England, on a map of the North and East ridings of Yorkshire; drawn by John Speed in 1610; from John Speed, *Theatre of the Empire of Great Britaine* (London, 1611). BM-M

FIGURE 6. *Plan of the Ancient Town of Winchelsea, Sussex.* Plan of Winchelsea, England, in 1853; engraved by J. H. Le Keux; from [John H. Parker], *Some Account of Domestic Architecture in England, from Edward I. to Richard II.* (Oxford, 1853). CU-FA

FIGURE 7. *Salesbvry.* Inset plan of Salisbury, England, on a map of Wiltshire; drawn by John Speed, engraved by Jodocus Hondius in 1610; from John Speed, *Theatre of the Empire of Great Britaine* (London, 1611). BM-M

FIGURE 8. Untitled, undated, and unsigned manuscript plan of Calais, France, ca. 1557. Cotton MS Aug. I. ii. 71. BM-MS

FIGURE 9. *Chichester.* Inset of Chichester, England, on a map of Sussex; drawn by John Norden; published in 1595. RGS

FIGURE 10. Untitled, unsigned, and undated manuscript plan of Armagh and the fort at Blackwater, Northern Ireland; drawn by Richard Bartlett ca. 1601. MS 2656. NLI

FIGURE 11. Untitled, undated, and unsigned plan of Londonderry, Northern Ireland; drawn in 1600 to show extensions proposed by Sir Henry Docwra; reproduced from the original manuscript in the library of Trinity College, Dublin, in Sir Thomas A. Larcom, *Ordnance Survey of the County of Londonderry*, vol. 1, *Memoir of the City and North Western Liberties of Londonderry.* (Dublin, 1837). BM-M

FIGURE 12. *The Plat of the Cittie of Londonderrie as it Stand Built and Fortyfyed.* Unsigned and undated manuscript plan of Londonderry, Northern Ireland; drawn in 1622; reproduced from the original in Lambeth Palace, London; from John T. Gilbert, ed., *Facsimiles of National Manuscripts of Ireland*, part 4, no. 2 (London, 1884). CU-O

FIGURE 13. *Colerane.* Plan of Coleraine, Northern Ireland; from William Petty, *Hiberniae Delineatio* (London, 1683). NBL

FIGURE 14. *A Gnnerall Plat of the lands Belonginge to the Cittie of London as they are devided and set out to the 12 Companies. . . .* Unsigned and undated manuscript map of Ulster, Northern Ireland; drawn in 1622; reproduced from the original in Lambeth Palace, London; from John T. Gilbert, ed., *Facsimiles of National Manuscripts of Ireland*, part 4, no. 2 (London, 1884). CU-O

FIGURE 15. *The Buildings Be Longing to the Company of Drapers at Monnemore.* Unsigned and undated manuscript plan of Moneymore, Northern Ireland; drawn in 1622; reproduced from the original in Lambeth Palace, London; from John T. Gilbert, ed., *Facsimiles of National Manuscripts of Ireland*, part 4, no. 2 (London, 1884). CU-O

FIGURE 16. *The Fishmongers Buildings at Ballekelle.* Unsigned and undated manuscript plan of Ballykelly, Northern Ireland; drawn in 1622; reproduced from the original in Lambeth Palace, London; from John T. Gilbert, ed., *Facsimiles of National Manuscripts of Ireland*, part 4, no. 2 (London, 1884). CU-O

FIGURE 17. *A Plan of the Cities of London and Westminster, and Borough of Southwark; with the Contiguous Buildings.* Portion of a plan of London in 24 sheets; drawn by John Rocque; published by John Pine and John Tinney (London, 1746). A

FIGURE 18. *A Plan of London . . . . Described by J. Evelyn, Esq F.R.S. A plan of the City of London . . . . of Sir Christopher Wren.* Plans for rebuilding London after the fire of 1666; by John Evelyn and Christopher Wren, engraved in 1748; from London Antiquarian Society, *Vetusta Monumenta* (London, 1789). A

FIGURE 19. *Americae pars, Nunc Virginia . . . .* Map of coastal North Carolina and adjacent areas; engraved by Theodore De Bry in 1590 from a drawing by John White of 1585; from Thomas Harriot, *Admiranda Narratio fida tamen, de Commodis et Incolarum Ritibus Virginiae* (Frankfurt, 1590). MMNN

FIGURE 20. *Anglorum in Virginiam aduentus.* Map of Roanoke Island, North Carolina, and vicinity; engraved by Theodore De Bry in 1590; from Thomas Harriot, *Admiranda Narratio fida tamen, de Commodis et Incolarum Ritibus Virginiae* (Frankfurt, 1590). MMNN

FIGURE 21. *Philippeville. Mariebourg.* Unsigned and undated plans of Philippsville and Mariebourg, Belgium; from Georg Braun and Frans Hogenberg, *Urbium Praecipuarum Totius Mundi* (Cologne, 1581), as reproduced in facsimile in Braun and Hogenberg, *Civitates Orbis Terrarum*, 1572–1618 (Amsterdam, 1965). A

FIGURE 22. *The forms of a fort . . . . in a parte of St. Johns Islande.* Unsigned manuscript plan of the fort designed by Ralph Lane in Puerto Rico; drawn by John White in 1585. BM-PD

FIGURE 23. *Plan of the fort as reconstructed.* Unsigned conjectural plan of Fort Raleigh, North Carolina, in 1585; prepared for the National Park Service in 1952, revised in 1962; from Jean Carl Harrington, *Search for the Cittie of Ralegh* (Washington, 1962). A

FIGURE 24. *Artist's reconstruction of the fort.* Unsigned and undated conjectural view of Fort Raleigh, North Carolina, in 1585; prepared for the National Park Service; from Jean Carl Harrington, *Search for the Cittie of Ralegh* (Washington, 1962). A

FIGURE 25. *Virginia.* Map of Virginia; drawn by Captain John Smith in 1608, engraved by William Hole; published in 1624 with alterations and additions to the original edition of 1612. LC-M

FIGURE 26. Untitled, undated and unsigned conjectural reconstruction of Jamestown, Virginia, in 1607; copied by Frances Dayton from a drawing prepared for the National Park Service. CW

FIGURE 27. Untitled, undated, and unsigned view of Fort Caroline, Florida, in 1564; engraved by Theodore De Bry in 1591 from a drawing by Jacques Le Moyne; from Jacques Le Moyne, *Brevis Narratio Eorum Quae in Florida Americae Provincia Gallis Acciderunt* (Frankfurt, 1591). BM-M

FIGURE 28. Untitled, undated, and unsigned manuscript plan of St. Augustine, Florida, in 1593; traced from the original in the Archives of the Indies, Seville,

Spain. Lowery Collection, WL 76; LC-M

FIGURE 29. *Virginiae Pars.* Map of the coast of Virginia and the James River in 1613; from Francus Jacobus (pseud. for Conrad Memmius). *Relations Historicae Continuatio, oder Warhafftige Beschreibunge aller . . . Historien . . . dieses* 1613 (Frankfurt, 1613). NY-R

FIGURE 30. Untitled, undated, and unsigned conjectural reconstruction of Jamestown, Virginia, ca. 1614; drawn by Sidney E. King for the National Park Service. CNHP

FIGURE 31. *A mapp of Virginia . . .* Map of Virginia and Maryland; drawn by John Farrer, engraved by John Goddard; from Edward Bland, *The Discovery of Nevv Brittaine* (London, 1651). WLC

FIGURE 32. *"New Towne" "A Part of old Jamestown, Virginia's Capital City."* Unsigned and undated conjectural plan prepared for the National Park Service, showing a portion of Jamestown, Virginia, as laid out by William Claiborne, ca. 1621. CNHP

FIGURE 33. Untitled, undated, and unsigned painting by Sidney E. King for the National Park Service, showing a conjectural reconstruction of structure 17 in Jamestown, Virginia. CNHP

FIGURE 34. Untitled and undated painting by Sidney E. King for the National Park Service, showing a conjectural reconstruction of structure 16 in Jamestown, Virginia. CNHP

FIGURE 35. Untitled, undated, and unsigned painting by Sidney E. King for the National Park Service, showing a conjectural reconstruction of structure 21 in Jamestown, Virginia. CNHP

FIGURE 36. Untitled painting by Sidney E. King in 1956 for the National Park Service, showing a conjectural reconstruction of structure 6 in Jamestown, Virginia. CNHP

FIGURE 37. Untitled and undated painting by Sidney E. King for the National Park Service showing a conjectural reconstruction of structure 115 in Jamestown, Virginia. CNHP

FIGURE 38. Untitled painting by Sidney E. King in 1957 for the National Park Service showing a conjectural reconstruction of the country house-Ludwell house-statehouse group in Jamestown, Virginia. CNHP

FIGURE 39. *Nova Terrae-Mariae tabula.* Map of Maryland in 1635, engraved by T. Cecill, from *A Relation of Maryland. . . .* London, 1635. CU-O

FIGURE 40. *Virginia and Maryland As it is Planted and Inhabited this present Year 1670.* Portion of a map of Virginia and Maryland, drawn by Augustine Herrman in 1670, engraved by W. Faithorne, published by Augustine Herrmann and Thomas Withinbrook. London, 1673. LC-M

FIGURE 41. *A Map of General Washington's Farm of Mount Vernon from a Drawing transmitted by the General.* Map of Mount Vernon, Virginia in 1793, drawn by George Washington, engraved by Neele, from *Letters from his Excellency Gen. Washington to Arthur Young.* London, 1801. LC-M

FIGURE 42. *Mount Vernon—The Home of Washington.* Portion of an illustration showing the plan of the grounds of Mount Vernon, Virginia, reproduced by R. von Glümer ca. 1892, from a drawing by George Washington ca. 1784, lithograph by N. Peters. Washington, D.C., ca. 1892. LC-M

FIGURE 43. Untitled, unsigned, and undated painting of a southern plantation ca. 1825. Garbisch collection. MMA

FIGURE 44. *A map Showing Ports Established in Virginia 1680 1691 1706.* Map of Virginia showing locations of new towns created by acts of the colonial General Assembly in 1680, 1691, and 1706, from Edward F. Heite, "Markets and Ports," *Virginia Cavalcade,* 16 (Autumn 1966). VSL

FIGURE 45. *The plott of New Plymouth Towne.* Manuscript plan of New Plymouth (now Tappahannock), Virginia; drawn by George Morris in 1680; from a photocopy of the original in Rappahannock County Deed Book No. 7, 1682–1688. VSL

FIGURE 46. *Tappahanock Town.* Manuscript plan of Tappahannock, Virginia; drawn by Harry Beverley in 1706. VSL

FIGURE 47. *Onancock, Virginia: 1681.* Redrawing in 1968 by John W. Reps of a plan of Onancock, Accomack County, Virginia, reproduced in Ralph T. Whitelaw, *Virginia's Eastern Shore* (Richmond, 1951), vol. 2; from a copy made ca. 1870 of a resurvey in 1761 by James Henry of the original plat of 1681 prepared by Colonel Daniel Jenifer. A

FIGURE 48. *Plan d'hampton pour Servir a l'Etablissement du Quartier d'hiver de la Legion de Lauzun. . . .* Manuscript plan of Hampton, Virginia; drawn by Louis-Alexandre Berthier in 1781. Berthier Papers, No. 28. PU-R

FIGURE 49. *Gray's New Map of Hampton.* Plan of Hampton, Virginia in 1878; published by O. W. Gray & Son (Philadelphia, 1878). VSL

FIGURE 50. *A Map of the Inhabited part of Virginia containing the whole Province of Maryland with Part of Pensilvania, New Jersey and North Carolina.* Portion of a map of Virginia and Maryland and adjoining areas; drawn in 1751 by Joshua Fry and Peter Jefferson; engraved and published by Thomas Jefferys (London, 1754[?]); from a facsimile of the original in the Tracy W. McGregor Library published in 1950 by the Princeton University Press for the Harry Clemons Publication Fund of the University of Virginia. UVMcL

FIGURE 51. *Plan of the Site of Norfolk Town 1680–1736.* Plan of Norfolk, Virginia, during the period 1680–1736; as reconstructed from records of survey by Rogers Dey Whichard in 1957; from his *The History of Lower Tidewater Virginia* (New York, 1959), vol. 1. CU-O

FIGURE 52. *Marlborough Town as surveyed by Theodorick Bland.* Manuscript copy drawn by John Savage in 1734 of a plan of Marlborough, Stafford County, Virginia; copied by Theodorick Bland in 1691 from the original plat drawn by William Buckner. John Mercer Letter Book. VSL

FIGURE 53. *The Town of Marlborough Surveyed by John Savage.* Manuscript plan of Marlborough, Stafford County, Virginia; drawn by John Savage in 1731. John Mercer Letter Book. VSL.

FIGURE 54. *Urbanna, Virginia: 1747.* Redrawing by John W. Reps in 1968 from a photocopy of a plan of Urbanna, Middlesex County, Virginia drawn by N. H. Towles in 1747, as copied in 1960 by Dr. Wesley M. Laing. VSL

FIGURE 55. *Carte detaillée de West point Sur la Riviere d'york au Confluent des Rivieres de Pamunkey et Matapony.* Unsigned, undated manuscript map of West Point, King William County, Virginia and vicinity; drawn ca. 1781. Rochambeau Collection, No. 54. LC-M

FIGURE 56. *Deleware Town.* Plan of Delaware Town, King William County, Virginia, surveyed by Harry Beverly in 1706; as reconstructed from records of survey by Malcolm H. Harris and drawn by G. L. Evans in 1934; from Malcolm H. Harris, " 'Delaware Town' and 'West Point' in King William County, Va.," *William and Mary Quarterly,* 2nd ser., 14 (1934). CU-O

FIGURE 57. *A Plat of fifty Acres of land surveyed for Yorke County for a Towne.* Manuscript survey of the boundary of Yorktown, York County, Virginia; drawn

by Lawrence Smith in 1691. YCRY

FIGURE 58. *A platt of the towne belonging to Yorke County.* Manuscript plan of Yorktown, York County, Virginia; drawn by Lawrence Smith in 1691. YCRY

FIGURE 59. *Plan of d'York-town . . . 1781.* Unsigned manuscript plan of a portion of Yorktown, York County, Virginia; drawn by Louis-Alexandre Berthier in 1781. Berthier Papers, No. 29. PU-R

FIGURE 60. *A View of the Town of York Virginia from the River.* Unsigned and undated manuscript view of Yorktown, York County, Virginia; drawn ca. 1755 by John Gauntlett; from *Voyage of H.M.S. Success & H.M.S. Norwich to Nova Scotia & Virginia 1754–6.* MMNN

FIGURE 61. *A Plan of York Town produced in York County Court the twenty first day of July 1788.* Manuscript plan of a portion of Yorktown, York County, Virginia; drawn by Robert Waller in 1788. YCRY

FIGURE 62. *A Plat of Gloucester County Town laid off and divided into Lotts . . . .* Manuscript plan of Gloucester Point, Virginia; surveyed April 19, 1707 by Niles Carey. Robert Reade Thruston Papers, 1653–1838, 1 bound volume, 217. FCL

FIGURE 63. *A View of the Town of Gloucester York River Virginia.* Unsigned and undated manuscript view of Gloucester Point, Gloucester County, Virginia; drawn ca. 1755 by John Gauntlett; from *Voyage of H.M.S. Success & H.M.S. Norwich to Nova Scotia & Virginia 1754–6.* MMNN

FIGURE 64. *Cobham, Virginia: 1738.* Redrawing by John W. Reps in 1968 of a manuscript survey by Richard Cocke in 1738; as reproduced in A. W. Bohannan, "The Old Town of Cobham," *Virginia Magazine of History and Biography*, 57 (1949). A

FIGURE 65. *Maryland Towns Established by Governor's Proclamations of 1668, 1669, and 1671.* Manuscript map of Maryland showing sites designated for new towns, 1668–1671; drawn by Richard L. Anglin in 1968. A

FIGURE 66. *Virginia and Maryland . . . .* Portion of a map of Virginia and Maryland and adjacent areas; drawn by Augustine Herrman in 1670, engraved by W. Faithorne; published by Augustine Herrman and Thomas Withinbrook (London, 1678). LC-M

FIGURE 67. *Maryland Towns Established by Legislative Enactments 1683, 1684, 1686, and 1688.* Manuscript map of Maryland showing sites designated for new towns, 1683–1688; drawn by Richard L. Anglin in 1968. A

FIGURE 68. *Maryland Towns Established by Legislative Enactments 1706, 1707, and 1708.* Manuscript map of Maryland showing sites designated for new towns, 1706–1708; drawn by Richard L. Anglin in 1968. A

FIGURE 69. *A Platt of Marleborough Town in Prince Geo. County 1706.* Manuscript plan of Upper Marlborough, Prince Georges County, Maryland; drawn by Thomas Truman Greenfield in 1706. MDHS

FIGURE 70. *St. Leonards Town.* Undated and unsigned manuscript plan of St. Leonards Town, Calvert County, Maryland; drawn ca. 1706. MDHS

FIGURE 71. *The Draught of Greene Hill Towne and Pourtt.* Manuscript plan of Green Hill, Somerset County, Maryland; drawn by William Whittington in 1707. MDHS

FIGURE 72. Untitled manuscript plan of Snow Hill, Worcester County, Maryland; drawn by Joshua Mitchell in 1793; photocopy of Worcester County land records, liber P, folio 293. MHR

FIGURE 73. *The Mappe of Vienna Towne in Nanticoke River.* Unsigned and undated manuscript plan of Vienna, Dorchester County, Maryland; drawn by Thomas Ennalls in 1706. MHR

FIGURE 74. Untitled manuscript plan of Cambridge, Dorchester County, Maryland; drawn in 1853 by Geo. Winthrop. MHR

FIGURE 75. *A Platt of the Towne & Port of Oxford.* Manuscript plan of Oxford, Talbot County, Maryland; drawn by William Turbutt in 1707; as reproduced from the original, owned by the commissioners of Oxford, in M. V. Brewington, *Chesapeake Bay: A Pictorial Maritime History* (Cambridge, Md. 1953). CU-O

FIGURE 76. *Oxford.* Plan of Oxford, Talbot County, Maryland in 1877; from Lake, Griffing & Stevenson, *An Illustrated Atlas of Talbot & Dorchester Counties, Md.* (Philadelphia, 1877). MDHS

FIGURE 77. *A Plat of Wye Town or Doncaster, Talbot County.* Plan of Wye, Talbot County, Maryland; redrawn by Henry Chandlee Forman from the original plat in Wye House surveyed by Philemon Hemsley in 1707; from Forman, *Tidewater Maryland Architecture and Gardens* (New York, 1956). A

FIGURE 78. *A Plot of Chester Town in Maryland.* Plan of Chestertown, Kent County, Maryland ca. 1850; traced in 1953 by Rolph Townshend, Jr., from a lithograph published by E. Sachse & Co. MHR

FIGURE 79. *Chestertown.* Plan of Chestertown, Kent County, Maryland in 1877; from Lake, Griffing & Stevenson, *An Illustrated Atlas of Kent & Queen Annes Counties, Md.* (Philadelphia, 1877). MDHS

FIGURE 80. *A Map of Virginia and Maryland.* Unsigned and undated map of Virginia and Maryland; engraved by F. Lamb; from John Speed, *Theatre of the Empire of Great Britain* (London, 1676). LC-M

FIGURE 81. *A Ground Plat of the City and Port of Annapolis.* Unsigned manuscript copy drawn in 1743 from the survey of Annapolis, Maryland in 1718 by James Stoddert. MHR

FIGURE 82. *Plan of Annapolis.* Plan of Annapolis, Maryland as surveyed by James Stoddert in 1718; redrawn in 1956 by Harry A. H. Ewald from a manuscript copy of the Stoddert survey drawn in 1743. MHR

FIGURE 83. *Plan of Annapolis, Maryland: 1718.* Manuscript plan of a portion of Annapolis, Maryland; drawn by John W. Reps in 1968 showing points of intersection of centerlines of streets; based on James Stoddert's resurvey of 1718 as copied in 1743. A

FIGURE 84. Untitled garden plan; from the English translation by John Evelyn of Jean de La Quintinie, *The Compleat Gard'ner . . . .* (London, 1693). CU-O

FIGURE 85. *London Restored Or Sir John Evelyn's Plan for Rebuilding that Ancient Metropolis after the Fire in 1666.* Plan for rebuilding London in 1666 by John Evelyn; from William Maitland, *The History and Survey of London from its Foundation to the Present Time. . . .* (London, 1756). A

FIGURE 86. *State House Annapolis, Md.* Unsigned and undated view of the statehouse in Annapolis, Maryland; published ca. 1863; after a view in the *Columbian Magazine*, February, 1789. PM-H

FIGURE 87. Untitled, unsigned, and undated manuscript view of Annapolis, Maryland; drawn ca. 1800. NY-S

FIGURE 88. *A Ground Plot of the City of Annapolis.* Unsigned and undated manuscript of Annapolis, Maryland; copied from the survey by James Stoddert in 1718 as redrawn in 1743. MHR

FIGURE 89. *Plan of the Harbor and City of Annapolis.* Portion of a manuscript plan of Annapolis, Maryland; drawn by Major Capitaine in 1781; from a photocopy of the original in the Dépot de la Guerre, Paris, France. LC-M

FIGURE 90. *The State House (at Annapolis Maryland).* Unsigned manuscript view of the statehouse at Annapolis, Maryland, and an untitled and unsigned manuscript view of McDowell Hall at St. John's College in Annapolis; drawn by G. W. Smith, ca. 1810. HSP

Rochambeau, avant le Siege de York en Virginie Mois d' 8bre 1781. Unsigned manuscript map of Williamsburg, Virginia and vicinity; drawn by Major Capitaine in 1781; from *Atlas de la Guerre à Amerique.* BCW

FIGURE 124. *Plan of That Part of the Virginia Canal from Colledge Creek to Williamsburg. . . .* Undated manuscript plan of the proposed canal from College Landing to Williamsburg, Virginia; drawn in 1818 by Thos. M. Ladd. VSL

FIGURE 125. *William and Mary College at Williamsburg, Va.* View of the College of William and Mary in Williamsburg, Virginia, from the east; drawn by Thomas Ch. Millington, lithograph by E. J. P. in 1840. NY-S

FIGURE 126. *Carte des Environs de Williamsburg en Virginia où les Armees Francoise et Americaine ont Campés en Septembre 1781.* Portion of an unsigned manuscript map of Williamsburg, Virginia, and vicinity, drawn in 1781; with the addition of the boundaries of the original town in 1699 and the 1971 boundaries of the area restored by Colonial Williamsburg. Rochambeau Collection, No. 57. LC-M

FIGURE 127. Untitled, unsigned, and undated plan of Manakin, Virginia, ca. 1700; from a reproduction of an unidentified manuscript in R. A. Brock, ed., *Documents. . . . Relating to the Huguenot Emigration to Virginia and to the Settlement at Manakin-Town* (Richmond, 1886). CU-O

FIGURE 128. *Eden in Virginia Von der Helvetischen Societet Er Kaufte 33400 Jucharten Land A° 1736.* Unsigned map of the land owned in Virginia by William Byrd II; with an inset plan of one of the proposed towns; from *Neu-gefundenes Eden. . . .* (Bern [?]), 1737. JCB

FIGURE 129. *Plan of the Town of Fredericksburg as first laid off in 50 Acres of Land by Royston & Buckman 1721.* Unsigned manuscript plan of Fredericksburg, Spotsylvania County, Virginia, as surveyed in 1721. VSL

FIGURE 130. Untitled manuscript plan of Fredericksburg, Spotsylvania County, Virginia, in 1769; as drawn by Caleb Smith in 1809; from Fredericksburg Court records, Land Causes and Appeals, 1808–1821. FCPR

FIGURE 131. *View of Fredericksburg, Va. Nov. 1862.* View of Fredericksburg, Spotsylvania County, Virginia from the east in 1862; drawn and published by E. Sachse & Co. (Baltimore, 1863). LC-P

FIGURE 132. *Fredericksburg.* Plans of Fredericksburg and Falmouth, Virginia, from a map of Fredericksburg and vicinity; surveyed and drawn by Maj. J. E. Weyss; printed by the New York Lithographing, Engraving & Printing Co. by order of the chief of Engineers, 1867. CU-O

FIGURE 133. Untitled, unsigned, and undated manuscript plan of Mercer Town, Stafford County, Virginia, ca. 1785. VSL

FIGURE 134. *A Plat of the Town of Newport on Potowmac River as laid out and Surveyed by Samuel Byrn. . . .* [title on reverse]. Manuscript plan of Newport, Prince William County, Virginia; drawn by Samuel Byrn in 1788; from Prince William County Legislative Petition, November 21, 1788. VSL

FIGURE 135. *Woodstock.* Manuscript copy drawn by Robert Bayly and W. P. Bayly in 1807 of an earlier survey of Woodstock, Stafford County, Virginia. VSL

FIGURE 136. *A Map of the Most Inhabited Part of Virginia Containing the Whole Province of Maryland. . . .* Portion of a map of Virginia and Maryland and adjacent areas; drawn by Joshua Fry and Peter Jefferson in 1751; engraved and published by Thomas Jeffreys (London, 1755). LC-M

FIGURE 137. *A Plan of Alexandria now Belhaven.* Unsigned, undated manuscript plan of Alexandria, Virginia; drawn by George Washington ca. 1749. LC-M

FIGURE 138. *Alexandria.* Unsigned and undated manuscript plan of Alexandria, Virginia; drawn ca. 1796. LC-M

FIGURE 139. *Plan of the Town of Alexandria in the District of Columbia.* Plan of Alexandria, Virginia; engraved by T. Clarke, published by I. V. Thomas in 1798. LC-M

FIGURE 140. *Birds Eye View of Alexandria, Va.* View of Alexandria, Virginia, from the east; published in 1862 by Charles Magnus (New York and Washington, 1862). LC-P

FIGURE 141. Untitled manuscript plan of Port Conway, King George County, Virginia; drawn by Aaron Thornley in 1783; from King George County Legislative Petition, December 5, 1783. VSL

FIGURE 142. *Plan of the Town of Smithfield in Isle of Wight County laid off by Jordon Thomas late surveyor of the said County.* Photocopy of a manuscript plan of Smithfield, Isle of Wight County, Virginia; drawn ca. 1752. VSL

FIGURE 143. Untitled manuscript plan of Norfolk, Virginia; drawn by George Nicholson in 1802. VSL

FIGURE 144. *Norfolk Harbor, Elizabeth River, Virginia.* Portion of a harbor chart showing Norfolk, Portsmouth, and Gosport, Virginia and vicinity in 1882; published by the U. S. Coast and Geodetic Survey (Washington, D. C., 1883). APSL

FIGURE 145. *Town of Portsmouth.* Manuscript plan of Portsmouth, Virginia; drawn by Gershom Nimmo in 1752. PNSM

FIGURE 146. *A View of Portsmouth in Virginia from the East Side of the River. . . .* Unsigned and undated manuscript plan of Portsmouth, Virginia; drawn ca. 1780. Public Records Office, A. O. 13/27, Bundle A, Folio 166, in Loyalist claims of Rev. John Agnew. PRO

FIGURE 147. *A Plan of Portsmouth Harbour in the Province of Virginia Shewing the Works Erected by the British Forces for its Defence 1781.* Portion of a manuscript map showing Portsmouth, Virginia, and vicinity in 1781; copied in 1782 from the original drawing by Lt. Stratton. Faden Collection, no. 92. LC-M

FIGURE 148. *Plat of the Town of Blandford* [title on reverse]. Unsigned manuscript plan of Blandford, Virginia; from petition to General Assembly of Baldwin Pierce, December 6, 1799. VSL

FIGURE 149. *Sketch of the Skirmish at Petersburg. . . .* Map of Petersburg and Blandford, Virginia, and vicinity in 1781; drawn by I. Hills; from Lieutenant-Colonel John Graves Simcoe, *A Journal of the Operations of the Queen's Rangers* (Exeter, [1787]). VHS

FIGURE 150. *The Plan of Wittontown in the County of Henrico.* Photocopy of an unsigned and undated manuscript plan of Wittontown (Pocahontas), Henrico County (now part of the city of Petersburg), Virginia; drawn ca. 1752. VSL

FIGURE 151. *Plan of Leesburg.* Photocopy of a manuscript plan of Leesburg, Loudoun County, Virginia; drawn by John Hough in 1759. LC-M

FIGURE 152. *Plan of Winchester.* Inset plan of Winchester, Frederick County, Virginia; from a map entitled *Frederick, Berkeley, & Jefferson Counties in the State of Virginia*; drawn by Charles Varlé; engraved by Benjamin Jones (Philadelphia, 1809). APSL

FIGURE 153. *Plan of the Town of Beverley.* Photocopy of a manuscript plan of Beverley, Henrico County, Virginia; drawn by Peter Jefferson in 1756; from the Ambler Papers in the Library of Congress. VHS

FIGURE 154. *A Plan of the Town of Lynchburg.* Photocopy of a manuscript plan of Lynchburg, Campbell County, Virginia; drawn by Richard Stith in 1790;

from Proceedings of the Trustees of the Town of Lynchburg, 1787–1817. VSL

FIGURE 155. Untitled, unsigned, and undated manuscript plan of Newcastle, Craig (then Botetourt) County, Virginia; drawn in 1834; from a Botetourt County Legislative Petition, February 5, 1834. VSL

FIGURE 156. Untitled, undated, and unsigned manuscript plan of Bath, Berkeley County, Virginia (now Berkeley Springs, Morgan County, West Virginia); drawn ca. 1777; from Fairfax Family Papers, Acc.No. 24052, Folder 101. VSL

FIGURE 157. *Plat of Joppa in 1725.* Plan of Joppa, Baltimore (now Harford) County, Maryland, in 1725; as redrawn in 1879; from J. Thomas Scharf, *History of Maryland* (Baltimore, 1879), vol. 1. CU-O

FIGURE 158. *A Plan of Charles-ton in Cecil County, Maryland.* Unsigned and undated manuscript plan of Charlestown, Cecil County, Maryland; drawn ca. 1743. LC-M

FIGURE 159. Untitled, unsigned, and undated manuscript plan of Charlestown, Cecil County, Maryland; drawn ca. 1743. LC-M

FIGURE 160. *A Map of the Head of Chesapeake Bay and Susquehanna River. A Plan of the Town of Havre de Grace* [inset]. Map of the northern end of Chesapeake Bay, with an inset plan of Havre de Grace, Maryland; drawn by C. P. Hauducoeur, engraved by Allardice; published in 1799. APSL

FIGURE 161. *Plat of Georgetown, Kent County, Maryland.* Unsigned and undated manuscript copy of a resurvey of Georgetown, Kent County, Maryland; drawn by William Humphrey in 1787. MDHS

FIGURE 162. *St. Michaels.* Plan of St. Michaels, Talbot County, Maryland, in 1877; from Lake, Griffing & Stevenson, *An Illustrated Atlas of Talbot & Dorchester Counties, Maryland* (Philadelphia, 1877). MDHS

FIGURE 163. *Town of Centre Ville.* Unsigned, undated manuscript plan of Centerville, Queen Annes County, Maryland; drawn in 1798; from a photocopy of the original in Queen Annes County Deed Record Book, S.T.W., No. 5, 1799 to 1802, 353. MHR

FIGURE 164. *Princess Anne.* Plan of Princess Anne, Somerset County, Maryland, from Lake, Griffing & Stevenson, *Atlas of Wicomico, Somerset & Worcester Cos., Md.* (Philadelphia, 1877). MDHS

FIGURE 165. *Port Tobacco—1894.* Undated and unsigned manuscript plan of Port Tobacco, Charles County, Maryland; drawn by R. G. Barbour in 1894. MDHS

FIGURE 166. *Map of the State of Maryland, laid down from an actual survey of all the principal waters, public roads and divisions of the Counties therein. . . .* Eastern portion of a map of Maryland; drawn by Dennis Griffith in 1794; engraved by J. Vallance (Philadelphia, 1795). MDHS

FIGURE 167. *A Plat of the Town of Bladensburg as Re-surveyed in 1787. . . .* Plan of Bladensburg, Prince Georges County, Maryland; traced by C. R. Beaumont in 1932 from a copy drawn by B. Rathbone in 1897 of a resurvey by John Frederick Augustus Priggs in 1787. MHR

FIGURE 168. *Plat of George-Town.* Unsigned and undated manuscript plan of Georgetown, Maryland (now the District of Columbia); drawn in 1751; from Georgetown Commissioners' Minutes, 1751–1789. LC-MS

FIGURE 169. *A Map of George Town with its Additions.* Manuscript plan of Georgetown, District of Columbia; drawn in 1796 by Geo. [illegible]; reproduced in 1915 from the original then owned by Miss Sally Somervell Mackall in Columbia Historical Society, *Records,* 18 (Washington, 1915). CU-O

FIGURE 170. Untitled, unsigned, and undated manuscript plan of Hamburg, Maryland; drawn ca. 1768. LC-M

FIGURE 171. *Plat of Carrollsburg.* Manuscript plan of Carrollsburg, Maryland; drawn by Francis Deakins in 1770. LC-M

FIGURE 172. *Territory of Columbia.* Map of the District of Columbia; drawn by Andrew Ellicott, published in 1793. LC-M

FIGURE 173. Untitled, undated and unsigned manuscript sketch by Thomas Jefferson in September, 1790, of a plan for a capital city on the site of Carrollsburg, Maryland. Papers of Thomas Jefferson. LC-MS

FIGURE 174. Untitled, undated, and unsigned manuscript plan for Washington, D. C.; drawn by Thomas Jefferson in 1791. Papers of Thomas Jefferson. LC-MS

FIGURE 175. *Sketch of Washington in Embryo.* Map showing the division of land on the site of the national capital in 1791; drawn by E.F.M. Faehtz and F.W. Pratt, based on research by Dr. Joseph M. Toner, with later manuscript additions (Washington, 1874). LC-M

FIGURE 176. Untitled, undated, and unsigned manuscript plan for Washington, D.C.; drawn by Pierre Charles L'Enfant in August, 1791, with later manuscript additions. LC-M

FIGURE 177. *Plan of the City Intended for the Permanent Seat of the Government of the United States.* Copy by the U.S. Coast and Geodetic Survey in 1887 of the manuscript plan for Washington, D.C. drawn by Pierre Charles L'Enfant in 1791. A

FIGURE 178. *Plan of the City of Washington in the Territory of Columbia. . . .* Central portion of a plan of Washington, D.C., drawn by Andrew Ellicott, engraved by Thackera & Vallance (Philadelphia, 1792). CU-O

FIGURE 179. *A Map of the City of Washington in the District of Columbia established as the permanent Seat of the Government of the United States of America.* Plan of Washington, D.C.; drawn by Robert King; engraved by C. Schwarz in 1803. LC-M

FIGURE 180. *Map exhibiting the property of the U.S. in the vicinity of the Capitol . . . with the manner in which it is proposed to lay off the same in building lots. . . .* Manuscript plan for land development in the vicinity of the Capitol in Washington, D.C.; drawn by Benjamin Henry Latrobe in 1815. LC-M

FIGURE 181. *Washington City 1821.* Painting by Madame Hyde de Neuville, wife of the French Minister, of the north front of the White House, *center,* the State and Treasury buildings, *left,* and the War and Navy buildings, *right.* NY-S

FIGURE 182. *City of Washington from beyond the Navy Yard.* View of Washington, D.C. from the southeast; drawn by W.J. Bennett from a painting by George Cooke; published by Lewis P. Clover (New York, 1834). LC-P

FIGURE 183. *View of Washington City, D.C.* View of the central portion of Washington, D.C. looking west from the Capitol; drawn and published by E. Sachse (Baltimore, 1862). MDHS

FIGURE 184. *Map of the City of Washington, D.C.* Portion of a plan of Washington, D.C.; drawn by James Keily; published by Lloyd van Derveer (Camden, 1850). LC-M

FIGURE 185. *An Exact Copy of a Plan of the Town of Richmond which appears to be taken in the Life time of William Byrd the Elder. . . .* Undated and unsigned manuscript plan of Richmond, Virginia; copied from a plan drawn prior to 1744. LC-MS

FIGURE 186. *Map of the Prize Lots of 100 Acres each in Byrds Lottery.* Inset plan of a portion of Richmond, Virginia; from *Plan of the City of Richmond,* drawn by Micajah Bates in 1835. VSL

Figure 187. *Manchester.* Inset plan of Manchester, Virginia, (now part of Richmond); from *Plan of the*
VSL
City of Richmond, drawn by Micajah Bates in 1835.

Figure 188. *Skirmish at Richmond Jan: 5th. 1781.* Plan of Richmond, Virginia, in 1781; drawn by Lt. Allans; from Lieutenant-Colonel John Graves Simcoe, *A Journal of the Operations of the Queen's Rangers.* . . . (Exeter, [1787]). VHS

Figure 189. *Map of a portion of Richmond, Va.* Unsigned and undated manuscript plan of a portion of Richmond, Virginia; drawn by Thomas Jefferson in 1780; from a reproduction of the original in the Massachusetts Historical Society, in Frederick Doveton Nichols, *Thomas Jefferson's Architectural Drawings* (Boston and Charlottesville, 1961). A

Figure 190. Untitled and undated manuscript plan for the public grounds of Richmond, Virginia; drawn by Thomas Jefferson in 1780. HM 9372. HEHL

Figure 191. *View of Richmond Virginia Taken by a French Gentlemen* [pencil title in upper right corner]. Undated etched view of Richmond, Virginia, from the south; drawn by C.B.J. Févret de Saint-Mémin ca. 1804. NY-S

Figure 192. *A Plan of the City of Richmond.* Undated plan of Richmond, Virginia; drawn in 1809 by Richard Young; as copied in 1932 by W. F. Beamon of the Richmond Bureau of Survey and Design, Department of Public Works. RDPW

Figure 193. *Plan of part of the city of Richmond, shewing the Situation of the proposed Building.* Undated and unsigned manuscript plan of a portion of Richmond, Virginia; drawn by Benjamin Henry Latrobe in 1798. LC-P

Figure 194. *Plan of the City of Richmond Drawn from Actual Survey and Original Plans.* Portion of a plan of Richmond, Virginia, showing the grounds of the state capitol as designed by Maximilian Godefroy in 1816; drawn by Micajah Bates in 1835. VSL

Figure 195. *Richmond, Va.* Undated view of the Capitol Square in Richmond, Virginia; drawn and published by L. A. Ramm (Richmond, ca. 1850). LC-P

Figure 196. *Richmond from the Hill Above the Waterworks.* View of Richmond, Virginia, from the west; engraved by W. G. Bennett in 1834 from a painting by G. Cooke. NY-S

Figure 197. *Baltimore.* Unsigned and undated manuscript map of Baltimore, Maryland, and vicinity; drawn in 1781. Rochambeau Collection, No. 13. LC-M

Figure 198. *Plan of Baltimore Town in 1729 Containing 60 Acres divided into 60 Lots.* Inset plan of Baltimore in 1730 on *Plan of the City of Baltimore as enlarged & laid out under the direction of the Commissioners Appointed by The General Assembly of Maryland in Feby 1818* . . .; drawn by Thomas H. Poppleton; engraved by C. P. Harrison (New York, 1823). PM-H

Figure 199. *Baltimore in 1752.* View of Baltimore, Maryland, from the south in 1752; from a drawing by John Moale; published ca. 1815. PM-H

Figure 200. Untitled, undated, and unsigned plan of Baltimore, Maryland, as surveyed by Nicholas Ruxton Gay in 1747. MDHS

Figure 201. *A New and Accurate Map of Baltimore Town.* . . . Manuscript plan of Baltimore, Maryland; drawn by G. Goulds. Presbury in 1780. MDHS

Figure 202. *Plan of the Town of Baltimore and it's Environs.* Plan of Baltimore, Maryland; drawn by A. P. Folie; engraved by James Poupard (Philadelphia, 1792). PM-G

Figure 203. *Plan of the City and Environs of Baltimore.* Plan of Baltimore, Maryland, in 1797 as reissued in 1801; engraved by Francis Shallus and published by Warner and Hanna; from a facsimile printed by the Meriden Gravure Co., published by the Peabody Institute Library (Baltimore, 1947). LC-M

Figure 204. *View of Baltimore City.* View of Baltimore, Maryland, from the north in 1850; drawn by E. Sachse, printed by E. Sachse & Co.; entered for copyright in 1850 by Casimir Bohn. PM-H

Figure 205. *Plan of the City of Baltimore as enlarged.* . . . Plan of Baltimore, Maryland, in 1823 with proposed extensions; drawn by Thomas H. Poppleton; engraved by C. P. Harrison (New York, 1823). MDHS

Figure 206. *Bird's Eye View of Baltimore City.* View of Baltimore, Maryland, in 1858 from the south; drawn by E. Sachse, printed and published by E. Sachse & Co. (Baltimore, 1858). PM-H

Index

Page numbers in boldface type denote illustrations.

TIDEWATER TOWNS

was composed by Coghill Composition Company, Richmond, Virginia, in Intertype Baskerville, lithographed by the Murray Printing Company, Forge Village, Massachusetts, and bound by Kingsport Press, Inc., Kingsport, Tennessee. The paper is Perkins & Squire Offset Lightone. The book was designed by Richard J. Stinely.

DATE DUE			